CELEBRATING

70

Mark McGwire's historic season

Editorial Direction

RON SMITH

Design

BILL WILSON

Photographic Coordination

ALBERT DICKSON

Prepress Project Coordinator

DAVID BRICKEY

Co-written by

BERNIE MIKLASZ
RON SMITH
MIKE EISENBATH
DAVE KINDRED

CONTRIBUTORS

Editorial Directors

Steve Meyerhoff, *The Sporting News;* Bob Rose, *St. Louis Post-Dispatch*;
Mike Smith, *St. Louis Post-Dispatch.*

Chief Copy Editor

Tom Klein, *St. Louis Post-Dispatch*

Copy Editors/Researchers

Todd Fitzpatrick, *The Sporting News;* Leslie Gibson McCarthy, *The Sporting News;*
Brendan Roberts, *The Sporting News;* Steve Siegel, *The Sporting News;*
Dave Sloan, *The Sporting News;* George Winkler, *The Sporting News.*

Graphics and Design

Ken Amos, *The Sporting News;* Amy Beadle, *The Sporting News;*
Michael Behrens, *The Sporting News.*

Prepress Director

Michael Bruner, *The Sporting News.*

Prepress Specialists

Steve Romer, *The Sporting News;* Ian Wilkinson, *The Sporting News.*

Contents

Foreword

by Jack Buck

It didn't take long

to plot the course for a memorable 1998 season. After four games, Mark McGwire had four home runs. At the end of May he had 27. By June 12, 65 games into the schedule for his St. Louis Cardinals, McGwire was halfway to the magic 62 figure that would make him the greatest single-season home run hitter of all time.

Strewn along the path of Big Mac's historic march were dramatic moments, 500-foot skidmarks, shellshocked pitchers and more standing ovations than a humble American folk hero could possibly endure. Waiting for him at the end was the emotional embrace of adoring fans and the unexpected challenge of Chicago Cubs right fielder Sammy Sosa, the shadow that wouldn't go away.

It was the perfect season for the near-perfect sports hero. And McGwire didn't shrink from his appointed rounds. He handled the media storm with calm and class, he charmed a nation with his values and humility and he helped baseball find forgiveness and rejuvenation with every powerful sweep of his bat.

Never in my 48 years in baseball had I seen anything like it. It was the most amazing thing, unparalleled—and not just in St. Louis. It was everywhere we went. It enveloped everybody in baseball, including all the Cardinals greats who rooted him on. McGwire brought everybody together, from Ozzie Smith to Bob Gibson, Lou Brock and Stan Musial. It was really fun to watch.

The following pages provide a homer-by-homer record of Mac's incredible journey. It's a celebration of the man as much as his feat. Every McGwire home run is captured photographically, but the ups and downs,

the highs and lows, the drama and routine of an exhausting season are captured in the words and pictures of The Sporting News and St. Louis Post-Dispatch reporters who were there.

The final chapter of this fascinating story deals with the race—the riveting Sosa-McGwire stretch run for baseball's single-season home run record after

THE DAY AFTER: *The McGwire aura took on a new dimension at Cincinnati's Cinergy Field the day after historic home run No. 62 .*

McGwire had won the sprint to 62. But when all was said and done, the final chapter was really the beginning of a more enduring relationship between baseball and its prodigal fans.

That's a message McGwire delivered over and over with every ovation and roar he generated during a historic season. The Summer of '98.

Jack Buck

BERNIE MIKLASZ

The Summer of '98

*Mark McGwire's power and magnetism
rejuvenated an ailing game*

Mark McGwire was riding in the back of a taxi, en route to Pittsburgh's Three Rivers Stadium, when he saw the police barricades. Hundreds of fans waited behind the sealed-off area near the players' entrance. They had stood for hours, patiently waiting to get a glimpse of their generation's Babe Ruth.

With four hours remaining before the scheduled first pitch, McGwire's green eyes twinkled in disbelief. He stepped out of the cab—the reason why so many had come so early, the reason why the stadium would be sold out on consecutive nights for the first time in 28 years, the reason why fans were falling in love with baseball again.

Cameras clicked. Mothers and fathers lifted their children to see him. Fans shouted McGwire's name, pleading for his autograph. Kids squealed.

"We love you Mark!"

"Hit one tonight!"

"Get the record, Mac!"

McGwire smiled and waved. Two security men rushed to his side and led him to the safety of the Cardinals' clubhouse. McGwire exhaled. This display of unconditional love had taken his breath away.

"Never in my wildest dreams," McGwire said, "did I ever think something like this would ever happen to me."

It was like this at every stop as McGwire barnstormed through the summer. St. Louis was his home base, his seat of power. But as he began sending home runs to the constellations, it became obvious: McGwire was much too large to be confined to one city, and no single ballpark could contain him. St. Louis understood, and America's best baseball town happily shared McGwire with the rest of the nation.

In the summer of 1998, baseball became a hit again—a home run that landed in the traditional soft spot of our national heritage. And more than any other player, McGwire was responsible for picking up the ailing game, slinging it across his wide shoulders and carrying it into living rooms across the country.

Mac got help in the season's first half from Seattle center fielder Ken Griffey Jr., who kept pace in the home-run fusillade. And when Griffey dropped off, a new power emerged: Chicago Cubs outfielder Sammy Sosa, who became McGwire's home-running mate in a joyful competition that charmed and captivated fans around the world. But if Sosa was baseball's middleweight champion, McGwire ruled the heavyweight division. He hit more homers, longer homers, and grabbed the larger share of headlines and attention.

When Big Mac came to town, it was a civic event. McGwire's batting practice was the best warmup act in sports. All across America, he hit cannon balls and took curtain calls. He pounded baseballs. He pounded baseball's bad image. The game was a brighter place, illuminated by a thousand camera flashes—those beautiful points of light—when he swung the bat.

"You're never going to see anything like him," said Cardinals broadcaster Mike Shannon, who has been with the team as a player and a radio voice since 1962. "In Mark McGwire, what you're talking about is John Wayne, Paul Bunyan and Superman rolled into one."

McGwire brought the fans back. And he brought families together, including his own. When McGwire hit his record-tying 61st homer, his father was in the seats at Busch Stadium, celebrating his 61st birthday. McGwire looked behind home plate and shouted, "Happy Birthday, Dad!" And McGwire's 10-year-old son, Matthew, observed the drama from his on-field perch as a Cardinals batboy. Three generations unified by one homer.

McGwire's feats became a shared interest between parents and children. Breakfast-table discussions

centered around box scores and McGwire's home-run tote board. At night, the families who couldn't watch or listen together provided home-run bulletins for each other with urgent phone calls.

The kids were wild about Big Mac. His stadium-rattling homers looked like something straight out of their video games and he bore a striking resemblance to the action figures that dominated afternoon television. It was cool the way he let his son hang with him at the ballpark, and how he fulfilled Matthew's spring-training prediction of 65 homers. He fought for other kids, too, donating $1 million annually to the foundation he established to combat child abuse.

Parents treasured him because he stressed the value of hard work, dedication and team-first play. And he shared himself, with remarkable grace. We especially were moved by the way McGwire reached out to the sons and daughters of the late Roger Maris, retroactively giving them the affection that had eluded their tormented father in 1961, when he defied New York's

wishes and broke Ruth's single-season home run record.

One August day at St. Louis' Busch Stadium, as McGwire left the field after batting practice, he looked into the stands. A 5-year-old boy was holding up a sign: "Hey Mark, It's My Birthday." McGwire walked over and handed the wide-eyed boy his first baseman's glove. There were similar scenes in other stadiums.

McGwire was the superhero that baseball needed after the destructive strike of 1994. But he was real. And he went from town to town spreading home runs, souvenirs and goodwill. Catcher Tom Lampkin, his teammate and friend, called McGwire's tour a "traveling salvation show."

And he was fun. The epic nature of his rocket-blast home runs satisfied our national craving for big, bigger, biggest. If you want to diagram the flight pattern of a typical McGwire homer, use St. Louis' Gateway Arch as your model.

McGwire's home runs dented signs and scoreboards at Busch Stadium. He caused $5,000 worth of damage to

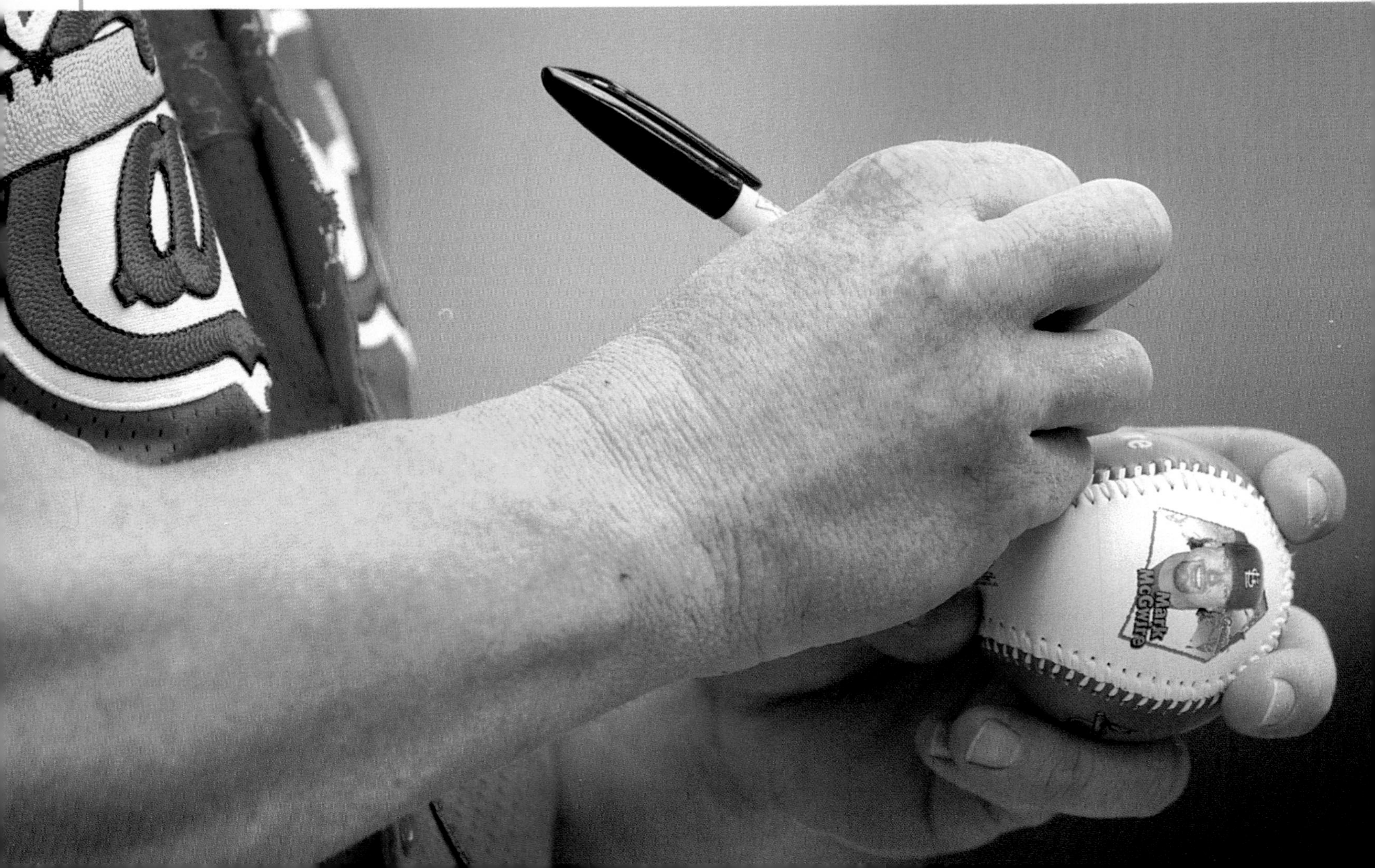

CROWD CONTROL: *With McGwire looking for home run No. 60, pregame activity outside Busch Stadium became a shoulder-bumping hazard.*

EVERYWHERE A SIGN: *Every direction McGwire turned, he encountered hordes of photographers, reporters and autograph-seeking fans. He tried hard to accommodate everybody and even tossed a few bones to the crowd.*

the scoreboard in Arizona. He struck a car in the players' parking lot at Coors Field in Colorado. He plunked a batting-practice ball off a bus on Waveland Avenue, beyond the left field bleachers at Chicago's Wrigley Field. He hit a stadium usher with an upper-deck batting-practice shot in Miami. He was dangerous.

"People say Babe Ruth hit them this way," Mets catcher Mike Piazza said. "But I really can't believe that Babe Ruth could hit them higher or longer than McGwire."

Rare is the athlete who consistently satisfies and delights the paying customer. But McGwire sent legions of babbling, bubbly people home from the ballpark to tell next-day tales of 500-foot homers around the coffee pot, or on the front steps of their church.

McGwire touched them all, young and old. Grandmothers baked him cookies. Grandfathers reminisced about baseball's good old days. Women sent him flowers. Kids pretended to be McGwire in their backyard games, launching the ball, just like Big Mac, over the rooftops.

McGwire emerged as a pop-culture curiosity. He attracted visits from celebrities, including Bruce Springsteen, Jerry Seinfeld, Tommy Hilfiger, Brett Favre, Dan Marino and other professional athletes. Sarah Ferguson, the Duchess of York, sat behind the Cardinals' dugout at Wrigley Field one day, waving an autographed McG-

wire bat.

"He's my favorite redhead," Fergie declared.

McGwire was baseball's equivalent of Michael Jordan. Everyone wanted to touch him, see him. And he responded with a natural showman's flair for the dramatic, an impeccable sense of timing.

On opening day, his grand slam knocked out the Dodgers. On April 14, Matthew made his season debut as a batboy and big daddy homered three times to destroy Arizona. On July 11, a slumping McGwire asked Matthew to kiss his bat for good luck, then walloped a 485-foot homer that zapped Houston and closer Billy Wagner. On August 19 in Chicago, Sosa hit his 48th home run to take a 1-stroke lead over McGwire, who allowed him to stay on top for exactly 58 minutes. Then Mac cranked two homers in the same game to reclaim the lead.

They left the park at a consistently furious pace. By the end of April, he had 11. By the end of May, he was resting on 27. June ended at 37, July closed at 45 and August at 55—one away from Hack Wilson's National League record and the homestretch of his remarkable quest—toward an eventual, unfathomable 70.

As he made his final approach to the record, McGwire's clutch touch was tested again. The Cardinals opened a five-game homestand September 4 with McGwire sitting on 59 home runs. He desperately wanted to bang three more and set the record in front of his adoring St. Louis fans.

Home run No. 60, which put him in company with the immortal Ruth, came in

Game 2 of the stand against the Cincinnati Reds. Homer 61, the Maris equalizer, came two days later, in a Labor Day showdown with the Cubs. He had one game left, one more chance to reward the city that had embraced him so lovingly and enthusiastically.

The date: September 8, 1998.

The time: 8:18 p.m.

With two out in the fourth inning, McGwire attacked the first pitch from Cubs starter Steve Trachsel. His 62nd home run was a streak of lightning. We barely had time to register the history that flashed before our eyes. The shot surged down the left field line, only 341 feet away, and barely cleared the wall in the corner as his shortest homer of the year.

Hey, why delay the celebration with a long-descending 500-footer? McGwire delivered, and Busch Stadium staged a nationally televised house party.

KEEP YOUR EYE ON THE BALL: *Under the watchful eye of Chicago rival Sammy Sosa (left), other fascinated players and thousands of McGwire-hungry fans, Big Mac put on a daily batting-practice show that played to rave reviews all over the country.*

"So much has been put on this guy," Cardinals manager Tony La Russa said. "Everywhere he goes, he's the center of attention. He's been given the responsibility for carrying the game on his shoulders. And I watch him thinking, 'There's no way we can expect one man to deliver like this. It's too much to ask. It isn't fair.' He has an anvil on his back. And then he swings the bat, and the ball goes over the fence. It's overwhelming."

But make no mistake, the home-run mission was never as easy as McGwire made it seem. Through the final month and a half, he had to deal with a serious challenge from the irrepressible Sosa, who stalked him down to the final weekend and made Mac's fans sweat through every swing.

Mac and Sammy, seemingly linked at the biceps, assaulted history together. And their duel brought out the best in each man. If Sosa homered, McGwire would respond. When McGwire pulled into a seemingly comfortable lead, Sosa would catch up with a stunning barrage. They exchanged these long-distance telegrams and

spectators packed ballparks at every stop, standing and straining to see every precious at-bat.

It was gripping theater, but not the only entertainment they provided. Mac and Sammy raised the level of sportsmanship on our playing fields. There was no trash talk or finger pointing and they openly rooted for each other. The shared experience drew them closer and they became fast friends, not hated foes. They were baseball's equivalent of Magic Johnson vs. Larry Bird.

Sosa was in right field when McGwire slipped No. 62 over the Busch Stadium wall in left. He ran in to embrace McGwire, who wrapped him in a bear hug. And then they exchanged their favorite post-homer rituals: McGwire threw playful punches to the stomach and Sosa blew kisses.

When McGwire made the comment, "Wouldn't it be great if we finished in a tie," no one smirked. We believed him, because Sosa and McGwire had a genuine camaraderie. And while chasing one of the most cherished records in all of sports, they cleaned up some pollution on the professional landscape.

What an unlikely duo: McGwire, the son of a California dentist who grew up near Disneyland; Sosa, the poor kid from the Dominican Republic who sold oranges and shined shoes to support his family after the death of his father.

Baseball brought McGwire and Sosa together. And they brought baseball back to its feel-good past.

We tingled through the final weeks, after Sosa had paused at 58 homers, allowing McGwire to reach 62 first. But Mac wasn't home free, not by a long shot.

Emotionally deflated after passing Maris, McGwire went a week without homering, and the opportunistic Sosa caught him at 62 with a dramatic four-homer weekend bombardment against Milwaukee at Wrigley Field. That's when the real race began. Sosa caught McGwire again at 63 and again at 65, thanks to another two-homer game against the Brewers on the final Wednesday of the season. And then, on the last Friday of the season, Sammy took another 1-stroke lead—for 45 minutes.

Sosa refused to go away and pushed McGwire to the end—a fitting conclusion to a remarkable season. In sports, the only way to certify greatness is to defeat greatness, the way Muhammad Ali fed off Joe Frazier, Affirmed responded to Alydar and the Lakers finally overcame the Celtics.

McGwire needed Sosa. But Sammy wasn't the only barrier.

During one grumpy stretch after the All-Star break, a mentally and physically fatigued McGwire resisted his own celebrity. He tried to disassemble his own bandwagon. He yearned for solitude, away from the autograph requests and the demands for interviews. Around midseason, flecks of gray appeared on his red goatee.

And this was appropriate; the personal angst gave him an extension to Maris. The proper historical connections were now established: McGwire, like Ruth, was an extra-large slugger who hit special-effects homers. McGwire, like Maris, squirmed in the public petri dish. To become baseball's new home run king, McGwire would need Babe's physical strength and Roger's mental fortitude.

McGwire's link to Ruth and Maris seemingly gave him peace. As he closed in on Ruth's 60 and Maris' 61, he felt them in his heart. He talked of wanting to meet them in heaven. And he offered this eloquent monologue—spoken September 5 after his 60th home run—as what he would say to Ruth and Maris, if given a chance:

"I would ask them if they ever felt the way I'm feeling right now.

"I would ask them if their heart beat a mile a minute, the way my heart is racing now.

"I'd ask them if the emotions ran through them, the way my emotions are right now. I have this incredible feeling inside. Did they feel this way, too?

"I would ask them how their life was away from the field, and if they could relax.

"I'd ask them about the media back then, and how it compared to what I'm going through now.

"I'd ask them how the pitchers were, what they faced, what was tough about hitting in their time.

"I'd ask them about the guys they played with, their teammates, and if they were as great as mine are now.

"I would ask them if they realized at the time that all of America was watching, the way I feel all the eyes are

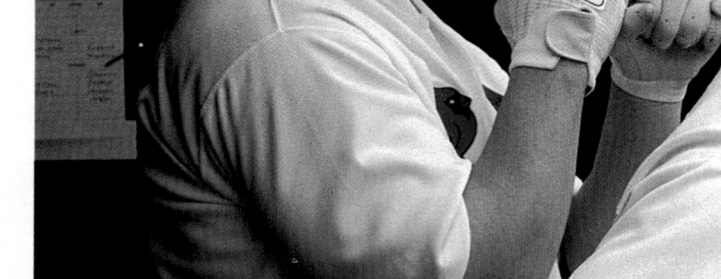

TONY AWARD: *Despite McGwire's long professional relationship with Tony La Russa (below right), everything he accomplished during the Summer of '98 amazed and impressed the Cardinals manager.*

watching me now.

"There's so much I'd want to talk to them about. And one day I will."

As soon as he overcame his emotional blockage, McGwire was home free. When he released his heart to America, it liberated him to make history.

As sports fans, we want our stars to have a human touch. When McGwire digs into the batter's box, he is as imposing as the Colossus of Rhodes. But there's vulnerable tissue under all those muscles.

McGwire has a bulging disk in his back. He has 20/500 eyesight. He has weak arches and wears a special shoe insert to keep his feet aligned. He has had three surgeries on his heels. His sinuses drip. McGwire has endured the agony of divorce. He went through psychological counseling to overcome a confidence crisis.

We could relate when an overly excited McGwire had to backtrack and touch first base to correct a misstep after his 62nd homer. Wouldn't you be dizzy, too? He aches, he stumbles—but he grinds on. Such visible adversity makes him even more endearing to everyday people.

"I've had enough adversity in my personal life, and in my professional life," McGwire said. "It would have been easy for me to turn around and to never be heard of again. But I decided to bust through the walls. My life has not been easy. I'm a perfect example of a person who is normal, who can conquer things if they can dream and believe in themselves."

Through all of the emotion and unrelenting acclaim, McGwire never stopped thinking of others. His press conferences in each city usually included a cheer-up message to those experiencing rough times. His pursuit of the record turned into a national parade, and he ignited the fireworks with his bat. He wanted everyone to join him, even those seemingly forgotten by society.

McGwire Mania was officially embraced as a national phenomenon August 20 at Shea Stadium in New York. McGwire homered in the first game of a doubleheader against the Mets, giving him 50 for the season and a major league record—no player had ever popped 50 homers for three consecutive seasons. As he rounded first base, he pumped his fists, clapped his hands; he paused at

the dugout to salute the cheering New York fans.

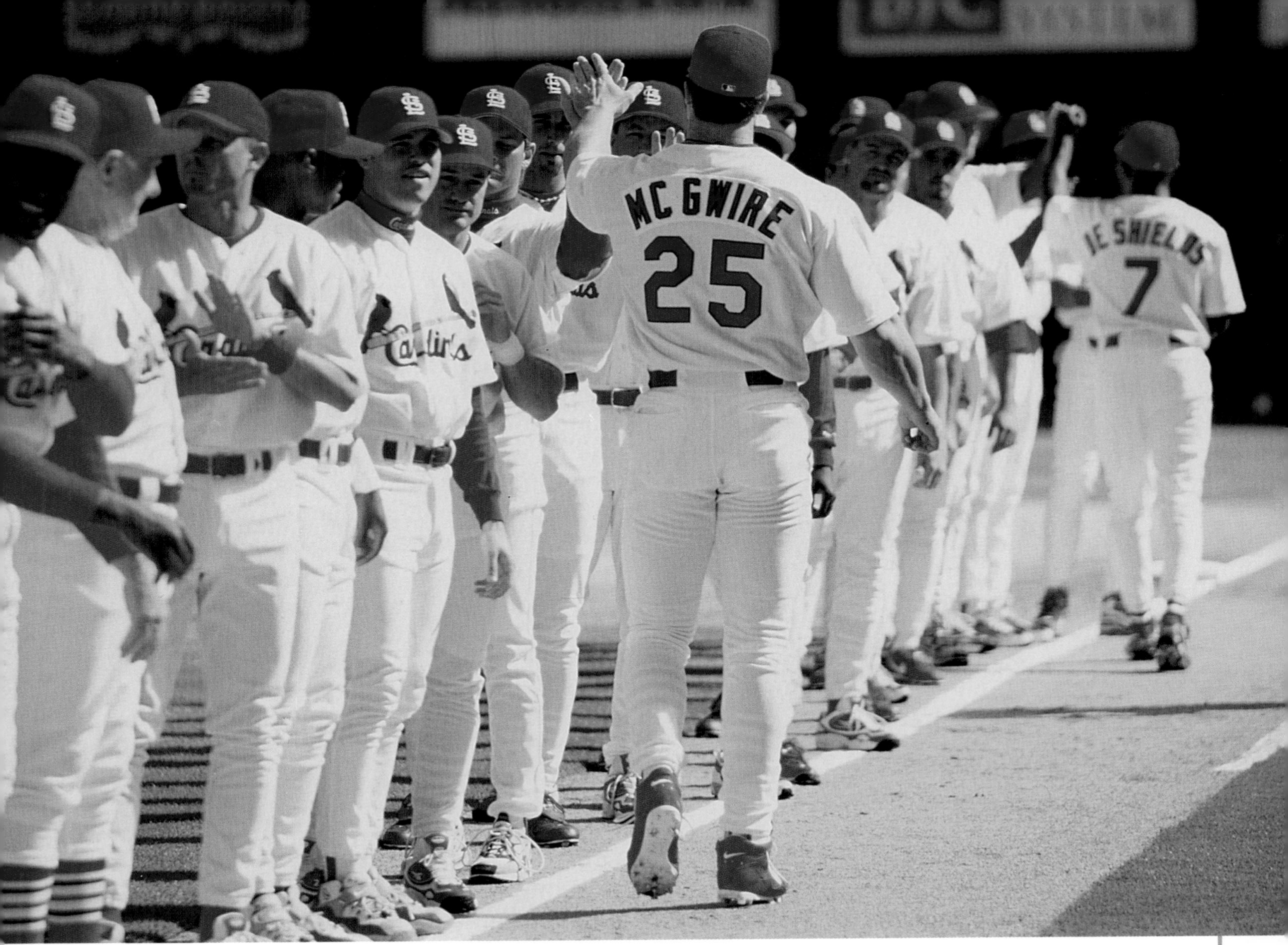

Big Mac put the Big Apple in his pocket.

Later that night, a thankful McGwire took a few cartons of baseballs to his hotel room and stayed awake until the wee small hours of the morning, personalizing autographed keepsakes for his teammates. He would do it again after hitting No. 62, scribbling on baseballs through the night to give his friends a piece of memorabilia, straight from his heart. "As great as he is as a player," La Russa said, "he's even a better person."

And he brought out the best in us, too. Late in the season, as he hit the various milestones of his record run, it was startling to see fans return the home run balls to McGwire, resisting the temptation to cash them in for a hefty ransom. He had that effect on people.

In the summer of 1998, Mark McGwire's home runs soared deep into our national consciousness. He hit those homers so high, so far, that they elevated the American spirit.

Bernie Miklasz is a sports columnist for the St. Louis Post-Dispatch.

The batting practice

THE KING OF SWING: *When McGwire takes batting practice, everybody listens—for the crack of the bat that comes with every ball he cranks into the upper deck of Busch Stadium and other big-league parks.*

It's not just for practice anymore.

Not when Mark McGwire steps into the cage.

Cardinals batting practice has become an event—whether McGwire is at Busch Stadium, or any other ballpark in America—something bordering on a rock concert. There's a certain choreography to it, with everything scheduled and no genuine surprises about what is supposed to take place.

But there also is an air of anticipation. Fans expect McGwire to play all the hits, cranked up to full blast, yet the live show always has a fresh feel.

Even if McGwire simply is jamming at rehearsal. The hype lets fans at every ballpark in America know a unique happening will be arriving at the ballpark. Thousands show up much earlier than normal. As soon as the gates open, fans flow down the aisles.

The crowds gather quickly and heavily in two prime locations: at the far corner of the Cardinals' dugout, because fans know McGwire almost always stops there to sign autographs on his way to the bat rack, and anywhere in left field, where chances are good they might come within diving distance of snaring one of the big

phenomenon

"When we were in Oakland, Mac wanted me to throw the ball as hard as I could. I think he was learning to be a hitter, going to battle in batting practice. So he didn't hit as many home runs. But every now and then when he did catch one, we'd stop and go, 'Wow.'

"Now he knows more about what he wants to do. He wants me to pitch a nice, easy comfortable ball over the plate. I get a little upset, not a lot but a little, when we go to a place like Colorado and they talk about the show coming to town. We're not trying to put a show on. He does practice what he does in the game.

"He's trying to get the ball in the air, to make the contact he does in a game."

redhead's towering drives.

"I've been doing this for 11 years, and no one ever made a big deal out of it before," a baffled McGwire said.

Suddenly, fans are making a big deal out of his every move. The routine finds people booing when he bunts the first pitch, groaning when he "only" smacks a hard line drive into left field or a fly ball that falls short of the fence, and screaming wildly

A CAGED LION: *Cardinal teammates like Ron Gant (left photo, right) found McGwire's batting-practice act fun, but tough to follow. But fans never tired of his prodigious home runs or friendly, accessible manner.*

when he sends a ball soaring into the upper reaches of the park.

Coach Dave McKay, who has thrown thousands of McGwire home runs in BP with Oakland and the Cardinals, has to make sure he fires pitches precisely on the outside part of the plate. McGwire has to lock in and try to please the fans with at least eight homers, which is only a regular day for him.

Players from the opposing team become fans, always making sure they're on the field during the show. Oh, they try to look busy by stretching or playing catch. But they are more like little boys during McGwire's 20 or so batting-practice swings.

And why not? They want to see baseballs soar in the heavens, too.

SHOWTIME: *McGwire's batting-practice routine included stretching, playful moments with teammates and coach Dave Parker (left) and the much-anticipated cage time, sometimes under the supervision of son Matt (above).*

Henry Rodriguez, Chicago Cubs:

"I made sure I wasn't in the clubhouse when he was taking batting practice. I wanted to be in that dugout, out there like everyone else. They want to see him swing. He's the King Kong of baseball. Everybody likes to watch somebody like that. He's a monster."

Ron Gant, St. Louis Cardinals:

"It's different taking batting practice in the same group as him. You go up there trying to hit the ball as far as he can, and you don't even come 150 feet close to it. That can be embarrassing if you think about it, because so many people are watching when you're in his group.

"But it's all in fun. I've always been able to get my work in, and I've been hitting in the same group as him a lot this year. It hasn't changed my batting practice at all.

"But I watch him where I don't always watch other guys I hit with. Even if I hit in the group before he does, I'll stay and watch his group hit. That's something you're not going to see for a long time."

The men who came before

BABE WATCH: *Maris (left) faced off with the Ruth mystique in 1961 and came out ahead, but it was not an enjoyable experience.*

It all starts with Babe Ruth, the ever-immortal Bambino who continues to dominate the baseball record books more than six decades after his final major league season.

When Ruth brought the home run into vogue in the 1920s and punctuated his amazing power feats with a 60-homer assault in 1927, nobody knew what plateaus might be within his reach. The number 60, it turned out, became magical in baseball lore and the target at which all future generations of power hitters would set their sights.

Several flirted with destiny, but

only one completed his mission. Roger Maris, daring to challenge the immortal Babe while wearing the same Yankees pinstripes and playing in the House That Ruth Built, battled teammate Mickey Mantle through a dramatic 1961 campaign in which the M&M boys powered 115 home runs—a record 61 by Maris and 54 by Mantle, the New York fans' favorite son.

The season was difficult for Maris, who reluctantly sacrificed his privacy to the media blitz that accompanies immortality. New York

BIG HITS: *The Ruth swing (left page) set an enduring standard in 1927, but the Maris home run routine (above, left) played to mixed reviews in the same New York market 34 years later.*

MEMORIES: *Ruth, immortalized (left) by a Hall of Fame plaque that Maris never earned, is greeted at the plate by teammate Lou Gehrig (below right) after a 1927 home run.*

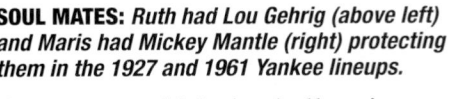

SOUL MATES: *Ruth had Lou Gehrig (above left) and Maris had Mickey Mantle (right) protecting them in the 1927 and 1961 Yankee lineups.*

fans resented Maris challenging their beloved Ruth, commissioner Ford Frick issued his infamous asterisk ruling (to get the record, Maris would have to hit his 61 in 154 games, the schedule Ruth played in 1927) and the media badgered him relentlessly, causing his hair to fall out by season's end. But he persevered and hit his record home run on the final day of the season against Boston.

Maris, who never again would approach such a lofty plateau in a career that fell short of Hall of Fame recognition, had his record, asterisk or not. It would last 37 years, three more than the span Ruth held the mark (1927-61).

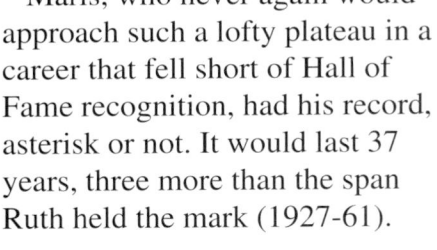

The Homers

"KING OF SWING"

1

"How can you not get chills? I was juiced up. I don't know my own strength. I hope I don't hurt anybody."

—McGwire

Two out, bases loaded in the fifth inning of a scoreless battle at Busch Stadium. Los Angeles Dodgers righthander Ramon Martinez, trying to block out memories of the fastball McGwire had transformed into a dramatic 517-foot home run in September 1997, delivers a 1-0 changeup and unwittingly sets the tone for a dramatic and unforgettable St. Louis summer.

Not only did McGwire begin his pursuit of Roger Maris' single-season home run record by launching a majestic 364-foot moonshot into the left field seats, he also served notice that all the preseason hype, all the long-discussed speculation about Ruthian-like feats and special moments, would be addressed in short order. The grand slam, the first ever by a Cardinals player on opening day, was delivered to a

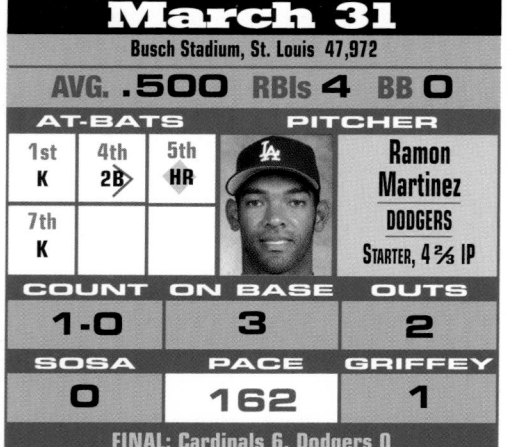

March 31
Busch Stadium, St. Louis 47,972

AVG. **.500**	RBIs **4**	BB **0**

AT-BATS			PITCHER
1st **K**	4th **2B**	5th **HR**	**Ramon Martinez**
7th **K**			DODGERS
			STARTER, 4⅔ IP

COUNT	ON BASE	OUTS
1-0	**3**	**2**

SOSA	PACE	GRIFFEY
0	**162**	**1**

FINAL: Cardinals 6, Dodgers 0

Cardinals' record: 1-0

364 ft.

Homer No. 1 landed in the left field seats just above Busch Stadium's visitors' bullpen.

hungry, sea-of-red sellout crowd with the fist-pumping, teammate-bumping enthusiasm of a Michael Johnson sprint to the finish line.

"People will be talking about that one for a while," said Cardinals manager Tony La Russa after a season-opening shutout that featured Todd Stottlemyre's seven-inning, three-hit pitching. A key defensive play by first baseman McGwire also was prominent, saving two runs in the fifth inning. McGwire's 10th career grand slam and his 25th home run in 52 games with the Cardinals was certainly a moment he will savor.

"It's a great feeling. How can you not acknowledge it?" he said when asked about his unusually animated curtain call. "I'm very flattered by the way (the St. Louis fans) have received me."

RUTH *The Babe's 1927 masterpiece, still considered by many the greatest home run season ever posted, began April 15 with a solo blast off Philadelphia A's righthander Howard Ehmke.*

MARIS *Homerless over his first 10 games, Maris began his 1961 assault on baseball's most cherished record April 26 with a fifth-inning solo shot off Detroit righthander Paul Foytack.*

■ "McGwire is the guy. If you give him an opportunity, if you make a bad pitch to him, he's going to hurt you. With the bases loaded, we had to pitch to him. You just can't afford to put yourself in that situation." *—Dodgers manager Bill Russell*

■ "You're not going to see many people hit a ball that high and have it leave the park. I'm sure he'll say he mishit it, but he's so strong, he can miss a pitch and still do that. I can't relate, because I don't have power like that." *—Dodgers outfielder Todd Hollandsworth*

A Grand Opening

The McGwire home run show opened to rave reviews, thanks to a fifth-inning grand slam that propelled the Cardinals to victory.

Big Mac watches the flight of his first 1998 home run (right) and begins the home run trot (below) that would become an almost nightly staple for national baseball fans. The greeting at home plate (above right) and the Busch Stadium curtain call (below right) would be repeated many times over the course of a record-setting summer.

2

"To get the record, you have to average 10 home runs a month. I believe it can be done, but it has to be a perfect season."

—McGwire

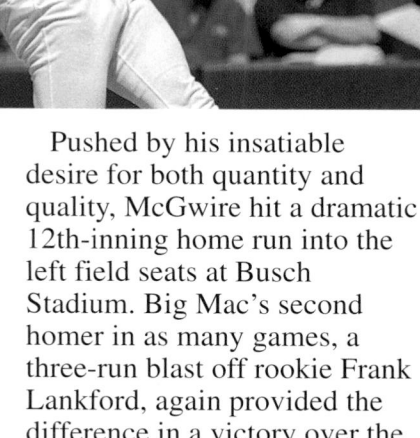

Pushed by his insatiable desire for both quantity and quality, McGwire hit a dramatic 12th-inning home run into the left field seats at Busch Stadium. Big Mac's second homer in as many games, a three-run blast off rookie Frank Lankford, again provided the difference in a victory over the Los Angeles Dodgers.

Still riding the crest of his opening day grand slam,

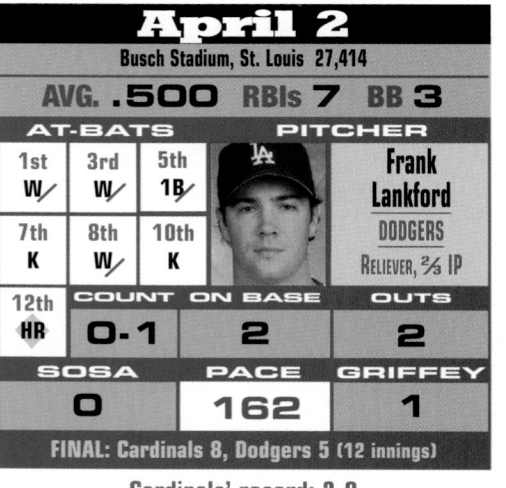

April 2
Busch Stadium, St. Louis 27,414

AVG. .500	RBIs 7	BB 3

AT-BATS			PITCHER	
1st W	3rd W	5th 1B		Frank Lankford
7th K	8th W	10th K		DODGERS
12th HR				Reliever, ⅔ IP

COUNT	ON BASE	OUTS
0-1	2	2

SOSA	PACE	GRIFFEY
0	162	1

FINAL: Cardinals 8, Dodgers 5 (12 innings)

Cardinals' record: 2-0

Homer No. 2 landed in the left field lower-deck seats at Busch Stadium.

368 ft.

McGwire punctuated his two-hit, three-walk Game 2 by hitting an 0-1 curveball, ending a seesaw battle that lasted more than four hours and required 14 pitchers. The Dodgers had worked a little magic of their own when pinch hitter Matt Luke singled with two out in the ninth and Thomas Howard hit a game-tying homer.

"You know anything is possible with him—is that amazing?" Cardinals manager Tony La Russa said after McGwire hit his 389th home run, tying Johnny Bench for 29th on the career list.

The homer prompted the first wave of can-you-break-the-record questions and inspired the comment that would become a regular feature of press conferences over the next five months: "If I have 50 going into September, talk to me then."

■ "It was a lollipop curve. I knew the minute it left my hand. I can't hang a curve to him. I don't think I'll throw that pitch to him again." —*Dodgers pitcher Frank Lankford*

■ "He (Lankford) got me out (opening day) with a breaking ball, so I was looking for another. He threw me a curve and I was able to get it all." —*McGwire*

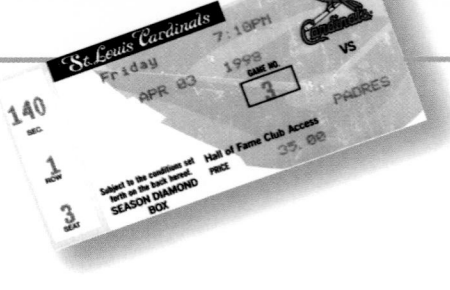

3

"He hits a baseball like no other human being. It takes off in a different way."

—*Padres manager Bruce Bochy*

After playing the dramatic lead for two St. Louis masterpieces, McGwire took on a subordinate role in the Cardinals' first loss of the season—a 13-5 San Diego blowout at Busch Stadium. On a damp, 44-degree night made even more frigid by a six-run Padres' opening inning, Big Mac provided one warm moment with a two-run homer, his third in as many 1998 games.

The fifth-inning blast, which cut the Padres' lead to 9-5, landed in the left field seats, just inside the foul pole, and gave McGwire home runs in

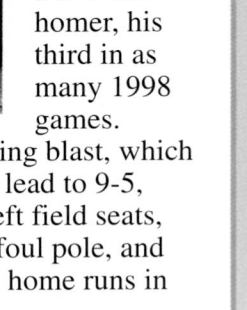

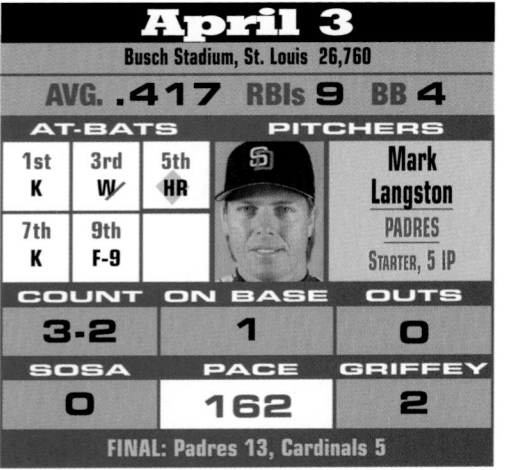

April 3
Busch Stadium, St. Louis 26,760

AVG. **.417**	RBIs **9**	BB **4**

AT-BATS			PITCHERS
1st K	3rd W	5th HR	**Mark Langston**
7th K	9th F-9		PADRES
			STARTER, 5 IP

COUNT	ON BASE	OUTS
3-2	1	0

SOSA	PACE	GRIFFEY
0	162	2

FINAL: Padres 13, Cardinals 5

Cardinals' record: 2-1

364 ft.

McGwire's third home run landed in the loge reserved level just inside the left field foul pole at Busch Stadium.

five straight games and 14 consecutive series dating to the 1997 season.

The homer was McGwire's 390th, tying him with Graig Nettles for 28th on baseball's career list.

"McGwire hit a two-run home run and it didn't really hurt us that bad," said Padres right fielder Tony Gwynn, aware of the dramatics that accompanied Big Mac blasts in the Cardinals' season-opening victories over Los Angeles. McGwire also walked and struck out twice, finishing his third 1998 game with a major league-leading nine RBIs.

The homer, McGwire's fifth off lefthander Mark Langston in 50 career at-bats, put him on an every-other-game homer pace since his July 31, 1997 trade to St. Louis. Big Mac finished the day with 27 home runs in 54 games with the Cardinals.

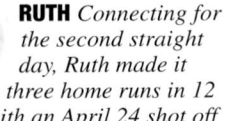

RUTH *Connecting for the second straight day, Ruth made it three home runs in 12 games with an April 24 shot off righthander Sloppy Thurston at Washington. It also was his third solo home run.*

MARIS *In his 20th game on May 6, Maris raised his unimpressive homer total to three. The fifth-inning solo blast came off Eli Grba in a game against the expansion Angels at Los Angeles.*

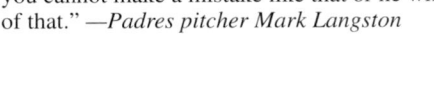 "I threw some pitches where I wanted to and some not. The one to McGwire was a changeup. I have faced him so many times, you cannot make a mistake like that or he will take advantage of that." —*Padres pitcher Mark Langston*

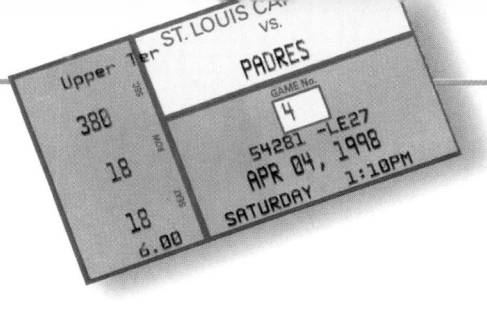

4

"I just go up there and look for the ball and try to hit it. You've got to simplify things."

—McGwire

McGwire, who pounded his way into a select power-hitting fraternity in 1997, made his first 1998 foray into exalted territory when he hit a home run in his fourth straight game, tying Willie Mays' record for consecutive homer games to begin a season.

"You put him in with Mr. Foxx and Mr. Ruth and now Mr. Mays," Cardinals manager Tony La Russa said, shaking his head. "That's serious company."

Like two of his first three homers, McGwire's shot, over the fence in left-center, was the big blow in a Cardinals' victory. It also was his first 400-foot-plus drive of the young season, a distance he soon would reach with amazing consistency. The 419-foot blast off San Diego reliever Don Wengert, a former Oakland teammate, keyed a decisive

April 4
Busch Stadium, St. Louis 34,292

AVG. **.438**	RBIs **12**	BB **5**

AT-BATS			PITCHER
1st **K**	3rd **W**	4th **1B**	**Don Wengert** PADRES RELIEVER, 0 IP
6th **HR**	7th **6-4-3**		

COUNT	ON BASE	OUTS
2-1	**2**	**0**

SOSA	PACE	GRIFFEY
1	**162**	**3**

FINAL: Cardinals 8, Padres 6

Cardinals' record: 3-1

This shot landed near the picture of the Cardinal at the edge of the left field bleachers.

five-run sixth inning.

Big Mac's season-opening outburst, which matched the homer streak compiled by a 39-year-old Mays in 1971, was enough to convince San Diego pitching coach Dave Stewart, a McGwire teammate for seven seasons in Oakland, that the best is yet to come. "I've seen him when he was not as good," Stewart said. "I've seen him when he's been good. And now you're going to get a chance to see him when he's great."

Amazingly, all of McGwire's major league-leading 12 RBIs were the result of his four home runs.

RUTH *No. 4, Ruth's third home run in four games, came in the fifth inning of an April 29 game against his old team, the Boston Red Sox. Slim Harriss was the victim of Babe's fourth straight solo shot.*

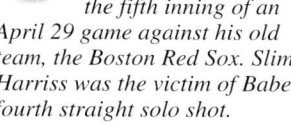

MARIS *Slowly but surely Maris inched forward, connecting for the fourth time in a May 17 game at Yankee Stadium against Washington. Maris' first lefthanded victim was Pete Burnside.*

■ "It's unbelievable. (McGwire) has a chance to hit the ball out of the ballpark every time he walks up to the plate."
—Cardinals catcher Tom Lampkin

■ "I'm glad to be in company with them (Mays, Foxx and Ruth). I think it's great. But it's just a day. I'm not going to sit back and dwell on what I've just done. I've got to think about what I'm going to do tomorrow." —McGwire

5/6/7

"He's unbelievable. No guy hits a ball like that."

—Cardinals outfielder John Mabry

All it took was some good, old-fashioned inspiration to get McGwire out of his first homerless funk of the young season. And that was provided by a 10-year-old Southern California kid who watched his dad take another giant stride in a record quest.

Matt McGwire, in from California to visit his father, spent his first night at Busch Stadium working as a batboy and watched Big Mac break an eight-game drought with three home runs against the expansion Arizona Diamondbacks.

"I tell him almost every day I talk to him that what I do in the game of baseball, I do for him," said McGwire, referring to the almost-daily phone conversations he has with his son.

But this time young Matt got a bird's-eye view of his father raking Arizona starter Jeff Suppan for third- and fifth-

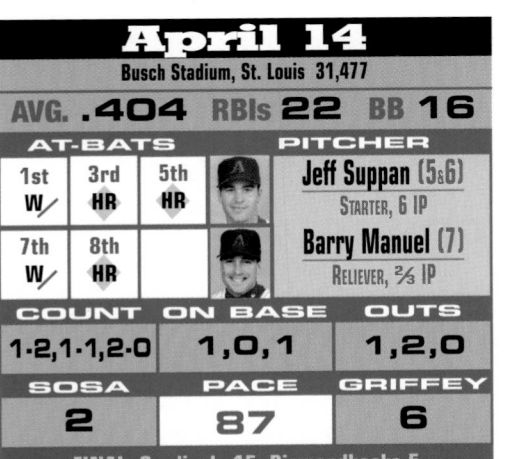

April 14
Busch Stadium, St. Louis 31,477

AVG. .404	RBIs 22	BB 16

AT-BATS			PITCHER
1st W/	3rd HR	5th HR	**Jeff Suppan (5&6)** STARTER, 6 IP
7th W/	8th HR		**Barry Manuel (7)** RELIEVER, ⅔ IP

COUNT	ON BASE	OUTS
1-2,1-1,2-0	1,0,1	1,2,0

SOSA	PACE	GRIFFEY
2	87	6

FINAL: Cardinals 15, Diamondbacks 5

Cardinals' record: 8-5

424 ft.
347 ft.
462 ft.

McGwire's first homer sailed over the visitors' bullpen, followed by shots off a pillar in left and near the giant Coke bottle in left center.

inning homers and connecting against Barry Manuel for a two-run, eighth-inning shot that helped the Cardinals pull away. The homers, which traveled 424, 347 and 462 feet, accounted for five RBIs. It marked Mac's third career three-homer game. Brian Jordan also homered and added four RBIs.

"The first year I played baseball in the big leagues, I played with Reggie Jackson," McGwire said. "He told me he always regretted that he never had a child who could watch him hit those 500 home runs."

The three-homer game was the first by a Cardinal since 1993, when Mark Whiten clubbed four against the Reds. It helped overcome a grand slam by Matt Williams, the first in Arizona's short history.

All of McGwire's first seven homers and 17 of his 22 RBIs came at Busch Stadium.

RUTH *After hitting two home runs in a May 1 game against Philadelphia, Ruth struggled through seven games before hitting his seventh homer in a May 10 game at St. Louis. The victim was Milt Gaston.*

MARIS *Homers 5, 6 and 7 were hit in consecutive games on May 19, 20 and 21. Cleveland's Jim Perry and Gary Bell and Baltimore's Chuck Estrada were the victims as Maris heated up.*

■ "I'm way past the point of something Mark McGwire does that's surprising. He's a very gifted young man who's in a perfect situation for him here. He's taking advantage of it. I hope he stays healthy." —Diamondbacks manager Buck Showalter

■ "I guess I tried to throw too hard. The thing you have to do with him is keep the ball down out of the strike zone." —Diamondbacks pitcher Jeff Suppan

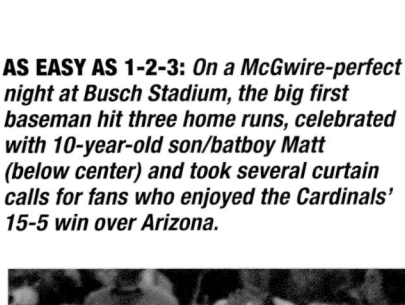

AS EASY AS 1-2-3: *On a McGwire-perfect night at Busch Stadium, the big first baseman hit three home runs, celebrated with 10-year-old son/batboy Matt (below center) and took several curtain calls for fans who enjoyed the Cardinals' 15-5 win over Arizona.*

Little Mac

One of the freshest faces to grace St. Louis' Busch Stadium in 1998 belonged to Matthew McGwire, the 10-year-old son of baseball's most revered slugger. Young Matt, who spent most of the time with his mother at their Southern California home, provided an inspiration that helped propel his father through several difficult stretches of his record-breaking season.

Young Matt, who enjoyed St. Louis so much during a 1997 visit that he encouraged his dad to re-sign with the Cardinals, made his major league debut as a batboy in an April 14 game against Arizona at Busch Stadium—after his father had endured an eight-game homer-less drought. Not only did he perform batboy functions, he became an official greeter for Big Mac on three home runs— the first of two three-homer games McGwire would enjoy in the first seven weeks of the season.

"He's just thrilled, first, to go out on the field to shag flies," Mark McGwire said of his son after a 15-5 win over the Diamondbacks. "And he got to be batboy for the first time."

Matt would don his Cardinals uniform off and on throughout the season, every time he could hook up with his father during a St. Louis visit or a Cardinals' West Coast swing. After a July 12 game in which McGwire hit two home runs, he looked at reporters and announced, "He kissed my bat." Matt had returned to his California home just prior to the game.

Coincidence or inspiration? There's little doubt Matt's presence did have a positive effect on dad. "I just feel fortunate that he is around to see me," McGwire said. "That makes it special."

8

"I've had success against him in the past. I didn't see any reason not to go right after him."

—*Phillies pitcher Matt Whiteside*

McGwire continued to give love-struck St. Louis fans every reason to remain that way when he drove a fourth-inning Matt Whiteside pitch into the bleachers in left-center field. The two-run shot broke a tie and set the stage for a victory over Philadelphia. Big Mac's league-leading eighth homer also was his eighth at Busch, where he finds the inspiration almost overwhelming.

"I love playing here," McGwire said. "It's a great baseball park. (Other players) just rave about how great it is to play here. So how can you not want to play with all the energy in the stands? It's a wonderful place."

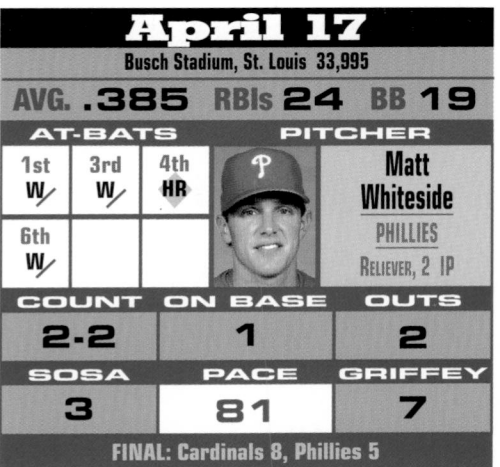

April 17

Busch Stadium, St. Louis 33,995

AVG. .385	RBIs 24	BB 19

AT-BATS		PITCHER
1st W✓	3rd W✓	4th HR
6th W✓		Matt Whiteside PHILLIES Reliever, 2 IP

COUNT	ON BASE	OUTS
2-2	1	2

SOSA	PACE	GRIFFEY
3	81	7

FINAL: Cardinals 8, Phillies 5

Cardinals' record: 10-6

419 ft.

Homer No. 8 landed high in the left field bleachers at Busch Stadium.

The numbers through nine games at Busch Stadium seemed to support McGwire's infatuation. He had a .429 average and eight homers in 28 at-bats and had outhomered several teams, including the Phillies. Since his arrival from Oakland on July 31, 1997, McGwire had 21 homers at Busch while averaging one every 5.3 at-bats.

The blast off Whiteside came with Delino DeShields at second and first base open, a situation that invariably results in a McGwire walk. But Whiteside had enjoyed success against McGwire (2-for-13, 0 homers) in his American League days and decided to take his chances.

One inning later, Ron Gant broke another tie with a three-run, pinch-hit homer that traveled 420 feet—1 foot longer than McGwire's.

RUTH *The Babe's eighth homer is a trivia footnote. The May 11 blast came off St. Louis Browns righthander Ernie Nevers, who went on to Hall of Fame glory—in the National Football League.*

MARIS *Picking up the pace, Maris connected for the fifth time in an eight-day span, this time off Boston righthander Gene Conley. The two-run homer was hit in the Yankees' 35th game.*

■ "I was looking just to drive it up the middle. It was a good pitch and I just got enough to get it out." —*McGwire*

■ "They need to start changing the measurement system for him. Using feet is getting too ridiculous. Quarter-miles would be good." —*Phillies outfielder Doug Glanville*

9

"He is definitely the premier power hitter in the game today and possibly of all time."

—Cardinals pitcher Todd Stottlemyre

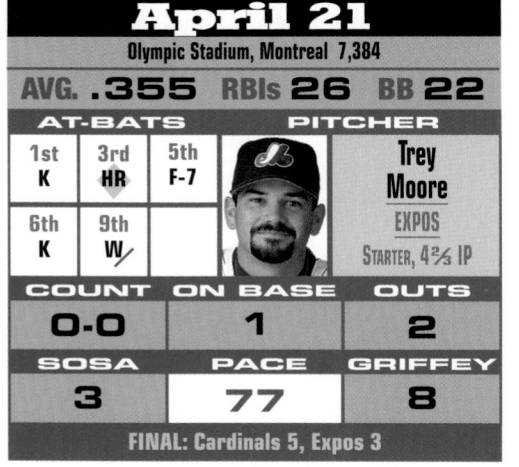

April 21

Olympic Stadium, Montreal 7,384

AVG. .355	RBIs 26	BB 22

AT-BATS			PITCHER	
1st K	3rd HR	5th F-7		Trey Moore
6th K	9th W			EXPOS STARTER, 4⅔ IP

COUNT	ON BASE	OUTS
0-0	1	2

SOSA	PACE	GRIFFEY
3	77	8

FINAL: Cardinals 5, Expos 3

Cardinals' record: 13-6

The long home run landed in the open area to the right of the seats in Olympic Stadium's left center field.

The McGwire home run show played to quiet reviews in Montreal, where only 7,384 fans were in attendance. But those who did find their way to Olympic Stadium were rewarded with a third-inning Big Mac bomb that traveled 437 feet to left-center field, giving the Cardinals a 2-0 lead.

McGwire's two-out shot off Montreal lefthander Trey Moore was his first road homer of the season and his first ever at Olympic Stadium. It also was his fifth of 400 or more feet and second-longest of the season.

"'Pops' used to say that Mantle hit the ball as far as anybody he's ever seen," said Cardinals starter and winning pitcher Todd Stottlemyre, referring to his father, former New York Yankees pitcher Mel Stottlemyre. "But I would say that Mac would put up a great argument. If somebody can hit the ball farther than Mac, I'd like to have seen him play."

Nobody could top McGwire for distance against the Expos, but teammate Ron Gant upstaged him for the second time in a week with a 414-foot homer that broke a 3-3 tie and lifted the Cardinals to a 5-3 victory.

It was Gant's third home run of the season and his third in games in which McGwire had also homered—all Cardinals' victories.

RUTH *The Babe waits until the eighth inning to contribute a solo home run in the Yankees' 9-2 victory over Detroit on May 17 at Navin Field. The victim was righthander Rip Collins.*

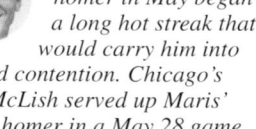

MARIS *His eighth homer in May began a long hot streak that would carry him into record contention. Chicago's Cal McLish served up Maris' ninth homer in a May 28 game at New York.*

■ "You can't hit a home run every at-bat every game. It just doesn't happen. But nobody ever writes that. They write how easy it is. That's what the national press is doing. But I like to do other things besides hitting a home run." —*McGwire*

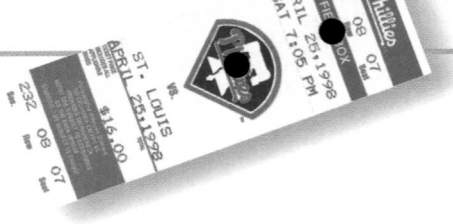

10

"I don't know what the pitch was. I was looking for anything."

—McGwire

What happens when a fastball from a 6-7, 240-pounder meets a 6-5, 250-pound swing? In the case of Philadelphia pitcher Jerry Spradlin vs. Mark McGwire, the answer was predictable—a monster 419-foot drive over the centerfield fence that capped a six-run, game-deciding rally in a victory over the Phillies.

McGwire's second road home run and his first ever at Veterans Stadium was a two-run shot that wiped out a 5-4 Phillies lead. It came off a big righthander Big Mac doesn't face with enthusiasm. "When you're that big, and

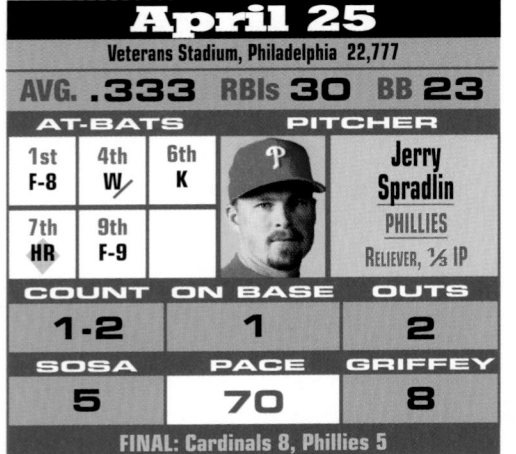

April 25

Veterans Stadium, Philadelphia 22,777

AVG. .333	RBIs 30	BB 23

AT-BATS			PITCHER
1st F-8	4th W	6th K	Jerry Spradlin PHILLIES RELIEVER, ⅓ IP
7th HR	9th F-9		

COUNT	ON BASE	OUTS
1-2	1	2

SOSA	PACE	GRIFFEY
5	70	8

FINAL: Cardinals 8, Phillies 5

Cardinals' record: 14-9

419 ft.

The ball hit the black tarp hanging in center field at Philadelphia's Veterans Stadium.

those arms and legs," McGwire said with a shake of his head. "He throws very, very hard. ... He's very tough."

McGwire, who had been homerless in 15 career at-bats at Veterans Stadium, put on quite a show for the enthusiastic Phillies fans. First he hit the ball out of the park on 20 batting-practice swings, including four drives into the upper deck. Then he provided the decisive blow during the game.

Veterans Stadium was the 28th park in which McGwire had homered, leaving Atlanta's Turner Field and New York's Shea Stadium as the only parks in which he had played without going deep.

Before the six-run seventh, Phillies starter Matt Beech, a lefthander with a career 5.58 ERA, had shut out the Cardinals on one hit.

RUTH *The methodical pace continued as Ruth connected for the 10th time, in a May 22 contest at Cleveland. The sixth-inning home run off righthander Benn Karr accounted for two Yankee runs.*

MARIS *Nearing the end of May with a bang, Maris touched off two home runs, his 10th and 11th, against Boston righthanders Gene Conley and Mike Fornieles on May 30 in a game at Fenway Park.*

■ "(The pitch) was not where I wanted it. You'd almost be surprised if he didn't hit it out." —*Phillies pitcher Jerry Spradlin*

■ "You can never be satisfied." —*McGwire, on why he took extra batting practice after the game*

CHILD'S PLAY: *Young, hopeful fans were tracking McGwire through every step of his record home run chase in baseball's dream season.*

11

"Not only is he a great player, but he's so humble. He's a gentle giant. He just takes all the hoopla in stride."

—Cubs first baseman Mark Grace

McGwire was obscured for seven innings by hard-throwing Chicago rookie Kerry Wood and a thick fog that enveloped Wrigley Field after a two-hour rain delay. But the fourth pitch from Cubs reliever Marc Pisciotta in the eighth became another notch for McGwire's growing reputation as the greatest pure power hitter since the days of Babe Ruth.

McGwire struck out twice and flied out once against the mid-90s deliveries of the 20-year-old Wood, who

April 30

Wrigley Field, Chicago 24,210

AVG. .318	RBIs 36	BB 27

AT-BATS			PITCHER
1st K	4th K	6th F-9	**Marc Pisciotta**
8th HR			CUBS RELIEVER, ⅓ IP

COUNT	ON BASE	OUTS
2-1	1	1

SOSA	PACE	GRIFFEY
6	66	11

FINAL: Cubs 8, Cardinals 3

Cardinals' record: 16-11

In a heavy Wrigley fog, McGwire hit a homer into the left center field bleachers, just in front of the chain-link fence behind the stands.

allowed only five hits and one run over seven innings. It didn't take long for McGwire to catch up with reliever Pisciotta, but his two-run, 371-foot drive over the left field wall was too little, too late.

McGwire's line drive literally disappeared into a fog that had thickened so much by the eighth inning that left fielder Henry Rodriguez could not pick the ball up and never left his position. Cardinals third baseman Gary Gaetti marveled at Rodriguez's predicament: "McGwire's ball, it could've hit him right in the face. The fog made it hard to play, but both teams had to do it."

Wood, who had been roughed up in his previous start against the Dodgers, attacked McGwire like a seasoned veteran. "I've got a lot of respect for him," Wood said, "but I didn't put too much emphasis on just him."

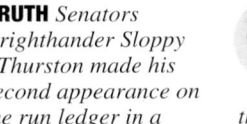

RUTH *Senators righthander Sloppy Thurston made his second appearance on Ruth's home run ledger in a May 23 game at Washington. Ruth's solo blast came in the Yankees' 34th game.*

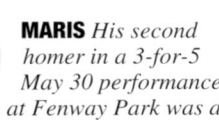

MARIS *His second homer in a 3-for-5 May 30 performance at Fenway Park was a three-run blast off Mike Fornieles in the eighth inning. His 10th and 11th homers came in the Yankees' 40th game.*

■ "Nobody hits the ball that far with an easy swing like he does. He has a short, easy swing and he's not trying to hit the ball out of the park." *—Cubs coach Billy Williams*

12

"He's a modern-day Babe Ruth. I have the ultimate respect for him. Everyone does."

—Cubs relief ace Rod Beck

Leave it to Chicago relief ace Rod Beck to put things in perspective after surrendering a two-run, ninth-inning home run to McGwire before closing out a 6-5 Cubs' victory.

"He gets paid to hit home runs and I get paid to save ballgames," Beck said. "We both did our jobs today."

Beck was more adventurous than his Chicago comrades, who pitched around the Cardinals' first baseman and the major league RBI leader (38), walking him three times as the Cubs built their lead.

Through 28 games, the ever-patient McGwire drew 30 bases on balls—putting him on a pace to break Babe Ruth's single-season walk record of 170—and compiled an impressive .484 on-base percentage. Such numbers might help the team's overall offensive production, but they were not

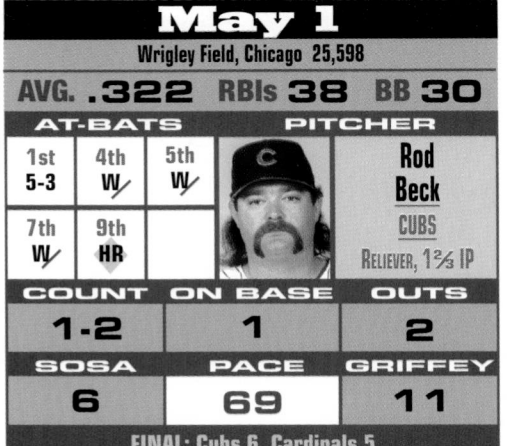

May 1		
Wrigley Field, Chicago 25,598		
AVG. .322	RBIs 38	BB 30

AT-BATS			PITCHER	
1st 5-3	4th W	5th W		Rod Beck
7th W	9th HR			CUBS RELIEVER, 1⅔ IP

COUNT	ON BASE	OUTS
1-2	1	2

SOSA	PACE	GRIFFEY
6	69	11

FINAL: Cubs 6, Cardinals 5

Cardinals' record: 16-12

362 ft.

This towering shot landed in the left center field bleachers at Wrigley Field, just in front of the chain-link fence behind the stands.

winning the favor of fans who pay to see him swing the bat.

"People don't want to see him walk," Cubs left fielder Henry Rodriguez admitted. "They want to see him swing. He's the King Kong of baseball."

McGwire's 362-foot drive into Wrigley Field's left field seats was the 399th home run of his career, leaving him one short of an exclusive club that includes only 25 other men. Even more exclusive was a Cardinals' 400-homer club that included only one player—Hall of Famer Stan Musial (475).

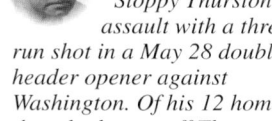

RUTH *The Babe continued his early Sloppy Thurston assault with a three-run shot in a May 28 double-header opener against Washington. Of his 12 homers, three had come off Thurston.*

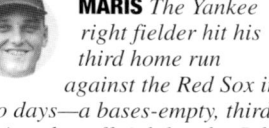

MARIS *The Yankee right fielder hit his third home run against the Red Sox in two days—a bases-empty, third-inning shot off righthander Billy Muffett in a May 31 game at Fenway Park.*

■ "I'm sure it will be special when it happens." —*McGwire, looking forward to his 400th career home run*

■ "Ray's the first guy who's ever protected me (in the lineup) my whole career. I never had anybody protect me in Oakland. I was always protecting them." —*McGwire, on Cardinals' cleanup hitter Ray Lankford*

13

"When people put my name next to Ruth's name, it still blows me away. I'm still in awe."

—McGwire

400!

McGwire carved his first major notch into the 1998 record books with a towering drive that stood up to a strong New York wind and settled into the left field seats, a paltry 358 feet from home plate and just inside the foul pole. What the home run lacked in distance and artistic merit it more than made up for with height and drama.

"I'm still not sure that ball ever came down," said Rick Reed, the Mets righthander who served up McGwire's milestone home run. "Anywhere you throw it, it's in his power."

McGwire's two-run blast, his first home run at Shea Stadium, came in the third inning with the Cardinals trailing 1-0. The ball appeared to be headed for straightaway left field, but the wind blew it toward the left

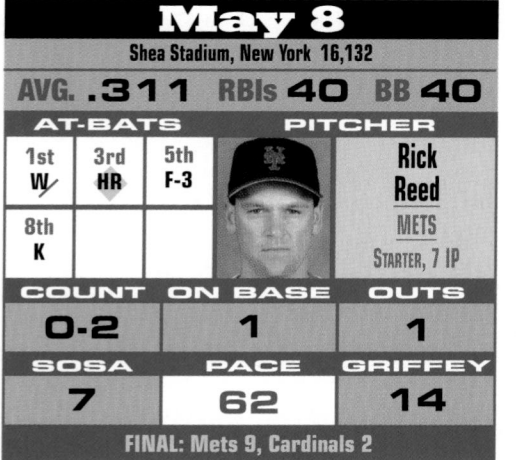

May 8
Shea Stadium, New York 16,132

AVG. .311	RBIs 40	BB 40

AT-BATS			PITCHER	
1st W/	3rd HR	5th F-3		Rick Reed
8th K				METS STARTER, 7 IP

COUNT	ON BASE	OUTS
0-2	1	1

SOSA	PACE	GRIFFEY
7	62	14

FINAL: Mets 9, Cardinals 2

Cardinals' record: 17-17

The ball landed in the seats just inside the left field foul pole at Shea Stadium.

field corner and McGwire stopped at the first base bag before getting umpire Sam Holbrook's home run signal. Big Mac's league-leading 39th and 40th RBIs were all the offense the Cardinals could muster in an otherwise disappointing loss to the Mets.

McGwire became the 26th player to reach the 400 plateau but the first to get there in fewer at-bats than Babe Ruth. McGwire achieved his milestone on at-bat No. 4,726, 128 fewer than The Bambino needed. No other player reached 400 home runs in fewer than 5,300 at-bats.

Shea Stadium became the 29th park in which McGwire had homered. That left only Turner Field, the Astrodome, Dodger Stadium, Cinergy Field and Bank One Ballpark on his N.L. hit list. McGwire had yet to play in the latter four parks.

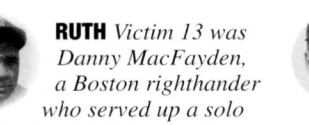

RUTH *Victim 13 was Danny MacFayden, a Boston righthander who served up a solo shot in the eighth inning of a May 29 game at Yankee Stadium. It was Ruth's second homer in as many days.*

MARIS *A heavy June home run barrage began on June 2 when Maris connected with two men on base in a game at Chicago. Maris' 13th homer was his second off White Sox righthander Cal McLish.*

■ "I don't know. I don't play the game for records. I play the game because I love it. It just happens to be a milestone." *—McGwire, on the significance of career homer No. 400*

■ "I knew I hit it well, but I didn't know if the wind was going to bring it back. It was howling. The flag was blowing straight in. When the ball left the infield, it looked as if it was dead left and it ended up over by the pole." *—McGwire*

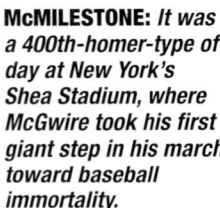

McMILESTONE: *It was a 400th-homer-type of day at New York's Shea Stadium, where McGwire took his first giant step in his march toward baseball immortality.*

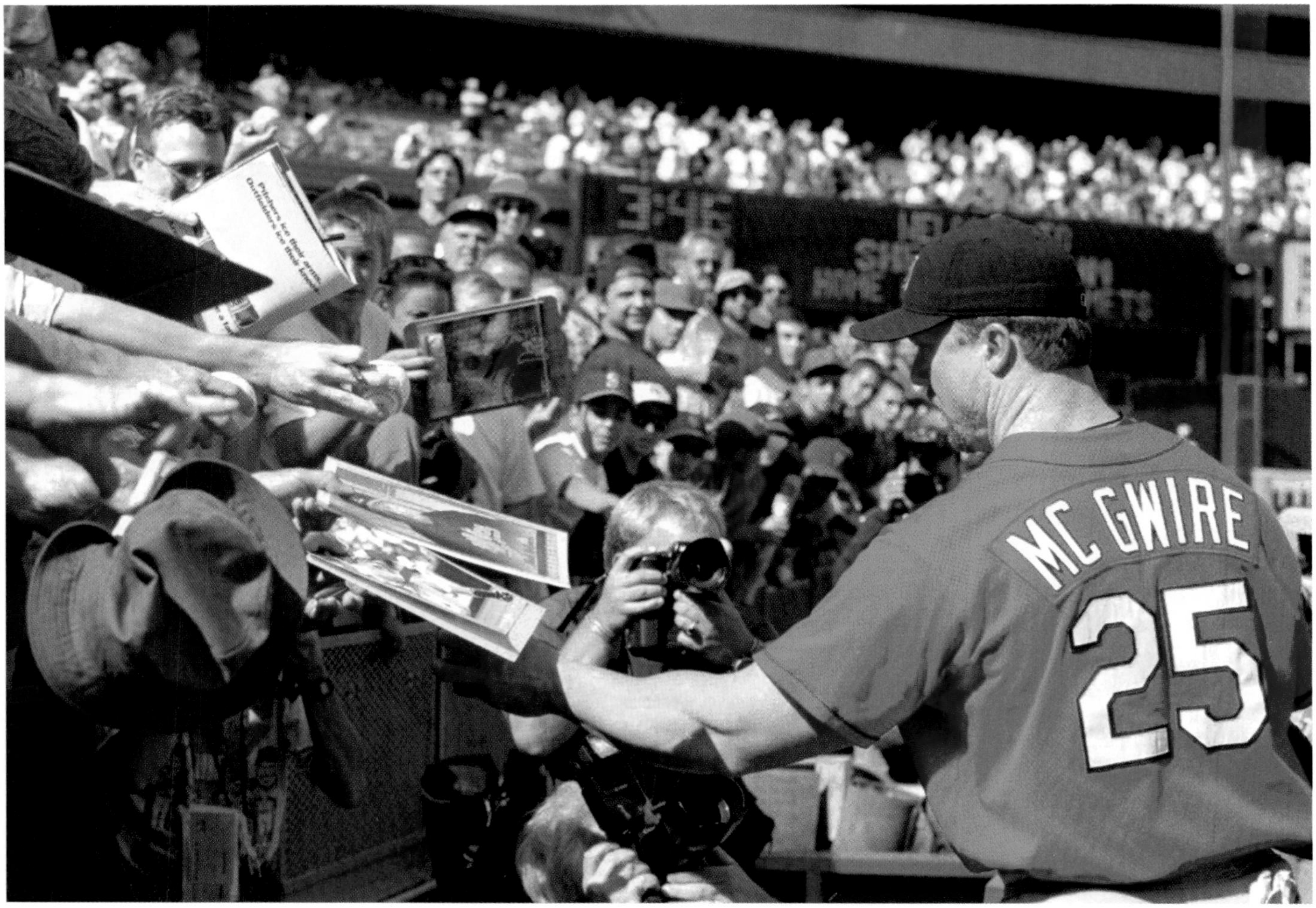

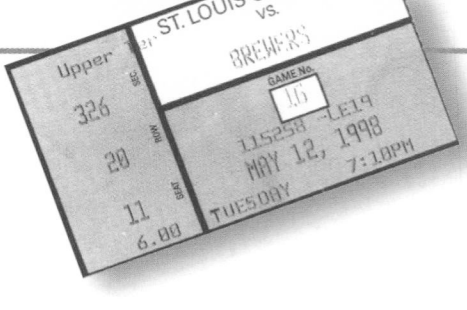

14

"If that one didn't get stopped by the bleachers, it probably would have gone in the river."

—*Cardinals teammate John Mabry*

McGwire, going where no man had gone before, sent a special-delivery missile that was retrieved by a young fan in the upper deck at Busch Stadium—the longest blow ever launched by a Cardinal or a visitor in the 32-year history of the St. Louis ballpark.

McGwire's fifth-inning, three-run blast traveled 527 feet to left-center and cleared the main scoreboard. Not only did the titanic blow stun the crowd of 25,680, it wiped out a 3-1 St. Louis deficit in a game the Cardinals would win in extra innings. The blow came off Milwaukee starter Paul Wagner, after Royce Clayton had singled and Ray Lankford had walked.

"I went to the well too many times with my fastball," Wagner said. "For him to hit it 550 feet, he must have guessed right. It was a great time for the

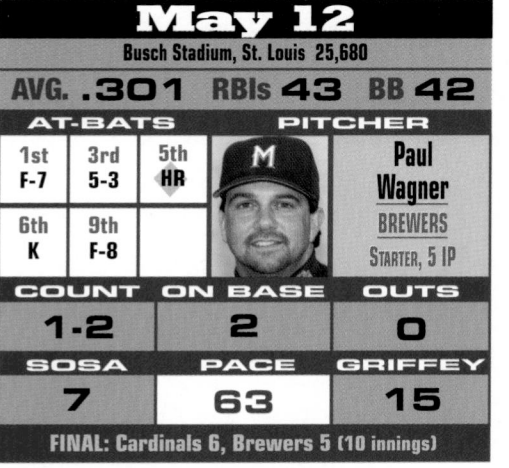

May 12
Busch Stadium, St. Louis 25,680

AVG. .301	RBIs 43	BB 42

AT-BATS / **PITCHER**

| 1st F-7 | 3rd 5-3 | 5th HR | | Paul Wagner |
| 6th K | 9th F-8 | | M | BREWERS STARTER, 5 IP |

COUNT	ON BASE	OUTS
1-2	2	0

SOSA	PACE	GRIFFEY
7	63	15

FINAL: Cardinals 6, Brewers 5 (10 innings)

Cardinals' record: 19-17

527 ft.

The longest measured home run at Busch Stadium landed in the upper deck in left center.

slider, but I stayed with the fastball."

McGwire's home run would have been another in his growing line of game-winners, but Milwaukee's Jeff Cirillo hit a two-run, ninth-inning homer that forced extra innings. A Delino DeShields 10th-inning single finally decided the issue.

The previous measured Busch Stadium distance record had been set in September 1997 by McGwire, on the memorable St. Louis day when he signed a three-year contract and then drove a pitch from Los Angeles righthander Ramon Martinez 517 feet in his first at-bat.

But Brewers manager Phil Garner remembered a Busch Stadium home run hit by Willie Stargell when they were Pittsburgh teammates.

"Those two (Mac's and Stargell's) are in another category," Garner said.

RUTH *The Bambino delivered in the 11th inning of a May 30 doubleheader nightcap at Philadelphia. The solo blast off lefty Rube Walberg, Ruth's 14th, gave the Yankees a 6-5 victory.*

MARIS *Roger's 14th homer, his second three-run blast in as many days against the White Sox, came at the expense of righthander Bob Shaw in a June 3 game at Chicago's Comiskey Park.*

■ "He has the power of three men. I've never faced anybody like him. He's a man among boys." —*Milwaukee pitcher Paul Wagner*

■ "It excites the people, but I have to look at it as one at-bat. I can't sit there and say, 'OK, great.' I have to worry about the next at-bat and worry about tomorrow." —*McGwire*

A LONG STORY: *Brewers righthander Paul Wagner fired and McGwire delivered—a mammoth 527-foot message to pitchers throughout the National League.*

15

"I don't manage (McGwire). I just tell him what time the game is and who we're playing."

—*Cardinals manager Tony La Russa*

The focus of this game was on home runs, but not of the McGwire ilk. Atlanta Braves followers would have been satisfied with just one, measly 330-footer over the left field fence—a garden variety shot

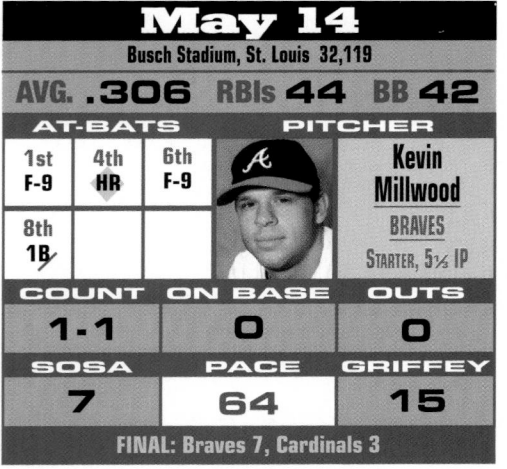

that would have enabled their team to establish a record (26) for consecutive games with at least one homer.

They didn't get it. But they were treated to an atypical home run by McGwire en route to a victory over the Cardinals.

"If we had hit a home run and lost, everybody would be dejected," Braves third baseman Chipper Jones said. "Tonight, being dominated for

May 14
Busch Stadium, St. Louis 32,119

AVG. .306	RBIs 44	BB 42

AT-BATS			PITCHER	
1st F-9	4th HR	6th F-9		Kevin Millwood
8th 1B				BRAVES STARTER, 5⅓ IP

COUNT	ON BASE	OUTS
1-1	0	0

SOSA	PACE	GRIFFEY
7	64	15

FINAL: Braves 7, Cardinals 3

Cardinals' record: 19-19

381 ft.

This unusual McGwire home run sailed into the Cardinals' bullpen—in right center.

seven innings, it was just nice to come back and win."

The Cardinals carried a 3-0 lead into the Braves' eighth, thanks in part to McGwire's fourth-inning home run—a 381-foot fly ball off Kevin Millwood that carried into the Cardinals' bullpen in right-center. It was Big Mac's first home run to the right of center field, and it gave him 23 homers in 41 career games at Busch Stadium.

Mark Petkovsek held the Braves to five hits through seven innings, but they broke through for seven eighth-inning runs against the Cardinals bullpen, winning for the 15th time in 17 games.

McGwire, who had captured national attention with his bat, showed a different side of his game in the fifth inning when he made two good plays on tricky grounders.

RUTH *The Babe finished May with a flourish, connecting in both games of a month-ending doubleheader at Philadelphia. Ruth's first-game, two-run shot, No. 15, was hit off righthander Jack Quinn.*

MARIS *After hitting his seventh homer in an eight-day span, Maris was on a roll. No. 15 was his third in as many games against the White Sox. The victim was Russ Kemmerer in a June 4 game at Chicago.*

■ "All of my success is due to hard work. I study pitchers. I spend extra time in the cage. It's an everyday process and it's made me a better, more experienced hitter. Hard work pays off. It gives me a better chance to succeed. I know that there is always someone behind you working harder, so that's what has kept me driven." —*McGwire*

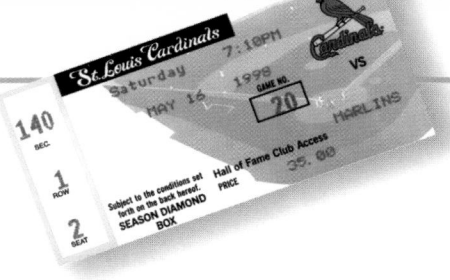

16

"They (McGwire homers) disappear and get real small, real quick. It's fortunate they only count as one run."

—Marlins manager Jim Leyland

The ball shot off his bat and soared toward the center field backdrop at Busch Stadium, instantly energizing the 41,464 fans who had hoped to witness another McGwire home run. The cheers reverberated through the stadium, and every body in every corner of the house rose in unison, straining to track an unfamiliar flight pattern.

As the ball rose up, up and away toward uncharted territory, so did the noisy din that enveloped the stadium. Ecstasy turned to disbelief when the ball, finally on a downward trajectory, banged high off the Post-Dispatch sign, just below the luxury boxes and

May 16
Busch Stadium, St. Louis 41,464

AVG. .310	RBIs 45	BB 46

AT-BATS / **PITCHER**

1st K	4th HR	5th W	Livan Hernandez
7th F-3			MARLINS STARTER, 6 IP

COUNT	ON BASE	OUTS
1-0	0	0

SOSA	PACE	GRIFFEY
8	65	15

FINAL: Cardinals 5, Marlins 4

Cardinals' record: 20-20

545 ft.

McGwire broke his own home run distance mark at Busch with a shot off a sign in center field. He had set the previous record four days earlier.

upper-deck seats that had always provided safe haven from guided missiles. Distance from home plate: 545 feet.

"It's the best ball I've ever hit," a stoic McGwire said after his team's victory over the Florida Marlins. "I don't think I can hit one better than that."

The home run, a solo shot off of 1997 World Series Most Valuable Player Livan Hernandez, was the longest drive ever measured at Busch Stadium. It was 18 feet longer than the 527-footer McGwire had stroked four days earlier against Milwaukee and 7 feet longer than his longest career blast—a 1997 homer off Seattle's Randy Johnson.

McGwire tied Colorado's Vinny Castilla for the major league homer lead, but teammate Brian Jordan secured the victory with a tie-breaking, seventh-inning homer.

RUTH *Home run No. 16 off Howard Ehmke in the second game of a May 31 doubleheader gives Ruth 11 home runs on the road. The Babe's 16 homers have been hit through 43 Yankee games.*

MARIS *A three-run homer off Minnesota righthander Ed Palmquist punctuates a four-RBI day in a June 6 game at Yankee Stadium. Maris' 16th comes in New York's 48th game.*

■ "I saw people in the upper deck ducking. You'd think a guy who has hit his longest home run would pull it. But this was to straight-away center. If he ever pulls one—and this is completely absurd—he may hit one out of the park." *—Marlins coach Rich Donnelly*

■ "If I stood at home ... and you said somebody was going to hit one in the center field upper deck, I'd have said, 'No way.' Well, I was right. He missed—by 6 inches." *—Cardinals catcher Tom Pagnozzi*

OUCH MARKS THE SPOT: *An oversized Band-Aid covers the dent on the center field sign off which McGwire bounced the longest recorded home run in Busch Stadium history. The shot off Florida's Livan Hernandez traveled 545 feet.*

17

"It's hard to believe that Babe Ruth could have hit balls higher and longer than that."

—Marlins catcher Mike Piazza

It was a case of inopportune timing.

Florida's Jesus Sanchez stopped the Cardinals on five hits over 7⅓ innings for his third win of the season, but he couldn't navigate around another gargantuan McGwire home run.

McGwire, in the midst of a stretch in which he would hit 16 homers in May, connected with the bases empty in the fourth inning—his fifth homer in nine games.

The towering drive to left hit the green facing in the upper deck at Busch Stadium, 478 feet from the plate. His 17th homer paled in comparison to the 527- and 545-foot shots he had recorded over the previous six-day span.

"I think you're seeing the guy that's probably the best power hitter in the history of the game," marveled Marlins

May 18
Busch Stadium, St. Louis 36,820

AVG. .301	RBIs 46	BB 48

AT-BATS			PITCHER
1st F-8	4th HR	6th F-9	**Jesus Sanchez** MARLINS STARTER, 7⅓ IP
8th F-9			

COUNT	ON BASE	OUTS
2-0	0	0

SOSA	PACE	GRIFFEY
8	66	16

FINAL: Marlins 7, Cardinals 3

Cardinals' record: 21-21

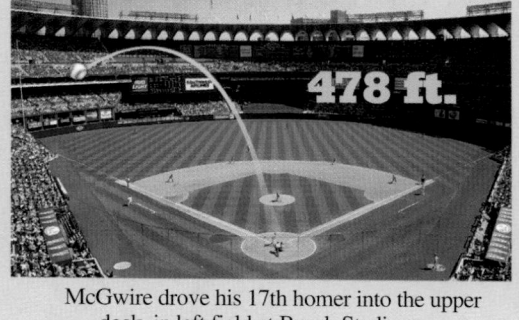

478 ft.

McGwire drove his 17th homer into the upper deck in left field at Busch Stadium.

catcher Mike Piazza. "I'm known to have hit some home runs myself, but never anything like the way he does it. I'm not even close to him. When you hear the sound as it comes off the bat, you can't believe it."

Piazza had a bird's-eye view of McGwire's memorable 517-foot shot off then-Los Angeles teammate Ramon Martinez in September 1997. Then he watched McGwire beat the Dodgers with an opening day grand slam and a 12th-inning, second-day homer to open the 1998 season. The 545- and 478-footers came after his trade to the Marlins.

Sanchez, however, got the last laugh, retiring McGwire twice. "It's good to see young pitchers like that, when they're real aggressive and go at hitters," McGwire said of the Marlins starter. "He doesn't mess around."

RUTH *Earl Whitehill of Detroit joined Rube Walberg as the only lefthanders to give up home runs to Ruth. Whitehill became a member of Babe's hit list in a June 5 game at Yankee Stadium.*

MARIS *The Maris surge continued June 7 when he drove a Pedro Ramos pitch over the Yankee Stadium fence for his second three-run homer in two days against the Minnesota Twins.*

■ "It was like a batting-practice fastball. I got good extension on it." —*McGwire*

■ "My kids play Babe Ruth League. In 15 years, it will be the Big Mac League. And a home run, from now on, shouldn't be a dinger or a bomb. It should just be a Mac." —*Marlins coach Rich Donnelly*

■ "To me, that's just a high line drive." —*Cardinals manager Tony La Russa*

18/19/20

"That's a nice way to win the game. But, hey, I'd have been just as happy if it had been a walk."

——*McGwire*

Big Mac took his batting-practice show to Philadelphia and then extended it into the game. When he was finished, the Cardinals first baseman had added three home runs and 1,362 feet to his ever-growing ledger.

McGwire's latest explosion was enough to ensure a Cardinals' victory—but just barely. The third of three tape-measure, two-run homers came in the eighth inning and provided the game-winning margin.

"I think he's only hit one this year where the game wasn't close," Cardinals manager Tony La Russa said. "He keeps hitting them in game situations."

Homer No. 1 was served up by Phillies starter Tyler Green and keyed a three-run Cardinals' third inning.

The 440-footer, which sailed over the fence in center field, was the baby of

May 19

Veterans Stadium, Philadelphia 16,541

AVG. .312	RBIs 52	BB 48

AT-BATS

1st K	3rd HR	5th HR
6th K	8th HR	

PITCHERS

Tyler Green — Matt Whiteside — Wayne Gomes
STARTER, 4⅔ IP — RELIEVER, 1⅓ IP — RELIEVER, 1 IP

COUNT	ON BASE	OUTS
2-0,0-2,0-0	1, 1, 1	1,0,0

SOSA	PACE	GRIFFEY
8	75	16

FINAL: Cardinals 10, Phillies 8

Cardinals' record: 22-21

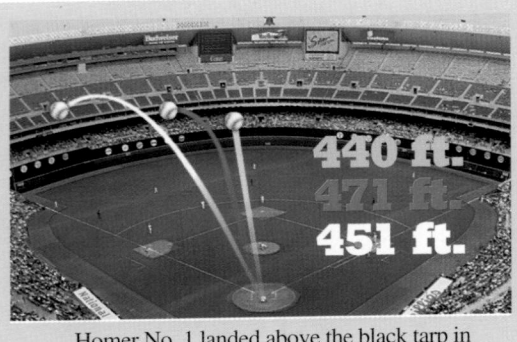

Homer No. 1 landed above the black tarp in center field; No. 2 hit the upper-deck facade; and No. 3 reached the upper deck.

Big Mac's trifecta.

McGwire's second two-run homer came in the fifth and helped the Cardinals build a five-run lead. This 471-foot bomb to center exploded in the face of reliever Matt Whiteside.

But the ultimate touch came in the eighth when McGwire sent a moonshot 451 feet into the left field upper deck on the first pitch from Wayne Gomes.

McGwire was saluted with standing ovations from the modest Veterans Stadium crowd and by his pitching victims afterward.

"Whether you're a Phillies fan or a Cardinals fan, you have to applaud the guy," Gomes said.

The outburst gave McGwire five home runs in four games and seven in eight. He became the 12th player in history to record two three-homer games in the same season.

RUTH *After hitting his 18th home run in a June 7 game against the Chicago White Sox, Ruth belted two more off Cleveland lefthander Garland Buckeye four days later at Yankee Stadium.*

MARIS *No. 18 on June 9 was followed on June 11 by Maris' second multihomer game—off Eli Grba and Johnny James at Yankee Stadium—two of the four he would hit against the expansion Angels.*

■ "He's a special player. What he did here tonight, he just kind of took it into his own hands." —*Phillies manager Terry Francona*

■ "If I came to see Mark McGwire and was sitting in the upper deck and he hit three home runs 450 feet, I might be cheering, too. I might have said, 'Wow.'" —*Phillies pitcher Wayne Gomes*

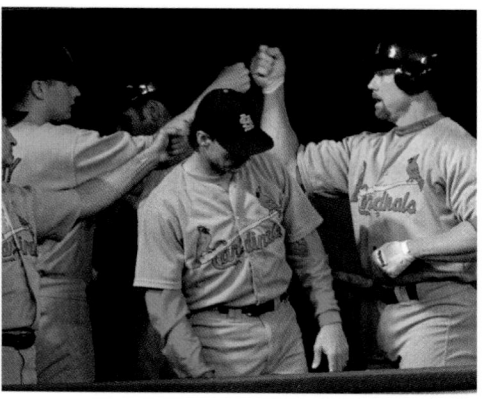

TRIFECTA: *Visions of another McGwire three-homer assault, the final of which left Philadelphia righthander Wayne Gomes (left) in a disconsolate mood. It was vintage McGwire: All three homers measured more than 400 feet.*

21

"I've never had (a Big Mac sandwich) in my whole life. ... I don't like that special sauce and all the other stuff."

—McGwire

Beanie Babies, Big Macs and a victory. McGwire's 21st home run, into the upper deck at Busch Stadium, helped complete a mammoth haul of rewards for the 47,549 fans who witnessed it.

McGwire's sixth-inning blast off righthander Mark Gardner, a two-run shot that gave the Cardinals a 2-1 lead over San Francisco on Beanie Babies night, landed in upper-deck Section 383, 425 feet from home plate.

That section is labeled "Big Mac Land" under terms of a McDonald's restaurant promotion that offers free Big Mac sandwiches to every person producing a ticket stub for a game in which McGwire homers into the specified area.

"It was a long game," said left fielder Ron Gant after delivering a game-winning single off Giants closer Robb Nen in

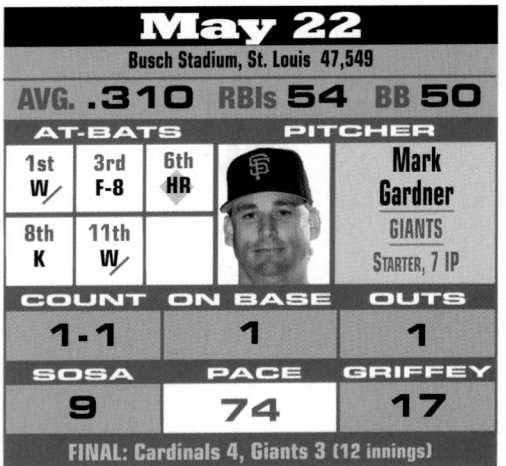

May 22
Busch Stadium, St. Louis 47,549

AVG. .310	RBIs 54	BB 50

AT-BATS			PITCHER	
1st W	3rd F-8	6th HR		Mark Gardner
8th K	11th W			GIANTS STARTER, 7 IP

COUNT	ON BASE	OUTS
1-1	1	1

SOSA	PACE	GRIFFEY
9	74	17

FINAL: Cardinals 4, Giants 3 (12 innings)

Cardinals' record: 24-22

425 ft.

McGwire crushed one into Big Mac Land, located in Busch Stadium's left field upper deck.

the 12th inning. "I'm kind of looking forward to one of those Big Macs."

The 425-foot drive was the shortest of McGwire's last six home runs and measured 3 feet shorter than the eighth-inning home run hit by teammate Ray Lankford. McGwire entered the game averaging a major league-best 421 feet per homer, and each of his previous five had traveled 440 feet or longer.

McGwire's major league-leading 21st homer would have been the game-winner if not for a dramatic two-run, ninth-inning home run by Giants' pinch hitter Bill Mueller off Cardinals reliever Jeff Brantley.

Mueller's drive, which followed a Barry Bonds double, tied the game and forced extra innings. It was Brantley's second blown save in nine opportunities.

RUTH *Three homers in two days: Ruth's latest victim was Cleveland righthander George Uhle in a June 12 game at Yankee Stadium. That gave him 21 home runs in 53 Yankee games.*

MARIS *The torrid pace continued when Maris pounded his 21st homer and his ninth in the first 13 days of June—a solo shot at Cleveland against tough righthander Jim Perry.*

■ "That was probably a short (home run) for him. I think he's locked in and he's guessing right and seeing the ball good. I don't know if it's going to last all year, but he's swinging the bat real well." —*Giants pitcher Mark Gardner*

HAMBURGER HEAVEN: *When McGwire hit Big Mac Land with a 425-foot drive against the Giants, he gave ecstatic Busch Stadium fans something to sink their teeth into.*

22/23

"At least I made *SportsCenter*."

—*Giants pitcher Rich Rodriguez*

After watching McGwire pound three home runs and lead the Cardinals past his Giants in consecutive games, San Francisco manager Dusty Baker came to a logical conclusion. "He hits the ball farther than anyone I've ever seen," Baker said.

Actually, McGwire's first home run, a bases-empty shot in the fourth inning off left-hander Rich Rodriguez, was a mini-blast by Big Mac standards—a 366-foot line drive that rocketed over the left field wall. But No. 2, a three-run homer in the fifth, was the stuff of which highlights are made. The drive off John Johnstone banged off the scoreboard in left-center, 477 feet from the plate.

The multihomer game was McGwire's third of the season and 45th of his career. And the four RBIs raised his league-

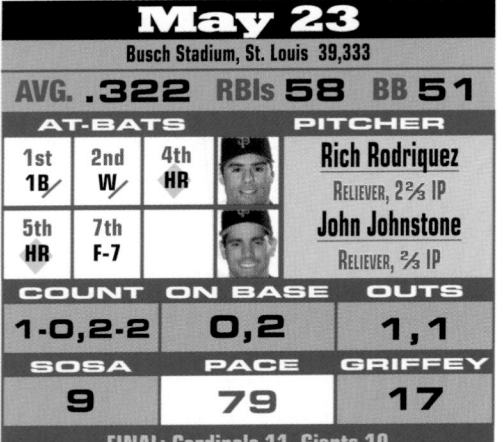

May 23
Busch Stadium, St. Louis 39,333

AVG. **.322**	RBIs **58**	BB **51**

AT-BATS			PITCHER
1st **1B**	2nd **W**	4th **HR**	**Rich Rodriquez** RELIEVER, 2⅔ IP
5th **HR**	7th **F-7**		**John Johnstone** RELIEVER, ⅔ IP

COUNT	ON BASE	OUTS
1-0,2-2	**0,2**	**1,1**

SOSA	PACE	GRIFFEY
9	**79**	**17**

FINAL: Cardinals 11, Giants 10

Cardinals' record: 25-22

477 ft.

366 ft.

McGwire's first homer landed in the loge reserved level in left field at Busch; his second bounced off the sign on the left field scoreboard.

leading count to 58. With 11 home runs in his last 13 games, he was on pace for an unlikely 79. The two home runs brought his Busch Stadium count to an almost unbelievable 28 in 47 games.

But of more importance to McGwire was the timing of his second blast, which broke an 8-8 tie and allowed the Cardinals to post a one-run victory. He was quick to point out that his battle with Johnstone was not as easy as it might have appeared.

"He made some good pitches on me," McGwire said. "I'm sitting behind in the count and I just reacted well to his slider."

The result was his seventh home run of 450 or more feet this season and his 14th over 400 feet. Two unbelievable shots topped the magical 500-foot barrier.

RUTH *Babe hit No. 22 off St. Louis lefty Tom Zachary, a name that would become prominent in his record season. But it took almost a week before he hit 23 and 24 in a June 22 doubleheader against Boston.*

MARIS *After a three-game drought, Maris started another hot streak with his 23rd home run—a bases-empty shot off Detroit lefthander Don Mossi in a June 17 game at Tiger Stadium.*

■ "I knew it was gone the minute I let it go. It was a slider that was too high." —*Giants pitcher John Johnstone*

■ "When I'm at the plate, I'm mentally locked in. This is a thinking-man's game. I don't care what anybody says. You've got to be able to use your mind. Sometimes you think right and sometimes you think wrong. But if you think wrong, you make adjustments." —*McGwire*

GIANT STRIDES: *Cardinals Brian Jordan (bottom left) and Ray Lankford (below left) provided fist-bumping partners after two more McGwire home runs—his second and third in two games against San Francisco.*

MARATHON MEN: *McGwire provided the dramatics with a 12th-inning equalizer against Robb Nen, but the Giants (above) got the last laugh in the 17th inning.*

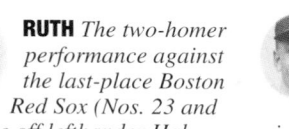

24

"Walk him. He's so locked in right now."

—Giants left fielder Barry Bonds when asked how to pitch to McGwire

When you're hot, you're hot. And not even a 98-mph Robb Nen fastball or the heavy shadows engulfing the home plate area at Busch Stadium could keep McGwire from his appointed rounds.

Big Mac, who had struck out with the bases loaded against San Francisco closer Nen in the 10th inning, was down to his final strike in the 12th when he sent a 397-foot drive into the left field seats for a two-run homer. That retied a game the Cardinals eventually would lose in the 17th.

McGwire's latest dramatic blast was set up by a Barry Bonds home run that tied the game in the ninth inning and a two-run homer by San Francisco second baseman Jeff Kent in the top of the 12th.

"None of us in the infield or outfield moved," left fielder Bonds said, referring to

May 24
Busch Stadium, St. Louis 45,864

AVG .323 RBIs 60 BB 54

AT-BATS			PITCHER
1st 1B/	3rd 5-3	5th W/	**Robb Nen** GIANTS Reliever, 2⅔ IP
7th K	9th W/	10th K	
12th HR	14th W/	17th K	

COUNT	ON BASE	OUTS
2-2	1	2

SOSA	PACE	GRIFFEY
9	81	18

FINAL: Giants 9, Cardinals 6 (17 innings)

Cardinals' record: 25-23

This one landed on the loge reserved level in left field at Busch Stadium.

McGwire's impressive home run. "The ballpark is too small for him."

The homer was McGwire's 12th in 14 games and seventh in his last five, including four against the Giants. Finally convinced that it makes little sense to play with fire, San Francisco manager Dusty Baker ordered his pitcher to walk McGwire intentionally in the 14th inning—with two out and nobody on base. It was McGwire's third intentional pass of the game.

The Giants finally ended the 5-hour, 45-minute marathon when they scored three times in the 17th inning off lefthander Kent Mercker, the sixth Cardinals pitcher and a desperation choice out of a depleted St. Louis bullpen. Mercker had worked into the ninth inning of his previous start two days earlier.

RUTH *The two-homer performance against the last-place Boston Red Sox (Nos. 23 and 24) came off lefthander Hal Wiltse in the opener of a June 22 doubleheader and keyed a New York sweep.*

MARIS *An eighth-inning, two-run shot provided the icing for a 9-0 Yankees victory June 18 at Tiger Stadium. Maris' 24th homer, off righthander Jerry Casale, came in New York's 62nd game.*

■ "Walk McGwire with nobody on? That's a legend. People will be wondering if they did that with Babe Ruth." —*Giants pitcher Orel Hershiser*

■ "Your first instinct is like, no. Then you realize it's him and you say, 'Oh well, I guess so.' He's going pretty good right now." —*Giants pitcher Jim Poole, who walked McGwire intentionally in the 14th inning*

25

"(McGwire) only hit one today. Evidently Thomson was very good."

—Cardinals manager Tony La Russa, on the work of Rockies starter John Thomson

McGwire's first-inning home run did not have much meaning in the context of a 6-1 loss to Colorado, but it did add fuel to his rise as the pre-eminent power hitter in today's game.

"It's the greatest show on Earth," said Rockies left fielder Dante Bichette. "It's fun to watch him hit."

Big Mac's 433-foot blast off righthander John Thomson bounced off the window of Busch's Stadium Club, a restaurant tucked just below the upper deck. "He probably scared the people in there," quipped Rockies right fielder Larry Walker. "They probably

May 25
Busch Stadium, St. Louis 42,038

AVG. .323	RBIs 61	BB 55

AT-BATS			PITCHER
1st HR	3rd F-3	6th F-7	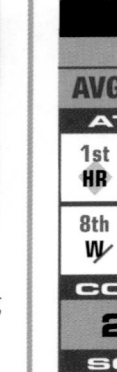 John Thomson ROCKIES STARTER, 7 IP
8th W			

COUNT	ON BASE	OUTS
2-2	0	2

SOSA	PACE	GRIFFEY
11	83	18

FINAL: Rockies 6, Cardinals 1

Cardinals' record: 25-24

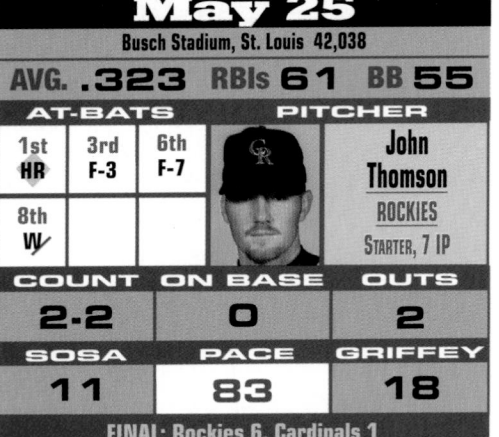

This home run ball bounced off the Stadium Club below Big Mac Land in left field.

dropped their lobster."

With the homer, McGwire became the only player in major league history to reach 25 home runs before June 1. It was his fifth homer in four games, ninth in seven and 13th in 15. It also gave Big Mac 30 homers in 49 games at Busch Stadium and a career mark of one home run every 11.60 at-bats—keeping him ahead of Babe Ruth's 11.76 pace.

McGwire's homer was the only major mistake Thomson made while working seven five-hit innings. He had entered the game with a 2-5 record and 6.47 ERA, but after allowing Mac's first-inning homer he retired him on a popup and a line drive. McGwire's homer also extended the Cardinals' team-record streak of games with at least one home run, to 17. Big Mac hit 13 of the team's 34 during that stretch.

RUTH *After an unusual nine-game drought, Ruth finally connected off Boston's Slim Harriss. Babe's 25th homer, a two-run shot, was hit on June 30 at Yankee Stadium, in the team's 70th game.*

MARIS *Continuing his relentless march, Maris pounded his 25th homer and third in as many days, off A's lefty Jim Archer, in a June 19 game at Kansas City. It was the 63rd game for the Yankees.*

■ "Sometimes guys think about the third hitter (McGwire) and forget about the first two. He's going to get his home runs, and you're not going to prevent them." —*Rockies manager Don Baylor*

■ "I'm very comfortable mentally. There's nobody who's going to get into my mind." —*McGwire*

26

"I've got to get my thesaurus out and look for synonyms for incredible. You have to be awestruck by what he's done."

——Cardinals catcher Tom Lampkin

May 29
Qualcomm Stadium, San Diego 36,648

AVG. .323	RBIs 65	BB 59

AT-BATS			PITCHER	
1st W✓	3rd K	6th K		**Dan Miceli** PADRES RELIEVER, 1 IP
8th 2B	9th HR			

COUNT	ON BASE	OUTS
0-1	1	1

SOSA	PACE	GRIFFEY
13	81	18

FINAL: Cardinals 8, Padres 3

Cardinals' record: 28-24

388 ft.

McGwire's 26th homer sailed over the palm trees that line the left center field seats at Qualcomm Stadium.

McGwire's bat continued to generate offensive headlines, but the big first baseman preferred to deflect attention toward a Cardinals pitcher after an impressive victory over San Diego.

"Petkovsek," McGwire said with a gesture toward the other side of the locker room, "had one hell of a game."

Big Mac was referring to righthander Mark Petkovsek, who shut out the Padres on four hits over eight innings while raising his record against them to 7-0. The Padres' runs were scored in the ninth inning, two on Greg Vaughn's 17th homer.

"If they flashed a stat like that about someone else, you'd say, 'Man, he's got their number,'" Petkovsek said. "But when it comes to yourself. ..."

Petkovsek's shutout pitching was in danger of going for naught after seven innings because San Diego starter Joey Hamilton was strangling the Cardinals' offense as well. But then McGwire and company broke the game open.

McGwire keyed a six-run Cardinals eighth with a two-run, bases-loaded double. He then drove an 0-1, ninth-inning pitch from Dan Miceli over the fence in left-center, after Delino DeShields had reached on an error. It was Big Mac's first homer in three games but his 10th in an 11-game span. The four RBIs raised his major league-leading total to 65.

RUTH *Homer No. 26 was delivered off Senators righthander Hod Lisenbee in a July 3 game at Washington. Lisenbee would go on to finish his best career season with an 18-9 record.*

MARIS *After hitting a homer in his fourth consecutive game, Maris stood at 26 through 64 games. The first-inning solo shot came in a June 20 at-bat against Kansas City lefty Joe Nuxhall.*

■ "It's really unbelievable what he's done with all the pressures he has to endure every day." —*Cardinals manager Tony La Russa*

■ "What he's done is unbelievable, because he hardly knows the pitchers in this league." —*Cardinals coach Carney Lansford*

FLIGHT PATTERN: *Young St. Louisans Phillip Hunt (yellow shirt) and Ryan Klippel watch home run No. 25 hit the Stadium Club at Busch Stadium—a 433-footer on the Big Mac charts.*

27

"I didn't know how good I hit it until it was gone."

—McGwire

May 30
Qualcomm Stadium, San Diego 54,089

AVG. .324	RBIs 66	BB 60

AT-BATS			PITCHER	
1st **HR**	3rd **W/**	5th **F-9**		**Andy Ashby**
8th **K**				**PADRES** STARTER, 9 IP

COUNT	ON BASE	OUTS
0-1	0	2

SOSA	PACE	GRIFFEY
13	83	18

FINAL: Padres 3, Cardinals 2

Cardinals' record: 28-25

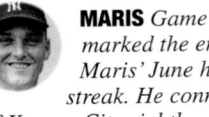

423 ft.

For the second straight game, Mac's left center field blast cleared the palm trees that line the outfield wall at Qualcomm Stadium.

The McGwire home run parade continued when he drove a first-inning pitch from San Diego starter Andy Ashby 423 feet over the fence in left-center. As the accolades piled up, so did the incredible statistical asides.

The home run gave Big Mac 16 for the month of May, a Cardinals' single-month record. It gave him 11 homers in his last 11 games and 15 over a 19-game span. After shattering the major league record for most home runs by the end of May, McGwire needed only five more to claim the June mark. But most of the talk about McGwire's feats still focused on quality over quantity.

"A guy that strong and the way he's swinging the bat, I mean he got the best of it," said Ashby after surrendering McGwire's 16th 1998 homer of 400 feet or better. Ashby issued McGwire's 60th walk in the third, got him on a fly ball in the fifth and retired him on a called third strike as the leadoff batter in the eighth inning with the Cardinals leading 2-1.

"I wasn't going to lay one in there," Ashby said. "Lord willing, it worked out that way that one didn't come back across the plate. He got me once and I got him once."

In the end, the Padres got the Cardinals by scoring an unearned ninth-inning run.

RUTH *Detroit right-hander Don Hankins served up Ruth's 27th home run in the nightcap of a July 8 doubleheader at Navin Field. The three-run shot propelled the Yankees to a 10-8 win.*

MARIS *Game No. 66 marked the end of Maris' June hot streak. He connected off Kansas City righthander Norm Bass in a June 22 game and brought to completion a run of nine homers in 12 games.*

■ "Any time a guy is that big, he kind of blocks out the sun. But any time you keep him in the ballpark the way he's swinging the bat, it's a moral victory." *—Padres pitcher Kevin Brown*

■ "He hits them out of sight. You can see mine." *—Cardinals outfielder Ron Gant*

28

"I knew Big Mac was going to play. He may have a bad back, but there is nothing wrong with his bat."

—Giants manager Dusty Baker

It didn't take long for the McGwire express to regain top speed after three days of preventive maintenance. After sitting out three games to keep minor back spasms from becoming a long-term problem, Big Mac made an agile defensive play in the top of the first against San Francisco and then hit a 409-foot home run in the bottom of the inning.

The two-run shot over the center field fence off Orel Hershiser validated Cardinals manager Tony La Russa's decision to put McGwire in the lineup after watching him drill several tape-measure homers in batting practice. The homer was all the offense the Cardinals could muster en route to a third consecutive loss, which dropped them a game below .500.

"It's not like I planned on having a break," McGwire said after hitting his 18th Busch

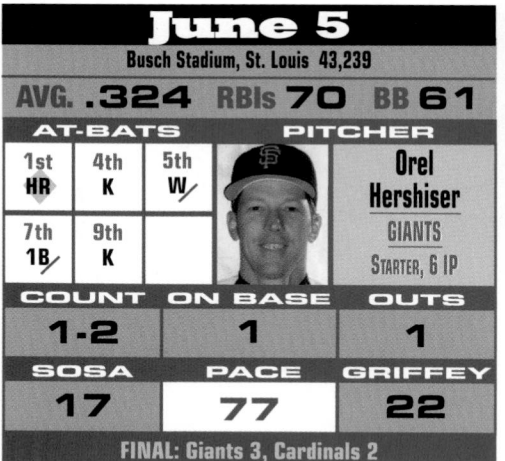

June 5
Busch Stadium, St. Louis 43,239

AVG. .324	RBIs 70	BB 61

AT-BATS			PITCHER
1st HR	4th K	5th W/	Orel Hershiser
7th 1B/	9th K		GIANTS STARTER, 6 IP

COUNT	ON BASE	OUTS
1-2	1	1

SOSA	PACE	GRIFFEY
17	77	22

FINAL: Giants 3, Cardinals 2

Cardinals' record: 29-30

409 ft.

This home run landed in the first row of bleachers behind the Cardinals logo in left center field.

Stadium home run, a Cardinals season record at Busch. "But sometimes they're good for you."

McGwire felt a twinge in his back while grounding out during a game at San Diego and immediately put himself on the shelf. The development was reminiscent of back problems that have cost him major chunks of seasons past.

But he looked healthy enough against the Giants, also drawing his eighth intentional walk and smashing a drive off the left field wall that netted him only a single.

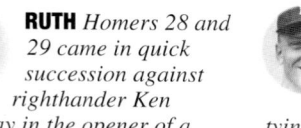

RUTH *Homers 28 and 29 came in quick succession against righthander Ken Holloway in the opener of a July 9 doubleheader at Detroit. This was the fourth multihomer game of the season for Ruth.*

MARIS *After seven homerless games, Maris resumed his march with a game-tying shot in the ninth inning of a July 1 game vs. Washington. Mickey Mantle followed with a game-ending homer.*

■ "I was a little too arrogant in thinking that I could get him out on that slider. I should have set him up better first." —*Giants pitcher Orel Hershiser*

■ "It's a mind game. If you say to yourself you're going to be slow, you're going to be slow. This game is mental and I was mentally prepared today." —*McGwire*

'A glimpse inside The Chase'

"Excuse me, Mark. I'm a writer. Can I have some of your time for a story I'm doing?"

It began tamely, though regularly. A steady parade that was maybe a nuisance at times, since so many of the reporters' questions got to be the same, about why he stayed in St. Louis instead of pursuing free agency, and whether anyone could break Roger Maris' record, and what he thought of as he ran the bases after a home run.

A nuisance like the incessant ring of the doorbell on Halloween. And then another ring. And another. But McGwire kept giving out the candy with a smile.

McGwire always had been a relatively shy man, and he couldn't understand what more there was to say about hitting home runs.

Understanding how miserable it had made Maris in 1961, he and the Cardinals decided it was best to organize the growing mob of reporters into a little party. The team would arrive in a new town and on the first day, McGwire would show up with a cup of coffee and lean against a wall in a hallway or the dugout or some out-of-the-way empty room at the stadium. Informally, he would answer many of the same questions he'd been answering since early March.

There would be five reporters, eight, a dozen. There soon would be 20, 25.

As the home runs piled up and the crush of bodies seemed to suffocate at times, the pressure to turn his daily job into an all-out pursuit of a record became more intense. Yet he knew he couldn't make it go away.

So he tried to laugh, joke, reveal a little of himself while protecting so much more. Reporters came looking for treats. He let them through the door, but they couldn't walk around and get anything more than what he dished out.

McGwire tried to keep his talks informal, even though he finally had to sit at a table in front of the 100 or so who wanted a glimpse inside The Chase.

And McGwire never seemed to run out of candy.

29

"They ought to charge people just to watch this."

—Utah Jazz basketball star Karl Malone, after watching McGwire's batting practice

As McGwire home runs kept sailing out of major league parks at a record pace, personal milestones provided little consolation for baseball's top gate attraction.

"We've been coming up short the last six games," he said after the Cardinals had lost their first 1998 interleague game, to the Chicago White Sox. "Nothing's clicking. It's not great and it's not fun. I don't care how you do individually, if you don't win as a team, it doesn't matter."

June 8
Comiskey Park, Chicago 23,087

AVG. .323	RBIs 73	BB 66

AT-BATS			PITCHER	
1st F-7	4th HR	6th 4-3		**Jason Bere**
7th F-5				WHITE SOX STARTER, 6 IP

COUNT	ON BASE	OUTS
0-0	1	0

SOSA	PACE	GRIFFEY
20	76	24

FINAL: White Sox 8, Cardinals 6

Cardinals' record: 29-33

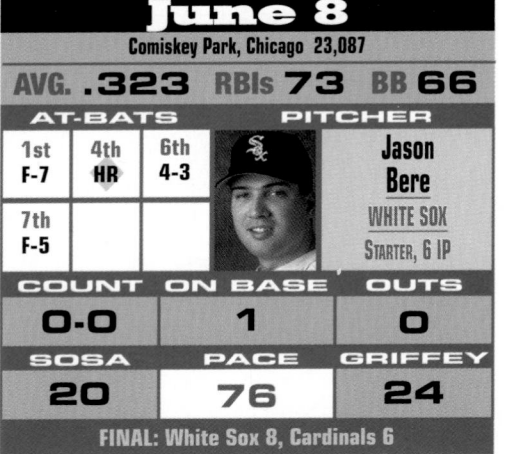

356 ft.

This towering fly ball barely cleared the wall and landed in the open area in front of Comiskey Park's left field seats.

In what had become a familiar 1998 routine, McGwire put on a batting-practice show, then homered in the game, but the Cardinals lost.

The defeat was their ninth in 10 games, dropping them to nine games behind the Chicago Cubs and Houston, co-leaders in the N.L. Central Division.

Big Mac's towering drive off Jason Bere in the fourth inning settled into the left field seats, a comparatively compact 356 feet from the plate. The two-run homer was his second shortest of the season.

It cut the Cardinals' deficit to 3-2, and they tied the game on a John Mabry homer an inning later before a five-run Chicago fifth broke it open. McGwire's home run was his eighth at new Comiskey Park and 12th overall against the White Sox in Chicago. It also brought his league-leading RBI total to 73.

RUTH *Babe's two-homer barrage against Ken Holloway fueled the Yankees' 19-run outburst in the opener of the team's July 9 doubleheader against the outmanned Detroit Tigers.*

MARIS *For the second straight day, Maris went 3-for-5 vs. Washington, and he spiced his July 2 effort with two home runs. The first, his 29th, came off Pete Burnside, a three-time victim in '61.*

■ "McGwire's probably the top home run threat in baseball. He must be seeing the ball very well." *—White Sox pitcher Jason Bere*

■ "He makes the place electric. Fans jump to their feet just to see him hit one. Players also, but not the opposing manager." *—White Sox manager Jerry Manuel*

30

"He hits the ball every day where you say, 'Wow, look at that one.' You never get tired of watching it, either."

—Cardinals third baseman Gary Gaetti

The routine was becoming disgustingly familiar, and McGwire wasn't in any mood to discuss home runs. The Cardinals blew a four-run, ninth-inning lead, lost to the Chicago White Sox in 11 innings, and then tried to come to grips with their seventh loss in eight games and 10th in 12.

"Absolutely meaningless," McGwire said, referring to his three-run, third-inning blast off White Sox rookie Jim Parque that helped the Cardinals storm to a 7-0 lead. "You take a two-, three-, four-run lead into the ninth inning, you have to win those games."

June 10
Comiskey Park, Chicago 16,151

AVG. .320	RBIs 76	BB 68

AT-BATS | **PITCHER**

| 1st K | 3rd HR | 5th W/ | **Jim Parque** |
| 7th 4-3 | 9th K | 11th W/ | **WHITE SOX** STARTER, 5 IP |

COUNT	ON BASE	OUTS
1-0	2	1

SOSA	PACE	GRIFFEY
20	76	25

FINAL: White Sox 10, Cardinals 8 (11 innings)

Cardinals' record: 30-34

409 ft.

The ball sailed just a few feet over the center field fence at Comiskey Park, landing in the open area behind the outfield wall.

With the help of McGwire's 409-foot drive into the center field backdrop at Comiskey Park, the Cardinals carried an 8-4 lead into the ninth. But Chicago's Albert Belle hit his second three-run homer of the game and Robin Ventura followed with a bases-empty shot that forced extra innings. Ventura's second homer, a two-run blast in the 11th, gave Chicago an unlikely victory.

McGwire's 18th homer in a 27-game span allowed him to reach the 30 plateau for the ninth time. It was the result of curious strategy by Chicago manager Jerry Manuel, who refused to take the normal course by walking Big Mac with runners on second and third and one out. The three RBIs lifted McGwire's N.L.-leading total to 76 and kept him on pace to top Hack Wilson's single-season record of 190.

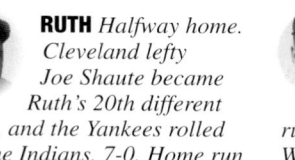

RUTH *Halfway home. Cleveland lefty Joe Shaute became Ruth's 20th different victim, and the Yankees rolled past the Indians, 7-0. Home run No. 30 came in the team's 83rd game on July 12.*

MARIS *The third multihomer game of Maris' season was punctuated by a two-run, seventh-inning blast off Washington's Johnny Klippstein. On July 2, after 75 games, he was halfway to 60.*

■ "I can remember over in the American League when they were saying if there was something up, he can't catch up with it. And you could pitch him there. But not any longer. You pitch McGwire up and you're going to allow more home runs than if you pitch him down." —*Cardinals manager Tony La Russa*

31

"He's a part of the game we should be proud of. There's something there people want to see."

—Diamondbacks manager Buck Showalter

McGwire reached the halfway point of his record-breaking home run quest the same way he started it—with a grand slam that keyed a Cardinals' victory. But until he had crossed the plate and performed his arm-bumping ritual with celebrating teammates, he didn't even realize what he had done.

"I don't want to be ignorant, but I didn't know it was a grand slam," McGwire said after helping the Cardinals post only their second win in nine games. "I was into trying to really mentally prepare myself against Andy (Benes) because he got me out the first time, so I wasn't aware of who was on base—and I guess maybe it helped me out."

McGwire's 438-foot blow into the seats in left-center at Arizona's Bank One Ballpark came off former teammate

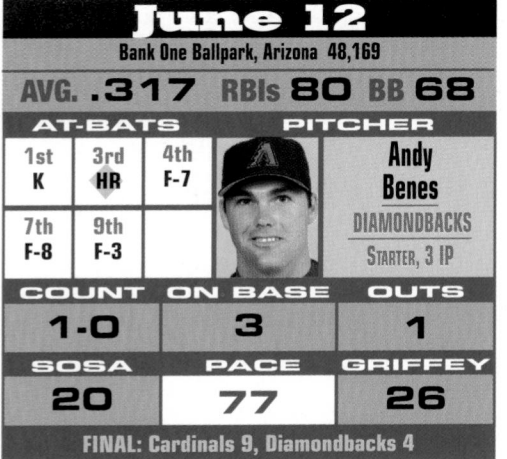

June 12

Bank One Ballpark, Arizona 48,169

AVG. .317	RBIs 80	BB 68

AT-BATS			PITCHER	
1st K	3rd HR	4th F-7		Andy Benes
7th F-8	9th F-3			DIAMONDBACKS STARTER, 3 IP

COUNT	ON BASE	OUTS
1-0	3	1

SOSA	PACE	GRIFFEY
20	77	26

FINAL: Cardinals 9, Diamondbacks 4

Cardinals' record: 31-34

438 ft.

McGwire hit his 31st homer deep into the seats in left center at Bank One Ballpark.

Benes, who had struck him out in the first inning. Benes, who was projected as the ace of the Cardinals' 1998 staff, chose instead to sign a big free-agent contract with the Diamond-backs in February.

The homer keyed an eight-run, third-inning uprising that also included a three-run homer by shortstop Royce Clayton, who scored two runs in the inning. McGwire's 11th career grand slam also was his 15th home run in 20 games.

Not only did the 48,169 fans get to see a memorable home run, many were present for a batting-practice wallop that landed on a ledge above the American flag in left-center field and bounced through a window onto Jefferson Street—the first ball to be hit out of the new park. The ledge is 483 feet from home plate and 89 feet above the field.

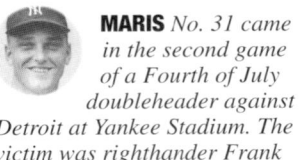

RUTH *White Sox righthander Tommy Thomas became a two-time victim when he served up Ruth's 31st home run, a third-inning solo shot, in a July 24 game at Chicago's Comiskey Park.*

MARIS *No. 31 came in the second game of a Fourth of July doubleheader against Detroit at Yankee Stadium. The victim was righthander Frank Lary, who would go on to post a 23-9 record in 1961.*

■ "The fans got to see what they wanted to see. I didn't see what I wanted to see. Maybe it took their attention away from a bad outing for me. It's just bad pitches and bad results." —*Diamondbacks pitcher Andy Benes*

■ "It's overwhelming. I've never seen it. I don't think any other baseball player has seen it." —*McGwire, on the intense fan interest engulfing him*

FLIGHT OF PHOENIX:
Big Mac's first visit to Bank One Ballpark attracted the usual expectant fans and featured his second grand slam of the season—this one off former teammate Andy Benes.

32

"They're showing batting practice on TV. ... They were broadcasting it play-by-play in Phoenix. Now that's psycho."

—McGwire

On a night in which they registered one of their most dramatic wins of the season, the Houston Astros felt the full impact of the McGwire phenomenon.

Many of the 37,147 fans who earlier had witnessed McGwire's major league-leading 32nd homer departed after his ninth-inning at-bat and didn't see the Astros rally with four ninth-inning runs.

"I understand that a lot of people come out to see Mark McGwire, but they should be out here to see the Houston Astros play the St. Louis Cardinals," said Astros first baseman Jeff Bagwell, who contributed a two-run homer to the winning rally. "For them to leave after Mark's last at-bat, I wouldn't say it was a slap in the face, but unfortunately for them, they missed a good inning."

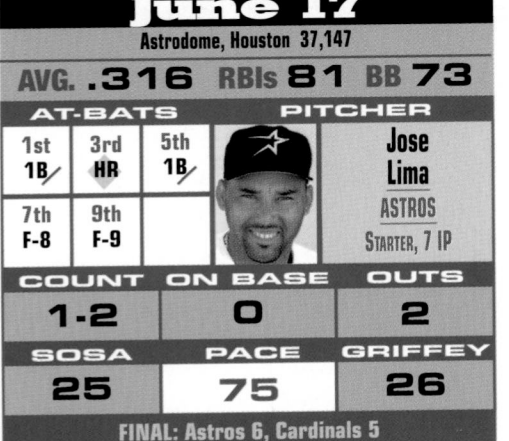

June 17
Astrodome, Houston 37,147

AVG. .316	RBIs 81	BB 73

AT-BATS — **PITCHER**

1st 1B	3rd HR	5th 1B
7th F-8	9th F-9	

Jose Lima
ASTROS
STARTER, 7 IP

COUNT	ON BASE	OUTS
1-2	0	2

SOSA	PACE	GRIFFEY
25	75	26

FINAL: Astros 6, Cardinals 5

Cardinals' record: 33-36

347 ft.

A low line drive cleared the top left corner of the Astrodome scoreboard in left field.

McGwire had helped the Cardinals build a 5-2 lead with a third-inning drive over the scoreboard in left. The 347-footer off righthander Jose Lima, which equaled McGwire's shortest of the season, broke a 12-at-bat homerless streak and was his first at the Astrodome.

But it wasn't enough to save the Cardinals, who slid further behind the division-leading Astros. Houston rallied against Jeff Brantley and Curtis King. "You can't describe what it feels like to lose this game," Cardinals manager Tony La Russa said.

 **RUTH** *The first of two July 26 home runs off righthander Milt Gaston came in the opener of a doubleheader against the St. Louis Browns at Yankee Stadium. It was Ruth's 11th first-inning homer.*

MARIS *Maris hit his 32nd home run in a July 5 game against Cleveland, the 78th game of the season for the Yankees. Frank Funk, a righthander, served up the seventh-inning blast.*

■ "If I hit a home run and we don't win, it doesn't matter. When you have a chance to be in two games and climb the ladder, especially against a team like Houston, it's really tough to lose one like this." —McGwire

■ "He's putting fans in the stands. They come to see him hit. Our job is to win and strike him out. He can keep putting fans in the seats and we can keep winning." —Astros outfielder Carl Everett

33

"He's the same as Aaron, Ruth or Williams. You've got to throw good stuff on the corners. Anything else is unacceptable."

—Astros manager Larry Dierker

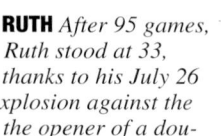

McGwire didn't want to discuss long home runs, but the one he hit into the fifth deck of the Astrodome had longtime Houston baseball watchers scratching their heads. The left field solo shot was measured at 449 feet, but most observers thought that figure was conservative.

"This was three outstanding games for us," said McGwire, deflecting talk toward the Cardinals' win, which gave them two of three vs. the Astros. "This is what baseball is all about. I just want to play baseball. I play this game for one reason—to win."

After relenting on his

June 18

Astrodome, Houston 43,806

AVG. .317	RBIs 82	BB 75

AT-BATS			PITCHER
1st 5-3	3rd W/	5th HR	**Shane Reynolds** ASTROS STARTER, 4⅓ IP
7th W/	9th F-9		

COUNT	ON BASE	OUTS
1-1	0	0

SOSA	PACE	GRIFFEY
25	76	27

FINAL: Cardinals 7, Astros 6

Cardinals' record: 34-36

This mammoth drive sailed into the left field upper deck at the Astrodome.

previous day's threat to stop taking batting practice because of the circus it had become, McGwire deposited 14 practice balls into the Astrodome seats, including four in the upper deck. He then ripped what might have been the longest home run in the history of the stadium. The fifth-inning shot, combined with home runs by Ron Gant and Ray Lankford, helped the Cardinals build a lead they never relinquished.

McGwire received a standing ovation from 43,806 fans as he rounded the bases. The homer was his sixth of the month and gave him the distinction of hitting more home runs than any player in history before the end of June.

That his homer apparently was mismeasured was the least of Big Mac's worries. "So be it," he said. "You don't win a prize for it."

 **RUTH** *After 95 games, Ruth stood at 33, thanks to his July 26 explosion against the Browns in the opener of a doubleheader. Milt Gaston became the fourth pitcher to serve up two homers in a game to him.*

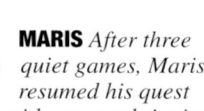 **MARIS** *After three quiet games, Maris resumed his quest with a seventh-inning homer off Bill Monbouquette in the opening game of a July 9 doubleheader against Boston at Yankee Stadium.*

■ "It (the June home run record) is a great honor, but I can't sit back and think about it. You've got to think about tomorrow. You don't have time to think about what you've done." —*McGwire*

Some days are better than others

McGwire's road to baseball's home run record was not traveled without some bumps and unexpected turns.

There were stretches when the remarkable consistency he exhibited through most of the season gave way to the angst suffered by any man on a mission.

After opening the season with four home runs in four games, the Cardinals first baseman struggled through an eight-game drought that ended with a three-homer purge against the Arizona Diamondbacks.

There were other slow times, but not many. One was a five-game homerless stretch between his June

18 homer at Houston and the 433-foot shot he hit at Cleveland off Jaret Wright June 24. And there was the early August slump that allowed Sammy Sosa to pull back into the home run chase.

But the frustration, the hard looks and the angst always ended with another home run barrage.

34

"I thought when he hit it, 'This ball is going to knock down the parking garage (behind the scoreboard).'"

—Indians manager Mike Hargrove

Five games and 18 at-bats after hitting home run No. 33, McGwire ended one of the longest droughts of his season with a 433-foot drive off Cleveland starter Jaret Wright. The ball fell just short of the massive Jacobs Field scoreboard in left field, but it looked short and unimportant on the scoreboard.

"It's really insignificant," McGwire said, after watching the Indians score seven runs in a marathon first inning en route to a lopsided victory. "We got a good butt-whipping today."

McGwire connected with the bases empty in the fourth inning, cutting the Cardinals' deficit to 7-1. The majestic fly ball settled just short of the scoreboard that only McGwire had reached during a regular-season game. He received a standing ovation from the sellout crowd of 43,321 as he circled the bases. Big Mac was removed

June 24
Jacobs Field, Cleveland 43,321

AVG. .316	RBIs 83	BB 78

AT-BATS / **PITCHER**

1st 1B	4th HR	6th F-4	Jaret Wright
			INDIANS STARTER, 6⅓ IP

COUNT	ON BASE	OUTS
1-1	0	1

SOSA	PACE	GRIFFEY
31	72	30

FINAL: Indians 14, Cardinals 3

Cardinals' record: 38-38

433 ft.

This home run landed near the top of the left field bleachers, just below the Jacobs Field scoreboard.

from the game in the sixth inning of a 12-2 blowout and, ironically, Brian Hunter, his replacement, stepped to the plate with the bases loaded in the seventh.

"So if McGwire hits a grand slam it's 12-7. So what?" Cardinals manager Tony La Russa told inquiring reporters. "We've been talking about needing to give Mark a day off between now and Monday, when we're off. What this means is, he can play now."

The homer was McGwire's 29th against the Indians, including 19 in Cleveland and eight at Jacobs Field. It brought back memories of the 485-foot rocket he hit off righthander Orel Hershiser in a 1997 game. That homer, which dented a beer advertisement on the scoreboard, was the longest in Jacobs Field history.

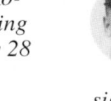 **RUTH** *Babe's two-run, eighth-inning homer in a July 28 game at Yankee Stadium helped the Bronx Bombers complete a four-game sweep of the Browns. Lefty Stewart was the victim.*

 **MARIS** *A July 13 home run off Early Wynn at Chicago carried extra significance because it was the only one Maris would hit off a future Hall of Famer. No. 34 came in New York's 84th game.*

■ "They're an outstanding team. When you give them a seven-run first inning, your backs are really against the wall." —McGwire

■ "If there's one guy in baseball who we want to do it, it's him. It's truly a pleasure to watch him, to watch how he handles himself. He's such a gentleman." —Indians first baseman Jim Thome

35

"I feel sorry for Burba. But I enjoyed this one as much as Hershiser's. It's amazing to see a ball travel that far."

—Indians shortstop Omar Vizquel

Cardinals fans trying to find a bright side to two one-sided losses in Cleveland needed look no further than the massive Jacobs Field scoreboard—more specifically, a steel support crossbeam connected to the structure.

"It makes your stomach feel funny when he hits them," said Indians manager Mike Hargrove, referring to the first-inning, 461-foot McGwire blast that struck the beam and bounced back onto the field, eluding the grasp of straining fans. "They just go so far and so high. I'd pay to watch him hit."

The homer, which gave the Cardinals a temporary 1-0 lead, was the second-longest ever hit at The Jake—24 feet shorter than the acclaimed 485-foot drive McGwire bounced off the scoreboard vs. Orel Hershiser in 1997. Only the beam, positioned between the left field foul pole and the scoreboard,

JUNE 25

Jacobs Field, Cleveland 43,309

AVG. .320	RBIs 84	BB 78

AT-BATS / **PITCHER**

1st HR	4th 1B/	6th F-2	Dave Burba
8th F-6			INDIANS
			STARTER, 7⅔ IP

COUNT	ON BASE	OUTS
2-2	0	2

SOSA	PACE	GRIFFEY
32	74	30

FINAL: Indians 8, Cardinals 2

Cardinals' record: 38-39

461 ft.

McGwire's towering blast hit the crossbeam that supports the Jacobs Field scoreboard in left field.

kept it from leaving the 5-year-old ballpark. It was McGwire's ninth homer at The Jake, more than any other visiting player.

"I thought it was foul," said Indians righthander Dave Burba. "I looked in for a new ball and Sandy (Alomar) was just staring. I never saw the ball. Apparently, it went pretty far."

McGwire was typically unimpressed by his latest strongman feat. "I just don't like losing," he said. "I'm sort of disappointed in the way it went here."

The two-game series was viewed by 86,630 Cleveland fans who were exposed to the best of both worlds—two long McGwire home runs as well as two routs by the Indians.

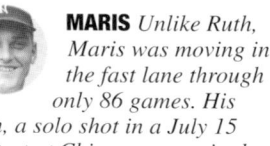

RUTH *A struggling Ruth finally broke his seven-game homer drought with an August 5 smash off Detroit righthander George Smith. With 35 homers in 106 games, Ruth needed to pick up his pace.*

MARIS *Unlike Ruth, Maris was moving in the fast lane through only 86 games. His 35th, a solo shot in a July 15 contest at Chicago, came in the third inning against righthander Ray Herbert.*

■ "(McGwire) is like the Empire State Building standing there with a bat in his hands. Words can't describe how good he is—to keep doing it day after day with the media pressure. I would have liked to see Ruth and him in the same era." —*Indians first baseman Jim Thome, who hit two home runs in the game*

■ "It's just not good losing. I don't think anybody enjoys it. We get on a roll, and then we come up to a brick wall. It's just not fun." —*McGwire*

36

"He's not just a power hitter, he's a great hitter. I had him 0-2 and he battled. He made it happen."

—Twins pitcher Mike Trombley

June 27
Metrodome, Minnesota 35,002

AVG. .313	RBIs 86	BB 79

AT-BATS			PITCHER
1st K	4th F-7	6th W✓	**Mike Trombley** TWINS RELIEVER, 1⅔ IP
7th HR	9th F-8		

COUNT	ON BASE	OUTS
2-2	1	2

SOSA	PACE	GRIFFEY
32	74	31

FINAL: Cardinals 7, Twins 2

Cardinals' record: 39-40

431 ft.

Fans in the left center field seats at the Metrodome swarmed to catch McGwire's 36th home run ball.

The McGwire home run and batting practice parade, weaving its way through major league ballparks throughout the country, was getting rave reviews as he maintained his record pace approaching the All-Star break. And Big Mac seemed a bit stunned by the emotional reaction of crowds in opposing ballparks.

"This has never happened to me and I don't know if it's happened to anybody else," he said after his 36th homer, at the Minneapolis Metrodome, was greeted by a roar that grew to a crescendo from 35,002 pumped-up Twins fans. "But it's a great feeling and I wish every ballplayer could feel the way I feel."

McGwire's seventh-inning blast, a towering 431-foot, two-run shot to left-center, extended a 4-1 Cardinals' lead and helped gain a much-needed victory. It was Big Mac's 60th home run in 124 games with the Cardinals and only his second hit in 10 career at-bats vs. the Twins' Mike Trombley.

The Cardinals ended a four-game losing streak and won for the first time ever at the Metrodome—site of their seventh-game World Series loss to the Twins in 1987. McGwire's 36th home run tied him for most by a Cardinals player since Hall of Famer Stan Musial hit that many in 1949.

RUTH *Snapping a three-game hitless skid, Ruth pounded his 36th homer, a three-run, third-inning shot off Senators lefty Tom Zachary in an August 10 game at Washington's Griffith Stadium.*

MARIS *After a five-game homer drought, Maris returned to form with a solo blast in a July 21 game at Boston. For the second time in two weeks, righthander Bill Monbouquette was the victim.*

■ "It amazes me. It's overwhelming. It's almost like I'm sort of speechless. What do you say? Basically, thank you." —*McGwire, on the reaction he was getting from opposing fans*

■ "The best thing going now in baseball is Mark McGwire. Baseball needs it. I think it's a great thing. The fans ought to be applauded for recognizing that he's got a chance to do something special every time he steps to the plate." —*Cardinals pitcher Todd Stottlemyre*

37

"It's pretty awesome. I'm sure we'll read all about it tomorrow."

—Cardinals third baseman Gary Gaetti

Kansas City lefthander Glendon Rusch shudders at the thought of giving up home runs, but he had to appreciate the one McGwire hit into the upper deck at Busch Stadium in an otherwise forgettable Cardinals loss. The blast was so majestic that the fireworks signaling a Cardinals' home run ignited even before the ball settled into the crowd.

"It was impressive," said Rusch, who had shut out the Cardinals for six innings before McGwire gave one of his fastballs a 472-foot ride. "I turned around and watched, just like everybody else did."

June 30
Busch Stadium, St. Louis 41,801

AVG. .319	RBIs 87	BB 79

AT-BATS			PITCHER
1st 2B⟩	4th 1B/	7th HR	**Glendon Rusch** ROYALS
9th 5-3			STARTER, 7⅔ IP

COUNT	ON BASE	OUTS
0-1	0	0

SOSA	PACE	GRIFFEY
33	74	33

FINAL: Royals 6, Cardinals 1

Cardinals' record: 39-42

472 ft.

This upper-deck home run landed on the Busch Stadium walkway behind and to the right of Big Mac Land.

The blast tied Reggie Jackson's record for home runs before the All-Star break—but in a lot fewer games. Jackson had 37 in 92 games for Oakland in 1969; McGwire's 37th came in the 81st game—with five games remaining before the midsummer classic. Jackson went on to hit only 10 more the rest of the season.

True to form, McGwire chose to focus on the Cardinals' sixth loss in seven games and dismal 3-8 interleague record, the worst in baseball. "You just hope that something clicks," he said. "Sometimes you think, 'What is it?' and then all of a sudden the next thing you know, you're on a 10-game winning streak. Anything can happen at any given time."

The homer was McGwire's 32nd in 60 career games at Busch Stadium.

RUTH *The Babe connected for a third time off White Sox righthander Tommy Thomas in an August 16 game at Chicago's Comiskey Park. The bases-empty homer ended a three-game homerless streak.*

MARIS *The biggest day of Maris' season began with a fourth-inning homer off Chicago lefty Frank Baumann in the opener of a July 25 doubleheader. He would hit three more before the day was over.*

■ "It says a lot when a guy's pitching a shutout against you and that's the only run you get. He's done it a lot of times against really good pitching. The pitch that he hit was no mistake—a fastball kind of up and on the inner part of the plate. That ties up a lot of hitters, but he hits it 400 feet." —*Cardinals manager Tony La Russa*

■ "McGwire is so focused and locked in right now, it's unbelievable. He may disagree, but I see him hit a ball out of the ballpark on *SportsCenter* every night." —*Royals manager Tony Muser*

McGwire shorts out in the All-Star homer contest

Everybody came to see Mark McGwire, but what they got was Ken Griffey Jr. That's not a bad consolation prize.

The event was baseball's annual home run-hitting contest, and the thought of McGwire lining up pitches in the rarefied air of home run-friendly Coors Field was enough to make expectant fans drool with delight. But as McGwire and his batting practice pitcher struggled to get in sync, other All-Stars took center stage.

Big Mac managed only four home runs on 14 swings and delivered only one of his trademark moonshots. But Griffey, a last-minute contest entry, hit several upper-deck drives en route to eventual victory.

McGwire was hitless in two at-bats in the All-Star Game the next day.

38

"I feel all right. I've just been a millimeter off. There hasn't been a guy alive who's been on all year. I'm human."

—McGwire

With the Houston Astros hovering above the pack in the National League Central Division, it was a bit easier for them to appreciate some good, old-fashioned drama at their expense.

"I don't like losing, but for a Cardinal fan, it doesn't get any more exciting than that," said first baseman Jeff Bagwell. "Extra innings. Team down by a run, man on base. Mark McGwire coming up against a guy throwing 98 miles per hour. That's classic."

So was the 485-foot bomb that exploded off his bat and landed above the Big Mac Land section of seats just inside the left field foul pole in Busch Stadium's upper deck. The distance seemed conservative, prompting Astros closer Billy Wagner, Mac's latest victim, to roll his eyes and suggest, "Somebody up

July 11
Busch Stadium, St. Louis 45,760

AVG. .306	RBIs 89	BB 91

AT-BATS			PITCHER
1st K	4th F-3	6th 1-3	**Billy Wagner**
9th W/	11th HR		ASTROS
			RELIEVER, ⅓ IP

COUNT	ON BASE	OUTS
0-2	1	1

SOSA	PACE	GRIFFEY
35	69	37

FINAL: Cardinals 4, Astros 3 (11 innings)

Cardinals' record: 42-47

485 ft.

This game-winning homer sailed into Busch's left field upper deck near Big Mac Land.

there can't count."

McGwire's first home run in eight games came in the bottom of the 11th inning, after the Astros had taken a 3-2 lead on Bill Spiers' bases-loaded sacrifice fly. McGwire pounded an 0-2 Wagner fastball clocked at 97 mph, sending the packed house of 45,760 into a wild celebration.

"Right at contact, I knew it was gone. It was the easiest swing I had all day," said McGwire, who had gone 21 at-bats without a homer, his second-longest drought of the season. In that stretch, Big Mac was walked 12 times and hit by a pitch.

Before ending Wagner's streak of 19 consecutive successful save chances, Big Mac had struck out, fouled out, grounded out and walked—his major league-leading 91st base on balls of the season.

RUTH *The Babe made No. 38 a dramatic one, connecting off Chicago righthander Sarge Connally in the 11th inning of an August 17 game at Comiskey Park. The homer gave New York a 3-2 win.*

MARIS *His second home run in the opener of the July 25 doubleheader was hit off former Yankee World Series hero Don Larsen, now with the White Sox. No. 38 was hit in the team's 95th game.*

■ "He hit the tar out of that ball. I looked up and I couldn't find it. I thought it was out of the stadium." —*Astros closer Billy Wagner*

■ "He had gone 20 or so at-bats without hitting one, so you knew he was about to explode on somebody. I was hoping we could sneak out of here before it happened." —*Astros first baseman Jeff Bagwell*

ST. LOUIS CARDINALS VS. ASTROS

Upper Ter
382
20
7
6.00

GAME No.
43
265125 -LE35
JUL 12, 1998
SUNDAY 1:10PM

39/40

"You've got to get that family of four out of the left field seats before he kills somebody."

—Astros second baseman Craig Biggio

Rejuvenated by his dramatic July 11 homer that beat Central Division-leading Houston, McGwire pounded two more in a series-ending victory over the Astros and became only the third player to reach the 40 plateau in the long history of the Cardinals franchise.

Big Mac connected for solo blasts off Sean Bergman, in the first inning, and rookie Scott Elarton, in the seventh. Both homers were 400-footers that easily cleared the left field wall. In reaching the 40-homer plateau for the fifth time, McGwire joined Rogers Hornsby (42 in 1922) and Johnny Mize (43 in 1940) as the only Cardinals to reach that figure. Stan Musial, the franchise's career home run leader, could do no better than 39 in 1948. No one in baseball history had reached the 40 mark in fewer at-bats

July 12
Busch Stadium, St. Louis 45,485

AVG. .310	RBIs 91	BB 92

AT-BATS | **PITCHER**

| 1st HR | 3rd K | 4th W/ | **Sean Bergman** STARTER, 5 IP |
| 7th HR | | | **Scott Elarton** RELIEVER, 2 IP |

COUNT	ON BASE	OUTS
0-0,2-1	0,0	2,0

SOSA	PACE	GRIFFEY
35	72	37

FINAL: Cardinals 6, Astros 4

Cardinals' record: 43-47

The first homer was a line drive off the back wall of the visitors' bullpen in left field; the second landed in the seats behind the bullpen wall.

405 ft.
415 ft.

(281) than McGwire.

"To have my name pass those is remarkable," McGwire said. "For somebody who never thought he would play in the National League. ... I'm very proud to be with those guys and surpass them."

McGwire attributed his surge to 10-year-old son Matt, an occasional Cardinals batboy who gave his dad a special good-luck present before leaving St. Louis for his home in Southern California prior to the game. "He kissed my bat," a smiling McGwire told reporters. "The last time he kissed it, I hit three home runs."

McGwire, who moved past Hall of Famer Billy Williams into 23rd place on the career home run list with 427, also was issued his major league-leading 19th intentional walk and 92nd overall.

RUTH *Babe's 40th homer, his second in three days, was not enough to keep the Yankees from dropping their fourth straight game to the Indians, a 9-4 loss on August 22 at Cleveland.*

MARIS *Chicago's Russ Kemmerer and Warren Hacker served up 39 and 40 in the nightcap of a July 25 twin bill, completing Maris' four-home run day. His homers accounted for seven runs.*

■ "Sixty-four (homers) in 135 games (as a Cardinal). He's a pretty good pickup." —*Cardinals manager Tony La Russa*

■ "I've not been around too long, but the home run he hit off me was the most impressive thing I've seen in my major league career." —*Astros pitcher Scott Elarton*

■ "The first two games he didn't swing the bat very well. He's swinging pretty good now." —*Astros manager Larry Dierker*

GOING, GOING, GONE:
McGwire connects with a Sean Bergman pitch, the first of two home runs he would hit in a July 12 game against the Houston Astros at Busch Stadium.

41/42

"You're not going to see a more beautiful swing on a home run than the first one. That was classic."

—Cardinals manager Tony La Russa

Two strikes, two more home runs. McGwire was the picture of efficiency as he keyed a Cardinals' victory over the Los Angeles Dodgers and kept his express rolling toward baseball's single-season home run record.

McGwire jumped on the first pitch from Brian Bohanon in the opening inning and connected with a 1-0 Antonio Osuna pitch in the eighth—the only strikes he would see during a game in which he drew his 98th and 99th walks. "I swung the bat twice tonight," McGwire said, "and I hit two home runs."

The first was a massive shot to left center that landed midway in the upper deck and was measured at 511 feet. The fourth-longest homer in Busch Stadium history (McGwire also hit the other three) was his fourth off Bohanon in nine big-league at-bats.

"It was early in the game and I wanted to challenge him," Bohanon said. "I made a bad pitch and he hit it out. ... We've got a history together. He's a guy I've struggled against."

So Bohanon took measures to make sure it wouldn't happen again.

"He got me in the first at-bat, and in the second at-bat I decided I wasn't going to let him hit," he said. "I decided to take my chances with (Brian) Jordan. I hate doing that, but I felt like it was the best situation."

McGwire's eighth-inning shot, which traveled 425 feet to left, completed his fifth multi-homer effort of the season and the 48th of his career. It also tied him with Hall of Famer Rogers Hornsby for most home runs in a season by a righthanded-hitting Cardinal.

July 17
Busch Stadium, St. Louis 39,191

AVG. **.306**	RBIs **93**	BB **99**

AT-BATS			PITCHER
1st **HR**	4th **W/**	6th **W/**	**Brian Bohanon** STARTER, 5⅔ IP
8th **HR**			**Antonio Osuna** RELIEVER, 2 IP

COUNT	ON BASE	OUTS
0-0, 1-0	0,0	2,1

SOSA	PACE	GRIFFEY
36	72	39

FINAL: Cardinals 4, Dodgers 1

Cardinals' record: 44-51

511 ft.
425 ft.

The first home run hit the upper-deck walkway in left center; the second landed in the left field seats below the Stadium Club.

RUTH *No. 42 was served up by lefty Ernie Wingard in an August 28 game at St. Louis. Wingard would go on to finish the season at 2-13, the worst record of any of Ruth's 1927 victims.*

MARIS *After hitting his 42nd home run in an August 11 game at Washington, Maris still trailed Yankees teammate Mickey Mantle (44) in the American League home run race.*

■ "I don't diagnose things like that. You see it and you swing. I'm not a player that sits around and diagnoses a swing." —*McGwire*

■ "He hits my fastball, he hits my changeup, he hits my curveball. ... With the power he has, Yellowstone ain't going to hold him." —*Dodgers pitcher Brian Bohanon*

DEEP, DEEP THOUGHTS: *By mid-July, McGwire was marching relentlessly toward his date with destiny. This two-home run performance against the Los Angeles Dodgers included a 511-foot bomb off shellshocked lefthander Brian Bohanon (above left).*

43

"McGwire is probably the strongest power hitter of all time."

—*Padres manager Bruce Bochy*

Something about San Diego seems to bring out the best in McGwire, who grew up in the Los Angeles area and played collegiate baseball at USC. "Southern California. It's like coming home," he said after collecting four hits and his major league-leading 43rd home run in a romp past the Padres.

With son Matt watching from the dugout, Big Mac hit a two-run shot off Brian Boehringer that landed in Qualcomm Stadium's second deck, 458 feet from home plate in left-center field. The four-hit night lifted his 1998 average against the Padres to .429, with

July 20
Qualcomm Stadium, San Diego 32,339

AVG. .311	RBIs 96	BB 103

AT-BATS			PITCHER	
1st 1B✓	3rd 1B✓	5th HR		Brian Boehringer
7th 1B✓	8th W✓			PADRES
				Reliever, 3⅓ IP

COUNT	ON BASE	OUTS
2-1	1	0

SOSA	PACE	GRIFFEY
36	71	39

FINAL: Cardinals 13, Padres 1

Cardinals' record: 46-52

458 ft.

The ball sailed into the left center field seats of Qualcomm Stadium's second deck.

five homers and 15 RBIs in eight games. Three of the homers came in San Diego.

"We've matched up with them pretty well through all the games we've played," McGwire said after the Cardinals had snapped San Diego's five-game winning streak. "We haven't won all of them, but we've been in every game."

The homer allowed Big Mac to tie Johnny Mize's single-season record for homers by a Cardinal. Mize hit 43 in 1940. Ray Lankford added a grand slam and Royce Clayton homered and tripled, giving the top three batters in the lineup nine hits, with three homers, nine RBIs and seven runs scored. McGwire's home run opened up some breathing room between him and fellow record-chasers Ken Griffey (39) and Sammy Sosa (36).

 **RUTH** *On the last day of August, Ruth connected off Boston righthander Tony Welzer. With 43 home runs in 127 Yankee games, the Bambino would need a big September finish.*

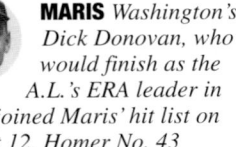 **MARIS** *Washington's Dick Donovan, who would finish as the A.L.'s ERA leader in 1961, joined Maris' hit list on August 12. Homer No. 43 pulled him to one behind A.L. leader Mickey Mantle.*

■ "There's no doubt he's a guy you can't make any mistakes against." —*Padres pitcher Mark Langston*

■ "I was sitting on the pitch and got hold of it. When you anticipate and get a good swing on it, you can drive it a long way." —*McGwire*

44

"The home run he hit was a slider. ... He's hit a lot of home runs. That's just his game."

—Rockies pitcher John Thomson

After he had seriously considered taking the day off, McGwire wrote a new page in the Cardinals' record book with a gargantuan 452-foot blast that gave 48,288 expectant fans at Colorado's Coors Field exactly what they had come to see.

Big Mac, who was struggling through an 0-for-16 slump that included the first two games of the Rockies series, drove a fourth-inning pitch from Colorado righthander John Thomson over the left field bleachers. The homer moved him past Hall of Famer Johnny Mize as the most prolific single-season slugger in the Cardinals' long history. Mize

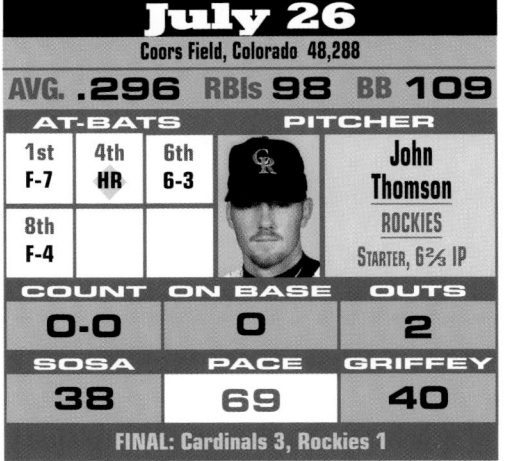

July 26
Coors Field, Colorado 48,288

AVG. .296	RBIs 98	BB 109

AT-BATS			PITCHER
1st F-7	4th HR	6th 6-3	John Thomson
8th F-4			ROCKIES
			STARTER, 6⅔ IP

COUNT	ON BASE	OUTS
0-0	0	2

SOSA	PACE	GRIFFEY
38	69	40

FINAL: Cardinals 3, Rockies 1

Cardinals' record: 49-55

McGwire's 44th home run, which cleared the left field bleachers at Coors Field, was caught by a fan in front of the concession stand.

posted his team-record 43 home runs in 1940.

"I would have loved to have had the day off today. But look what happened. I ran into one," said McGwire, who had played 18 straight games since the All-Star break. "I was dead. I should have had an off day sometime during this road trip, but we didn't do it. Sometimes a day off goes a long way. ..."

Johnny Mize

Thomson had retired 11 straight Cardinals when McGwire broke a scoreless tie, jump-starting a St. Louis victory.

It was his only hit of the night and his first home run at long ball-friendly Coors Field in six 1998 games. He had hit four in four games there after his 1997 trade to the Cardinals.

RUTH *Philadelphia lefty Rube Walberg, bringing out the best in Ruth for the fourth time, served up home run No. 44 as the September assault began during a 12-2 Yankees' victory.*

MARIS *Another multihomer day. His 44th came in the opener of an August 13 doubleheader at Washington and added righthander Bennie Daniels to Maris' ever-growing hit list.*

■ "I'm just learning the history of the Cardinals. I was stuck on the West Coast for 11 years and didn't really know much about the history of the Cardinals, but now I do and I'm happy to be a part of it." —*McGwire, after setting the team single-season home run record*

■ "You'd better go talk to those pitchers over there who don't throw me many strikes. You guys think they put it on a tee for me, and they don't." —*McGwire, explaining his recent slump*

45

"He can hit it anywhere in this ballpark against any type of pitching."

—Cardinals manager Tony La Russa, on McGwire's opposite-field homer

In a game that featured eighth- and ninth-inning grand slams and another blown ninth-inning lead by the Cardinals, McGwire's bases-empty, opposite-field homer was more of an aside. But that doesn't mean it went unnoticed.

The 36,812 McGwire-hungry fans at Busch Stadium took great delight when he drove a pitch from Milwaukee reliever Mike Myers 408 feet to right-center field, completing the Cardinals' scoring in a five-run eighth inning.

Ray Lankford, the batter preceding McGwire, had given the Cardinals a 9-8 lead with a grand slam.

But the Brewers countered with their own rally. The big hit against reliever Rick Croushore in their five-run ninth inning was a grand slam by late-inning defensive replacement Darrin Jackson. It

July 28
Busch Stadium, St. Louis 36,812

AVG. **.300**	RBIs **100**	BB **110**

AT-BATS			PITCHER
1st 1B/	3rd SF-8	6th W/	**Mike Myers** BREWERS Reliever, 0 IP
7th F-7	8th **HR**		

COUNT	ON BASE	OUTS
2-2	**0**	**1**

SOSA	PACE	GRIFFEY
41	**69**	**40**

FINAL: Brewers 13, Cardinals 10

Cardinals' record: 49-56

408 ft.

The ball landed in the right center field seats, just to the left of the Cardinals' bullpen.

marked the seventh time the Cardinals had blown a lead in the ninth inning.

"We were down after those two home runs," Brewers manager Phil Garner said, "but you wouldn't believe how up we were after Darrin's hit."

McGwire's homer was his 25th at Busch Stadium, which tied a team record for home runs at home. Johnny Mize hit 25 of his 43 homers at St. Louis' Sportsman's Park in 1940. McGwire also had a third-inning sacrifice fly and finished the day with 100 RBIs. One walk lifted his major league-leading total to 110.

"I don't want to talk about (the home run)," a subdued McGwire said after the ninth-inning collapse. "This is the way the year's gone. If you want to be a playoff-contending team, you have to win those games."

RUTH *The Babe heated up in a September 6 doubleheader, a splurge that would catapult him toward 60. No. 45 came in the sixth inning of the opener, vs. Boston's Tony Welzer.*

MARIS *After homering in both games of an August 13 doubleheader at Washington, Maris was tied with teammate Mickey Mantle atop the major league home run charts.*

■ "Mark has such discipline of mind. ... He's doing great, he's concentrating great. He doesn't need anyone to give him incentive, he doesn't need a target number. He's really got the perfect focus." —*Cardinals manager Tony La Russa*

■ "I know it's tough. Everybody in baseball knows it's tough. I'm just going to give it my best shot." —*McGwire, on hitting home runs*

SLAMMED: *McGwire's 45th home run made a rare appearance in right-center field, but the Brewers got the last laugh in a game that featured two grand slams and a five-run, ninth-inning rally.*

46

"There are more important things to worry about than Mark McGwire hitting home runs. Let's talk about the game."

—McGwire

After seeing his formerly comfortable major league home run lead shrink to two during a season-high 29 at-bat drought, McGwire connected in the fourth inning against Chicago righthander Mark Clark.

But Sammy Sosa, the Cubs right fielder who had taken advantage of Big Mac's slump to close the gap in the homer chase, delivered an in-your-face response with a game-tying, ninth-inning homer. That set the stage for a wild ending to another classic game in the long series between archrivals.

Sosa, who had trailed McGwire 44-38 after games of July 26, continued his surge with a two-run shot off Rick Croushore to force extra innings. The Cubs took leads in both the 11th and 12th innings, but Cardinals Ray Lankford and Eli Marrero answered each

August 8
Busch Stadium, St. Louis 48,064

AVG. .288	RBIs 103	BB 119

AT-BATS / **PITCHER**

1st F-8	4th HR	6th W
7th W	9th W	11th K
13th W		

Mark Clark
CUBS
STARTER, 6⅓ IP

COUNT	ON BASE	OUTS
2-1	0	0

SOSA	PACE	GRIFFEY
44	65	41

FINAL: Cardinals 9, Cubs 8 (13 innings)

Cardinals' record: 55-60

374 ft.

This home run barely reached the first row of Busch Stadium's loge reserved level in left field.

time with tying home runs off closer Rod Beck. Lankford, who had struck out five times in the game before hitting his homer, finally ended the wild affair with a 13th-inning, bases-loaded single.

"I've never seen anything like it," Cardinals manager Tony La Russa said.

"It's one of the greatest games I've ever been associated with," Cubs manager Jim Riggleman said. "They thought they had it and we came back. We thought we had it and they came back."

Lost in the dramatics was another McGwire record—he became the first Cardinals player to homer 26 times at home. McGwire also walked four times, bringing his season total to 119. Sosa, the N.L. leader with 114 RBIs, also singled home the Cubs' go-ahead run in the 12th.

 **RUTH** *The second of Ruth's two home runs in the opener of a September 6 doubleheader gave him 46 in 132 games. The victim for both blasts was Boston righthander Tony Welzer.*

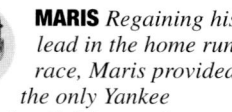 **MARIS** *Regaining his lead in the home run race, Maris provided the only Yankee scoring in a 2-1 loss to the Chicago White Sox at Yankee Stadium. The August 15 victim was Juan Pizarro.*

■ "It had a little bit of everything. Both Mac and Sammy went deep, and that's what the fans came to see. It was just a fun game to be in." —*Cardinals second baseman Pat Kelly*

■ "When he hits a home run, I'm happy. He was struggling a little and he hadn't had a home run in a long time." —*Sammy Sosa*

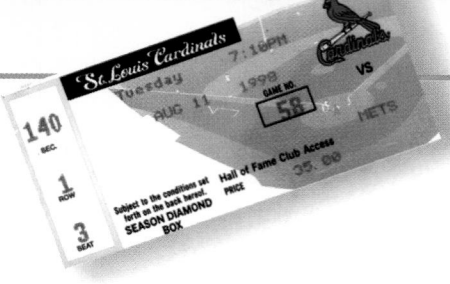

47

"I knew when he hit it that it was gone. I turned around and admired it. He hit it a long way."

—Mets pitcher Bobby Jones

McGwire, tied in the home run race with Chicago right fielder Sammy Sosa for about 21 hours, powered a shot off the base of the Busch Stadium scoreboard in left-center to regain the advantage. But the fourth-inning, bases-empty homer could not prevent another lop-sided loss.

After Sosa had pulled into a tie with a two-homer game against San Francisco the night before, Big Mac responded against New York Mets righthander Bobby Jones.

The 464-foot drive gave McGwire the National League record for home runs by the end of August, and he barely missed No. 48 in the sixth

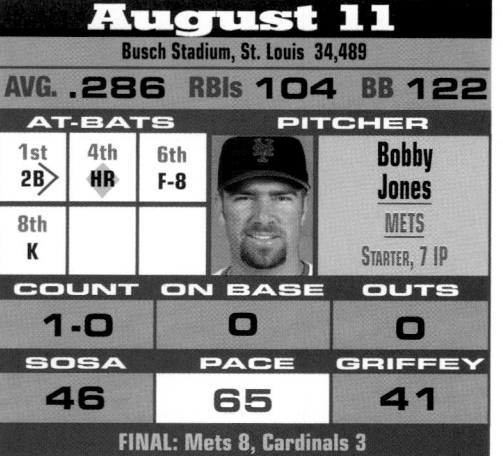

August 11
Busch Stadium, St. Louis 34,489

AVG. .286	RBIs 104	BB 122

AT-BATS

1st 2B▷	4th HR	6th F-8
8th K		

PITCHER

Bobby Jones
METS
STARTER, 7 IP

COUNT	ON BASE	OUTS
1-0	0	0

SOSA	PACE	GRIFFEY
46	65	41

FINAL: Mets 8, Cardinals 3

Cardinals' record: 56-62

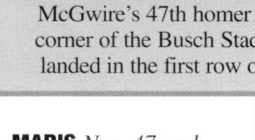

464 ft.

McGwire's 47th homer bounced off the bottom left corner of the Busch Stadium scoreboard sign and landed in the first row of the left field bleachers.

inning when he drove a Jones changeup to the warning track.

"When you pitch against McGwire, you want to move the ball in and out," Jones said. "But it's not like he's not going to hit a home run off you when you pitch him away. He can hit a low pitch and a high pitch. He's so strong that he hits just about everything in the air, no matter where you throw it."

The game was McGwire's 162nd in a Cardinals uniform, the equivalent of a season. The homer was his 71st over that span and his 40th in 81 games at Busch Stadium. He bettered Hack Wilson's N.L. mark for homers by September 1. That was set in 1930, when Wilson had 46 by the end of August.

McGwire's first-inning double ended a streak of 13 plate appearances in which he either had struck out or drawn a base on balls.

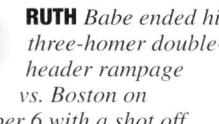

RUTH *Babe ended his three-homer double-header rampage vs. Boston on September 6 with a shot off Jack Russell in the nightcap. It was the ninth of 11 homers he would hit vs. his former team.*

MARIS *Nos. 47 and 48 came on the afternoon of August 16 at Yankee Stadium vs. Chicago. Lefthander Billy Pierce was the victim both times as Maris completed a stretch of seven homers in six games.*

■ "They booed when I threw him a strike. They booed when I threw him a ball. Strike. Booooo. Ball. Boooo. They just want to see him hit a home run." —*Mets pitcher Al Leiter, on fan reaction when he pitched to McGwire earlier in the series*

48/49

"That's why he's The Man. That's why I keep telling you that Mark McGwire is The Man."

—Sammy Sosa

It was a story right out of scriptwriter's heaven. Cubs vs. Cardinals. Sosa vs. McGwire. A race for baseball immortality.

The 39,689 pumped-up fans who ventured to Wrigley Field for this dramatic showdown involving the Cubs and Cardinals got everything they expected—and more. In the fifth inning, Sosa hit his 48th homer off Cardinals starter Kent Bottenfield, moving past McGwire and into the lead for the first time in the 1998 home run derby and setting off chants of "Sam-mee, Sam-mee" as he circled the bases to a standing ovation.

But the best was yet to come. With his team trailing 6-5 in the eighth, Big Mac responded. He drove a Matt Karchner pitch 430 feet over the left field wall and onto Waveland Avenue, tying the game and reclaiming a share of the home

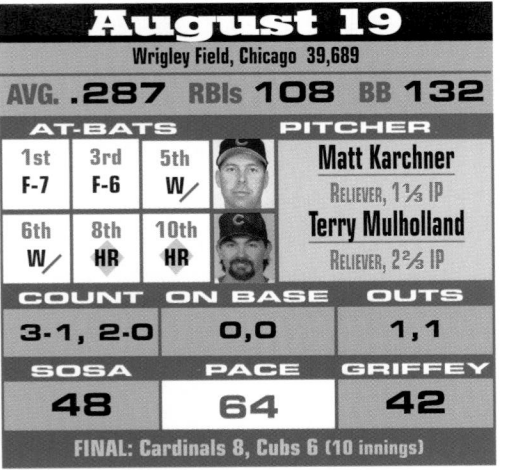

August 19
Wrigley Field, Chicago 39,689

AVG. **.287**   RBIs **108**   BB **132**

AT-BATS			PITCHER
1st F-7	3rd F-6	5th W/	**Matt Karchner** RELIEVER, 1⅓ IP
6th W/	8th HR	10th HR	**Terry Mulholland** RELIEVER, 2⅔ IP

COUNT	ON BASE	OUTS
3-1, 2-0	0,0	1,1

SOSA	PACE	GRIFFEY
48	64	42

FINAL: Cardinals 8, Cubs 6 (10 innings)

Cardinals' record: 60-64

430 ft.
402 ft.

The first homer sailed over Wrigley's left field fence and onto Waveland Avenue; the second landed in the center field shrubbery.

run lead Sosa had held for 58 minutes. Then, in the 10th, McGwire powered a 2-0 Terry Mulholland pitch 402 feet over the center field fence to give the Cardinals a lead they would not relinquish. Challenge accepted.

"Apparently," Cardinals catcher Tom Lampkin said, "the big fellow took it personally."

Before the game, a slumping McGwire had looked tired and confused. But he seemed rejuvenated after his eighth-inning blast. "The last week or so, it was the most frustrated I've ever seen him," said Brian Jordan. "It's been getting to him, everything. The frustration set in. You could see it in his face. It was good to see him relaxed like that."

Juan Acevedo escaped a 10th-inning, bases-loaded jam to pick up the victory.

RUTH *Danny Mac-Fayden and Slim Harriss were the victims of another two-homer game at Boston, giving Ruth five homers in two days. His last 24 games would be played at Yankee Stadium.*

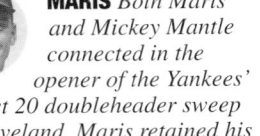

MARIS *Both Maris and Mickey Mantle connected in the opener of the Yankees' August 20 doubleheader sweep at Cleveland. Maris retained his three-homer lead with a two-run blast off Jim Perry.*

■ "What a thrill to be at the park as a fan or a teammate to see both those guys come through." —*Cardinals manager Tony La Russa*

■ "Every move we make, every swing we take, every home run we hit. ... he's in the lead, no, he's in the lead. ... it's going to be that way every day till the end of the season." —*McGwire*

WRIGLEY TIME: *As the Sosa-McGwire home run battle heated up, so did the sights and sounds of venerable Wrigley Field. Mac won the unofficial August 19 homer duel, but he didn't diminish the feverish excitement fans were feeling for their resurgent Cubs.*

50

"It's ironic breaking Babe's record just right down the street from where he played."

—McGwire

It was an unusual sight. McGwire, epitome of subdued home run trots, pumped his fist into the air and clapped twice before he'd touched second base.

He punched his fist into the air again as he approached the plate and yet again before disappearing into the dugout. But even after he'd vanished, a standing ovation continued at Shea Stadium.

The reason for Big Mac's exuberance: home run No. 50, a modest 369-footer that loomed large in historical significance.

The drive over the left field wall gave him a distinction no other player in baseball history can claim. McGwire became the first to hit 50 or more home runs in three consecutive seasons, breaking the record he shared with Babe Ruth. The moment was not lost on him.

"Obviously, it's history,"

August 20
Shea Stadium, New York 45,308

AVG. .286	RBIs 109	BB 132

AT-BATS / **PITCHER**

| 1st K | 4th F-5 | 7th HR | Willie Blair |
| 9th F-8 | | | METS STARTER, 7 IP |

COUNT	ON BASE	OUTS
2-1	0	0

SOSA	PACE	GRIFFEY
48	65	42

FINAL: Cardinals 2, Mets 0

Cardinals' record: 61-64

369 ft.

McGwire hit his 50th home run into the bottom left corner of Shea Stadium's left center field bleachers.

McGwire said. "First baseball player to do it three consecutive years. There's been thousands of power hitters to play this game, and nobody's ever done it. ... And I'm pretty proud of it."

McGwire's seventh-inning home run, off Willie Blair, followed a solo shot by teammate Brian Jordan and provided all the scoring Donovan Osborne and Juan Acevedo would need for their four-hit shutout in the opener of a doubleheader.

McGwire, who became the oldest player to reach the 50-homer plateau at 34 years, 324 days, had been 2-for-16 with nine strikeouts vs. Blair entering the game.

"I just made a mistake," Blair said. "I've gotten him out a lot on that pitch (slider). But that one wasn't where I wanted it."

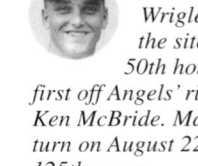

RUTH *Babe's September 11 solo home run was his 50th of the season and his fourth off St. Louis Browns righthander Milt Gaston. Ruth reached the homestretch in the Yankees' 138th game.*

MARIS *Los Angeles' Wrigley Field was the site of Maris' 50th home run, his first off Angels' righthander Ken McBride. Maris made the turn on August 22, in his team's 125th game.*

■ "I'd like to see him break the record. I think he deserves it. He respects the game. He works hard." *—Mets pitcher Willie Blair*

■ "It was almost like a relief. I got to 49 and you need one more, and it can take some time to get that extra one. This time it took only one day. It was a relief." *—McGwire*

■ "I have to thank the fans here in New York. It was tremendous. I mean, wow, what a reception!" *—McGwire*

HAPPY 50TH:
After becoming the first player in history to hit 50 home runs in three consecutive years, McGwire stayed up half the night signing special 50-50-50 balls for teammates and others associated with the team.

51

"He (10-year-old son Matt) was the first person I called. But he already knew."

—McGwire

Rejuvenated and suddenly ready to focus on the record he had been reluctant to discuss for much of the season, McGwire punctuated 4 hours 44 minutes of baseball at Shea Stadium with his second homer of the day and 51st of the season.

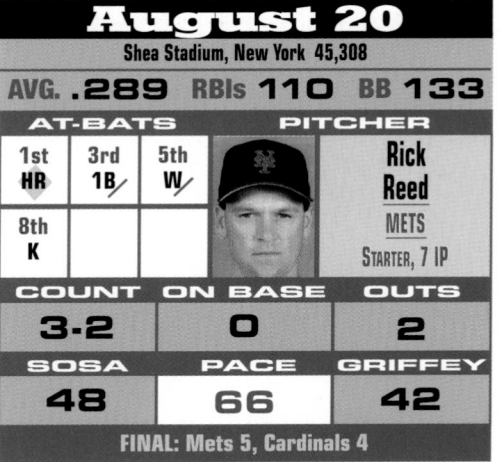

August 20
Shea Stadium, New York 45,308

AVG. .289	RBIs 110	BB 133

AT-BATS   **PITCHER**

1st HR	3rd 1B/	5th W/	Rick Reed
8th K			METS STARTER, 7 IP

COUNT	ON BASE	OUTS
3-2	0	2

SOSA	PACE	GRIFFEY
48	66	42

FINAL: Mets 5, Cardinals 4

Cardinals' record: 61-65

Having hit his record-setting 50th homer in a Cardinals' victory in the opener of a doubleheader against the Mets, McGwire went deep again in the nightcap. In his first-inning at-bat against righthander Rick Reed, he smashed a 385-foot drive that bounced off of the left field foul pole. His fourth home run in seven at-bats over a two-day

Homer No. 51 bounced off Shea Stadium's left field foul pole, about 15 feet above the first row of seats.

span gave the Cardinals an early lead in a game they eventually would lose.

After the doubleheader, fulfilling a promise he had been making all season, McGwire discussed his prospects of breaking Roger Maris' single-season home run record.

"I have to say I do have a good shot," he said. "But I know it's going to be tough. I truly believe that if someone gets to 50 by September 1, they have a legitimate shot down the stretch run."

McGwire, who had hit career homer No. 400 earlier in the season off Reed, pulled three home runs ahead of Chicago right fielder Sammy Sosa. And McGwire created a different kind of excitement in the third inning of Game 2 when he stole his first base of the season, the 11th of his 13-year career and his third with the Cardinals.

RUTH *A two-run homer off Cleveland righthander Willis Hudlin got Ruth off to a good start in the opener of what would become a festive September 13 doubleheader at Yankee Stadium.*

MARIS *His final August homer was hit off righthander Jerry Walker in the sixth inning vs. the A's at Kansas City. He moved five homers ahead of Mickey Mantle in the great home run chase.*

■ "I had no problem with what they (the fans) did. If we win, he can hit all the home runs he wants. I'd cheer, too, if I was one of them." *—Mets pitcher Rick Reed*

■ "I've got my second wind." *—McGwire*

52

"I'm just going to try and enjoy what's going on. I don't know if I'll ever be in this situation again."

—McGwire

Onward and upward. Having shaken an early-August dry spell, McGwire continued a relentless record march with a towering 477-foot homer off Francisco Cordova in a lopsided loss to the Pirates.

The game seemed to be secondary for 45,082 fans who filled many seats that usually go unoccupied at Three Rivers Stadium.

McGwire delivered for them in the first inning, when he hit a Cordova pitch into the stands in right-center. It was his third opposite-field homer of the season.

"That was by accident, believe me," McGwire said. "I

August 22				
Three Rivers Stadium, Pittsburgh 45,082				
AVG. .292		RBIs 112		BB 135
AT-BATS			PITCHER	
1st HR	3rd W/	5th 1B/		Francisco Cordova
7th F-8				PIRATES STARTER, 6 IP
COUNT		ON BASE		OUTS
0-2		0		2
SOSA		PACE		GRIFFEY
49		65		42
FINAL: Pirates 14, Cardinals 4				

Cardinals' record: 62-67

The ball went over Three Rivers Stadium's right center field fence and disappeared into a sea of screaming fans.

477 ft.

wasn't sure if I'd hit it hard enough. Last weekend, I was guessing against (Cordova) too much, so I just tried to react to the ball."

The home run, the fifth in McGwire's last 14 at-bats, was greeted by a standing ovation—much louder than any the Pirates received. The reaction was hard to ignore.

"Oh, yeah, you can feel it," McGwire said. "It takes me off guard when you hear it on the road. I don't think any visiting player is used to playing before different crowds, all of them cheering for you."

The homer was Mac's 162nd over three seasons, moving him one ahead of Babe Ruth's three-season record set in 1926-28. The 52 total equaled the third-highest total in N.L. history and the most by a National Leaguer since George Foster hit that many in 1977.

RUTH *Babe's second home run of the September 13 twin bill helped the Yankees complete their sweep of Cleveland and clinch the A.L. pennant. Joe Shaute became a three-time victim.*

MARIS *The Yankee right fielder continued his march by posting his seventh multihomer game of the season. His first homer in the September 2 game was hit off Detroit's Frank Lary.*

■ "I would think that a majority of America is watching. To know that every eye in the country, every eye in the stadium is watching, and every move that you make is critiqued, that's pressure. But I'll deal with it." *—McGwire*

■ "The buzz is so alive, so real, you can almost touch it. I just want to listen. And then you look into the stands, and you see the look of joy on all those faces." *—Cardinals manager Tony La Russa*

53

"I guarantee you that 47,000 people didn't come out to see me play baseball here today."

—Pirates first baseman Kevin Young

The snowballing magnetism of McGwire mania rolled through Pittsburgh, leaving normally hard-to-impress Pirates fans gasping in the wake of another Big Mac power surge. McGwire's 1998 home run parade inspired the first consecutive regular-season sell-outs in the 28-year history of Three Rivers Stadium—and the Cardinals' big first baseman didn't disappoint.

Moments after Cubs rival Sammy Sosa had hit homer 50 against Houston in Chicago, and minutes before Sosa would connect again for 51, McGwire drove an eighth-inning pitch from lefthander Ricardo Rincon 393 feet into the left field seats and joined Hack Wilson and Ralph Kiner as the only N.L. players to hit as many as 53 homers in a season.

The Pittsburgh crowd roared as McGwire circled the bases

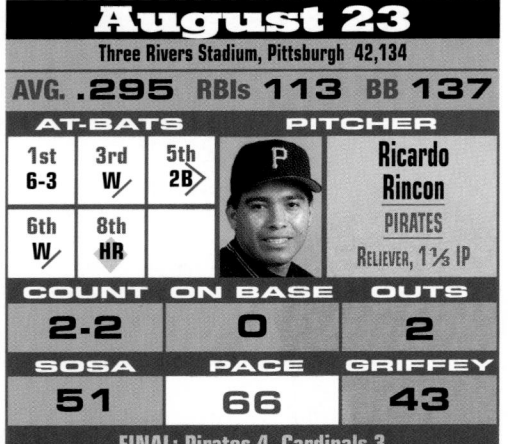

August 23
Three Rivers Stadium, Pittsburgh 42,134

AVG. **.295**   RBIs **113**   BB **137**

AT-BATS			PITCHER	
1st 6-3	3rd W/	5th 2B▷	P	Ricardo Rincon
6th W/	8th HR			PIRATES RELIEVER, 1⅓ IP

COUNT	ON BASE	OUTS
2-2	0	2

SOSA	PACE	GRIFFEY
51	66	43

FINAL: Pirates 4, Cardinals 3
Cardinals' record: 62-68

Pittsburgh fans got another Mac souvenir when homer 53 landed in the seats just above the fence in left field.

and returned to the dugout. But as the cheering picked up steam, teammates nudged him back onto the field for a rare honor—an opposing-park curtain call.

"When a crowd responds like that, the professional thing to do is acknowledge it," said Cardinals manager Tony La Russa. "He wasn't kicking and screaming, but he wasn't going to do it without being reminded."

McGwire's sixth homer in five days came amid a controversy over his use of androstenedione, a legal testosterone-producing, strength-enhancing substance that is permitted by baseball. It also came in a losing cause as the Pirates won their seventh straight game.

McGwire extended his own record for home runs by a righthanded batter over two seasons to 111.

RUTH *A homer off Ted Blankenship in the third inning propelled the Yankees to a 7-2 victory in the September 16 opener of a five-game sweep of Chicago. With 11 games remaining, Ruth had 53.*

MARIS *A two-run, eighth-inning blow off Detroit's Hank Aguirre capped Maris' two-homer September 2 game and gave him 53 home runs with 28 games remaining on the Yankees' schedule.*

■ "He deserves that ovation, and he deserves to be able to come out like that. He's chasing history, and we won the ballgame. It worked out fine. I didn't mind it." —*Pirates catcher Jason Kendall*

■ "I felt uncomfortable doing that (making a curtain call) as a visiting player, in all due respect for the Pirates. But a couple of teammates said I should go out there, so I did." —*McGwire*

MAN OF STEEL: *All eyes (bottom photo) watch the flight of home run 53, a special treat for McGwire-crazy fans who packed Pittsburgh's Three Rivers Stadium on consecutive days.*

54

"I can only take care of myself. Let's just have fun watching until the end of the season."

—McGwire, on his battle with Sammy Sosa

McGwire's eighth-inning home run was a thing of beauty. What happened thereafter to the Cardinals was not—at least in the view of McGwire and 30,004 stunned fans at Busch Stadium.

Big Mac stepped into a pitch from Florida Marlins rookie Justin Speier and sent a majestic drive that bounced off the top of the 35-foot backdrop in center field. The 509-footer was his fourth home run of the season at Busch Stadium that measured more than 500 feet.

The home run extended the Cardinals' lead to 3-0 and seemingly unnerved Speier, who served up a three-run homer to John Mabry later in the inning.

But the celebrating was short-lived. Florida's Derrek Lee, Cliff Floyd and Kevin Orie hit consecutive ninth-inning

August 26
Busch Stadium, St. Louis 30,004

AVG. .293 RBIs 116 BB 138

AT-BATS			PITCHER	
1st F-8	4th K	6th F-8		**Justin Speier**
8th HR	9th 1B/			MARLINS RELIEVER, ⅓ IP

COUNT	ON BASE	OUTS
0-1	1	0

SOSA	PACE	GRIFFEY
52	66	44

FINAL: Marlins 7, Cardinals 6 (10 innings)

Cardinals' record: 62-70

509 ft.

This majestic drive to straightaway center field bounced off the top of Busch Stadium's 35-foot backdrop.

homers off reliever John Frascatore, and pinch-hitter Mark Kotsay tied the game with a three-run blow off Jeff Brantley. The Marlins won the game in the 10th on Randy Knorr's double.

"I'm not even sure what I saw," Cardinals manager Tony La Russa said. "I certainly don't know how to describe it. Pretty horrible."

McGwire called the emotional swing "probably one of the worst I've ever had in my career." But the media focus continued to be the great home run chase that had heated up earlier in the day, when Chicago right fielder Sammy Sosa hit No. 52.

"I know what America is watching," a disappointed McGwire conceded. "They're not watching the Cardinals, they're watching me. And that's hard to accept."

RUTH *Homer No. 54 was hit off Chicago's Ted Lyons in the second game of a September 18 doubleheader. Lyons was the first of two future Hall of Famers who would serve up Ruth homers.*

MARIS *Washington righthander Tom Cheney became Maris victim No. 54 on September 6 in a game at Yankee Stadium. The blow gave Maris a three-homer lead over teammate Mickey Mantle.*

■ "I wouldn't want to be in his shoes day in and day out. Personally, I wouldn't like all that attention. It takes a special person to handle it." —*Marlins third baseman Kevin Orie*

■ "I knew it was gone. You want to challenge a hitter like him and go right after him, and if he hits one off you, oh well." —*Marlins pitcher Justin Speier*

FOLLOW THE BOUNCING BALL: *That's what Marlins reliever Justin Speier was doing (above) after McGwire bounced a 509-foot shot off the backdrop in straightaway center field at Busch Stadium for home run No. 54.*

The ejection

Somewhere between home runs 54 and 55, McGwire lost his patience and St. Louis fans threw a nationally televised temper tantrum.

The August 29 game at Busch Stadium against the Atlanta Braves was devoid of McGwire home runs, but not of the fireworks that normally follow his at-bats. Big Mac took a Saturday afternoon off from the Great Home Run Chase and reminded the world that he is indeed human.

The game got off to a temperamental start when McGwire took a called third strike from pitcher Tom Glavine, a pitch that appeared low and inside to the big first baseman. He questioned umpire Sam Holbrook's judgment and when the conversation became animated, manager Tony La Russa and third base coach Rene Lachemann rushed to intercede.

But McGwire, restrained by Lachemann, refused to back off and was ejected, along with La Russa and coach Dave Duncan. The ejection was not accepted gracefully by the capacity crowd, which tossed considerable debris onto the field—prompting a threat of forfeit. Peace was restored and McGwire had an afternoon off, courtesy of Holbrook.

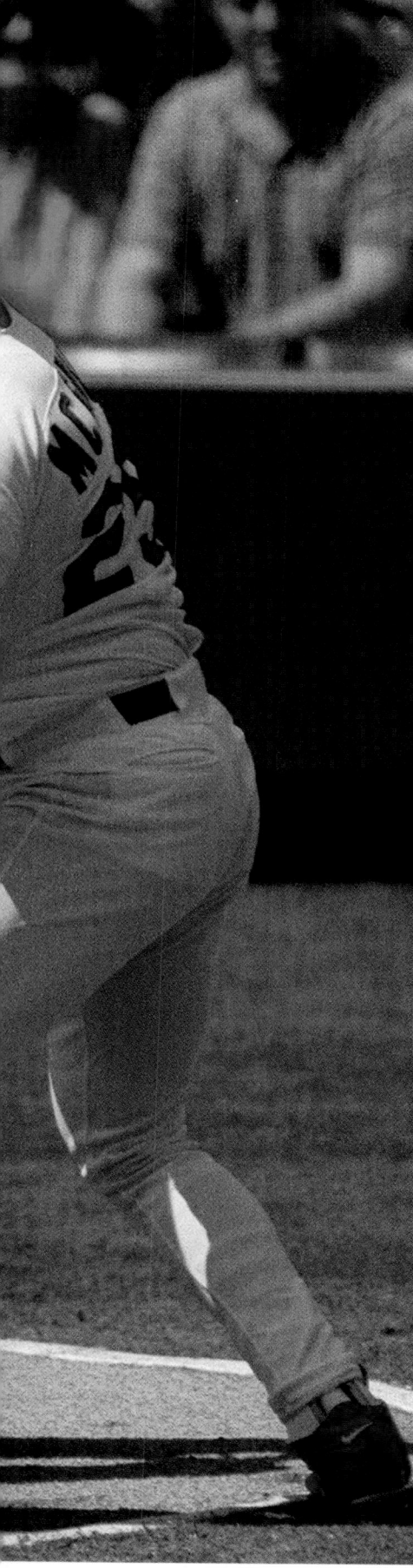

OUT PATTERN:
As McGwire (above) argues with Holbrook, LaRussa nears the plate and Lachemann runs up the third-base line. Lachemann's attempts to restrain Mac couldn't stop the ejection.

55

"This is a Mark McGwire show. No matter what happened, I believe he's going to come back—as always."

—Chicago's Sammy Sosa, after tying McGwire briefly at 54 home runs

Like two great boxers looking for a late-round knockout, Mac and Sammy continued to jab and counterpunch their way through the myth and legend that surrounds one of baseball's most cherished feats.

Reflecting a pattern of the previous two weeks, Chicago right fielder Sammy Sosa hit his 54th home run in an afternoon game at Colorado, tying him with McGwire for the major league lead. But Mac answered with a game-winning, three-run blast against the Atlanta Braves in a Sunday night game at St. Louis. It marked the third straight McGwire home run that had come on the same day as Sosa homers.

"I've said it time and time again. I can only take care of Mark McGwire, period," McGwire said after his

August 30

Busch Stadium, St. Louis 44,051

AVG. **.295**   RBIs **119**   BB **141**

AT-BATS			PITCHER
1st W	4th 1B	5th 2B	Dennis Martinez
7th HR			BRAVES RELIEVER, 2 IP

COUNT	ON BASE	OUTS
1-0	2	0

SOSA	PACE	GRIFFEY
54	66	47

FINAL: Cardinals 8, Braves 7

Cardinals' record: 64-72

501 ft.

The latest McGwire cannon shot fell between the backdrop and Coke bottle sign in straightaway center field.

dramatic seventh-inning homer had completed the Cardinals' comeback from a 6-0 deficit. "This is not a challenge, this is not a race to whatever. We don't get an Oscar at the end for like best actor. He takes care of himself, I take care of myself and wherever the chips fall at the end of the season, that's where it is."

McGwire's 501-foot shot to center field off veteran righthander Dennis Martinez came the day after he had been ejected in the first inning of a nationally televised game against the Braves for arguing a called third strike.

The homer moved McGwire past former Pittsburgh star Ralph Kiner into second place on the National League's single-season home run charts. He needed only one more to match the 1930 record of Chicago Cubs outfielder Hack Wilson.

 **RUTH** *A ninth-inning home run against Detroit's Sam Gibson kept the Yankees from suffering their first home shutout loss of the season. Homer No. 55 came September 21 in the team's 148th game.*

 **MARIS** *Continuing a run of five homers in nine games, Maris belted his 55th on September 7 vs. Cleveland's Dick Stigman at Yankee Stadium. After 141 games, he was five short of Ruth's record.*

■ "Sammy always says I'm The Man. But he's The Man, too. He's right there. I was asked today, 'What if we both finish up with over 62?' What can you do except say what a great year? A historical year. I mean, there's a good possibility that might happen." —McGwire

■ "I'm extremely happy for Sammy. Sammy is having a magical year, a way better year than I'm having. His team is right there in the wild-card race, he's driven in quite a few more runs than I have, he's hit for a higher average. You tip your hat to him." —McGwire

55 AND COUNTING:
The Atlanta Braves and veteran righthander Dennis Martinez got 'McGwired' in a nationally televised Sunday night game at Busch Stadium. Big Mac ignited the crowd with a three-run, seventh-inning blast that carried the Cardinals to a dramatic come-from-behind victory.

56/57

"The bat felt pretty good tonight. America is watching very closely. It's become enjoyable, and it's become fun."

—McGwire

After 68 years and a host of unsuccessful challenges, Hack Wilson finally surrendered his National League single-season home run record, giving way to that man named McGwire.

The Cardinals' first baseman scarcely had time to savor the moment after blasting a Livan Hernandez pitch 450 feet in the seventh inning. The homer, McGwire's 56th, traveled into the tarp-covered center field seats at Florida's Pro Player Stadium.

Two innings later, he hit the first pitch from reliever Donn Pall into the same area, a 472-footer for record-setting homer No. 57 as the Cardinals eased past the Marlins.

"It's a pretty awesome feat," McGwire acknowledged. "I didn't realize till the other day that (56) was the record. Almost everybody in the dugout congratulated me and hugged

me, and the fans here in south Florida gave me two curtain calls, which is unbelievable."

In his rapid-fire move past Wilson, McGwire answered another Sammy Sosa challenge. Sosa, the Chicago right fielder, had hit his 55th home run one day earlier and entered the Cubs' night game against Cincinnati tied with McGwire. But Sosa went 0-for-4 while Big Mac was making history.

"I think one of the reasons he is going to do it (break Roger Maris' record) is because I'm right there with him," Sosa said. "He is a competitive guy, and I think he responds to a challenge."

The multihomer game was McGwire's seventh of the season and 50th of his career.

Ray Lankford and Ron Gant also homered for the Cardinals, and Matt Morris pitched five-hit ball over seven innings.

September 1
Pro Player Stadium, Florida 37,014

AVG. .296	RBIs 121	BB 143

AT-BATS			PITCHER
1st F-8	3rd 1B/	5th 4-3	**Livan Hernandez** STARTER, 7 IP
7th HR	9th HR		**Donn Pall** RELIEVER, 1 IP

COUNT	ON BASE	OUTS
1-1,0-0	0,0	0,1

SOSA	PACE	GRIFFEY
55	67	47

FINAL: Cardinals 7, Marlins 1

Cardinals' record: 66-72

McGwire's two home runs landed within a few feet of each other on a tarp that covered seats in straightaway center field.

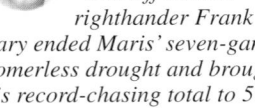

RUTH *A September 27 grand slam off future Hall of Famer Lefty Grove touched off the closing four-homers-in-three-games surge that lifted the Bambino to his season total of 60.*

MARIS *A September 16 two-run shot off Detroit righthander Frank Lary ended Maris' seven-game homerless drought and brought his record-chasing total to 57 with 12 games remaining.*

■ "He's going to do it. He's going to get the record, and I think everyone knows he's going to do it now. This is an incredible man." *—Cardinals catcher Tom Lampkin*

■ "I've never seen anything like this in my life. I saw Nolan Ryan win his 300th game, and throw two no-hitters, and get his 5,000th strikeout, but this is unbelievable what (McGwire's) doing. He just gets people so excited. He's like a movie star and a rock 'n' roll star rolled into one." *—Cardinals pitcher Bobby Witt*

HACKING AWAY:
McGwire Mania hit record heights during an eventful trip to Florida when he struck twice in a game against the Marlins and claimed the N.L. single-season homer mark previously held by Chicago's Hack Wilson (right).

TWO PLUS TWO: *The sign (below) relayed the feeling of Marlins fans for McGwire, who delivered with his second two-homer salvo in as many days at Florida's Pro Player Stadium. He returned to St. Louis and Busch Stadium on the brink of history.*

58/59

"I'll be able to sit back with my grandkids and tell them all about this."

—Cardinals second baseman Delino DeShields

With two more flicks of his powerful wrists, McGwire crossed into territory charted by only two players among the more than 15,000 who have played the game. After pushing Hack Wilson to the sideline with a dramatic two-homer effort the previous night, Big Mac did the same to Jimmie Foxx and Hank Greenberg with a Herculean two-homer encore at Florida's Pro Player Stadium. After the game, only Babe Ruth and Roger Maris stood between McGwire and what appeared to be his destiny.

McGwire's second consecutive two-homer night followed script. In becoming the most prolific single-season home run hitter in National League history the night before, he connected in the seventh and ninth innings. Home runs 58 and 59 were hit to left and left-center in the seventh and eighth, the

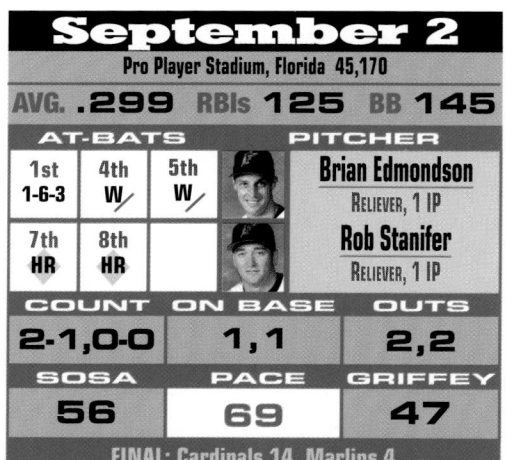

September 2
Pro Player Stadium, Florida 45,170

AVG. .299	RBIs 125	BB 145

AT-BATS			PITCHER
1st 1-6-3	4th W	5th W	**Brian Edmondson** RELIEVER, 1 IP
7th HR	8th HR		**Rob Stanifer** RELIEVER, 1 IP

COUNT	ON BASE	OUTS
2-1,0-0	1,1	2,2

SOSA	PACE	GRIFFEY
56	69	47

FINAL: Cardinals 14, Marlins 4

Cardinals' record: 67-72

497 ft.
458 ft.

McGwire's first homer was an upper-deck shot to left; his second went into the lower deck in left center at Pro Player Stadium.

first a 497-foot, upper-deck shot off rookie Brian Edmondson and the second a first-pitch 458-footer off Rob Stanifer.

"What's going on is pretty big," McGwire conceded after making two more curtain calls for a large Florida crowd. "It's quite amazing. It almost blows me away."

McGwire's second straight big night helped ensure an easy victory that also featured pitcher Kent Mercker's fourth-inning grand slam. His encore effort answered another challenge by Chicago's Sammy Sosa, who had homered for the 56th time earlier in the day. On the single-season chart, McGwire moved past Foxx, Greenberg and McGwire himself—all of whom had hit 58—and into a tie with Ruth, who hit 59 in 1921.

McGwire left Florida with 12 homers in a 17-game span.

RUTH *Hod Lisenbee and Paul Hopkins, two Washington righthanders, served up homers 58 and 59 to Ruth in his second-last game of the season. No. 59 was his second grand slam in two games.*

MARIS *Creeping ever closer to his destiny, Maris hit No. 58 against Detroit and 59 against Baltimore in a four-day span. His September 20 blow off Milt Pappas came in New York's 155th game.*

■ "The pitch was probably three inches off the ground. I amazed myself that I went down and got it." —*McGwire, on his 58th homer*

■ "He crushed it. It's amazing. You can't throw the guy any pitch he can reach or he hits it 500 feet. It's a little unfair at times. He's like the Michael Jordan of baseball." —*Marlins pitcher Rob Stanifer on homer No. 59*

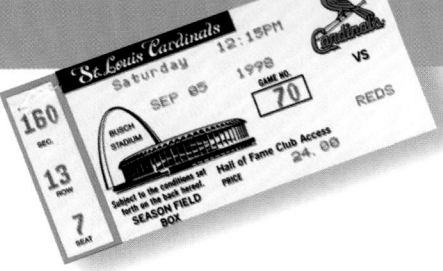

60

"For me, it's just another homer. I don't want to be the last one and I wasn't the first one."

——Reds pitcher Dennis Reyes, after surrendering homer No. 60 to McGwire

It started as an over-hyped dream in January and became an early-September reality.

When McGwire launched a 2-0 fastball from Cincinnati lefthander Dennis Reyes into Busch Stadium's left field seats, he took his place along-side Babe Ruth and Roger Maris as the only 60-home run bashers in history.

McGwire achieved the 60-homer plateau, a standard by which sluggers have been measured since Ruth hit that many in 1927, on his first swing of a festive Saturday afternoon. The high drive sailed just inside the foul pole and sent a crowd of 47,994 into a prolonged roar.

Big Mac's homer gave the Cardinals a 2-0 lead, and Donovan Osborne secured a Cardinals win with a three-hit shutout that was witnessed by numerous baseball dignitaries and more than 700 media mem-

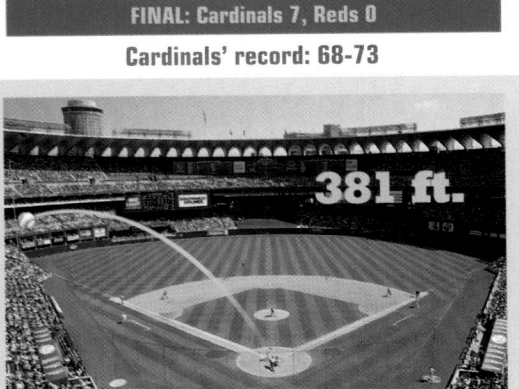

September 5
Busch Stadium, St. Louis 47,994

AVG. .296	RBIs 127	BB 146

AT-BATS			PITCHER	
1st HR	2nd K	5th K		**Dennis Reyes** REDS Starter, 4 IP
7th K				

COUNT	ON BASE	OUTS
2-0	1	1

SOSA	PACE	GRIFFEY
58	69	48

FINAL: Cardinals 7, Reds 0

Cardinals' record: 68-73

381 ft.

Historic home run No. 60 disappeared into the seats just inside the left field foul pole.

bers from around the world.

McGwire stepped onto the Ruthian plateau in the team's 142nd game, 12 fewer than Ruth needed to reach 60. And he got there against the only National League team that had not surrendered a home run to him in 1998. Against Reds pitching, Big Mac had managed two singles in 16 previous at-bats, with 12 walks.

As he moved one swing shy of Maris' 1961 record of 61, McGwire surpassed his wildest expectations. "Babe Ruth," he repeated over and over. "You are almost speechless when people put your name alongside his."

Despite McGwire's historic effort, the shadow of Chicago right fielder Sammy Sosa remained. Hours after Big Mac had hit his 60th homer, Sosa recorded his 58th, in Three Rivers Stadium at Pittsburgh.

 **RUTH** *Tom Zachary, who was traded at midseason from St. Louis to Washington, joined Ruth in the record books when he served up home run No. 60 in the Babe's 154th and final regular-season game.*

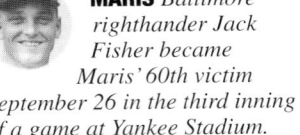 **MARIS** *Baltimore righthander Jack Fisher became Maris' 60th victim September 26 in the third inning of a game at Yankee Stadium. The record-tying homer was hit in game No. 159.*

■ "Let's just accept what is happening, enjoy it, ride the wave. I mean, look what it has done to baseball. If you want to say it has brought America together, it has." —*McGwire*

■ "He motivates me. I motivate him. And this is fun. ... We're pushing each other. We're not going to stop now. We're doing a great job together." —*Cubs right fielder Sammy Sosa*

"One day, we will meet."

The discomfort of an early-September heat wave couldn't diminish the happiness and harmony that filled Busch Stadium. And while the temperature for Cardinals game No. 142 hovered in the mid-90s, the degree of fan and player

anticipation rose to a feverish pitch.

Every McGwire move, every gesture, every expression was cheered with an almost-religious fervor while being chronicled for posterity. As more than 700 media representatives prepared to analyze shots that would be heard around the world, millions of fans were brought to attention by radio and television announcers who dared compare the challenger to baseball's ultimate

heavyweight: Babe Ruth.

Yes, the immortal Babe Ruth, who had blasted his way through the 1920s and into the record book with a 60-homer 1927 season, setting a standard by which future generations of sluggers would be measured.

And when McGwire brought down the house with a first-inning swing that sent the baseball world into an uncontrollable spin, the sanctity of the Ruthian accomplishment and the torment suffered by Roger Maris, the only previous challenger to match Ruth's 60 homers, was not lost on the Cardinals first baseman.

"I truly believe that ... they're both watching," McGwire said after home run No. 60 in a Cardinals' victory over Cincinnati. "I can feel it. And one day, we will meet."

Their paths crossed in the record books on McGwire's first at-bat. Responding to the standing, roaring ovations that had greeted his every at-bat since home run No. 59, he touched off a citywide celebration with a high drive that settled comfortably into the seats just inside the left field foul pole.

As the normally low-key McGwire made a fist-pumping trot around the bases, ecstatic fans hugged, leaped and danced in Busch Stadium's aisles and living rooms throughout the country.

They were participating in the magic of McGwire while paying tribute to the glory of Ruth.

"Obviously, he was the most important sports figure in the world of that time," said McGwire, who moved two swings away from one of the most cherished records in sports. "Babe Ruth. What can you say? You are almost speechless when people put your name alongside his name.

"I wish I could go back in time and meet him. Hopefully when I pass away, I'll get to meet him and then I can truly find out what he was really like."

SEEING RED: *Interested observers of homer No. 60 included St. Louis Hall of Famers Red Schoendienst and Stan Musial, who serenaded fans on his harmonica. Reds pitcher Dennis Reyes was not in a celebratory mood after serving up the record-tying blast.*

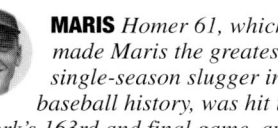

61

"That's storybook stuff. ... And he actually did it. It's like Star Wars, with Luke (Skywalker). The Force was with him."

—Cardinals left fielder Ron Gant

The missile descended at 1:22 p.m., a split second after banging off the glass that protected diners in the Stadium Club, located between the upper and lower decks in left field at Busch Stadium.

As it disappeared into a sea of Cardinal red, so did the last vestiges of doubt about McGwire's assault on one of baseball's most cherished records.

"It's been a long, rough road," McGwire said after his 61st home run, a solo shot in the first inning, matched the 37-year-old, single-season record of Roger Maris. "I go back to, I don't know, January, talking about it into spring training, and here we are, tied at 61. I am one swing away from breaking it."

The 430-foot blast off of Chicago righthander Mike Morgan moved McGwire past

another former Yankee, Babe Ruth, on the single-season home run chart. Ruth needed 154 games to hit 60 in 1927; McGwire needed only 144 to hit 61. Maris hit his 61st on the final day of the 1961 season, the team's 163rd game.

The home run was doubly sweet because it helped the Cardinals defeat longtime rival Chicago. And Big Mac's primary challenger, Sammy Sosa, watched the historic moment from his position in right field. Later, after Sosa had singled, he hugged McGwire in a touching scene at first base.

After McGwire hit Morgan's third pitch, he stood near the plate, watched the ball leave the park in fair territory and began his record-tying celebration. "As soon as it left my bat, I just threw my hands up," McGwire said. "I knew it at that time. What a feeling that was."

September 7
Busch Stadium, St. Louis 50,530

AVG. .296	RBIs 128	BB 147

AT-BATS | **PITCHER**

| 1st HR | 3rd 1B/ | 5th F-8 | Mike Morgan |
| 7th F-8 | | | CUBS STARTER, 6 IP |

COUNT	ON BASE	OUTS
1-1	0	2

SOSA	PACE	GRIFFEY
58	69	50

FINAL: Cardinals 3, Cubs 2

Cardinals' record: 70-73

430 ft.

The record-tying home run bounced off a Stadium Club window just inside the left field foul pole and landed in the first row of loge reserved seats.

MARIS *Homer 61, which made Maris the greatest single-season slugger in baseball history, was hit in New York's 163rd and final game, an October 1 victory over Boston at Yankee Stadium. The history-making pitch was served up by Tracy Stallard.*

■ "This guy is doing everything, isn't he? It's like I've always said. He's a better person than he is a player." *—Cardinals manager Tony La Russa*

■ "It has been quite amazing. I think I have amazed myself. I think I have amazed other people. So it is hard not to have emotions for this." *—McGwire*

■ "I told him that I got to 61, so he should be able to do it, too." *—John McGwire, who was celebrating his 61st birthday when Mark hit homer No. 61*

"Swing and look at there! Look at there! Look at there! McGwire's No. 61! McGwire's Flight 61 headed for planet Maris! Home run McGwire, 61. ... Pardon me while I stand and applaud."

—The historic 61st-homer call from Hall of Fame broadcaster Jack Buck

A family affair

It was the birthday bash of the century, but few of the celebrants even knew that's what it was. But, oh, what a present!

"I didn't call him today to say happy birthday, because I was driving to the ballpark," McGwire said. "I said this is meant to be his birthday present. Sixty-first home run on his 61st birthday. Happy birthday, Dad! I mean, you can't ask for anything better than that."

John McGwire got the message, loud and clear. It was delivered with a first-inning crack of the bat that echoed through the baseball world and lifted his son onto the 61-homer plateau previously occupied by only Roger Maris. The message was reinforced by a triumphant home run trot that punctuated his son's ascension to record heights, followed by a birthday salute into the stands.

The wild, emotional celebration, played out in front of 50,530 raucous Busch Stadium fans and a national television audience, was very much a family affair.

ALL IN THE FAMILY: *Birthday boy John McGwire (left) got a special gift from son Mark—homer No. 61 on birthday No. 61. Mac also enjoyed a home-plate family reunion (right photo) with son Matt and a postgame hug (above) with the children of Roger Maris, whose record he matched.*

After receiving congratulatory slaps and bashes from Cubs Mark Grace and Gary Gaetti and Cardinals coach Rene Lachemann and center fielder Ray Lankford during a fist-pumping romp around the bases, Mark McGwire looked down into the wide eyes of his 10-year-old son, who had arrived from his southern California home in the first inning.

"I didn't see him there in the top of the first inning," McGwire said. "I went to the hole to get my bat and

PLAY IT AGAIN, SAMMY: *Seven innings after his 61st homer, McGwire and Chicago's Sammy Sosa enjoyed an impromptu celebration at first base.*

there he is. I told him I loved him. I gave him a kiss."

And then, after circling the bases, he gave young Matt a bear hug and carried him halfway to the dugout. "Next thing I knew I see him at home plate and what a wonderful feeling a father could have."

McGwire also attended to the business of another family with an emotional salute to the children of Roger Maris, who were seated along the first-base line. "I pointed to my heart and said, 'Roger's with me,' " McGwire said. "I would love to meet with them some day when this is all over and tell them the feeling what their father was going through at the time because it is an amazing feeling."

A feeling that will never go away.

"I don't think you ever let go of the moment," McGwire said. "I don't know if I'll ever be here again, so how can you let it go? What I've done is fabulous. I'm going to enjoy it right now. The whole time, I just thought, 'What a great birthday present for my father.' "

62

"It was a sweet, sweet run around the bases. ... I hope I didn't act foolish, but this was history."

——McGwire, after his record-breaking home run

It was a line drive into the corner, not your average, everyday McGwire production. The 341-foot shot barely cleared the wall, well below the lower left field seats, and fell unmolested into a storage area below the stands.

Ordinarily, Big Mac might have been tempted to throw this minnow back. But on this special night at Busch Stadium, everything was a keeper.

62!

The number flashed through the minds of baseball fans throughout the world as McGwire made one of the most memorable and historic home run trots in the game's history. He missed first base and had to return to the scene of the crime. He bashed, mashed and hugged everybody in sight, friends and opponents alike. He danced, he jumped, he yelled and he celebrated the

September 8		
Busch Stadium, St. Louis 49,987		
AVG. **.297** RBIs **129** BB **149**		

AT-BATS		PITCHER	
1st 6-3	4th HR	6th W/	Steve Trachsel
8th W/			CUBS STARTER, 5⅔ IP

COUNT	ON BASE	OUTS
0/0	0	2
SOSA	PACE	GRIFFEY
58	70	50

FINAL: Cardinals 6, Cubs 3

Cardinals' record: 71-73

341 ft.

The record-breaker, McGwire's shortest home run of the season, barely cleared the left field wall and landed in an open area under the stands.

record-breaking moment as a wave of jubilation cascaded through the stadium, the streets of St. Louis, the country and points beyond.

McGwire's history-making moment came in the fourth inning on the first pitch he saw from Chicago righthander Steve Trachsel. The bases-empty blow lifted him onto a single-season plateau that hadn't been ascended in baseball history, and it came in his 145th game, nine fewer than Babe Ruth needed to hit 60 in 1927 and a whopping 18 fewer than Roger Maris needed to hit 61 in 1961.

It also came in a Cardinals victory over the hated Cubs, with Sammy Sosa, Mac's chief challenger with 58 homers, watching from his right field position. The record-breaker was McGwire's 50th off righthanded pitching and only his 19th of less than 400 feet.

■ "What a perfect way to end the homestand, by hitting 62 for the city of St. Louis and all the fans. I truly wanted to do it here, and I did. Thank you, St. Louis." —*McGwire*

■ "It's just a home run. We lost the ballgame. That's what is most disappointing. ... I'm hoping they'll be talking about Steve Trachsel (years from now) helping the Cubs get to the World Series. I hope that's what they will be talking about." —*Cubs pitcher Steve Trachsel, McGwire victim No. 62*

■ "I jumped and yelled and screamed like everybody else. It brings back the little kid in you. We're teammates, but we're fans, too. It brings back the great emotions of playing baseball as a kid, the positive things about the game that have been overshadowed." —*Cardinals infielder Pat Kelly*

"Swing and a shot into the corner. It might make it! There it is: 62, folks! It just got over the left field wall in the corner. And we have a new home run champion! A new Sultan of Swat! It's Mark McGwire! He touches them all. Unbelievable."

—The historic call of homer 62 by Cardinals radio broadcaster Mike Shannon

PARTY OF ONE: *One of the few unhappy faces at Busch Stadium September 8 belonged to Cubs righthander Steve Trachsel (above), who fumed as Big Mac (in the background) danced around the bases after his record-breaking 62nd homer. The blow over the left field wall (above left) brought both tears and cheers (right page, below) from the older and younger Cardinals faithful.*

Homer **62** Quick Facts

- 50th off righthanded pitching
- 19th of less than 400 feet
- 32nd at Busch Stadium
- 15th on a Tuesday
- 11th in the fourth inning

- 30th with the bases empty
- 9th on the first pitch
- 46th in night games
- 7th against the Cubs
- 25th since the All-Star Game
- 145th game of the season
- 1st time a non-Yankee has held the record since 1919
- 341 feet, McGwire's shortest of the season

HAVING A BALL: *Not lost in the excitement of a magical moment was home run ball No. 62, which was returned to McGwire by Tim Forneris (right), a member of the Busch Stadium grounds crew, during a postgame ceremony that honored baseball's new home run king. Mac's father, John McGwire (second from right), commissioner Bud Selig (left) and broadcaster Jack Buck (second from left) were center stage for the festivities.*

"Unbelievable ... class"

For 11 glorious minutes on the night of September 8, the baseball world stood still. Or, more accurately, Mark McGwire held it motionless in the palms of his powerful hands.

As the new home run king, the first heir to the throne in 37 years, Big Mac wielded that kind of power. His magic wand had driven away all the negative remnants and hard feelings left over from the 1994 baseball strike and his sense of drama and accommodating personality had returned the game to its feel-good past. Now it was time to enjoy the fruits of his labor.

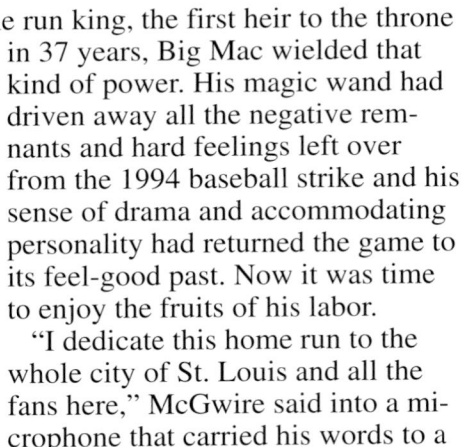

"I dedicate this home run to the whole city of St. Louis and all the fans here," McGwire said into a microphone that carried his words to a packed house at Busch Stadium. "Thanks for all your support. It's unbelievable. All my family, everybody. Chicago Cubs. Sammy Sosa. Unbelievable ... class."

The words triggered another in a long line of roars from fans, players, officials and any other living being that had found an empty nook in a Busch Stadium

RECORD HUGS: *An emotional McGwire delivered home-run hugs to his parents (above) and former wife Kathy Williamson (left) after trotting into uncharted territory.*

cranny. Among those paying tribute were such Cardinals of yesteryear as Stan Musial, Lou Brock, Red Schoendienst and Ozzie Smith.

"I think this is the biggest thrill I've ever had in baseball," said Hall of Fame broadcaster Jack Buck, the Cardinals' radio voice for 44 years. "This was the most monumental home run in the history of the game. I don't think anything that's ever happened in this ballpark compares to what we've just observed."

The most anticipated home run since Hank Aaron hit No. 715 in 1974 was only the start of McGwire's victory parade. After "a sweet, sweet run around the bases," McGwire picked up his 10-year-old son Matthew near home plate, gave him a bear hug and planted a big kiss that seemed to punctuate the moment. Then he was mobbed by Cardinals teammates and congratulated by Chicago rival Sammy Sosa, who joined the celebration from his right field position to exchange bashes and hugs with the enemy.

NICE RIDE: *Roger Maris' children (top photo) inspect the bat their father used to set his homer mark in 1961. The ultimate victory laps were taken in Mac's Cardinal-red '62 Corvette, a gift from the team.*

After blowing more kisses into the stands and saluting his parents, McGwire jogged triumphantly over to the first-base box seats in a gesture that would cement his status as a genuine American hero. He stepped over the railing and shared his moment with the children of Roger Maris, hugging them and giving them the respect their father had never received during the 1961 season in which he surpassed Babe Ruth's 34-year-old single-season homer record.

"My body's still numb. I'm extremely happy for Mark. For all he's done for baseball. ...I couldn't be happier," said Roger Jr. "For Mark to be the person he is and to mean what he means to baseball and to the fans of America, I couldn't think of a better person to be the new home run king for a single season.

"I think Dad would be happy for Mark and proud of

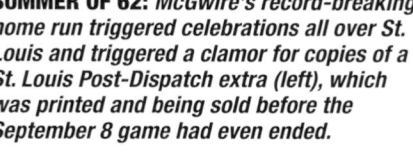

SUMMER OF 62: *McGwire's record-breaking home run triggered celebrations all over St. Louis and triggered a clamor for copies of a St. Louis Post-Dispatch extra (left), which was printed and being sold before the September 8 game had even ended.*

MASS CONFUSION: *McGwire, who has never been far from the maddening crowd, saw the relentless media (below) and expectant fans (right) swell to record proportions in anticipation of a record night at Busch Stadium.*

him for his accomplishments. He would've been very proud of Mark as a player, but I think more so as a person."

Earlier in the day, Mac had made another Maris connection—with Roger's bat, which was brought from Cooperstown as a Hall of Fame gesture for the moment that was about to unfold.

"I touched it," McGwire said. "I touched it with my heart. Now I can honestly say my bat's going right next to his and I'm damn proud of it.

"Thanks to Babe, Roger and everybody who's watching up there."

The rest of the game, played amid a

steady roar, merely set the stage for postgame festivities that included McGwire's triumphant trip around Busch Stadium in a 1962 Cardinal-red Corvette convertible—the team's gift to the new home run champion—and a memorable tribute from commissioner Bud Selig that labeled it "one of the most historic nights in baseball history" and St. Louis as "the crown jewel of baseball franchises."

But National League president Leonard Coleman might have put the home run into more accurate perspective.

"The shot heard 'round the world was Bobby Thomson's home run in 1951 to win the pennant for the New York Giants," Coleman said. "This was the shot seen 'round the world."

PLAY IT AGAIN, SAM: *Sharing the 62 moment with McGwire was Cubs right fielder Sammy Sosa, who had more than a passing interest.*

THE DAY AFTER: *McGwire's 62nd home run was not taken lightly by St. Louis fans, who celebrated the feat with a downtown party the next day. Among the party hearty congregation were 3-year-old Brittney Dunworth (above middle, right) and 5-year-old sister Taylor.*

The Race

Sosa's

Weekend

"I have to admit, I was one of them," said Cubs teammate Mark Grace, who ended the Sunday game with a 10th-inning home run—while Sosa waited in the on-deck circle. "It was chilling when McGwire did it. I was dumbfounded. That put him four ahead and I pretty much thought the home run race was over.

"But when my friend Sammy gets hot, he gets them in a hurry. And right now, he's hot."

Sosa's Sunday effort highlighted a wild, emotional day at Wrigley Field. It started with a record crowd of 40,846 hoping for a Sosa home run and a victory that would inch the Cubs closer to a post-season berth and it ended with jubilant Chicago players carrying Sosa around the field on their shoulders. The fans got everything they wanted—and then some. The moment was not lost on the man who would be king.

"For the first time, I'm so emotional," a choked-up Sosa said after the Sunday game. "When I got to 62, I have to say it was something unbelievable, something I can't believe what I'm doing. I said to Mark McGwire, 'Wait for me.' Now we're together."

The Cubs were trailing 6-3 in the fifth inning when Sosa rocketed a Bronswell Patrick changeup onto Waveland Avenue, triggering a wild scramble by souvenir-seeking fans who had gathered with hopes of catching homer No. 61. "It was just an unbelievable feeling, an emotional moment for me," said Sosa, who was embraced by Grace after his stutter-stepping home run trot and overwhelmed by a roaring crowd that demanded the customary curtain call.

But the real celebration was triggered by a ninth-inning solo blast off Eric Plunk that sailed onto Waveland Avenue and cut the Chicago deficit to 10-9. Only two curtain calls would appease the crowd and the game had to be delayed so ushers could gather up debris thrown onto the field. The inspired Cubs rallied to force extra innings and set up Grace's 10th-inning heroics.

"That was the greatest series of baseball I've ever been involved in," Grace said. "I'll remember this series until my deathbed. I'm just sorry that I hit the home run and that Sammy didn't get to come up and do it himself. I know that's what the fans wanted to see."

The three-day, four-homer blitz gave Sosa 10 home runs off the Milwaukee pitching staff and ended his five-game homerless drought.

DON'T LOOK BACK: *The hot breath McGwire felt on the back of his neck September 13 belonged to Sosa, who assaulted the Brewers and claimed a share of the single-season home run record.*

Down but not out after watching McGwire hit his record-breaking 62nd home run in a September 8 game at St. Louis, Chicago's Sammy Sosa drilled four homers in a three-game weekend series against Milwaukee and set the stage for the most dramatic home run race in baseball history.

Sosa connected for homer No. 59 in a 13-11 Friday night loss to the Brewers and joined McGwire, Ruth and Roger Maris in the exclusive 60-something club the next day as the Cubs rallied for a 15-12 victory. But the best was yet to come. Sosa delivered a pair of 480-foot lightning bolts in a wild 11-10 Sunday victory that shot him past Maris' previous record of 61 and tied McGwire's all-time mark of 62.

63

"A home run is an earned run and that upsets me any time. ... It really doesn't matter if it's a guy's first homer or his 100th."

—Pirates pitcher Jason Christiansen

It was a cameo appearance, a gift at-bat for the Busch Stadium faithful who had not expected to see McGwire in the opener of a doubleheader against the Pittsburgh Pirates. But, like he had done so many times in a movie-like season, Big Mac attached a memory to the moment.

"It was just a moment," Cardinals manager Tony La Russa said after watching McGwire deliver his 63rd home run in an unusual pinch-hit role. "How do you do that? You've seen it. He's been doing that for a year and two months. People cheer him, 'C'mon Mark, we want you to hit one.' Boom. He hits it."

McGwire's 450th career homer, a towering 385-foot drive into the left-center field

September 15

Busch Stadium, St. Louis 41,271

AVG. .294	RBIs 132	BB 154

AT-BATS		PITCHER
9th HR		**Jason Christiansen** PIRATES RELIEVER, ⅓ IP

COUNT	ON BASE	OUTS
1-0	0	1

SOSA	PACE	GRIFFEY
62	68	52

FINAL: Pirates 8, Cardinals 6

Cardinals' record: 74-77

385 ft.

McGwire's first pinch-hit homer of the season landed in the left-center field bleachers at Busch Stadium.

bleachers, came on a 1-0 pitch from Pirates lefthander Jason Christiansen and allowed him to reclaim the single-season home run record from Sammy Sosa, who had caught Big Mac at 62. McGwire, who had been battling minor back spasms, batted in the ninth inning with the bases empty and the Cardinals trailing by three runs, a situation that normally would not pry him from the bench.

"Under ordinary circumstances, you wouldn't send McGwire up in that situation," Pirates manager Gene Lamont said. "But I understood why Tony did it. It was a good idea."

McGwire played the second game of the doubleheader, a 9-3 St. Louis victory, and collected a double and two walks. His first-game homer, which came one week after his festive 62nd record-breaker, overshadowed the two-homer effort of Cardinals rookie J.D. Drew.

SOSA'S 63rd *One day after McGwire had hit his record 63rd homer, Sammy Sosa pulled back into a tie with a game-deciding grand slam in the eighth inning of a 6-3 victory at San Diego.*

Sosa's dramatic 434-foot drive off Brian Boehringer landed in the upper deck and snapped a 2-2 tie. He had doubled home the Cubs' first two runs and drove in all six runs in the game. The win gave Chicago a half-game lead over the New York Mets in the race for the N.L. wild-card berth.

"I never thought I would get No. 63 with the bases loaded," Sosa said.

■ "Whatever I end up with, I end up with. I've done what I've done. Does it make it any less if I don't lead? No. Because what I've done and what Sammy has done is fantastic." *—McGwire*

64

"Never forget how amazing this man is. I keep searching for a way to describe it."

—Cardinals manager Tony La Russa

Turnabout is fair play. Sammy Sosa used a four-homer weekend blitz against Milwaukee to spring back into baseball's Great Home Run Race, so it seemed only fitting McGwire should break a tie at 63 and reclaim the single-season record in the opener of a three-game series against the Brewers.

McGwire regained his one-homer edge with a 417-foot fourth-inning shot over the left-center field fence at County Stadium and then barely missed two more with towering upper-deck drives that hooked foul in the sixth and eighth innings. The message was clear: Mac's post-62 lull was over and his home run battery was recharged.

"He put three great swings on the ball," said manager Tony La Russa after watching his team win its third straight game and reach the .500 mark for the first time since June 24. "That last one was really, really close."

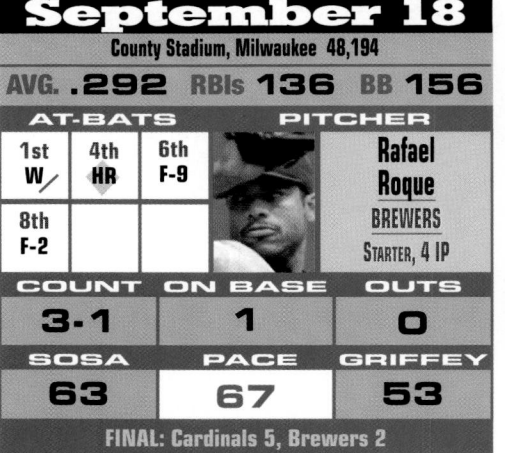

September 18

County Stadium, Milwaukee 48,194

AVG. .292	RBIs 136	BB 156

AT-BATS			PITCHER
1st W/	4th HR	6th F-9	**Rafael Roque** BREWERS STARTER, 4 IP
8th F-2			

COUNT	ON BASE	OUTS
3-1	1	0

SOSA	PACE	GRIFFEY
63	67	53

FINAL: Cardinals 5, Brewers 2

Cardinals' record: 77-77

The ball sailed over the left-center field fence and down a runway at Milwaukee's County Stadium.

McGwire's 64th homer came in the Cardinals' 154th game—the schedule Babe Ruth played in 1927 when he hit 60 for the Yankees. It was his second home run in 24 at-bats since hitting record-breaking 62.

"There's such a buildup to what I did—and you do it. I basically didn't know where I was for a couple of days," McGwire said. "I think that's explainable."

McGwire's record-breaker came against rookie Rafael Roque and a staff that had surrendered 10 home runs to Sosa.

SOSA *The Chicago Cubs dropped a tough-to-swallow 6-4 decision to Cincinnati on September 18 and Sammy Sosa completed his second straight game without a home run, falling one behind McGwire in the Great Race.*

"I have to say they pitch me real carefully," said Sosa, who was 0-for-4 and failed to get a ball out of the infield against Reds pitchers. "They didn't give me much to hit today."

Despite the loss, the Cubs remained a game ahead of the New York Mets in their pursuit of the N.L. wild-card berth. The Mets lost to Florida.

■ "There's nothing better than playing a baseball game in front of a full house. I know for quite some time now that a lot of fans across America have come specifically to watch me. At first, it was very overwhelming, but I got used to it. ... You don't come to a baseball game to watch one guy. But I've learned to accept it." *—McGwire*

65

"I couldn't care less if he hits 150 home runs. As an umpire, you can't get caught up in that."

—Umpire Bob Davidson, after ruling McGwire's potential 66th home run a double

No. 65 was a gift for Matthew. No. 65A was a little spice for the previously controversy-free great home run celebration of 1998.

"I asked him how many home runs he wanted his dad to hit," said McGwire, referring to a conversation he had with 10-year-old son Matt just before leaving for spring training. "He looked me in the eye and said, 'Sixty-five.'"

No problem. Big Mac filled Matt's order in the first inning of an easy win at Milwaukee's County Stadium when he drilled a Scott Karl pitch 423 feet into the left field seats, raising the single-season home run bar to 65—two ahead of Chicago's Sammy Sosa. The home run, which lifted

McGwire's career total to 452 and tied him with Carl Yastrzemski for 20th place on the all-time list, was one of five struck by the Cardinals.

"Sixty-five had a big meaning because that's the number my son set before spring training, so it means a lot to me," McGwire said. "That's all I thought about when I was running around the bases."

The two-run blow was just an appetizer. In the fifth inning, McGwire drove a pitch from Rod Henderson toward the seats in left-center. The ball appeared to clear the yellow bar atop the outfield wall, but umpire Bob Davidson stopped McGwire at second base, ruling a fan had reached over the fence and interfered with its flight. The crowd roared its disapproval, but McGwire had to be satisfied with his ground-rule double and still-uncomfortable home run lead over Sosa.

September 20

County Stadium, Milwaukee 52,831

AVG. .294	RBIs 138	BB 157

AT-BATS			PITCHER	
1st HR	3rd 1B	5th 2B		Scott Karl
7th K	9th W			BREWERS STARTER, 3 IP

COUNT	ON BASE	OUTS
2-1	1	1

SOSA	PACE	GRIFFEY
63	68	53

FINAL: Cardinals 11, Brewers 6

Cardinals' record: 79-77

No. 65 sailed high into the left field seats at Milwaukee's County Stadium.

SOSA *On Sammy Sosa Day at Chicago's Wrigley Field, Cubs fans saluted their Dominican star and threw a festive pregame party in his honor. But an 0-for-5 day by Sosa and a 7-3 Chicago loss to Cincinnati threw a damper on the occasion.*

Adding to everybody's discomfort was news McGwire had homered again in Milwaukee, increasing his lead over Sosa to 65-63.

Sosa, who saw his hitless streak reach 17 at-bats, failed to get a ball out of the infield for a third straight game.

■ "You're not supposed to hit 65 homers. We know how important Matthew is to him, but you can't just hit 65 homers because your son asks you to. But here we are with six games left and he has 65. It's unbelievable. Sixty-five?" *—Cardinals catcher Tom Lampkin*

DOUBLE TALK: *Fans battle for potential homer No. 66 as Brewers center fielder Marquis Grissom looks for the ball. Umpire Bob Davidson ruled fan interference and stopped McGwire at second.*

66

The ball screamed toward the left-center field seats as more than 50,000 sets of eyes strained to see its final destination. Home run No. 66 would be icing on the cake for the near-capacity Milwaukee County Stadium crowd that already had witnessed No. 65 in the ever-growing legacy of Mac moments.

The ball disappeared, touching off a mighty roar and the now-familiar melding of bodies in search of the ultimate souvenir. But as McGwire rounded second base, he was suddenly halted in mid-home run trot by umpire Bob Davidson, who delivered some startling news. Route 66 would end at second—a ground-rule double instead of a home run—because a fan had reached over the yellow-topped outfield fence and interfered with a ball that would not have reached the seats.

"The ball got out there in about half a second," Davidson explained after the game. "When I saw it, the fan was leaning over and the ball hit him below the yellow line. I saw the ball good. To me, the fan was over."

Television replays and fan testimonials disputed Davidson's judgment. It appeared the only "leaning" that took place was over an inside fence, thanks to the crush of ball-seekers pushing from behind.

"It was definitely a home run," said Allan Riesbeck, a partially paralyzed Iowa man who got a hand on the ball but couldn't hold it. "I was careful not to get my hands over the field. It was a home run. I went numb when they gave him a double."

Michael Chapes, who caught the ball but had it snatched out of his glove, was even more numb, thanks to the escort he received out of the park and a $518 fine he got for interfering with a ball in play. "It was definitely a home run. This whole thing makes me sick," he said.

Although the fans roared their disapproval, the Cardinals did not put up much of an argument at the time. But the team appealed to the National League after the game—an appeal that was denied the next day. The Cardinals argued that their victory over the Brewers was lopsided and McGwire scored anyway on Brian Jordan's single.

"After further review, it looked like a home run. The replay shows it. I didn't see the ball come back in play," said McGwire, who had to settle for a 65-63 home run advantage over Sammy Sosa entering the final week of the season. "(Davidson) said (the fan) came over the fence. I didn't see it running, but when I saw it on videotape, the man who caught the ball never came over the yellow line."

STOP SIGN: *Mac lost home run 66 when umpire Bob Davidson ruled that overzealous fans had given his ball an illegal lift into the stands.*

Ready for the Grand Finale

Two down, four games to play. No problem, at least not for Cubs right fielder Sammy Sosa in the magic Summer of '98.

The unshakable Sosa, hitless in his last 21 at-bats and seemingly on the verge of being closed out in the Great Home Run Chase, climbed out of his funk and delivered a 1-2 punch that set up a dramatic finale to one of the greatest chapters in baseball history. Sosa hit homers 64 and 65 in consecutive innings of a game at Milwaukee, drawing even with McGwire in the race for baseball's most exalted single-season record.

"This is my lucky team," said a smiling Sosa after hitting his 11th and 12th homers of the season against the Brewers. "Whatever has happened with the Brewers, how can you explain? I have to say I was strong. I came back today and felt great today."

Sosa ended his five-day struggle with style. Home run 64 came in the fifth off left-hander Rafael Roque, the same pitcher who had allowed McGwire's 64th. The opposite-field solo shot was followed by a bases-empty drive over the center field fence in the sixth off Rod Henderson, the pitcher who had surrendered McGwire's disallowed 66th homer.

"On the second, (Henderson) threw me a lot of breaking pitches," Sosa said. "I was fighting for that at-bat. He got two strikes, I relaxed, waited to see a good pitch and then he threw me a fastball."

Sosa's homers helped the playoff-hungry Cubs build a 7-0 lead, but Milwaukee fought back and handed Chicago a devastating defeat when left fielder Brant Brown dropped a two-out, bases-loaded fly ball that allowed three runs to score in the ninth inning. The shocking conclusion put a damper on Sosa's heroics.

"If I finish first or if I finish last (in home runs), it is no different," Sosa said. "I have another thing to do. It is the playoffs."

SOMETHING'S BREWING: *Sosa's unyielding challenge to McGwire stirred patriotic emotions, both at home in the Dominican Republic and among the Dominican flag-waving fans he encountered at every National League stop.*

The Final Weekend

66

"One thing about this game is that you don't usually get to choose your fame."

—Espos pitcher Shayne Bennett, who gave up homer 66

After a week filled with disallowed home runs, foul homers and drives to the warning track, McGwire finally broke through against the Montreal Expos— and his 375-foot shot into Busch Stadium's left field seats came just in the nick of time.

No. 66, unlike the four that preceded it, was not a major league record because 45 minutes earlier Sammy Sosa had connected for his 66th home run in a game at Houston. It was the first time Sosa had beaten him to a record milestone and the long-distance duel was waged in the third-to-last games for both McGwire's Cardinals and Sosa's Cubs.

"It was pretty obvious, of course. How could you not? The crowd said something," said McGwire when asked if he knew Sosa had jumped ahead in the home run chase. "But then again, like I've said 1,000 times, it really doesn't matter."

He controls his destiny, and I control my destiny."

Big Mac's fifth-inning at-bat against Shayne Bennett appeared to be destined for more of the frustration that had been coming in steady doses. He jumped on Bennett's first pitch and sent a towering drive toward the left field corner, but the ball settled into the upper deck, inches foul.

"It was foul, but it wasn't foul far," umpire Joe West said. "I think (it) went over the pole."

Four pitches later, McGwire ended his three-game homerless skid and keyed a victory that also featured a pair of homers by rookie J.D. Drew.

September 25
Busch Stadium, St. Louis 48,159

AVG. .293	RBIs 140	BB 161

AT-BATS			PITCHER
1st W/	3rd F-7	5th HR	Shayne Bennett
7th 1B/	9th K		EXPOS Reliever, ⅔ IP

COUNT	ON BASE	OUTS
1-2	1	2

SOSA	PACE	GRIFFEY
66	67	56

FINAL: Cardinals 6, Expos 5

Cardinals' record: 82-78

375 ft.

McGwire's record-tying 66th homer landed in the left field seats at Busch Stadium.

SOSA *Homer 66 temporarily lifted Sosa past McGwire, but it couldn't lift his Cubs to a much-needed victory over Houston. The Cubs, trying to keep pace in the race for the N.L. wild-card spot, lost to the Astros, 6-2, and finished the day in a three-way tie with the New York Mets and San Francisco.*

Sosa's fourth-inning blast, which gave him the distinction of reaching the 66 plateau before McGwire, tied the game 2-2, but that's all the scoring the Cubs could manage. The Mets dropped a 6-5 decision to Atlanta and the Giants defeated the Rockies, 8-6, to force the tie with two games remaining.

■ "I am going to have fun. I'm going to do my best at whatever I can do. I'm not going away hanging my head at all. If (Sosa's) up by one or we're tied or whatever may happen, it's going to be an exciting weekend." —McGwire, looking ahead to the season's final two games.

The leader—for less than an hour

August 19. Chicago's Wrigley Field. Sammy Sosa vs. Mark McGwire in baseball's 1998 production of Home Run Derby. Sosa blasts a fifth-inning homer off St. Louis' Kent Bottenfield and passes McGwire for the first time all season. But the lead lasts only 58 minutes as Big Mac responds with his tying 48th home run in the eighth and a game-winning 49th homer in the 10th.

September 25. The final weekend at St. Louis' Busch Stadium and Houston's Astrodome, 750 miles apart. Sosa pounds a pitch from Astros righthander Jose Lima 462 feet for his major league-record 66th home run, breaking a 2-day-old tie with McGwire. But this lead lasts only 45 minutes as Big Mac responds with a fifth-inning, 375-foot blast off Montreal righthander Shayne Bennett.

"A classic. It's like *Gone With the Wind*," said Cardinals outfielder John Mabry. "It's an amazing thing to look up and see the flash that Sammy just hit 66, and then Mac hits one, too. You wouldn't believe it unless you were here to see it. It's like one of those bad baseball movies that people make."

But great theater in baseball's season of hope. It marked the 21st time Sosa and McGwire had homered on the same day and the fourth time they had been tied (at 62, 63, 65 and 66) since Big Mac broke Roger Maris' single-season home run record. Turnabout was

fair play for No. 66. After being stalked relentlessly through the second half of the season by Sosa, it seemed only fair that McGwire should return the favor.

"He's been doing things like that since opening day," Cardinals manager Tony La Russa said of his big first baseman. "When has Mark done anything that's anywhere near normal and natural?"

While that flair for the dramatic kept fans and teammates on the edge of the seats, McGwire and Sosa remained true to their emotions.

"My feeling is that what (Sosa) and I have done, nobody should be disappointed," McGwire said. "We're two guys who have done something that's never been done in the history of the game."

Sosa agreed. "I'm not here to chase anybody, just to do my job," he said. "I felt great when I hit mine and then when Mark McGwire hit No. 66, too."

McGwire even went so far as to suggest that a home run tie might be the perfect ending. But not everybody shared that sentiment.

"As far as I'm concerned—I'm not speaking for the ownership or the coaches or the front office—Mark McGwire's home run record is the most important thing the next two days," said La Russa. "That sounds like heresy for me to say it. But he deserves everything we've got behind him. We're pulling for him real, real hard. We're probably more excited than he is."

67/68

"I had a feeling that he was going to explode. He was so locked in, so relaxed ... and he just crushed two balls."

——*Cardinals catcher Tom Lampkin*

With two more swings, McGwire cut an 838-foot swath in the 1998 home run race and staked yet another claim as the greatest single-season home run hitter in history.

While Sammy Sosa was going 2-for-4 without a homer at Houston, Big Mac muscled up twice against Montreal and broke the home run record for the fifth and sixth times.

"Does it look like he's under pressure? He hit two today," marveled catcher Tom Lampkin when asked about McGwire's state of mind entering the season's final day. "The mental aspect of his game is amazing. Nobody knows what he's going through because no one has hit 68 home runs before. I can't even fathom what goes through that guy's mind."

After he'd struck out against Expos starter Dustin Hermanson in his first at-bat, Big Mac hit

September 26
Busch Stadium, St. Louis 48,212

AVG. .294	RBIs 143	BB 161

AT-BATS			PITCHER
1st K	4th HR	5th F-9	**Dustin Hermanson** STARTER, 4 IP
7th HR	9th 5-3		**Kirk Bullinger** RELIEVER, ⅓ IP

COUNT	ON BASE	OUTS
0-0, 1-1	0,1	1,2

SOSA	PACE	GRIFFEY
66	68	56

FINAL: Expos 7, Cardinals 6

Cardinals' record: 82-79

403 ft.
435 ft.

Home run 67 sailed into the left field seats and No. 68 prompted a souvenir scramble in the left center field bleachers.

Hermanson's first pitch of the fourth inning 403 feet to left field. He pumped his fist into the air on his way to first, and was congratulated by Expos third baseman Shane Andrews on his way home.

In the seventh, McGwire drilled a low sinker from Kirk Bullinger 435 feet to left-center, marking his ninth multihomer game of 1998 and giving him a 2-stroke lead over Sosa. As he approached first, McGwire found himself still holding the bat, high in the air to celebrate the moment—like an artist who'd supplied the final stroke to a canvas.

The Expos, however, pushed across a ninth-inning run and escaped with a victory. But not before retiring McGwire on a grounder to third for the last out of the game. After which, he received yet another standing ovation.

SOSA *Neither of Sosa's hits were homers, but he was instrumental in a 3-2 Cubs victory over Houston that kept them tied with San Francisco for the N.L. wild-card playoff position entering the season's final day.*

Sosa's one-out single in the eighth inning set up a two-run Cubs rally that broke a 1-1 tie and gave them their second victory in seven games. That was good enough for Sammy on a day when Big Mac was having deep thoughts. "I've always said that I'm more interested in the wild card. ... However it finishes, it's been a great year," Sosa said.

■ "I completely forgot the bat was still in my hand. I said, 'I've got to get rid of this thing.' " —*McGwire, on his bat-raising home run trot after homer 68*

■ "It's not the physical grind; it's the mental grind. ... I've never used my mind any more than this year." —*McGwire*

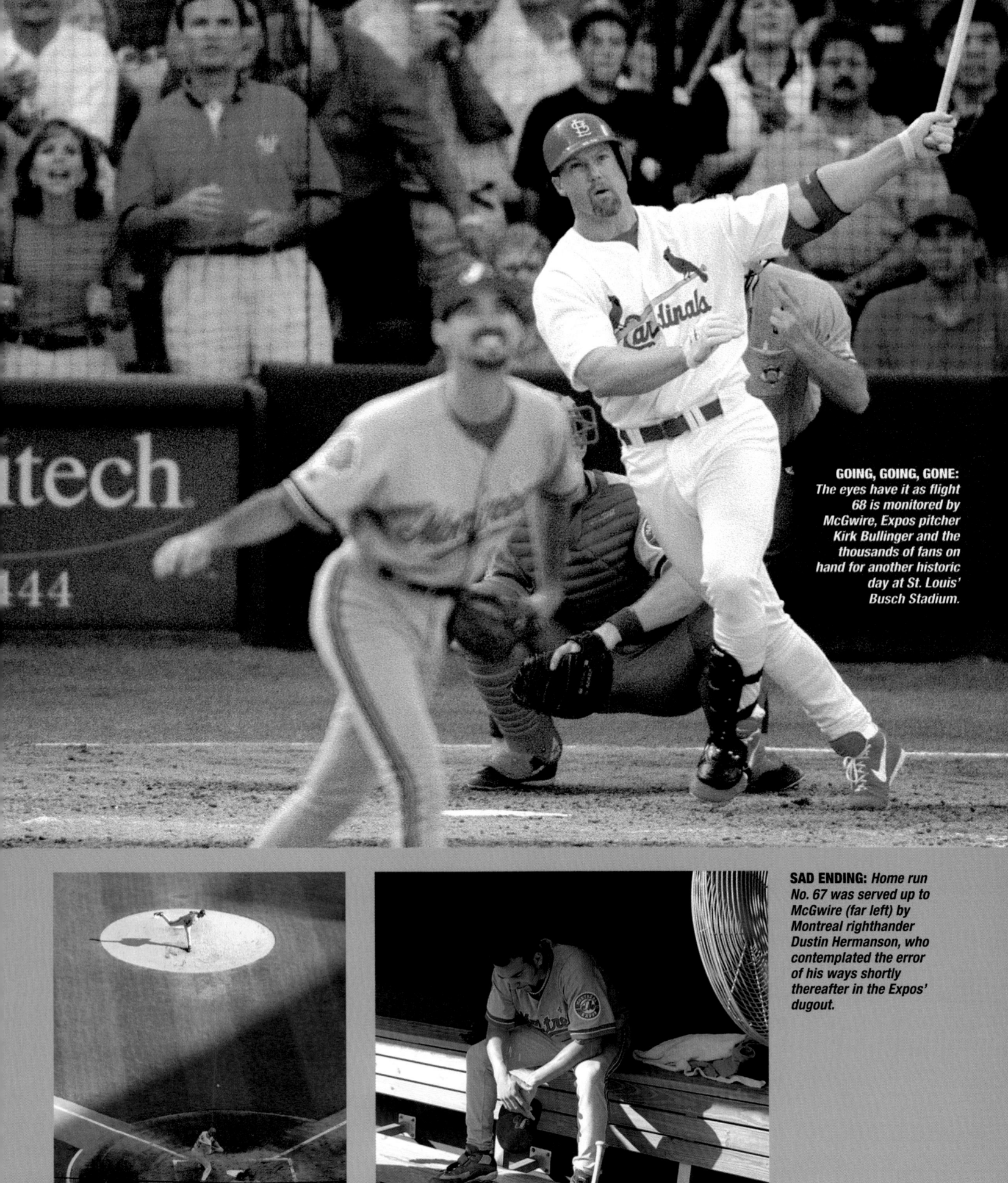

GOING, GOING, GONE: *The eyes have it as flight 68 is monitored by McGwire, Expos pitcher Kirk Bullinger and the thousands of fans on hand for another historic day at St. Louis' Busch Stadium.*

SAD ENDING: *Home run No. 67 was served up to McGwire (far left) by Montreal righthander Dustin Hermanson, who contemplated the error of his ways shortly thereafter in the Expos' dugout.*

69/70

"If Mac wrote this script, then he'll get more nominations than *Titanic*."

——Cardinals outfielder John Mabry

Like a great actor taking his final bow, McGwire closed the most sensational single-season home run performance in major league history by lifting his record into a new dimension.

McGwire, who had been locked in a neck-and-neck home run race with Sammy Sosa with two games to play, turned the season's final weekend into a riveting and joyous victory trot at St. Louis' Busch Stadium.

With Mac-crazed fans roaring their approval, he slammed homers 69 and 70 on the final day of the season to bring his weekend total to five in three games and finish four ahead of the defeated but still amazing Sosa.

"To say the least, I'm amazed," McGwire said. "Hitting 70, I've never thought about it or dreamt about it. ... I'm speechless, really. I can't

believe I did it. Can you? It blows me away."

Relaxed and zoned in after trailing Sosa for 45 minutes only two days earlier, McGwire smashed a breaking pitch from Montreal's Mike Thurman into the left field seats in the third inning for No. 69.

And he completed his second straight multihomer game in the seventh with a line drive off Carl Pavano—a three-run shot that broke a 3-3 tie. After what would prove to be the game-winning homer, McGwire was congratulated by Montreal catcher Mike Barrett and the entire Expos infield.

McGwire also singled to raise his final average to .299. "That (.300) is something nobody's really talked about— I've hit a lot of home runs but I've maintained an average," McGwire said. "And I'm proud of it."

September 27
Busch Stadium, St. Louis 46,110

AVG. .299	RBIs 147	BB 162

AT-BATS

1st 1B/	3rd HR	5th W/
7th HR		

PITCHER
Mike Thurman
STARTER, 5 IP
Carl Pavano
RELIEVER, 2 IP

COUNT	ON BASE	OUTS
1-1, 0-0	0,2	2,2

SOSA	PACE	GRIFFEY
66	70	56

FINAL: Cardinals 6, Expos 3

Cardinals' record: 83-79

McGwire's towering 69th homer landed in the left field seats; historic No. 70 was a line drive into a party room just above the left field fence.

SOSA *While McGwire was distancing himself from Sosa in the home run chase, Sammy was enjoying the satisfaction of helping his team claim a wild-card playoff berth.*

Sosa, who was homerless over his final three games, went 2-for-5 and drove in his major league-leading 158th run in an 11-inning, 4-3 final-day loss to Houston. Then he was 2-for-4 (two singles) in Chicago's 5-3 victory over San Francisco in the one-game playoff for the N.L. wild-card berth. Sosa finished with a .308 average.

■ "I'm like in awe of myself right now." —*McGwire*

■ "He's a massive human being. He's a big dude ... and he hit a good pitch. I didn't lay it in there. I was going after him. He went right after me and hit a home run. I guess he won." —*No. 70 victim Carl Pavano*

"Swing and it's ... get up, baby! Get up, get up, get up.

HOME RUN. He's done it again!

Seventy home runs. Take a ride on that for history! ... How can you end a season better than Mark McGwire has just done?"

—*The historic call of homer 70 by Cardinals broadcaster Mike Shannon*

'Stranger than fiction'

It started with a distant thud and ended with fireworks. In between, the final weekend of the 1998 season was filled with enough drama, excitement, amazement and emotional thunder to overwhelm even the most hardened and grizzled of baseball fans.

The thud was provided by Sammy Sosa when he drove a Jose Lima pitch into the fourth deck of Houston's Astrodome and startled the St. Louis fans who had gathered at Busch Stadium to watch McGwire complete the final leg of his record home run journey. The fireworks started 45 minutes later when Big Mac answered with his 66th home run, reclaiming a share of the major league record he had held for almost three weeks.

| 25 | MC GWIRE | 70 |
| 21 | SOSA | 66 |

UNCHARTED TERRITORY: *The scoreboard homer count (left page, below) seemed like something right out of a fairy tale when McGwire hit No. 70 and enjoyed a dugout celebration with coach Dave Parker (right, left photo) and teammates. On the at-bat before his history-making blow, Mac had dipped and dodged away from Mike Thurman pitches (photos below) while drawing his 162nd walk.*

"I just think he's been incredible all year long. And somehow the next three days he's going to do whatever he has to do—some way, somehow," Cardinals manager Tony La Russa had predicted before the Friday night game against Montreal.

Having taken and answered Sosa's best punch, a suddenly relaxed McGwire drove La Russa's crystal ball into the outer reaches of everybody's wildest dreams. First he took the lead with home runs 67 and 68 in a memorable Saturday afternoon game against the Expos.

68!

"He came into the dugout after he hit his (66th) home run, and he looked at me and just exhaled," said Cardinals catcher Tom Lampkin, one of McGwire's closest friends. "It was like he just had the biggest weight lifted off his shoulder. He didn't say anything, but it was like he finally got over the hump. He tied Sammy again.

"And I came in (Saturday), and I never had as good a feeling as I did about him hitting two home runs. Because after he gave me that little sign on the bench, I had a feeling that he was going to explode. He was so locked in, so relaxed, as if he had no pressure on him at all. And he just crushed two balls."

The first, a fourth-inning shot off Expos ace Dustin Hermanson, traveled 403 feet and prompted a

MASTERPIECE THEATER:
Home run No. 68 was worthy of a special bat-tossing gesture (right) on Saturday. Homer 69, which was saluted by first base coach Dave McKay (below left), was merely a Sunday appetizer for the grand finale Mac would deliver a few innings later. A special 69 salute was delivered by Kerry Woodson Jr. (white shirt, bottom photo), the St. Louis fan who caught the ball.

"I'll never let this season go," McGwire said during

fist-pumping trot reminiscent of his 60th, 61st and 62nd homers. The second, a 435-footer off Kirk Bullinger in the seventh inning, was watched by McGwire as he trotted down the first-base line, bat extended in the air like a magic wand, and he was escorted around the bases by another wave of cheers from the roaring crowd.

Then, before the Saturday excitement could even reach a level pitch, McGwire punctuated his big finish with another two-homer barrage—69 and 70—in a Sunday afternoon party at Busch Stadium.

70!

"It's one of the most special things we'll ever see in our lives," said Drew Baur, one of the Cardinals' owners.

"I'm speechless, really," McGwire said. "I can't believe I did it."

The impact of the moment, the creation of a new monument in baseball's record book, was not lost on Cardinals outfielder John Mabry.

"This is something you can tell your kids you were a part of," Mabry said. "You can't say enough about it, what it's meant to the game and the people who have been around it. He's not only in the hearts of St. Louis, but he's in the hearts of the country and even around the world."

It seemed only fitting that Big Mac would break ground on his own lofty plateau on his final swing of the incredible season with a three-run, game-winning blow. Homer 69 had sent the Busch Stadium crowd into another tizzy, complete with two curtain calls. But No. 70—a vicious line drive to left that shot out of the park in a blink of the eye—generated a whole new feeling of euphoria from a crowd and a city that should have been running low on emotional energy.

The 70 celebration, while lacking the electricity generated by 62, was more like a sustained canonization of a baseball god. McGwire tipped his cap, saluted, smiled and waved to the St. Louis faithful

the final series. "It might never happen again."

In perspective...

Quick facts to contemplate while trying to digest McGwire's 70-home run season:

■ McGwire reached his amazing milestone on 509 official at-bats, 31 fewer than Babe Ruth needed to hit 60 homers in 1927 and 81 fewer than Roger Maris needed to raise the single-season record bar to 61 in 1961.

■ McGwire has averaged 60 home runs over the last three seasons and his three-year total of 180 is 19 more than Ruth's best three-year run. It is, in fact, better than Ruth's best non-consecutive three years (173).

■ McGwire didn't play favorites, hitting home runs off 65 different pitchers. The only repeat victims were Arizona's Jeff Suppan, Philadelphia's Tyler Green, New York's Rick Reed, Colorado's John Thomson and Florida's Livan Hernandez.

■ McGwire finished the season with nine more home runs than singles.

■ Mac's homer total was three better than Earl Webb's 1931 record for doubles in a season.

■ The 70-homer total was three higher than the Cardinals team hit in 1982 en route to a World Series championship.

■ McGwire hit 38 home runs at Busch Stadium. Only three Cardinals in history (Johnny Mize, Rogers Hornsby and Stan Musial) have hit that many in a single season—home and away.

■ McGwire hit a major league record-tying 32 home runs on the road. Only seven Cardinals (Mize, Hornsby, Musial, Rip Collins, Jack Clark, Dick Allen and Ken Boyer) have hit that many in a season.

■ Big Mac hit 27 more home runs than previous Cardinals record-holder Johnny Mize, in 1940. Only 14 Cardinal players have hit as many as 27 in a season.

■ Only four players on the Cardinals' final-day 1998 roster (Ron Gant, Willie McGee, Brian Jordan and Ray Lankford) had hit as many as 70 home runs in their career.

■ McGwire's 70 home runs traveled a combined distance of 29,598 feet—higher than Mount Everest.

■ McGwire and Sammy Sosa combined for 136 home runs, topping the best two-player single-season total of 115 by Yankees Maris and Mickey Mantle in 1961.

■ McGwire homered every 7.3 at-bats in 1998, Sosa every 9.7. Ruth homered every 9.0 at-bats in 1927 and Maris every 9.7 at-bats in 1961.

■ McGwire's 162 walks equaled the second-highest total in major league history—by Ted Williams in 1947 and '49. Ruth, the record-holder, hit 41 homers when he walked 170 times in 1923. When Ruth put his 60 on the board in '27, he walked 138 times.

■ Despite going to greater lengths than any other hitter, McGwire had 317 occasions in which he didn't put the ball in play: He had 155 strikeouts to go with his 162 walks.

■ McGwire's .752 slugging percentage ranked second in National League history, behind only Hornsby's .756 of 1925. McGwire's total ranked seventh overall.

AND THE WINNER IS...: *Cardinals Hall of Fame broadcaster Jack Buck did the postgame honors (above) when McGwire was presented with the prestigious St. Louis Award.*

who remained long after the final out to honor him in postgame ceremonies. After all was said and done on an 83-79 season that became special because of McGwire's exploits, La Russa grasped unsuccessfully for the words to describe what he had witnessed.

"I've tried, believe me, because he provided moment after moment after moment after moment," La Russa said. "You stutter and you search. What you're thinking, I can't explain.

"I wish somebody was able to say it or write it correctly so that everybody could share it. But I tell you, I've struggled. I've even written stuff down. It never comes out even close to the moment, so I give up.

"The guy is ... it's even stranger than fiction, what this man has done and become."

McGwire vs. Sosa: A statistical

HR	Date	Opposing pitcher, Club	Place	Inn.	On base
1	March 31	Ramon Martinez (righthander), Los Angeles	H	5	3
2	April 2	Frank Lankford (righthander), Los Angeles	H	12	2
3	April 3	Mark Langston (lefthander), San Diego	H	5	1
1	April 4	Marc Valdes (righthander), Montreal	H	3	0
4	April 4	Don Wengert (righthander), San Diego	H	6	2
2	April 11	Anthony Telford (righthander), Montreal	A	7	0
5	April 14	Jeff Suppan (righthander), Arizona	H	3	1
6	April 14	Jeff Suppan (righthander), Arizona	H	5	0
7	April 14	Barry Manuel (righthander), Arizona	H	8	1
3	April 15	Dennis Cook (lefthander), New York Mets	A	8	0
8	April 17	Matt Whiteside (righthander), Philadelphia	H	4	1
9	April 21	Trey Moore (lefthander), Montreal	A	3	1
4	April 23	Dan Miceli (righthander), San Diego	H	9	0
5	April 24	Ismael Valdes (righthander), Los Angeles	A	1	0
10	April 25	Jerry Spradlin (righthander), Philadelphia	A	7	1
6	April 27	Joey Hamilton (righthander), San Diego	A	1	1
11	April 30	Marc Pisciotta (righthander), Chicago Cubs	A	8	1
12	May 1	Rod Beck (righthander), Chicago Cubs	A	9	1
7	May 3	Cliff Politte (righthander), St. Louis	H	1	0
13	May 8	Rick Reed (righthander), New York Mets	A	3	1
14	May 12	Paul Wagner (righthander), Milwaukee	H	5	2
15	May 14	Kevin Millwood (righthander), Atlanta	H	4	0
8	May 16	Scott Sullivan (righthander), Cincinnati	A	3	2
16	May 16	Livan Hernandez (righthander), Florida	H	4	0
17	May 18	Jesus Sanchez (lefthander), Florida	H	4	0
18	May 19	Tyler Green (righthander), Philadelphia	A	3	1
19	May 19	Tyler Green (righthander), Philadelphia	A	5	1
20	May 19	Wayne Gomes (righthander), Philadelphia	A	8	1
9	May 22	Greg Maddux (righthander), Atlanta	A	1	0
21	May 22	Mark Gardner (righthander), San Francisco	H	6	1
22	May 23	Rich Rodriguez (lefthander), San Francisco	H	4	0
23	May 23	John Johnstone (righthander), San Francisco	H	5	2
24	May 24	Robb Nen (righthander), San Francisco	H	12	1
25	May 25	John Thomson (righthander), Colorado	H	1	0
10	May 25	Kevin Millwood (righthander), Atlanta	A	4	0
11	May 25	Mike Cather (righthander), Atlanta	A	8	2
12	May 27	Darrin Winston (lefthander), Philadelphia	H	8	0
13	May 27	Wayne Gomes (righthander), Philadelphia	H	9	1
26	May 29	Dan Miceli (righthander), San Diego	A	9	1
27	May 30	Andy Ashby (righthander), San Diego	A	1	0
14	June 1	Ryan Dempster (righthander), Florida	H	1	1
15	June 1	Oscar Henriquez (righthander), Florida	H	8	2
16	June 3	Livan Hernandez (righthander), Florida	H	5	1
17	June 5	Jim Parque (lefthander), Chicago White Sox	H	5	1
28	June 5	Orel Hershiser (righthander), San Francisco	H	1	1
18	June 6	Carlos Castillo (righthander), Chicago White Sox	H	7	0
19	June 7	James Baldwin (righthander), Chicago White Sox	H	5	2
20	June 8	LaTroy Hawkins (righthander), Minnesota	A	3	0
29	June 8	Jason Bere (righthander), Chicago White Sox	A	4	1
30	June 10	Jim Parque (lefthander), Chicago White Sox	A	3	2
31	June 12	Andy Benes (righthander), Arizona	A	3	3
21	June 13	Mark Portugal (righthander), Philadelphia	A	6	1
22	June 15	Cal Eldred (righthander), Milwaukee	H	1	0
23	June 15	Cal Eldred (righthander), Milwaukee	H	3	0
24	June 15	Cal Eldred (righthander), Milwaukee	H	7	0
25	June 17	Bronswell Patrick (righthander), Milwaukee	H	4	0
32	June 17	Jose Lima (righthander), Houston	A	3	0
33	June 18	Shane Reynolds (righthander), Houston	A	5	0
26	June 19	Carlton Loewer (righthander), Philadelphia	H	1	0
27	June 19	Carlton Loewer (righthander), Philadelphia	H	5	1
28	June 20	Matt Beech (lefthander), Philadelphia	H	3	1
29	June 20	Toby Borland (righthander), Philadelphia	H	6	2
30	June 21	Tyler Green (righthander), Philadelphia	H	4	0
31	June 24	Seth Greisinger (righthander), Detroit	A	1	0
34	June 24	Jaret Wright (righthander), Cleveland	A	4	0
35	June 25	Dave Burba (righthander), Cleveland	A	1	0
32	June 25	Brian Moehler (righthander), Detroit	A	7	0
36	June 27	Mike Trombley (righthander), Minnesota	A	7	1

Categories	McGwire	Sosa
vs. RHP	55	54
vs. LHP	15	12
Home	38	35
Away	32	31
Day	21	33
Night	49	33
Sunday	10	10
Monday	5	14
Tuesday	16	2
Wednesday	8	14
Thursday	7	3
Friday	11	13
Saturday	13	10
1st inning	11	12
2nd inning	0	2
3rd inning	8	8
4th inning	13	5
5th inning	9	12
6th inning	2	8
7th inning	10	6
8th inning	9	9
9th inning	4	4
10th inning	1	0
11th inning	1	0
12th inning	2	0
Solo	33	37
Two-run	28	19
Three-run	7	7
Grand slams	2	3
2-HR games	8	10
3-HR games	2	1
No outs	23	16
One out	21	20
Two outs	26	30
With team losing	25	28
Score tied	25	17
Team leading	20	21
Team record	34-24	30-24
Game-tying HRs	6	7
Go-ahead HRs	30	20
March	1	0
April	10	6
May	16	7
June	10	20
July	8	9
August	10	13
September	15	11
vs. D'backs	4	5
vs. Braves	2	3
vs. Cubs	7	0
vs. ChiSox	2	3

profile

Categories	McGwire	Sosa
vs. Reds	1	4
vs. Indians	2	0
vs. Rockies	2	3
vs. Tigers	0	2
vs. Marlins	7	4
vs. Astros	5	4
vs. Royals	1	0
vs. Dodgers	4	1
vs. Brewers	4	12
vs. Twins	1	1
vs. Expos	6	3
vs. Mets	4	2
vs. Phillies	5	8
vs. Pirates	3	2
vs. Cardinals	0	3
vs. Padres	5	3
vs. Giants	5	3
On grass	60	57
On turf	10	9
Pre-All Star	37	33
Post-All Star	33	33
0-0 Count	11	3
1-0 Count	8	12
2-0 Count	5	2
3-0 Count	0	0
0-1 Count	6	10
1-1 Count	9	2
2-1 Count	8	8
3-1 Count	2	4
0-2 Count	4	3
1-2 Count	7	5
2-2 Count	8	8
3-2 Count	2	9
To LF	34	12
To LCF	20	22
To CF	13	10
To RCF	3	12
To RF	0	10
Total distance (feet)	29598	26869
Average (by feet)	422.8	407.1
Longest (by feet)	545	500
350 and below	3	5
351-375	12	15
376-400	8	10
401-425	16	14
426-450	11	14
451-475	10	3
476-500	5	5
501-525	3	0
526 and longer	2	0

HR	Date	Opposing pitcher, Club	Place	Inn.	On base
37	June 30	Glendon Rusch (lefthander), Kansas City	H	7	0
33	June 30	Alan Embree (lefthander), Arizona	H	8	0
34	July 9	Jeff Juden (righthander), Milwaukee	A	2	1
35	July 10	Scott Karl (lefthander), Milwaukee	A	2	0
38	July 11	Billy Wagner (lefthander), Houston	H	11	1
39	July 12	Sean Bergman (righthander), Houston	H	1	0
40	July 12	Scott Elarton (righthander), Houston	H	7	0
41	July 17	Brian Bohanon (lefthander), Los Angeles	H	1	0
36	July 17	Kirt Ojala (lefthander), Florida	A	6	1
42	July 17	Antonio Osuna (righthander), Los Angeles	H	8	0
43	July 20	Brian Boehringer (righthander), San Diego	A	5	1
37	July 22	Miguel Batista (righthander), Montreal	H	8	2
38	July 26	Rick Reed (righthander), New York Mets	H	6	1
44	July 26	John Thomson (righthander), Colorado	A	4	0
39	July 27	Willie Blair (righthander), Arizona	A	6	1
40	July 27	Alan Embree (lefthander), Arizona	A	8	3
41	July 28	Bob Wolcott (righthander), Arizona	A	5	3
45	July 28	Mike Myers (lefthander), Milwaukee	H	8	0
42	July 31	Jamey Wright (righthander), Colorado	H	1	0
43	Aug. 5	Andy Benes (righthander), Arizona	H	3	1
46	Aug. 8	Mark Clark (righthander), Chicago Cubs	H	4	0
44	Aug. 8	Rick Croushore (righthander), St. Louis	A	9	1
45	Aug. 10	Russ Ortiz (righthander), San Francisco	A	5	0
46	Aug. 10	Chris Brock (righthander), San Francisco	A	7	0
47	Aug. 11	Bobby Jones (righthander), New York Mets	H	4	0
47	Aug. 16	Sean Bergman (righthander), Houston	A	4	0
48	Aug. 19	Kent Bottenfield (righthander), St. Louis	H	5	1
48	Aug. 19	Matt Karchner (righthander), Chicago Cubs	A	8	0
49	Aug. 19	Terry Mulholland (lefthander), Chicago Cubs	A	10	0
50	Aug. 20 (1)	Willie Blair (righthander), New York Mets	A	7	0
51	Aug. 20 (2)	Rick Reed (righthander), New York Mets	A	1	0
49	Aug. 21	Orel Hershiser (righthander), San Francisco	H	5	1
52	Aug. 22	Francisco Cordova (righthander), Pittsburgh	A	1	0
50	Aug. 23	Jose Lima (righthander), Houston	H	5	0
53	Aug. 23	Ricardo Rincon (lefthander), Pittsburgh	A	8	0
51	Aug. 23	Jose Lima (righthander), Houston	H	8	0
52	Aug. 26	Brett Tomko (righthander), Cincinnati	A	3	0
54	Aug. 26	Justin Speier (righthander), Florida	H	8	1
53	Aug. 28	John Thomson (righthander), Colorado	A	1	0
54	Aug. 30	Darryl Kile (righthander), Colorado	A	1	1
55	Aug. 30	Dennis Martinez (righthander), Atlanta	H	7	2
55	Aug. 31	Brett Tomko (righthander), Cincinnati	H	3	1
56	Sept. 1	Livan Hernandez (righthander), Florida	A	7	0
57	Sept. 1	Donn Pall (righthander), Florida	A	9	0
56	Sept. 2	Jason Bere (righthander), Cincinnati	H	6	0
58	Sept. 2	Brian Edmondson (righthander), Florida	A	7	1
59	Sept. 2	Rob Stanifer (righthander), Florida	A	8	1
57	Sept. 4	Jason Schmidt (righthander), Pittsburgh	A	1	0
60	Sept. 5	Dennis Reyes (lefthander), Cincinnati	H	1	1
58	Sept. 5	Sean Lawrence (lefthander), Pittsburgh	A	6	0
61	Sept. 7	Mike Morgan (righthander), Chicago Cubs	H	1	0
62	Sept. 8	Steve Trachsel (righthander), Chicago Cubs	H	4	0
59	Sept. 11	Bill Pulsipher (lefthander), Milwaukee	H	5	0
60	Sept. 12	Valerio De Los Santos (lefthander), Milwaukee	H	7	2
61	Sept. 13	Bronswell Patrick (righthander), Milwaukee	H	5	1
62	Sept. 13	Eric Plunk (righthander), Milwaukee	H	9	0
63	Sept. 15 (1)	Jason Christiansen (lefthander), Pittsburgh	H	9	0
63	Sept. 16	Brian Boehringer (righthander), San Diego	A	8	3
64	Sept. 18	Rafael Roque (lefthander), Milwaukee	A	4	1
65	Sept. 20	Scott Karl (lefthander), Milwaukee	A	1	1
64	Sept. 23	Rafael Roque (lefthander), Milwaukee	A	5	0
65	Sept. 23	Rod Henderson (righthander), Milwaukee	A	6	0
66	Sept. 25	Jose Lima (righthander), Houston	A	4	0
66	Sept. 25	Shayne Bennett (righthander), Montreal	H	5	1
67	Sept. 26	Dustin Hermanson (righthander), Montreal	H	4	0
68	Sept. 26	Kirk Bullinger (righthander), Montreal	H	7	1
69	Sept. 27	Mike Thurman (righthander), Montreal	H	3	0
70	Sept. 27	Carl Pavano (righthander), Montreal	H	7	2

St. Louis played 163 games in 1998 (one tie on August 24), with McGwire participating in 155 games.

Chicago played 163 games in 1998 (one game playoff on September 28), with Sosa participating in 159 games.

Riding the wave

In case a ground ball comes bouncing through the house, I have my old baseball glove within reach. My wife one day asked, "Why do you keep that old glove on your desk? And don't give me that stuff about ground balls rebounding through the house."

The Wilson A2000 is a masterpiece of man's creative urge. It sits atop a computer tower—enthroned, beautiful, shimmering with memories. The leather is golden under a patina of black dirt carried away from infields all over central Illinois.

Slide your hand into the A2000. It's 36 years old and a little dry. Yet the leather is soft to the touch. Soft enough to bring back a kid's dreams. The kid imagines the A2000 carrying him toward a ground ball behind second base. To touch the glove after all this time is to. ...

"Honey, I've figured it out, about my ball glove."

"And?"

"It reminds me of when I had hair."

Yes, and hooray! Baseball lets us be kids forever. The novelist W.P. Kinsella wrote: "Within the baselines, anything can happen. Tides can reverse, oceans can open. That's why they say, 'The game is never over until the last man is out.' Colors can change, lives can alter, anything is possible in this gentle, flawless, loving game." Of all that, Mark McGwire is proof.

Throughout the 1998 season, with grace, warmth, passion and inimitable skill, he showed us how much fun the game can be. He put a smile on America's face.

He did it by hitting baseballs higher and farther than anyone else ever had. He became the very incarnation of that great American mythological hero, the home run hitter.

Best of all, the hero made us smile in the most human way of all. He shared his emotions. "What I've accomplished," he said, "is fabulous." True, and said with a tone of wonder, as if someone else had done it.

He touched us with sentiment and generosity. After hopping onto home plate the night of his 62nd home run, the big man lifted high and kissed his young son, Matt, who was in uniform as the Cardinals' batboy. Time and again, McGwire figuratively embraced Roger Maris even as he literally embraced Sammy Sosa. "Riding the wave," McGwire said of his moment, "along with America."

Astonishing, McGwire's work. More astonishing, his effect on the game. Who'd have thought baseball ever again would be happy front-page news?

The 1998 season began less than four years after major league owners, unable to settle a players' strike, canceled a World Series. Neither Hitler nor an earthquake had ever caused so foul a deed. The owners also made plans to play the 1995 season with strikebreakers/incompetents recruited from God only knows where. Such arrogance. Go back to the Black Sox scandal of 1921. Only then was baseball's connection to its fans more tenuous.

Long embittered by two decades of player-owner wars, fans decided that a pox should fall on both their houses. Attendance, interest and prestige were driven down by anger born of betrayal and abandonment.

A lesser game might have foundered. Baseball, as always, simply outlasted the fools who run it. McGwire himself had foreshadowed the game's comeback. He did it late in the 1997 season.

Though he would be a free agent at season's end and had spent less than two months in St. Louis, he signed a three-year contract extension with the Cardinals. His signing came as a surprise at many levels.

Saying he liked playing for St. Louis fans, he did not conduct a bidding war. His contract averages $9.5 million per year, perhaps about $5 million under the value of a player who had hit 110 home runs for the two previous seasons. McGwire also announced he would donate $1 million per year to fund a foundation for abused children. At a press conference, when he came to the part about children, the strongest man in baseball wept.

Whoa. An athlete who honors his city's fans? Who leaves $5 million on the table? Who gives $1 million to kids whose lives bring him to tears? Who does all this and can hit home runs out of any park, including Yellowstone?

Small wonder, then, that as McGwire chased Babe Ruth's 60 and Roger Maris' 61, baseball fans opened wide their arms to him. And all of baseball profited from the example. Suddenly, those scoundrels of '94 became heroes in '98.

Even in Chicago, it happened for the delightful Sosa. Cubs fans used to call him a whiner who struck out too often and produced too little to earn the adulation and money he demanded. But by the end of the '98 season, when he had chased McGwire across the landscape, he took Wrigley Field curtain calls to chants of "Sam-mee! Sam-mee!" He owned those parts of Chicago not taken by Michael Jordan.

Such a summer, 1998, the sweetest ever in baseball, so sweet that for a neat little while, baseball heroes bumped a presidential scoundrel to the bottom of our front pages.

This is life as life should be.

Thank you, Mr. McGwire.

Dave Kindred is a contributing editor for THE SPORTING NEWS.

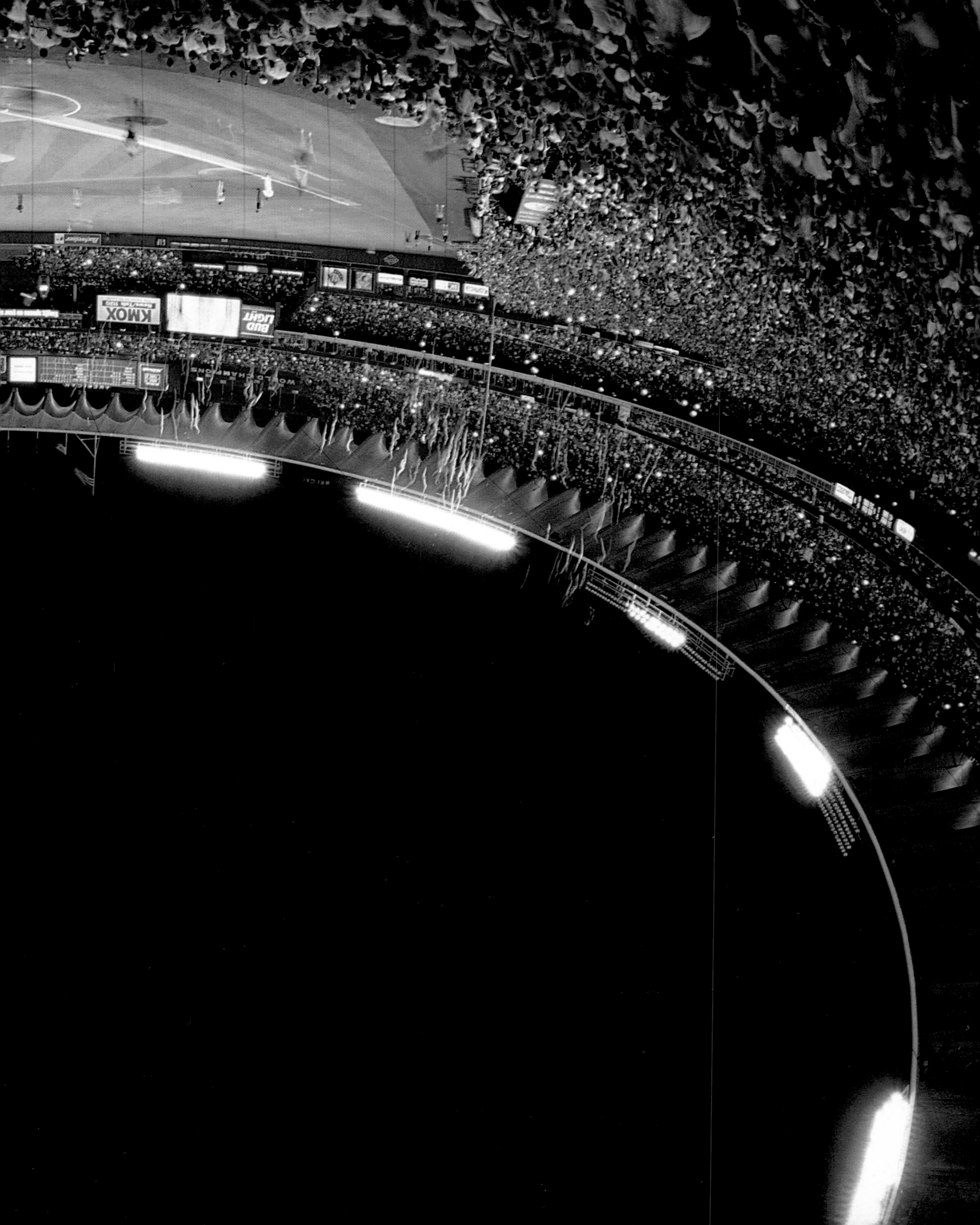

Photographer Credits

Page Photo Appears *T=top, B=bottom, L=left, R=right, M=middle*

Albert Dickson/The Sporting News — Rear cover, 17, 21T, 25T, 29T, 38-39, 40(all), 41(all), 133 TL, 135TR, BR; 136-137, 140T, BL; 142-143, 144-145, 146-147, 148TR, 150T, MR; 151ML, BR; 153, 154 TR, 164R, 165L, 167BL, 169, 172(2), 174R, 177, 184

Ed Nessen/The Sporting News — 4TL, 5, 6-7, 18T, 19B, 21B, 22, 23M, T, 27R, 28, 29M, B; 30(2), 31BL, 37, 42, 45, 47R, T; 48, 49, 53, 62-3, 79, 81, 97, 107, 108, 109, 114-115, 123B, 127TR, 139T, 140BR, 141R, 155, 158L, 159B, R; 160L, B; 162(3), 163, 170L, BR; 173(3),

Robert Seale/The Sporting News — Front cover, 14-15, 117B, 138, 144-145, 150BR, 151TR

Bob Leverone/The Sporting News — 4ML, 19T, 94(3), 95, 129(3), 130(5), 133TR, 134(2), 139B, 141L, 150L, 180

Fred Barnes/The Sporting News — 133B

Bill Wilson/The Sporting News — 152(3)

Michael Behrens/The Sporting News — 154L,TR, MR;

Steve Romer/The Sporting News — 154BR

The Sporting News Archives — 32, 33,34,35,36, 103R, 129BL,

Odell Mitchell Jr./St. Louis Post-Dispatch — 61, 171, 173T, 174BL,

Karen Elshout/St. Louis Post-Dispatch — 64, 72T, 72BR, 149BL,BR;

Jerry Naunheim Jr./St. Louis Post-Dispatch — 20TL, 117(3), 119, 121(3)

Laurie Skrivan/St. Louis Post-Dispatch — 16, 23(4) 112 TL, BL, BM, LR(4); 175R,

Chris Lee/St. Louis Post-Dispatch — 2-3, 4BL, 18B, 20BL, 25B, 26-7, 31TR, 80B, 88(3), 93, 99, 101BL, 101BR, 105(2), 110-111, 112ML, BL; 113T, B; 123T, 124(2), 125MR, BR; 127TL, ML, B

J.B. Forbes/St. Louis Post-Dispatch — 31TM, 76-77, 80B, 125TR, 148TL, ML, BL; 167BR, 176

Jacob Ware/St. Louis Post-Dispatch — 166-167

Dilip Vishwanat/St. Louis Post-Dispatch — 8-9, 10-11, 182-183

Wayne Crosslin/St. Louis Post-Dispatch — 149T, 174TL

Kevin Manning/St. Louis Post-Dispatch — 24, 43, 44, 47BL, BM; 50, 147BR

Wesley Law/St. Louis Post-Dispatch — 89

Ryan Remiorz/Associated Press — 51
Pat Sullivan/Associated Press — 87, 165R
Jamie Yanak/Associated Press — 90, 91
David Sherman/Associated Press — 92
Lenny Ignelzi/Associated Press — 102
Harold Jenkins/Associated Press — 101TR
John Gaps III/Associated Press — 80TL
Fred Jewell/Associated Press — 82
Jay Crihfield/Associated Press — 83
Ken Levine/Associated Press — 85(2)
Joan C. Fahrenthold/Associated Press — 78
Rusty Kennedy/Associated Press — 52, 67MR,
Denis Poroy/Associated Press — 75
Osamu Honda/Associated Press — 57TR, 57MR, 118
Mark Lennihan/Associated Press — 57TL
John Dunn/Associated Press — 57B
Leon Algee/Associated Press — 59T, 59L, 59B, 69TL, 71BR 71MR, 72BL

Tom Gannam/Associated Press — 59R, 60
Mary Butkus/Associated Press — 74, 101TL
George Widman/Associated Press — 67BL,TR
James Finley/Associated Press — 69TR
Eric Risberg/Associated Press — 158BL
Jeffrey Phelps/Associated Press — 161BR
David J. Phillip/Associated Press — 164BL
Tim Nordmann/Associated Press — 71BL, 71TL
Doug Collier/Agency France Presse — 103
Jim Gehrz/Milwaukee Journal Seninel — 161TL
Tom Cruze/Chicago Sun-Times — 54
David Fahleson/Houston Chronicle — 86
Stephen Green/Chicago Cubs — 157
Andie Giapaglione/Chicago Cubs — 156
Ron Vesely — 55
Bill Greenblatt/United Press International — 69B
Jery Lodriguss/Philadelphia Inquirer — 67TL

Stadium Photos

Shea Stadium, New York — Marc Levine/NY Mets
Bank One Ballpark, Phoenix — Jason Wise for The Sporting News
Busch Stadium, St. Louis — Ed Nessen/The Sporting News
Wrigley Field, Chicago — Jerry Naunheim Jr./St. Louis Post-Dispatch
Qualcomm Stadium, San Diego — J. Zwink/San Diego Padres
Houston Astrodome — Robert Seale/The Sporting News

Jacobs Field, Cleveland — Albert Dickson/The Sporting News
Metrodome, Minneapolis — Rick Orndorf
Veterans Stadium, Philadelphia — Jeff Hixon/Allsport
Coors Field, Denver — Albert Dickson/The Sporting News
Pro Player Stadium, Miami — Bob Leverone/The Sporting News
Olympic Stadium, Montreal — Phil Norton

The BIG BOOK of DESIGN IDEAS

editor
DAVID E. CARTER

art director
SUZANNA M.W.

designers
CYNTHIA B. COMBS
ANTHONY B. STEPHENS

HD
HARPER
DESIGN

An Imprint of HarperCollins*Publishers*

THE BIG BOOK OF DESIGN IDEAS
Copyright © 2000 by HARPER DESIGN and David E. Carter

First published in 2000 by:
Harper Design,
An Imprint of HarperCollins*Publishers*
10 East 53rd Street
New York, NY 10022
Tel: (212) 207-7000
Fax: (212) 207-7654
HarperDesign@harpercollins.com
www.harpercollins.com

Distributed throughout the world by
HarperCollins International
10 East 53rd Street
New York, NY 10022
Fax: (212) 207-7654

HarperCollins books may be purchased for educational, business, or sales
promotional use. For information, please write: Special Markets Department,
HarperCollins Publishers Inc., 10 East 53rd Street, New York, NY 10022.

Library of Congress Control Number: 2004115429

ISBN: 0-06-008763-3

Printed in Hong Kong by Everbest Printing Company through Four Colour Imports,
Louisville, Kentucky.

Third Printing, 2005

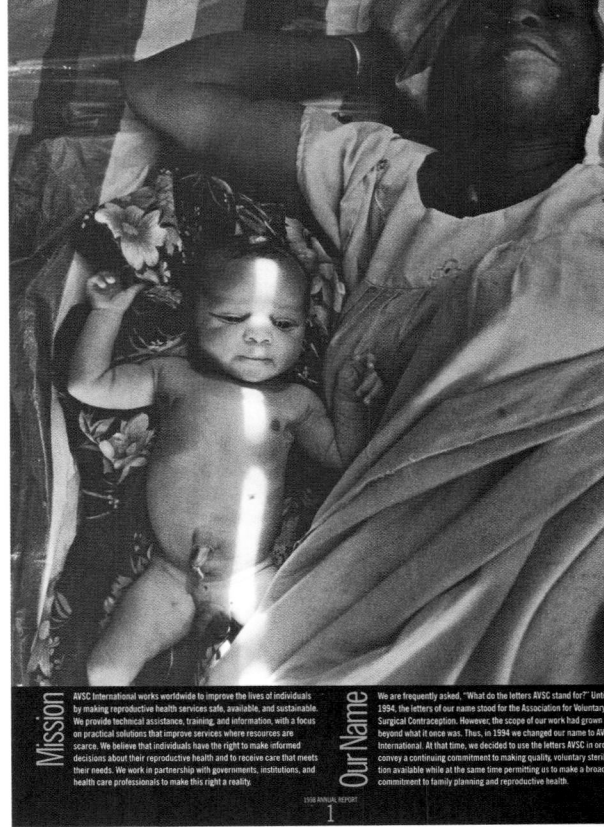

creative firm
**EMERSON,
WAJDOWICZ
STUDIOS**
New York, New York
creative director
JUREK WAJDOWICZ
senior art director
LISA LaROCHELLE
client
AVSC INTERNATIONAL

creative firm
LOUEY/RUBINO DESIGN GROUP, INC.
Santa Monica, California
creative director
ROBERT LOUEY
client
KAUFMAN AND BROAD HOME CORPORATION

creative firm
SIBLEY PETEET DESIGN
Dallas, Texas
designer
DAVID BECK
photographers
JOHN PARRISH, GREG BOOTH
client
ZALE CORPORATION

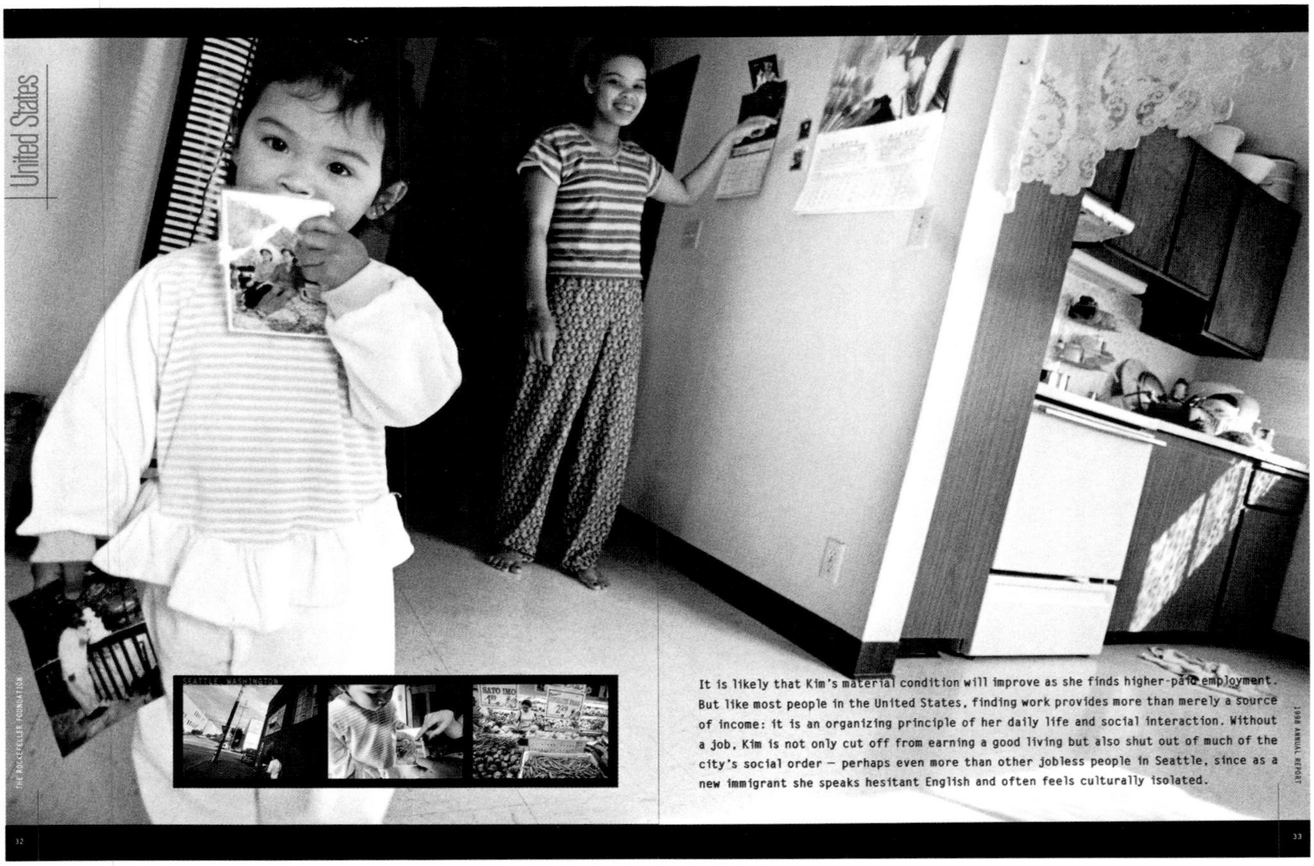

United States
SEATTLE, WASHINGTON
SATO IMO
It is likely that Kim's material condition will improve as she finds higher-paid employment. But like most people in the United States, finding work provides more than merely a source of income: it is an organizing principle of her daily life and social interaction. Without a job, Kim is not only cut off from earning a good living but also shut out of much of the city's social order — perhaps even more than other jobless people in Seattle, since as a new immigrant she speaks hesitant English and often feels culturally isolated.
THE ROCKEFELLER FOUNDATION
1998 ANNUAL REPORT
32
33

creative firm
EMERSON, WAJDOWICZ STUDIOS
New York, New York
creative director
JUREK WAJDOWICZ
senior art director
LISA LaROCHELLE
client
THE ROCKEFELLER FOUNDATION

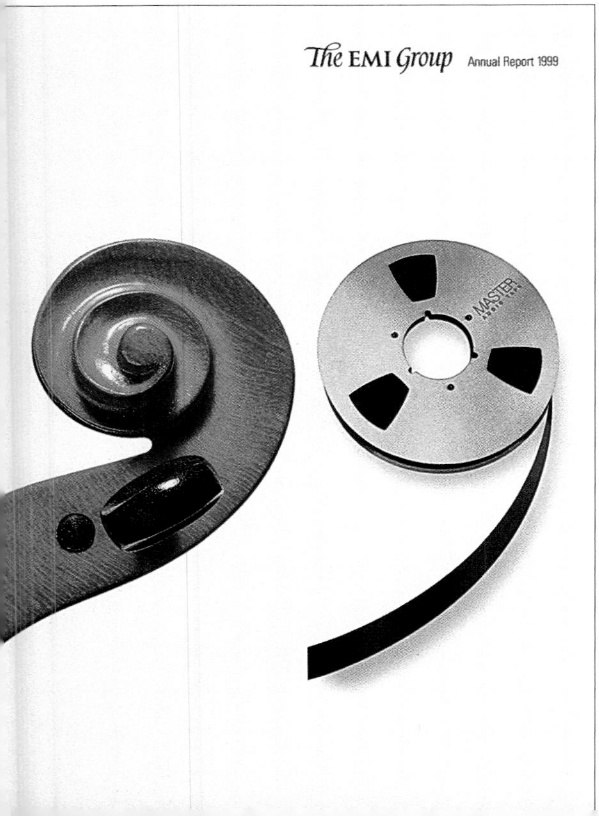

The EMI Group Annual Report 1999
MASTER

creative firm
TOR PETTERSEN
& PARTNERS
London, England
designers
JEFF DAVIS, JIM ALLSOPP
client
THE EMI GROUP

creative firm
ARNOLD SAKS
ASSOCIATES
New York, New York
creative director
ARNOLD SAKS
designer
MICHELLE NOVAK
client
GENERAL CHEMICAL

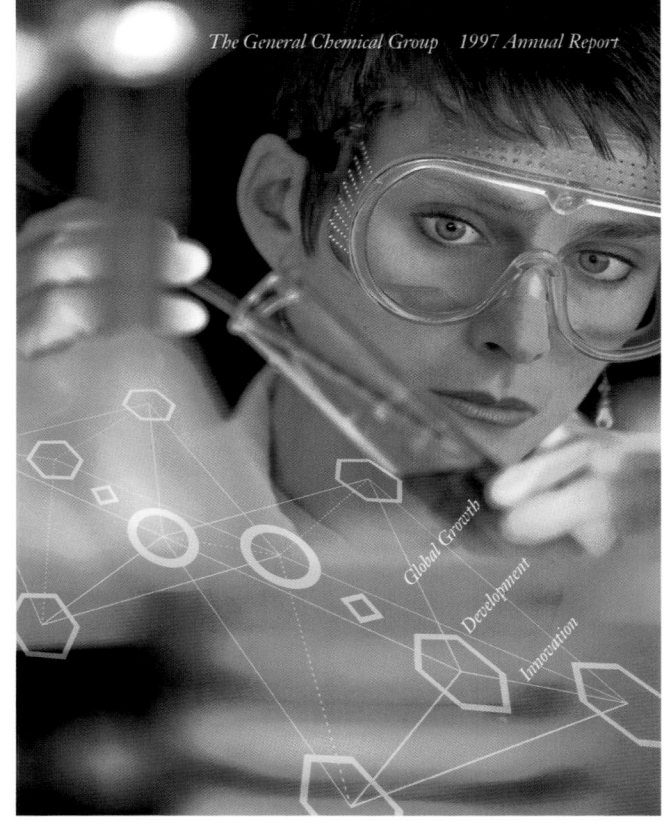

The General Chemical Group 1997 Annual Report
Global Growth
Development
Innovation

creative firm
    HEINEY & CRAIG, INC.
    San Francisco, California
creative director
    TIM CRAIG
senior designer
    SHARON BACKURZ
client
    PUMA TECHNOLOGIES

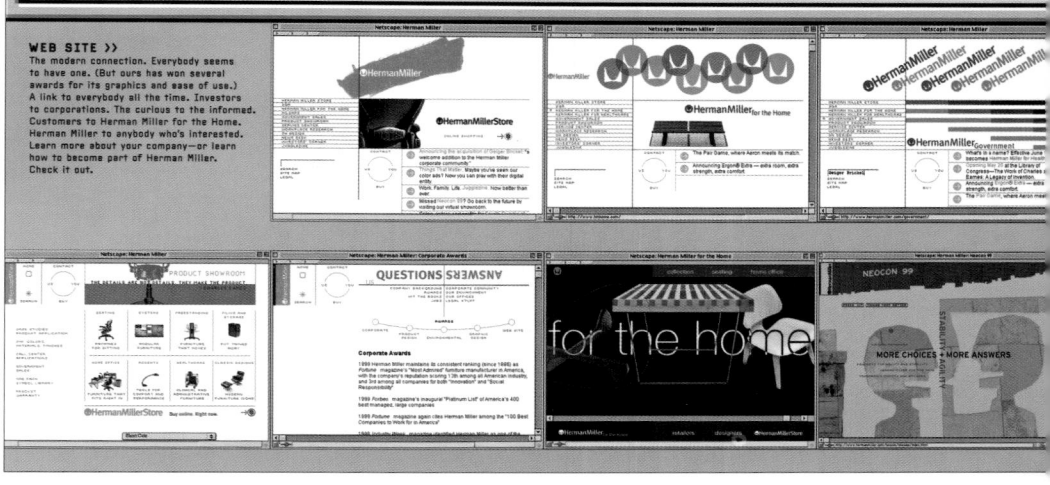

creative firm
    BBK STUDIO INC.
    Grand Rapids, Michigan
creative director
    STEVE FRYKHOLM
designer
    YANG KIM
copywriter
    CLARK MALCOLM
typesetter
    KIM LAPP
client
    HERMAN MILLER INC.

The Hybrid Strategy: Superior Technology/Customer Focus

True broadband solutions for any environment or user need

The superior broadband Internet access of wireless and cable represents an important new value-added revenue opportunities for wireless and cable companies, network systems integrators, resellers, and even traditional telephone-access

Work...
that are...
ing stron...
as RCN...
tomorrow...

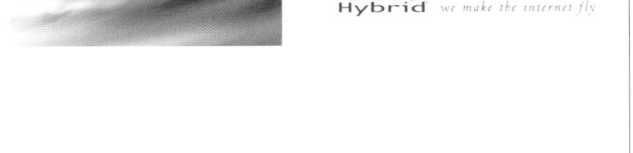

Hybrid Networks, Inc. Annual Report 1997

download in seconds rather than minutes

Hybrid ® *we make the internet fly*

creative firm
  HEINEY & CRAIG, INC.
  San Francisco, California
creative director
  TIM CRAIG
senior designer
  JANET CARPINELLI
client
  HYBRID NETWORKS, INC.

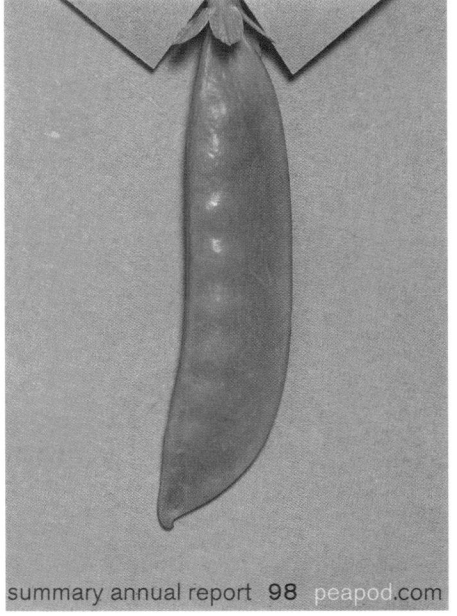

summary annual report **98** peapod.com

creative firm
  PARAGRAPHS DESIGN
  Chicago, Illinois
designer
  SCOTT HICKMAN
client
  PEAPOD

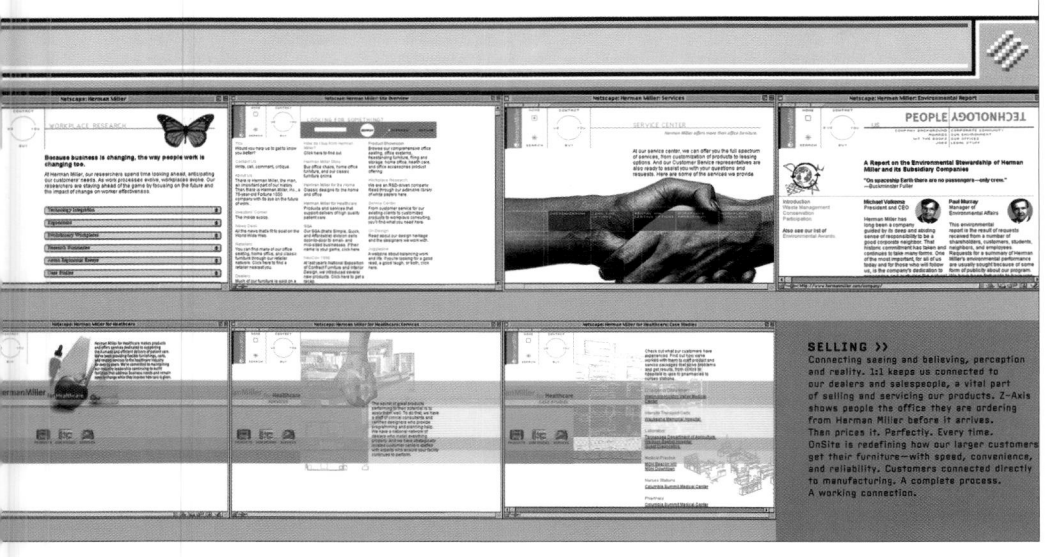

CTIONS   NOW

SELLING >>
Connecting seeing and believing, perception
and reality. 1:1 keeps us connected to
our dealers and salespeople, a vital part
of selling and servicing our products. Z-Axis
shows people the office they are ordering
from Herman Miller before it arrives.
Then prices it. Perfectly. Every time.
OnSite is redefining how our larger customers
get their furniture—with speed, convenience,
and reliability. Customers connected directly
to manufacturing. A complete process.
A working connection.

1998 HIGHLIGHT

creative firm
DEVER DESIGNS
Laurel, Maryland
art director
JEFFREY L. DEVER
designer
AMY WHITE SUCHERMAN
client
U.S. DEPT OF LABOR

creative firm
HEINEY & CRAIG, INC.
San Francisco, California
creative director
TIM CRAIG
senior designer
SHARON BACKURZ
client
UNION BANK

creative firm
HEINEY & CRAIG, INC.
San Francisco, California
creative director
TIM CRAIG
designer
KRIS MATSUYAMA
client
APEX PC SOLUTIONS

Can you help
keep my global
trade *spinning*?

"We need an international correspondent that has an extensive
network and can deliver all types of trade-related services, from
foreign exchange to letters of credit. We insist upon high quality,
competitive pricing and overall value. Our domestic clients depend
upon us for fast payment and processing of their transactions.
Union Bank of California's quality and efficient services make
my life easier and our clients happier."

Harry Tang, General Manager
International Bank of China and a Satisfied Customer

UNION
BANK OF
CALIFORNIA

The Company continues to increase its presence as one of North America's premier specialty retailers of men's tailored apparel by offering customers a shopping experience that combines quality merchandise, value pricing and a high level of customer service. At the end of 1998, the Company operated 431 stores in 40 states. Through a merger completed in early 1999, the Company also operates Moores Retail Group Inc. under the name Moores the Suit People, which has 107 stores throughout Canada.

Even with the changing look of business, taste still remains **in style.**

$298.2
$226.0
159.1

DERS' EQUITY
millions
96 97 98

$767.9
$631.1
$483.5
$406.3
337.1

NET SALES
in millions
94 95 96 97 98

$40.9
$28.9
$21.1
$16.5
$12.1

NET EARNINGS
in millions
94 95 96 97 98*

10.4%
8.5%
8.9%

ABLE STORE GROWTH
millions
96 97 98

$1.17
$.87
$.67
$.54
$.42

DILUTED EARNINGS PER SHARE
94 95 96 97 98*

431
396
345
278
231

NUMBER OF STORES
94 95 96 97 98

* Before extraordinary item.

creative firm
HEINEY & CRAIG, INC.
San Francisco, California
creative director
TIM CRAIG
senior designer
SHARON BACKURZ
client
THE MEN'S WEARHOUSE

creative firm
CASPER DESIGN GROUP
Berkeley, California
creative director, designer
BILL RIBAR
photographer
DAVID POWERS
client
PROBUSINESS SYSTEMS

Jenny Craig

Personal support makes the difference.

Jenny Craig, Inc. is one of the most successful weight management service companies in the world. What truly sets it apart is an emphasis on personal support. Consultants help clients one-on-one to develop a healthy relationship with food, build an active lifestyle, and create a more balanced approach to living.

In turn, Jenny Craig, Inc. relies on expert personal support from ProBusiness to automate its payroll processing and payroll tax filings for more than 2,900 employees at 524 company-owned Centres in the United States.

"We've been extremely pleased with the level of service provided by ProBusiness," says Jim Kelly, vice president and CFO for Jenny Craig, Inc. "ProBusiness has enabled us to save time and focus our resources on more strategic initiatives."

Jamie Filippone, director of finance, has found several tangible benefits to working with ProBusiness. "One of the challenges that we had in the past was a lack of direct access to our own information," she says. "We were with another payroll provider, and we always had to go through them to get any type of detailed report. With ProBusiness, we're able to generate detailed reports at the push of a button. Before, it took days to generate these reports—now it takes minutes."

"Working with ProBusiness has been a very positive experience—from the people to the product to the training," says Filippone. "If I call them with questions, they get back to me right away. They do quality work. It's always 'How can we do that better?' It's been great."

ProBusiness Account Team for Jenny Craig:
Dave Kenther, Tom Lamb,
and Kimberly Haring

Powering businesses by empowering people.

Personal motivation is key to the success of Jenny Craig, both with its clients and with its employees. The company reengineered the commission process to reward performance on an individual basis — and to teams of employees — who meet their goals. Monthly team commissions apply to everyone in a Centre, from consultants to program directors to the Centre director, even to support staff. ProBusiness has allowed Jenny Craig to reduce processing time for the entire payroll process — including commissions, vacation accruals, benefits administration, and tax deposits — by a day and a half each pay period.

creative firm
MCNULTY & CO.
Thousand Oaks, California
creative director
DAN McNULTY
designer
EUGENE BUSTILLOS
illustrator
LIZ WHEATON
copywriter
GERRY FREISLEBEN
client
CALAVO GROWERS OF CALIFORNIA

creative firm
ARNOLD SAKS ASSOCIATES
New York, New York
creative director
ARNOLD SAKS
designer
MICHELLE NOVAK
client
VF CORPORATION

a strong diversified customer base,

creative firm
LOUEY/RUBINO DESIGN GROUP, INC.
Santa Monica, California
creative director
ROBERT LOUEY
client
RELIANCE STEEL & ALUMINUM COMPANY

1998 Annual Report

Harvest

Grow

Fertilize

Protect

TREETOP

creative firm
HORNALL ANDERSON DESIGN WORKS
Seattle, Washington
art director
KATHA DALTON
designers
KATHA DALTON, JANA NISHI
client
TREE TOP

creative firm
MULLER + CO.
Kansas City, Missouri
creative executive officer
JOHN MULLER
creative director, copywriter
DAVID MARKS
designer
MARK VOSS
client
BOY SCOUTS OF AMERICA

creative firm
MINALE TATTERSFIELD + PARTNERS
Richmond, England
creative director
PAUL ASTBURY
senior designers
GRANT RUSSELL, ROBIN CHAPMAN
client
EXPRESS DAIRIES

1998 Annual Report UnionBanCal Corporation

creative firm
HEINEY & CRAIG, INC.
San Francisco, California
creative director
TIM CRAIG
senior designer
JANET CARPINELLI
client
UNION BANK OF CALIFORNIA

"It means having access to affordable health care."

creative firm
CASPER DESIGN GROUP
Berkeley, California
creative director
BILL RIBAR
designer
CHRISTOPHER BUEHLER
photographer
DAVID POWERS
client
THE CALIFORNIA ENDOWMENT

creative firm
MULLER + CO.
Kansas City, Missouri
creative directors
JOHN MULLER, MARK EINER
art director
MARK EINER
designer
JENNIFER JAHDE
client
UTILICORP UNITED

ESTERLINE TECHNOLOGIES
1998
NYSE ESL
ANNUAL REPORT

creative firm
LEIMER CROSS DESIGN
Seattle, Washington
creative director, art director
KERRY LEIMER
designers
KERRY LEIMER, MARIANNE LI
photographers
JEFF CORWIN, TYLER BOLEY
copywriters
KERRY LEIMER, BRIAN KEOGH
client
ESTERLINE TECHNOLOGIES, INC.

creative firm
 SQUIRES & COMPANY
  Dallas, Texas
designer
 BRANDON MURPHY
photographer
 JAY ROUSQUICH
client
 BELLWETHER

creative firm
 BONNIE MATHER DESIGN
  Edmunds, Washington
graphic designer
 BONNIE MATHER
client
 EVERETT PARKS FOUNDATION

kf *knowledge keeps like fish*

creative firm
PARAGRAPHS DESIGN
Chicago, Illinois
designer
SCOTT HICKMAN
client
DIAMOND TECHNOLOGY—JULIA POTTER

creative firm
LOUEY/
RUBINO
DESIGN
GROUP,
INC.
Santa Monica,
California
creative director
ROBERT LOUEY
client
FREMONT
GENERAL

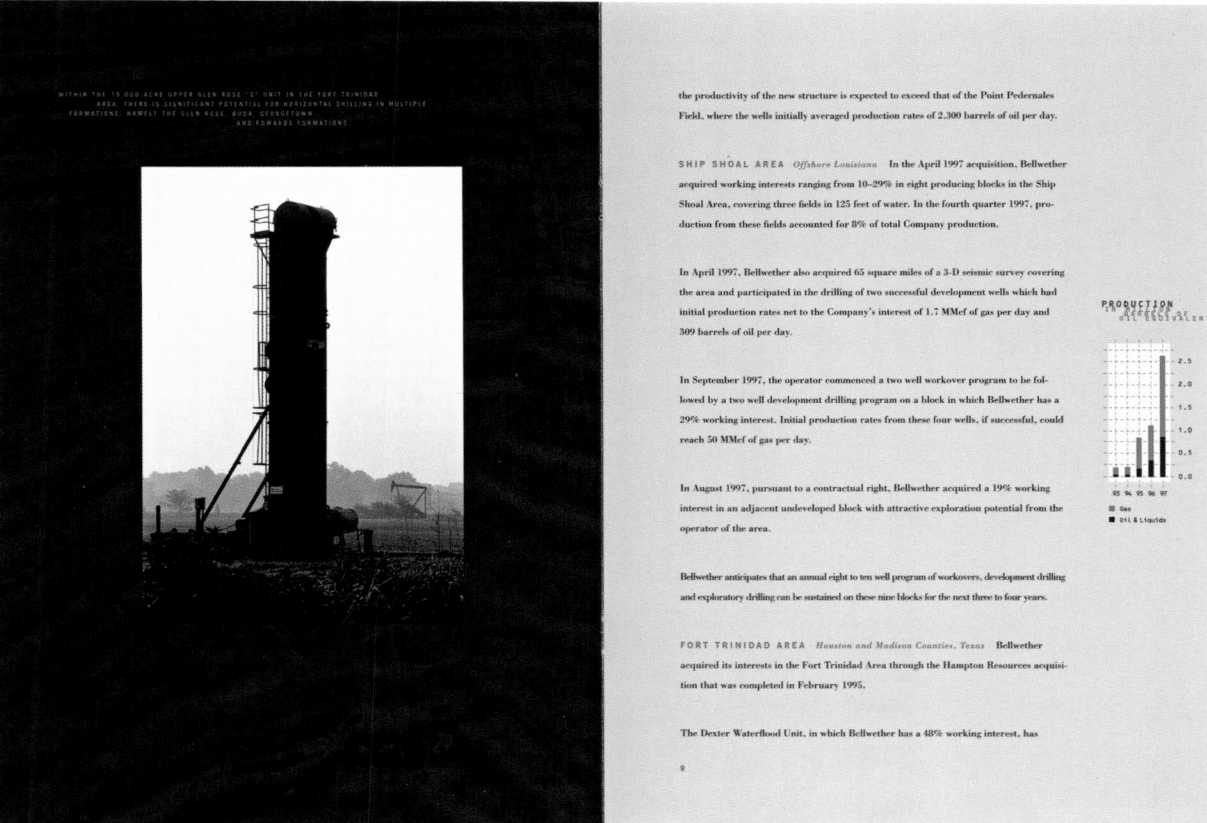

the productivity of the new structure is expected to exceed that of the Point Pedernales Field, where the wells initially averaged production rates of 2,300 barrels of oil per day.

SHIP SHOAL AREA *Offshore Louisiana*   In the April 1997 acquisition, Bellwether acquired working interests ranging from 10–29% in eight producing blocks in the Ship Shoal Area, covering three fields in 125 feet of water. In the fourth quarter 1997, production from these fields accounted for 8% of total Company production.

In April 1997, Bellwether also acquired 65 square miles of a 3-D seismic survey covering the area and participated in the drilling of two successful development wells which had initial production rates net to the Company's interest of 1.7 MMcf of gas per day and 309 barrels of oil per day.

In September 1997, the operator commenced a two well workover program to be followed by a two well development drilling program on a block in which Bellwether has a 29% working interest. Initial production rates from these four wells, if successful, could reach 50 MMcf of gas per day.

In August 1997, pursuant to a contractual right, Bellwether acquired a 19% working interest in an adjacent undeveloped block with attractive exploration potential from the operator of the area.

Bellwether anticipates that an annual eight to ten well program of workovers, development drilling and exploratory drilling can be sustained on these nine blocks for the next three to four years.

FORT TRINIDAD AREA *Houston and Madison Counties, Texas*   Bellwether acquired its interests in the Fort Trinidad Area through the Hampton Resources acquisition that was completed in February 1995.

The Dexter Waterflood Unit, in which Bellwether has a 48% working interest, has

creative firm
SQUIRES & COMPANY
Dallas, Texas
designer
PAUL BLACK
photographers
GARY McCOY, KIETH WOOD
client
BELLWETHER

McWhorter Technologies, Inc.
Annual Report 1998

Growth through Technology

creative firm
  PARAGRAPHS DESIGN
  Chicago, Illinois
designer
  SCOTT HICKMAN
client
  McWHORTER

creative firm
  CASPER DESIGN GROUP
  Berkeley, California
creative director
  BILL RIBAR
designer
  CHRISTOPHER BUEHLER
illustrator
  WARD SCHUMAKER
photographers
  LONNIE DUKA, SLAN MUSILEK,
  KINGMOND YOUNG
client
  PEOPLESOFT

We work in your world.

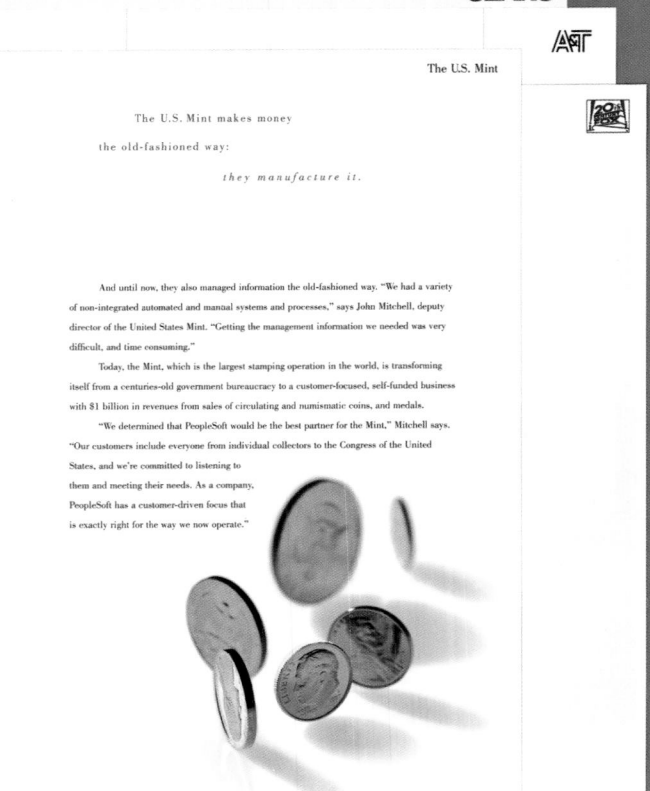

SEARS

ART

The U.S. Mint

The U.S. Mint makes money

the old-fashioned way:

they manufacture it.

And until now, they also managed information the old-fashioned way. "We had a variety
of non-integrated automated and manual systems and processes," says John Mitchell, deputy
director of the United States Mint. "Getting the management information we needed was very
difficult, and time consuming."

Today, the Mint, which is the largest stamping operation in the world, is transforming
itself from a centuries-old government bureaucracy to a customer-focused, self-funded business
with $1 billion in revenues from sales of circulating and numismatic coins, and medals.

"We determined that PeopleSoft would be the best partner for the Mint," Mitchell says.
"Our customers include everyone from individual collectors to the Congress of the United
States, and we're committed to listening to
them and meeting their needs. As a company,
PeopleSoft has a customer-driven focus that
is exactly right for the way we now operate."

Community Involvement

"Logan Airport is as much at the center of local and regional economic development as were the shipyards of Donald McKay in the late 1800s."

DAVID MIGLIACCIO

PRESIDENT,

EAST BOSTON CHAMBER

OF COMMERCE

The continued strength of New England's economy in the 21st century is the reason Massport is investing so heavily to improve its facilities. But the burden of those improvements is borne most directly by those living and working near these vital transportation facilities. As it pursues business opportunities around the globe, Massport also works hard in its own backyard to ensure Massport's neighbors benefit directly from the economic growth its facilities generate.

In Chelsea, Massport forged a far-ranging economic development compact this year that guarantees $2.5 million over five years for the city. The agreement also creates joint economic ventures that combine Chelsea's economic goals with Logan's need for additional parking, maintenance and freight forwarding space as the airport gets ready for the crush of as many as 10 to 15 million new passengers a year by 2010.

In East Boston, Massport is collaborating with the community on a waterfront development agenda that keeps maritime uses alive, and opens the waterfront to the public while providing economically feasible development opportunities needed to drive new building.

For many local businesses, Massport can be their best customer. Massport's on-going "Logan and Beyond" contract forums give local businesses the information they need to begin a profitable relationship supplying Massport's many needs.

With South Boston A to Z, and The Local Advantage Massport helps open doors for East Boston and South Boston vendors who want to do business with companies located at Logan Airport and the Port of Boston. The second edition of Massport's popular Taste of Eastie East Boston restaurant guide doubled the number of listings. And with its support for the new "Eastie Express" shuttle service, Massport is making it even easier for Logan's 17,000 workers to patronize East Boston businesses.

While it continues to support local businesses, Massport hasn't forgotten the important investment in young people. Each summer, Massport sponsors Student Internship and Community Summer Jobs programs that help get young people off to a good start. Students are put to work in every department at Massport and throughout their local communities as maintenance workers, camp counselors, peer leaders, and lifeguards. Massport-sponsored students work with at-risk youngsters, in day care centers, senior centers and in Head Start programs. Through these programs, young people get the chance to build a brighter future for themselves and their community.

14

15

creative firm

KOR GROUP

Boston, Massachusetts

art director

ANNE CALLAHAN

designer

JIM GIBSON

photographer

BETSY CULLEN

client

MASSPORT

creative firm

EDWARD WALTER DESIGN

New York, New York

designer

MARTIN BRYNELL

client

MERCURY COMPUTER SYSTEMS

MERCURY Computer Systems, Inc.

1999 ANNUAL REPORT

17

"Did you get Tony's message?"

PORTICO. NEW PRODUCTIVITY FROM AN OLD CONNECTION.
As the pace of business quickens, so does the opportunity to fall behind. Staying in touch, staying in the
loop, becomes ever harder. Particularly when you're on
the road. So you juggle phones and pagers, PDAs and
computers, unsure whether to check voice mail or email
when time is tight, worrying that you might not get the
message. Why can't a device you already own connect you
to both? Now it can, with Portico.

We've developed an integrated voice and data communication
service that acts as a second-generation virtual assistant for mobile
professionals. Our service, Portico, offers subscribers access to all of their
important information at any time, from any location, using just a phone
or a favorite Web browser. But that's only the beginning. The real productivity of Portico comes from its ability to link the world of voice and data.
Subscribers accessing Portico will use natural language – just as they
would talk to another person – to direct a virtual assistant to read emails
and voice mails, forward phone calls and look up contacts. No awkward
menus. No irritating prompts. Because voice and data are integrated, the
subscriber is in the driver's seat. And that's not all. Portico will offer a rich
array of access services. It will answer subscribers' inbound calls, try to
find them, have them paged, or simply take a message. Follow-me routing
will maximize a subscriber's availability to callers. Intelligent filtering will
screen calls and emails per the subscriber's directions, and will forward only
priority messages to the subscriber's cell phone. Accessing Portico
through a Web browser will be just as convenient.

creative firm
HORNALL ANDERSON DESIGN WORKS
Seattle, Washington
art directors
JACK ANDERSON, JANA NISHI
designers
JACK ANDERSON, JANA NISHI, MARY CHIN HUTCHISON, MICHAEL BRUGMAN
client
GENERAL MAGIC

TECHNOLOGY

that connects.

creative firm
HEINEY & CRAIG, INC.
San Francisco, California
creative director
TIM CRAIG
senior designer
JANET CARPINELLI
client
SILICON VALLEY GROUP

Silicon Valley Group / **10**

BIOGEN

DELIVERING ON THE PROMISE OF BIOTECHNOLOGY

1998 Annual Report

creative firm
GILL FISHMAN ASSOCIATES, INC.
Cambridge, Massachusetts
creative director
GILL FISHMAN
designer
MICHAEL PERSONS
photographer
JOHN EARLE
client
BIOGEN, INC.

creative firm
HORNALL ANDERSON DESIGN WORKS
Seattle, Washington
art directors
JOHN HORNALL, LISA CERVENY
designers
JOHN HORNALL, LISA CERVENY, HEIDI FAVOUR, BRUCE BRANSON-MEYER
client
AIRBORNE EXPRESS

creative firm
SIBLEY PETEET DESIGN
Dallas, Texas
designer
DON SIBLEY
photographer
PETER KRAEMER
client
TEXAS UTILITIES

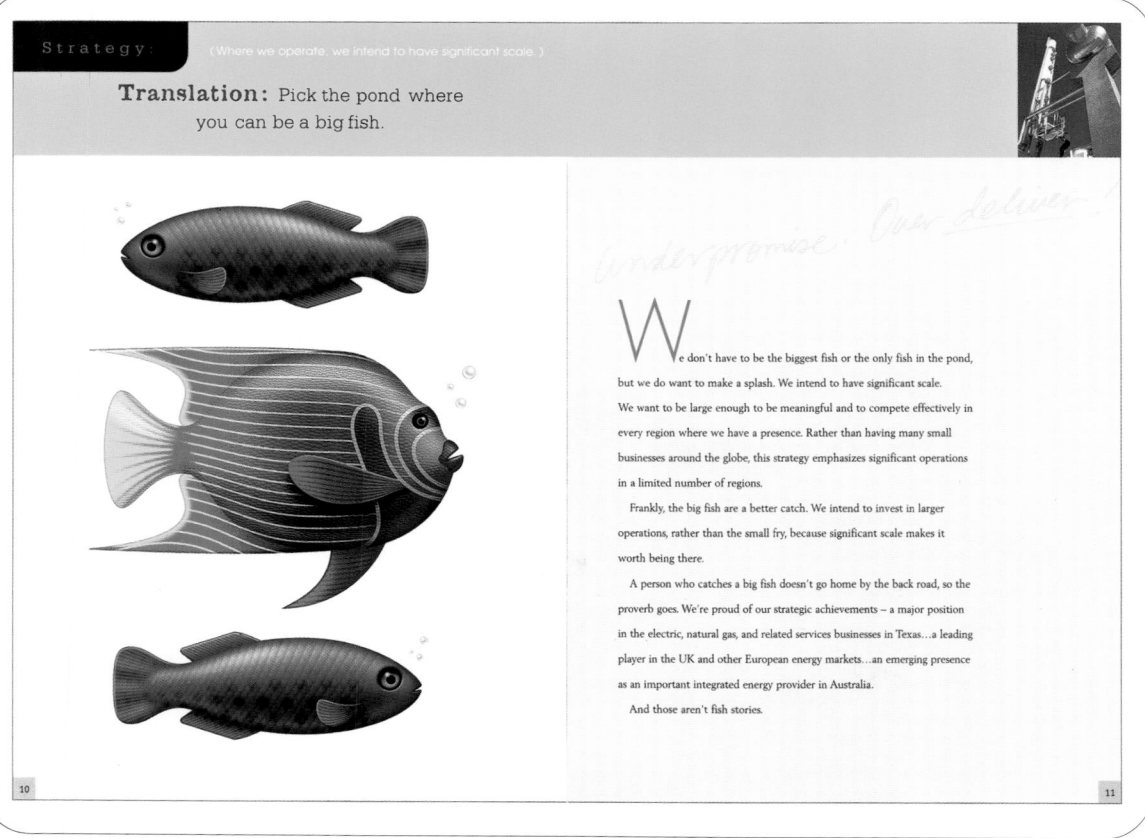

Strategy: (Where we operate, we intend to have significant scale.)

Translation: Pick the pond where you can be a big fish.

We don't have to be the biggest fish or the only fish in the pond, but we do want to make a splash. We intend to have significant scale. We want to be large enough to be meaningful and to compete effectively in every region where we have a presence. Rather than having many small businesses around the globe, this strategy emphasizes significant operations in a limited number of regions.

Frankly, the big fish are a better catch. We intend to invest in larger operations, rather than the small fry, because significant scale makes it worth being there.

A person who catches a big fish doesn't go home by the back road, so the proverb goes. We're proud of our strategic achievements – a major position in the electric, natural gas, and related services businesses in Texas…a leading player in the UK and other European energy markets…an emerging presence as an important integrated energy provider in Australia.

And those aren't fish stories.

10

11

creative firm
PEPE GIMENO—PROYECTO GRÁFICO
Valencia, Spain
designer
SUSO PÉREZ
client
EXPERIMENTA EDICIONES DE DISEÑO

John Steinbeck (1902–1968) was born in Salinas, California. He studied at Stanford University but left without taking a degree and, after a series of jobs, began to write. His first book, *Cup of Gold*, was published in 1929.

Popular success came to him in 1935 with *Tortilla Flat*. That book's promise was confirmed by succeeding works—*In Dubious Battle*, *Of Mice and Men*, and especially *The Grapes of Wrath*, a novel so powerful that it remains an enduring American classic. Often set in California, Steinbeck's later books include *Cannery Row*, *The Wayward Bus*, *East of Eden*, and *Travels with Charley*.

In 1962, Steinbeck received the Nobel Prize for Literature. In announcing the award, the Swedish Academy declared: "He had no mind to be an unoffending comforter and entertainer. Instead, the topics he chose were serious and denunciatory, for instance, the bitter strikes on California fruit and cotton plantations. . . . His literary power steadily gained impetus . . . [until] the great work . . . the epic chronicle *The Grapes of Wrath*."

"To the red country and part of the gray country of Oklahoma, the last rains came gently, and they did not cut the scarred earth . . ."

THE GRAPES OF WRATH

John **STEINBECK**

First published in 1939, *THE GRAPES OF WRATH* is a landmark of American literature. This Pulitzer Prize–winning epic of the Great Depression chronicles the Dust Bowl migration of the 1930s and tells the story of one Oklahoma farm family, the Joads—driven from their homestead by the "land companies" and forced to travel west to the promised land of California. A portrait of conflict between the powerful and the powerless, the novel captures the horrors of the Depression and probes the very nature of equality in America.

"It is Steinbeck's best novel, i.e., his roughest and tenderest, his roughest written and most mellifluous, his most realistic and, in its ending, his most melodramatic, his angriest and most idyllic. It is great in the way that *Uncle Tom's Cabin* was great. One of the most impassioned and exciting books of the year." —*Time*

"One comes away moved, indignant, protesting, pitying. A fiery document of protest and compassion, as a story that had to be told, as a book that must be read." —LOUIS KRONENBERGER, *The Nation*

A PENGUIN BOOK
Literature
U.S. $14.95
CAN. $19.99

ISBN 0-14-028162-2

PENGUIN GREAT BOOKS OF THE 20TH CENTURY   PENGUIN GREAT BOOKS OF THE 20TH CENTURY   http://www.penguinputnam.com

creative firm
PENGUIN PUTNAM INC.
New York, New York

creative firm
PENGUIN
PUTNAM INC.
New York, New York

[continued from front flap]

what is lost. Or, failing that, to exact a little revenge. Phineas is savvy and sharp, but he's unraveling at the edges. A fierce but tender killer, Jude allows him to catch up with her—perhaps too easily. Phineas soon falls warily, reluctantly in love with her and must fight to avoid becoming her accomplice as well as her victim. A hallucinatory journey unfolds, taking the unlikely couple from Denver to Las Vegas to a final reckoning in the stark countryside outside of El Paso, Texas.

Laced with shocks and surprises, *KISS ME, JUDAS* is a stylish, ingeniously constructed novel, a meditation on love, sorrow, and redemption that entertains in a fearsomely intelligent way. Baer's writing glitters with corrosive wit and razor-sharp images that invade the mind with the arrogance and sexual intimacy of film. He doesn't so much describe arousal and vertigo and the shifting waves of danger and ecstasy that course through this novel as cause them in the reader—through the back-lit smoke of noir. This is a strong and bold debut, from an immensely talented writer.

WILL CHRISTOPHER BAER lives in California.

JACKET DESIGN BY PAUL BUCKLEY / COVER PHOTOGRAPH BY JASON FULFORD / AUTHOR PHOTOGRAPH BY BRAD WILSON

A member of Penguin Putnam Inc.
375 Hudson Street, New York, N.Y. 10014
http://www.penguinputnam.com

viking

"*KISS ME, JUDAS* IS INGENIOUSLY PLOTTED, A PERFECT NOIR NOVEL, RIGHT UP THERE WITH CHANDLER'S *THE BIG SLEEP*." —*Madison Smartt Bell, author of All Souls' Rising*

WILL CHRISTOPHER BAER
kiss me, judas
viking

"A DECONSTRUCTION OF AN URBAN L[...]
A DARK UNRAVELING OF MYSTERY [...]
MYSTERY *KISS ME, JUDAS* IS A FI[...]
DANGEROUS WORK." —*Peggy Z. Brite, author of Exquisite*

"If you want to live, call 91[...]

Phineas Poe—an ex-cop just released fro[...] state psychiatric ward—wakes up in a De[...] hotel room in a bathtub full of ice, with [...] soggy note in a seductive, girlish script s[...] in his hand. A day, or was it two days ear[...] he was lured into bed by a beautiful but m[...] acing woman named Jude. Now he must [...] rushed to the hospital, for Jude, who co[...] amateur surgery among her unusual tale[...] has stolen one of his kidneys.

"Don't worry," she whispers in his drea[...] "you really only need one."

kiss me, judas, Will Christoph[...] hypnotic novel of paranoia and sexu[...] sion, explodes from these bloody [...] pages and spins the reader into a wor[...] perversion and betrayal are simply [...] granted. This phantasmagoric tal[...] Poe—a fractured, deeply vulnerable [...] who is still mourning the unresolve[...] his wife—as he pursues the myster[...] and is plunged into an edgy, dra[...] underworld inhabited by a gleeful c[...] ister characters. Phineas believes [...] intends to sell his kidney on the b[...] ket, and he's grimly determined to [...]

[continued on back flap]

U.S.
CANADA

WILL CHRISTOPHER BAER

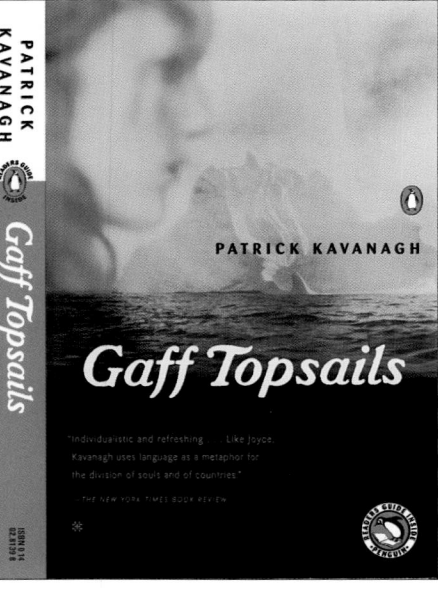

creative firm
PENGUIN PUTNAM INC.
New York, New York

creative firm
FROST DESIGN LTD
London, England
creative director
VINCE FROST
client
D&AD

(continued from front flap)

RAW, EXPLOSIVE, STEAMY,
marked by searing action and bold thought. *Me*
stands head, shoulders, and torso above Dan
Quayle's *Standing Erect*, Newt Gingrich's *Things
I Finally Figured Out*, and Colin Powell's *My
Trips Around the U.S.*

Jacket design by Paul Buckley & Mark Melnick
Jacket illustration by C. F. Payne
Photo: Underwood Photo Archives / Superstock

Pink Boas, Spangly Tights,
Dangly Earrings,
AND NOW
Governor of Minnesota —
WHAT A GUY!

ISBN 0-670-88796-X
9 780670 887965
90000>

A member of Penguin Putnam Inc.
375 Hudson Street, New York, N.Y. 10014
VIKING   http://www.penguinputnam.com

Me
—BY—
**JIMMY
(BIG BOY)
VALENTE**

A POLITICAL SATIRE

As told to
Garrison Keillor

VIKING

Abandoned by his mother at
little Clifford Oxnard grows up i
Minneapolis, tormented by bullies and
by big dogs until an encounter with t
Man of Borneo and a mail-order body-l
course changed his life. Transformed i
six-foot-four 300-pound he-man Jimm
Boy) Valente, he enlists in the U.S. Nav
Walrus program and is trained to use exp
speak in code, navigate unfamiliar terra
know the darkness of the human heart
sent to Vietnam.

In Vietnam, his Walrus unit vanc
hordes of Viet Cong, fighting off tar
artillery and even the Lost Squadro
Rising Sun (the last surviving Japane
from World War II), assisted by J
defector buddy, Victor Charlie, better
as The Rodent.

Returning to the Sta
Jimmy finds his way to Alaska, 'man's cc
where, after a few wrong turns, he
professional wrestling troupe, replac
Duke of Dubuque and the Dauphin L
Louie, embarking on a career that take
the pinnacle of International World W
bringing him fame and fortune and intr
him to his hero, Arnold Schwarzenegge
also brings him into conflict with a da
death-dealing foe who stalks him relent

(continued on back flap)

creative firm
  PENGUIN PUTNAM INC.
  New York, New York

creative firm
  MIRIELLO GRAFICO INC.
  San Diego, California
designers
  MICHELLE ARANDA, MAXIMO ESCOBEDO, DAN RENNER
client
  HARCOURT BRACE

Jean-Noël Indergand
Suzanne Vitacco
Jürgen Sell

Holzhausbau
Qualität+Detail

EMPA
Lignum
Baufachverlag

creative firm
  ALBERT GOMM SGD
  Basel, Switzerland
graphic designer
  ALBERT GOMM
architect
  CHARLES VON BUEREN
client
  BAUFACHVERLAG

THROWING THINGS
DAVID KASPAREK

REVIVAL
ROBERT DRY

creative firm
KINETIK COMMUNICATION GRAPHICS, INC.
    Washington, D.C.
designer
    BETH CLAWSON
client
    NORTH CAROLINA STATE UNIVERSITY

Wallowa Llamas

Raz and Louise Rasmussen • Steve Backstrom
Rt. 1 Box 84 • Halfway, OR 97834
phone: (541) 742-2961 • email: wallama@pdx.oneworld.com

Since 1985, Wallowa Llamas has conducted guided tours of small groups into the state's largest wilderness area, the Eagle Cap. Here, at the southern edge of Eastern Oregon's spectacular Wallowa Mountains, amid towering peaks, glacier-sculpted valleys and sparkling mountain streams, our llamas carry the amenities, unburdening hikers to experience ease and luxury normally unavailable to backcountry travelers in such rugged environs.

Packing with even-tempered llamas, we can enjoy delightful meals prepared without freeze-dried ingredients. Wallowa Llamas provides tents, eating utensils, and all meals, beginning with lunch the first day and ending with lunch the last day.

The llamas will carry up to 20 pounds of each guest's personal gear. Anything above that must be carried by the guest. A daypack is highly recommended for carrying cameras, binoculars or rain gear.

"One of the highlights of my life" Deanna Watkins

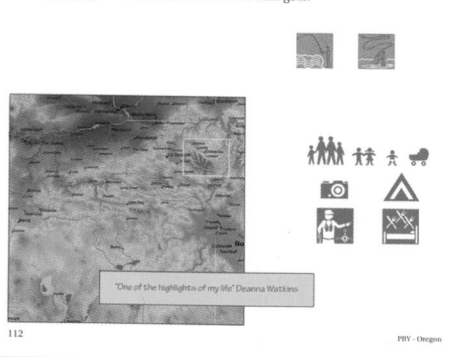

WALLOWA LLAMAS

PBY - Oregon

PBY - Oregon

creative firm
    FIFTH STREET DESIGN
    Berkeley, California
production
    ALLISON VALERIO
copywriter
    MAURIZIO VALERIO
client
    PICKED-BY-YOU

creative firm
  JILL TANENBAUM GRAPHIC DESIGN & ADVERTISING
  Bethesda, Maryland
creative director
  JILL TANENBAUM
art director
  SUE SPRINKLE
designers
  LEAH GERMAN, HANNA CHANG
client
  U.S. POSTAL SERVICE

creative firm
  PEPE GIMENO—PROYECTO GRÀFICO
  Valencia, Spain
designer
  JOSE P. GIL
client
  FERIA INTERNACIONAL DEL MUEBLE DE VALENCIA

creative firm
THE RIORDON
DESIGN GROUP INC.
Oakville, Canada
designer, illustrator
DAN WHEATON
client
FRONTIER RESEARCH
PUBLICATIONS

creative firm
PENGUIN PUTNAM BOOKS
New York, New York
designer
JENNIFER HEISEY
client
VIKING

Glarner und St. Galler Alpen, Alpstein

Tödi, Glärnisch, Walensee, Churfirsten

creative firm
ALBERT GOMM SGD
Basel, Switzerland
designer
ALBERT GOMM
typesetter
MARCO VOLKEN
illustrator
GUIDO KOEHLER
photographer
REMOKUNDERT
client
SWISS ALPINE CLUB

A sexy and funny cross-cultural tale of two seemingly disparate women that is "a feast that leaves you hungry for whatever Ozeki cooks up next." —*Newsweek*

Ruth Ozeki's mesmerizing debut novel has captivated readers and reviewers worldwide. When documentarian Jane Takagi-Little finally lands a job producing *My American Wife!*, a Japanese television show sponsored by an American meat-exporting business, she discovers some unsavory truths about love, fertility, and a hormone called DES. Meanwhile, on the other side of the globe, Akiko Ueno, a beleaguered Japanese housewife, struggles to escape from her child-craving husband. When Jane's and Akiko's lives intersect, the deepest concerns of our time are illuminated: how the past informs the present, and how we live and love in an ever-shrinking world.

"It's juicy, it's tender, it's bloody, it's sizzling."
—*St. Louis Post Dispatch*

"There is an ardent passion to the center of this novel . . . rare and provocative."
—*USA Today*

RUTH L. OZEKI

my **Year** of **Meats**

"A comical-satirical-farcical-epical-tragical-romantical novel . . . delicious . . . up-to-the-minute."
—JANE SMILEY, *Chicago Tribune*

RUTH L. OZEKI

MY YEAR OF MEATS

A PENGUIN BOOK
Fiction

ISBN 0-14-028046-4

U.S. $12.95
CAN. $18.99

http://www.penguinputnam.com

9 780140 280463

creative firm
  PENGUIN PUTNAM BOOKS
  New York, New York
designer
  JENNIFER HEISEY
client
  PENGUIN

creative firm
  PENGUIN PUTNAM BOOKS
  New York, New York

PRAISE FOR
My Year of Meats

"This is a very cool book, satirical but never mean, funny, peopled by fully in-habited characters who are both blind and self-aware. Ruth Ozeki's *My Year of Meats* reassures us that media and culture, though bound inextricably, will never become one." —John Sayles, Former member, Amalgamated Meat Packers and Butcher Workers of North America, and director of *Matewan* and *Men With Guns*

Lamb Too

ISBN 0-670-87904-5

9 780670 879045

My Year of Meats

Ruth L. Ozeki

VIKING

My Year of Meats

a novel

Ruth L. Ozeki

creative firm
PENGUIN PUTNAM BOOKS
New York, New York

creative firm
PENGUIN PUTNAM BOOKS
New York, New York

All
Is
Calm

REFLECTIONS FOR ADVENT AND OTHER BUSY SEASONS

Donna Schaper

creative firm
  ST. MARY'S PRESS
  Winona, Minnesota
cover designer
  STEPHAN NAGEL
cover painting
  CHARLES PERKALIS
manuscript editor
  REBECCA FAIRBANK
client
  ST. MARY'S PRESS

creative firm
  ST. MARY'S PRESS
  Winona, Minnesota
art director
  MAURINE R. TWAIT
typesetter
  HOLLACE STORKEL
copy editor
  LAURIE A. BERG
client
  ST. MARY'S PRESS

Woman
Un-Bent

Irene Zimmerman

Each
New
Sunrise
Meditations
in Maturity

MARGARET
ALDERMAN

creative firm
  ST. MARY'S PRESS
  Winona, Minnesota
cover designer
  CINDI RAMM
cover illustrator
  ROSEAN TISHMAN
copy editor
  LAURIE A. BERG
client
  ST. MARY'S PRESS

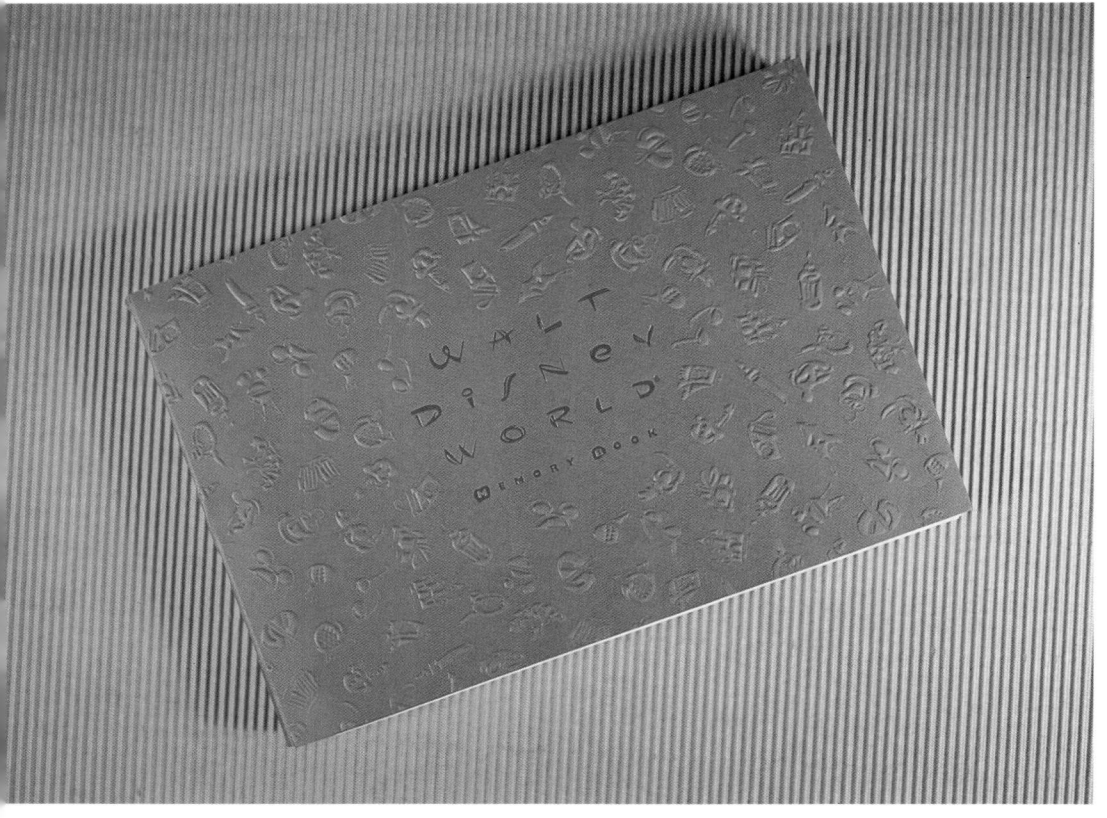

creative firm
DISNEY DESIGN GROUP
Lake Buena Vista, Florida
creative director
MICHELE KEATING
art director
MARK SEPPALA
designer
THOMAS SCOTT
illustrators
LARRY MOORE, CHRISTIAN MILDH
client
WALT DISNEY WORLD SALES & MARKETING

creative firm
SAYLES GRAPHIC DESIGN
Des Moines, Iowa
art director, illustrator
JOHN SAYLES
client
HOTEL PATTEE

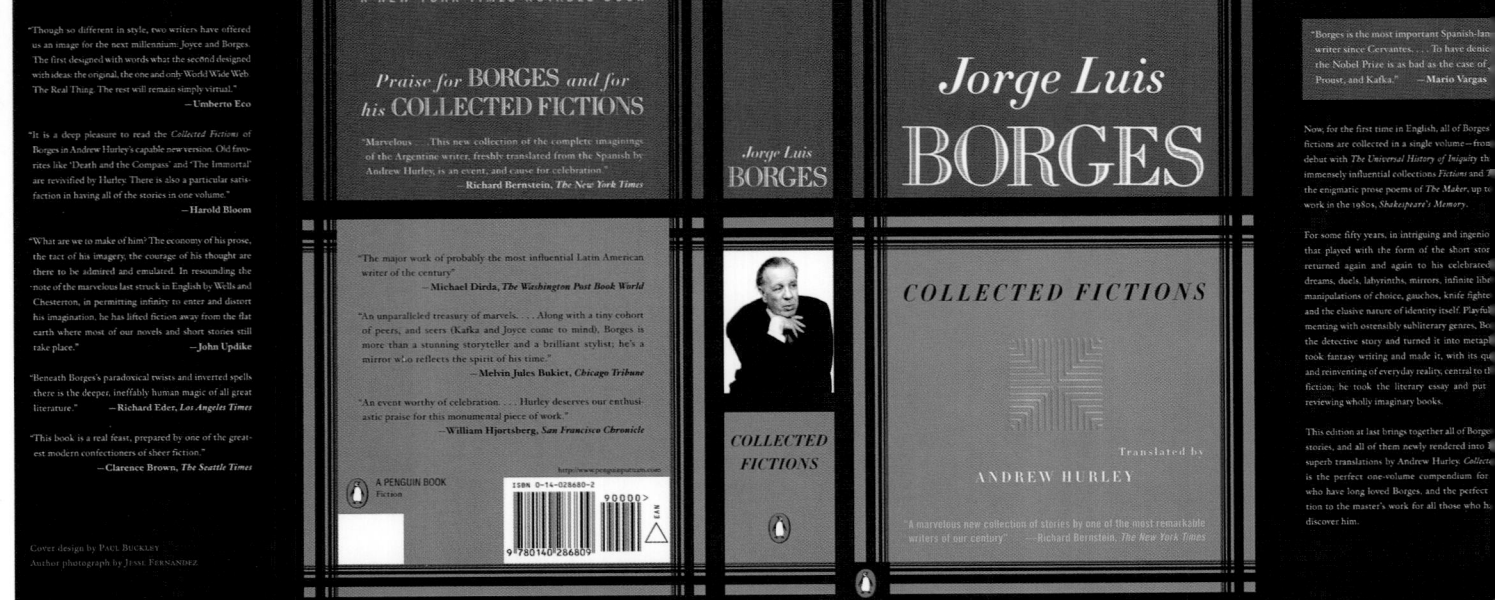

Top cover — Collected Fictions:

A *NEW YORK TIMES* NOTABLE BOOK

THE NATIONAL BESTSELLER

Praise for BORGES *and for his* COLLECTED FICTIONS

"Marvelous.... This new collection of the complete imaginings of the Argentine writer, freshly translated from the Spanish by Andrew Hurley, is an event, and cause for celebration."
—Richard Bernstein, *The New York Times*

"The major work of probably the most influential Latin American writer of the century."
—Michael Dirda, *The Washington Post Book World*

"An unparalleled treasury of marvels.... Along with a tiny cohort of peers, and seers (Kafka and Joyce come to mind), Borges is more than a stunning storyteller and a brilliant stylist; he's a mirror who reflects the spirit of his time."
—Melvin Jules Bukiet, *Chicago Tribune*

"An event worthy of celebration.... Hurley deserves our enthusiastic praise for this monumental piece of work."
—William Hjortsberg, *San Francisco Chronicle*

A PENGUIN BOOK
Fiction

http://www.penguinputnam.com

ISBN 0-14-028680-2

9 780140 286809

"Though so different in style, two writers have offered us an image for the next millennium: Joyce and Borges. The first designed with words what the second designed with ideas: the original, the one and only World Wide Web The Real Thing. The rest will remain simply virtual."
—Umberto Eco

"It is a deep pleasure to read the *Collected Fictions* of Borges in Andrew Hurley's capable new version. Old favorites like 'Death and the Compass' and 'The Immortal' are revisited by Hurley. There is also a particular satisfaction in having all of the stories in one volume."
—Harold Bloom

"What are we to make of him? The economy of his prose, the tact of his imagery, the courage of his thought are there to be admired and emulated. In resounding the note of the marvelous last struck in English by Wells and Chesterton, in permitting infinity to enter and distort his imagination, he has lifted fiction away from the flat earth where most of our novels and short stories still take place."
—John Updike

"Beneath Borges's paradoxical twists and inverted spells there is the deeper, ineffably human magic of all great literature."
—Richard Eder, *Los Angeles Times*

"This book is a real feast, prepared by one of the greatest modern confectioners of sheer fiction."
—Clarence Brown, *The Seattle Times*

Cover design by PAUL BUCKLEY.
Author photograph by JESSE FERNANDEZ.

Jorge Luis BORGES

COLLECTED FICTIONS

Translated by
ANDREW HURLEY

"A marvelous new collection of stories by one of the most remarkable writers of our century"
—Richard Bernstein, *The New York Times*

Now, for the first time in English, all of Borges' fictions are collected in a single volume—from his debut with *The Universal History of Iniquity* to the immensely influential collections *Fictions* and *The Aleph*, the enigmatic prose poems of *The Maker*, up to his work in the 1980s, *Shakespeare's Memory*.

For some fifty years, in intriguing and ingenious fictions that played with the form of the short story, Borges returned again and again to his celebrated themes: dreams, duels, labyrinths, mirrors, infinite libraries, the manipulations of choice, gauchos, knife fighters, and the elusive nature of identity itself. Playfully experimenting with ostensibly subliterary genres, Borges took the detective story and turned it into metaphysics; he took fantasy writing and made it, with its questioning and reinventing of everyday reality, central to the craft of fiction; he took the literary essay and put it to reviewing wholly imaginary books.

This edition at last brings together all of Borges' stories, and all of them newly rendered into English in superb translations by Andrew Hurley. *Collected Fictions* is the perfect one-volume compendium for those who have long loved Borges, and the perfect introduction to the master's work for all those who have yet to discover him.

"Borges is the most important Spanish-language writer since Cervantes.... To have denied him the Nobel Prize is as bad as the case of Proust, and Kafka."
—Mario Vargas

creative firm
PENGUIN PUTNAM BOOKS INC.
New York, New York

creative firm
PENGUIN PUTNAM BOOKS INC.
New York, New York

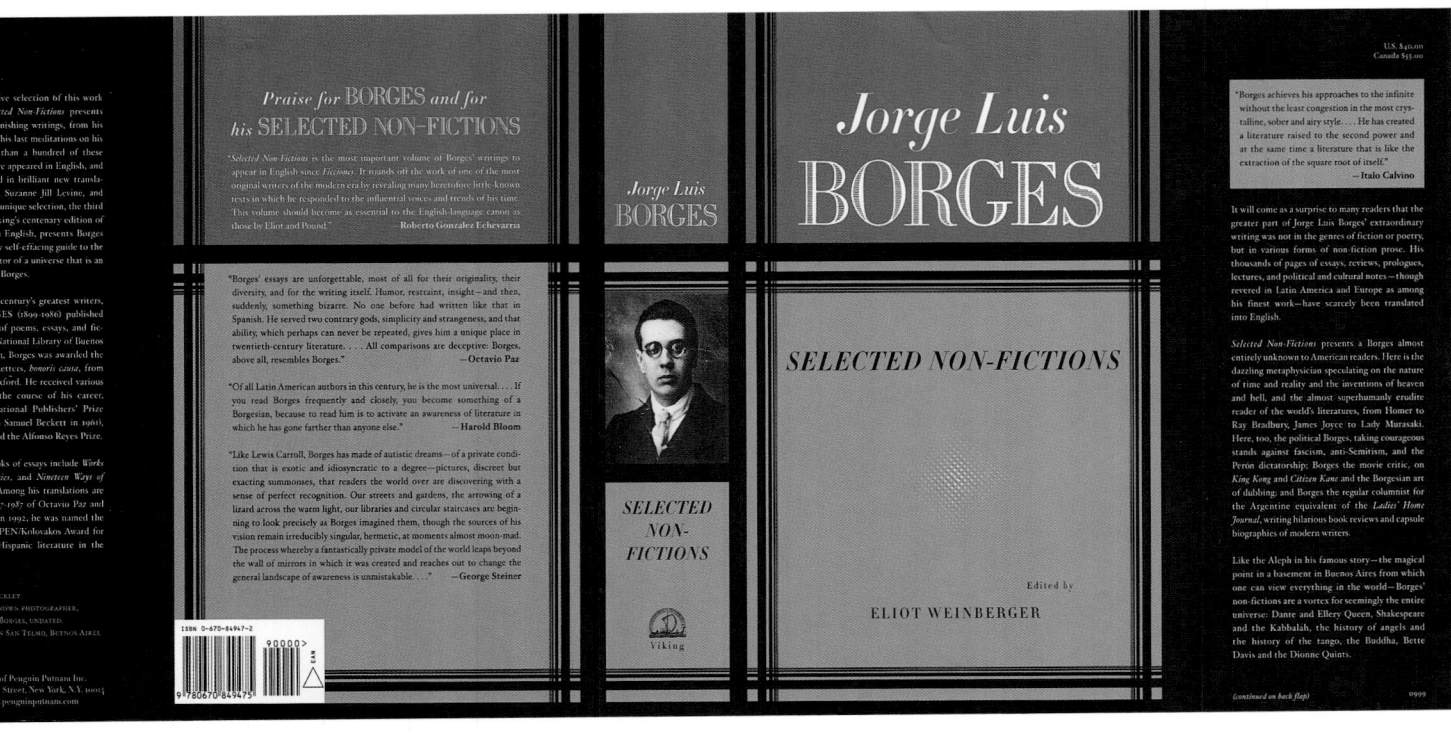

Bottom cover — Selected Non-Fictions:

...ped from front flap)

...first comprehensive selection of this work ...y language, *Selected Non-Fictions* presents ...ion of these astonishing writings, from his ...ul manifestos to his last meditations on his ...te books. More than a hundred of these ...s have never before appeared in English, and ...ve been rendered in brilliant new transla-...by Esther Allen, Suzanne Jill Levine, and ...Weinberger. This unique selection, the third ...nal volume in Viking's centenary edition of ...Collected Work in English, presents Borges ...ce as a deceptively self-effacing guide to the ...rse and the inventor of a universe that is an ...pensable guide to Borges.

...of the twentieth century's greatest writers, ...E LUIS BORGES (1899-1986) published ...rous collections of poems, essays, and fic-...Director of the National Library of Buenos ...from 1955 to 1973, Borges was awarded the ...e of Doctor of Letters, *honoris causa*, from ...Columbia and Oxford. He received various ...ry awards over the course of his career, ...ding the International Publishers' Prize ...h he shared with Samuel Beckett in 1961), ...erusalem Prize, and the Alfonso Reyes Prize.

...Weinberger's books of essays include *Works ...per*, *Outside Stories*, and *Nineteen Ways of ...ng at Wang Wei*. Among his translations are ...Collected Poems 1957-1987* of Octavio Paz and ...gs' *Seven Nights*. In 1992, he was named the ...recipient of the PEN/Kolovakos Award for ...ork promoting Hispanic literature in the ...ed States.

...design by PAUL BUCKLEY.
...photograph: UNKNOWN PHOTOGRAPHER, ...AIT OF JORGE LUIS BORGES, UNDATED, ...OGRAPH: FUNDACIÓN SAN TELMO, BUENOS AIRES.

ISBN 0-670-84947-2

9 780670 849475

A member of Penguin Putnam Inc.
...375 Hudson Street, New York, N.Y. 10014
http://www.penguinputnam.com

Praise for BORGES *and for his* SELECTED NON-FICTIONS

"*Selected Non-Fictions* is the most important volume of Borges's writings to appear in English since *Fictions*. It rounds off the work of one of the most original writers of the modern era by revealing many heretofore little-known texts in which he responded to the influential voices and trends of his time. This volume should become as essential to the English-language canon as those by Eliot and Pound."
—Roberto Gonzalez Echevarria

"Borges' essays are unforgettable, most of all for their originality, their diversity, and for the writing itself. Humor, restraint, insight—and then, suddenly, something bizarre. No one before had written like that in Spanish. He served two contrary gods, simplicity and strangeness, and that ability, which perhaps can never be repeated, gives him a unique place in twentieth-century literature.... All comparisons are deceptive: Borges, above all, resembles Borges."
—Octavio Paz

"Of all Latin American authors in this century, he is the most universal.... If you read Borges frequently and closely, you become something of a Borgesian, because to read him is to activate an awareness of literature in which he has gone farther than anyone else."
—Harold Bloom

"Like Lewis Carroll, Borges has made of autistic dreams—of a private condition that is exotic and idiosyncratic to a degree—pictures, discreet but exacting summonses, that readers the world over are discovering with a sense of perfect recognition. Our streets and gardens, the arrowing of a lizard across the warm light, our libraries and circular staircases are beginning to look precisely as Borges imagined them, though the sources of his vision remain irreducibly singular, hermetic, at moments almost moon-mad. The process whereby a fantastically private model of the world leaps beyond the wall of mirrors in which it was created and reaches out to change the general landscape of awareness is unmistakable...."
—George Steiner

Jorge Luis BORGES

SELECTED NON-FICTIONS

Edited by
ELIOT WEINBERGER

Viking

U.S. $40.00
Canada $55.00

"Borges achieves his approaches to the infinite without the least congestion in the most crystalline, sober and airy style.... He has created a literature raised to the second power and at the same time a literature that is like the extraction of the square root of itself."
—Italo Calvino

It will come as a surprise to many readers that the greater part of Jorge Luis Borges' extraordinary writing was not in the genres of fiction or poetry, but in various forms of non-fiction prose. His thousands of pages of essays, reviews, prologues, lectures, and political and cultural notes—though revered in Latin America and Europe as among his finest work—have scarcely been translated into English.

Selected Non-Fictions presents a Borges almost entirely unknown to American readers. Here is the dazzling metaphysician speculating on the nature of time and reality and the inventions of heaven and hell, and the almost superhumanly erudite reader of the world's literatures, from Homer to Ray Bradbury, James Joyce to Lady Murasaki. Here, too, the political Borges, taking courageous stands against fascism, anti-Semitism, and the Perón dictatorship; Borges the movie critic, on *King Kong* and *Citizen Kane* and the Borgesian art of dubbing; and Borges the regular columnist for the Argentine equivalent of the *Ladies' Home Journal*, writing hilarious book reviews and capsule biographies of modern writers.

Like the Aleph in his famous story—the magical point in a basement in Buenos Aires from which one can view everything in the world—Borges' non-fictions are a vortex for seemingly the entire universe: Dante and Ellery Queen, Shakespeare and the Kabbalah, the history of angels and the history of the tango, the Buddha, Bette Davis and the Dionne Quints.

(continued on back flap)

0999

THE NORTH AFRICAN CAMPAIGN
1940–1943

★ DESERT WAR ★

"ONE OF THE MOST REMARKABLE BOOKS OF THIS OR ANY OTHER MODERN WAR."
—New Statesman

Alan Moorehead

WITH AN INTRODUCTION BY **JOHN KEEGAN**

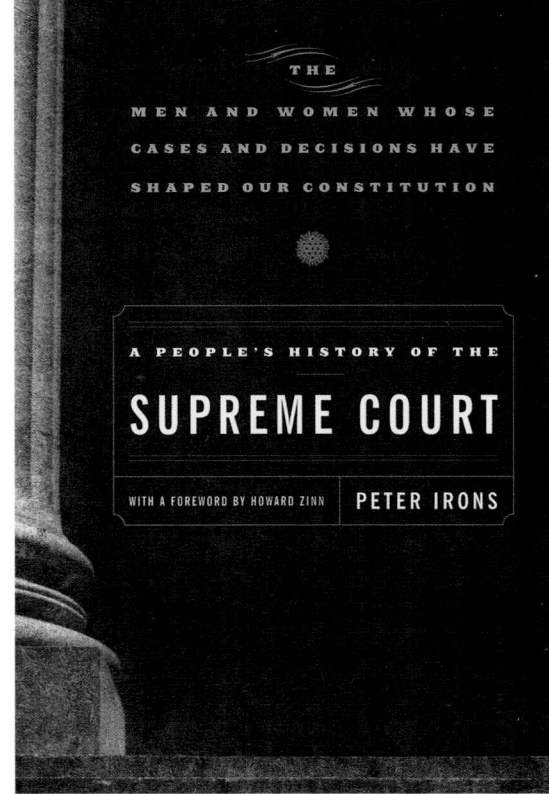

THE
MEN AND WOMEN WHOSE
CASES AND DECISIONS HAVE
SHAPED OUR CONSTITUTION

A PEOPLE'S HISTORY OF THE

SUPREME COURT

WITH A FOREWORD BY HOWARD ZINN | PETER IRONS

creative firm
PUTNAM PENGUIN INC.
New York, New York
designer
JENNIFER HEISEY
client
PENGUIN

creative firm
PUTNAM PENGUIN INC.
New York, New York
designer
JENNIFER HEISEY
client
VIKING BOOKS

"*Billy Dead* is a brave, heartwrenching debut. I couldn't look away."
—ALICE MUNRO

"This is a compelling work, reminiscent of both Dorothy Allison and Caroline Chute, that evokes empathy for those who lead bleak, savage lives and even finds a measure of dignity and love in people raised in a world where all the rules and taboos are broken on a daily basis."
—PUBLISHERS WEEKLY

BILLY DEAD

LISA REARDON

a novel by
LISA REARDON

VIKING

ISBN 0-670-88224-0
90000>
9 780670 882243

creative firm
PUTNAM PENGUIN INC.
New York, New York
designer
MAGGIE PAYETTE
client
VIKING BOOKS

creative firm
 NIKLAUS TROXLER DESIGN
  Willisau, Switzerland
designer, typographer, illustrator
 NIKLAUS TROXLER
client
 LARS MÜLLER PUBLISHERS

creative firm
 DESIGN GUYS
  Minneapolis, Minnesota
art director
 STEVEN SIKORA
illustrator
 JAY THEIGE
copywriter
 AMIE VALENTINE
client
 TARGET STORES

creative firm
 JACK SCHECTERSON ASSOCIATES
  Little Neck, New York
concept
 BARBARA HARRIS
design director
 JACK SCHECTERSON
illustrator
 THERESA DELLA CERRA
copywriter
 LIANE ONISH
client
 EURPSVILLE, USA, INC.

creative firm
 PLATINUM DESIGN, INC.
  New York, New York
art director, designer
 VICTORIA STAMM
client
 CLARKSON POTTER/PUBLISHERS
 (BEAUTIFUL AMERICAN ROSE GARDENS)

creative firm
 SIBLEY PETEET DESIGN
  Dallas, Texas
designer
 BRENT McMAHAN
photographer
 MICHAEL ROYTEK
client
 BOY SCOUTS OF AMERICA

MARY TONETTI DORRA

BEAUTIFUL AMERICAN ROSE GARDENS

Beautiful American
ROSE GARDENS

MARY TONETTI DORRA
Photographs by Richard Felber

POTTER

creative firm
DISNEY DESIGN GROUP
Lake Buena Vista, Florida
creative director
MICHELE KEATING
designer
MIKE WOOD
photographers
JOE BROOKS, WALT DISNEY WORLD PHOTOGRAPHY
client
WALT DISNEY ATTRACTIONS MERCHANDISE

creative firm
**UKULELE DESIGN
CONSULTANTS PTE LTD**
Singapore
design director
KIM CHUN-WEI
designer
LYNN LIM
client
THE ASIA INSURANCE CO. LTD

creative firm
WARNER BOOKS
New York, New York
designer, artist
DANIEL PELAVIN
client
WARNER BOOKS

Count on This

The castle was in Buffalo and the king was in the castle. The car was in the pine woods of Georgia and Parker was on the move: slowly plotting his attack on the head of the powerful criminal outfit that had put a contract on his life. Armed with a new face and the old iron will, Parker is declaring coast-to-coast war. And after Parker's associates pull off twelve robberies in five days against Outfit targets, the man in the castle starts to get the picture. All except one part: with a hot car and a cold tenacity, Parker is coming after him…

"AS DONALD E. WESTLAKE OR RICHARD STARK, THIS CRIME NOVELIST GIVES THE BEST LINES TO THE BAD GUYS."—*TIME*

"WESTLAKE KNOWS PRECISELY HOW TO GRAB A READER, DRAW HIM OR HER INTO THE STORY, AND THEN SLOWLY TIGHTEN HIS GRIP UNTIL ESCAPE IS IMPOSSIBLE."—*Washington Post Book World*

Visit our Web site at http://warnerbooks.com

$12.00 US / $14.99 CAN.
ISBN 0-446-67467-2

9 780446 674676

CRIME FICTION

RICHARD STARK
The Outfit

A PARKER NOVEL
RICHARD STARK
The Outfit

"PARKER IS A TRUE TREASURE.…THE MASTER THIEF IS BACK, ALONG WITH RICHARD STARK (AKA DONALD WESTLAKE)."
—MARILYN STASIO, *NEW YORK TIMES BOOK REVIEW*

MYSTERIOUS PRESS

creative firm
WARNER BOOKS
New York, New York
designers
JACKIE MEYER, JON VALK
client
WARNER BOOKS

the neighbors

a novel by carol smith author of *Charmed Circle*

creative firm
WARNER BOOKS
New York, New York
designer
JACKIE MERRI MEYER
photographer
ALEXA GABANINO
client
WARNER BOOKS

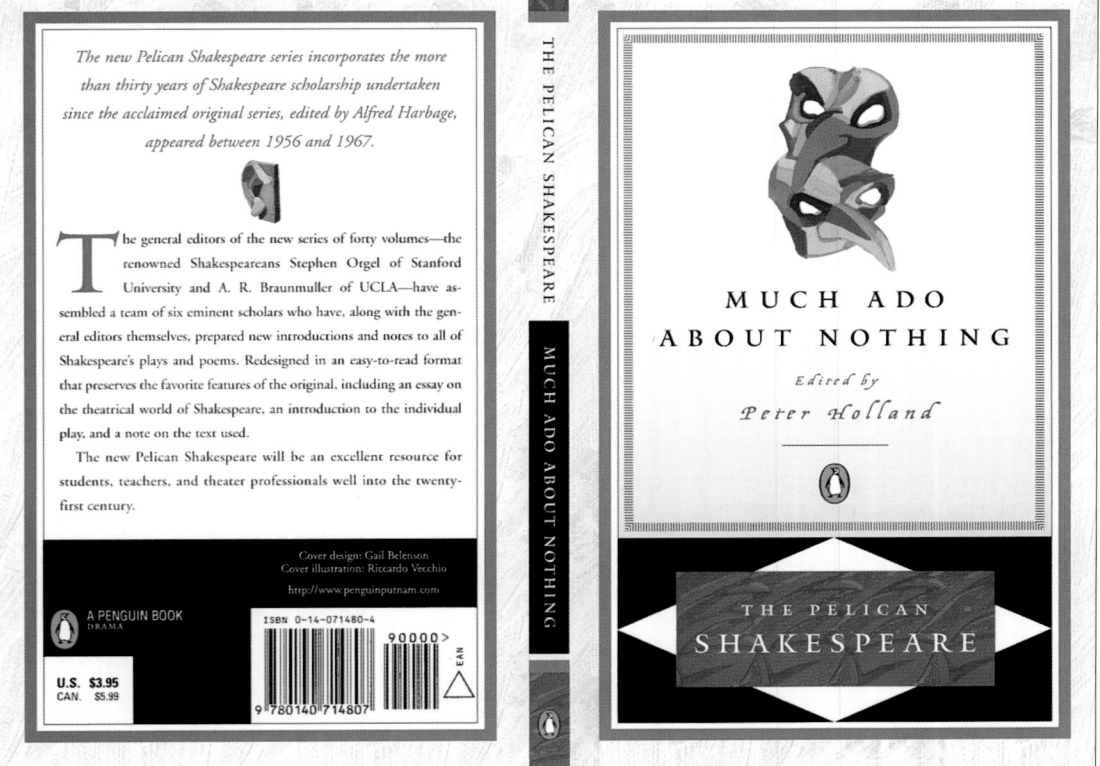

The new Pelican Shakespeare series incorporates the more than thirty years of Shakespeare scholarship undertaken since the acclaimed original series, edited by Alfred Harbage, appeared between 1956 and 1967.

The general editors of the new series of forty volumes—the renowned Shakespeareans Stephen Orgel of Stanford University and A. R. Braunmuller of UCLA—have assembled a team of six eminent scholars who have, along with the general editors themselves, prepared new introductions and notes to all of Shakespeare's plays and poems. Redesigned in an easy-to-read format that preserves the favorite features of the original, including an essay on the theatrical world of Shakespeare, an introduction to the individual play, and a note on the text used.

The new Pelican Shakespeare will be an excellent resource for students, teachers, and theater professionals well into the twenty-first century.

THE PELICAN SHAKESPEARE

MUCH ADO ABOUT NOTHING

MUCH ADO ABOUT NOTHING

Edited by Peter Holland

THE PELICAN SHAKESPEARE

Cover design: Gail Belenson
Cover illustration: Riccardo Vecchio
http://www.penguinputnam.com

A PENGUIN BOOK
DRAMA

ISBN 0-14-071480-4

90000>

U.S. $3.95
CAN. $5.99

9 780140 714807

creative firm
PENGUIN PUTNAM INC.
New York, New York

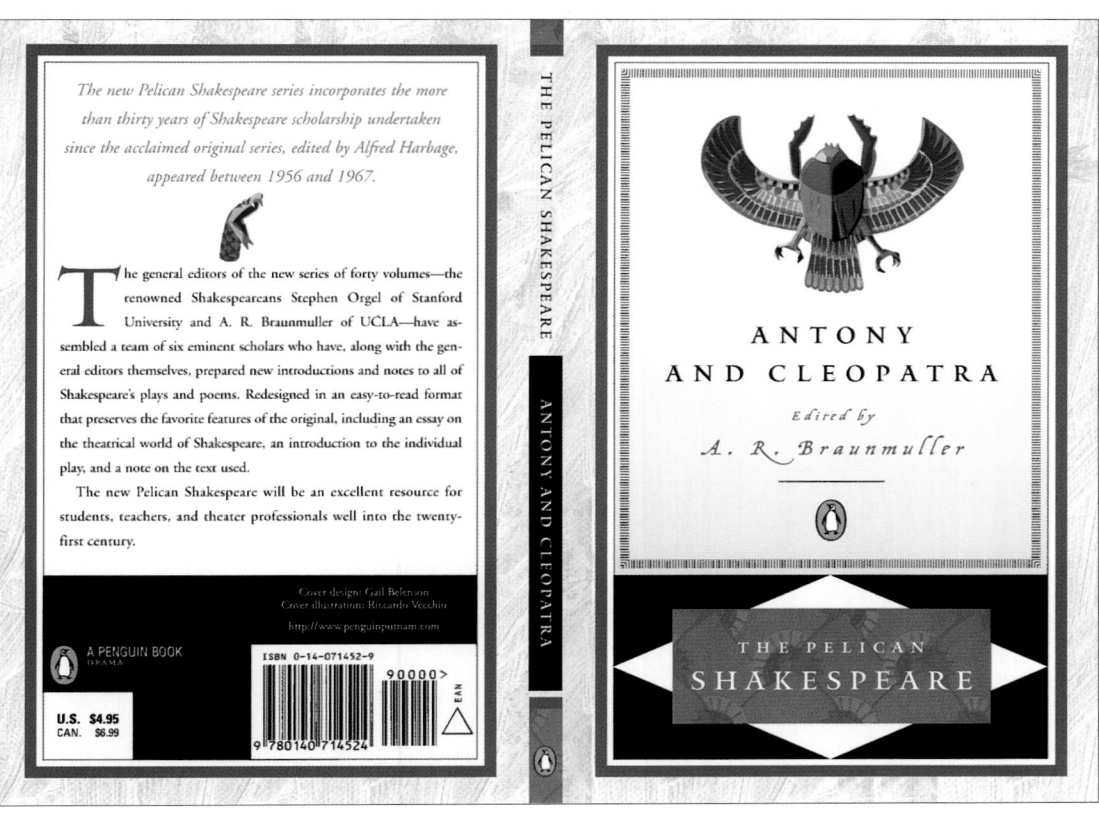

The new Pelican Shakespeare series incorporates the more than thirty years of Shakespeare scholarship undertaken since the acclaimed original series, edited by Alfred Harbage, appeared between 1956 and 1967.

The general editors of the new series of forty volumes—the renowned Shakespeareans Stephen Orgel of Stanford University and A. R. Braunmuller of UCLA—have assembled a team of six eminent scholars who have, along with the general editors themselves, prepared new introductions and notes to all of Shakespeare's plays and poems. Redesigned in an easy-to-read format that preserves the favorite features of the original, including an essay on the theatrical world of Shakespeare, an introduction to the individual play, and a note on the text used.

The new Pelican Shakespeare will be an excellent resource for students, teachers, and theater professionals well into the twenty-first century.

THE PELICAN SHAKESPEARE

ANTONY AND CLEOPATRA

ANTONY AND CLEOPATRA

Edited by A. R. Braunmuller

THE PELICAN SHAKESPEARE

Cover design: Gail Belenson
Cover illustration: Riccardo Vecchio
http://www.penguinputnam.com

A PENGUIN BOOK
DRAMA

ISBN 0-14-071452-9

90000>

U.S. $4.95
CAN. $6.99

9 780140 714524

creative firm
PENGUIN PUTNAM INC.
New York, New York

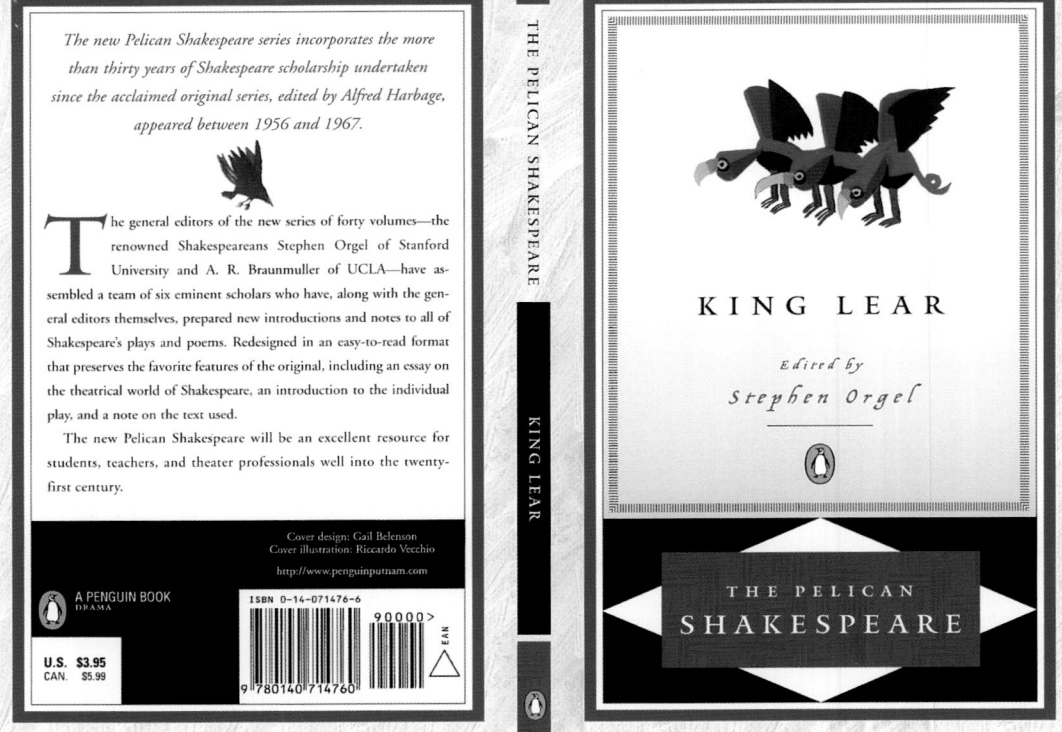

The new Pelican Shakespeare series incorporates the more than thirty years of Shakespeare scholarship undertaken since the acclaimed original series, edited by Alfred Harbage, appeared between 1956 and 1967.

The general editors of the new series of forty volumes—the renowned Shakespeareans Stephen Orgel of Stanford University and A. R. Braunmuller of UCLA—have assembled a team of six eminent scholars who have, along with the general editors themselves, prepared new introductions and notes to all of Shakespeare's plays and poems. Redesigned in an easy-to-read format that preserves the favorite features of the original, including an essay on the theatrical world of Shakespeare, an introduction to the individual play, and a note on the text used.

The new Pelican Shakespeare will be an excellent resource for students, teachers, and theater professionals well into the twenty-first century.

Cover design: Gail Belenson
Cover illustration: Riccardo Vecchio
http://www.penguinputnam.com

A PENGUIN BOOK
DRAMA

U.S. $3.95
CAN. $5.99

ISBN 0-14-071476-6

90000>

9 780140 714760

THE PELICAN SHAKESPEARE

KING LEAR

KING LEAR

Edited by
Stephen Orgel

THE PELICAN
SHAKESPEARE

creative firm
PENGUIN PUTNAM INC.
New York, New York

creative firm
PENGUIN PUTNAM INC.
New York, New York

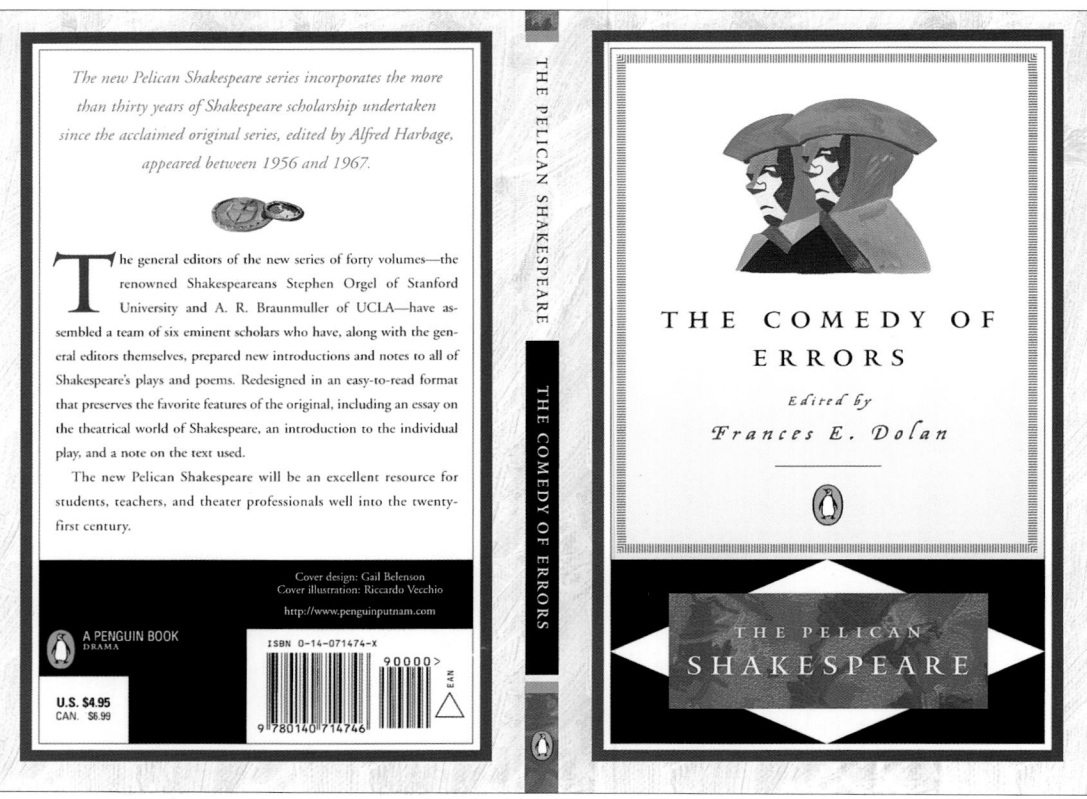

The new Pelican Shakespeare series incorporates the more than thirty years of Shakespeare scholarship undertaken since the acclaimed original series, edited by Alfred Harbage, appeared between 1956 and 1967.

The general editors of the new series of forty volumes—the renowned Shakespeareans Stephen Orgel of Stanford University and A. R. Braunmuller of UCLA—have assembled a team of six eminent scholars who have, along with the general editors themselves, prepared new introductions and notes to all of Shakespeare's plays and poems. Redesigned in an easy-to-read format that preserves the favorite features of the original, including an essay on the theatrical world of Shakespeare, an introduction to the individual play, and a note on the text used.

The new Pelican Shakespeare will be an excellent resource for students, teachers, and theater professionals well into the twenty-first century.

Cover design: Gail Belenson
Cover illustration: Riccardo Vecchio
http://www.penguinputnam.com

A PENGUIN BOOK
DRAMA

U.S. $4.95
CAN. $6.99

ISBN 0-14-071474-X

90000>

9 780140 714746

THE PELICAN SHAKESPEARE

THE COMEDY OF ERRORS

THE COMEDY OF
ERRORS

Edited by
Frances E. Dolan

THE PELICAN
SHAKESPEARE

creative firm
  WARNER BOOKS
  New York, New York
designer
  JACKIE MERRI MEYER
illustrator
  FRANCO ACCORNERO
client
  WARNER BOOKS

creative firm
  WARNER BOOKS
  New York, New York
designer
  FLAG
client
  WARNER BOOKS

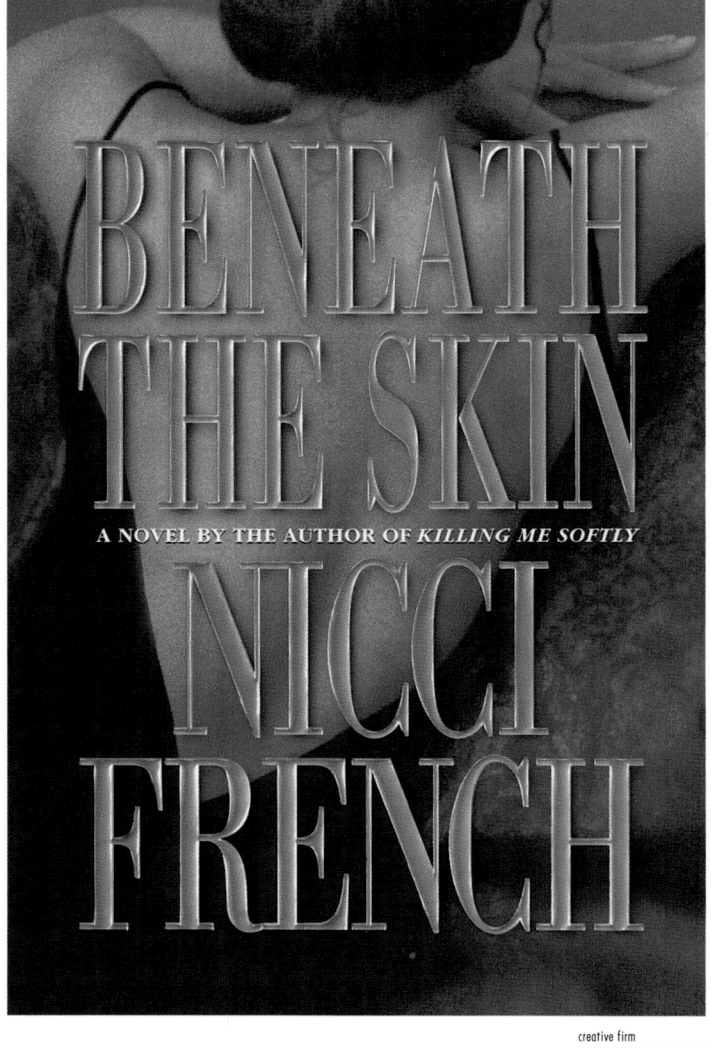

BENEATH THE SKIN

A NOVEL BY THE AUTHOR OF *KILLING ME SOFTLY*

NICCI FRENCH

creative firm
  WARNER BOOKS
  New York, New York
designer
  LOUISE FILI
photographer
  ALICE GANIK
client
  WARNER BOOKS

TRAVELING LIGHT

A NOVEL

KATRINA KITTLE

creative firm
  WARNER BOOKS
  New York, New York
designer
  DIANE LUGER
photographer
  FRANCO ACCORNERO
client
  WARNER BOOKS

creative firm
   WATERSDESIGN.COM
   New York, New York
creative director
   JOHN WATERS
designer
   DIRK ROWNTREE
client
   LAZARD FRERES

TUESD. 1990

A True-Life Journey into the Mind of the Serial Killer

THE LAST VICTIM

JASON MOSS

WITH JEFFREY KOTTLER, PH.D.

creative firm
   WARNER BOOKS
   New York, New York
designer
   FLAG
client
   WARNER BOOKS

AMPERSAND ISSUE 3 JANUARY/FEBRUARY 1999 BRITISH DESIGN & ART DIRECTION

creative firm
  FROST DESIGN LTD.
    London, England
creative director
  VINCE FROST
client
  D&AD

creative firm
  WARNER BOOKS
    New York, New York
designer
  JACKIE MERRI MEYER
image courtesy of
  ALEXANDER'S ANTIQUES OF NEW YORK CITY
client
  WARNER BOOKS

creative firm
  WARNER BOOKS
  New York, New York
designer
  RACHEL McCLAIN
illustrator
  JOHN MARTINEZ
client
  WARNER BOOKS

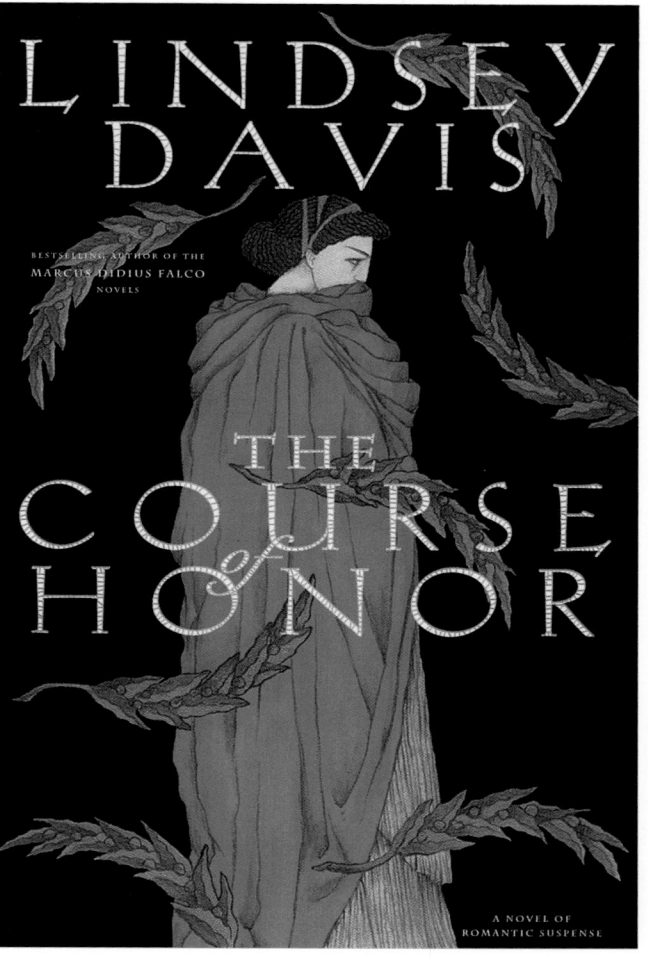

creative firm
  WARNER BOOKS
  New York, New York
designer
  RICHARD FAHEY
client
  WARNER BOOKS

creative firm
  WARNER BOOKS
  New York, New York
designer
  RACHEL McLAIN
illustrator
  JOHN MARTINEZ
client
  WARNER BOOKS

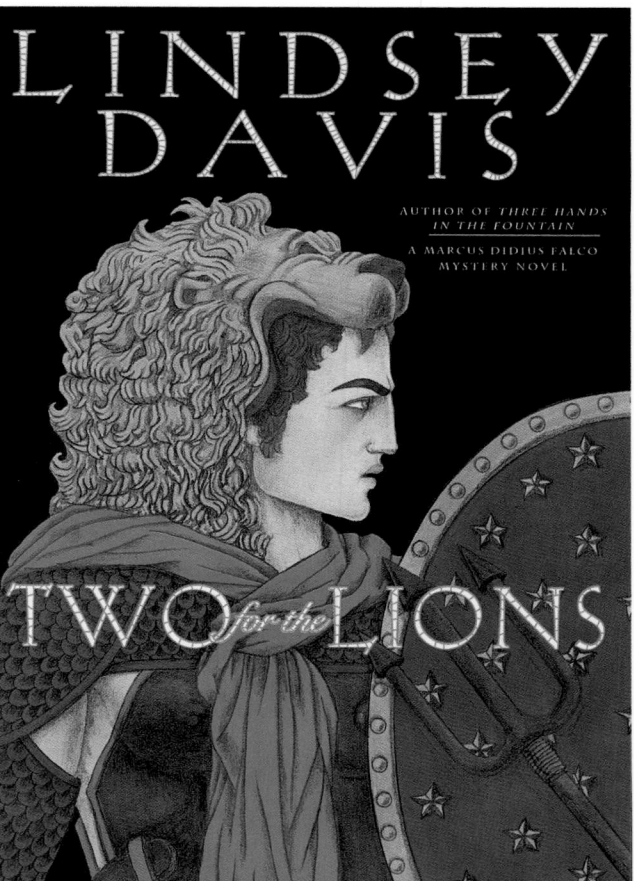

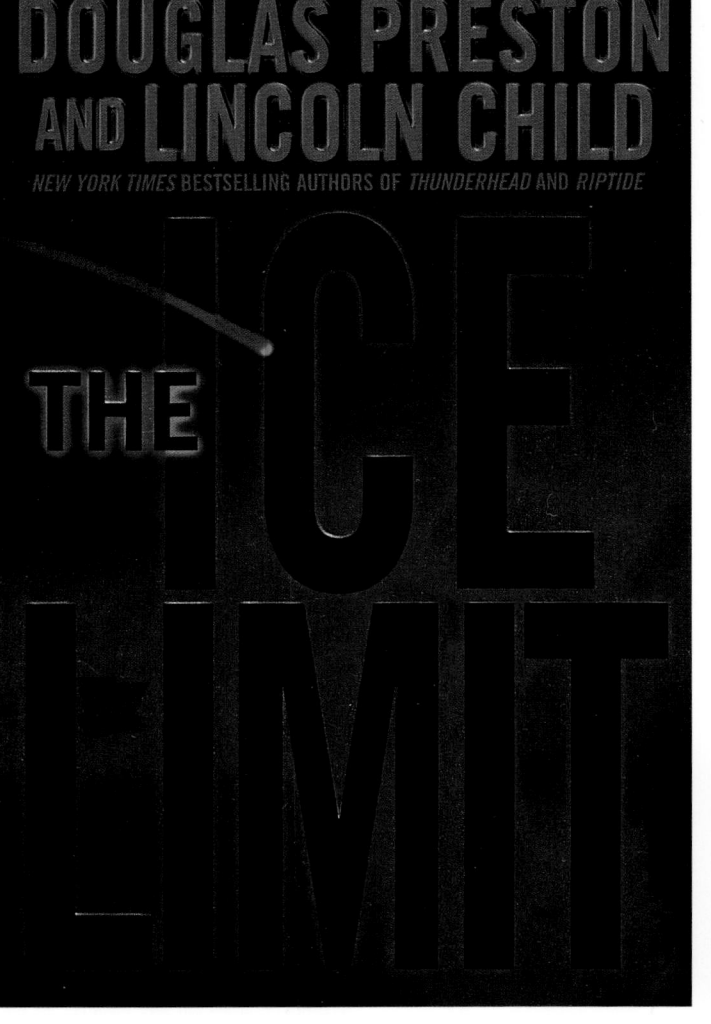

creative firm
    WARNER BOOKS
    New York, New York
designer
    FLAG
illustrator
    FRANCO ACCORNERO
client
    WARNER BOOKS

creative firm
    WARNER BOOKS
    New York, New York
designer
    DIANE LUGER
client
    WARNER BOOKS

creative firm
   VIVA DOLAN COMMUNICATIONS AND DESIGN INC.
   Toronto, Canada
designers
   FRANK VIVA, DOMINIC AYRE, JOHN GUDELJ
photographers
   RON BAXTER SMITH (cover),
   BRIAN BOYEL (interior)
copywriters
   PETER GIFFEN, ROBERT STACEY
client
   THE ADVERTISING AND DESIGN CLUB OF CANADA

creative firm
   SIBLEY PETEET DESIGN
   Dallas, Texas
designer
   DON SIBLEY
client
   BELLAGIO RESORT & CASINO

creative firm
BRUNAZZI & ASSOCIATI/
IMAGE + COMMUNICATION
Turin, Italy
art director
GIOVANNI BRUNAZZI
client
MALGRÉ TOUT...LA PITTURE

Malgré tout...
la pittura

Aimone
Artias
Avondoglio
Casorati
Castella
De Alexandris
Dekerle
Fanelli
Giorda
Griffa
Jaillet
Lambert
Mader
Mamet
Mantovani

Payet
Ramella
Soffiantino
Surbone
Thorens

james harte

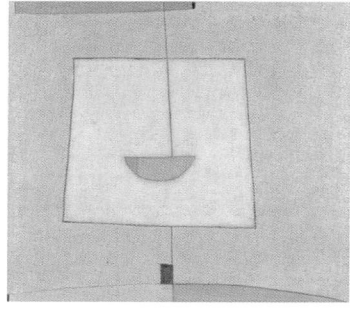

new paintings

creative firm
ALBERT GOMM
Basel, Switzerland
graphic designer
ALBERT GOMM
painter
JAMES HARTE
client
JAMES HARTE

creative firm
PENGUIN PUTNAM INC.
New York, New York

FORTHCOMING TITLES IN THE PENGUIN LIVES SERIES

Edna O'Brien on James Joyce
Jonathan Spence on Mao Zedong
Jane Smiley on Charles Dickens
Carol Shields on Jane Austen
Mary Gordon on Joan of Arc
Karen Armstrong on the Buddha
Patricia Bosworth on Marlon Brando
R. W. B. Lewis on Dante
Janet Malcolm on Anton Chekhov
Marshall Frady on Martin Luther King, Jr.
Elizabeth Hardwick on Herman Melville
John Keegan on Winston Churchill
Wayne Koestenbaum on Andy Warhol
Roy Blount, Jr., on Robert E. Lee
David Quammen on Charles Darwin
Sherwin Nuland on Leonardo da Vinci
Nigel Nicolson on Virginia Woolf
Bobbie Ann Mason on Elvis Presley
Louis Auchincloss on Woodrow Wilson
Douglas Brinkley on Rosa Parks
Francine du Plessix Gray on Simone Weil

PETER GAY

PETER GAY

Mozart

Mozart

Penguin LIVES

Viking

ISBN 0-670-88238-0
9 780670 882380   90000>

LOUIS AUCHINCLOSS

Woodrow Wilson

Penguin LIVES

creative firm
PENGUIN PUTNAM INC.
New York, New York

creative firm
ST. MARY'S PRESS
Winona, Minnesota
cover designer
CINDI RAMM
copy editor
REBECCA FAIRBANK

Tales
from a
Real
Life

Everyday Essays by Jim Doyle

UNIVERSAL

"Psycho" 1960

UNIVERSAL

"The Birds" 1963

| 8 mon | 9 tue | 10 wed | 11 thu | 12 fri | 13 sat | 14 sun | 15 mon | 16 tue | 17 wed | 18 thu | 19 fri | 20 sat | 21 sun | 22 mon | 23 tue | 24 wed | 25 thu | 26 fri | 27 sat | 28 sun | 29 mon | 30 tue | 31 wed |
| 8 thu | 9 fri | 10 sat | 11 sun | 12 mon | 13 tue | 14 wed | 15 thu | 16 fri | 17 sat | 18 sun | 19 mon | 20 tue | 21 wed | 22 thu | 23 fri | 24 sat | 25 sun | 26 mon | 27 tue | 28 wed | 29 thu | 30 fri | |

UNIVERSAL

"Vertigo" 1958

SEPTEMBER
| 2 thu | 3 fri | 4 sat | 5 sun | 6 mon | 7 tue | 8 wed | 9 thu | 10 fri | 11 sat | 12 sun | 13 mon | 14 tue | 15 wed | 16 thu | 17 fri | 18 sat | 19 sun | 20 mon | 21 tue | 22 wed | 23 thu | 24 fri | 25 sat | 26 sun | 27 mon | 28 tue | 29 wed | 30 thu | |

OCTOBER
| 2 sat | 3 sun | 4 mon | 5 tue | 6 wed | 7 thu | 8 fri | 9 sat | 10 sun | 11 mon | 12 tue | 13 wed | 14 thu | 15 fri | 16 sat | 17 sun | 18 mon | 19 tue | 20 wed | 21 thu | 22 fri | 23 sat | 24 sun | 25 mon | 26 tue | 27 wed | 28 thu | 29 fri | 30 sat | 31 sun |

creative firm
AREA STRATEGIC DESIGN/ROME
Rome, Italy
creative director
ANTONIO ROMANO
art director
KEVIN MOULT
photographer
MASSIMO PIERSANTI
client
UNIVERSAL STUDIO/ROME-LOS ANGELES

creative firm
TOM FOWLER, INC.
Stamford, Connecticut
art director, designer, illustrator
ELIZABETH P. BALL
client
GRAPHICS THREE, INC.

THEY GROW AND SURVIVE
WITH LITTLE HELP FROM MANKIND
FINDING THEIR OWN WAY

SUN	MON	TUE	WED	THU	FRI	SAT
			1	2	3	4
5	6	7	8	9	10	11
12	13	14	15	16	17	18
19	20	21	22	23	24	25
26	27	28	29	30		

SKAGIT WATERSHED COUNCIL
A Community Partnership for Salmon

november

creative firm
BONNIE MATHER DESIGN
Edmunds, Washington
graphic designer
BONNIE MATHER
client
SKAGIT WATERSHED COUNCIL
(a community partnership for salmon)

creative firm
AERIAL
San Francisco, California
designer, copywriter
TRACY MOON
client
AERIAL

creative firm
ARеA STRATEGIC
DESIGN/ROME
Rome, Italy
creative director
ANTONIO ROMANO
art director
STEFANO AURELI
illustrator
FRANCESCA MONTOSI
photographers
MARCO TEMPERA, GIUSEPPE FADDA
client
ARеA STRATEGIC DESIGN/ROME

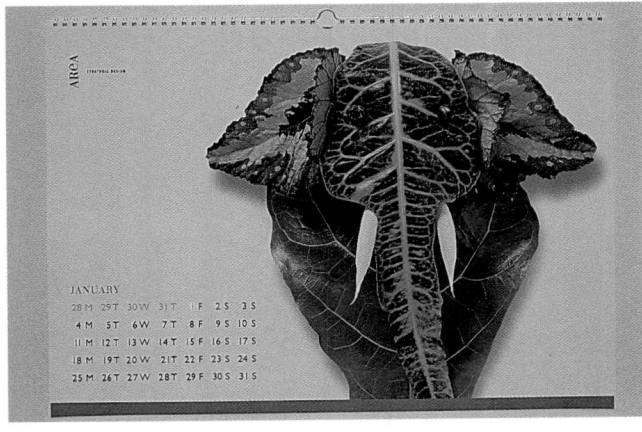

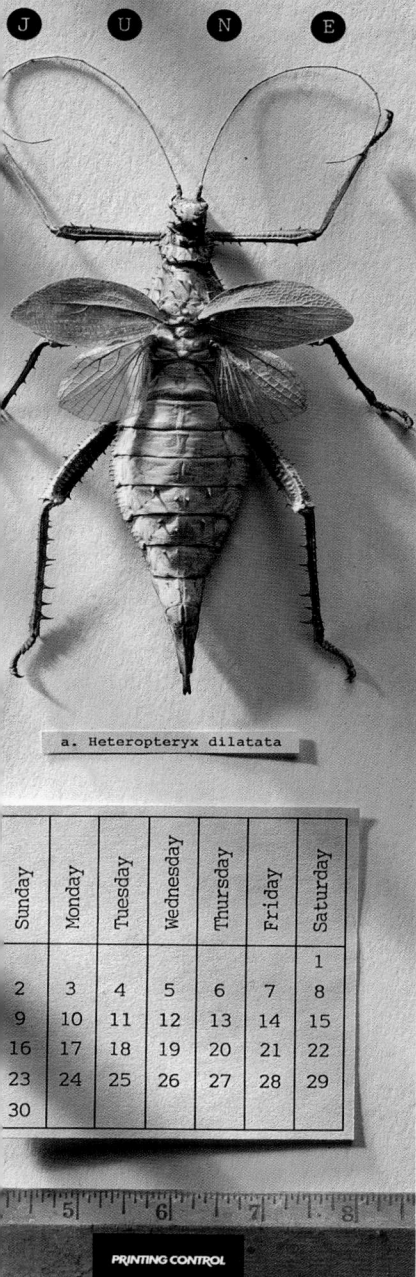

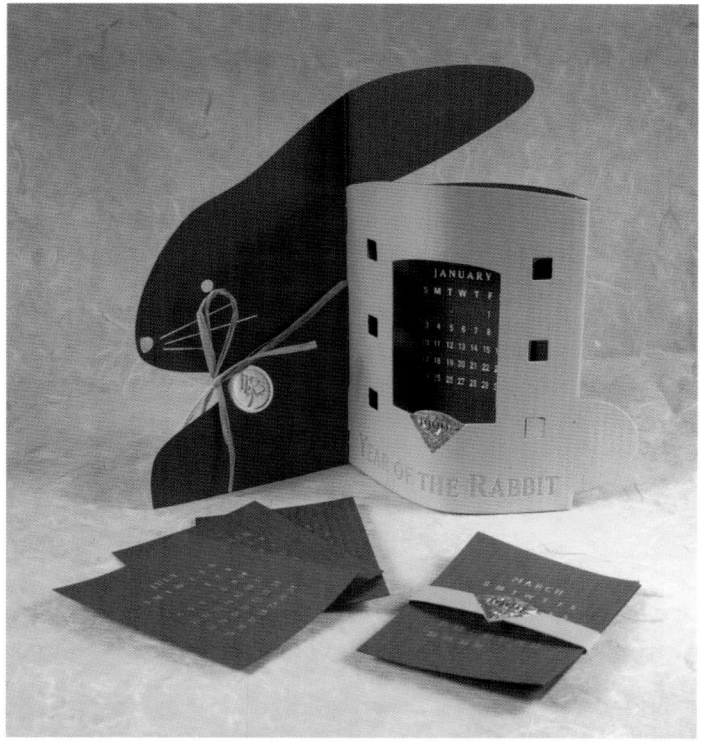

creative firm
JULIA TAM DESIGN
Palos Verdes, California
client
JULIA TAM DESIGN

creative firm
BELYEA
Seattle, Washington
art director
PATRICIA BELYEA
designer
RON LARS HANSEN
letterer
JOCELYN CURNY
photographer
ROSANNE OLSEN
client
BELYEA

creative firm
GREG WALTERS DESIGN
Seattle, Washington
designer
GREG WALTERS
photographer
TOM COLLICOTT
client
PRINTING CONTROL

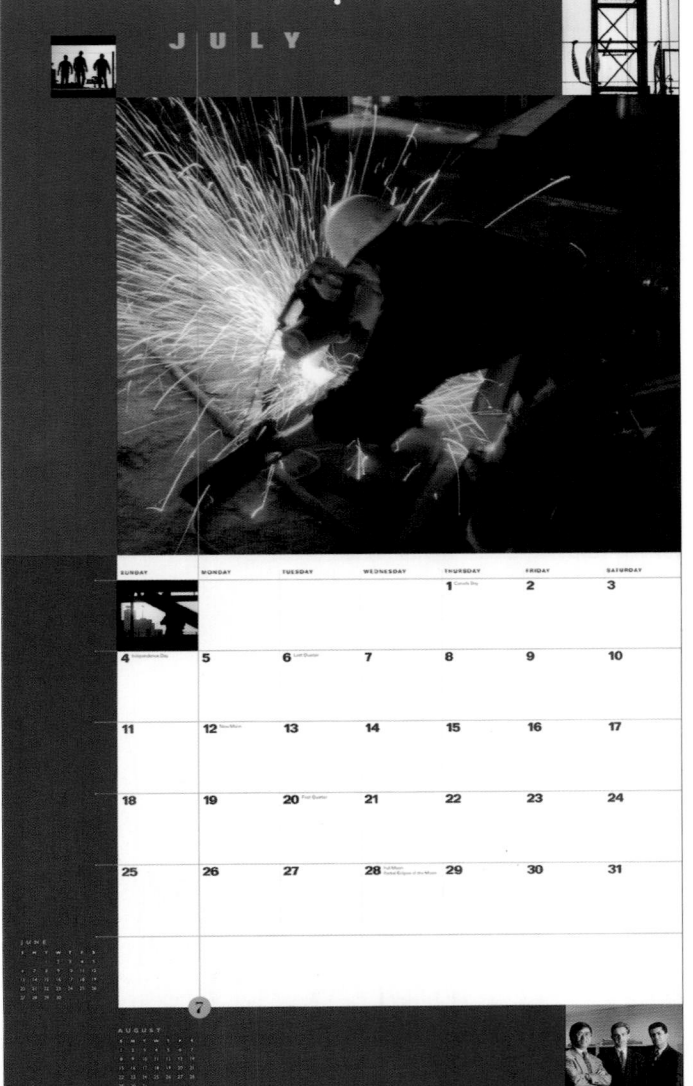

JULY

SUNDAY	MONDAY	TUESDAY	WEDNESDAY	THURSDAY	FRIDAY	SATURDAY
				1 Canada Day	2	3
4 Independence Day	5	6 Last Quarter	7	8	9	10
11 New Moon	12	13	14	15	16	17
18	19	20 First Quarter	21	22	23	24
25	26	27	28 Full Moon / Partial Eclipse of the Moon	29	30	31

creative firm
  BIG CAT
  MARKETING
  COMM.
  Colorado Springs, Colorado
designer
  ANNA BARNES
client
  COLORADO SPRINGS
  UTILITIES

Ollie's Words on Water Conservation:

Save 4-10 gallons per day by turning off the faucet while brushing your teeth.

Save 2 gallons per day by keeping a container full of tap water in your refrigerator.

August '99

Sunday	Monday	Tuesday	Wednesday	Thursday	Friday	Saturday
1	2	3	4	5	6	7
8	9	10	11	12	13	14
15	16	17	18	19	20	21
22	23	24	25	26	27	28
29	30	31				

See where our water comes from!
See our "Elementary Presentations and Program Guide" in the back of this calendar for more information.

creative firm
  SACKETT DESIGN ASSOCIATES
  San Francisco, California
creative director
  MARK SACKETT
designers
  JAMES SAKAMOTO, ERIC SIEMENS
photographers
  HOLLY STEWART PHOTOGRAPHY, MENUEZ PICTURES
client
  SAN FRANCISCO INTERNATIONAL AIRPORT

July

creative firm
  TRICKETT & WEBB LTD
  London, England
designers
  LYNN TRICKETT, BRIAN WEBB, MARCUS TAYLOR
client
  FOREIGN & COMMONWEALTH OFFICE

DECEMBER 2000

Grumman F8F-1 Bearcat
SPECIFICATIONS

		SUNDAY	MONDAY	TUESDAY	WEDNESDAY	THURSDAY	FRIDAY	SATURDAY

creative firm
  30SIXTY DESIGN, INC.
   Los Angeles, California
creative director
  HENRY VIZCARRA
art director
  JAIME FLORES
designers
  ANNA KALINKA, RICKARD OLSSON,
  THOMAS GUNDRED
client
  MUSEUM OF FLYING

creative firm
  BRUNAZZI & ASSOCIATI/
  IMAGE + COMMUNICATION
   Turin, Italy
photo editor
  ADA BRUNAZZI
client
  CARTIERE BURGO

Novembre November Novembre November Noviembre

1 2 3 4 5 6 7 8 9 10 11 12 13 14 15 16
17 18 19 20 21 22 23 24 25 26 27 28 29 30

A DISCOUNT STORE WITH STYLE

"TARGET IS THE DISCOUNT ANSWER TO THE DEPARTMENT STORE EXPERIENCE."
—New York Times Reporter

THE SECOND YOU WALK INTO A TARGET STORE, YOU'LL KNOW YOU'VE DISCOVERED SOMETHING UNIQUE. "IS THIS A DISCOUNT STORE?" YOU'LL FIND THE DISCOUNT STORE BASICS. SODA POP TO TOOTHPASTE. TOILET PAPER TO UNDERWEAR. (And yes, we have very competitive prices.) "OR A DEPARTMENT STORE?" YOU'LL ALSO FIND FASHION-FORWARD APPAREL JUST LIKE YOU'VE SEEN IN THOSE DEPARTMENT STORE WINDOWS. AND TREND-RIGHT HOME FASHIONS LIKE THOSE FOUND IN MAGAZINES. (But take a look at the price tag. Lower than you expected, huh?) DO SOME RESEARCH AND YOU'LL DISCOVER THAT TARGET IS THE LARGEST CHARITABLE CONTRIBUTOR IN THE RETAIL INDUSTRY. (All this and nice too.) I GUESS YOU COULD SAY, WE'VE FOUND OUR NICHE RIGHT SMACK DAB IN THE MIDDLE OF IT ALL. AND WE KIND OF LIKE IT HERE. FOR NOW, WE'LL SAY WE'RE A MULTI-DEPARTMENTAL/UPSCALE DISCOUNT STORE. BUT YOU CAN JUST CALL US BY OUR FIRST NAME...TARGET. (Or "Tar-zhay" as our loyal guests have nicknamed us.)

creative firm
GRAPHICULTURE
Minneapolis, Minnesota
designer
CHERYL WATSON
illustrator
ROBIN ZINGONE
client
TARGET

creative firm
DOTZLER CREATIVE ARTS
Omaha, Nebraska
client
JOHN DAY COMPANY

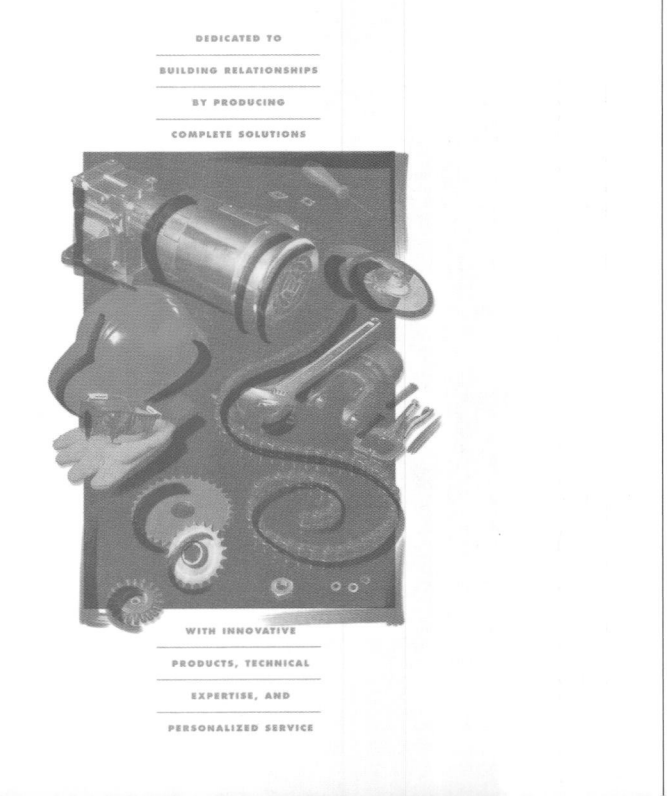

DEDICATED TO

BUILDING RELATIONSHIPS

BY PRODUCING

COMPLETE SOLUTIONS

WITH INNOVATIVE

PRODUCTS, TECHNICAL

EXPERTISE, AND

PERSONALIZED SERVICE

creative firm
  SIGN
  Frankfurt, Germany
creative director
  KARL W. HENSCHEL
client
  SIGN I TOKYO

creative firm
  DEVER DESIGNS
  Laurel, Maryland
creative director
  JEFFERY L. DEVER
art director
  EMILY MARTIN KENDALL
designer
  EMILY MARTIN KENDALL,
  CHRISTINE DRAUGHN
client
  INSTITUTE OF MUSEUM AND LIBRARY SERVICES

National Award *for* Museum Service

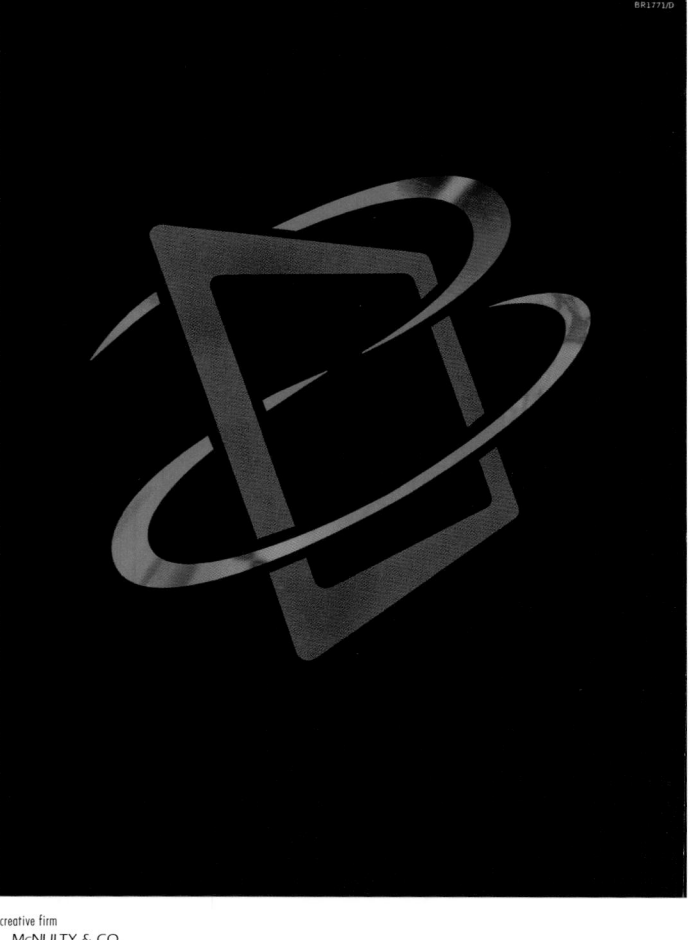

BR1771/D

creative firm
  McNULTY & CO.
  Thousand Oaks, California
creative director
  DAN McNULTY
designer
  BRIAN JACOBSON
client
  MOTOROLA

DEFINING THE **FUTURE** OF NORTHERN VIRGINIA

ONE
FREEDOM
SQUARE

AT RESTON TOWN CENTER

TECHNOGYM SYSTEM®

SOFTWARE

WELLNESS

W

IN MOTION

creative firm
HORNALL ANDERSON DESIGN WORKS
Seattle, Washington
art director
JACK ANDERSON
designers
LARRY ANDERSON, MARY HERMES, MARY CHIN HUTCHISON
client
TECHNOGYM (WELLNESS)

creative firm
KINETIK COMMUNICATION GRAPHICS, INC.
Washington D.C.
designers
JEFFREY FABIAN,
SCOTT RIER,
SAM SHELTON
client
BOSTON PROPERTIES

creative firm
AMY NEIMAN DESIGN
Berkley, California
designer
AMY NEIMAN
photographer
WES WALKER
client
INCA (INTERNATIONAL NATURE &
CULTURAL ADVENTURES)

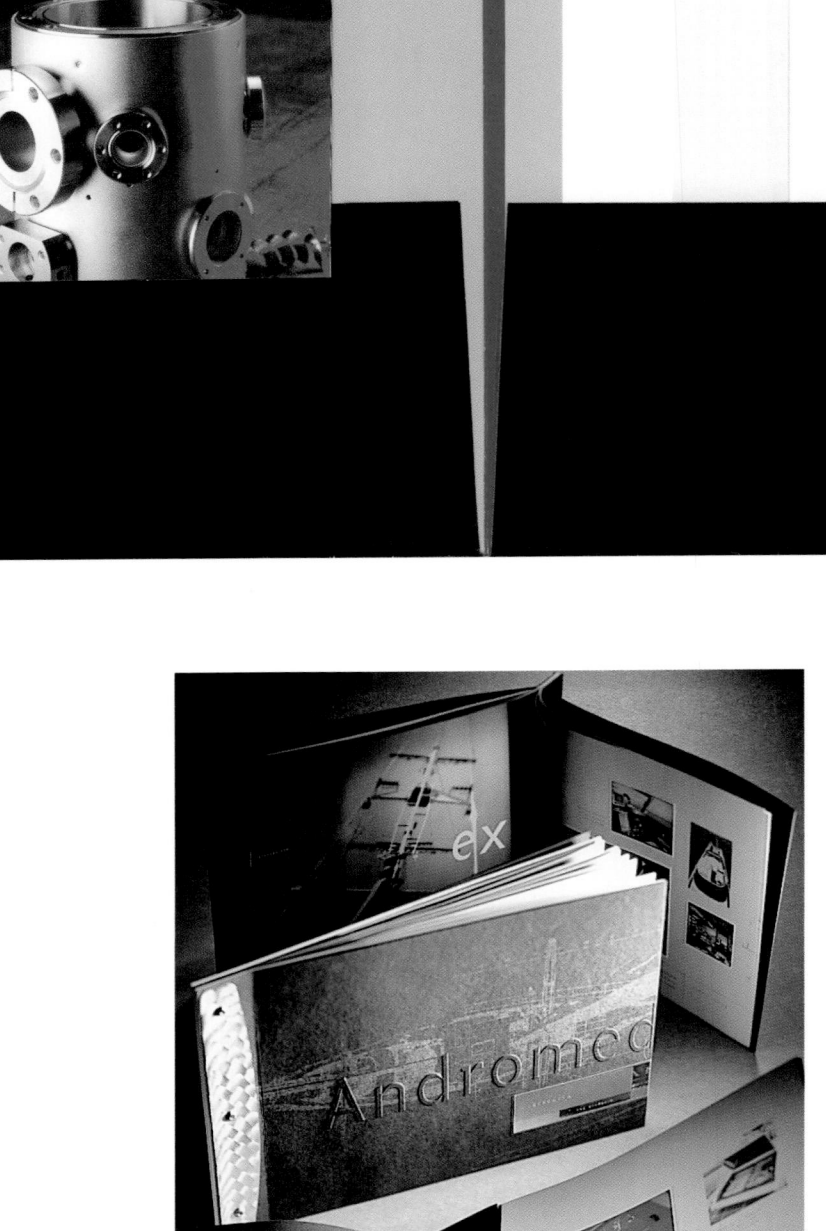

creative firm
KLUNDT HOSMER DESIGN
Spokane, Washington
designers
BRIAN GAGE,
DARIN KLUNDT
client
MacKAY

creative firm
MIRIELLO GRAFICO INC.
San Diego, California
designers
MAXIMO ESCOBEDO,
DENNIS GARCIA
client
OMEGA MARINE

Tom Uglow

Bruce Naumann. Ed Ruscha: Clive Phillpot bought the Ruscha and I bought its companion piece from Marcus Campbell whilst researching of burning pages from Ruscha's Various Small Fires (1964).

my book, Artists' Books, in 1994. There is a future for a medium that can humorously reflect on itself: Burning Small Fires [1968] consists

creative firm
 TRICKETT & WEBB LTD
  London, England
designers
 LYNN TRICKETT,
 BRIAN WEBB,
 KATJA THIELEN
client
 THE LONDON INSTITUTE

creative firm
 GARDNER DESIGN
  Wichita, Kansas
art directors
 BILL GARDNER,
 BRIAN MILLER
designer
 BRIAN MILLER
client
 EXCEL

Butcher & Cook's precooked meats are perfect for any day of the week. The partnership between the trained butcher and chef has resulted in carefully selected cuts of meat that have been slow-cooked to ensure tenderness and great taste time after time. Convenient and easy to prepare at home, ready in minutes. Butcher & Cook's — the everyday home meal solution.

Garlic-Peppered

BUTCHER & COOK'S

creative firm
  GARDNER DESIGN
  Wichita, Kansas
art directors
  BILL GARDNER, TRAVIS BROWN, BRIAN MILLER
designer
  TRAVIS BROWN
client
  EXCEL

至上歡迎　　賓至如歸

歡
迎

Fidelity Investments
富達投資

creative firm
  WONG WONG BOYACK, INC.
  San Francisco, California
art director
  BEN WONG
calligrapher
  H.W. WONG
copywriters
  BEN WONG, SHINY HUANG
client
  FIDELITY INVESTMENTS

creative firm
  HORNALL ANDERSON
  DESIGN WORKS
  Seattle, Washingtona
art directors
  JACK ANDERSON, LARRY ANDERSON
designers
  JACK ANDERSON, LARRY ANDERSON,
  MARY HERMES, MIKE CALKINS,
  MICHAEL BRUGMAN
client
  U.S. CIGAR

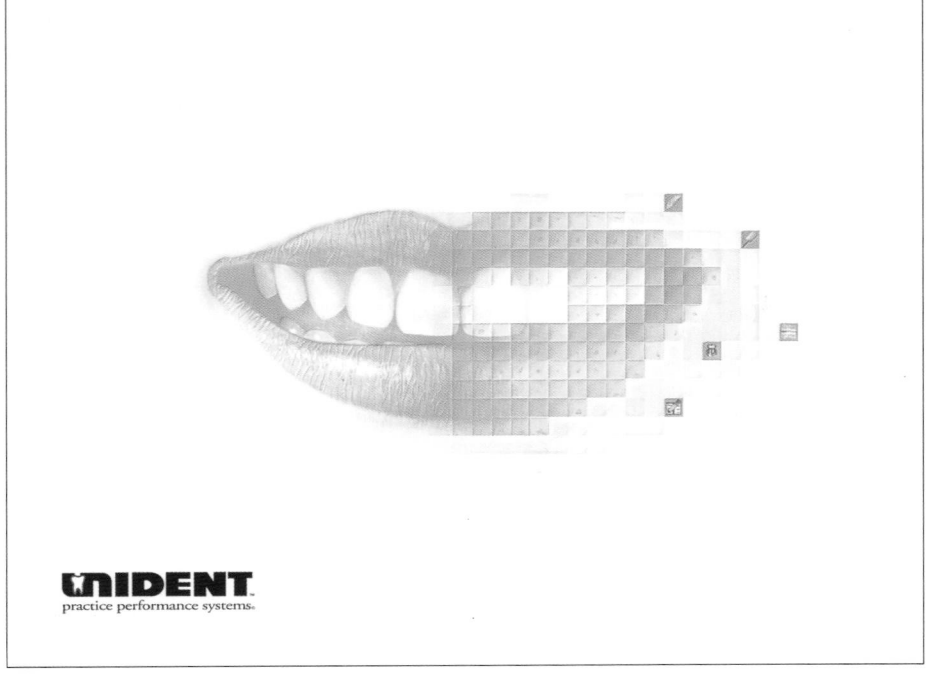

UNIDENT.
practice performance systems.

creative firm
DOTZLER CREATIVE ARTS
Omaha, Nebraska
client
UNIDENT

creative firm
NAKATSUKA DAISUKE, INC.
Tokyo, Japan
designers
DAISUKE NAKATSUKA, TOM NAKATSUKA,
KENJI INOUE, JUNKO NAKATSUKA,
YOSHIFUMI NAKASHIMA, FUMIYO KITAZUME,
HIROMI YAMADA, TOMOKO KANOU
photographers
FRANCOIS GILLET, GORO ARIZONA,
SHOZO NAKAMURA, ERNST HAAS
client
H+B LIFESCIENCE CO., LTD.

HAYASHIBARA
GROUP

creative firm
WAGES DESIGN
Atlanta, Georgia
designer
RANDY ALLISON
photographer
JERRY BURNS
client
CADMUS

creative firm
WDA PINFOLD
Leeds, England
art directors
MYLES PINFOLD,
RICHARD HUNT
design manager
ANDY PROBERT
designer
PHIL MOMSON
client
WATERFORD-WEDGEWOOD

GET ME TO THE CHURCH ON **TIME**

Floral Tapestry is a fruitful marriage of the traditions of fine needlework and great ceramic design.
The pattern is inspired by the richly detailed embroidery of Tudor and Stuart times.
Here it is worked with Sage Green Jasper, an original Wedgwood colour now enjoying a splendid renaissance in this varied range of giftware.

creative firm
PIVOT DESIGN, INC.
Chicago, Illinois
creative director
BROCK HALDEMAN
designer
HOLLE ANDERSON
client
BAKER & McKENZIE

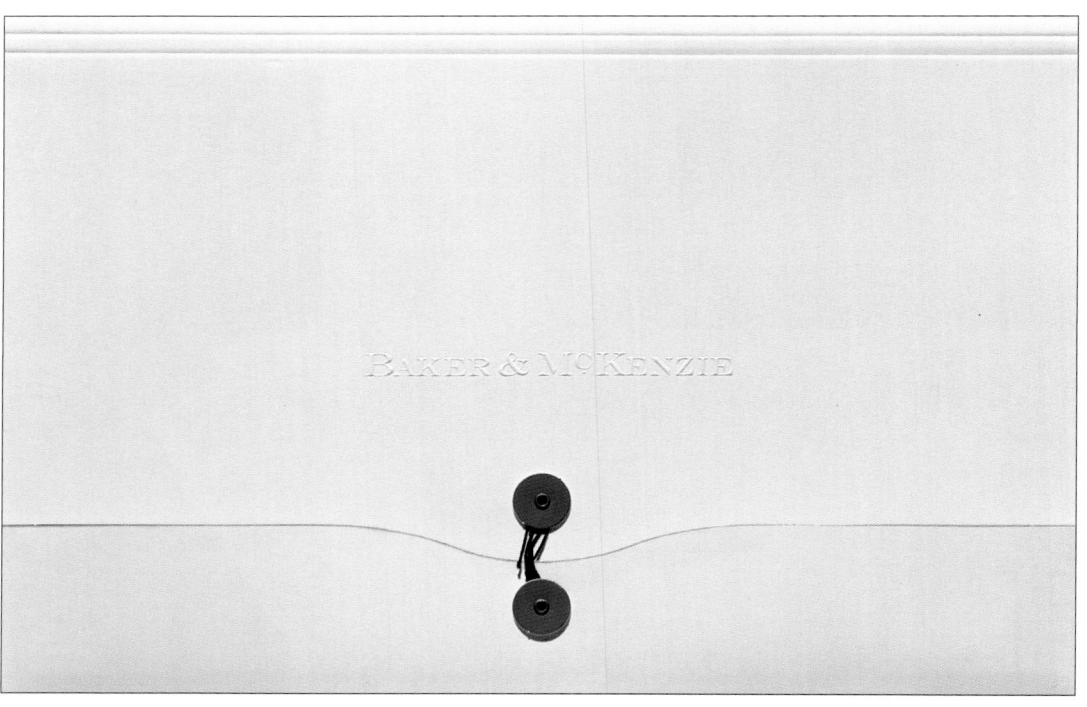

creative firm
HORNALL ANDERSON DESIGN WORKS
Seattle, Washington
art directors
JACK ANDERSON,
JANA NISHI
designers
JACK ANDERSON,
JANA NISHI,
MARY CHIN HUTCHINSON
client
INFERENCE

creative firm
SHEILA HART DESIGN, INC.
Strongsville, Ohio
art director
SHEILA HART
client
MIDWEST CURTAINWALLS

creative firm
ARNOLD SAKS ASSOCIATES
New York, New York
creative director
ARNOLD SAKS
designer
ROBERT YASHARIAN
client
CONSOLIDATED PAPERS

creative firm
  5D STUDIO
  Malibu, California
art director, designer
  JANE KOBAYASHI
client
  BROWN JORDAN

creative firm
  MacVICOR DESIGN + COMMUNICATION
  Arlington, Virginia
art director, designer
  CATHY BROADWELL
illustrator
  CHRIS O'CONNOR
photographer
  CHRIS USHER
client
  EU SERVICES
  (COLLATERAL)

creative firm
  DOUGLAS JOSEPH PARTNERS
  Los Angeles, California
art director
  DOUG JOSEPH
designer
  JULIE SLOTO-MELLEN
illustrators
  JULIE SLOTO-MELLEN, JOHN HERSEY
photographers
  RICK BRIAN, JERRY GARNES
copywriter
  MARK SCAPICCHIO
client
  3D SYSTEMS CORPORATION

creative firm
  JAMES ROBIE DESIGN ASSOCIATES
  Los Angeles, California
creative director
  JAMES ROBIE
design director
  WAYNE FUJITA
designer
  WAYNE FUJITA
photographer
  HENRY BLACKHAM
client
  JAMES ROBIE DESIGN ASSOCIATES

What is

good graphic design

?

R
JAMES ROBIE DESIGN ASSOCIATES

creative firm
  HORNALL ANDERSON DESIGN WORKS
  Seattle, Washington
art director
  JACK ANDERSON
designers
  JACK ANDERSON, LISA CERVENY,
  HEIDI FAVOUR, JANA WILSON ESSER
client
  NOVELL, INC.

CORPORATE PROFILE

Novell

creative firm
  DISNEY DESIGN GROUP
  Lake Buena Vista, Florida
creative director
  MICHELE KEATING
art director
  MARK SEPPALA
designers
  THOMAS SCOTT, DARREN WILSON
illustrators
  THOMAS SCOTT, DARREN WILSON, MARK SEPPALA,
  COSTA ALAVEZOS, JON BISHOP, DAVID WHITAKER,
  ALEX MAHER, MONTY MALDOVAN, CODY REYNOLDS,
  JOHN TRENT, ROBERT VANN, BRIAN BLACKMORE,
  DOUG STRAYER, KERI MURPHY, RICHARD SZNERCH,
  MICHAEL MOJHER
production coordinator
  CHRISTINE MacFARLANE
client
  WALT DISNEY WORLD SPECIAL EVENTS DEVELOPMENT

creative firm
  ROSS ADVERTISING
creative director
  SKIP DAMPIER
art director
  MICK JIBBEN
copywriter
  JOHN RUEBUSH
client
  CATERPILLAR

creative firm
 DOUGLAS JOSEPH PARTNERS
 Los Angeles, California
art directors
 DOUG JOSEPH, SCOTT LAMBERT
designer
 SCOTT LAMBERT
illustrators
 DAVID PLUNKERT, AUGUST STEIN
photographer
 ERIC TUCKER
copywriter
 SCOTT LAMBERT
client
 SPICERS PAPER

creative firm
 GRETEMAN GROUP
 Wichita, Kansas
creative director
 SONIA GRETEMAN
art director
 SONIA GRETEMAN, JAMES STRANGE
designer
 CRAIG TOMSON
client
 LEARJET

creative firm
 DISNEY DESIGN GROUP
 Lake Buena Vista, Florida
creative director
 MICHAEL KEATING
designers
 MIKE WOOD, DARREN WILSON
illustrators
 BRIAN BLACKMORE, ALEX MAHER
client
 WALT DISNEY WORLD SPECIAL EVENTS DEVELOPMENT

Learjet 31A

creative firm
  HORNALL ANDERSON DESIGN WORKS
  Seattle, Washington
art directors
  JACK ANDERSON, KATHA DALTON
designers
  JACK ANDERSON, KATHA DALTON,
  RYAN WILKERSON, BELINDA BOWLING
client
  BOULLION AVIATION SERVICES

creative firm
  HORNALL ANDERSON DESIGN WORKS
  Seattle, Washington
art director
  JACK ANDERSON
designers
  JACK ANDERSON, BRUCE BRANSON-MEYER,
  HEIDI FAVOUR, MARGARET LONG
client
  DDB SEATTLE

The Sony of Canada story, like so many great stories, begins with a stroke of luck. It is October 1955. Albert Cohen, a 41-year-old entrepreneur from Winnipeg, is in his room at Tokyo's Imperial Hotel. It is his second trip to Japan at a time when few Westerners come here. He is shopping for products to expand his distributing business: watches, lighters, any kind of reasonably priced gadget that will appeal to Canadian consumers.

Browsing through the English-language *Nippon Times*, Cohen notices an item on Japan's first transistor radio. He has been following the new transistor technology with interest, looking for an alternative to battery-powered tube radios (whose short life span cost him profits on an earlier import deal). Of course, it isn't likely that a small, unknown company, Tokyo Tsushin Kogyo (TTK) Ltd., will have the solution. But it's worth a shot. He calls and sets up a meeting for the following afternoon.

Arriving by taxi, Cohen feels his hopes sink still lower when he sees TTK's office, a ramshackle wooden house in the Shinagawa district. He is greeted by a Mr. Naruse, who informs him cautiously that the news story was a bit premature: the new radio is not quite ready for market. Without fanfare, he presents this historic Japanese first: the TR-55.

Cohen is intrigued. The five-transistor set measures 5" by 3" by 1.25" and is powered by four inexpensive penlight batteries with a fairly long life span. Canadian consumers will buy this, provided the price is right. Mr. Naruse allows that TTK has not considered exporting the new radio. After some calculations, he arrives at a wholesale price of $27. Cohen is taken aback: that becomes $79.95 retail, far more than the $25 people typically pay for a tube radio. Still, the distributor is impressed by the TR-55's compactness and long battery life — and even more so by a brief meeting with one of TTK's founders, a gentleman named Akio Morita.

4 / 5

creative firm
VIVA DOLAN COMMUNICATIONS ANDDESIGN, INC.
Toronto, Canada
designer
FRANK VIVA
illustrator
MICHAEL BARTALOS
photographer
HILL PEPPARD
copywriter
DOUG DOLAN
client
SONY CANADA

creative firm
VIVA DOLAN COMMUNICATIONS AND DESIGN, INC.
Toronto, Canada
art director
FRANK VIVA
designers
FRANK VIVA, JIM RYCE
client
GOLDEN BOOKS FAMILY ENTERTAINMENT

creative firm
  McELVENEY + PALOZZI DESIGN GROUP, INC.
  Rochester, New York
creative director
  WILLIAM McELVENEY
art director
  LISA WILLIAMSON
client
  ATWATER FOODS, INC.

creative firm
  SIGN KOMMUNIKATION GMBH
  Frankfurt, Germany
creative director
  KARL W. HENSCHEL
client
  SIGN KOMMUNIKATION GMBH

creative firm
  BBK STUDIO, INC.
  Grand Rapids, Michigan
art director, designer, calligrapher
  KEVIN BUDELMANN
editor
  DICK HOLM
photographer
  BOB NEUMANN
copywriter
  KATE CONVISSOR
client
  HERMAN MILLER INC.

creative firm
PENGUIN PUTNAM, INC.
New York, New York

creative firm
CASPER DESIGN GROUP
Berkeley, California
creative director
BILL RIBAR
designer
CHRISTOPHER BUEHLER
photographer
DAVID POWERS
client
ALZA CORPORATION 1998 ANNUAL REPORT

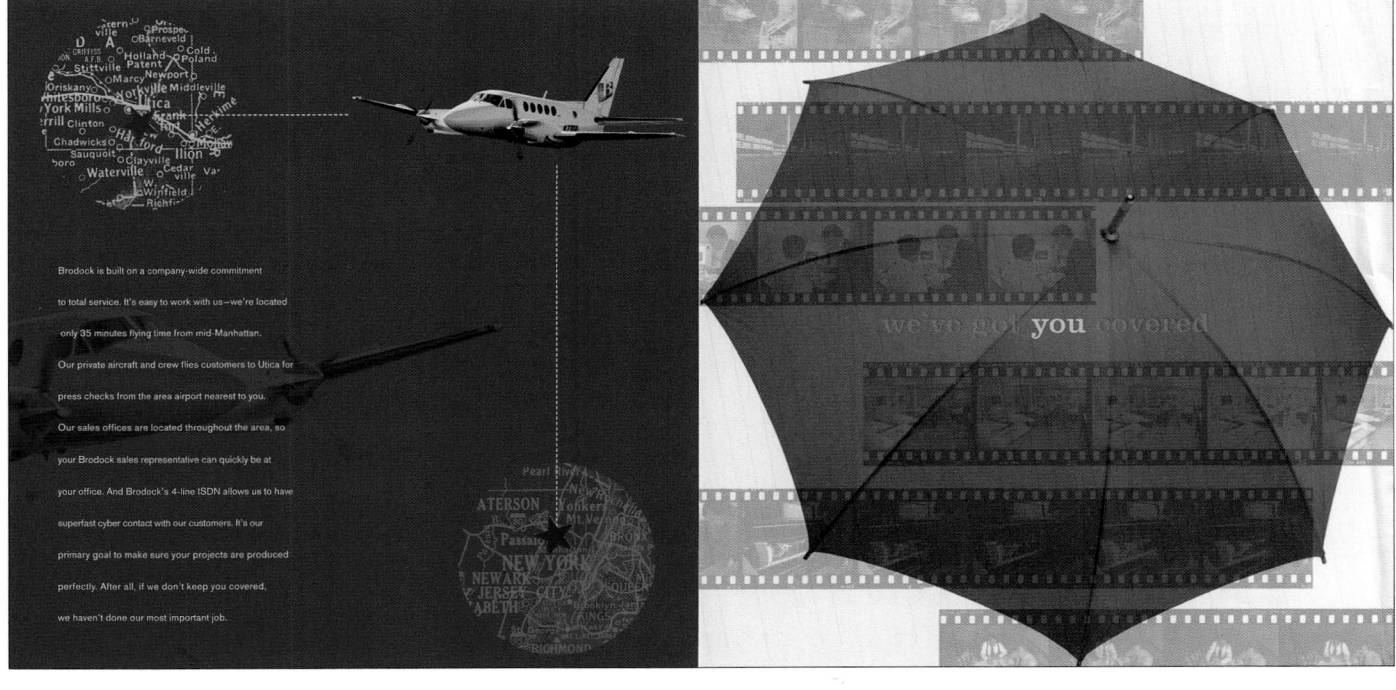

creative firm
PLATINUM DESIGN, INC.
New York, New York
art director
VICTORIA STAMM
designers
KELLY HOGG, MIKE JOYCE
photographer
BART GORIM
copywriter
ARTHUR LEBOW
client
BRODOCK PRESS

creative firm
PARAGRAPHS DESIGN
Chicago, Illinois
designer
JENNIFER ESPOSITO
client
COOL SAVINGS

creative firm
PARAGRAPHS DESIGN
Chicago, Illinois
designer
SCOTT HICKMAN
client
CSC

creative firm
  DESIGN GUYS
  Minneapolis, Minnesota
art director
  STEVEN SIKORA
designer
  JAY THEIGE
client
  TARGET STORES

creative firm
  SIGN KOMMUNIKATION GMBH
  Frankfurt, Germany
creative director
  KARL W. HENSCHEL
client
  DEBIS SYSTEMHAUS

IT services on
an international
scale

creative firm
  JILL TANENBAUM GRAPHIC DESIGN & ADVERTISING
  Bethesda, Maryland
creative director
  JIM TANENBAUM
senior designer
  LEAH GERMANN
client
  KELLERT HECKMAN

People

The people of Harb, Levy & Weiland are working for you. We carefully select a service team comprised of HLW people with experience and expertise tailored to the needs of each client. The service team is headed by an engagement partner who is directly involved with every aspect of your account.

The experience and specialized knowledge of everyone at HLW is available for assistance as needed, while the combined resources of Nexia International, the twelfth largest accounting organization in the world, are available to serve your international needs and to extend our accounting, tax and consulting capability.

Our partners average more than twenty years of public accounting experience, including many years with international accounting firms. This combined experience includes substantial work in most industries and functional specialties in all aspects of audit, accounting and taxation, and many elements of consulting.

HLW people have the highest academic and professional credentials, and we expect a work ethic and spirit committed to quality and timely service. Our formal training typically exceeds the forty hours per year required for CPA licensing. Additional training allows our firm's professionals to update and expand their skills to better serve our clients.

*Audit
&
Accounting*

creative firm
STRATFORD DESIGN ASSOCIATES
Brisbane, California
designer
G.W. STRATFORD, SR.
photographers
GERALD L. FRENCH,
KERRICK JAMES
client
HARD LEVY & WEILAND

BIKING 1999
Butterfield & Robinson
The World's Great Biking Journeys

creative firm
VIVA DOLAN COMMUNICATIONS AND DESIGN, INC.
Toronto, Canada
designer
FRANK VIVA
illustrator
DOUG ROSS
photographer
ED CHIN
editor
DALI CASTRO
production artist
SONJA KLOSS
client
BUTTERFIELD & ROBINSON

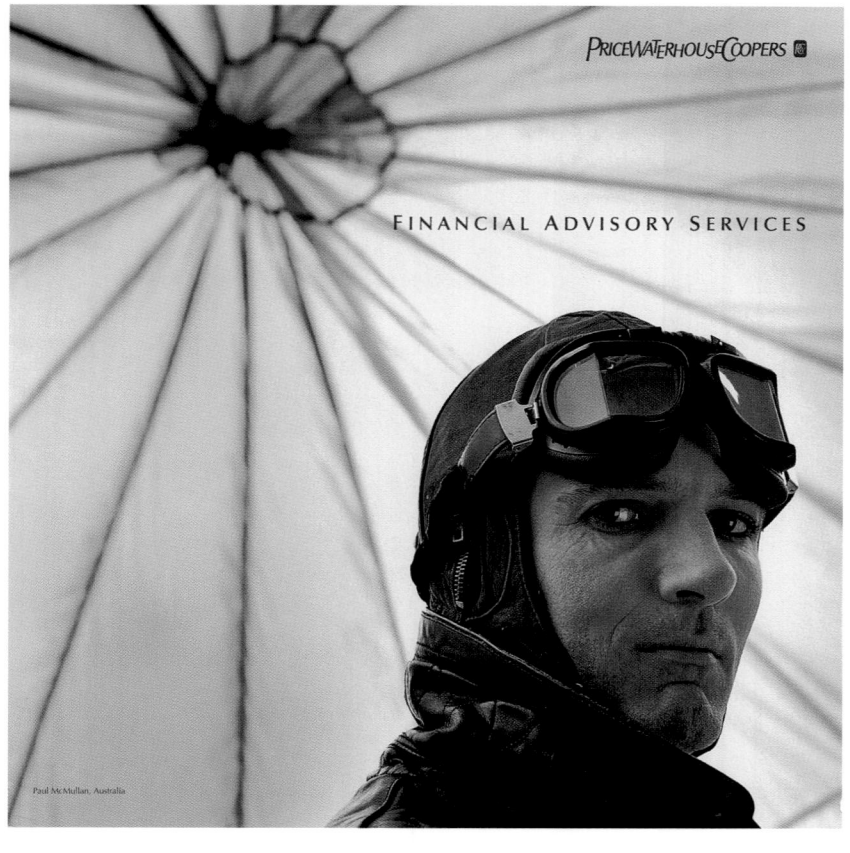

Paul McMullan, Australia

FINANCIAL ADVISORY SERVICES

PRICEWATERHOUSECOOPERS

creative firm
EDWARD WALTER DESIGN
New York, New York
designer
MARTIN BRYNELL
client
PRICEWATERHOUSECOOPERS

GAUDNEK
MUSEUM &
SAMMLUNG

creative firm
CHAVDA GRAPIX
Oviedo, Florida
designer
JAGDISH J. CHAVDA
client
DR. WALTER GAUDNEK

creative firm
FROST DESIGN LTD
London, England
creative director
VINCE FROST
client
PHOTONICA

creative firm
A TO Z COMMUNICATIONS, INC.
Pittsburgh, Pennsylvania
senior graphic designer
JOE TOMKO
client
PERSAD

creative firm
HARPER & CASE LTD
New York, New York
creative director
LISSA TOOLE
designer
JEANNE McMANAMAN
client
CHILDREN'S AID SOCIETY

RENEWING A BLOCK
IN HARLEM

PHASE II — AFTER THE RENOVATIONS
The Children's Aid Society/
Carmel Hill Project: Years 5 and 6

Photographs by Bill Foley
Text by Terry Quinn

creative firm
  VIVA DOLAN COMMUNICATIONS AND DESIGN, INC.
  Toronto, Canada
art director, designer
  FRANK VIVA
illustrator
  MALCOLM HILL
photographers
  RON BAXTER SMITH, MacDUFF EVERTON,
  HILL PEPPARD, STEVEN ROTHFELD
copywriter
  DOUG DOLAN
client
  BUTTERFIELD & ROBINSON

creative firm
  WPA PINFOLD
  Leeds, Yorks, United Kingdom
art director
  MYLES PINFOLD
design manager
  ANDY PROBERT
designer
  PHIL MOMSON
client
  JOHN SMITH'S LTD

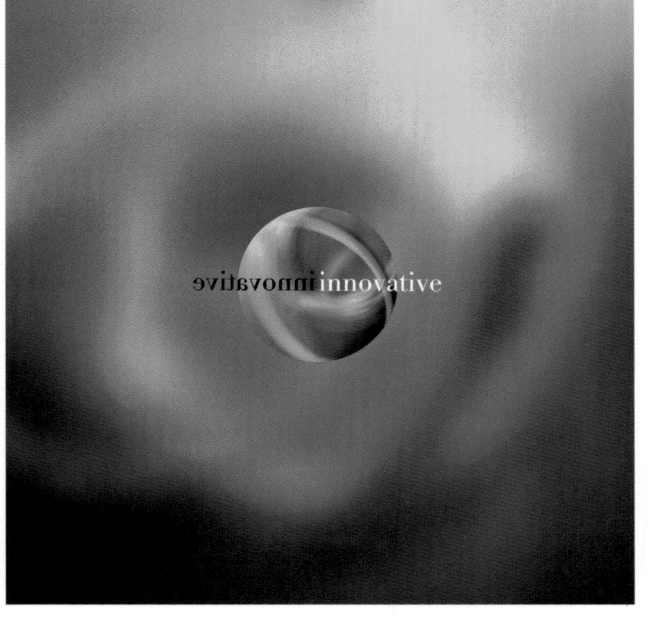

creative firm
  EMERSON, WAJDOWICZ STUDIOS
  New York, New York
creative director
  JUREK WAJDOWICZ
senior art director
  LISA LaROCHELLE
client
  DOMTAR, EDDY SPECIALTY PAPERS

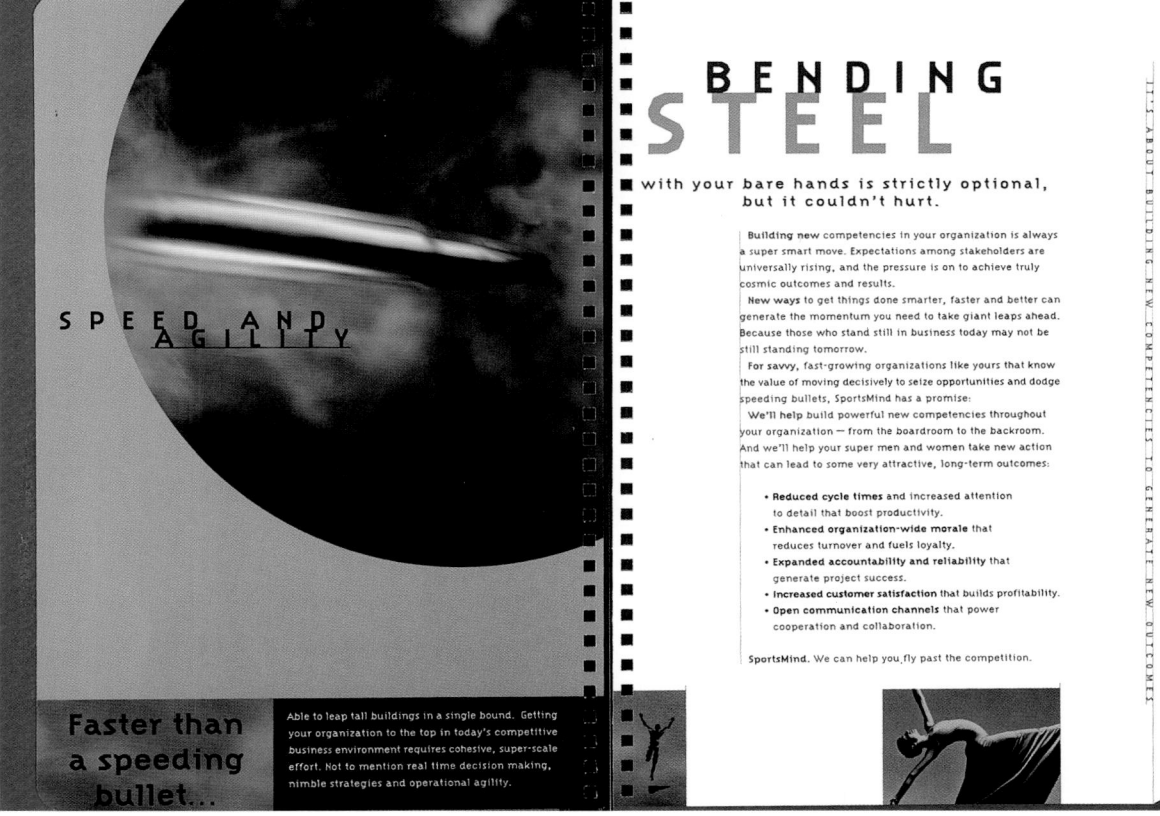

SPEED AND AGILITY

Faster than a speeding bullet...

Able to leap tall buildings in a single bound. Getting your organization to the top in today's competitive business environment requires cohesive, super-scale effort. Not to mention real time decision making, nimble strategies and operational agility.

BENDING STEEL

with your bare hands is strictly optional, but it couldn't hurt.

Building new competencies in your organization is always a super smart move. Expectations among stakeholders are universally rising, and the pressure is on to achieve truly cosmic outcomes and results.

New ways to get things done smarter, faster and better can generate the momentum you need to take giant leaps ahead. Because those who stand still in business today may not be still standing tomorrow.

For savvy, fast-growing organizations like yours that know the value of moving decisively to seize opportunities and dodge speeding bullets, SportsMind has a promise:

We'll help build powerful new competencies throughout your organization — from the boardroom to the backroom. And we'll help your super men and women take new action that can lead to some very attractive, long-term outcomes:

- **Reduced cycle times** and increased attention to detail that boost productivity.
- **Enhanced organization-wide morale** that reduces turnover and fuels loyalty.
- **Expanded accountability and reliability** that generate project success.
- **Increased customer satisfaction** that builds profitability.
- **Open communication channels** that power cooperation and collaboration.

SportsMind. We can help you fly past the competition.

IT'S ABOUT BUILDING NEW COMPETENCIES TO GENERATE NEW OUTCOMES

creative firm
KLUNDT HOSMER DESIGN
Spokane, Washington
designers
JUDY DAVIS-HEGGEM,
DAREN KLUNDT,
RICK HOSMER
client
SPORTS MIND

WALKING 1999

Butterfield & Robinson

The Great Walks of the World

creative firm
VIVA DOLAN COMMUNICATIONS AND DESIGN, INC.
Toronto, Canada
designer
FRANK VIVA
illustrator
DOUG ROSS
photographer
ED CHIN
copywriter
DOUG DOLAN
editor
DALI CASTRO
production artist
SONJA KLOSS
client
BUTTERFIELD & ROBINSON

creative firm
   DESIGN GUYS
   Minneapolis, Minnesota
creative director
   LYNETTE ERICKSON-SIKORA
art director
   STEVEN SIKORA
designers
   GARY PATCH , JAY THEIGE
photographer
   PATRICK FOX
client
   THYMES LIMITED

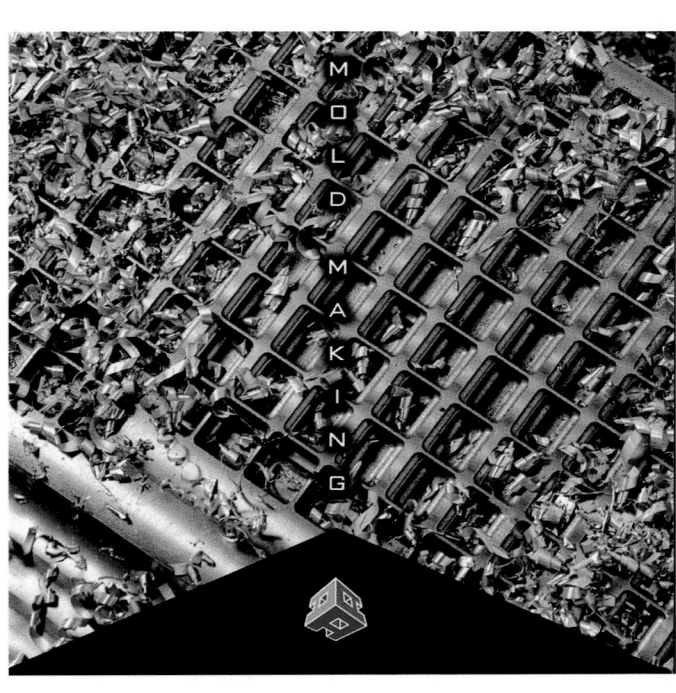

MOLD MAKING

creative firm
   KLUNDT HOSMER DESIGN
   Spokane, Washington
designers
   BRIAN GAGE,
   DARIN KLUNDT
client
   ALTEK

creative firm
  GREENFIELD/BELSER LTD
  Washington D.C.
art director, designer
  BURKEY BELSER
copywriter
  LISEANNE SCHWARTZ
client
  WILLIAMS & JENSEN

creative firm
  ROSE SREBRO DESIGN
  Waban, Massachusetts
creative director, designer
  ROSE SREBRO
illustrator
  CHRIS GALL
client
  BALDWIN BROTHERS

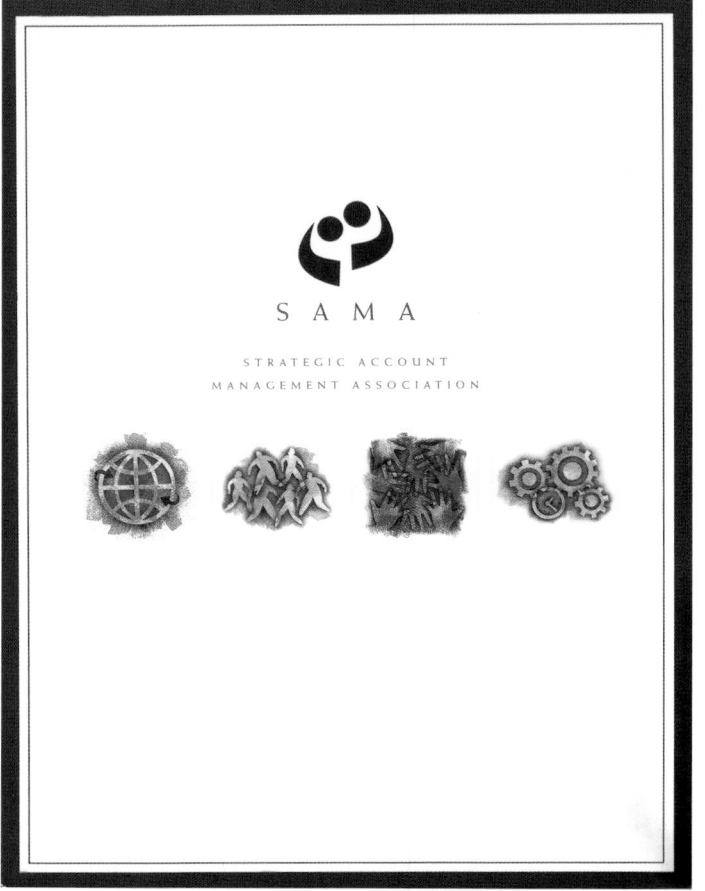

creative firm
  HARPER + CASE, LTD
  New York, New York
creative director, designer
  LISSA TOOLE
client
  SAMA

77

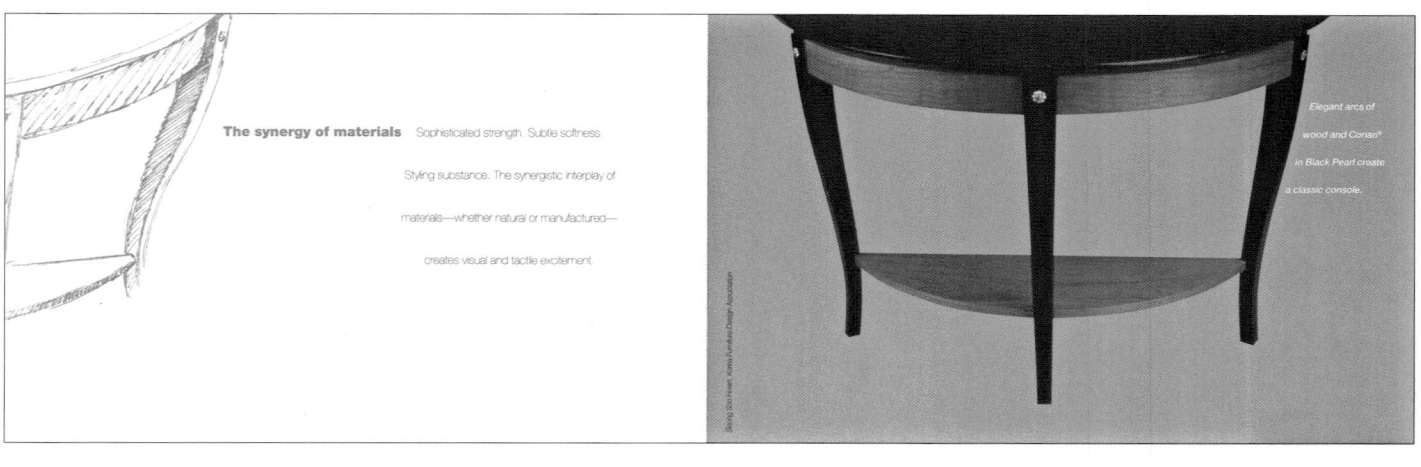

The synergy of materials Sophisticated strength. Subtle softness
Styling substance. The synergistic interplay of
materials—whether natural or manufactured—
creates visual and tactile excitement.

Elegant arcs of
wood and Corian®
in Black Pearl create
a classic console.

creative firm
  REESE, TOMASES, & ELLICK
  Wilmington, Delaware
creative director
  RICK CLEMONS
designer
  CINDY DUMONT
client
  DUPONT CORIAN

creative firm
  WAGES DESIGN
  Atlanta, Georgia
designer
  MATT TAYLOR
photographer
  RALPH DANIELS
copywriter
  PAT WAGES
client
  SWARTZ INSTITUTIONAL FINANCE

PRIVATE
PLACEMENT
FUNDING
for the NEXT MILLENNIUM

What will the next 100 years bring for your company? As the 21st
century unfolds, no doubt it will present unique situations and unexpected
opportunities. Imagine facing those years with the confidence your
capital requirements will be met thoroughly and swiftly, allowing your
management team to stay focused on its core competencies. With the right
partner, private equity financing can strengthen your position in the
competitive business environment. With our history of pioneering private
equity instruments, Swartz is uniquely positioned to be a vital resource,
leveraging your growth potential throughout the critical years to come.
Now small and mid-cap companies have access to big financial resources.

*"With the right partner, private equity financing can strengthen
your position in the competitive business environment."*

THE MAGIC OF SHARING

THE DISNEYLAND RESORT

creative firm
  DISNEYLAND CREATIVE SERVICES
  Anaheim, California
creative director
  SCOTT STARKEY
photographer
  WALTER URIE
copywriter
  TONY SERNA
client
  DISNEYLAND COMMUNITY AFFAIRS–BILL ROSS

Butterfield & Robinson

BIKING & WALKING SINCE 1966

trip guide 2000

creative firm
  VIVA DOLAN COMMUNICATIONS AND DESIGN
  Toronto, Canada
art director, designer
  FRANK VIVA
illustrators
  FRANK VIVA, TERRY SHOFFNER
photographers
  ROB HOWARD, ED CHIN, MacDUFF EVERTON, JOHN KANE,
  KINDRA CLINEFF, TOM KIRKENDALL, ROB CRANDELL, HOWARD GARETT,
  CHARLIE SCOTT, DAVID SWALES, DENIS PAGÉ, PHILIPPE BROWN,
  ROBERT MINNES, MICHAEL LISS
copywriter
  DOUD DOLAN
editor
  DALI CASTRO
production artist
  SONJA KLOSS
client
  BUTTERFIELD & ROBINSON

WHY JACK CHARLTON IS NOT A BIG BELIEVER IN FRICTION

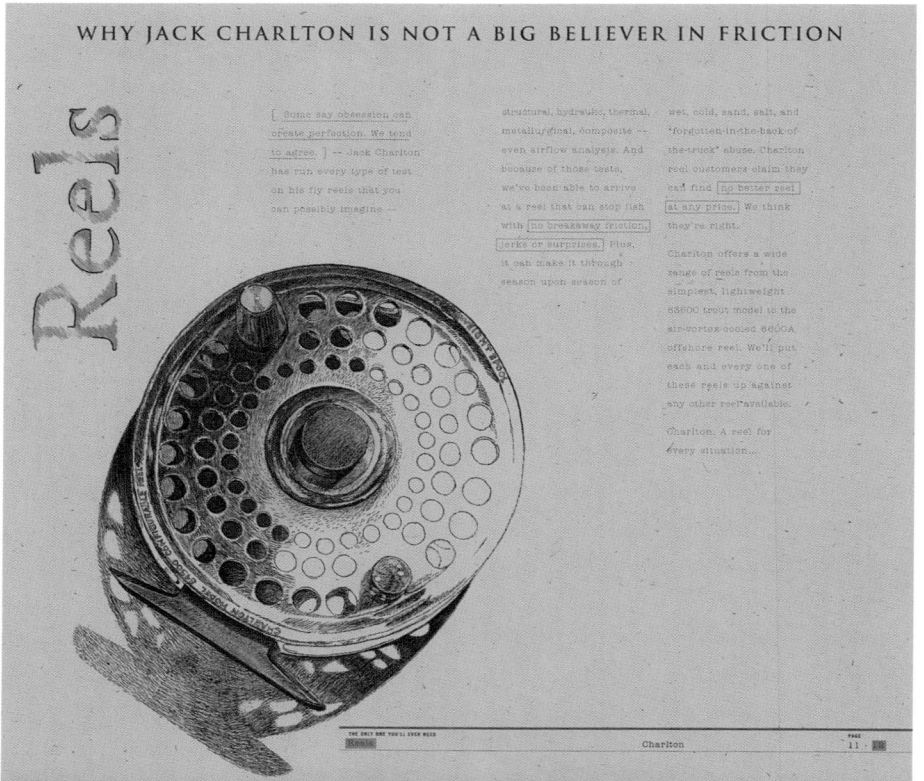

Reels

[Some say obsession can
create perfection. We tend
to agree.] -- Jack Charlton
has run every type of test
on his fly reels that you
can possibly imagine --

structural, hydraulic, thermal,
metallurgical, composite --
even airflow analysis. And
because of those tests,
we've been able to arrive
at a reel that can stop fish
with [no breakaway friction,
jerks or surprises.] Plus,
it can make it through
season upon season of

wet, cold, sand, salt, and
"forgotten-in-the-back of
the-truck" abuse. Charlton
reel customers claim they
can find [no better reel
at any price.] We think
they're right.

Charlton offers a wide
range of reels from the
simplest, lightweight
83600 trout model to the
air-vortex-cooled 6600A
offshore reel. We'll put
each and every one of
these reels up against
any other reel available.

Charlton. A reel for
every situation....

creative firm
  HORNALL ANDERSON DESIGN WORKS
  Seattle, Washington
art director
  JACK ANDERSON
designers
  JACK ANDERSON, BELINDA BOWLING,
  ANDREW SMITH, ED LEE
client
  STREAMWORKS

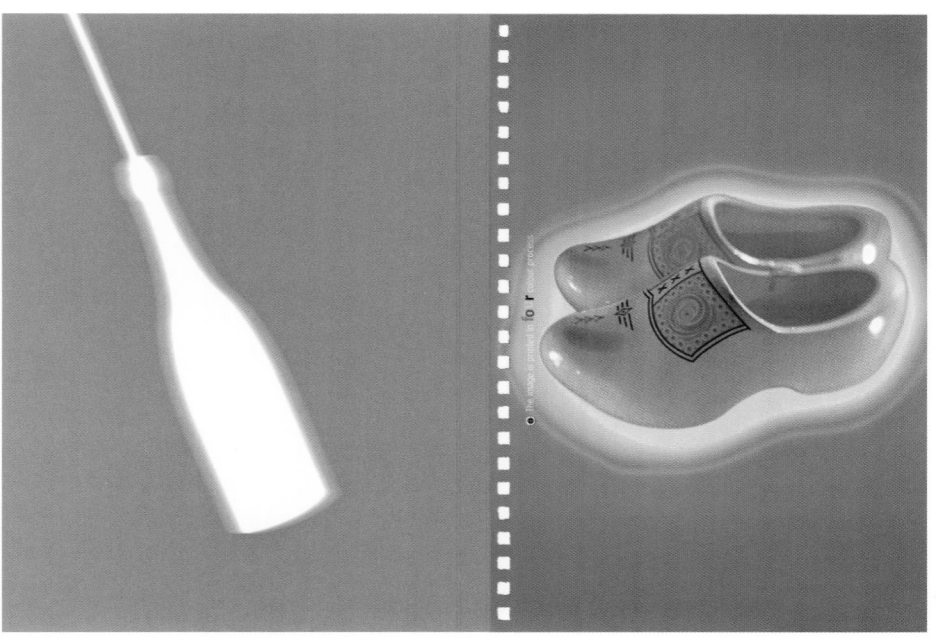

creative firm
 TRICKETT & WEBB LTD
 London, England
designers
 LYNN TRICKETT,
 BRIAN WEBB,
 MARCUS TAYLOR
photographer
 ANDREW HALL
copywriter
 NEIL MATTINGLEY
client
 ISTD FINE PAPER LTD

creative firm
 PLATINUM DESIGN, INC.
 New York, New York
art director
 MIKE JOYCE
designer
 MIKE JOYCE
copywriter
 PAMELA COOK
client
 ENTERCOM

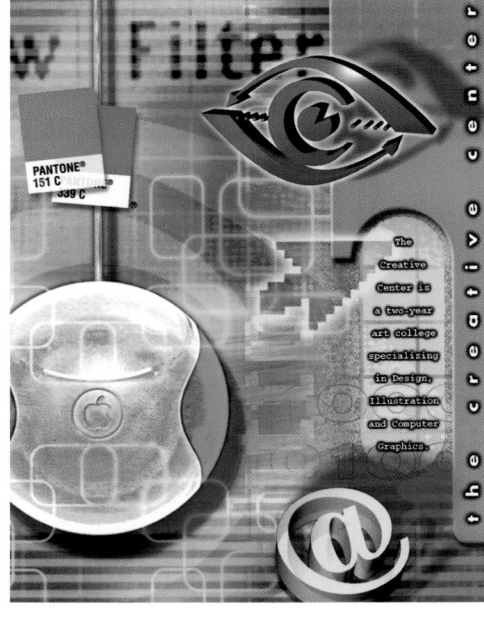

creative firm
  DOTZLER CREATIVE ARTS
  Omaha, Nebraska
client
  THE CREATIVE CENTER

creative firm
  KLUNDT HOSMER DESIGN
  Spokane, Washington
designers
  JUDY HEGGEM-DAVIS,
  DARIN KLUNDT
client
  ICM MANAGEMENT, INC.

creative firm
  HORNALL ANDERSON
  DESIGN WORKS
  Seattle, Washington
art director
  JACK ANDERSON
designers
  JACK ANDERSON, KATHY SAITO,
  JULIE LOCK, ED LEE,
  HEIDI FAVOUR, VIRGINIA LE
client
  GROUND ZERO

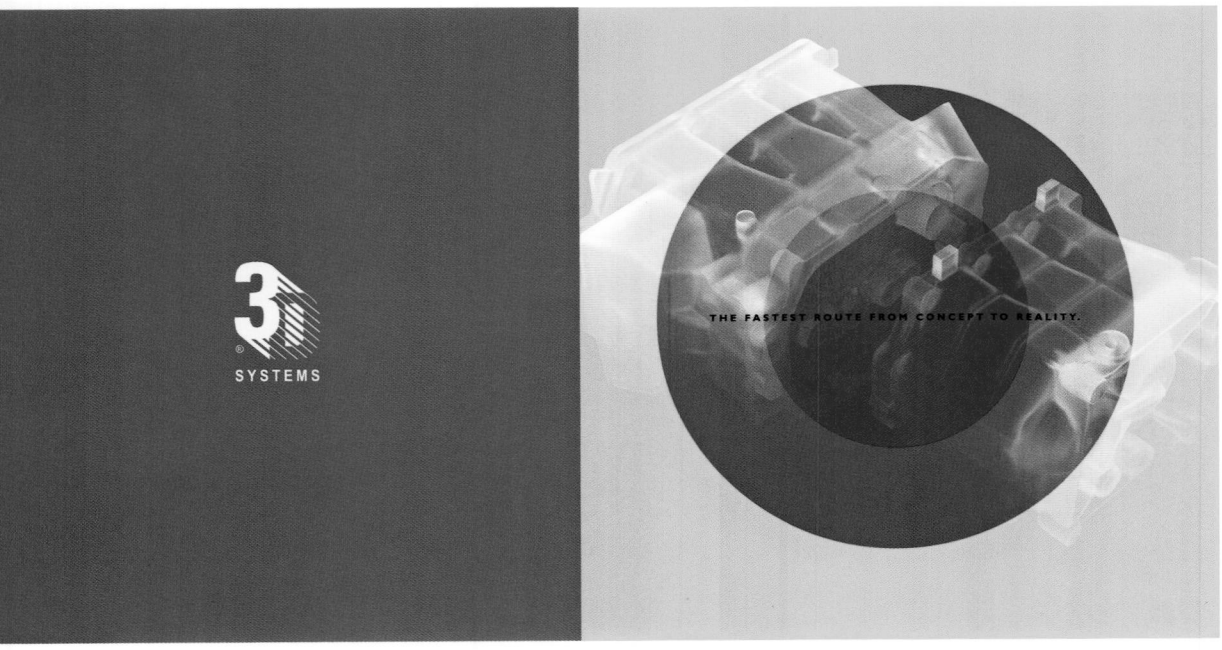

creative firm
   DOUGLAS JOSEPH PARTNERS
   Los Angeles, California
art director
   DOUG JOSEPH
designer
   JULIE SLOTO-MELLEN
copywriter
   MARK SCAPICCHIO
client
   3D SYSTEMS CORPORATION

4 | **SMALL SLENDER CABINET** (1 bottom shelf) *Also available as...*
TALL SLENDER CABINET (2 bottom shelves)

SLENDER FLOOR CABINET | 5

creative firm
   AIRE DESIGN COMPANY
   Tucson, Arizona
creative director
   CATHARINE M. KIM
art director
   SHARI RYKOWSKI
client
   KNF DESIGNS

creative firm
   AIRE DESIGN COMPANY
   Tucson, Arizona
creative director
   CATHARINE M. KIM
art director
   SHARI RYKOWSKI
client
   ARIZONA-SONORA DESERT MUSEUM

creative firm
  TANGRAM STRATEGIC DESIGN
    Novara, Italy
creative director, art director, designer
  ENRICO SEMPI
client
  RIBES

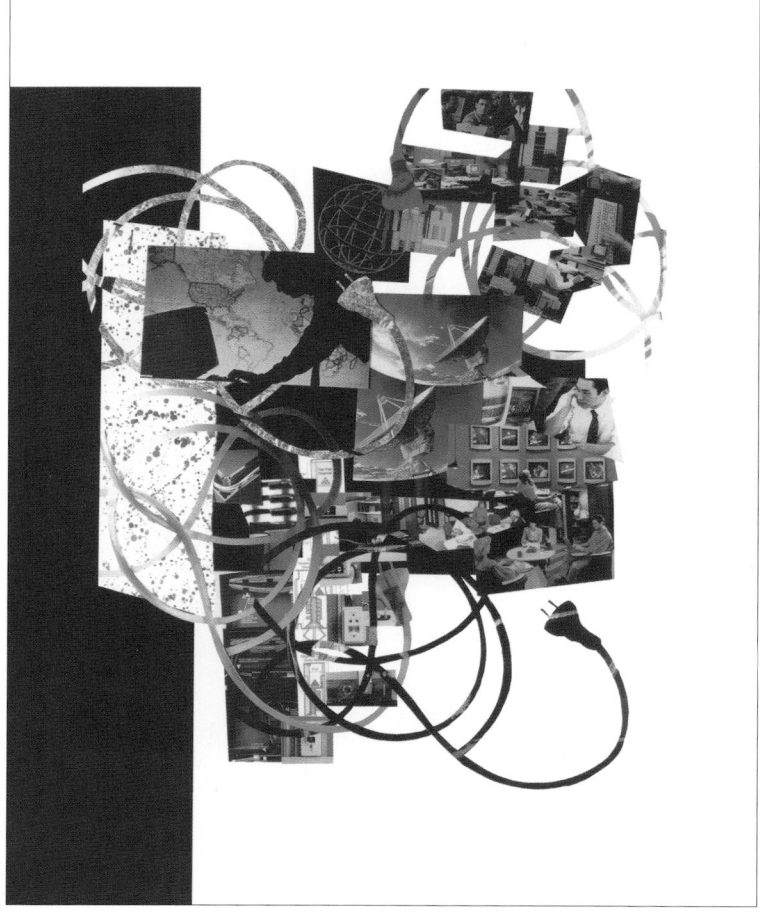

creative firm
  BBK STUDIOS INC.
  Grand Rapids, Michigan
designer
  MICHAEL BARILE
illustrators
  MICHAEL BARILE,
  ALLEN McKINNEY
copywriter
  BOB TOBIN
client
  STEELCASE, INC.

Sutherland
Asbill &
Brennan LLP
ATTORNEYS AT LAW

National focus
international perspective

creative firm
  GREENFIELD/BELSER LTD
  Washington, D.C.
art director, designer
  BURKEY BELSER
client
  SUTHERLAND ASBILL & BRENNAN

creative firm
  VIVA DOLAN COMMUNICATIONS AND DESIGN
  Toronto, Canada
art director, designer
  FRANK VIVA
illustrator
  MALCOLM HILL
photographers
  RON BAXTER SMITH, MacDUFF EVERTON,
  HILL PEPPARD, STEVEN ROTHFELD
copywriter
  DOUG DOLAN
client
  BUTTERFIELD & ROBINSON

BIKING 1998

Butterfield & Robinson

The World's Great Biking Journeys

creative firm
  WPA PINFOLD
  Leeds, England
design manager
  ANDY PROBERT
designer
  PHIL MOMSON
client
  WINPAC GROUP

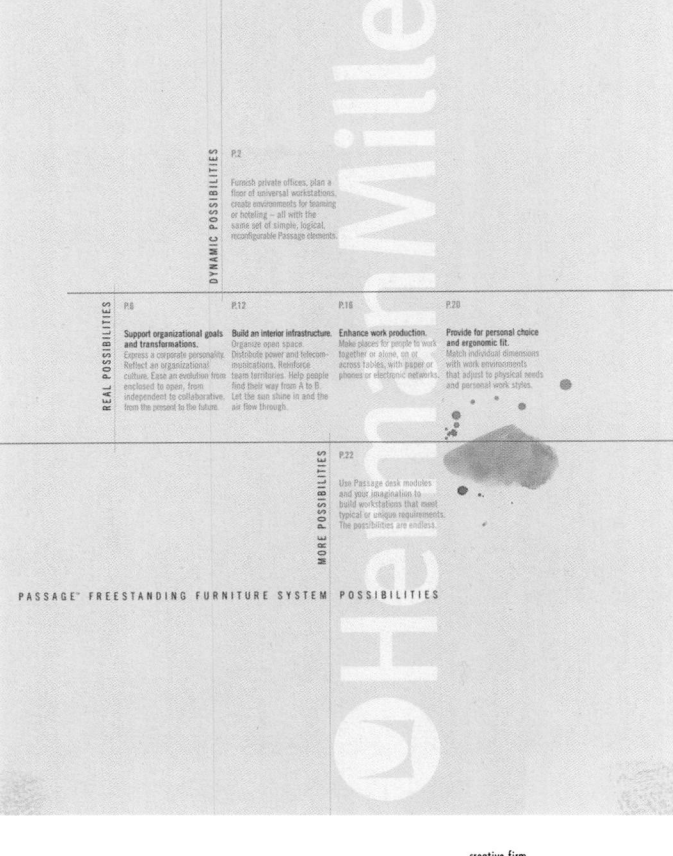

creative firm
  BBK STUDIO INC.
  Grand Rapids, Michigan
creative director
  KEVIN BUDELMANN
designer
  ALLISON POPP
illustrators, photographers
  NICK MERRICK, BOB NEUMANN, SUSAN CARR
copywriter
  DEB WIERENGA
client
  HERMAN MILLER INC.

Imagine...No Limits

creative firm
  THE WYANT SIMBOLI GROUP
  Norwalk, Connecticut
creative director
  JULIE WYANT
production manager
  KAREN OLENSHI
designers
  PAUL M. NEEL, SHERI CIFALDI, LANCE HERTZBACH
client
  GE CAPITAL

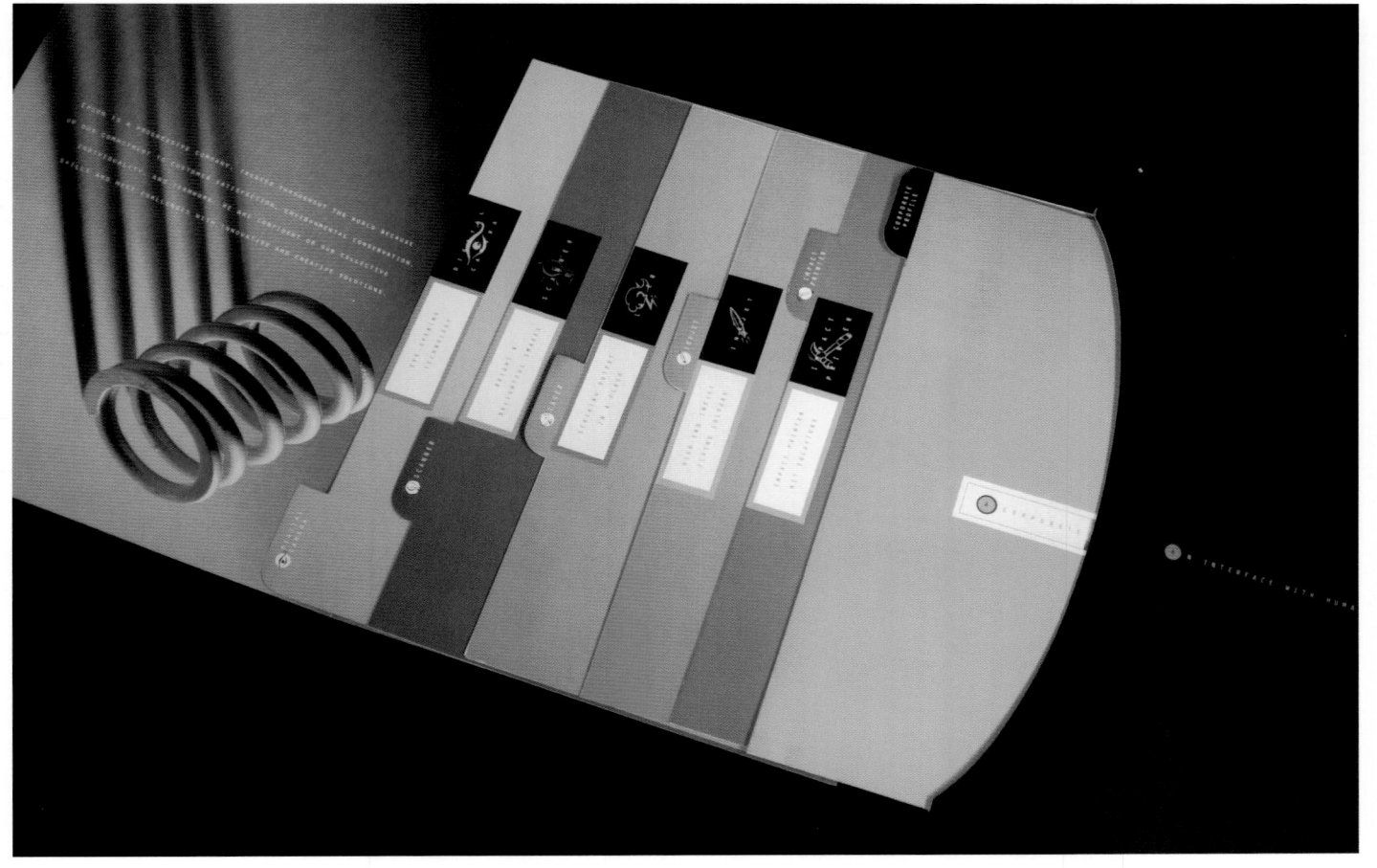

creative firm
  UKULELE DESIGN CONSULTANTS PTE LTD
   Singapore
design director
  KIM CHUN-WEI
designer
  LYNN LIM
copywriter
  EVELYN TENG
client
  EPSON SINGAPORE PTE LTD

creative firm
  HORNALL ANDERSON DESIGN WORKS
  Seattle, Washington
art directors
  JACK ANDERSON, LISA CERVENY
designers
  LISA CERVENY, DAVID BATES, ALAN FLORSHEIM
client
  LEATHERMAN TOOK GROUP

creative firm
  KINETIK COMMUNICATION GRAPHICS, INC.
  Washington, D.C.
designers
  BETH CLAWSON,
  JEFFREY FABIAN,
  SCOTT RIER,
  KAMOMI SOLIDUM
client
  SMITHSONIAN INSTITUTION

creative firm
  HORNALL ANDERSON DESIGN WORKS
  Seattle, Washington
art directors
  JOHN HORNALL, KATHA DALTON
designers
  JOHN HORNALL, KATHA DALTON,
  MARY HERMES, STEPHANIE LORIG,
  ALAN COPELAND, MICHAEL BRUGMAN
client
  FOSTER PEPPER SHEFELMAN

creative firm
 WATERSDESIGN.COM
 New York, New York
creative director
 JOHN WATERS
content
 JACQUELINE STOLTE
designer
 LAURA SAUTER
client
 WALTER P. SAUER

creative firm
 5D STUDIO
 Malibu, California
art director
 JANE KOBAYASHI
designer
 ANNE COATES
client
 WALKER ZANGER

creative firm
KLUNDT HOSMER DESIGN
Spokane, Washington
designer
DARIN KLUNDT
client
COPELAND DESIGN & CONSTRUCTION

creative firm
SQUARE ONE DESIGN
Grand Rapids, Michigan
art director
MIKE GORMAN
designer
ELENA TISLEVICS
client
JOHN WIDDICOMB

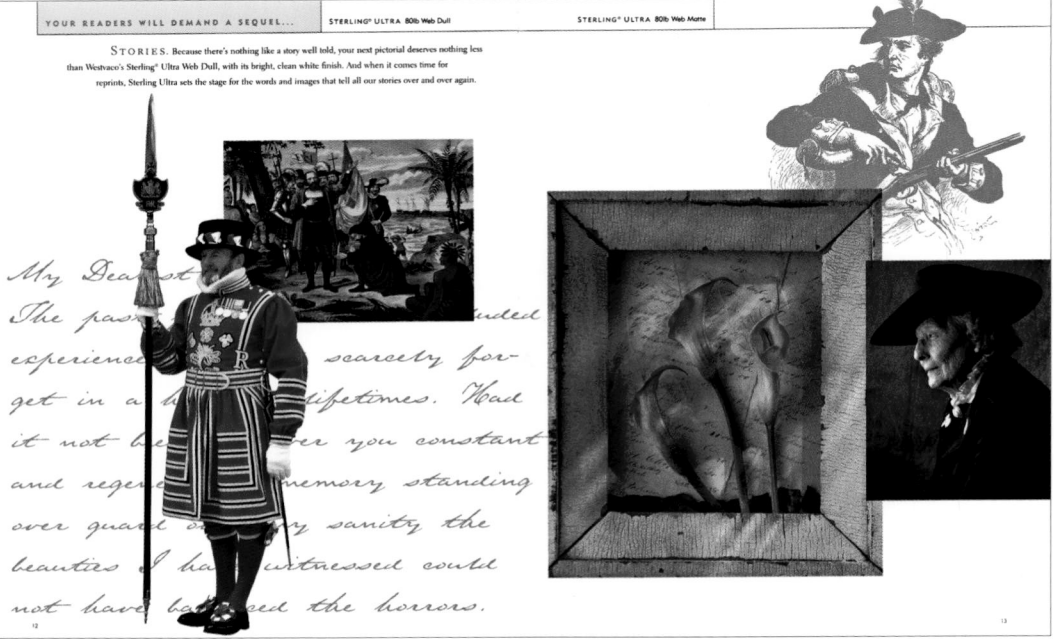

creative firm
WATERSDESIGN.COM
New York, New York
creative director
JOHN WATERS
producer
SUSAN DeMIRJIAN
content director
ANDY AUSTIN
designers
DIRK ROWNTREE, SUSAN HILDEBRAND
client
WESTVACO

creative firm
  30SIXTY DESIGN, INC.
  Los Angeles, California
creative director
  HENRY VIZCARRA
art director, illustrator
  PÄR LARSSON
designers
  RICKARD OLSSON, PÄR LARSSON,
  PEGGY MARTIN, SUPPASAK VIBOONLARP
client
  VIACOM CONSUMER PRODUCTS

creative firm
  O&J DESIGN INC.
  New York, New York
art director
  ANDRZEJ J. OLEJNICZAK
designer
  LESLIE NAYMAN
client
  NEW YORK UNIVERSITY SCHOOL OF CONTINUING AND PROFESSIONAL STUDIES

creative firm
  ROLF HARDER & ASSOC. INC.
  Beaconsfield, Canada
designer
  ROLF HARDER
client
  ENGLISH MONTREAL SCHOOL BOARD

creative firm
OH&CO
IN COLLABORATION WITH
IDEO
New York, New York
creative director
BRENT OPPENHEIMER
strategy director
ROBIN HAUETER
designer
ROBERT HOMACK
client
AMTRAK

creative firm
MORTENSEN DESIGN
Mountain View, California
art director
GORDON MORTENSEN
designers
GORDON MORTENSEN, PJ NIDECKER
client
HANDSPRING, INC

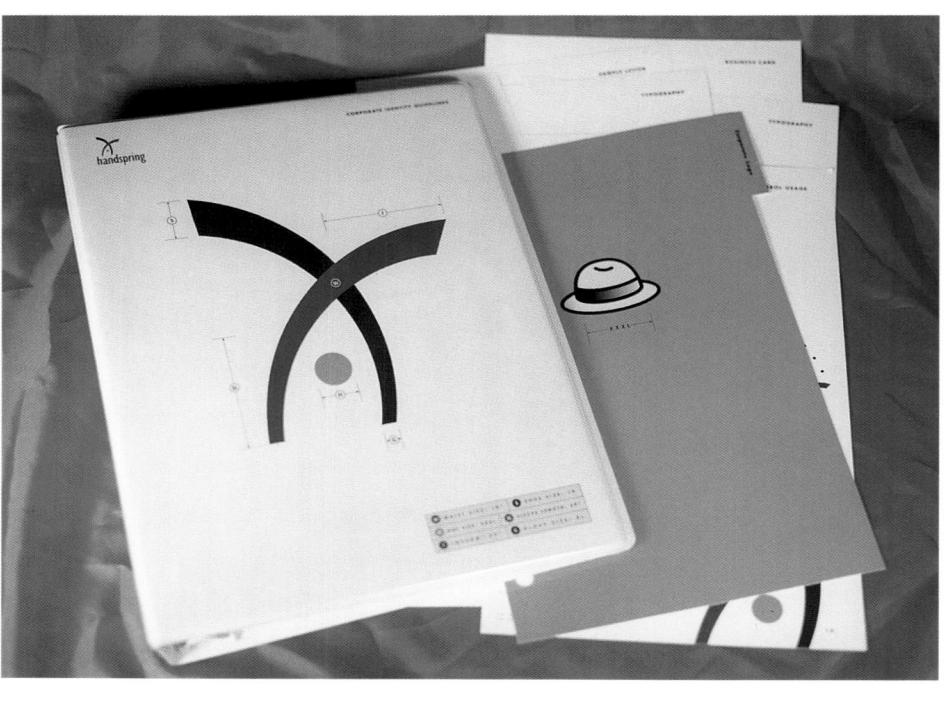

creative firm
O&J DESIGN INC.
New York, New York
art director
ANDRZEJ J. OLEJNICZAK
designers
**LIA CAMARA-MARISCAL,
CHRISTINA MUELLER,
SASHA SWETSCHINSKI**
client
AVON PRODUCTS INC.

creative firm
LARSEN DESIGN
+ INTERACTIVE
Minneapolis, Minnesota
creative director, designer
TODD MANNES
client
MINNESOTA PARKS &
TRAILS COUNCIL

creative firm
  McELVENEY + PALOZZI DESIGN GROUP, INC.
  Rochester, New York
creative director
  WILLIAM McELVENEY
art director
  ELLEN JOHNSON
client
  THE LODGE AT WOODCLIFF

creative firm
  MICHAEL COURTNEY DESIGN
  Seattle, Washington
art director, designer
  MICHAEL COURTNEY
illustrator
  DENISE WEIR
client
  EVERGREEN PRINTING

creative firm
  McELVENEY + PALOZZI
  DESIGN GROUP, INC.
  Rochester, New York
creative director
  WILLIAM McELVENEY
art director
  ELLEN JOHNSON
client
  THE LODGE AT WOODCLIFF

G-FORCE
COLLABORATIONS

creative firm
  McELVENEY + PALOZZI
  DESIGN GROUP, INC.
  Rochester, New York
creative director
  WILLIAM McELVENEY
art director
  MATT NOWICKI
designer
  DILLON CONSTABLE
client
  G-FORCE COLLABORATIONS

creative firm
  BUTLER KEMP DESIGN
  North Adelaide, Australia
art director
  DEREK BUTLER
designer
  HELLEN KIPRIZLOGLOV
client
  DAISHSAT

DAISHSAT
GEODETIC SURVEYORS

GNIBUS
PUBLIC RELATIONS

creative firm
  THE WECKER GROUP
  Monterey, California
designer
  MATT GNIBUS
client
  GNIBUS PUBLIC RELATIONS

the
Children's
Museum

creative firm
BIG CAT MARKETING COMM.
Colorado Springs, Colorado
designer
NORMANDINA SNOW
client
THE CHILDREN'S MUSEUM

BLUEPRINT

creative firm
SIBLEY PETEET DESIGN
Dallas, Texas
designer
BRENT McMAHAN
client
SABRE GROUP

™

AQUAFUTURE

creative firm
THE WECKER GROUP
Monterey, California
designers
ROBERT WECKER, MATT GNIBUS
client
AQUA FUTURE, INC.

AUREA

creative firm
KEVIN AKERS
—DESIGNER
San Rafael, California
designer
KEVIN AKERS
client
AUREA HEADSET
MANUFACTURER

ALCOA

creative firm
ARNOLD SAKS ASSOCIATES
New York, New York
designer
ARNOLD SAKS
client
ALCOA

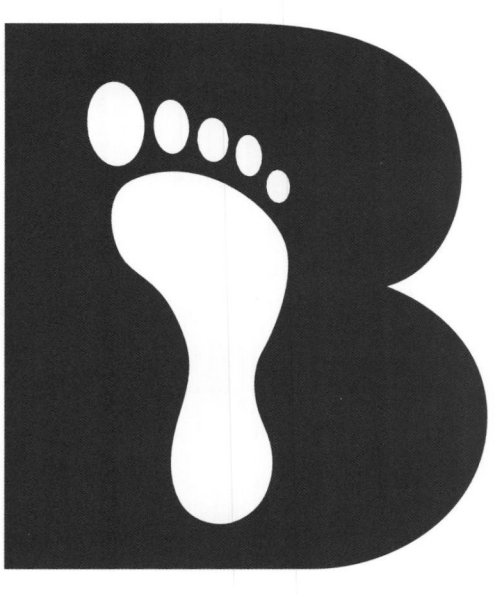

creative firm
McMILLIAN DESIGN
Woodside, New York
art director
WILLIAM McMILLIAN
client
DR. RICHARD BELLI

creative firm
DEVER DESIGNS
Laurel, Maryland
art director
JEFFREY L. DEVER
designers
JEFFREY L. DEVER, EMILY KENDALL
client
CARNEGIE ENDOWMENT FOR INTERNATIONAL PEACE

creative firm
HORNALL ANDERSON DESIGN WORKS
Seattle, Washington
art director
JACK ANDERSON
designers
MARGARET LONG, JASON HICKNER
client
GETTUIT

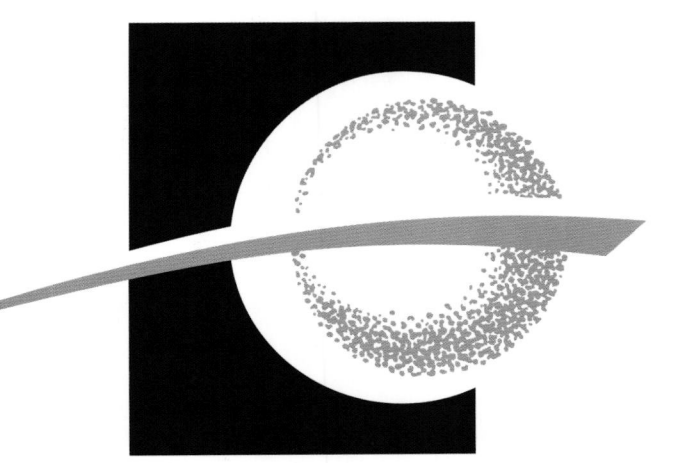

gettuit.com™

creative firm
  MIRIELLO GRAFICO, INC.
  San Diego, California
designers
  CHRIS KEENEY, DENNIS GARCIA
client
  NEWPORT COMMUNICATIONS

creative firm
  ROBERT MEYERS DESIGN
  Fairlawn, Ohio
designer
  ROBERT MEYERS
client
  PITTSBURGH ST. PATRICK'S DAY

creative firm
  KEVIN AKERS—DESIGNER
  San Rafael, California
designer
  KEVIN AKERS
client
  SUSAN SARGENT
  (textile designer)

creative firm
  HORNALL ANDERSON DESIGN WORKS
  Seattle, Washington
art director
  JACK ANDERSON
designers
  JACK ANDERSON, KATHY SAITO,
  GRETCHEN COOK, JAMES TEE,
  JULIE LOCK, HENRY YIU
client
  GETTUIT (WORKENGINE)

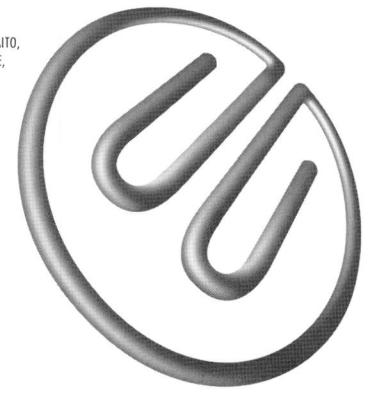

workengine℠

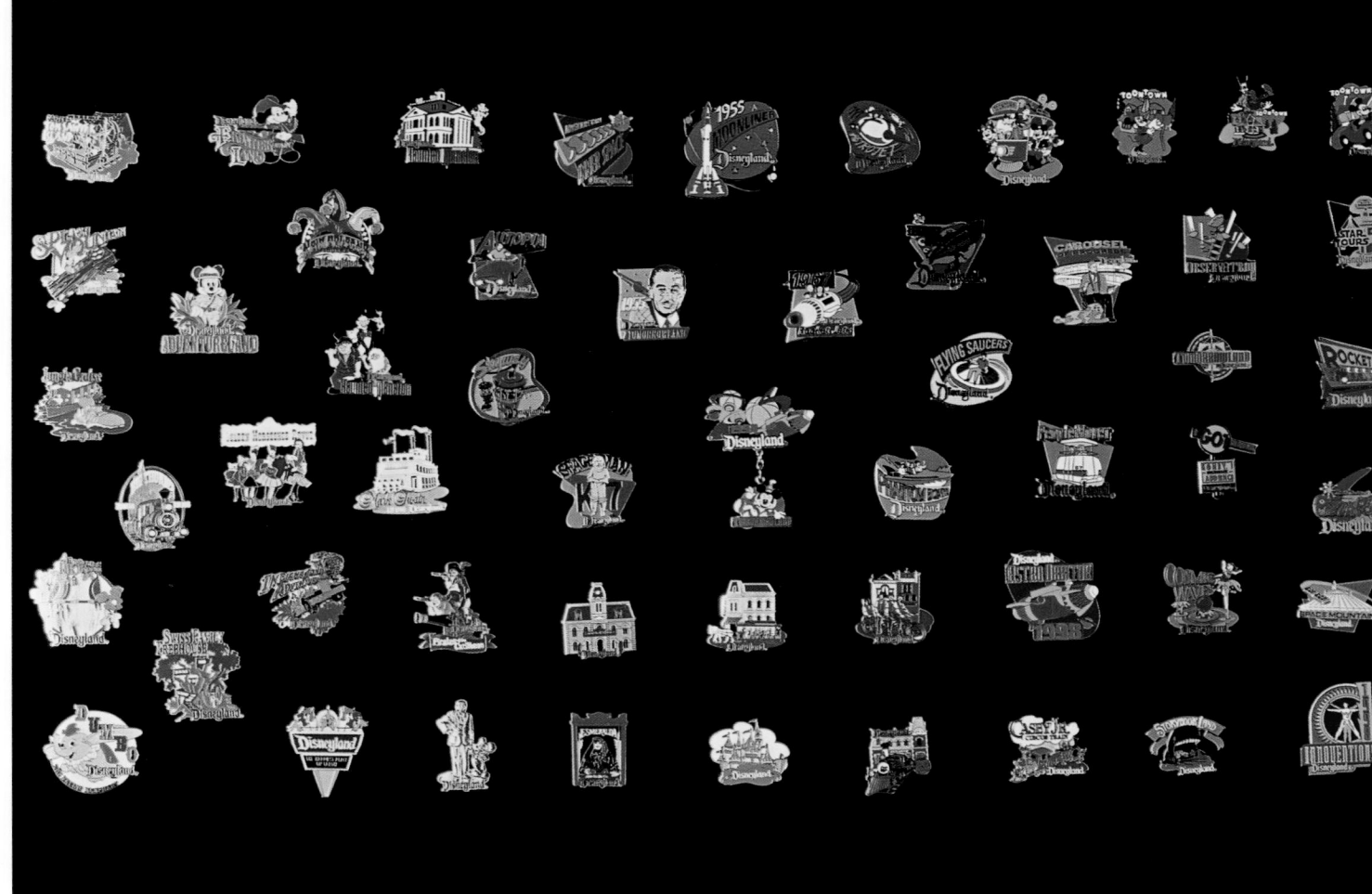

creative firm
  DISNEYLAND CREATIVE SERVICES
    Anaheim, California
creative director
  SCOTT STARKEY
designers
  MIKE PUCHALSKI, DATHAN SHORE,
  DAVID RILEY & ASSOCATES, BARTON/KOMAI/DUNNAHOE
client
  DISNEYLAND MERCHANDISE

creative firm
THE RIORDON DESIGN GROUP
Oakville, Canada
art director
RIC RIORDON
designer, illustrator
DAN WHEATON
client
CHUCK GAMMAGE ANIMATION

creative firm
ROBERT MEYERS DESIGN
Fairlawn, Ohio
designer
ROBERT MEYERS
client
SHADYSIDE CHAMBER OF COMMERCE

creative firm
THE WECKER GROUP
Monterey, California
art director
ROBERT WECKER
designer
MATT GNIBUS
client
DAVID LOOP EUROPEAN

creative firm
SAYLES GRAPHIC DESIGN
Des Moines, Iowa
art director, illustrator
JOHN SAYLES
client
MEREDITH CORPORATION

creative firm
  BECKER DESIGN
  Milwaukee, Wisconsin
designer
  NEIL BECKER
client
  MILWAUKEE BALLET NUTCRACKER

creative firm
  SHOOK DESIGN GROUP, INC.
  Charlotte, North Carolina
graphic designer
  JEFF CAMILLO
client
  BACK TO THE FIFTIES SODA SHOPPE

creative firm
  WAGES DESIGN
  Atlanta, Georgia
designer
  MATT TAYLOR
client
  UTILITIES PROTECTION CENTER

creative firm
  SHIELDS DESIGN
  Fresno, California
designer
  CHARLES SHIELDS
client
  FRESNO METROPOLITAN MUSEUM

creative firm
  SQUIRES & COMPANY
  Dallas, Texas
designer
  CHRISTIE GROTHEIM
client
  DEEP ELLUM DASH '98

creative firm
  SHIELDS DESIGN
  Fresno, California
designer
  CHARLES SHIELDS
photographer
  CAMERAD,INC.
client
  CHARLES SHIELDS

creative firm
  BRYNELL DESIGN
  New York, New York
designer
  MARTIN BRYNELL
client
  WHERE

creative firm
  SHIELDS DESIGN
  Fresno, California
designer
  CHARLES SHIELDS
photographer
  PHIL RUDY
client
  PHIL RUDY PHOTOGRAPHY

One Hilton
One Place to Stay

creative firm
 KEVIN AKERS—DESIGNER
 San Rafael, California
designer
 KEVIN AKERS
client
 HILTON HOTELS

creative firm
 BOBCO DESIGN, INC.
 Irvine, California
designer
 ROBERT S. NENNINGER
client
 THE GOLDEN GATE BREAD CO.
 (sourdough bread exporter)

About Face

Salon & Boutique

creative firm
 BECKER DESIGN
 Milwaukee, Wisconsin
designer
 NEIL BECKER
client
 ABOUT FACE

DakotaCom.net

creative firm
AIRE DESIGN COMPANY
Tucson, Arizona
creative director
CATHARINE M. KIM
art director
SHARI RYKOWSKI
client
DAKOTACOM.NET

NAPA VALLEY CELEBRATES

CLIMB AGAINST THE ODDS

AN ASSAULT ON BREAST CANCER

creative firm
DESIGN SOLUTIONS
Napa, California
art director, designer
DEBORAH MITCHELL
client
THE BREAST CANCER FUND

creative firm
MacVICAR DESIGN + COMMUNICATIONS
Arlington, Virginia
senior designer
WILLIAM A. GORDON
client
IDS—INTERACTIVE DIGITAL SYSTEMS

creative firm
BRYNELL DESIGN
New York, New York
designer
MARTIN BRYNELL
client
WHERE

BAR
CENTRO
Madrid
©European Bar

ids

creative firm
  SAYLES GRAPHIC DESIGN
  Des Moines, Iowa
art director, illustrator
  JOHN SAYLES
client
  VINO VICCINO'S RISTORANTE

r i s t o r a n t e

innoVisions™

creative firm
  HORNALL ANDERSON
  DESIGN WORKS
  Seattle, Washington
art director
  JACK ANDERSON
designers
  JACK ANDERSON, KATHY SAITO, ALAN COPELAND
client
  WELLS FARGO (INNOVISIONS)

creative firm
  THE WECKER GROUP
  Monterey, California
designers
  ROBERT WECKER, MATT GNIBUS
client
  DOUBLETREE MONTEREY

creative firm
  THE WECKER GROUP
  Monterey, California
designer
  ROBERT WECKER
client
  THE HEARTH SHOP

creative firm
  BRUNAZZI & ASSOCIATI/
  IMAGE + COMMUNICATION
  Turin, Italy
art director
  GIOVANNI BRUNAZZI
designer
  ADA BRUNAZZI
client
  AUGUSTA BAGIENNORUM

creative firm
  INTERBRAND
  GERSTMAN + MEYERS
  New York, New York
creative director
  JEFF ZACK
client
  KELLOGG'S

creative firm
GARDNER DESIGN
Wichita, Kansas
designers
BILL GARDNER, BRIAN MILLER
client
TALLGRASS BEEF

creative firm
SAYLES GRAPHIC DESIGN
Des Moines, Iowa
art director, illustrator
JOHN SAYLES
client
THE POWER TEAM

freetv
FReeDoMIZe

creative firm
THE RIORDON DESIGN GROUP INC.
Oakville, Canada
art director
RIC RIORDON
designer
DAN WHEATON
client
FREE T.V.

BLACK CAT

creative firm
McMILLIAN DESIGN
Woodside, New York
art director
WILLIAM McMILLIAN
client
McMILLIAN DESIGN

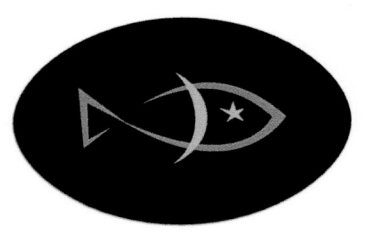

S U S H I   N I G H T S

creative firm
SQUIRES & COMPANY
Dallas, Texas
designer
CHRISTIE GROTHEIM
client
SUSHI NIGHTS

creative firm
BOBCO DESIGN, INC.
Irvine, California
designer
ROBERT S. NENNINGER
client
THE CRAZY HORSE STEAKHOUSE RESTAURANT

creative firm
KEVIN AKERS—DESIGNER
San Rafael, California
designer
KEVIN AKERS
client
SAVE HEADWATERS FOREST

creative firm
GARDNER DESIGN
Wichita, Kansas
designers
BILL GARDNER, BRIAN MILLER
client
COWLEY COUNTY COMMUNITY COLLEGE

HEARTLAND ARTS SERIES

LOGOS

The JOURNEY is ABOUT to BEGIN

creative firm
  PRIMO ANGELI INC.
  San Francisco, California
creative director
  CARLO PAGODA
project director
  RICH SCHEVE
senior designer
  TERRENCE TONG
illustrator
  MARK JONES
client
  SILICON GAMING (ODYSSEY)

creative firm
  McGAUGHY DESIGN
  Falls Church, Virginia
designer
  MALCOLM McGAUGHY
client
  McGAUGHY DESIGN

creative firm
  DOTZLER CREATIVE ARTS
  Omaha, Nebraska
client
  HOPE CENTER

creative firm
  WALLACE CHURCH ASS. INC.
  New York, New York
designers
  STAN CHURCH, CRAIG SWANSEN
client
  LYCOS

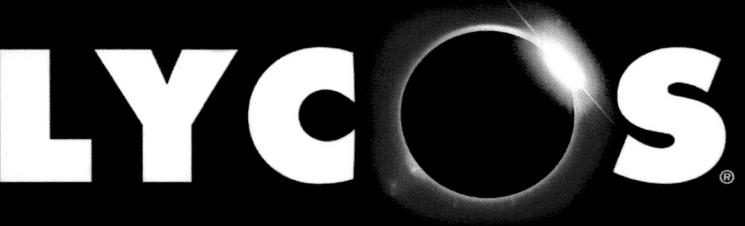

creative firm
SABINGRAFIK, INC.
Carlsbad, California
art director
MARILEE BANKERT
designer, illustrator
TRACY SABIN
client
OLIVER McMILLIN

creative firm
SHOOK DESIGN GROUP, INC.
Charlotte, North Carolina
graphic designer
JEFF CAMILLO
client
THE SUNSET CLUB

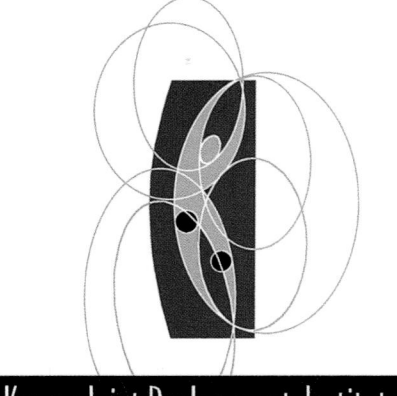

creative firm
GARDNER DESIGN
Wichita, Kansas
designer
BILL GARDNER
client
KANSAS JOINT REPLACEMENT INSTITUTE

creative firm
 THE WECKER GROUP
 Monterey, California
designer
 ROBERT WECKER
client
 UNIVERSAL INTERNET

creative firm
 GARDNER DESIGN
 Wichita, Kansas
designers
 BILL GARDNER, KAREN HOGAN
client
 GLORY

GLORY

creative firm
 ROSS ADVERTISING
 Peoria, Illinois
creative directors
 BRIAN BRUSH, SKIP DAMPIER
designer
 BRIAN BRUSH
client
 WAHL

creative firm
 AIRE DESIGN COMPANY
 Tucson, Arizona
creative director
 CATHARINE M. KIM
art director
 SHARI RYKOWSKI
client
 COMMUNITY FOUNDATION FOR SOUTHERN ARIZONA

COMMUNITY
FOUNDATION
for SOUTHERN ARIZONA

creative firm
    TELMET DESIGN ASSOCIATES
    Toronto, Canada
designer
    TIIT TELMET
client
    IONS WORLD CORP.

creative firm
    HORNALL ANDERSON DESIGN WORKS
    Seattle, Washington
art director
    JACK ANDERSON
designers
    JACK ANDERSON, MIKE CALKINS
illustrator
    MIKE CALKINS
client
    HAMMERQUIST & HALVERSON

creative firm
    MADDOCKS & CO.
    Carlsbad, California
art director
    CLAIRE SEBENIUS
illustrator
    TRACY SABIN
client
    EL CHOLO

creative firm
MICHAEL NIBLETT DESIGN
Fort Worth, Texas
designer
MICHAEL NIBLETT
client
J.M. MOUDY EXHIBITION HALL

creative firm
MICHAEL COURTNEY DESIGN
Seattle, Washington
art director
MICHAEL COURTNEY
designers
MICHAEL COURTNEY, DAN HOANG, HEIDI FAVOUR, BRIAN O'NEILL
client
FLEISCHMANN OFFICE INTERIORS

creative firm
KEVIN AKERS—DESIGNER
San Rafael, California
designer
KEVIN AKERS
client
SAN FRANCISCO SYMPHONY
(Grateful Dead Members SFS Concert t-shirt logo)

PALMER | GOLF

BUILT TO HIT IT

creative firm
MIRIELLO GRAFICO, INC.
San Diego, California
designers
CHRIS KEENEY, COURTNEY MEYER
client
ARNOLD PALMER GOLF

creative firm
KEVIN AKERS—DESIGNER
San Rafael, California
designer
KEVIN AKERS
client
SAN FRANCISCO SYMPHONY
(Grateful Dead Members SFS Concert t-shirt logo)

creative firm
SHOOK DESIGN
GROUP, INC.
Charlotte, North Carolina
graphic designer
JEFF CAMILLO
client
THE TOWN OF CORNELIUS, NC

creative firm
DEVER DESIGNS
Laurel, Maryland
art director, designer
JEFFREY L. DEVER
client
DEVER DESIGNS

113

creative firm
  ROSS ADVERTISING
  Peoria, Illinois
senior art director
  NICK JIBBEN
client
  UPPER LIMITS TEAM CHALLENGE

creative firm
  THE WECKER GROUP
  Monterey, California
designer
  ROBERT WECKER
client
  SAN JUAN BAUTISTA CHAMBER OF COMMERCE

creative firm
  McELVENEY + PALOZZI
  DESIGN GROUP, INC.
  Rochester, New York
creative director
  STEVE PALOZZI
client
  SPRING STREET SOCIETY

creative firm
  TIM SMITH DESIGN
  Loveland, Ohio
designers
  TIM SMITH, LESLIE BURNS
client
  BURNS AUTO PARTS

creative firm
SIBLEY PETEET DESIGN
Dallas, Texas
designer
BRENT McMAHAN
client
JOHN HUTTON

DESIGN GROUP INC.

creative firm
McELVENEY + PALOZZI
DESIGN GROUP, INC.
Rochester, New York
creative directors
WILLIAM McELVENEY, STEVE PALOZZI
senior art director
JON WESTFALL
client
McELVENEY + PALOZZI DESIGN GROUP, INC.

LeRoy Village Green

RESIDENTIAL HEALTHCARE FACILITY

creative firm
McELVENEY + PALOZZI DESIGN GROUP, INC.
Rochester, New York
creative director
WILLIAM McELVENEY
art director
LISA PARENTI
designer
JAN MARIE GALLAGHER
client
LEROY VILLAGE GREEN

creative firm
DEUTSCH DESIGN WORKS
San Franicsco, California
creative director
BARRY DEUTSCH
senior designer
LORI WYNN
client
BELLAGIO RESORT & HOTEL, LAS VEGAS

BELLAGIO

creative firm
KEVIN AKERS—DESIGNER
San Rafael, California
designer
KEVIN AKERS
client
MONACO COSMETICS

creative firm
THE WECKER GROUP
Monterey, California
designer
ROBERT WECKER
client
BLUE FIN BILLIARDS

creative firm
ROSS ADVERTISING
Peoria, Illinois
creative directors
BRIAN BRUSH, SKIP DAMPIER
client
ARCHER DANIELS MIDLAND

creative firm
GARDNER DESIGN
Wichita, Kansas
designer
CHRIS PARKS
client
SAFETEMP

creative firm
  TYLER BLIK DESIGN
  Carlsbad, California
art director, designer
  RON FLEMING
illustrator
  TRACY SABIN
client
  OTAY RANCH

creative firm
  KEVIN AKERS—DESIGNER
  San Rafael, California
designer
  KEVIN AKERS
client
  COUNTRY GROWERS
  (nursery)

creative firm
  KEVIN AKERS—DESIGNER
  San Rafael, California
designer
  KEVIN AKERS
client
  INKWELL
  (print brokers)

creative firm
  HORNALL ANDERSON DESIGN WORKS
  Seattle, Washington
art directors
  JACK ANDERSON, LISA CERVENY
designers
  JACK ANDERSON, LISA CERVENY, SONJA MAX, MARY HERMES
illustrator
  MARY HERMES
client
  TIGERLILY

creative firm
GARDNER DESIGN
Wichita, Kansas
designer
CHRIS PARKS
client
CARLOS O'KELLYS

ILI<D ℠

creative firm
SIBLEY PETEET DESIGN
Dallas, Texas
designer
TOM HOUGH
client
CHASE BANK

HAUTe DECOR .COM

creative firm
TOM FOWLER, INC.
Stamford, Connecticut
art directors, designers
THOMAS G. FOWLER, ELIZABETH P. BALL
client
HAUTE DECOR.COM

creative firm
COMPASS
DESIGN
Minneapolis, Minnesota
designers
MITCHELL LINDGREN,
TOM ARTHUR,
RICH McGOWEN
client
SUNRISE GOURMET

SUNRISE GOURMET™

The CALIFORNIA Grill

creative firm
THE WECKER GROUP
Monterey, California
designer
ROBERT WECKER
client
DOUBLETREE MONTEREY

creative firm
GREENFIELD/BELSER LTD
Washington, D.C.
art director, designer
BURKEY BELSER
client
MORRIS JAMES

MorrisJames
DELAWARE

garbs
clothing   accessories   jewelry

creative firm
BECKER DESIGN
Milwaukee, Wisconsin
designer
NEIL BECKER
client
GARBS

NIKOLA'S BISCOTTI

creative firm
COMPASS DESIGN
Minneapolis, Minnesota
designers
MITCHELL LINDGREN, TOM ARTHUR, RICH McGOWEN
client
NIKOLA'S SPECIALTY FOODS

creative firm
McELVENEY + PALOZZI DESIGN GROUP, INC.
Rochester, New York
creative director
STEVE PALOZZI
art director
MATT NOWICKI
designer
PAUL REISINGER, JR.
client
LPA SOFTWARE

creative firm
BAILEY DESIGN GROUP, INC.
Plymouth Meeting, Pennsylvania
creative director
DAVID FIEDLER
designers
STEPHEN PERRY, WENDY SLAVISH
client
MARRIOTT

creative firm
ESTUDIO RAY
Phoenix, Arizona
art directors
CHRISTINE RAY, JOE RAY
designers
CHRISTINE RAY, JOE RAY, LESLIE LINK
client
RESTAURANT OCEANA

creative firm
MORTENSEN DESIGN
Mountain View, California
art director
GORDON MORTENSEN
designer
PJ NIDECKER
client
HANDSPRING, INC.

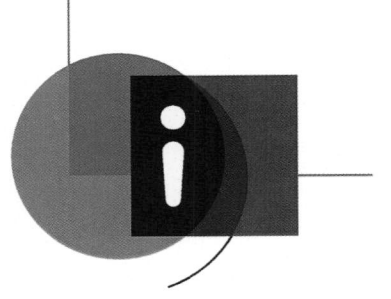

INTELLIGENT/DIGITAL

creative firm
   WAGES DESIGN
   Atlanta, Georgia
designer
   DOMINGA LEE
client
   INTELLIGENT DIGITAL

MIRAPOINT

creative firm
   MORTENSEN DESIGN
   Mountain View, California
art director
   GORDON MORTENSEN
designer
   PJ NIDECKER
client
   MIRAPOINT, INC.

CENTRE EUROPEEN LASER

creative firm
   TANGRAM STRATEGIC DESIGN
   Novara, Italy
creative director
   ENRICO SEMPI
art director, designer
   ANTONELLA TREVISAN
client
   CENTRE EUROPEEN DU LASER

SwiftTouch

creative firm
   GILL FISHMAN ASSOCIATES, INC.
   Cambridge, Massachusetts
creative director
   GILL FISHMAN
designer, illustrator
   ALICIA OZYJOWSKI
client
   SWIFT TOUCH CORP.

conversā

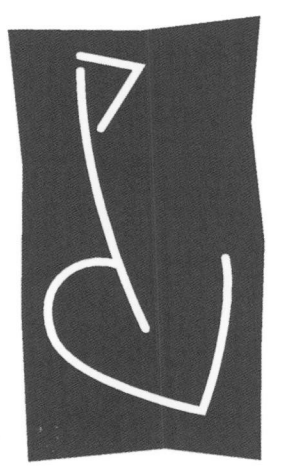

LINKS FOR LIFE

creative firm
 McMILLIAN DESIGN
 Woodside, New York
art director
 WILLIAM McMILLIAN
client
 GOLF DIGEST MAGAZINE

Center Trust

creative firm
 JAMES ROBIE DESIGN ASSOCIATES
 Los Angeles, California
creative director, designer
 JAMES ROBIE
client
 CENTER TRUST, INC.

creative firm
 GARDNER DESIGN
 Wichita, Kansas
designer
 BRIAN MILLER
client
 BALANCE

creative firm
 COMPASS DESIGN
 Minneapolis, Minnesota
designers
 MITCHELL LINDGREN,
 TOM ARTHUR, RICH McGOWEN
client
 WORLD WIDE SPORTS

123

creative firm
  FIVE VISUAL COMMUNICATION & DESIGN
  West Chester, Ohio
designers
  DENNY FAGAN, RONDI TSCHOPP
client
  DOUBLE TREE HOTEL DAYTON DOWNTOWN

creative firm
  BRUCE YELASKA DESIGN
  San Francisco, California
art director, designer
  BRUCE YELASKA
client
  BIKRAM'S YOGA COLLEGE

creative firm
  GARDNER DESIGN
  Wichita, Kansas
designers
  CHRIS PARKS, BILL GARDNER
client
  SERGEANT'S

STREAMWORKS

creative firm
  HORNALL ANDERSON DESIGN WORKS
  Seattle, Washington
art director
  JACK ANDERSON
designers
  JACK ANDERSON, BELINDA BOWLING, ANDREW SMITH, ED LEE
client
  STREAMWORKS

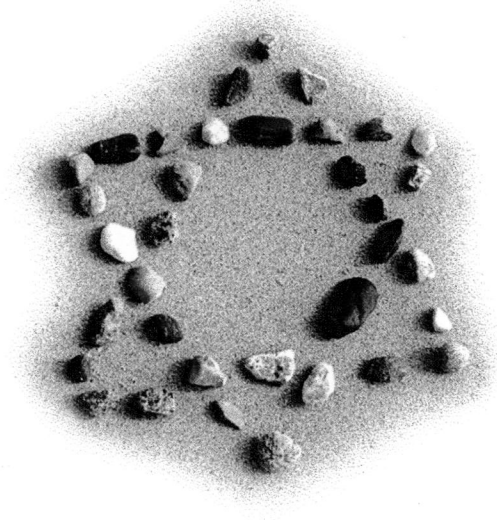

WRIGHT
WILLIAMS
&KELLY

creative firm
GILL FISHMAN ASSOCIATES, INC.
Cambridge, Massachusetts
creative director
GILL FISHMAN
designer
TAMMY TORREY
photographer
THOMAS TORREY
client
ISRAEL'S 50TH BIRTHDAY CELEBRATION

creative firm
THE WECKER GROUP
Monterey, California
designers
ROBERT WECKER, MATT GNIBUS
client
WRIGHT WILLIAMS & KELLY

The Refinery

creative firm
MINALE TATTERSFIELD + PARTNERS
Richmond, England
creative director
DIMITRI KARAVIAS
designer
LEE NEWHAM
client
THE REFINERY
(grooming emporium for men)

creative firm
MULLER + CO.
Kansas City, Missouri
creative director
JOHN MULLER
art director, designer
MARK VOSS
client
KANSAS CITY BLUES & JAZZ FESTIVAL

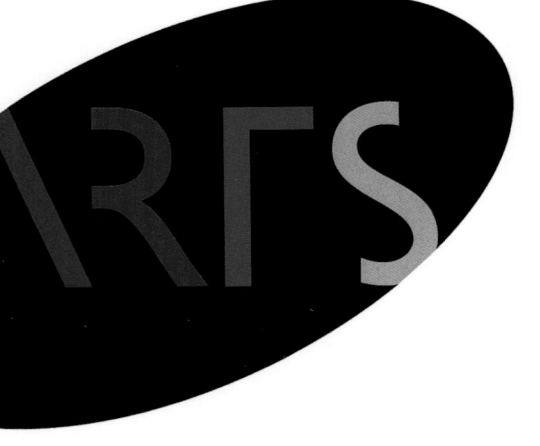

creative firm
PEG FAIMON DESIGN
Oxford, Ohio
designer
PEG FAIMON
client
MIAMI UNIVERSITY

creative firm
KEVIN AKERS—DESIGNER
San Rafael, California
designer
KEVIN AKERS
client
CHRISTIAN TEEN MAGAZINE

creative firm
SAYLESS GRAPHIC DESIGN
Des Moines, Iowa
art director, designer, illustrator
JOHN SAYLES
client
GLAZED EXPRESSIONS

SOUTHWEB PRINTING

creative firm
BUTLER KEMP DESIGN
North Adelaide, Australia
art director
DEREK BUTLER
designer
HELLEN KIPRIZLOGLOV
client
SOUTHWEB PRINTING
(web printers)

ORGANIC
S Y S T E M S

creative firm
GILL FISHMAN ASSOCIATES, INC.
Cambridge, Massachusetts
creative director
GILL FISHMAN
designer
TAMMY TORREY
client
ORGANIC SYSTEMS, INC.

Opteon

creative firm
GILL FISHMAN ASSOCIATES, INC.
Cambridge, Massachusetts
creative director
GILL FISHMAN,
designer
TAMMY TORREY
client
OPTEON

michael's
A RESTAURANT

creative firm
THE WECKER GROUP
Monterey, California
art director
ROBERT WECKER
designers
RUTH MINERVA, CRAIG RADER
client
MICHAELS

Logal.net

creative firm
GILL FISHMAN ASSOCIATES, INC.
Cambridge, Massachusetts
creative director
GILL FISHMAN
designer, illustrator
ALICIA OZYJOWSKI
client
LOGAL.NET

LOGOS

creative firm
    THE WECKER GROUP
    Monterey, California
designer
    ROBERT WECKER
client
    GREAT EXPECTATIONS LIGHTING

creative firm
    PRIMO ANGELI, INC.
    San Francisco, California
creative director
    CARLO PAGODA
project director
    RICH SCHEVE
senior designer
    KELSON MAU
client
    CALIFORNIA ACADEMY OF SCIENCE

creative firm
    DEUTSCH DESIGN WORKS
    San Francisco, California
creative director
    BARRY DEUTSCH
senior designer
    GREGG PERIN
client
    SILICON ENTERTAINMENT—
    NASCAR SILICON MOTOR SPEEDWAY

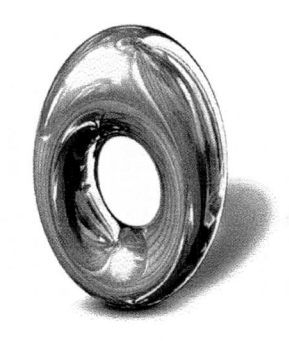

ORGANIC
S Y S T E M S

creative firm
  GILL FISHMAN ASSOCIATES, INC.
  Cambridge, Massachusetts
creative director
  GILL FISHMAN
designer
  TAMMY TORREY
client
  ORGANIC SYSTEMS, INC.

Opteon

creative firm
  GILL FISHMAN ASSOCIATES, INC.
  Cambridge, Massachusetts
creative director
  GILL FISHMAN,
designer
  TAMMY TORREY
client
  OPTEON

michael's
A RESTAURANT

creative firm
  THE WECKER GROUP
  Monterey, California
art director
  ROBERT WECKER
designers
  RUTH MINERVA, CRAIG RADER
client
  MICHAELS

Logal.net

creative firm
  GILL FISHMAN ASSOCIATES, INC.
  Cambridge, Massachusetts
creative director
  GILL FISHMAN
designer, illustrator
  ALICIA OZYJOWSKI
client
  LOGAL.NET

creative firm
 FIVE VISUAL COMMUNICATION & DESIGN
 West Chester, Ohio
designers
 DENNY FAGAN, RONDI TSCHOPP
client
 DOUBLETREE HOTEL DAYTON DOWNTOWN

creative firm
 DESIGN SOLUTIONS
 Napa, California
designer
 DEBORAH MITCHELL
client
 LIGHTHOUSE RELOCATION SYSTEMS

creative firm
 SAYLES GRAPHIC DESIGN
 Des Moines, Iowa
art director, illustrator
 JOHN SAYLES
client
 MEREDITH CORPORATION "INDUSTRIAL REVOLUTION"

creative firm
 DOTZLER CREATIVE ARTS
 Omaha, Nebraska
client
 CHRIST FOR THE CITY

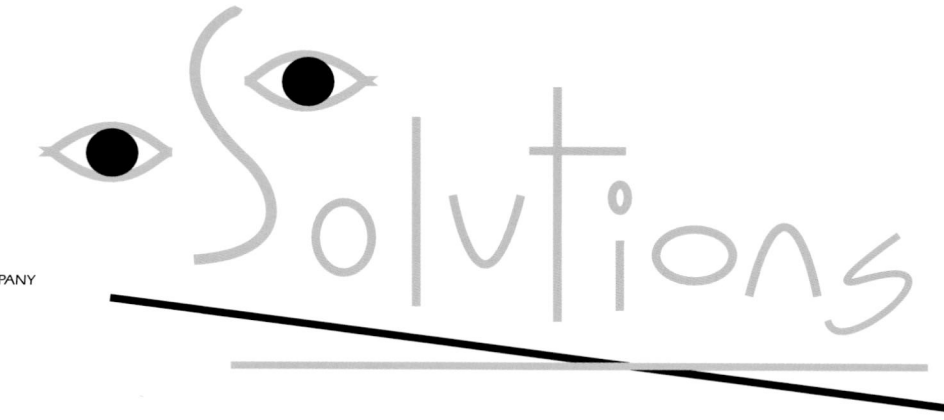

creative firm
AIRE DESIGN COMPANY
Tucson, Arizona
creative director
CATHARINE M. KIM
art director
SHARI RYKOWSKI
client
SOLUTIONS

creative firm
HORNALL ANDERSON DESIGN WORKS
Seattle, Washington
art director
JACK ANDERSON
designers
JACK ANDERSON, KATHY SAITO, ALAN COPELAND
client
WELLS FARGO (ATREVA)

personify

creative firm
HORNALL ANDERSON DESIGN WORKS
Seattle, Washington
art director
JACK ANDERSON
designers
JACK ANDERSON, DEBRA McCLOSKEY, HOLLY CRAVEN
client
PERSONIFY

GREAT
EXPECTATIONS
LIGHTING Co.

creative firm
THE WECKER GROUP
Monterey, California
designer
ROBERT WECKER
client
GREAT EXPECTATIONS LIGHTING

CALIFORNIA
ACADEMY
OF
SCIENCES

creative firm
PRIMO ANGELI, INC.
San Francisco, California
creative director
CARLO PAGODA
project director
RICH SCHEVE
senior designer
KELSON MAU
client
CALIFORNIA ACADEMY OF SCIENCE

creative firm
DEUTSCH DESIGN WORKS
San Francisco, California
creative director
BARRY DEUTSCH
senior designer
GREGG PERIN
client
SILICON ENTERTAINMENT—
NASCAR SILICON MOTOR SPEEDWAY

AVON
the company for women

creative firm
O&J DESIGN, INC.
New York, New York
art director
ANDRZEJ OLEJNICZAK
designer
HEISHIN RA
client
AVON PRODUCTS, INC.

ristorante

creative firm
SAYLES GRAPHIC DESIGN
Des Moines, Iowa
art director, illustrator
JOHN SAYLES
client
BASIL PROSPERI

creative firm
BIG CAT MARKETING COMM
Colorado Springs, Colorado
designer
ANNA BARNES
client
SKYLANDS MUSIC & ARTS ALLIANCE

creative firm
TOR PETTERSEN & PARTNERS
London, England
designer
JEFF DAVIS
client
MAP COMMUNICATIONS

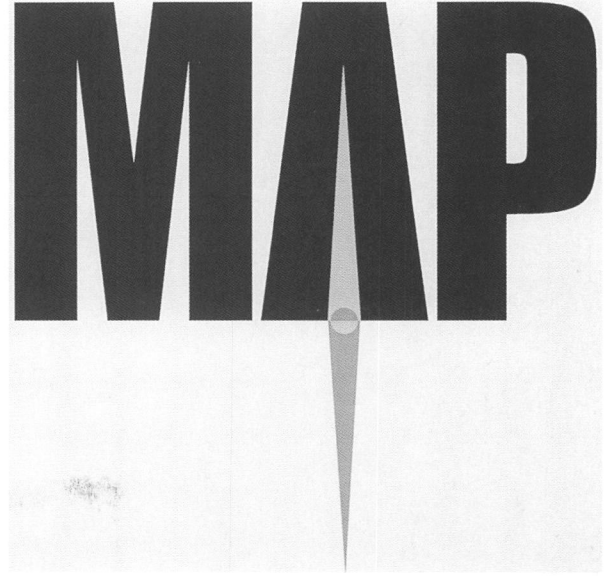

creative firm
  COMPASS DESIGN
  Minneapolis, Minnesota
designers
  MITCHELL LINDGREN, TOM ARTHUR, RICH McGOWEN
client
  GREAT WATERS BREWING CO.

creative firm
  LOVE PACKAGING GROUP
  Wichita, Kansas
designers
  BRIAN MILLER, CHRIS WEST
client
  THE FANTASTIC WORL OF GOURMET CHOCOLATE
  (chocolate manufacturer)

creative firm
  TANGRAM STRATEGIC DESIGN
  Novara, Italy
creative director
  ENRICO SEMPI
art director, designer
  ANTONELLA TREVISAN
illustrator
  GUIDO ROSA
client
  CAMERA DI COMMERCIO DI VICENEA

creative firm
  WAGES DESIGN
  Atlanta, Georgia
designer
  DOMINGA LEE
client
  AIGA (BIG NIGHT)

creative firm
  HORNALL ANDERSON DESIGN WORKS
  Seattle, Washington
art directors
  JACK ANDERSON, LARRY ANDERSON
designers
  JACK ANDERSON, LARRY ANDERSON, MARY HERMES,
  MIKE CALKINS, MICHAEL BRUGMAN
client
  U.S. CIGAR

creative firm
  ADKINS/BALCHUNAS
  Providence, Rhode Island
creative director
  JERRY BALCHUNAS
designers
  SUSAN DE ANGELIS, JERRY BALCHUNAS
client
  SBARRO

creative firm
  DESIGN GUYS
  Minneapolis, Minnesota
art director
  STEVEN SIKORA
designers
  AMY KIRKPATRICK, ANNE PETERSON
letterer
  TODD AP JONES
client
  TARGET STORES

THE SAINT JOHN'S BIBLE

creative firm
  SABINGRAFIK, INC.
  Carlsbad, California
art director
  MARILEE BANKERT
designer, illustrator
  TRACY SABIN
client
  OLIVER McMILLIN

creative firm
  GREENFIELD/BELSER LTD.
  Washington, D.C.
art director
  BURKEY BELSER
designer
  JANET MORALES
client
  IN2BOOKS

MONTEREY SPORTS CENTER

creative firm
  THE WECKER GROUP
  Monterey, California
designer
  ROBERT WECKER
client
  MONTEREY SPORTS CENTER

creative firm
  McELVENEY + PALOZZI
  DESIGN GROUP, INC.
  Rochester, New York
creative director
  WILLIAM McELVENEY
art director
  LISA PARENTI
client
  ABBOTTS FROZEN CUSTARD

creative firm
TELMET DESIGN ASSOCIATES
Toronto, Canada
art director
TIIT TELMET
designers
JOSEPH GAULT, MARKO BARAC
illustrator
JOSEPH GAULT
client
EVERYWARE DEVELOPMENT CORP.

™

creative firm
THE WECKER GROUP
Monterey, California
designer
ROBERT WECKER
client
DELTA POINT, INC.

creative firm
GILL FISHMAN ASSOCIATES, INC.
Cambridge, Massachusetts
creative director
GILL FISHMAN
designer
MICHAEL PERSONS
client
ORIDION MEDICAL

creative firm
DEVER DESIGNS
Laurel, Maryland
art director, designer
JEFFREY L. DEVER
client
DIAMANTI, INC.

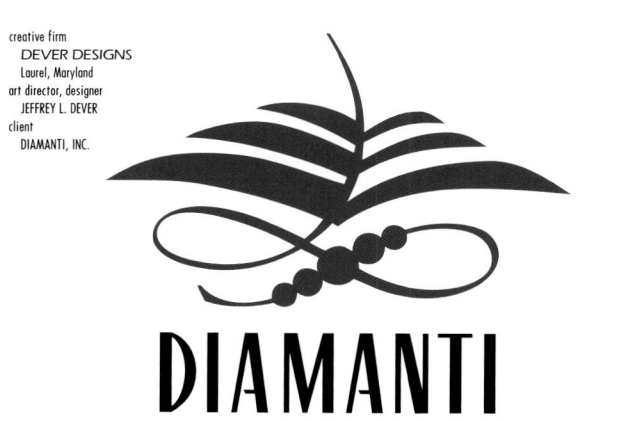

DIAMANTI

Oridion

creative firm
  GARDNER DESIGN
  Wichita, Kansas
designer
  BILL GARDNER
client
  BUZZCUTS MAXIMUM LAWNCARE

creative firm
  SIBLEY PETEET DESIGN
  Dallas, Texas
designer
  DONNA ALDRIDGE
client
  CATHEDRAL OF HOPE

creative firm
  SQUIRES & COMPANY
  Dallas, Texas
designers
  BRANDON MURPHY, AMY CHANG
client
  POPULI

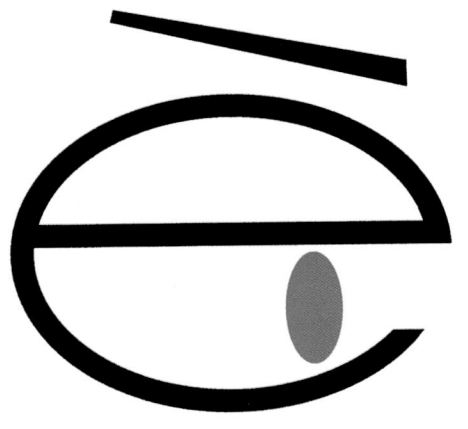

creative firm
  KEVIN AKERS—DESIGNER
  San Rafael, California
designer
  KEVIN AKERS
client
  BILL EMBERLEY
  (video producer)

MUSIC PUBLISHING
still going strong at No.1

THE FULL MONTY

Operating and financial review continued

Copacabana catalogue was acquired giving EMI the worldwide rights to 4,300 master recordings encompassing a range of genres, including Samba, Sertaneja and regional music.

In Europe, EMI acquired 100% of CMC Records, a Danish record company specialising in local pop/dance repertoire. EMI also acquired an additional 30% of Minos-EMI S.A. specialising in Greek local repertoire, increasing its interest in the company to 90%.

In addition, EMI Recorded Music established new companies in the emerging music markets of Bolivia, Ecuador, Paraguay, Peru, and Uruguay.

1998/99 Recorded Music release schedule

Major artist releases scheduled for 1998/99 include: new studio albums from Smashing Pumpkins, Beastie Boys, Blur, Backstreet Boys, Lenny Kravitz, Enigma, Roxette, Deana Carter, Luther Vandross, Fun Lovin' Criminals, Ice Cube and Massive Attack; "Live" albums from Garth Brooks, Bob Seger and The Rolling Stones; a "Greatest Hits" album from Meat Loaf and major Japanese releases by Dreams Come True, Yumi Matsutoya, Kuroyume, Hotei and Aska.

EMI Music Publishing

Music Publishing, the world's leader with over one million copyrights, maintained its track record of continued sales and profit growth despite the lower growth in major developed markets.

Major successes this year included The Prodigy, The Verve, Jamiroquai, Matchbox 20, Savage Garden, Puff Daddy & the Family, Eros Ramazzotti, The Notorious B.I.G., Third Eye Blind, Deana Carter, Counting Crows and Texas.

Once again this year, EMI Music Publishing received numerous industry awards, including Billboard's Pop, R&B and Country Publisher of the Year in the US, and top music publisher in the US, UK, Germany and Canada.

In one of the most significant music publishing arrangements, EMI Music Publishing acquired a 50% interest in the Jobete Music publishing companies. Jobete's catalogues contain the great hit songs of the Motown era, including "My Girl", "I'll Be There", "I Heard it Through the Grapevine", "You Are the Sunshine of My Life" and "I Just Called to Say I Love You". Jobete's 15,000 copyrights include more than 100 number one songs, recorded by such legendary artists as Stevie Wonder, Marvin Gaye, The Temptations, Diana Ross and the Supremes and Smokey Robinson.

In another major deal, EMI Music Publishing secured a long term publishing arrangement with Sting, and will represent his entire back catalogue (both solo works and as a member of The Police) and current and future material throughout the world on a long term basis. Other significant deals included Keith Sweat, Cleopatra, Usher, Matchbox 20, Meredith Brooks and Chumbawamba, and the renewal of publishing arrangements with Aerosmith, Janet Jackson and Carlton TV.

Throughout the year, EMI Music Publishing entered new markets, opening offices in Taiwan and South Korea – firsts for an international publisher – and entered into an agreement with the Music Copyright Society of China to represent our music in mainland China.

Expansion also continued into Eastern Europe with direct operations being

1,000,000+ world's most **popular songs**

On-line customers wax lyrical

creative firm
TOR PETTERSEN & PARTNERS
London, England
designers
JEFF DAVIS, JIM ALLSOPP
client
THE EMI GROUP

---

creative firm
DEVER DESIGNS
Laurel, Maryland
art director, designer
JEFFREY L. DEVER
photographer
TIM BARNWELL
client
THE ROSEN GROUP/AMERICANSTYLE

NATURAL ReSOURCES
BY SUE WASSERMAN

Mornings in Penland, N.C., are filled with moments of quiet lingering, watching the sunlight play softly against the subtle blue-gray shadows of the vast Blue Ridge mountain range or waving casual greetings to the conductor as the first train of the day chugs slowly past the shore of the gurgling Toe River. The richness of this rural community's natural resources first attracted computer consultant Mignon Durham, who loved exploring the wealth of hiking trails and fishing holes, finding it the perfect weekend escape from never-ending phone calls and faxes. Before long, however, the Winston-Salem native discovered that the region's finest natural resources aren't the rivers and mountains but the local artists who have forged a small, tightly knit community around the prestigious Penland School of Crafts.

MIGNON DURHAM finds countless treasures right in her own backyard

The region's artistic spirit springs to life in Durham's home, a rustic log cabin lovingly filled to capacity with a kaleidoscopic array of handcrafted glass, wood, metal and ceramic objects. "When I decided to build this cabin," Durham reflects, "I wanted it to be a celebration of everything handmade, especially a celebration of Penland's artists." The expanding list of artists whose works brighten her home includes such recognized names as Harvey Littleton, Ginny Ruffner, Jon Kuhn, Rob Levin, Marvin Jensen and Ed and Philip Moulthrop.

The cabin itself is a marvel, the result of Durham's impassioned efforts to restore and join three pre-Civil War cabins while incorporating the finest elements of contemporary craft. "My challenge and joy was in commissioning artists to do work they had never done before," she says.

PHOTOGRAPHY BY TIM BARNWELL

Sue Wasserman is a freelance writer specializing in the arts and design. She is based in Atlanta, Ga.

Michael Croft's snake walking stick, right, might have slithered right out of Randy Sual's Garden of Eden staircase. Torchères by Marvin Jensen frame the chenille sofa by James Taylor. A jaunty doll by Akira Blount holds court. Far left, the whimsical man toting his marble teapot is the brainchild of Wesley Anderson.

the rainbow coalition

The spring/summer season will see rich fabrics and even richer colours. The future is bright

creative firm
   THE OBSERVER
   London, England
art director
   WAYNE FORD
photographer
   FRANCESCA SORRENTI
fashion editor
   JO ADAMS
editor
   SHERYL GARRATT
client
   THE OBSERVER LIFE MAGAZINE

creative firm
   COMMTEK COMMUNICATIONS CORPORATION
   Fairfax, Virginia
art director
   LIZ RICHARDS
illustrator
   GEORGE TOOMER
client
   SATELLITE DIRECT

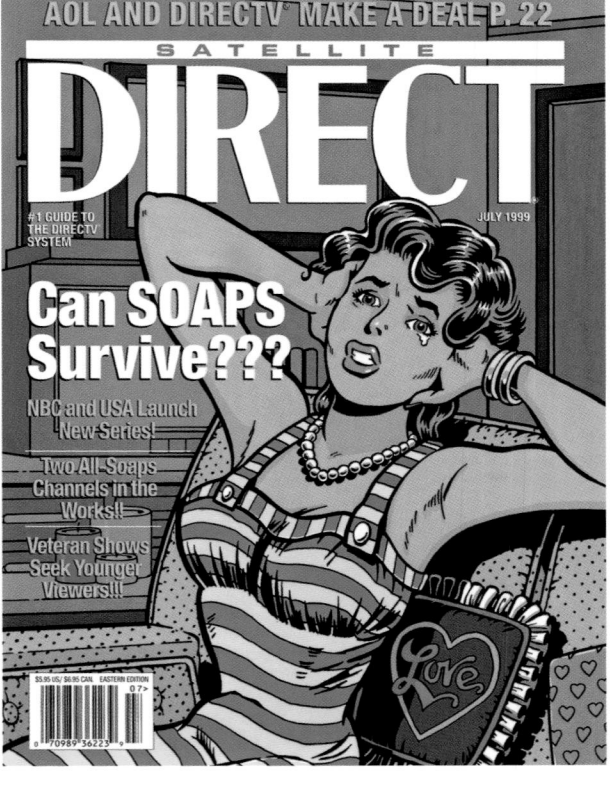

FREE! PRO BASKETBALL TV SCHEDULE

SATELLITE **ORBIT**

OCTOBER 1999

COMPLETE NATIONAL TV PROGRAMMING GUIDE

TV PREVIEW

BOUNCING BACK

Watching The NBA's Road To Recovery

PLUS:
College Basketball's Top 10

$3.95 US/$6.95 CAN

creative firm
    COMMTEK COMMUNICATIONS CORP.
    Fairfax, Virginia
design director
    POLLY JOHNSON
illustrator
    STUART SIMONS
client
    SATELLITE ORBIT

creative firm
    THE OBSERVER
    London, England
art director
    WAYNE FORD
photographer
    HEATHER FAVELL
fashion editor
    JO ADAMS
editor
    SHERYL GARRATT
client
    THE OBSERVER LIFE MAGAZINE

Fashion editor **Jo Adams** Photographs **Heather Favell**

Sequin dress, £39.99, from Kays Catalogue (inquiries 08000 681689). Cream jacket, De La Guarda costume wardrobe. Shoes, £69.95, by Rockport, from Selfridges, 400 Oxford Street, London W1 (stockist inquiries 01524 580400)

Swinging in the rain

High-flying performance group De La Guarda, whose act is a mix of trapeze, dancing, drumming and dramatics, has been enthralling audiences since it opened this summer at the Roundhouse, in London's Camden. The costumes – everyday clothes that make the performers look as if they have been pulled out of the audience – are customised to allow total freedom of movement. To spruce up the act, we raided the stores in search of relaxed suits for men, mismatched skirts and tops, a bit of sparkle, and some good old, practical Rockport shoes – an eclectic blend of the sensible and the frivolous...

W.Y.S.I.W.Y.G.

(what you see is what you get)

Australian beef – prepared to your exact specifications.
You want beef cuts that come well trimmed – saving you valuable time and money.
Well, Australia has them. And they really are as good as they look.

You can be sure they're safe, too. Australian beef is processed under HACCP programs
that measure up to all Australian Quarantine Inspection Service (AQIS), USDA/FSIS and
Canadian Food Inspection Agency requirements. The Australian beef industry is
committed to delivering safe, wholesome beef products to our customers worldwide.

For more information, call (212) 486-2405 ext. 303 or visit our website
@ www.australian-beef.com

australian beef | The highest standards. Worldwide.

creative firm
  RISE AGENCY, INC.
  New York, New York
art director, creative director
  CAROLINA RODRIGUEZ
designer
  ROBERT ZWASCHKA
copywriter
  CATHERINE PENFOLD
client
  AUSTRALIAN BEEF

creative firm
  BOLDRINI & FICCARDI
  Mendoza, Argentina
art director
  LEONARDO FICCARDI
designer
  VICTOR BOLDRINI
client
  REVISTA

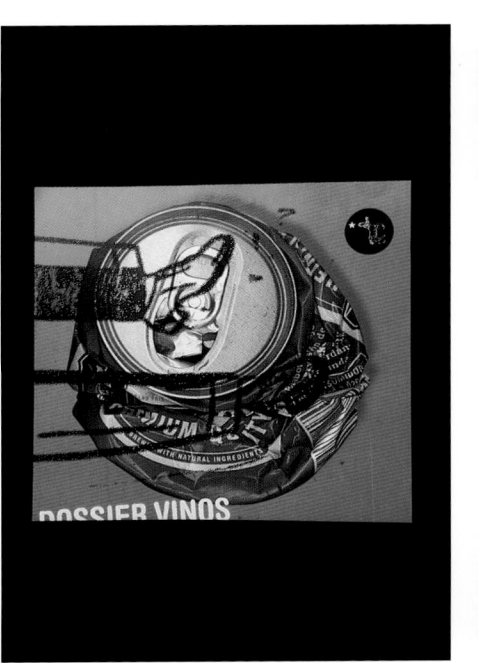

creative firm
THE OBSERVER
London, England
art director
WAYNE FORD
photographer
ZED NELSON
picture editor
JENNIE RICKETTS
editor
SHERYL GARRATT
client
THE OBSERVER LIFE MAGAZINE

Pastor Bill Oudemolen of the Foothills Bible Church, in Littleton, gave the sermon at the funeral of 16-year-old John Tomlin. 'What happened at Columbine High School was the work of Satan,' he said

A sign in Littleton in response to the tragedy

Tom Mauser, whose son Daniel was shot dead at Columbine High, addresses an 8,000-strong crowd on the steps of the Denver State Capitol Building. The protest condemned the timing of the National Rifle Association's annual meeting in Denver only a week and a half after the killings

Jason Norn, 25, (above, right) buys a handgun at the Firing Line gun store in Aurora, Colorado, one week after the massacre. He chose a Kimber .45 calibre compact, and in the while-you-wait background check, he explained it was for 'home defence'. He left the store with the gun. His friend Kirk Smith, 19, accompanied him. Both are from Littleton

Charlton Heston, president of the National Rifle Association, addresses a crowd of 2,000 pro-gun members at a meeting in Denver on 1 May. Responding to calls for tighter gun control after the tragedy at Columbine High School, he said: 'Those who would give up their freedom to purchase a little security... deserve neither freedom nor security'

A day after the shooting, a television journalist in the grounds of Columbine High reports to camera. In the background, shocked students wander across the school playing fields

Ten days after the shooting the victims' cars remain in the school car park, piled high with wilting flowers. The vehicles became shrines to their young owners

Posters advertising military-designed assault weapons in the window of Paladin Arms. For local gun stores, it's business as usual

creative firm
COMMTEK COMMUNICATIONS CORP.
Fairfax, Virginia
art director
LIZ RICHARDS
client
SATELLITE DIRECT

THE MASTER OF SUSPENSE WAS BORN 100 YEARS AGO THIS MONTH, BUT THE SHADOW HE HAS CAST OVER AMERICAN FILMS WILL LAST MUCH LONGER.

The Hitchcock Legacy
BY PAT DOWELL

MOVIE THRILLERS were being made before Alfred Hitchcock first sat in the director's chair in 1925, but nearly 75 years later his name still defines the ultimate in big-screen excitement. It comes in many shadings—the sheer terror of *Psycho* as meek Anthony Perkins unravels; the sleek, sophisticated thrill of Cary Grant landing just one graceful step ahead of pursuers across half a continent in *North by Northwest*; the gathering doom of James Stewart's dark obsession with a woman he must bring back to life in *Vertigo*.

Hitchcock's thrillers were so unforgettable that "Hitchcockian" is just about the nicest word any critic can apply to a movie that keeps you guessing, not about whodunit but rather how and why, and will they get caught? That's the difference between a mystery, which Hitchcock disdained, and suspense, which he understood like no other filmmaker before or since.

Hitchcock was born on August 13, 1899, and to mark his centennial Encore (ch. 526) has created an original documentary, *Dial H for Hitchcock: The Genius Behind the Showman*, which airs at 8 p.m. ET on his birthday. It anchors a 24-hour festival of some of Hitchcock's greatest hits, including *Shadow of a Doubt*, *The Trouble With Harry*, *Vertigo* and *Psycho*. (Check the daily listings for show times.) →

ALFRED HITCHCOCK'S IMPOSING FIGURE IS AS FAMILIAR TO MOVIEGOERS AS IMAGES FROM *PSYCHO* (TOP) AND *VERTIGO* (RIGHT).

While a student at the University of Alabama in 1952, I interned with a national public accounting firm in Atlanta. On my way to work I sometimes passed what was probably the first "adult" store I had ever seen. I remember a large sign out front with quotes from opinions of U.S. Supreme Court associate justice Hugo L. Black. In recent years my office has been in the Hugo L. Black U.S. Courthouse in Birmingham, Alabama. The foyer walls have bronze plaques, also containing quotes from Justice Black.

I have often wondered what made Justice Black tick. I realize that he is an icon to many in law, the media, and academia,* but my study of his career and his judicial reasoning raises questions about the First Amendment jurisprudence that he is significantly credited with establishing. "Expedience" is a continuous theme in his career.

The Pre-Court Years

After he became a lawyer in Birmingham, Alabama, Black joined the Ku Klux Klan. In the early 1920s he represented a preacher charged with murdering a Catholic priest who had married the defendant's daughter to a Puerto Rican. Black appealed to both the religious and racial prejudices of the jury (he gave the Klan members on the jury the Klan sign), which acquitted the defendant. He had similar success in less notorious but similar cases.

In 1924, when U.S. senator Oscar W. Underwood from Alabama denounced the Ku Klux Klan, he knew that he could not retain his seat in 1926. John F. Kennedy's book *Profiles in Courage* recognizes Underwood's courage. Kennedy's book quotes another writer: "Had Senator Underwood played the game in Alabama in accord with the sound political rule of seeming to say something without doing so, there would have been no real opposition to his remaining in the Senate for the balance of his life." Black did not denounce the Klan, but joined it instead and was given a lifetime membership. He gave a letter of resignation to be disclosed when convenient. The oath he took included a promise to "preserve by any and all justifiable means and methods . . . white supremacy" (Roger K. Newman, *Hugo Black, A Biography*, pp. 91, 92). He made open appeals to its members and received its support when he ran for and was elected to the U.S. Senate, taking Underwood's position in 1926. During the campaign he addressed nearly all the 148 Klan Klaverns in Alabama (*Ibid.*, p. 104). His total votes received closely paralleled the total Alabama Klan membership (*Ibid.*, p. 115). He acknowledged that he owed his victory to the Klan. To a Klan gathering he stated: "I desire to impress upon you as representatives of

Robert B. Propst is a senior U.S. district judge in Alabama.

A U.S. District Judge From Alabama Takes On Justice Hugo Black, Liberty Magazine, and Judicial Activism

K U · K L U X

By ROBERT B. PROPST

ILLUSTRATION BY MARC BURCKHARDT

ICON

creative firm
DEVER DESIGNS
Laurel, Maryland
art director, designer
JEFFREY L. DEVER
illustrator
MARC BURCKHARDT
client
LIBERTY MAGAZINE

Life The Observer Magazine

25 July 1999

On Being an Angel (detail), Rhode Island, 1977 a self-portrait by Francesca Woodman

the woman who disappeared

the extraordinary art of Francesca Woodman

creative firm
THE OBSERVER
London, England
art director
WAYNE FORD
photographer
FRANCESCA WOODMAN
picture editor
JENNIE RICKETTS
editor
SHERYL GARRATT
client
THE OBSERVER LIFE MAGAZINE

creative firm
  RISE AGENCY, INC.
  New York, New York
creative director
  CAROLINA RODRIGUEZ
art director, copywriter
  CATHERINE PENFOLD
client
  SWATCH U.S.

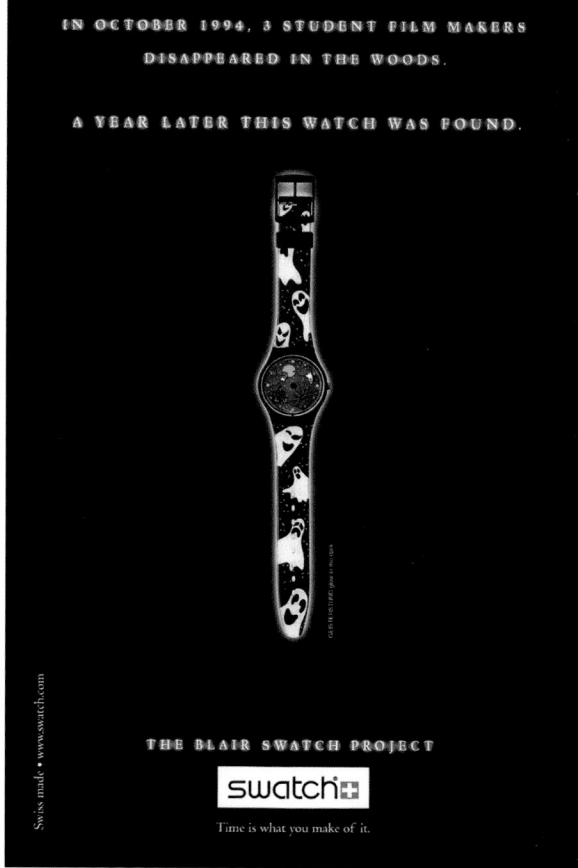

creative firm
  THE OBSERVER
  London, England
art director
  WAYNE FORD
photographer
  BEN INGHAM
fashion editor
  JO ADAMS
editor
  SHERYL GARRATT
client
  THE OBSERVER LIFE MAGAZINE

creative firm
  COMMTEK COMMUNICATIONS CORP.
  Fairfax, Virginia
design director
  POLLY JOHNSON
client
  SATELLITE ORBIT

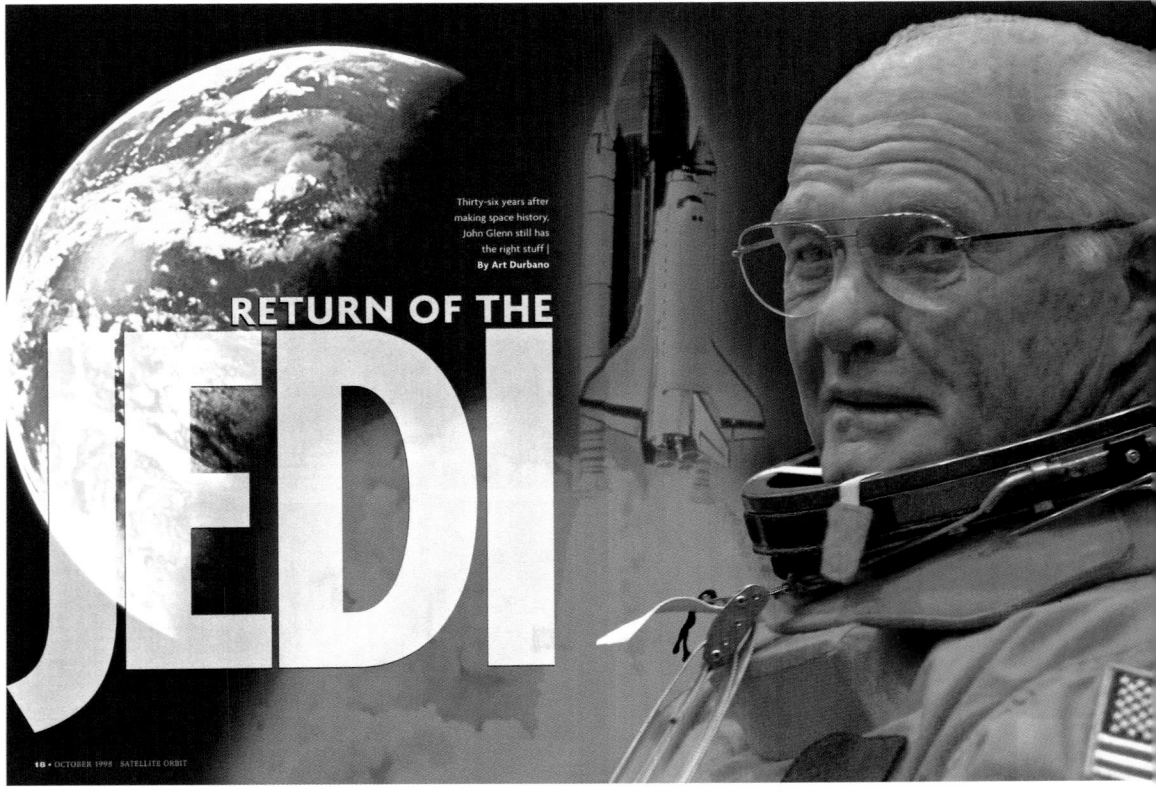

Thirty-six years after making space history, John Glenn still has the right stuff |
By Art Durbano

RETURN OF THE
JEDI

16 · OCTOBER 1998 · SATELLITE ORBIT

creative firm
  DEVER DESIGNS
  Laurel, Maryland
art director, designer
  JEFFREY L. DEVER
client
  FAMILY THERAPY NETWORK

creative firm
  BIG CAT MARKETING COMMUNICATIONS
  Colorado Springs, Colorado
designer
  MATT DUNCAN
client
  THE CHRISTIAN MEDICAL + DENTAL SOCIETY

March/April 1999 $5.00 U.S./$6.00 Canada

FAMILY THERAPY
NETWORKER
Psychotherapy & Modern Life

The
Chemistry of
Sex
The Alchemy
of **Love**

AN EARLY WARNING SYSTEM FOR YOUR PRACTICE

0 74470 75672 9

THE JOURNAL OF THE CHRISTIAN MEDICAL & DENTAL SOCIETY

TODAY'S
CHRISTIANDOCTOR

VOLUME XXX, NO.3 FALL 1999

OUR NATIONAL HEALTH CARE SYSTEM CONTINUES TO CHANGE AT AN UNPRECEDENTED RATE— WITH NO DECELERATION IN SITE. THE CURRENT MEDICAL PARADIGM IS CRACKING UNDER ENORMOUS LEVELS OF FISCAL, POLITICAL, AND COGNITIVE DISSONANCE. DOCTORS ARE REELING UNDER THE IMPACT, DESPERATELY TRYING TO GAIN SOME FOUNDATION, A FOOTHOLD IN THE SHIFTING LANDSCAPE.

Facing
the
Future

fear or faith?

creative firm
UKULELE DESIGN CONSULTANTS PTE LTD
  Singapore
design director
  KIM CHUN-WEI
designer
  LYNN LIM
client
  SINGAPORE TELEVISION TWELVE PTE LTD

creative firm
  DEVER DESIGNS
  Laurel, Maryland
art director
  JEFFREY L. DEVER
designer
  AMY WHITE SUCHERMAN
illustrator
  DAVID KLEIN
client
  LIBERTY MAGAZINE

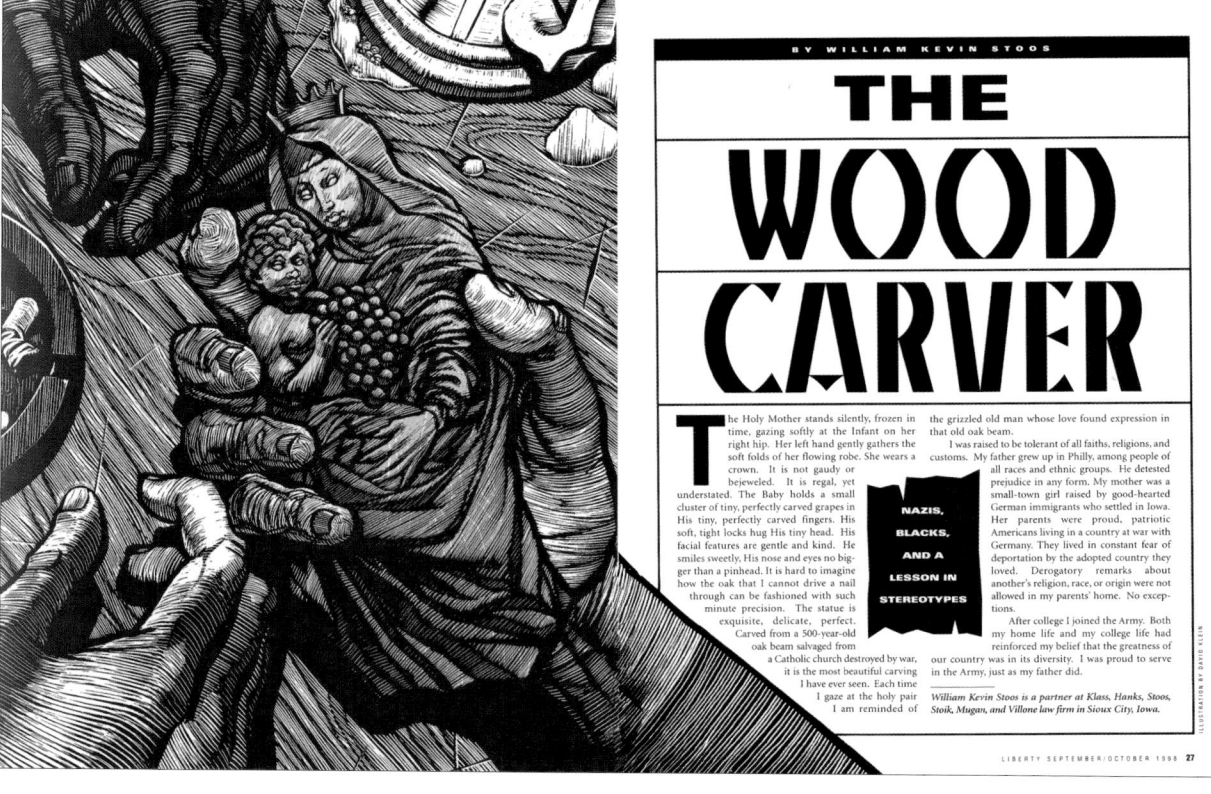

BY WILLIAM KEVIN STOOS

THE WOOD CARVER

NAZIS, BLACKS, AND A LESSON IN STEREOTYPES

The Holy Mother stands silently, frozen in time, gazing softly at the Infant on her right hip. Her left hand gently gathers the soft folds of her flowing robe. She wears a crown. It is not gaudy or bejeweled. It is regal, yet understated. The Baby holds a small cluster of tiny, perfectly carved grapes in His tiny, perfectly carved fingers. His soft, tight locks hug His tiny head. His facial features are gentle and kind. He smiles sweetly, His nose and eyes no bigger than a pinhead. It is hard to imagine how the oak that I cannot drive a nail through can be fashioned with such minute precision. The statue is exquisite, delicate, perfect. Carved from a 500-year-old oak beam salvaged from a Catholic church destroyed by war, it is the most beautiful carving I have ever seen. Each time I gaze at the holy pair I am reminded of

the grizzled old man whose love found expression in that old oak beam.

I was raised to be tolerant of all faiths, religions, and customs. My father grew up in Philly, among people of all races and ethnic groups. He detested prejudice in any form. My mother was a small-town girl raised by good-hearted German immigrants who settled in Iowa. Her parents were proud, patriotic Americans living in a country at war with Germany. They lived in constant fear of deportation by the adopted country they loved. Derogatory remarks about another's religion, race, or origin were not allowed in my parents' home. No exceptions.

After college I joined the Army. Both my home life and my college life had reinforced my belief that the greatness of our country was in its diversity. I was proud to serve in the Army, just as my father did.

William Kevin Stoos is a partner at Klass, Hanks, Stoos, Stoik, Mugan, and Villone law firm in Sioux City, Iowa.

creative firm
DEVER DESIGNS
Laurel, Maryland
art director, designer
JEFFREY L. DEVER
illustrator
JOEL SPECTOR
client
LIBERTY MAGAZINE

creative firm
DEVER DESIGNS
Laurel, Maryland
art director, designer
JEFFREY L. DEVER
client
THE ROSEN GROUP/AMERICANSTYLE

creative firm
TOR PETTERSEN & PARTNERS
London, England
designers
JEFF DAVIS, JIM ALLSOP
client
THE EMI GROUP

creative firm
SAYLES GRAPHIC DESIGN
Des Moines, Iowa
art director, illustrator
JOHN SAYLES
client
ALPHABET SOUP TOY STORE

creative firm
BRUNAZZI & ASSOCIATI/IMAGE + COMMUNICATION
Turin, Italy
art director
ANDREA BRUNAZZI
designer
SILVIA ZANETTI
client
MONETTI

creative firm
THE RIORDON DESIGN GROUP, INC.
Oakville, Ontario, Canada
creative director
DAN WHEATON
planet productions
GARY CAPON
client
IN-SPIRATION

creative firm
  SPAGNOLA & ASSOCIATES
    New York, New York
art director
  TONY SPAGNOLA
designer
  BOB CALLAHAN
architects
  DAVIS BRODY BOND LLP
client
  NEW YORK PUBLIC LIBRARY

creative firm
  HORNALL ANDERSON DESIGN WORKS
    Seattle, Washington
art director
  CLIFF CHUNG
designers
  CLIFF CHUNG, ALAN FLORSHEIM
client
  NEXTRX CORPORATION

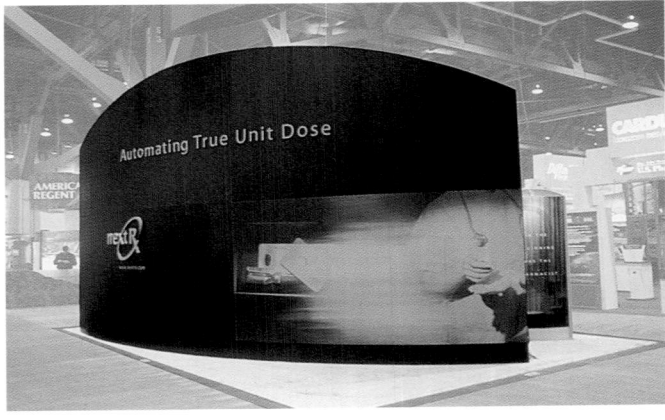

creative firm
HORNALL ANDERSON DESIGN WORKS
Seattle, Washington
art directors
JACK ANDERSON, CLIFF CHUNG
designers
CLIFF CHUNG, ALAN FLORSHEIM,
DAVID BATES, MIKE CALKINS
client
NOVELL, INC.

creative firm
SABINGRAFIK, INC.
Carlsbad, California
art director
LAURA BECKER
illustrator
TRACY SABIN
mosaicist
MIOTTE MOSAICS
marketing director
CHERI WALKER
client
UNIVERSITY TOWNE CENTRE

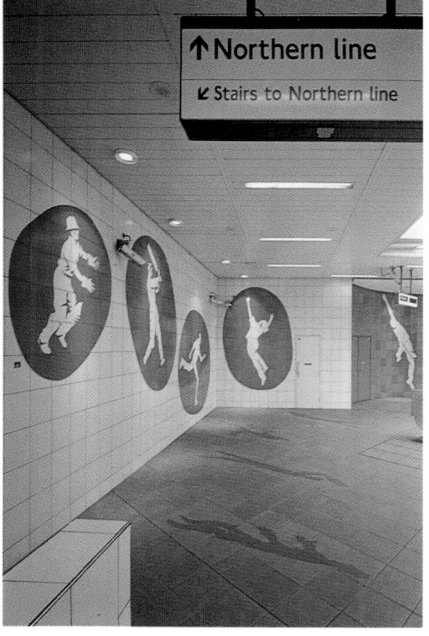

creative firm
MINALE TATTERSFIELD + PARTNERS
Richmond, Surrey, United Kingdom
creative director
BRIAN TATTERSFIELD
designer
PAUL ASTBURY
client
LONDON TRANSPORT

creative firm
TEAMWORK DESIGN LTD.
Hong Kong
design director
GARY TAM
senior designer
JOEL ONG
designers
ALEX CHAN, IVY WONG
client
PEAK TRAMWAYS CO. LTD.

creative firm
BLUMLEIN ASSOCIATES, INC.
Greenvale, New York
exhibit designers
WILLIAM ARBIZU, CHRIS LEONARDI
designer
MICHAEL KASE
client
SONY ELECTRONICS

creative firm
LORENC + YOO DESIGN
Roswell, Georgia
design director
JAN LORENC
project manager
DAVID PARK
designer
STEVE McCALL
client
FIRST UNION MANAGEMENT JOURNEY COMMUNICATIONS

creative firm
 MICHAEL COURTNEY DESIGN
 Seattle, Washington
art director, designer
 MICHAEL COURTNEY
photographer
 J.F. HOUSEL
client
 ROSCHE SERVICES

creative firm
 SQUARE ONE DESIGN
 Grand Rapids, Michigan
art directors
 MIKE GORMAN, LIN VERMEULEN
designer
 GRANT CARMICHAEL
fabrication
 BOB WARDLOW
client
 HERMAN MILLER, INC.

15

creative firm
    DESIGN GUYS
    Minneapolis, Minnesota
art director
    STEVEN SIKORA
designers
    DAWN SELG, AMY KIRKPATRICK
client
    TARGET STORES

creative firm
    DESIGN GUYS
    Minneapolis, Minnesota
art director
    STEVEN SIKORA
creative director
    LYNETTE ERICKSON-SIKORA
designer
    GARY PATCH
client
    TARGET STORES

creative firm
ELLEN BRUSS DESIGN
Denver, Colorado
designers
ELLEN BRUSS,
CHARLES CARPENTER,
JASON C. OTERO
client
CHERRY CREEK SHOPPING CENTER
(RACE FOR THE CURE)

creative firm
SABINGRAFIK, INC.
Carlsbad, California
art directors
LAURA BECKER
marketing director
CHERI WALKER
illustrator
TRACY SABIN
client
UNIVERSITY TOWNE CENTRE

ILLUSTRATION

DON * IVAN * PUNCHATZ
ILLUSTRATION
A * TEXAS * TRADITION

DON IVAN PUNCHATZ RETROSPECTIVE EXHIBITION • FEBRUARY 15 THROUGH MARCH 10 • TCU MOUDY EXHIBITION HALL

creative firm
  WET PAPER BAG GRAPHIC DESIGN
  Fort Worth, Texas
art director, designer, copywriter
  LEWIS GLASER
illustrator
  DON IVAN PUNCHATZ
client
  TCU ART DEPARTMENT

creative firm
  CHAVDA GRAPIX
  Oviedo, Florida
designer
  JAGDISH J. CHAVDA
client
  UNIVERSITY OF CENTRAL FLORIDA PRESIDENT'S OFFICE

creative firm
SELFRIDGE DESIGN, LTD.
Plainfield, Illinois
art director
SAM TAKAHASHI
illustrator
M.C. SELFRIDGE
client
NORTHEASTERN UNIVERSITY, BOSTON

creative firm
CHAVDA GRAPIX
Oviedo, Florida
designer
JAGDISH J. CHAVDA
client
UNIVERSITY OF CENTRAL FLORIDA PRESIDENT'S OFFICE

creative firm
  GEORGOPULOS
  West Chester, Pennsylvania
designer
  JONATHAN GEORGOPULOS
client
  NEOS/SUNGARD PRODUCT

creative firm
  SABINGRAFIK, INC.
  Carlsbad, California
art director
  BLAIZE MEKINNA
illustrator
  TRACY SABIN
client
  SCRIPPS INSTITUTE OF OCEANOGRAPHY

creative firm
 SABINGRAFIK, INC.
 Carlsbad, California
art director
 JOHN BALL
illustrator
 TRACY SABIN
client
 INTEL

creative firm
 SELFRIDGE DESIGN, LTD.
 Plainfield , Illinois
illustrator
 M.C. SELFRIDGE
client
 SELFRIDGE DESIGN, LTD.

creative firm
  SABINGRAFIK, INC.
  Carlsbad, California
art director
  CHARLIE CARR
illustrator
  TRACY SABIN
client
  SANTANA MANAGEMENT

creative firm
  SABINGRAFIK, INC.
  Carlsbad, California
art directors
  TOM BURKE, TOM MORRISON
illustrator
  TRACY SABIN
client
  MORRISON AND BURKE

creative firm
  SABINGRAFIK, INC.
  Carlsbad, California
art directors
  TOM BURKE, TOM MORRISON
illustrator
  TRACY SABIN
client
  MORRISON AND BURKE

creative firm
  MIRES DESIGN
  Carlsbad, California
art director
  JOHN BALL
illustrator
  TRACY SABIN
client
  HARCOURT AND COMPANY

creative firm
  MIRES DESIGN
  Carlsbad, California
art director
  JOHN BALL
illustrator
  TRACY SABIN
client
  HARCOURT AND COMPANY

creative firm
  McELVENEY + PALOZZI DESIGN GROUP, INC.
  Rochester, New York
art director
  MATT GARRITY
creative director
  STEPHEN PALOZZI
illustrator
  MIKE JOHNSON
client
  GENESEE BREWING CO.

creative firm
  McELVENEY + PALOZZI DESIGN GROUP, INC.
  Rochester, New York
art director
  MATT GARRITY
creative director
  STEPHEN PALOZZI
illustrator
  NICK WOYCIESJES
client
  GENESEE BREWING CO.

creative firm
  McELVENEY + PALOZZI DESIGN GROUP, INC.
  Rochester, New York
art director
  MATT GARRITY
creative director
  STEPHEN PALOZZI
illustrators
  MIKE JOHNSON, NICK WOYCIESJES
client
  GENESEE BREWING CO.

creative firm
  CYD DESIGN
  Milwaukee, Wisconsin
designer
  CORY DEWALT
illustrator
  DAVID WELKY
client
  STARK IMAGES

creative firm
BIG CAT MARKETING COMMUNICATIONS
Colorado Springs, Colorado
illustrator
PATER SPEACH
client
STERLING RESOURCES, INC.

creative firm
RAY BESSERDIN, PAPER SCULPTURE ARTIST
Mentone, Australia
art director
HENRY BIRMAN
designer
RAY BESSERDIN
client
BOOMERANG PAPER

creative firm
SELFRIDGE DESIGN, LTD.
Plainfield, Illinois
illustrator
M.C. SELFRIDGE
client
SELFRIDGE DESIGN, LTD.

creative firm
  RAY BESSERDIN, PAPER SCULPTURE ARTIST
    Mentone, Australia
art director, designer
  RAY BESSERDIN
client
  RAY BESSERDIN

creative firm
  RAY BESSERDIN, PAPER SCULPTURE ARTIST
    Mentone, Australia
art director
  REBECCA LLOYD
designer
  RAY BESSERDIN
client
  BRW MEDIA/CPA MAGAZINE

creative firm
  ESTUDIO RAY
   Phoenix, Arizona
art directors
  CHRISTINE & JOE RAY
designers
  CHRISTINE RAY, JOE RAY, LESLIE LINK
illustrator
  JOE RAY
typographer
  LESLIE LINK
client
  AIGA ARIZONA

creative firm
  THE RIORDON DESIGN GROUP, INC.
   Oakville, Canada
illustrators
  DAN WHEATON, DAVID BATHURST
client
  FCB DIRECT/IBM B.A.N.D.

creative firm
  THE RIORDON DESIGN GROUP, INC.
  Oakville, Canada
creative director
  DAN WHEATON,
illustrator
  SHARON PORTER
client
  AETNA HEALTH

creative firm
  THE RIORDON DESIGN GROUP, INC.
  Oakville, Canada
art director
  CLAUDE DUMDULIN
illustrators
  DAN WHEATON, SHARON PORTER
client
  FCB DIRECT/IBM (JAVA CAMPAIGN)

creative firm
  SABINGRAFIK, INC.
  Carlsbad, California
art director
  SCOTT MIRES
illustrator
  TRACY SABIN
client
  INTEL

creative firm
  SABINGRAFIK, INC.
  Carlsbad, California
art director
  JOHN BALL
illustrator
  TRACY SABIN
client
  ANACOMP, INC.

creative firm
TELMET DESIGN ASSOCIATES
Toronto, Canada
design/production
MARKO BARAC
designer
TILT TELMET
client
CANADA POST CORPORATION

creative firm
TELMET DESIGN ASSOCIATES
Toronto, Canada
designer
TILT TELMET
illustrator
GARY LAY
design assistant
MARKO BARAC
client
CANADA POST CORPORATION

167

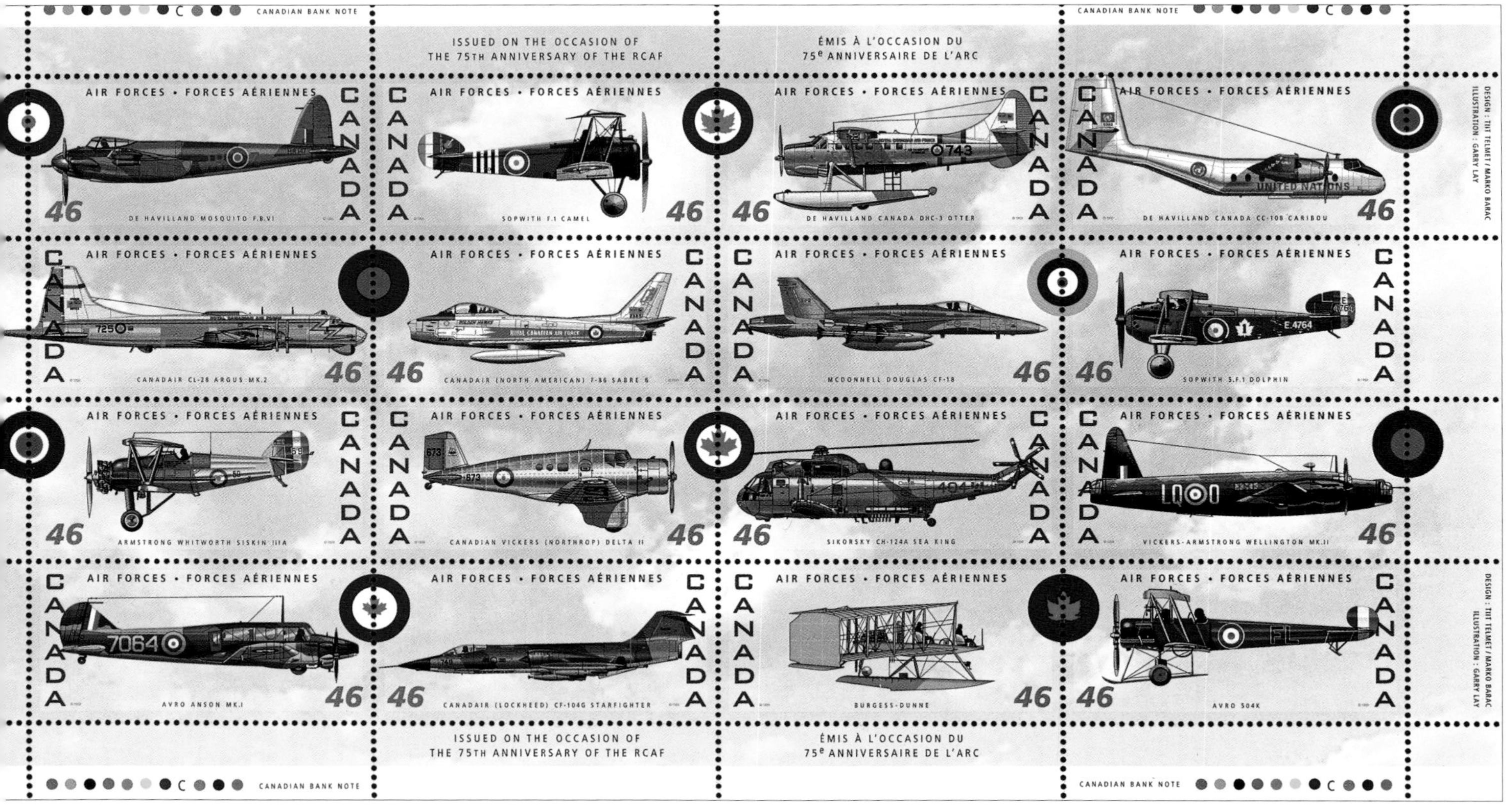

creative firm
RAY BESSERDIN, PAPER SCULPTURE ARTIST
Mentone, Australia
art director
SQEEZ D'SOUZA
designer
RAY BESSERDIN
client
AUSTRALIAN GEOGRAPHIC MAGAZINE

creative firm
RAY BESSERDIN, PAPER SCULPTURE ARTIST
Mentone, Australia
art director, designer
RAY BESSERDIN
client
MacQUARIE BANK LTD

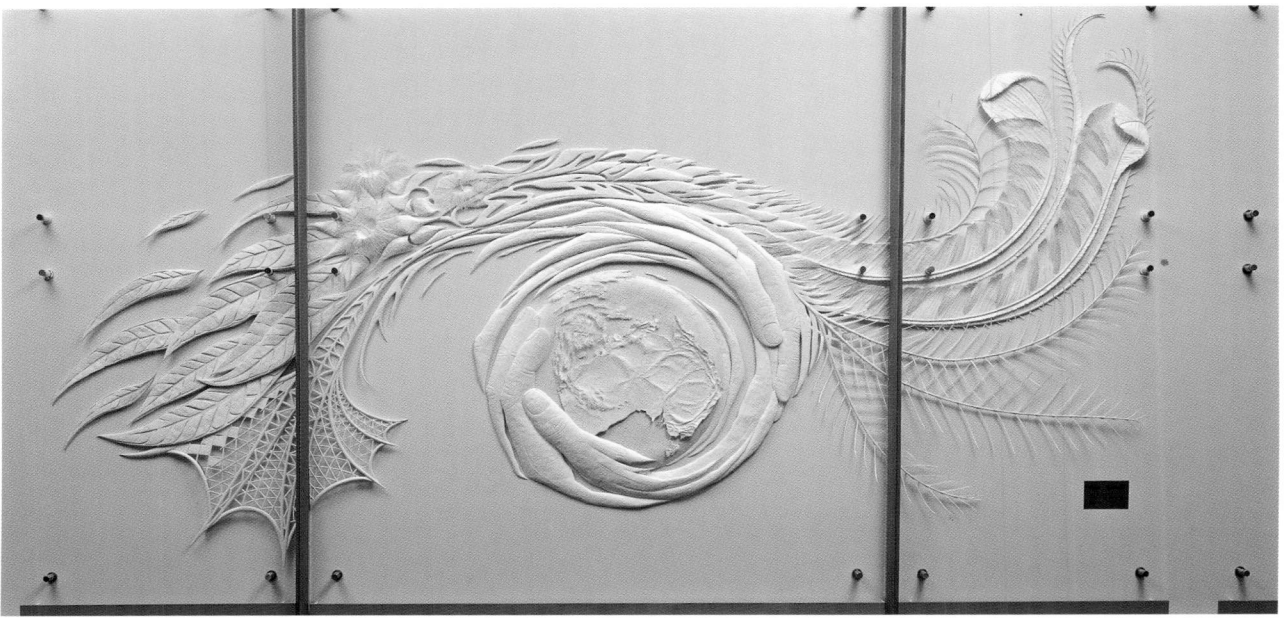

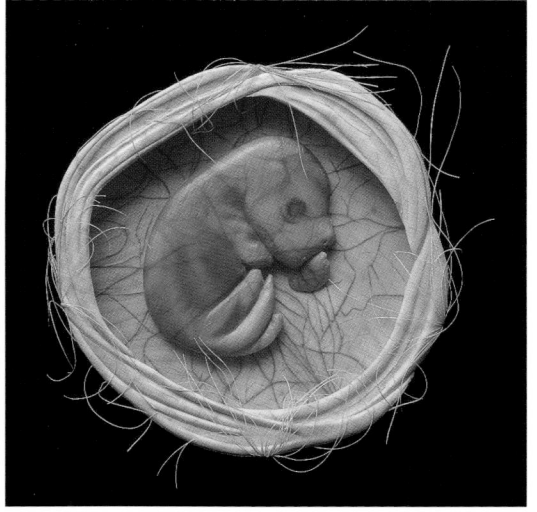

creative firm
    RAY BESSERDIN, PAPER SCULPTURE ARTIST
    Mentone, Australia
art director
    KARL ERIKOVIC
designer
    RAY BESSERDIN
client
    CROW MEDIA/TECHNICAL GROUP N.T.

creative firm
    RAY BESSERDIN, PAPER SCULPTURE ARTIST
    Mentone, Australia
art director
    KARL ERIKOVIC
designer
    RAY BESSERDIN
client
    CROW MEDIA/TECHNICAL GROUP N.T.

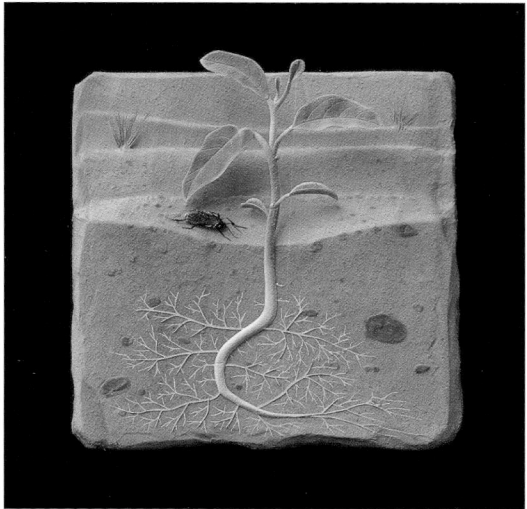

creative firm
  TANGRAM STRATEGIC DESIGN
  Novara, Italy
art director, designer
  ANTONELLA TREVISAN
creative director
  ENRICO SEMPI
illustrator
  SERGIO QUARANTA
client
  STANDA

creative firm
  TANGRAM STRATEGIC DESIGN
  Novara, Italy
art directors
  ANTONELLA TREVISAN, ENRICO SEMPI
designer
  ANTONELLA TREVISAN
creative director
  ENRICO SEMPI
illustrator
  SERGIO QUARANTA
client
  E. VISHARA DI A. BIFFI ("SUGHI D'AUTORE)

creative firm
  HORNALL ANDERSON DESIGN WORKS
  Seattle, Washington
art directors
  JACK ANDERSON, JANA NISHI
designers
  JANA NISHI, BRUCE BRANSON-MEYER
client
  MOCAFE

creative firm
  LMS DESIGN
  Stamford, Connecticut
designers
  RICHARD SHEAR, ALEX WILLIAMS
client
  BC-USA

creative firm
  McELVENEY + PALOZZI DESIGN GROUP, INC.
  Rochester, New York
art director
  GRETCHEN BYE
creative director
  STEPHEN PALOZZI
client
  CANANDAIGUA WINE CO.

creative firm
  ANTISTA FAIRCLOUGH
  Atlanta, Georgia
art directors
  TOM ANTISTA, THOMAS FAIRCLOUGH
designers
  TOM ANTISTA, THOMAS FAIRCLOUGH, JAMEY WAGNER
client
  ANHEUSER, BUSCH, INC.

creative firm
  McELVENEY + PALOZZI DESIGN GROUP, INC.
  Rochester, New York
art director
  DENNIS DeSILVA
creative directors
  STEPHEN PALOZZI, WILLIAM McELVENEY
client
  CANANDAIGUA WINE CO.

creative firm
  BOLDRONI FICCARDI
  Mendoza, Argentina
art director
  VICTOR BOLDRINI
designer
  LEONARDO FICCARDI
client
  VINITERRA WINERY

CLEARDATA.NET

CLASSIC CREST

CLEARDATA.NET

5956 Sherry Lane   Dallas, TX 75225

CLEARDATA.NET

CLEARDATA.NET

John D. Hartley, Jr.
Executive V. P. Finance, Treasurer
5956 Sherry Lane   Dallas, TX 75225
phone 214 750 1595 ext 200
fax 214 750 7696
email john.hartley@cleardata.net

creative firm
 AFTER HOURS CREATIVE
 Phoenix, Arizona
client
 CLEARDATA.NET

creative firm
 JAMES ROBIE DESIGN ASSOCIATES
 Los Angeles, California
design director, designer
 WAYNE FUJITA
creative director
 JAMES ROBIE
client
 BECKSON DESIGN ASSOCIATES

B   D
B   D   A
B   D
B   D
B   D
A
A

Beckson Design Associates 933 North La Brea Ave. Suite 300 Los Angeles, CA 90038

A

Beckson Design Associates

Beckson Design Associates 933 North La Brea Ave. Suite 300 Los Angeles, CA 90038   323.874.6144 Fax 323.874.6148 info@becksondesign.com

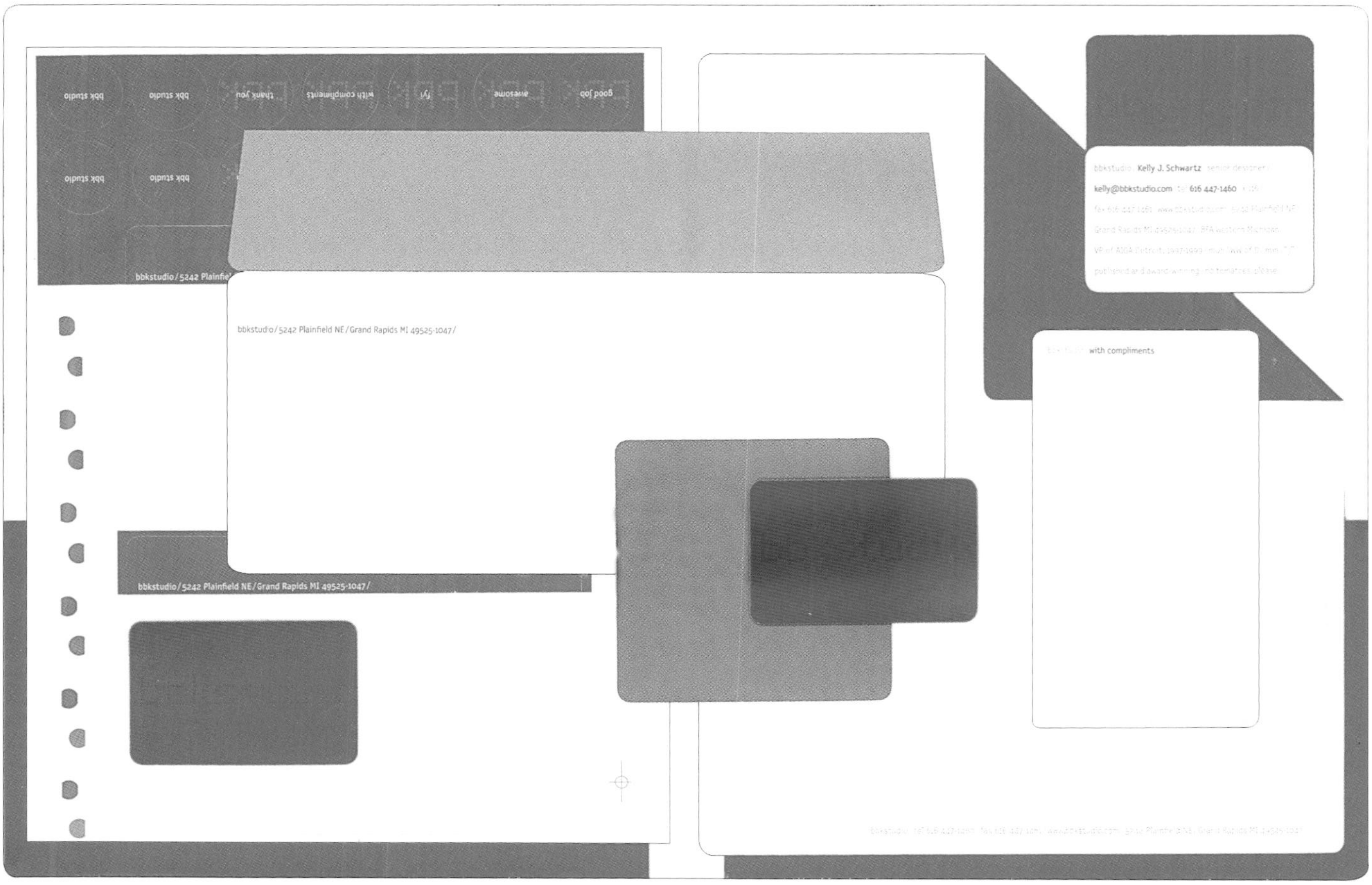

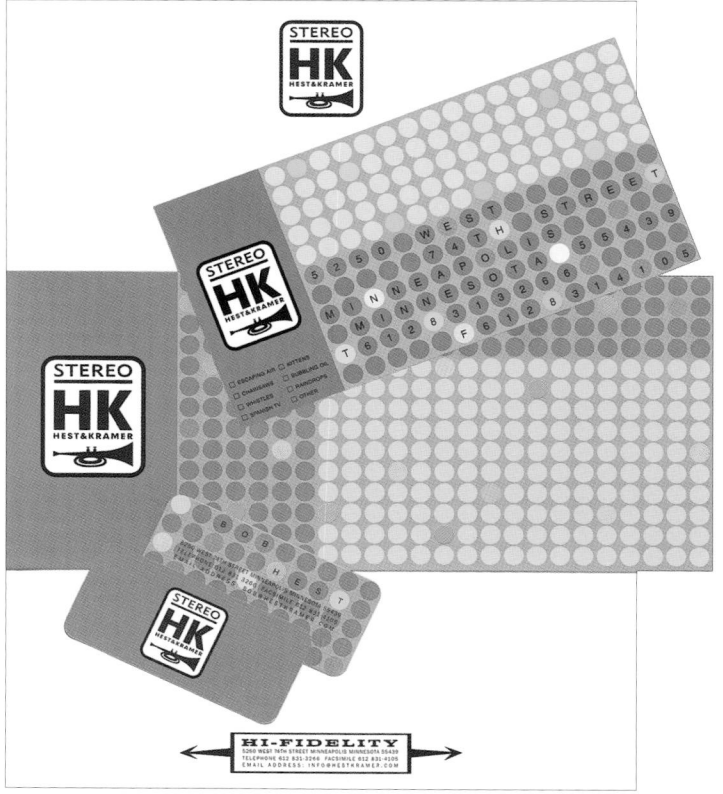

creative firm
  BBK STUDIO INC.
  Grand Rapids, Michigan
creative director, designer
  YANG KIM
client
  BBK STUDIO INC.

creative firm
  DESIGN GUYS
  Minneapolis, Minnesota
art director
  STEVEN SIKORA
designer
  SCOTT THARES
client
  HEST & KRAMER

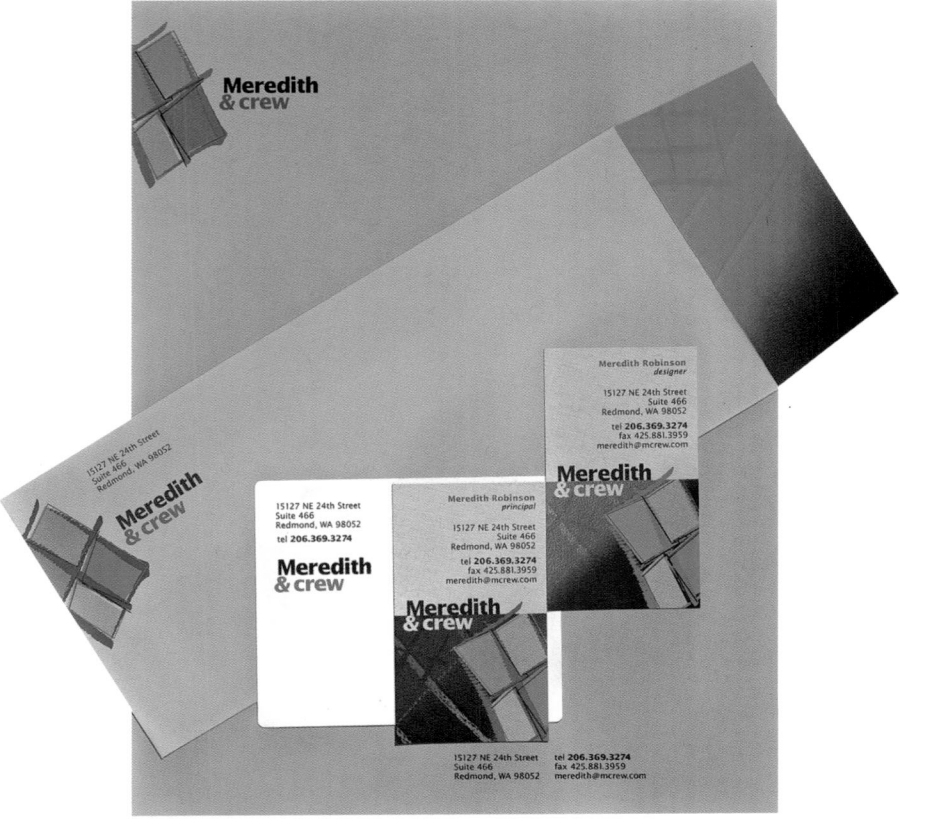

creative firm
  BELYEA
  Seattle, Washington
art director
  PATRICIA BELYEA
designer, illustrator
  NAOMI MURPHY
client
  MEREDITH & CREW

creative firm
  McELVENEY + PALOZZI DESIGN GROUP, INC.
  Rochester, New York
art director
  ELLEN JOHNSON
creative director
  WILLIAM McELVENEY
client
  THE LODGE AT WOODCLIFF

GOLfOTO
The Source for Golf Photography
2116 W. Willow • Enid, OK 73703
Tel 405.234.8284 • Fax 405.234.8335 • E-mail golfoto@ionet.net • www.golfoto.com
Mike Klemme

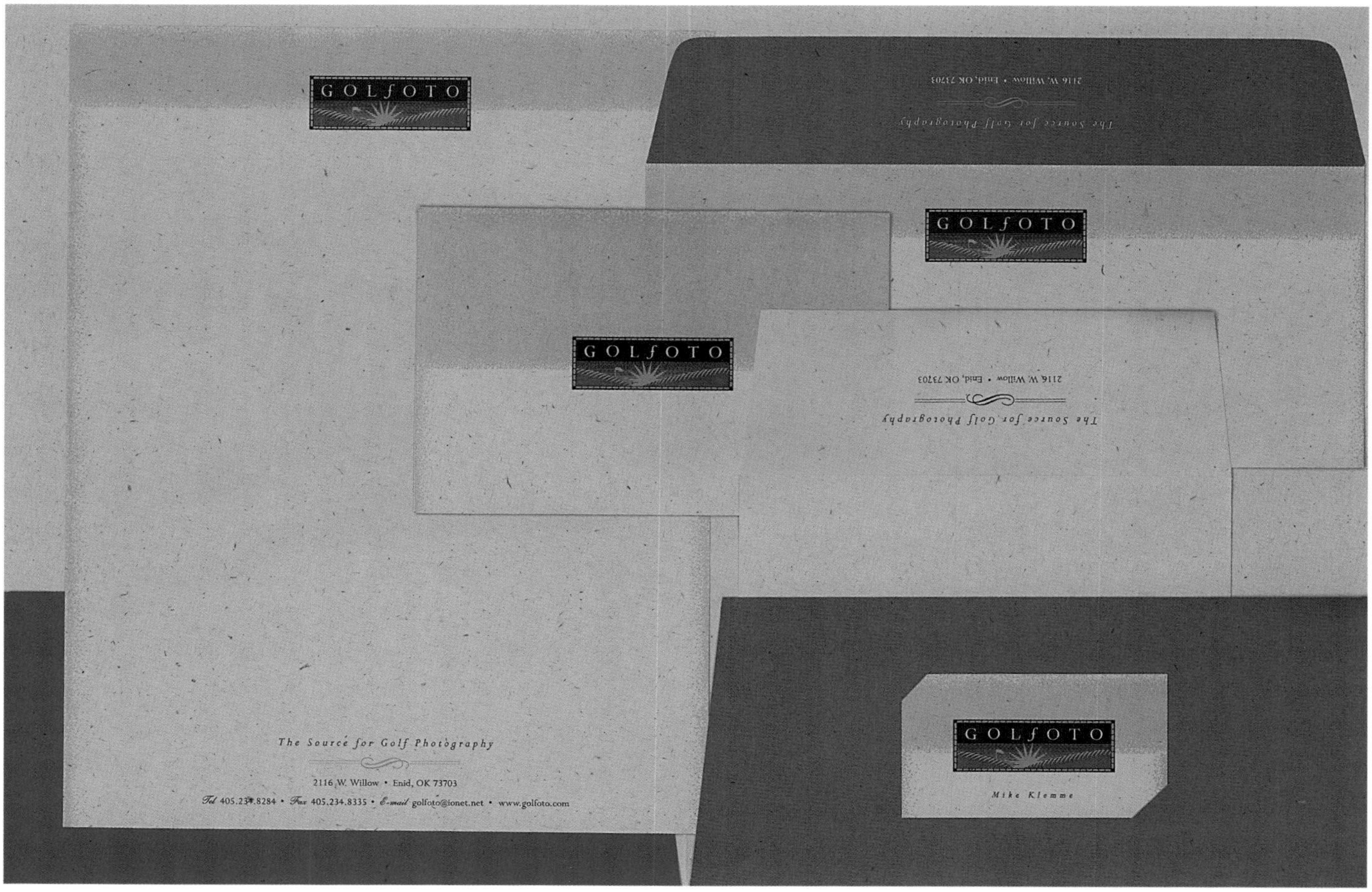

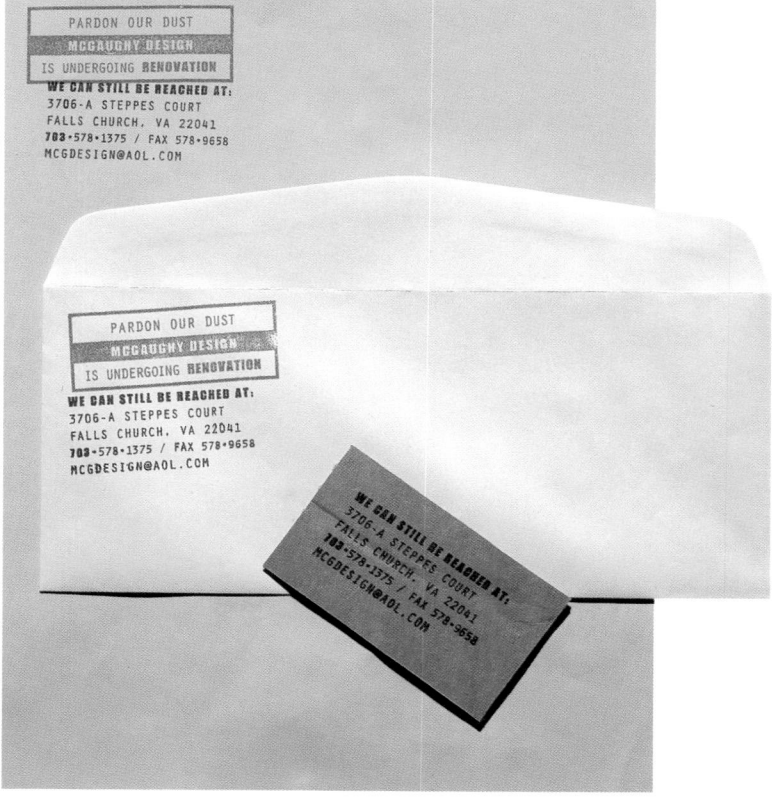

creative firm
GRETEMAN GROUP
Wichita, Kansas
art director, creative director
SONIA GRETEMAN
designer
JAMES STRANGE
client
GOLFOTO

PARDON OUR DUST
McGAUGHY DESIGN
IS UNDERGOING RENOVATION
WE CAN STILL BE REACHED AT:
3706-A STEPPES COURT
FALLS CHURCH, VA 22041
703•578•1375 / FAX 578•9658
MCGDESIGN@AOL.COM

creative firm
McGAUGHY DESIGN
Falls Church, Virginia
designer
MALCOLM McGAUGHY
client
McGAUGHY DESIGN

creative firm
   H2D
   Milwaukee, Wisconsin
creative director
   JOSEPH HAUSCH
client
   CHRISTINE KEMPTER

Surface Design Association PO Box 300286 Kansas City, MO 64130 816.836.0913 Fax 816.254.8521 wetmore@earthlink.net

Surface Design Association PO Box 300286 Kansas City, MO 64130

creative firm
   MULLER + CO.
   Kansas City, Missouri
creative executive officer
   JOHN MULLER
designer
   JEFF MILLER
client
   SURFACE DESIGN ASSOCIATION

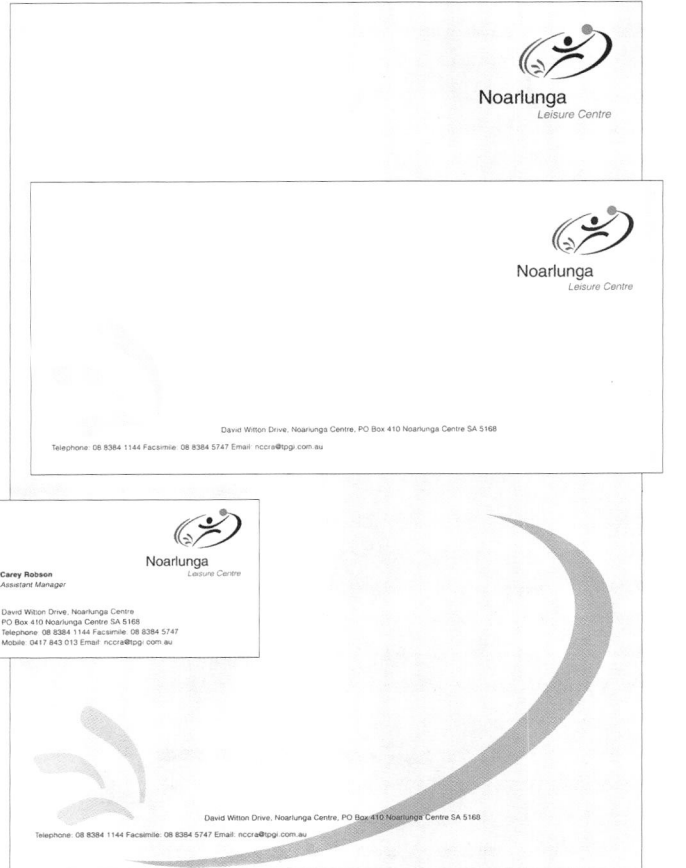

David Witton Drive, Noarlunga Centre, PO Box 410 Noarlunga Centre SA 5168

Telephone: 08 8384 1144 Facsimile: 08 8384 5747 Email: nccra@tpgi.com.au

Carey Robson
Assistant Manager

David Witton Drive, Noarlunga Centre
PO Box 410 Noarlunga Centre SA 5168
Telephone: 08 8384 1144 Facsimile: 08 8384 5747
Mobile: 0417 843 013 Email: nccra@tpgi.com.au

David Witton Drive, Noarlunga Centre, PO Box 410 Noarlunga Centre SA 5168

Telephone: 08 8384 1144 Facsimile: 08 8384 5747 Email: nccra@tpgi.com.au

creative firm
  BUTLER KEMP DESIGN
    North Adelaide, Australia
art director
  DEREK BUTLER
designer
  JULIE KEMP
client
  NOARUINGA LEISURE CENTRE

creative firm
  FIFTH STREET DESIGN
    Berkeley, California
designers
  J. CLIFTON MEEK,
  BRENTON BECK
client
  INDIAN ROCK IMAGESETTING

IRI
Indian Rock Imagesetting

professional digital imaging & prepress

IRI
Indian Rock Imagesetting
2115 Fourth Street
Berkeley
California
94710

(510) 843-8973

2115 Fourth Street
Berkeley
California
94710
fax (510) 843-4991
data (510) 843-1527
www.indianrock.com

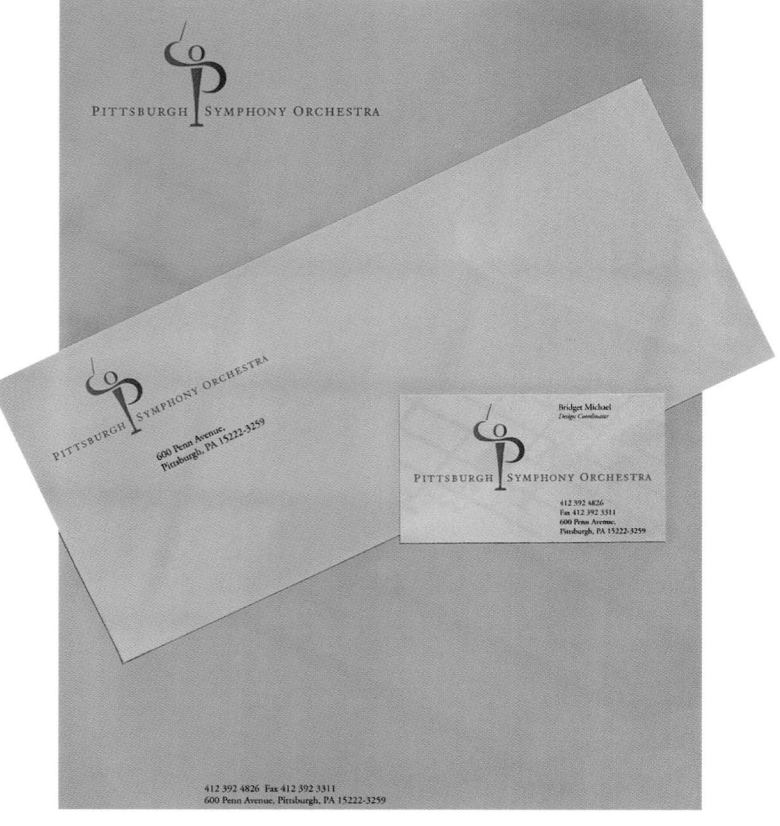

PITTSBURGH SYMPHONY ORCHESTRA

PITTSBURGH SYMPHONY ORCHESTRA
600 Penn Avenue,
Pittsburgh, PA 15222-3259

Bridget Michael
Design Coordinator

PITTSBURGH SYMPHONY ORCHESTRA
412 392 4826
Fax 412 392 3311
600 Penn Avenue,
Pittsburgh, PA 15222-3259

412 392 4826 Fax 412 392 3311
600 Penn Avenue, Pittsburgh, PA 15222-3259

creative firm
  ROBERT MEYERS DESIGN
  Fairlawn, Ohio
designer
  ROBERT MEYERS
client
  PITTSBURGH SYMPHONY ORCHESTRA

creative firm
  CHAVDA GRAPIX
  Oviedo, Florida
designer
  JAGDISH J. CHAVDA
client
  DR. DEENDAYAL KHANDELWAL, FOUNDER

creative firm
   RANDI WOLF DESIGN, INC.
   Glassboro, New Jersey
graphic designer
   RANDI WOLF
client
   RANDI WOLF DESIGN

creative firm
   ROBERT MEYERS DESIGN
   Fairlawn, Ohio
designer
   ROBERT MEYERS
client
   INDIANER COMPUTER CORPORATION

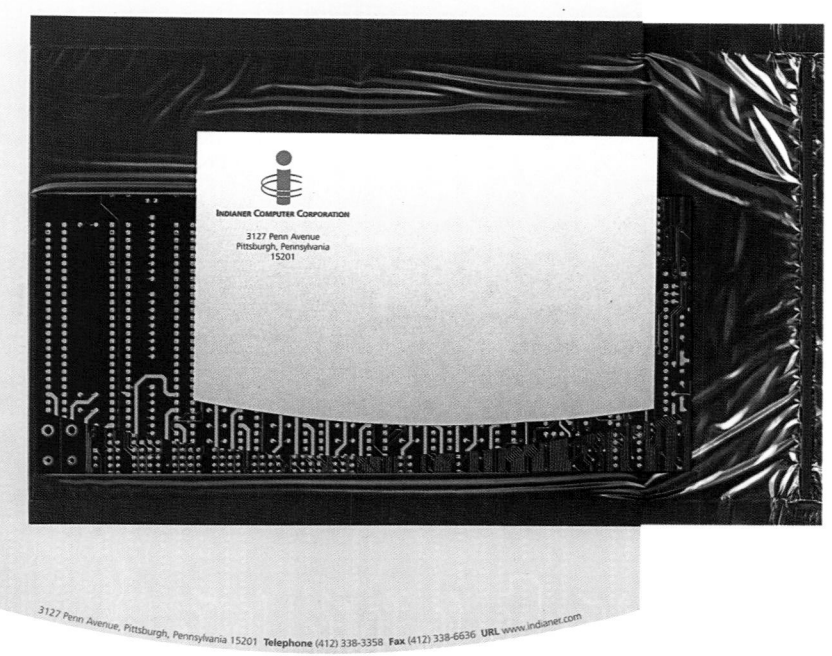

1779

creative firm
SQUIRES & COMPANY
Dallas, Texas
designer
CHRISTIE GROTHEIM
client
MacGUIFFIN MANAGEMENT

creative firm
GARDNER DESIGN
Wichita, Kansas
art director, designer
BILL GARDNER
client
GRIDER & CO.

creative firm
FROST DESIGN , LTD.
London, England
creative director
VINCE FROST
client
FOUR HUNDRED FILMS LTD

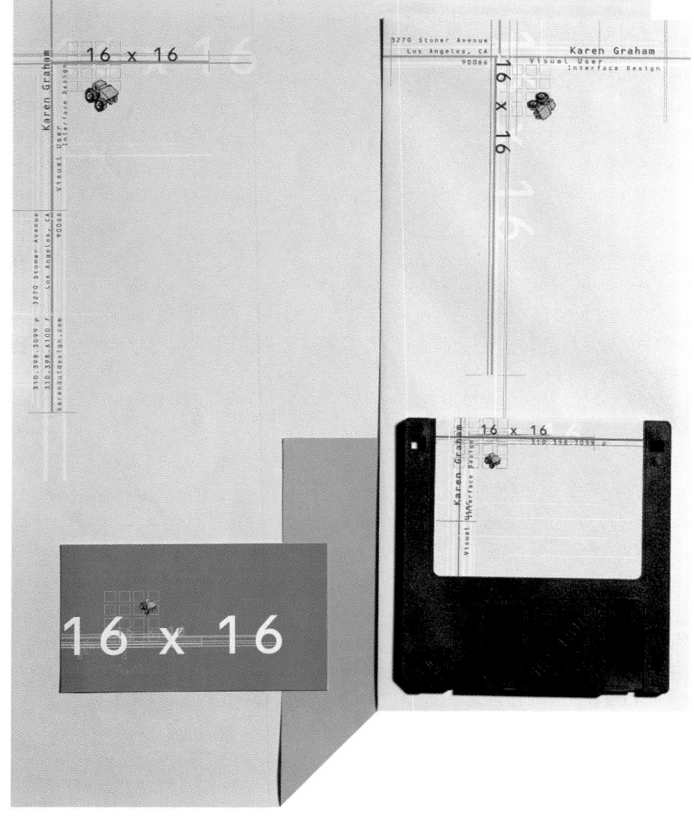

creative firm
5D STUDIO
Malibu, California
art director
JANE KOBAYASHI
designer
VICTOR CORPUZ
client
16 X 16

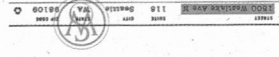

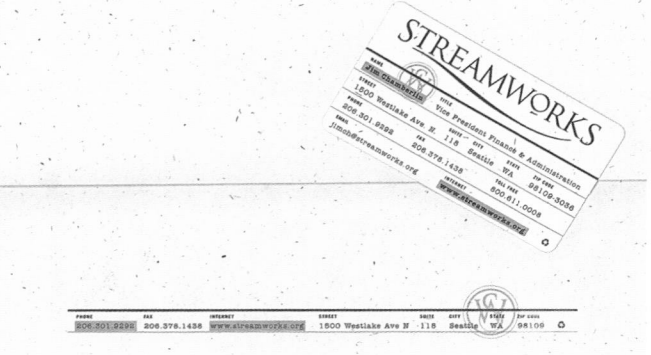

creative firm
   HORNALL ANDERSON DESIGN WORKS
   Seattle, Washington
art director
   JACK ANDERSON
designers
   JACK ANDERSON, BELINDA BOWLING, ANDREW SMITH
client
   STREAMWORKS

creative firm
   THE RIORDON DESIGN GROUP INC.
   Oakville, Canada
creative director, designer, illustrator
   DAN WHEATON
art director
   RIC RIORDON
client
   CHUCK GAMMAGE ANIMATION INC.

creative firm
MULLER + CO.
Kansas City, Missouri
creative executive officer
JOHN MULLER
designer
JEFF MILLER
client
REES MASILIONIS TURLEY ARCHITECTURE

REES

REES MASILIONIS TURLEY
ARCHITECTURE
THE STUDIO BUILDING 210 W. 19TH TERRACE
KANSAS CITY, MO 64108
WWW.REES-STUDIO.COM
816.842.1292
816.842.1878

REES

REES MASILIONIS TURLEY
ARCHITECTURE
THE STUDIO BUILDING 210 W. 19TH TERRACE, KANSAS CITY, MO 64108
WWW.REES-STUDIO.COM
816.842.1292
816.842.1878

creative firm
WAGES DESIGN
Atlanta, Georgia
designer
JOANNA TAK
client
PREVAIL

PREVAIL

PREVAIL
P.O. Box 100 Marietta, GA 30061-0100
THINKING SKILLS THAT FACILITATE INNOVATION

"Ideas are the
currency of success.
They separate you from
your competition."

– Dr. Edward deBono.

THINKING SKILLS THAT FACILITATE INNOVATION
TJ 770 426 1008 | FJ 770 426 8001

GRANT E. TODD president

PREVAIL
P.O. Box 100 Marietta, GA 30061-0100
TJ 770 426 1008 | FJ 770 426 8001 www.prevail.org

creative firm
    HORNALL ANDERSON DESIGN WORKS
    Seattle, Washington
art director
    JACK ANDERSON
designers
    JACK ANDERSON, HEIDI FAVOUR, MARGARET LONG
client
    MAHLUM ARCHITECTS

creative firm
    GARDNER DESIGN
    Wichita, Kansas
art directors
    BILL GARDNER, BRIAN MILLER
designer
    BRIAN MILLER
client
    BUTCHER & COOK'S

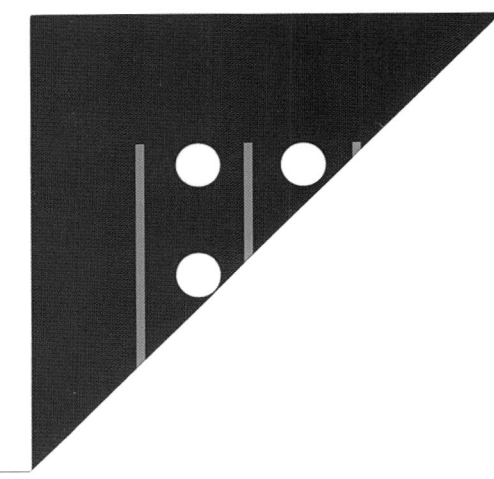

zero.zero five design
5354 Muirfield Court
Boulder Colorado 80301
p 303.530.5505
f 303.530.5504
zero.zerofivedesign@gte.net

creative firm
ELLEN BRUSS DESIGN
Denver, Colorado
designer
ELLEN BRUSS
client
0.05 DESIGN • DAVID NICKEL

creative firm
GARDNER DESIGN
Wichita, Kansas
art directors, designers
BILL GARDNER, BRIAN MILLER
client
TALLGRASS BEEF

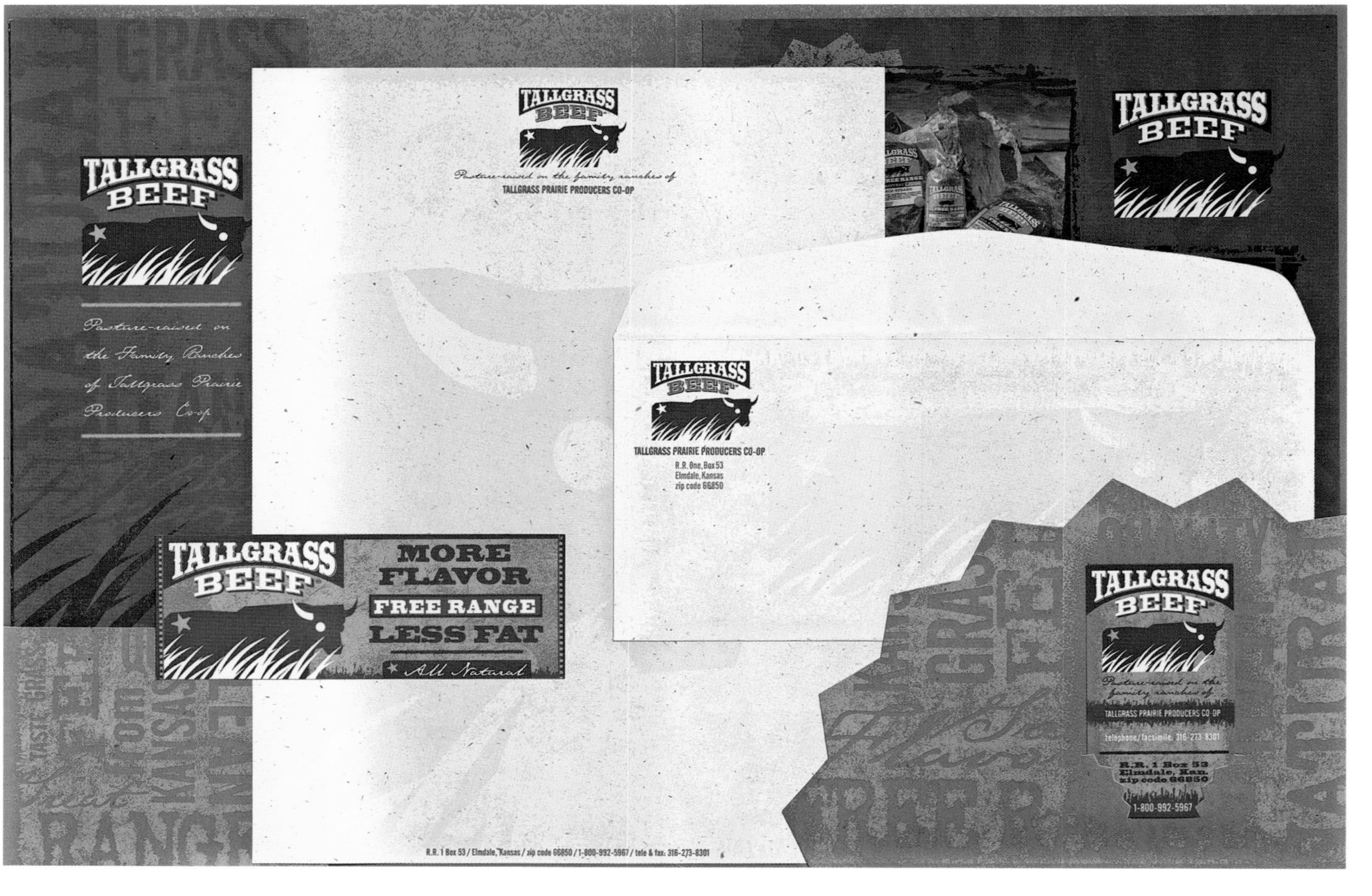

creative firm
  MULLER + CO.
    Kansas City, Missouri
creative director
    JOHN MULLER
art director, designer
    MARK VOSS
client
    KANSAS CITY BLUES + JAZZ FESTIVAL

creative firm
    RANDI WOLF DESIGN, INC.
      Glassboro, New Jersey
graphic designer, illustrator
      RANDI WOLF
client
      OLD STREET MARKET

OLD MARKET STREET

OLD MARKET STREET

OLD MARKET STREET

Lynn Martin Haren, Ph.D.
Chairman

OLD MARKET STREET

134 Arch Street
★
Philadelphia, PA
19106
★
Telephone
215-440-9166
Fax
215-440-0793

134
Arch
Street
★
Philadelphia
Pennsylvania
19106

134
Arch
Street
★
Philadelphia
Pennsylvania
19106
★
Telephone
215-440-9166
Fax
215-440-0793

OLD MARKET STREET

134
Arch
Street
★
Philadelphia, PA
19106
★
Telephone
215-440-9166
Fax
215-440-0793

creative firm
   NBBJ GRAPHIC DESIGN
   Seattle, Washington
designer
   PAM GILLIS
client
   NBBJ GRAPHIC DESIGN

Allbritton Art Institute
B A Y L O R   U N I V E R S I T Y

Allbritton Art Institute
B A Y L O R   U N I V E R S I T Y

Department of Art • 1401 S. University Parks Drive
P.O. Box 97263 • Waco, TX 76798-7263

Department of Art • 1401 S. University Parks Drive
P.O. Box 97263 • Waco, TX 76798-7263
(254) 710-6387 • Fax: (254) 710-1566

creative firm
   TERRY M. ROLLER, GRAPHIC DESIGNER
   Hewitt, Texas
designer
   TERRY M. ROLLER
client
   ALLBRITTON ART INSTITUTE

m

robert meyers
communication design and planning

The Times Building, 336 Fourth Avenue
Pittsburgh, Pennsylvania 15222

m

robert meyers
communication design
and planning

Jane Brooke Mason

m

robert meyers
communication design
and planning

412 391 1150
412 391 1120 Facsimile
The Times Building, 336 Fourth Avenue
Pittsburgh, Pennsylvania 15222

Telephone 412 391 1150

Facsimile 412 391 1120

nue, Pittsburgh, Pennsylvania 15222

creative firm
ROBERT MEYERS DESIGN
Fairlawn, Ohio
designer
ROBERT MEYERS
client
ROBERT MEYERS DESIGN

creative firm
JAMES ROBIE DESIGN ASSOCIATES
Los Angeles, California
design director
WAYNE FUJITA
designer
KAREN NAKATANI
client
JAMES ROBIE DESIGN ASSOCIATES

JAMES ROBIE DESIGN ASSOCIATES

JAMES ROBIE DESIGN ASSOCIATES

152-½ N. La Brea Avenue
Los Angeles, California
90036-2912

JAMES ROBIE
CREATIVE DIRECTOR

152-½ N. La Brea Avenue
Los Angeles, California
90036-2912

PHONE
323.939.7370 Ext.12
FAX
323.937.9728
E MAIL
jrobie@robie.com
WEB SITE
www.robie.com

JAMES ROBIE DESIGN ASSOCIATES

152-½ N. La Brea Avenue
Los Angeles, California
90036-2912

R

152-½ N. La Brea Avenue   Los Angeles, California   90036-2912   PHONE   FAX   E MAIL   WEB SITE
323.939.7370   323.937.9728   jrda@robie.com   www.robie.com

creative firm
  LOUEY/RUBINO DESIGN GROUP, INC.
    Santa Monica, California
designer
  ROBERT LOUEY
client
  CALIFORNIA COUNCIL ON ECONOMIC EDUCATION

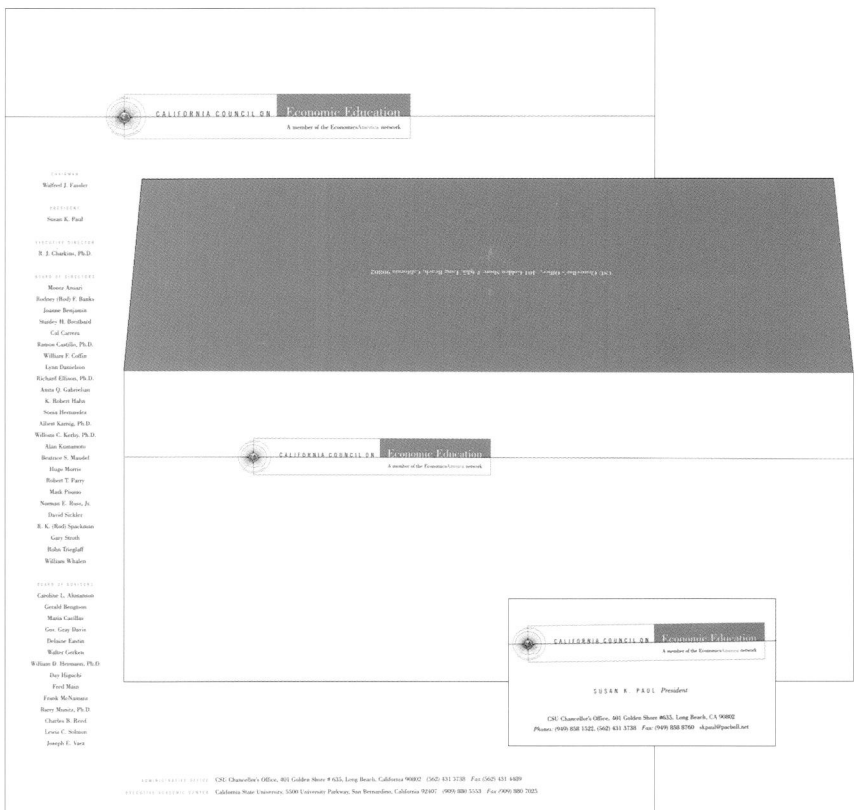

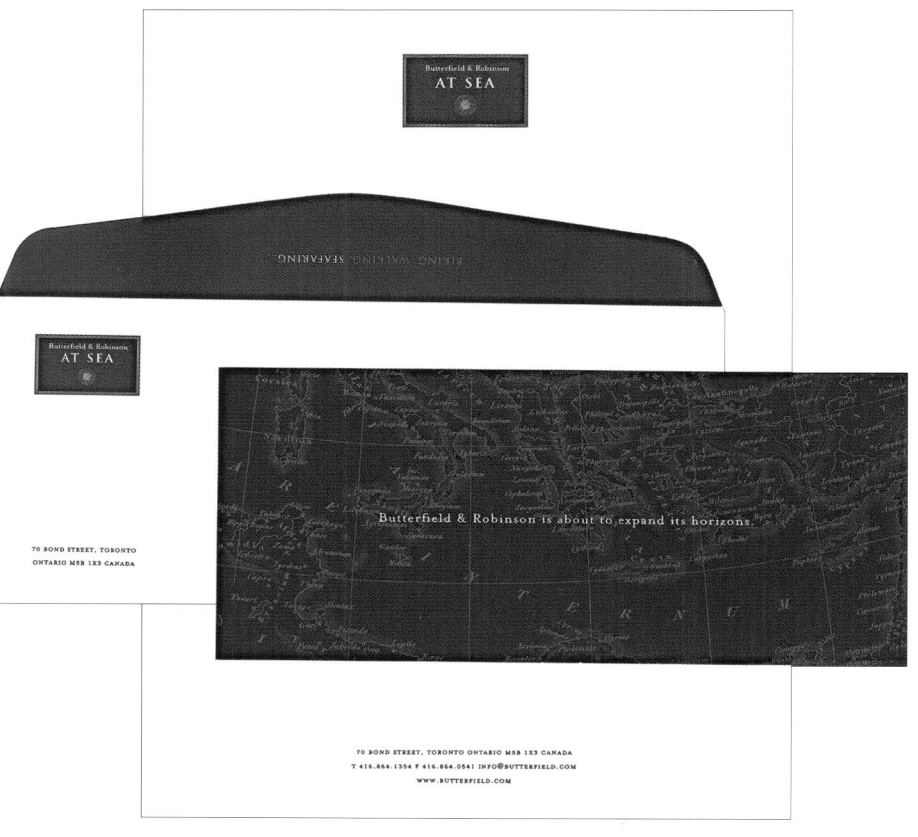

creative firm
  TEIKNA GRAPHIC DESIGN INC.
    Toronto, Canada
creative director, designer
  CLAUDIA NERI
production
  GARRY CAMPBELL
client
  BUTTERFIELD & ROBINSON

creative firm
FIFTH STREET DESIGN
Berkeley, California
designers
J. CLIFTON MEEK, BRENTON BECK
client
COMPUTER ACCESS SYSTEMS

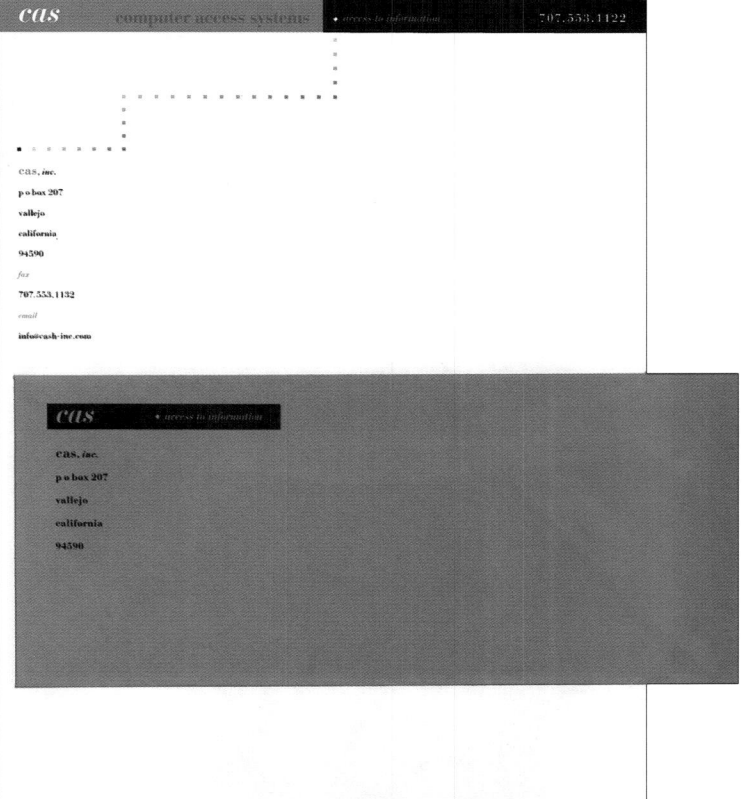

creative firm
GARDNER DESIGN
Wichita, Kansas
art director, designer
BRIAN MILLER
client
SCRIPT MASTER

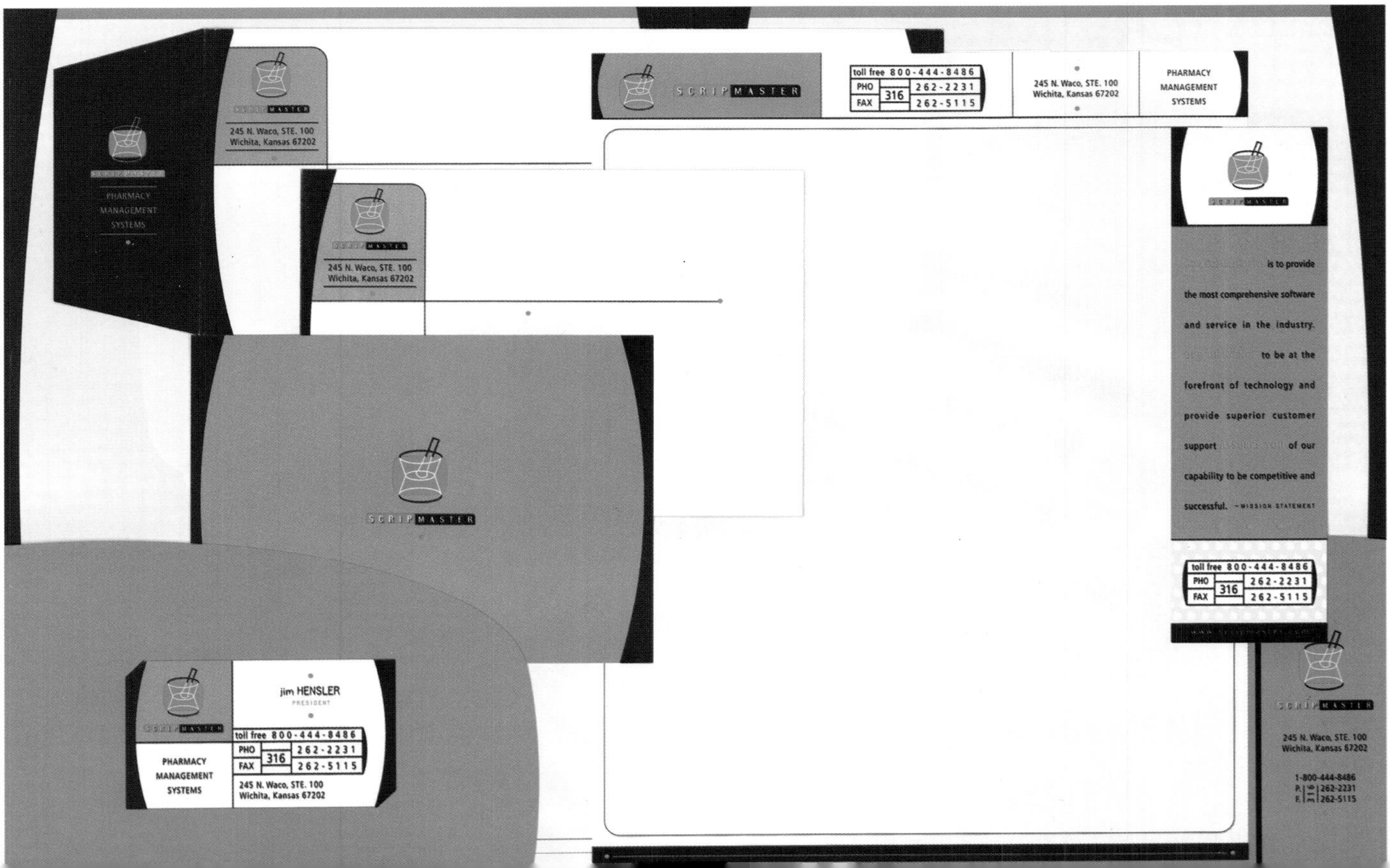

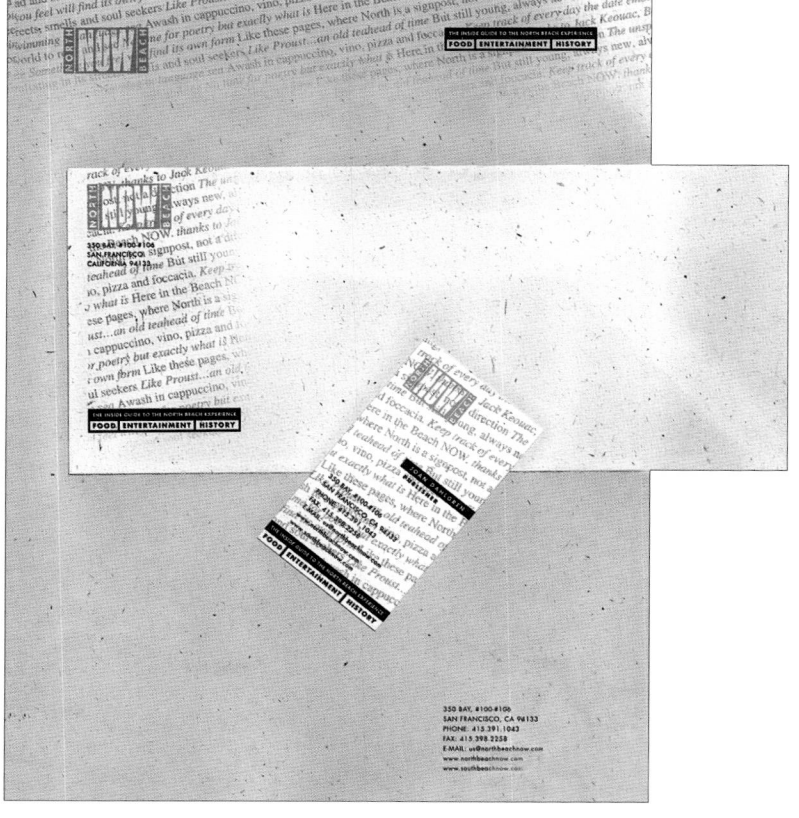

creative firm
  GRETEMAN GROUP
  Wichita, Kansas
creative director
  SONIA GRETEMAN
art directors
  SONIA GRETEMAN, JAMES STRANGE
designer
  JAMES STRANGE
client
  LAHAM DEVELOPMENT

creative firm
  BRUCE YELASKA DESIGN
  San Francisco, California
art director
  BRUCE YELASKA
designers
  BRUCE YELASKA, KELLY LOW
writer
  JOAN DAULGREN

creative firm
  HORNALL ANDERSON DESIGN WORKS
  Seattle, Washington
art director
  JACK ANDERSON
designers
  KATHY DALTON, HOLLY CRAVEN
client
  TRANSPOINT

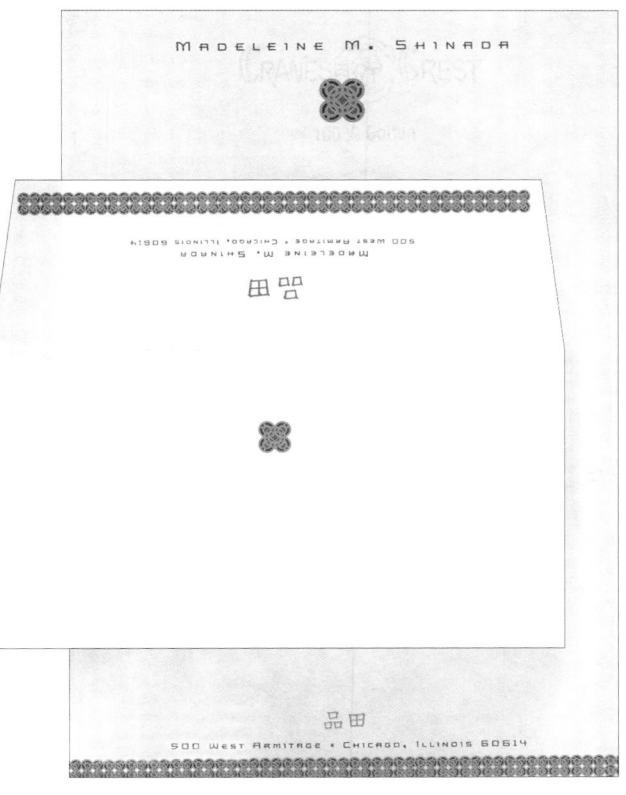

creative firm
  AIRE DESIGN COMPANY
  Tucson, Arizona
creative director
  CATHARINE M. KIM
art director
  SHARI RYKOWSKI
client
  MADELEINE M. SHINADA

creative firm
  AIRE DESIGN COMPANY
    Tucson, Arizona
creative director
  CATHARINE M. KIM
art director
  SHARI RYKOWSKI
client
  AIRE DESIGN COMPANY

creative firm
  SEWICKLEY GRAPHICS & DESIGN, INC.
    Sewickley, Pennsylvania
graphic designer
  STEVE CYPHER
client
  AEROLINK INTERNATIONAL

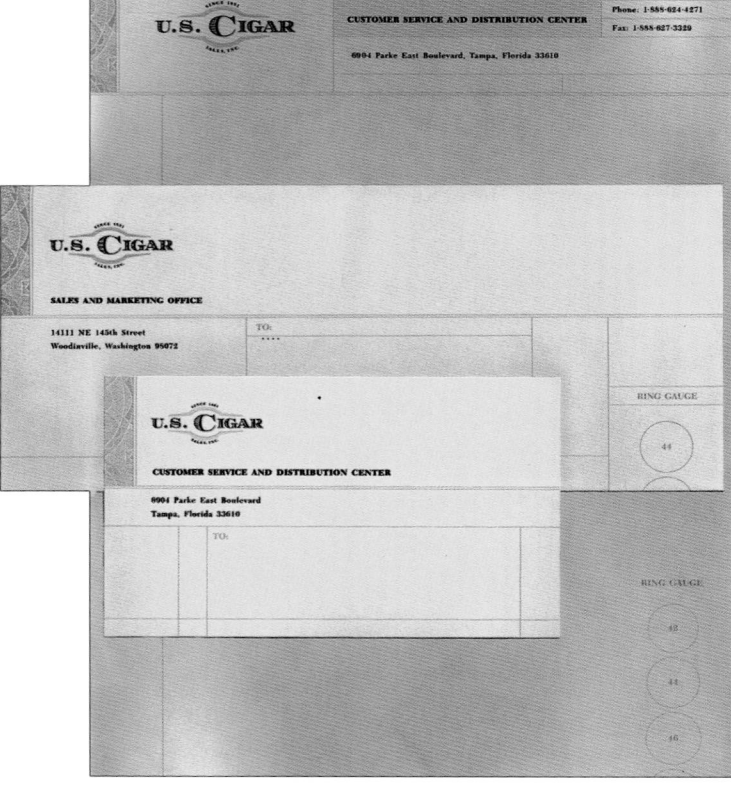

creative firm
  HORNALL ANDERSON DESIGN WORKS
  Seattle, Washington
art directors
  JACK ANDERSON, LARRY ANDERSON
designers
  JACK ANDERSON, LARRY ANDERSON, MARY HERMES,
  MIKE CALKINS, MICHAEL BRUGMAN
client
  U.S. CIGAR

creative firm
  JOHN K. LANDIS GRAPHIC DESIGN
  Kutztown, Pennsylvania
art director
  JOHN K. LANDIS
client
  BARBARA SCHULMAN, FIBER ARTIST

creative firm
JULIA TAM DESIGN
Palos Verdes, California
designer
JULIA TAM
client
JANE BROWN INTERIORS

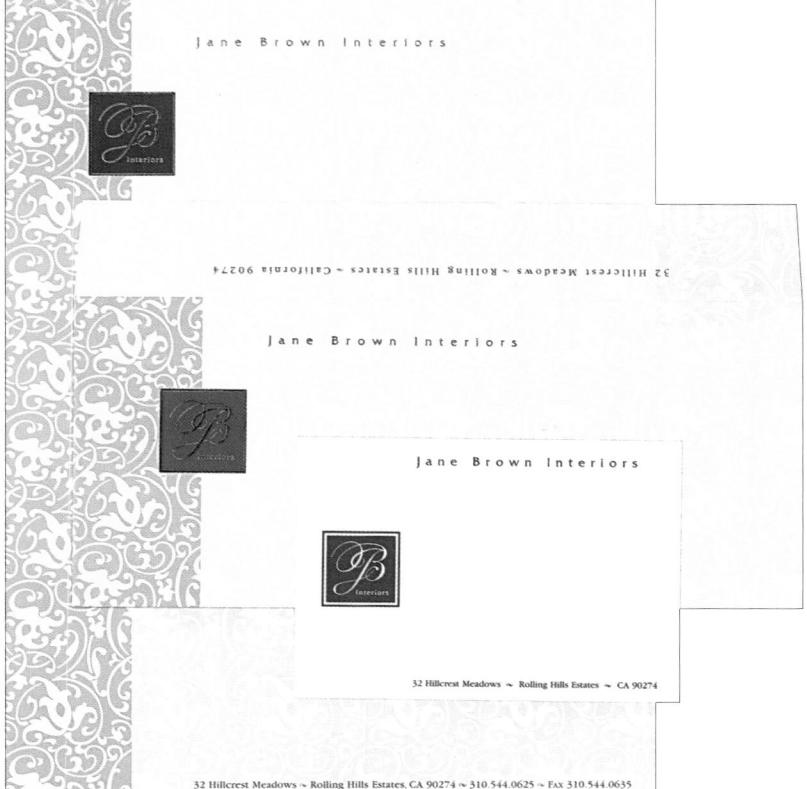

Jane Brown Interiors
interiors
32 Hillcrest Meadows ~ Rolling Hills Estates ~ California 90274
Jane Brown Interiors
Jane Brown Interiors
interiors
32 Hillcrest Meadows ~ Rolling Hills Estates ~ CA 90274
32 Hillcrest Meadows ~ Rolling Hills Estates, CA 90274 ~ 310.544.0625 ~ Fax 310.544.0635

creative firm
PARAGRAPHS
Chicago, Illinois
client
ORCHESTRA 33

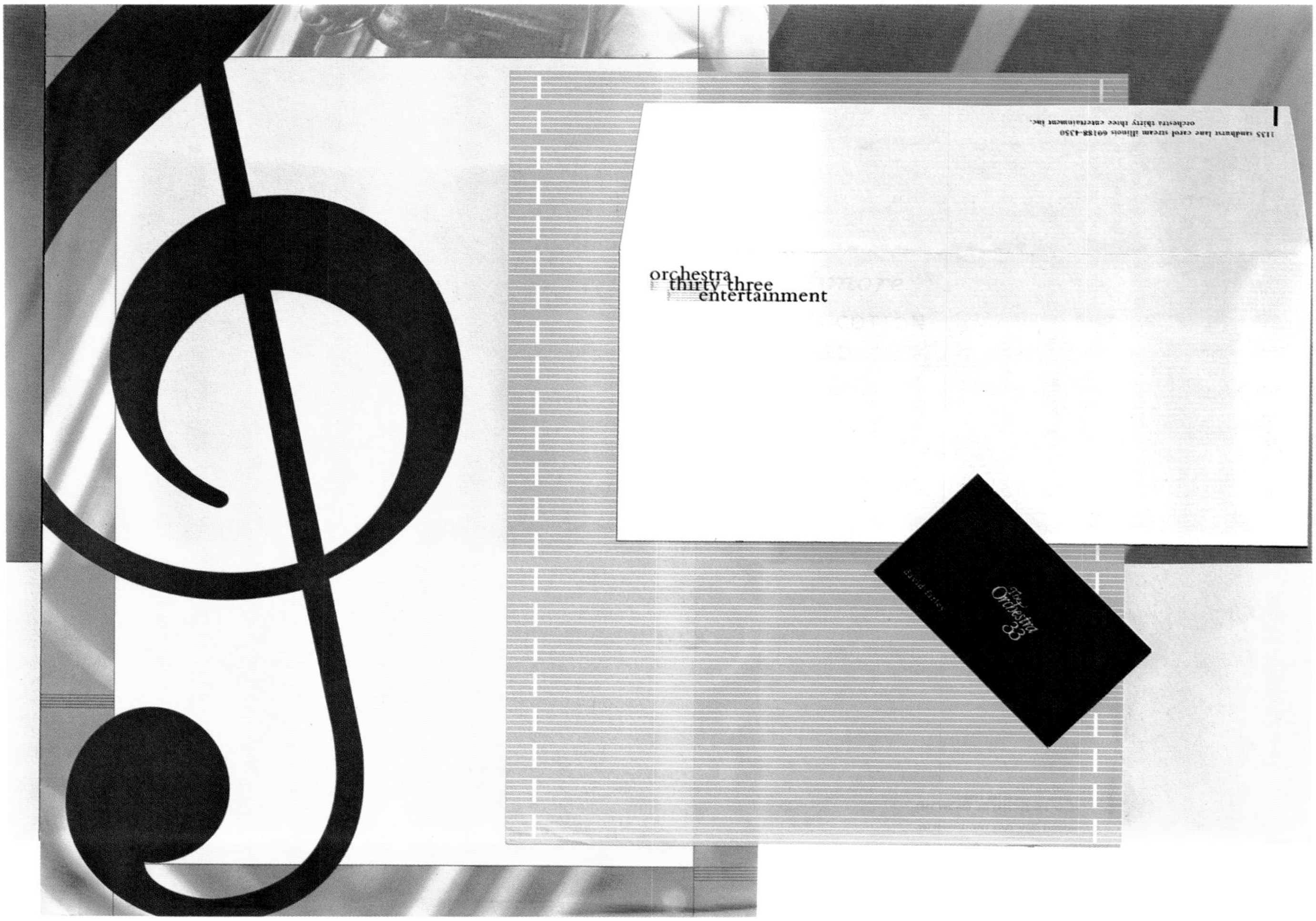
1135 sandhurst lane carol stream illinois 60188-4350
orchestra thirty three entertainment inc.
orchestra
thirty three
entertainment
Orchestra 33

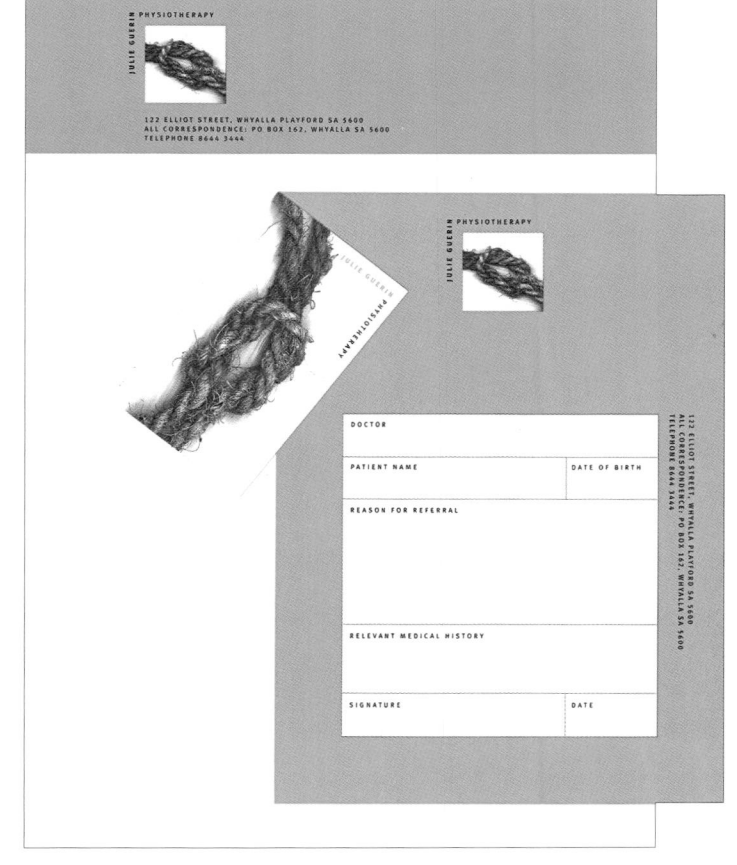

creative firm
BUTLER KEMP DESIGN
North Adelaide, Australia
designers
DEREK BUTLER, HELLEN KIPRIZLOGLOU
client
JULIE GUERIN PHYSIOTHERAPY

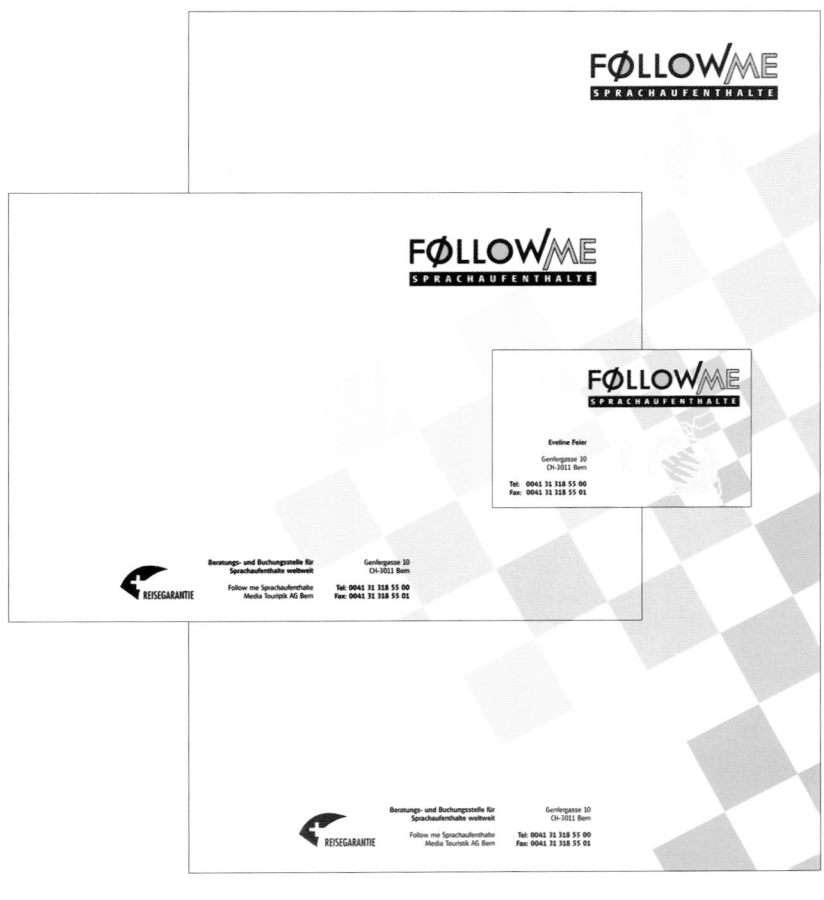

creative firm
REVOLUZION
Neuhausen do Eck, Germany
art director, designer
BERND LUZ DIPL
client
FOLLOW ME SPRACHREISEN

creative firm
  BOLDRINI & FICCARDI
  Mendoza, Italy
designers
  VICTOR BOLDRINI, LEONARDO FICCARDI
photographer
  CRISTIAN LAZZARI
client
  GUILLERMO CORVALAN

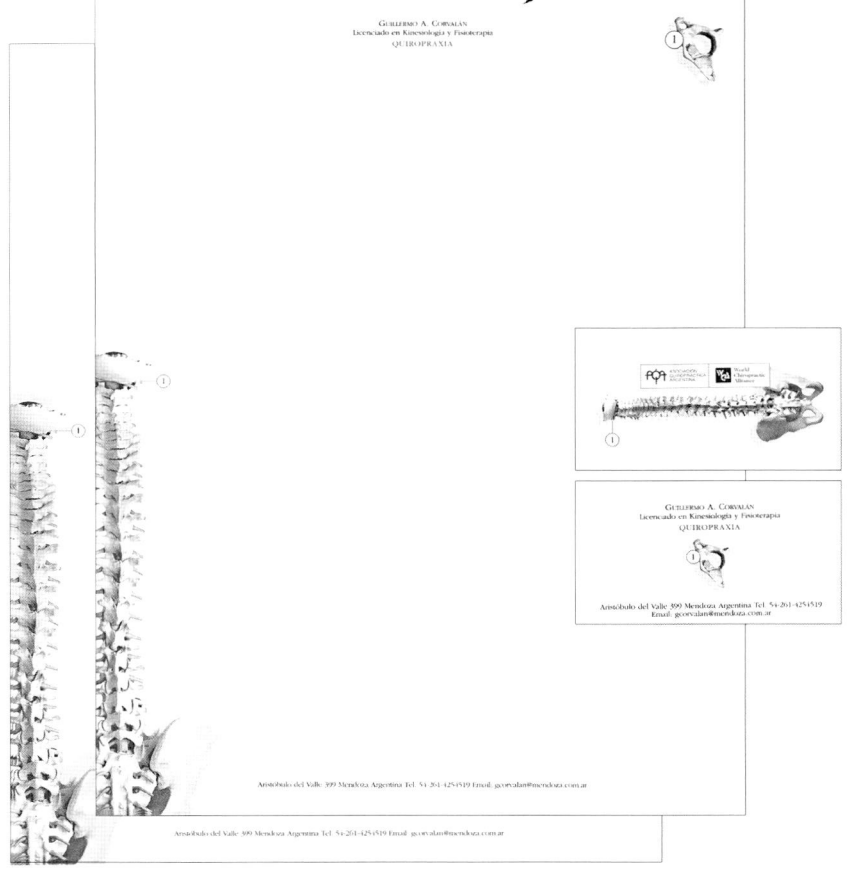

creative firm
  H2D
  Milwaukee, Wisconsin
creative director
  JOSEPH HAUSCH
creative specialist
  JENNIFER PECK
client
  WISCONSIN HUMANE SOCIETY

1997

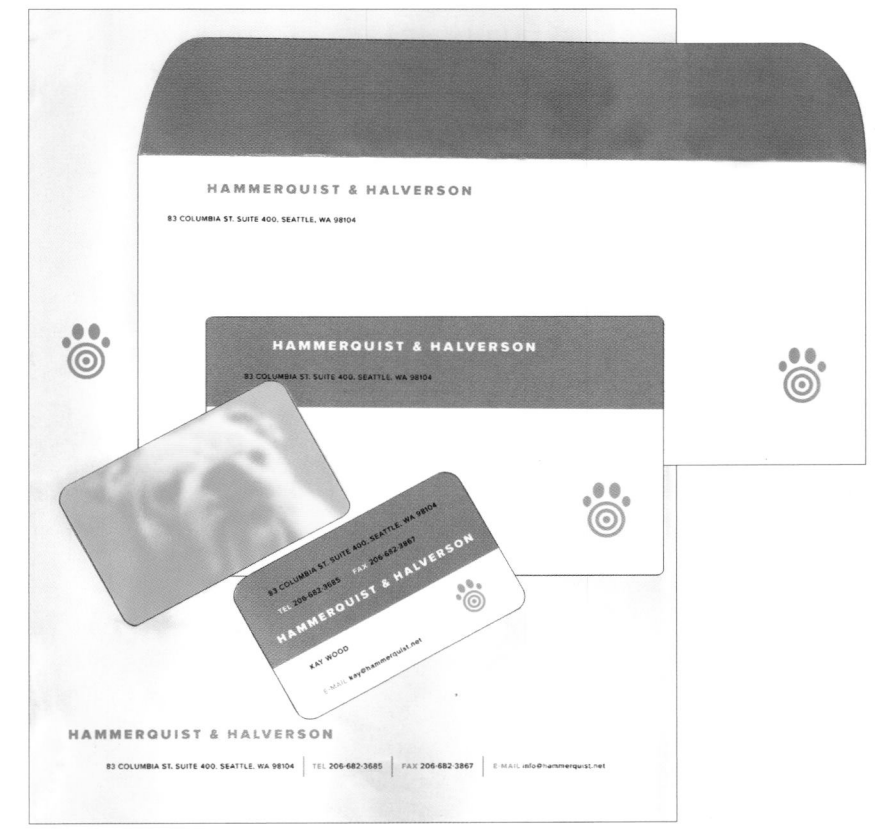

creative firm
  HORNALL ANDERSON DESIGN WORKS
  Seattle, Washington
art director
  JACK ANDERSON
designers
  JACK ANDERSON, MIKE CALKINS
client
  HAMMERQUIST & HALVERSON

creative firm
  AERIAL VISUAL IDENTITY DESIGN
  San Francisco, California
designers
  TRACY MOON, STEPHANIE WEST, KIMBERLY GROSS
client
  TRIBE PICTURES

creative firm
   FIFTH STREET DESIGN
   Berkeley, California
designers
   J. CLIFTON MEEK, BRENTON BECK
client
   POSTERDOCS

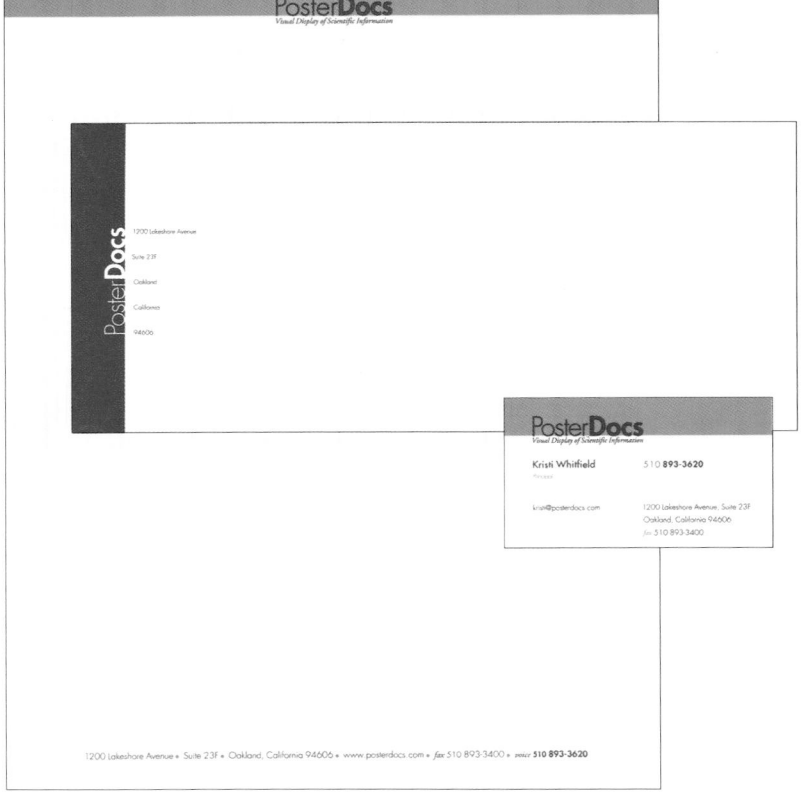

creative firm
   FIFTH STREET DESIGN
   Berkeley, California
designers
   J. CLIFTON MEEK, BRENTON BECK
client
   FIFTH STREET DESIGN

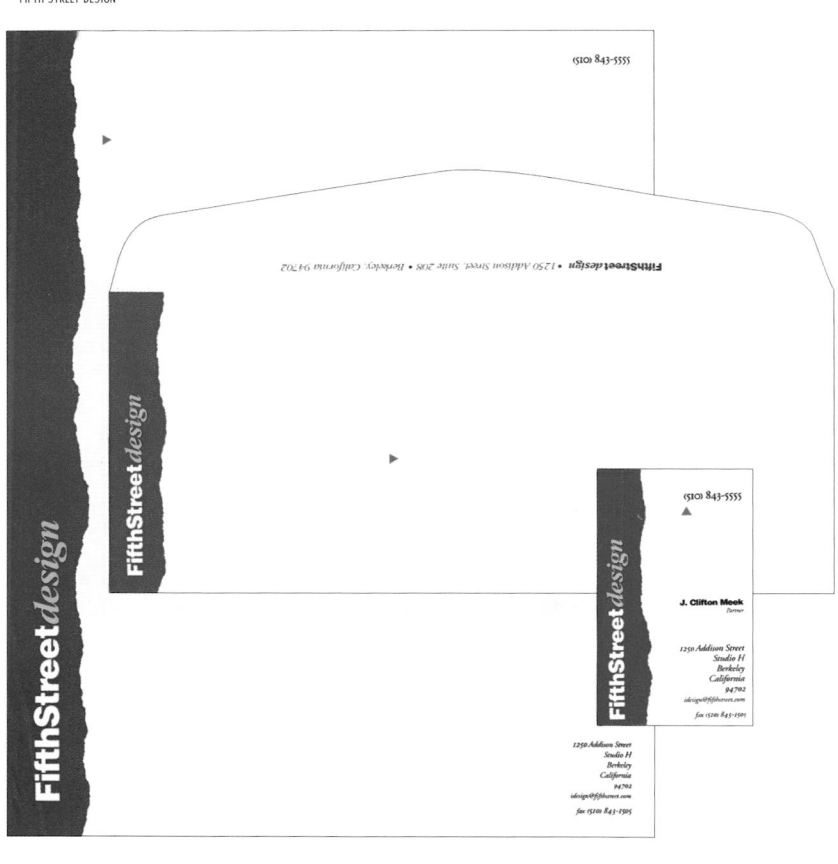

LETTERHEAD SETS

creative firm
GARDNER DESIGN
Wichita, Kansas
art directors
BILL GARDNER, BRIAN MILLER
designer
BRIAN MILLER
client
PAUL CHAUNCEY PHOTOGRAPHY

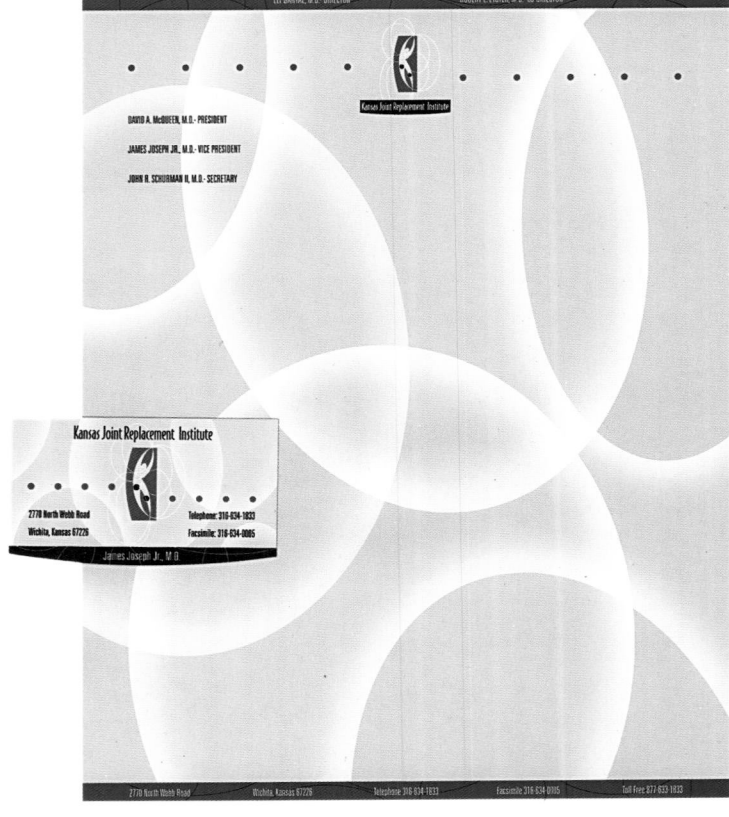

creative firm
GARDNER DESIGN
Wichita, Kansas
art directors
TRAVIS BROWN, BRIAN MILLER
designer
TRAVIS BROWN
client
KANSAS JOINT REPLACEMENT INSTITUTE

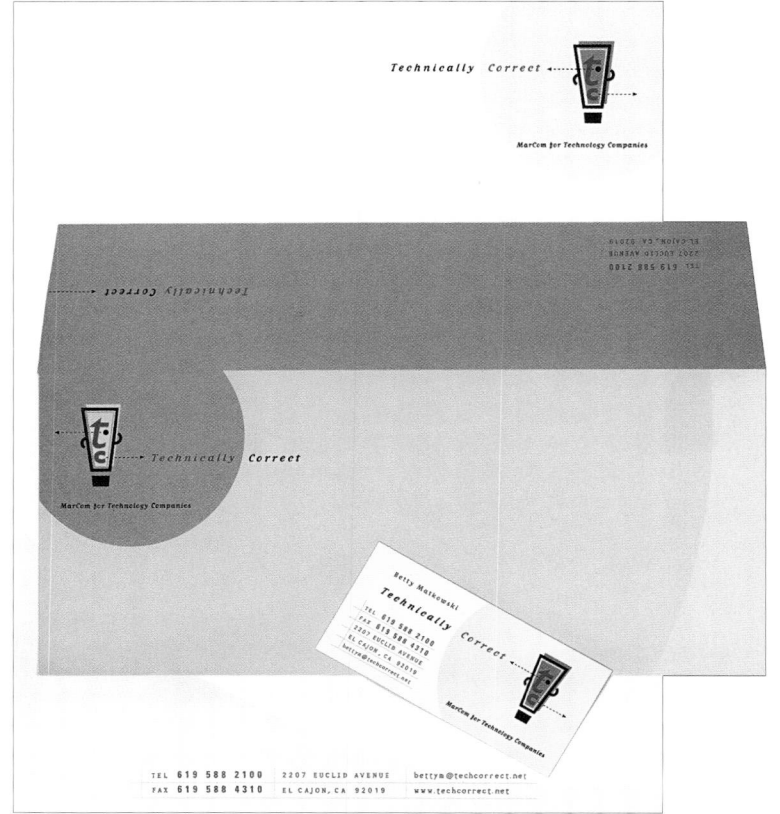

creative firm
MIRIELLO GRAFICO INC.
San Diego, California
designer
DENNIS GARCIA
client
TECHNICALLY CORRECT

TEL **619 588 2100**   2207 EUCLID AVENUE   bettym@techcorrect.net
FAX **619 588 4310**   EL CAJON, CA 92019   www.techcorrect.net

creative firm
MIRIELLO GRAFICO INC.
San Diego, California
designer
CHRIS KEENEY
client
DR. VISSER

michael regnier photography

shawnee mission, ks. 66202
5627 newton

michael regnier photography

michael regnier photography
5627 newton
shawnee mission, ks. 66202
mike@regnierphotography.com
www.regnierphotography.com
tel:[913]362.5222
fax:[913]362.5222

5627 newton
shawnee mission, ks. 66202
mike@regnierphotography.com
tel: 913 362.5599

(www)regnierphotography.com

5627 newton
shawnee mission, ks. 66202
mike@regnierphotography.com
tel: [913] 362.5599
fax:[913]362.5222

creative firm
MULLER + CO.
Kansas City, Missouri
creative director
JOHN MULLER
designer
JEFF MILLER
client
MICHAEL REGNIER PHOTGRAPHY

deca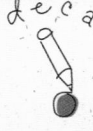

deca

deca

deep ellum center for the arts
2808 commerce street
dallas, texas 75226

deep ellum center for the arts
2808 commerce street
dallas, texas 75226
phone 214.744.arts (744.2787)
facsimile 214.744.2789

melissa white sauvage
executive director

deca

deep ellum center for the arts
2808 commerce street
dallas, texas 75226
phone 214.744.arts (744.2787)
facsimile 214.744.2789

creative firm
SQUIRES & COMPANY
Dallas, Texas
designer
CHRISTIE GROTHEIM
client
DECA

deep ellum center for the arts
2808 commerce street
dallas, texas 75226
phone 214.744.arts (744.2787)
facsimile 214.744.2789

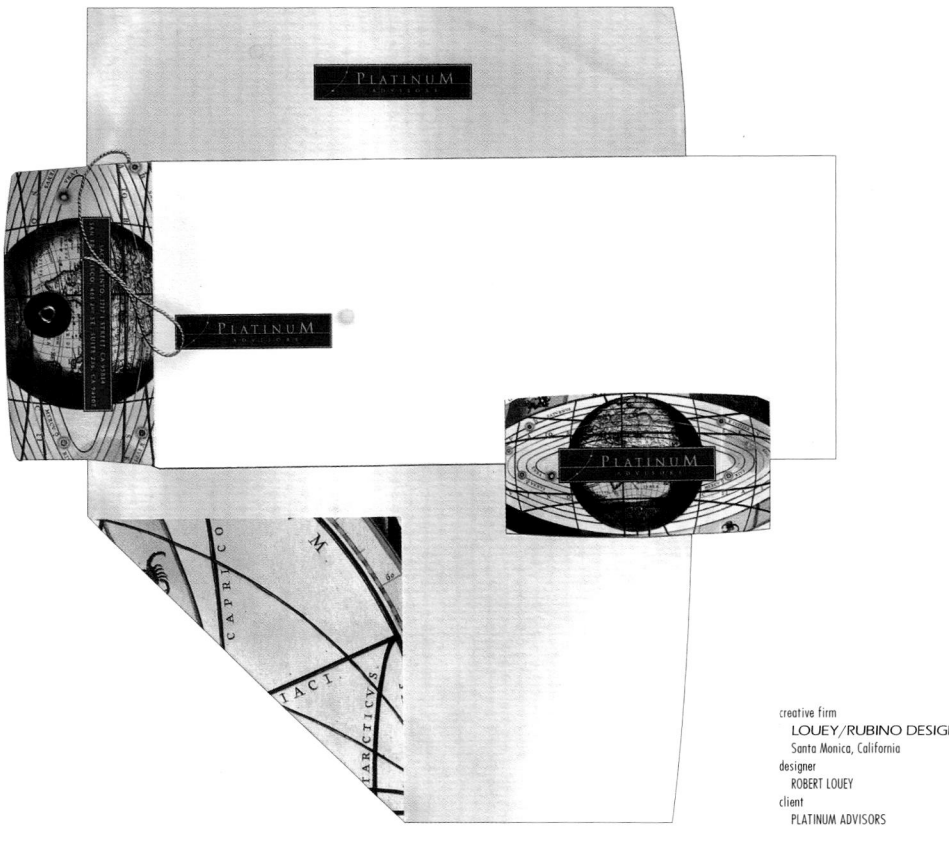

creative firm
   LOUEY/RUBINO DESIGN GROUP, INC.
   Santa Monica, California
designer
   ROBERT LOUEY
client
   PLATINUM ADVISORS

creative firm
   30 SIXTY DESIGN, INC.
   Los Angeles, California
creative director, art director
   HENRY VIZCARRA
designer
   ANNA KALINKA
photographer
   SCOTT HENSEL
copywriter
   HILLEL WASSERMAN
client
   30 SIXTY DESIGN, INC.

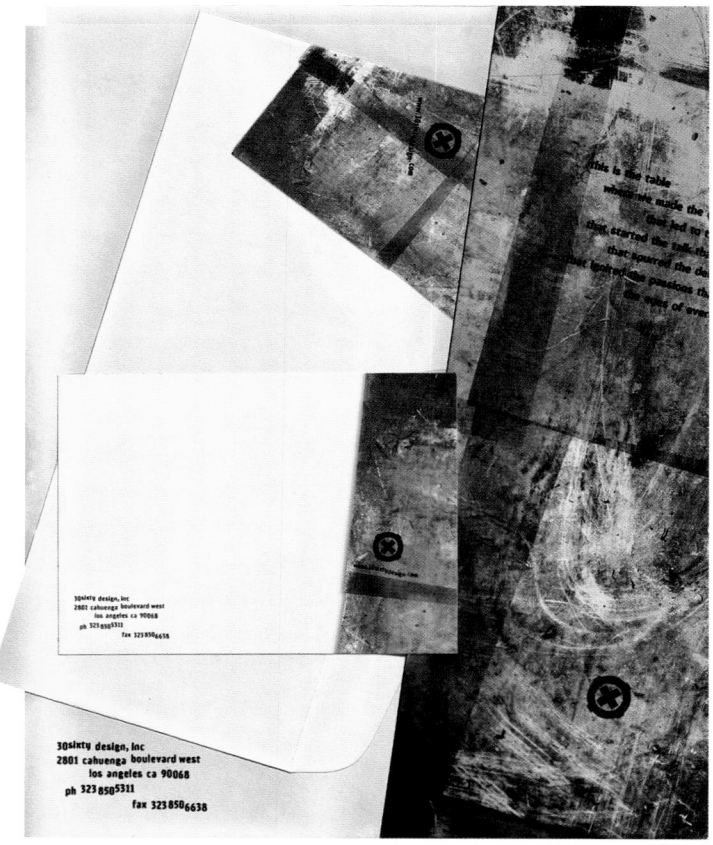

creative firm
    HORNALL ANDERSON DESIGN WORKS
    Seattle, Washington
art directors
    JOHN HORNALL, LARRY ANDERSON
designers
    JOHN HORNALL, LARRY ANDERSON,
    MARY CHIN HUTCHISON, BRUCE STIGLER
client
    COPPER SKY GRILL

creative firm
    HORNALL ANDERSON DESIGN WORKS
    Seattle, Washington
art director
    JACK ANDERSON
designers
    JACK ANDERSON, MARY HERMES,
    GRETCHEN COOK, JULIE LOCK
client
    SPACE NEEDLE

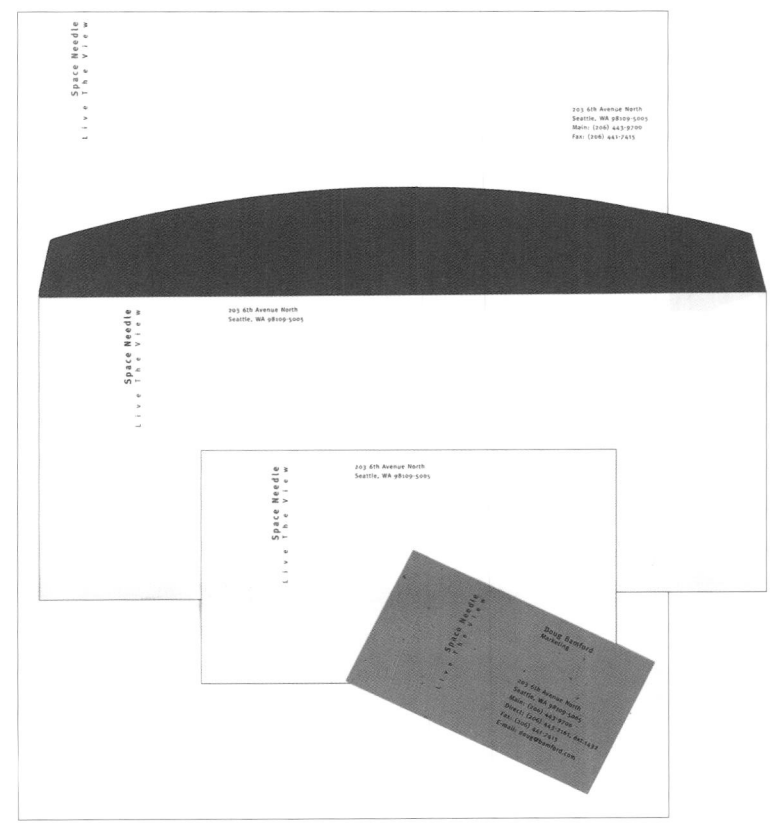

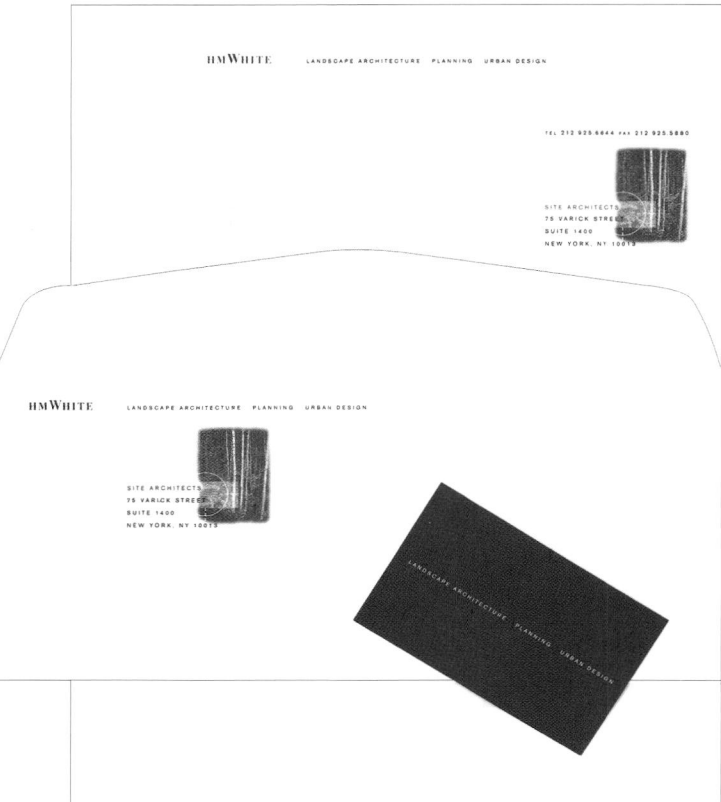

creative firm
  SHOOK DESIGN GROUP, INC.
  Charlotte, North Carolina
designer
  STEVE FENTON
client
  HM WHITE LANDSCAPE ARCHITECTS

creative firm
  BRUCE YELASKA DESIGN
  San Francisco, California
art director, designer
  BRUCE YELASKA
client
  BRUCE YELASKA DESIGN

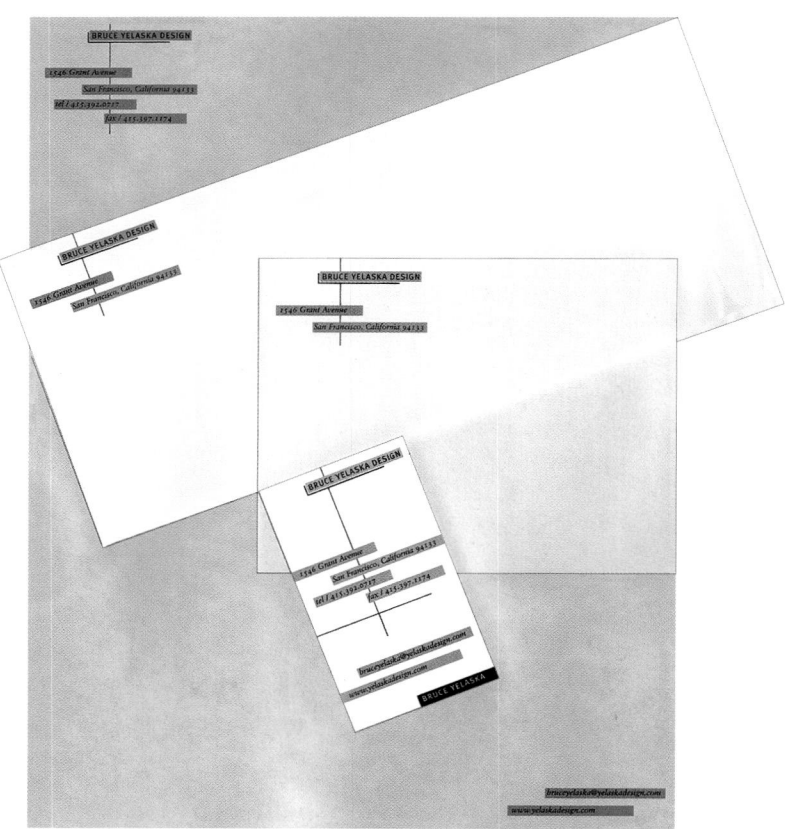

HEIDI GILMORE

HEIDI GILMORE

343 North Broadway
Milwaukee, WI 53202

343 North Broadway, Milwaukee, WI 53202. Phone 414.224.0871 Fax 414.224.0872 info@heidigilmore.com www.heidigilmore.com

Heidi Gilmore CEO
343 North Broadway
Milwaukee, WI 53202
Phone 414.224.0871
Fax 414.224.0872
heidi@heidigilmore.com
www.heidigilmore.com

H|G

creative firm
  BECKER DESIGN
  Milwaukee, Wisconsin
designer
  NEIL BECKER
client
  HEIDI GILMORE

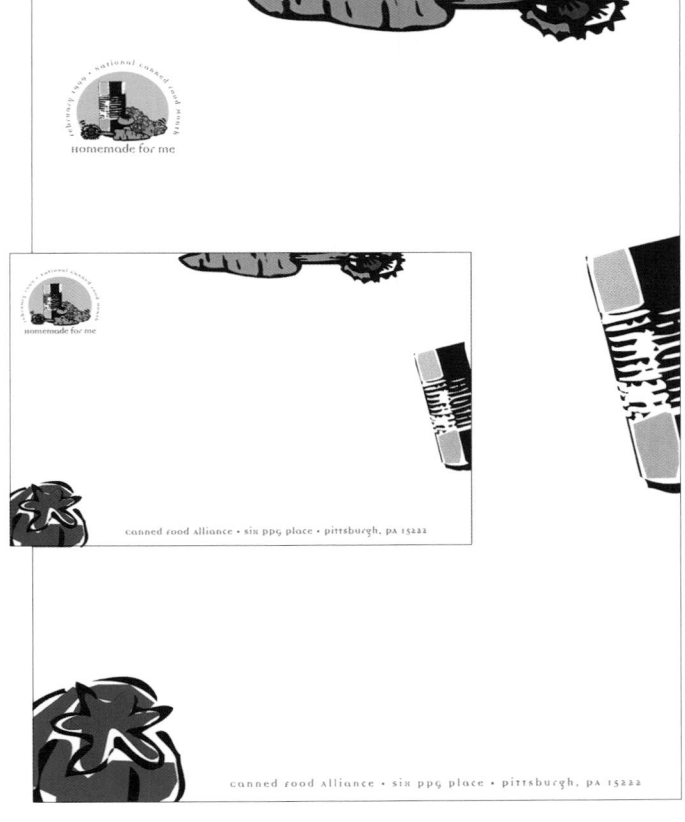

homemade for me

canned food Alliance · six ppg place · pittsburgh, pa 15222

creative firm
  A TO Z COMMUNICATIONS, INC.
  Pittsburgh, Pennsylvania
creative director
  ALAN BOARTS
designer
  VONNIE HORNBURG
client
  KETCHUM PR

creative firm
  ROSS ADVERTISING
  Peoria, Illinois
executive creative director
  SKIP DAMPIER
senior art director
  NICK JIBBEN
client
  GRIDIRON

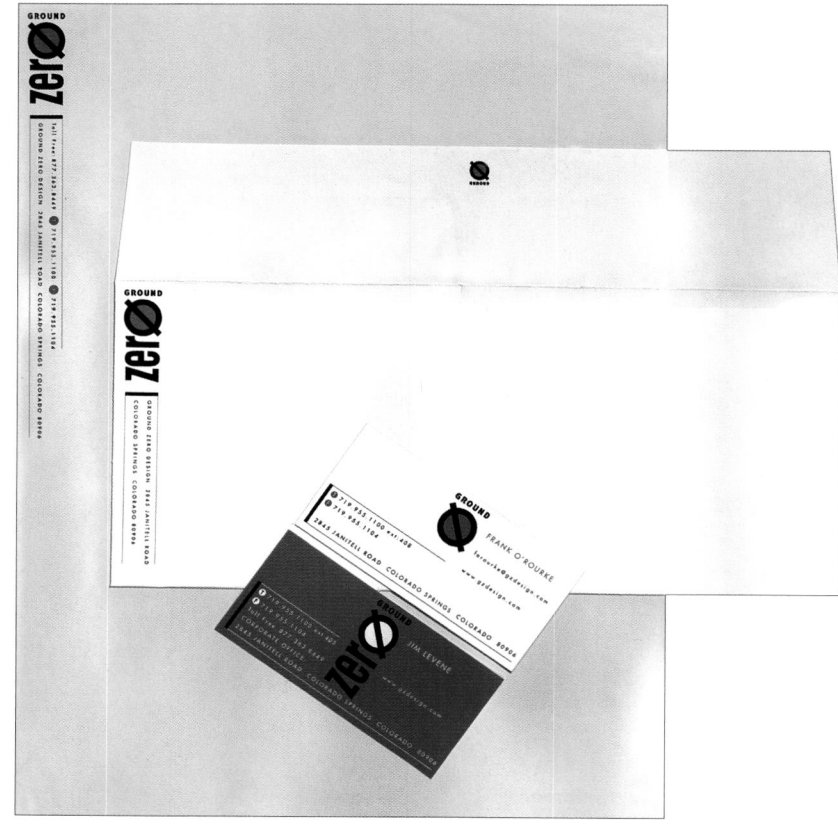

creative firm
  HORNALL ANDERSON DESIGN WORKS
  Seattle, Washington
art director
  JACK ANDERSON
designers
  JACK ANDERSON, KATHY SAITO, JULIE LOCK,
  ED LEE, HEIDI FAVOUR, VIRGINIA LE
client
  GROUND ZERO

207

creative firm
DIRECTION DESIGN
Los Angeles, California
creative director, designer
ANJA MUELLER
managing director
TERESA A. LOPEZ

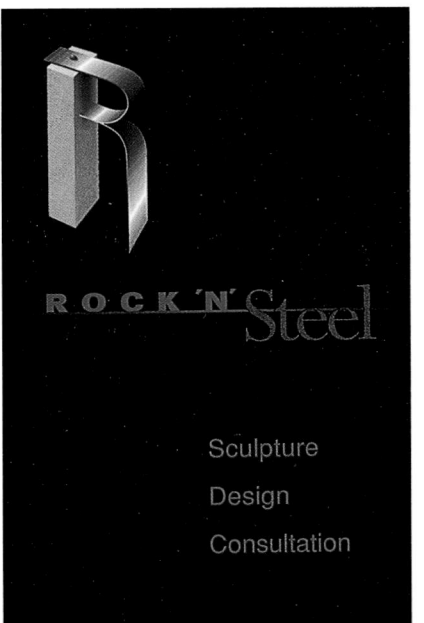

creative firm
GRETEMAN GROUP
Wichita, Kansas
creative director, art director
SONIA GRETEMAN
designers
SONIA GRETEMAN, CRAIG TOMSON
client
ROCK 'N' STEEL

creative firm
GRETEMAN GROUP
Wichita, Kansas
creative director
SONIA GRETEMAN
art directors
SONIA GRETEMAN, JAMES STRANGE
designer
JAMES STRANGE
client
GRANT TELEGRAPH

creative firm
  GRETEMAN GROUP
  Wichita, Kansas
creative director
  SONIA GRETEMAN
art directors
  SONIA GRETEMAN, JAMES STRANGE
designers
  SONIA GRETEMAN, JAMES STRANGE, GARRETT FRESH
client
  HOTEL AT OLD TOWN

creative firm
  GRETEMAN GROUP
  Wichita, Kansas
creative director, art director
  SONIA GRETEMAN
designers
  SONIA GRETEMAN, JO QUILLIN
client
  ERIC FISHER SALON

209

creative firm
   BONNIE MATHER DESIGN
   Edmonds, Washington
designer
   BONNIE MATHER
client
   WYMAN PARK, SPECIALTY GIFTS

creative firm
   BONNIE MATHER DESIGN
   Edmonds, Washington
designer
   BONNIE MATHER
client
   BETH DUNTON, HAIR STYLIST

creative firm
   GRETEMAN GROUP
   Wichita, Kansas
creative director
   SONIA GRETEMAN
art directors
   SONIA GRETEMAN, JAMES STRANGE
designer
   JAMES STRANGE
client
   POLO CLUB

creative firm
  SAYLES GRAPHIC DESIGN
  Des Moines, Iowa
art director, illustrator
  JOHN SAYLES
client
  BARRICK ROOFING

Lewis Glaser
Coordinator of Graphic Design
Associate Professor

TEXAS CHRISTIAN UNIVERSITY
TCU Box 298000
Fort Worth, Texas 76129
817.257.7697 *voice* ★ 817.257.7780 *fax*
http://gamma.is.tcu.edu/~glaser
l.glaser@tcu.edu

creative firm
  WET PAPER BAG GRAPHIC DESIGN
  Fort Worth, Texas
art director, designer, illustrator, copywriter
  LEWIS GLASER
client
  TCU GRAPHIC DESIGN PROGRAM

creative firm
  PIVOT DESIGN, INC.
  Chicago, Illinois
creative director
  BROCK HALDEMAN
designer
  ELIZABETH JOHNSON
client
  UPPERCASE BOOKS

UPPERCASE BOOKS, INC. 233 WEST ERIE STREET 4SW CHICAGO ILLINOIS 60610
TELEPHONE 312 280 3232 FACSIMILE 312 280 3233 WWW.UPPERCASEBOOKS.COM

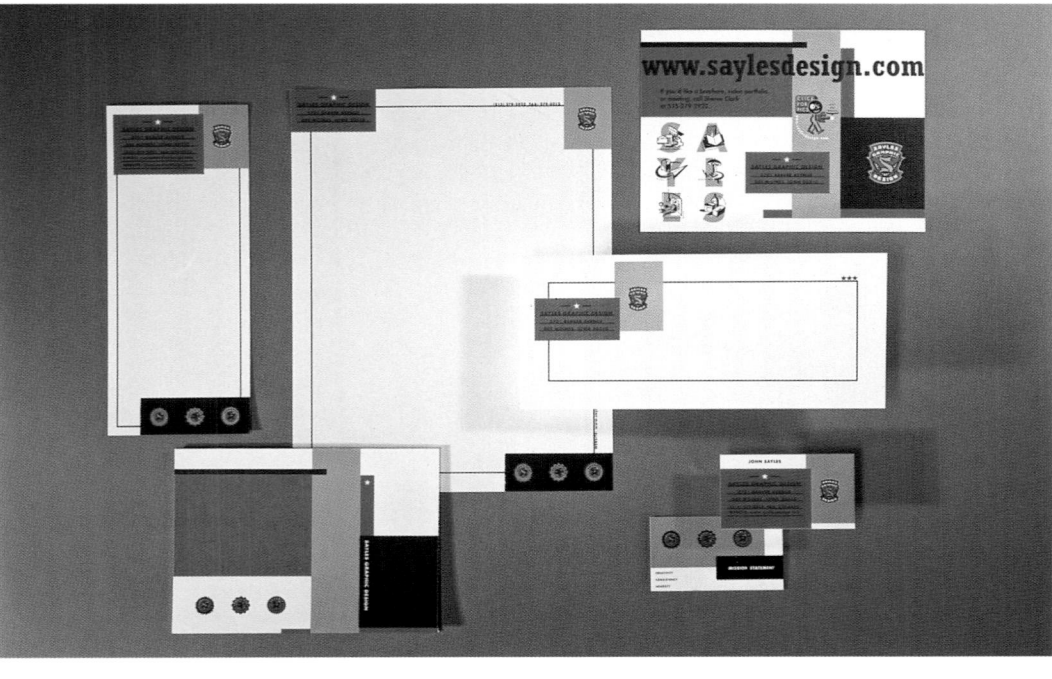

creative firm
  SAYLES GRAPHIC DESIGN
  Des Moines, Iowa
art director, illustrator
  JOHN SAYLES
client
  SAYLES GRAPHIC DESIGN

creative firm
  SIBLEY PETEET DESIGN
  Dallas, Texas
designer
  TOM KIRSCH
client
  AGI KLEARFOLD

creative firm
SAYLES GRAPHIC DESIGN
Des Moines, Iowa
art director, illustrator
JOHN SAYLES
client
CASA BONITA

creative firm
SAYLES GRAPHIC DESIGN
Des Moines, Iowa
art director, illustrator
JOHN SAYLES
client
CONSOLIDATED CORRECTIONAL FOOD SERVICES

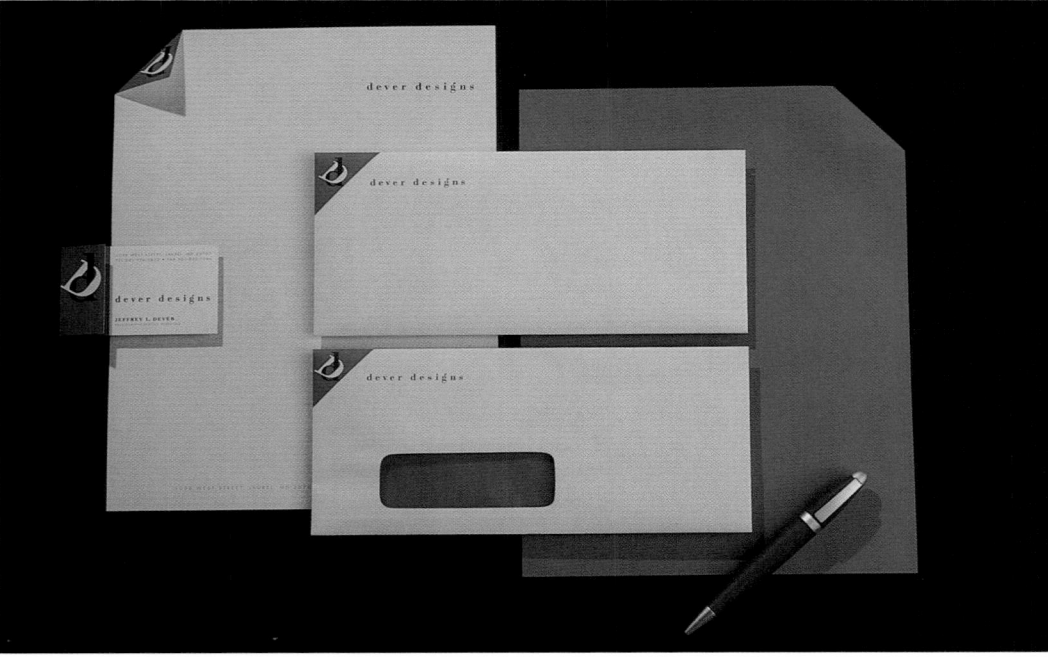

creative firm
DEVER DESIGNS
Laurel, Maryland
art director, designer
JEFFREY L. DEVER
client
DEVER DESIGNS

creative firm
BBK STUDIO, INC.
Grand Rapids, Michigan
creative director, designer
YANG KIM
copywriter
CHRISTINE MacLEAN
client
CONTENT STUDIO

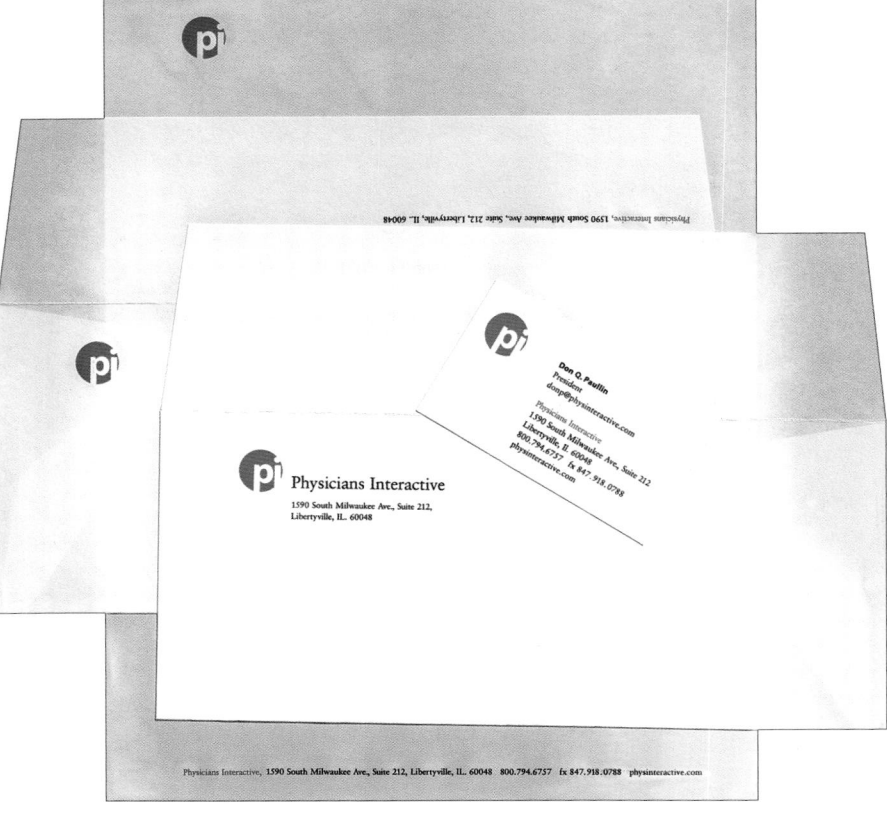

creative firm
 PARAGRAPHS DESIGN
 Chicago, Illinois
designer
 CRISPIN PREBYS
client
 PHYSICIANS INTERACTIVE

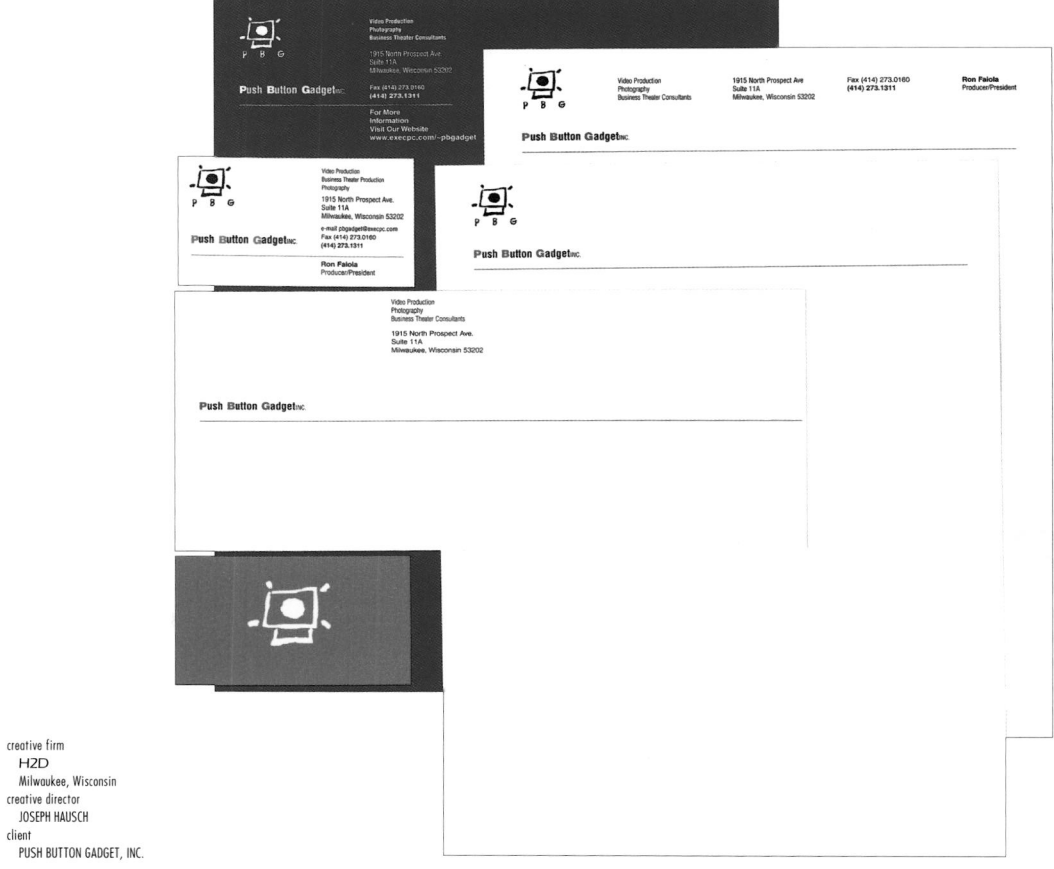

creative firm
 H2D
 Milwaukee, Wisconsin
creative director
 JOSEPH HAUSCH
client
 PUSH BUTTON GADGET, INC.

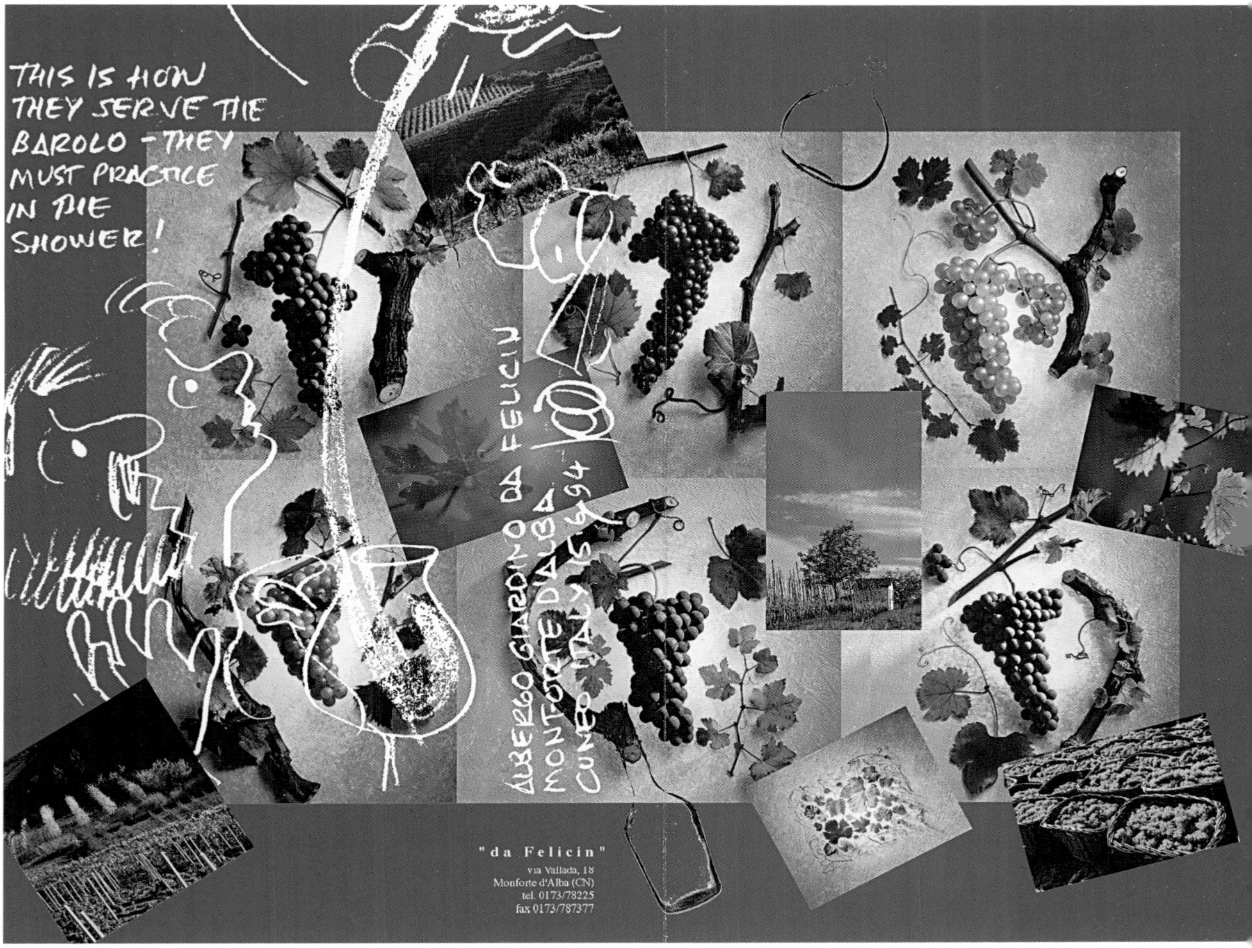

THIS IS HOW
THEY SERVE THE
BAROLO - THEY
MUST PRACTICE
IN THE
SHOWER!

ALBERGO GIARDINO DA FELICIN
MONFORTE D'ALBA
CUNEO ITALY 5.6.94

"da Felicin"
via Vallada, 18
Monforte d'Alba (CN)
tel. 0173/78225
fax 0173/787377

creative firm
    BRUNAZZI & ASSOCIATI/
    IMAGE + COMMUNICATION
    Turin , Italy
designers
    SILVIA ZANETTI, GIOVANNI BRUNAZZI
client
    FELICIN

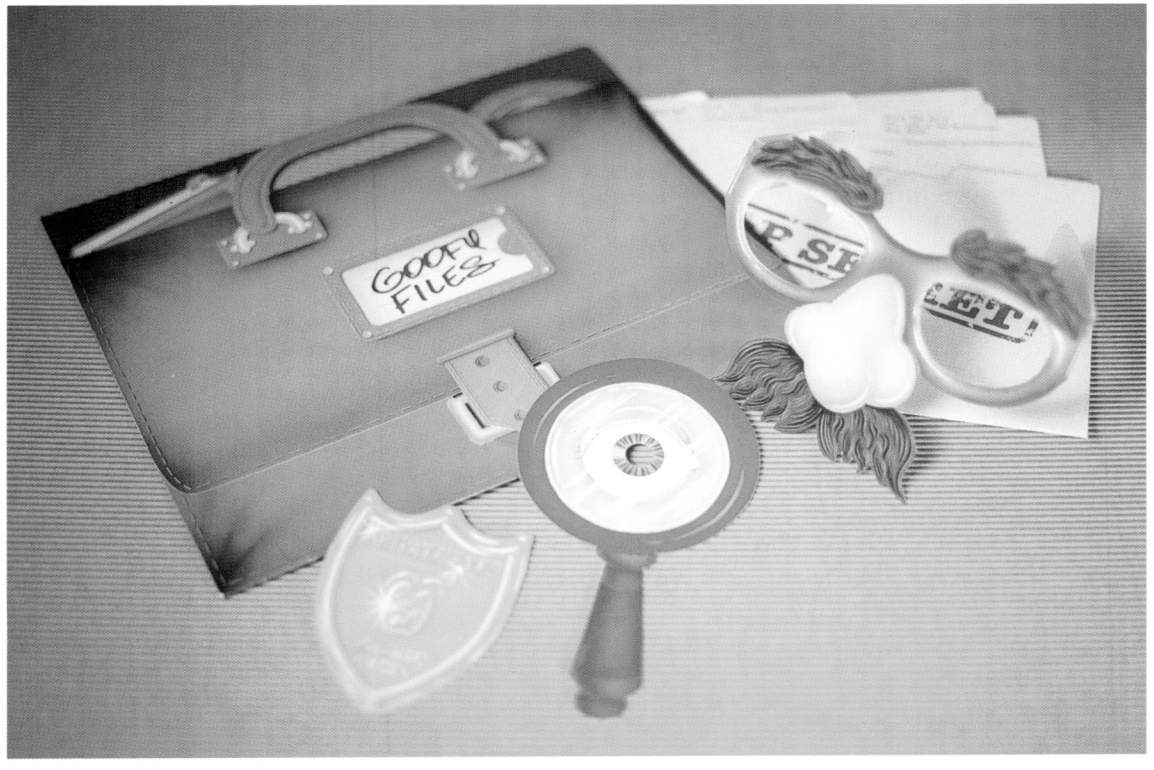

creative firm
    DISNEY DESIGN GROUP
    Lake Buena Vista, Florida
creative director
    MICHELE KEATING
designer
    MIKE WOOD
client
    DISNEY CRUISE LINE

creative firm
JAMES ROBIE DESIGN ASSOCIATES
  Los Angeles, California
creative director
  JAMES ROBIE
designer
  KAREN NAKATANI
client
  THE HUMP SUSHI BAR & RESTAURANT

creative firm
DISNEY DESIGN GROUP
  Lake Buena Vista, Florida
creative director
  MICHELE KEATING
designer
  MARK FRANKEL
illustrator
  JOYCE STIGLICH
client
  DISNEY CRUISE LINE

creative firm
THE RIORDON DESIGN GROUP, INC.
Oakville, Ontario, Canada
designer
SHIRLEY RIORDON
photographer
DAVID GRAHAM WHITE
client
TAMARA MORGAN CHAFFEE

creative firm
CREATIVE SERVICES
New York, New York
art director, designer
GIULIO TURTURRO
client
SONY CLASSICAL

creative firm
CREATIVE SERVICES
New York, New York
art director, designer
GIULIO TURTURRO
client
SONY CLASSICAL

creative firm
CREATIVE SERVICES
New York, New York
art director
ALLEN WEINBERG
designer
NICKY LINDEMAN
client
SONY CLASSICAL

creative firm
   THE RIORDON DESIGN GROUP, INC.
   Oakville, Ontario, Canada
art director
   TONI FITZPENN
designer
   SHIRLEY RIORDON
illustrator
   SHARON PORTER
client
   VINEYARD MUSIC GROUP

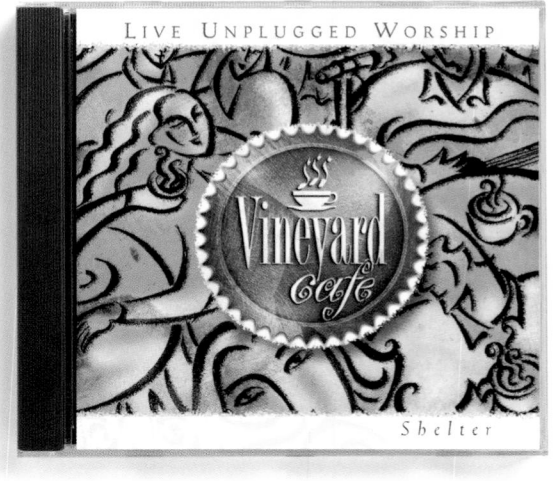

creative firm
   DISNEY CONSUMER PRODUCTS
   Burbank, California
art director
   LUIS M. FERNANDEZ
designers
   TIFFANY QUON, MARCELLA WONG
client
   THE DISNEY STORE

creative firm
   CREATIVE SERVICES
   New York, New York
art director
   ALLEN WEINBERG
designer
   RISA NOAH
photographer
   CHRISTIAN MICHAELS/FPG INTERNATIONAL
client
   SONY CLASSICAL

creative firm
   CREATIVE SERVICES
   New York, New York
art director, designer
   GIULIO TURTURRO
illustrator
   MATT MAHURIN
client
   SONY CLASSICAL

creative firm
  AFTER HOURS CREATIVE
  Seattle, Washington
photography
  TIM LANTERMAN
digital manipulation
  JUDY MILLER
client
  ARIZONA MILLS

You only live once.

175 value retailers.   5 minutes away.   Exit #155, Baseline Road.

ARIZONA MILLS

creative firm
  GRETEMAN GROUP
  Wichita, Kansas
creative director
  SONIA GRETEMAN
art directors
  SONIA GRETEMAN, CRAIG TOMSON, JAMES STRANGE
designers
  CRAIG TOMSON, JAMES STRANGE
client
  LAN KINGDON

creative firm
  GRETEMAN GROUP
  Wichita, Kansas
creative director, art director
  SONIA GRETEMAN
designers
  CRAIG TOMSON, JAMES STRANGE
client
  HAMILTON PLACE

creative firm
  GRETEMAN GROUP
    Wichita, Kansas
creative directors, art directors
  SONIA GRETEMAN, CHRIS BRUNNER
designers
  SONIA GRETEMAN, CHRIS BRUNNER,
  CRAIG TOMSON, JAMES STRANGE
client
  CITY ARTS

creative firm
  MULLER + CO.
    Kansas City, Missouri
art director
  JOANN OTTO
client
  NORTH KANSAS CITY HOSPITAL DAY CARE CENTER

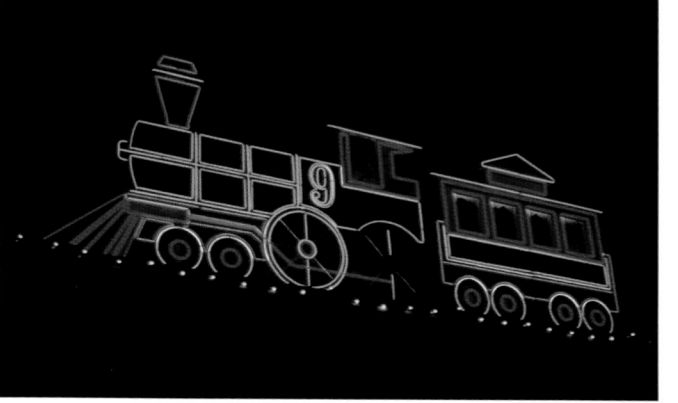

creative firm
  WAGES DESIGN
    Atlanta, Georgia
designers
  RANDY ALLISON, JOANNA TAK
client
  GEORGIA STATE UNIVERSITY

creative firm
SEWICKLEY GRAPHICS & DESIGN, INC.
Sewickley, Pennsylvania
senior designer
JIM REYBEIN
client
SLIPPERY ROCK UNIVERSITY OF PENNSYLVANIA

creative firm
MULLER +CO.
Kansas City, Missouri
creative directors
JOHN MULLER, DAVID MARKS
art director, designer
MARK VOSS
copywriter
DAVID MARKS
client
KANSAS CITY BLADES HOCKEY CLUB

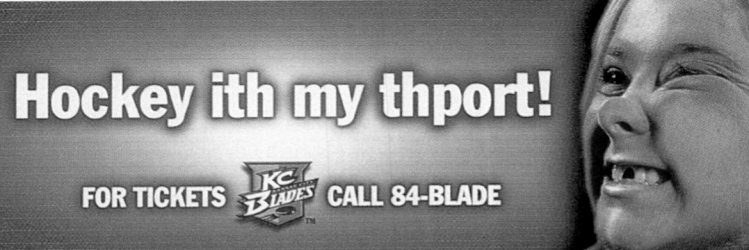

creative firm
MULLER +CO.
Kansas City, Missouri
creative director
JOHN MULLER
art director, designer
MARK VOSS
copywriter
ROB HOLMES
client
MISSOURI DIVISION OF TOURISM

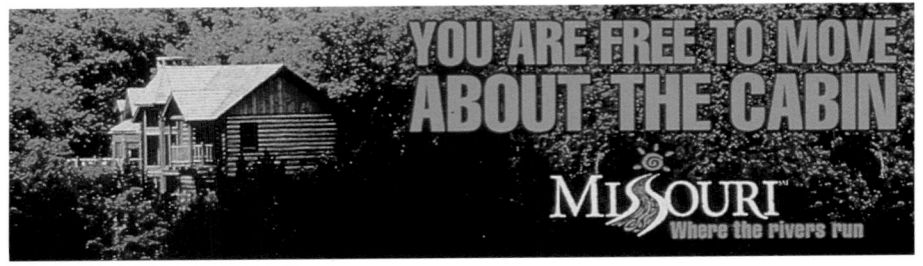

creative firm
 LORENC + YOO DESIGN
 Roswell, Georgia
design director
 JAN LORENC
designer
 STEVE McCALL
client
 HINES-COOL SPRINGS

creative firm
 LORENC + YOO DESIGN
 Roswell, Georgia
design director
 JAN LORENC
designer
 STEVE McCALL
architect
 GARY FLESHER
client
 WORLD GOLF VILLAGE-DAVIDSON DEVELOPMENT

creative firm
 LORENC + YOO DESIGN
 Roswell, Georgia
design director
 JAN LORENC
designers
 STEVE McCALL, DAVID PARK
client
 GENERAL GROWTH PROPERTIES/JJR

creative firm
  WPA PINFOLD
  Leeds, England
designers
  JAMES LITTLEWOOD, PAUL PHILLIPS
client
  RANK HOLIDAYS

creative firm
  MICHAEL COURTNEY DESIGN
  Seattle, Washington
art director
  MICHAEL COURTNEY
designers
  MICHAEL COURTNEY, DAN HOANG
client
  CORIXA CORPORATION

creative firm
  DESIGN GUYS
  Minneapolis, Minnesota
art director
  STEVEN SIKORA
designers
  GARY PATCH, ANNE PETERSON
client
  TARGET STORES

creative firm
  MULLER + CO.
  Kansas City, Missouri
art director
  JOANN OTTO
illustrator
  JIM PAILLOT
writer
  JEFF SOBUL
client
  NORTH KANSAS CITY HOSPITAL DAY CARE CENTER

creative firm
SPENCER ZAHN & ASSOCIATES
Philadelphia, Pennsylvania
creative director
SPENCER ZAHN
designer
ED McHUGH
client
KEENAN MOTORS

creative firm
GREGORY GROUP
Dallas, Texas
creative director
JON GREGORY
client
EDS

creative firm
TANAGRAM, INC.
Chicago, Illinois
designer
LANCE RUTTER
client
NIKETOWN SEATTLE

creative firm
SQUIRES & COMPANY
Dallas, Texas
designer
THOMAS VASQUES
client
ST. PETE'S

creative firm
SBG ENTERPRISE
San Francisco, California
creative director
THOMAS BOND
designer
IRATXE MUMFORD
illustrator
RIK OLSEN
client
THE LEARNING COMPANY

creative firm
DEUTSCH DESIGN WORKS
San Francisco, California
creative director
BARRY DEUTSCH
designers
JOHN LUCAS, ERIC PINO, JACQUES ROSSOUW
client
RED ORB DIVISION-BRODERBUND SOFTWARE AGES OF MYST

creative firm
DEUTSCH DESIGN WORKS
San Francisco, California
creative director
BARRY DEUTSCH
designer
JACQUES ROSSOUW
client
RED ORB DIVISION-BRODERBUND SOFTWARE PRINCE OF PERSIA 3D

creative firm
  HUGHES DESIGN INC.
  Norwalk, Connecticut
client
  IBM VIAVOICE

creative firm
  HORNALL ANDERSON DESIGN WORKS
  Seattle, Washington
art director
  JACK ANDERSON
designers
  JACK ANDERSON, KATHA DALTON,
  JANA WILSON ESSER, JANA NISHI,
  JULIE LOCK
client
  ADOBE

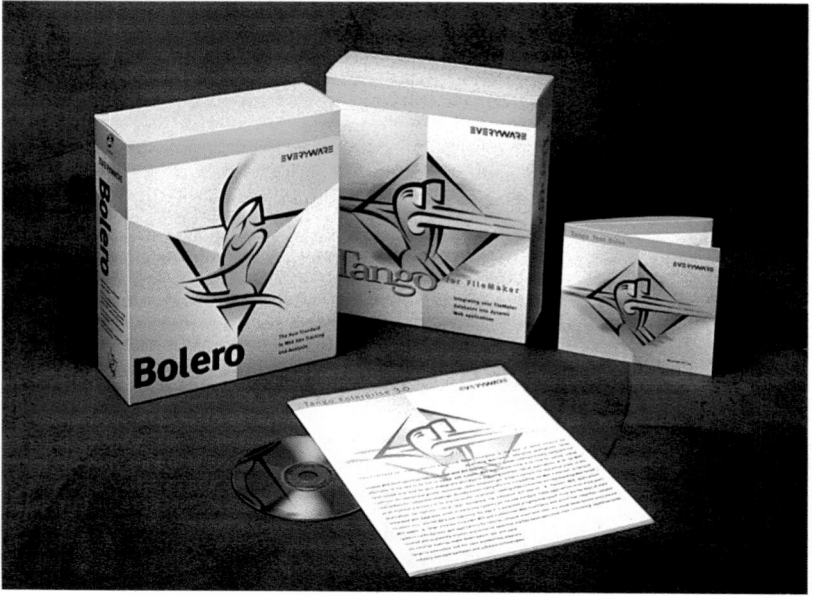

creative firm
  TELMET DESIGN ASSOCIATES
  Toronto, Canada
art director
  TIIT TELMET
designers
  JOSEPH GAULT, MARKO BARAC
client
  EVERYWARE DEVELOPMENT CORPORATION

227

creative firm
  LMS DESIGN
  Stamford, Connecticut
designers
  RICHARD SHEAR, ALEX WILLIAMS
client
  DELORME INC

creative firm
  BAILEY DESIGN GROUP, INC.
  Plymouth Meeting, Pennsylvania
creative director
  DAVID FIEDLER
designer
  LAURA MARKLEY
client
  C.F. MARTIN & COMPANY

creative firm
  BAILEY DESIGN GROUP, INC.
  Plymouth Meeting, Pennsylvania
creative director
  DAVID FIEDLER
designer
  LAURA MARKLEY
client
  C.F. MARTIN & COMPANY

What else lights up New York City like the Empire State Building

swatch

creative firm
  RISE AGENCY, INC.
  New York, New York
creative director
  CAROLINA RODRIGUEZ
art director
  ROBERT ZWASCHKA
client
  SWATCH U.S.

creative firm
  FARENGA DESIGN GROUP
  New York, New York
designer
  ANTHONY FARENGA
client
  WATSON-GUPTILL PUBLICATIONS

creative firm
  VAN NOY GROUP
  Torrance, California
creative director
  BILL MURAWSKI
designer
  JOE HUIZAR
client
  PENTEL OF AMERICA, LTD.

creative firm
  DEUTSCH DESIGN WORKS
  San Francisco, California
creative director
  BARRY DEUTSCH
senior designer
  LORI WYNN
client
  ANHEUSER-BUSCH MICHELOB HOLIDAY

creative firm
  DEUTSCH DESIGN WORKS
  San Francisco, California
creative director
  BARRY DEUTSCH
senior designers
  LORI WYNN, GREGG PERIN
client
  ANHEUSER-BUSCH MILLENIUIM GIFT BOX

creative firm
  DEUTSCH DESIGN WORKS
  San Francisco, California
creative director
  BARRY DEUTSCH
designer
  JACQUES ROSSOUW
client
  ANHEUSER-BUSCH MICHELOB MAPLE BROWN ALE

creative firm
  DEUTSCH DESIGN WORKS
  San Francisco, California
creative director
  BARRY DEUTSCH
designers,
  LORI WYNN, KATE GREENE
client
  ANHEUSER-BUSCH MILLENIUM TWELVE PACKS

creative firm
  DEUTSCH DESIGN WORKS
  San Francisco, California
creative director
  BARRY DEUTSCH
senior designer
  LORI WYNN
client
  ANHEUSER-BUSCH MICHELOB SAMPLER PACK

creative firm
  COMPASS DESIGN
  Minneapolis, Minnesota
designers
  MITCHELL LINDGREN,
  TOM ARTHUR,
  RICH McGOWEN
client
  AUGUST SCHELL BREWING COMPANY

creative firm
GARDNER DESIGN
Wichita, Kansas
art director, designer
BRIAN MILLER
client
HEMMEN WINES

creative firm
VAN NOY GROUP
Torrance, California
creative director
JIM VAN NOY
art director, designer
BILL MURAWSKI
illustrator
MIKE WEPLO
client
GAETANO SPECIALTIES, LTD.

creative firm
ANTISTA FAIRCLOUGH
Atlanta, Georgia
art directors, designers
TOM ANTISTA, THOMAS FAIRCLOUGH
client
FETZER VINEYARDS

creative firm
 KLIM DESIGN, INC.
 Avon, Connecticut
creative director
 MATT KLIM
client
 CASA CUERVO, S.A. DE C.V.

creative firm
 BUTLER KEMP DESIGN
 North Adelaide, Australia
art directors
 DEREK BUTLER, JULIE KEMP
designer
 HELLEN KIPRIZLOGLOU
client
 BROWNS' OF PADTHAWAY

creative firm
 WALLACE CHURCH ASSOCIATES INC.
 New York, New York
designer
 NIN GLAISTER
client
 WALLACE CHURCH

creative firm
BUTLER KEMP DESIGN
North Adelaide, Australia
art director
DEREK BUTLER
designers
HELLEN KIPRIZLOGLOU, JULIE KEMP
client
BROWNS' OF PADTHAWAY

creative firm
DESIGN SOLUTIONS
Napa, California
designer
DEBORAH MITCHELL
Illustrator
JOHN BURNS
client
TREFETHEN VINEYARDS

creative firm
McELVENEY + PALOZZI DESIGN GROUP, INC.
Rochester, New York
creative directors
STEPHEN PALOZZI, WILLIAM McELVENEY
art director
GRETCHEN BYE
client
CANANDAIGUA WINE COMPANY

creative firm
ANTISTA FAIRCLOUGH
Atlanta, Georgia
art directors, designers
TOM ANTISTA, THOMAS FAIRCLOUGH
client
BELL ARBOR VINEYARDS

creative firm
PEARLFISHER
London, England
creative director
JONATHAN FORD
designer
IAN CATLING
client
THE ABSOLUT COMPANY

creative firm
PEARLFISHER
London, England
creative director
JONATHAN FORD
designer
SHAUN BOWEN
client
THE ABSOLUT COMPANY

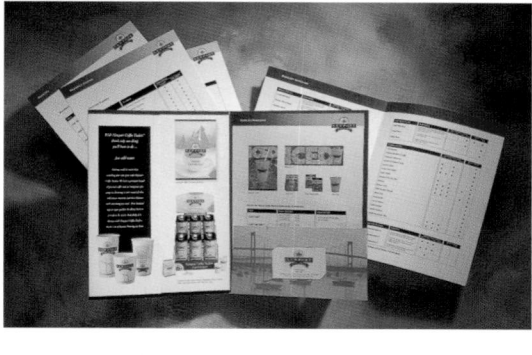

creative firm
ESTUDIO RAY
Phoenix, Arizona
art directors
CHRISTINE RAY, JOE RAY
designers
CHRISTINE RAY, JOE RAY, LESLIE LINK
illustrator
JOE RAY
client
COFFEE PLANTATION

creative firm
ADKINS/BALCHUNAS
Providence, Rhode Island
creative director
JERRY BALCHUNAS
designers
MICHELLE PHANEUF, JERRY BALCHUNAS,
SUSAN DeANGELIS
client
AUTOCRAT, INC.

creative firm
COMPASS DESIGN
Minneapolis, Minnesota
designers
MITCHELL LINDGREN,
TOM ARTHUR,
RICH McGOWEN
client
NIKOLA'S SPECIALTY FOODS

creative firm
  ROSS ADVERTISING
  Peoria, Illinois
creative directors
  SKIP DAMPIER, BRIAN BRUSH
designer
  BRIAN BRUSH
copywriter
  JOHN RUEBUSH
client
  ILLINOIS POWER

creative firm
  COMPASS DESIGN
  Minneapolis, Minnesota
designers
  MITCHELL LINDGREN,
  TOM ARTHUR,
  RICH McGOWEN
client
  AUNT GUSSIE'S COOKIES + CRACKERS

creative firm
  TANGRAM STRATEGIC DESIGN
  Novara, Italy
creative director, art director
  ENRICO SEMPI
designers
  ENRICO SEMPI, ANNA GRIHALDI
illustrator
  GUIDO ROSA
client
  STANDA

creative firm
  ADKINS/BALCHUNAS
  Providence, Rhode Island
creative director
  JERRY BALCHUNAS
senior designer
  MATTHEW FERNBERGER
client
  BYBLOS

creative firm
  THE WYANT SIMBOLI GROUP
  Norwalk, Connecticut
creative director, designer
  JULIA WYANT
illustrator
  JULIE BERSON
client
  PODS-OF-PLEASURE

creative firm
  HORNALL ANDERSON DESIGN WORKS
  Seattle, Washington
art director,
  JANA NISHI
designers
  JANA NISHI, SONJA MAX
client
  STICKY FINGERS BAKERY

creative firm
  TANGRAM STRATEGIC DESIGN
  Novara, Italy
creative director
  ENRICO SEMPI
art directors
  ENRICO SEMPI, ANTONELLA TREVISAN
designer
  ANTONELLA TREVISAN
illustrator
  SERGIO QUARANTA
client
  E. VISMARA DI A. BIFFI ("CREME DI AUTORE")

creative firm
  TANGRAM STRATEGIC DESIGN
  Novara, Italy
creative director
  ENRICO SEMPI
art director, designer
  ANTONELLA TREVISAN
photographer
  STEFANACCI & CIARLO
client
  CONSILIA

creative firm
  PRIMO ANGELI INC.
  San Francisco, California
creative director
  CARLO PAGODA
designers
  HARUMI KUBO, SANDY RUSSELL, KOJI MIYAKE
client
  PARAMOUNT FARMS, INC.

creative firm
  SBG ENTERPRISE
  San Francisco, California
creative director
  MARK BERGMAN
illustrator
  JUSTIN CARROLL
photographer
  DAVID CAMPBELL
client
  DEL MONTE FOODS

creative firm
  BRUNAZZI & ASSOCIATI/IMAGE + COMMUNICATION
  Turin, Italy
creative director
  ANDREA BRUNAZZI
designer
  KATIA STABILE
client
  CRAI

creative firm
  RGB GRAPHIC DESIGN
  Rio De Janeiro, Brazil
designer
  MARIA LUIZA GONCALUES VEIGA BRITO
client
  DE MILLUS IND E COM. S.A.

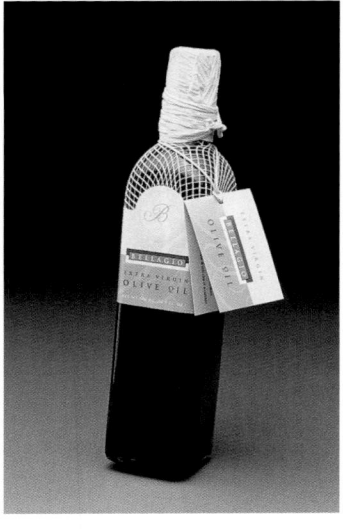

creative firm
  SIBLEY PETEET DESIGN
  Dallas, Texas
designers
  DON SIBLEY, TOM HOUGH,
  DAVID BECK
client
  BELLAGIO HOTEL & CASINO

creative firm
SAYLES GRAPHIC DESIGN
Des Moines, Iowa
art director, illustrator
JOHN SAYLES
client
GIANNA ROSE "WATERCOLOUR"

creative firm
BAILEY DESIGN GROUP, INC.
Plymouth Meeting, Pennsylvania
creative director
DAVID FIEDLER
designers
LAUREN DUNOFF, TISHA ARMOUR,
CHRISTIAN WILLIAMSON
client
CULTIVATIONS

creative firm
DISNEY DESIGN GROUP
Lake Buena Vista, Florida
creative director
MICHELE KEATING
designer
THOMAS SCOTT
illustrator
MICHAEL MOJHER
client
DISNEY CRUISE LINE

creative firm
  PEARLFISHER
  London, England
creative director
  JONATHAN FORD
designer
  SARAH BUTLER
client
  SUPERDRUG STORES PLC

creative firm
  NAKATSUKA DAISUKE INC.
  Tokyo, Japan
designers
  SHU UEMURA, DAISUKE NAKATSUKA,
  KANNA NUMAJIRI
client
  SHU UEMURA COSMETICS INC.

creative firm
  NAKATSUKA DAISUKE INC.
  Tokyo, Japan
designers
  DAISUKE NAKATSUKA, JUNKO NAKATSUKA,
  TOMOKO KANOU, RYOKO YAGITA,
  KOICHIROU IKEDA, RYOKEI KURABA
client
  SHU UEMURA COSMETICS INC.

creative firm
  DESIGN GUYS
  MInneapolis, Minnesota
art director
  STEVEN SIKORA
designer
  JAY THEIGE
client
  BATH & BODY WORKS

creative firm
  LMS DESIGN
  Stamford, Connecticut
designers
  RICHARD SHEAR, RICK MAPES, ALEX WILLIAMS
client
  J.B. WILLIAMS

creative firm
  WALLACE CHURCH ASSOCIATES INC.
  New York, New York
creative director
  STAN CHURCH
designers
  WENDY CHURCH, PAULA BUNNY
client
  SCHROEDER & TREMAYNE

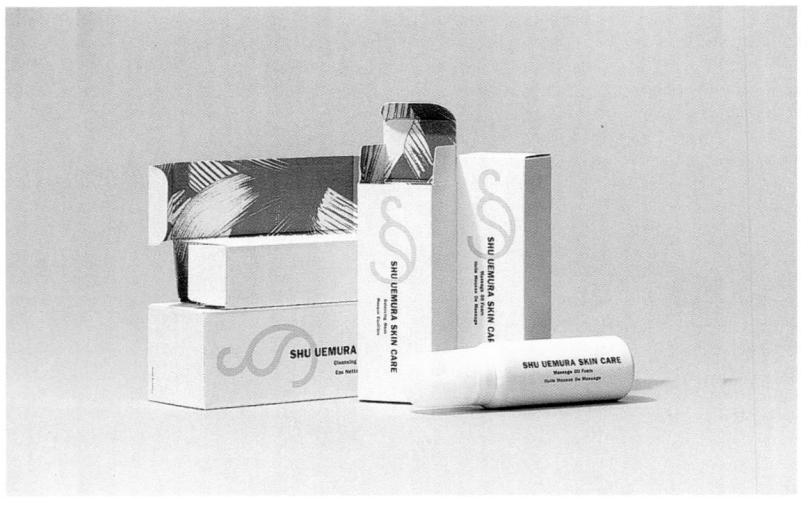

creative firm
  NAKATSUKA DAISUKE INC.
  Tokyo, Japan
designers
  SHU UEMURA, DAISUKE NAKATSUKA,
  JUNKO NAKATSUKA, TOM NAKATSUKA,
  KANNA NUMAJIRI, OSAMU KUWATA
client
  SHU UEMURA COSMETICS INC.

creative firm
  SAYLES GRAPHIC DESIGN
  Des Moines, Iowa
art director, illustrator
  JOHN SAYLES
client
  SUMER DISTRIBUTING

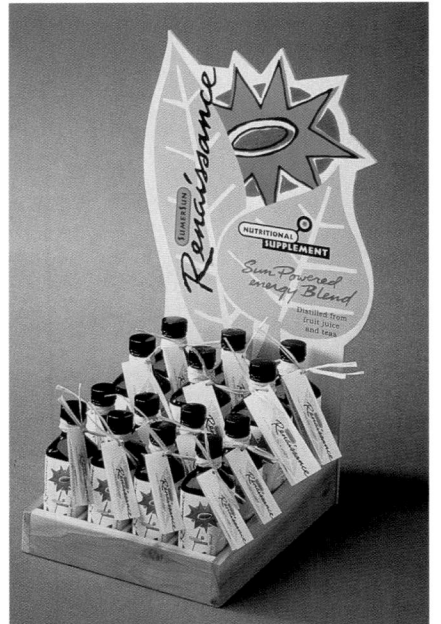

creative firm
  SIBLEY PETEET DESIGN
  Dallas, Texas
designer
  JOY PRICE
client
  SKIN CEUTICALS

creative firm
 WALLACE CHURCH ASSOCIATES INC.
 New York, New York
creative director
 STAN CHURCH
designers
 WENDY CHURCH, DEREK SAMUEL
client
 INSTEAD

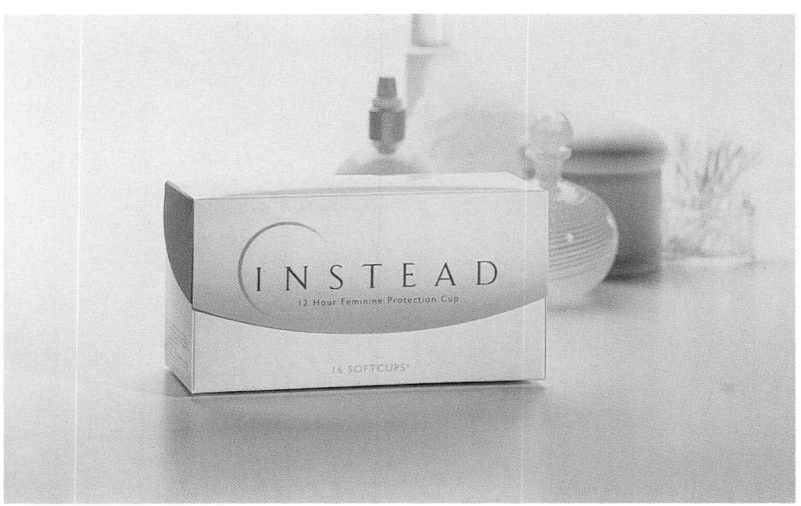

creative firm
 UKULELE DESIGN CONSULTANTS PTE LTD
 Singapore
design director
 KIM CHUN-WEI
designer
 LYNN LIM
client
 HIO SENG CO. PTE LTD

creative firm
 TANGRAM STRATEGIC DESIGN
 Novara, Italy
creative director, art director, designer
 ENRICO SEMPI
client
 GOLDEN LADY

creative firm
  INTERBRAND GERSTMAN + MEYERS
  New York, New York
creative director
  RAFAEL FELICIANO
client
  WHITEHALL ROBBINS

creative firm
  WALLACE CHURCH ASSOCIATES INC.
  New York, New York
creative director
  STAN CHURCH
designer
  JOE CUTICONE
illustrator
  LUCIAN TOMA
client
  GILLETTE

creative firm
  INTERBRAND GERSTMAN + MEYERS
  New York, New York
creative director
  CHRIS SANDERS
design director
  MICHAEL ENDY
senior designer
  MELISSA MULLIN
client
  PROCTOR & GAMBLE

creative firm
  INTERBRAND GERSTMAN + MEYERS
  New York, New York
creative director
  RAFAEL FELICIANO
client
  WHITEHALL ROBINS

creative firm
  INTERBRAND GERSTMAN + MEYERS
  New York, New York
creative director
  RAFAEL FELICIANO
client
  LANDER COMPANY

creative firm
  WALLACE CHURCH ASSOCIATES INC.
  New York, New York
creative directors
  STAN CHURCH, NIN GLAISTER
designer
  PAULA BUNNY
client
  TAYLOR MADE

creative firm
  INTERBRAND GERSTMAN + MEYERS
  New York, New York
creative directors
  JUAN CONCEPCION, MITCH GOTTLIEB
senior designer
  MELISSA MULLIN
client
  SCHERING PLOUGN

creative firm
  INTERBRAND GERSTMAN + MEYERS
  New York, New York
creative director
  JUAN CONCEPCION
client
  GENERAL MOTORS

creative firm
  INTERBRAND GERSTMAN + MEYERS
  New York, New York
creative director
  MITCH GOTTLIEB
client
  SHERWIN WILLIAMS

creative firm
  COMPASS DESIGN
  Minneapolis, Minnesota
designers
  MITCHELL LINDGREN, TOM ARTHUR, RICH McGOWEN
client
  TARGET STORES

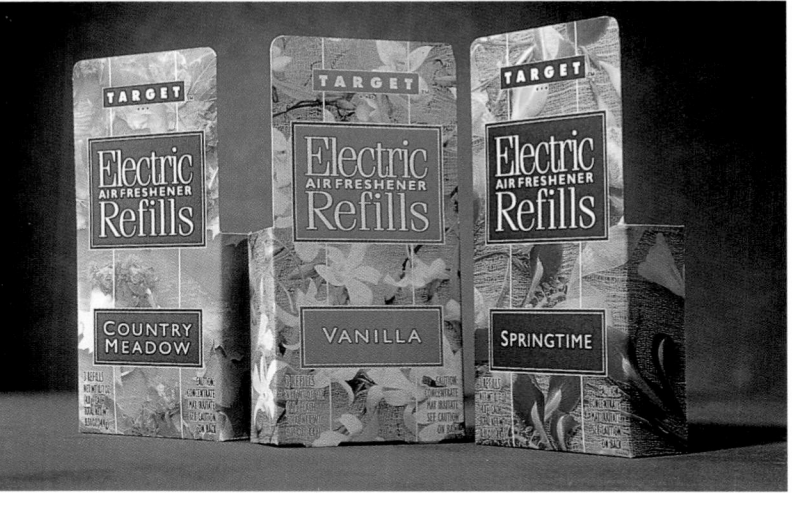

creative firm
  COMPASS DESIGN
  Minneapolis, Minnesota
designers
  MITCHELL LINDGREN, TOM ARTHUR, RICH McGOWEN
client
  TARGET STORES

creative firm
  INTERBRAND GERSTMAN + MEYERS
  New York, New York
creative director
  RAFAEL FELICIANO
client
  MIRACLE GRO

creative firm
  PHILLIPS DESIGN GROUP
  Boston, Massachusetts
creative director
  STEVE PHILLIPS
senior designer
  SUSAN LOGCHER
client
  OPUS

creative firm
  TANGRAM STRATEGIC DESIGN
  Novara, Italy
creative director, art director
  ENRICO SEMPI
designers
  ENRICO SEMPI, ANTONELLA TREVISAN,
  ANNA GRIMALDI
photographer
  LA FOTOGRAPHIA DIE. MARI
client
  BRICO

creative firm
  ROSS ADVERTISING
  Peoria, Illinois
executive creative director
  SKIP DAMPIER
art directors
  NICK JIBBEN, BRAD PASCUAL
copywriter
  JOHN RUEBUSH
client
  GRIDIRON

creative firm
  TELMET DESIGN ASSOCIATES
  Toronto, Ontario, Canada
designer
  TILT TELMET
client
  IONS WORLD CORPORATION

creative firm
THOMPSON & COMPANY
Memphis, Tennesee
creative director
TRACE HALLOWELL
art director
KENNY PATRICK
illustrator
ADAM McCAULEY
client
MEMPHIS REDBIRDS

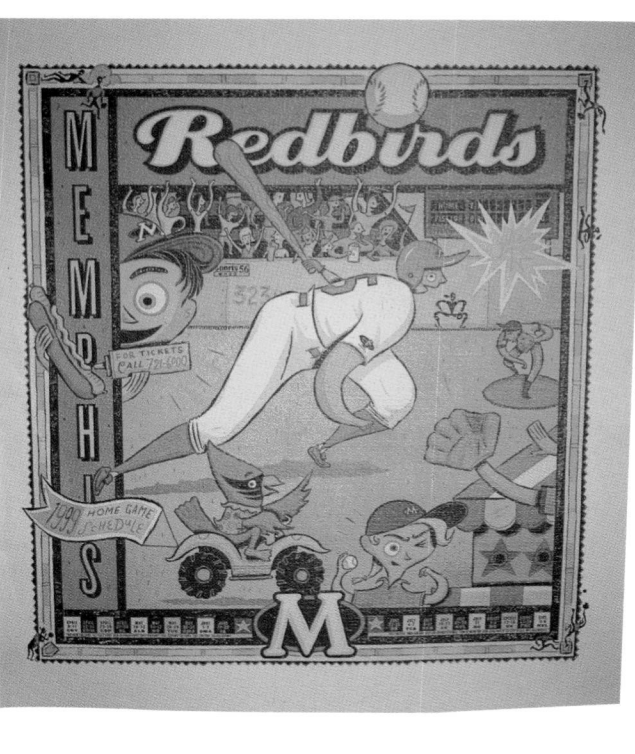

THE NEW ATTACK SUBMARINE. IT'S ALL COMING TOGETHER.

ELECTRIC BOAT CORPORATION
A GENERAL DYNAMICS COMPANY

creative firm
KEILER & COMPANY
Farmington, Connecticut
designer
JEFF LIN
client
ELECTRIC BOAT

creative firm
OH&CO IN COLLABORATION WITH **IDEO**
New York, New York
creative director
BRENT OPPENHEIMER
strategy director
ROBIN HAUETER
design director
MARY ELLEN BUTTNER
copywriter
GINGER STRAND
client
AMTRAK

creative firm
KIRK DESIGN
Prescott, Arizona
designer
MARY JO KIRK
client
WHISKEY ROW MARATHON 1998

creative firm
NAKATSUKA DAISUKE INC.
Tokyo, Japan
designers
**DAISUKE NAKATSUKA, TOM NAKATSUKA,
HIROMI YAMADA, SHOZO NAKAMURA**
client
YAMASA CORPORATION

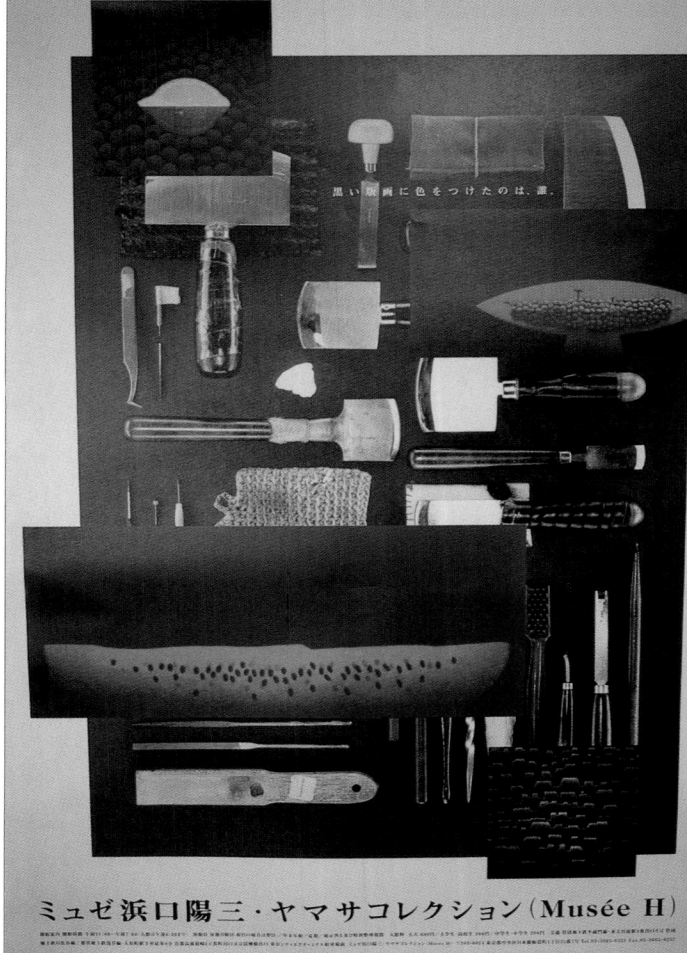

creative firm
  NESNADNY & SCHWARTZ
  Cleveland, Ohio
designer
  GREGORY OZNOWICH
client
  CLEVELAND ZOOLOGICAL SOCIETY

creative firm
  NIKE, INC.
  Beaverton, Oregon
designer
  JASON BACON
client
  NIKE EVENTS

creative firm
  NESNADNY & SCHWARTZ
  Cleveland, Ohio
designer
  TIMOTHY LACHINA
client
  ROCK AND ROLL HALL OF FAME MUSEUM

creative firm
  SAYLES GRAPHIC DESIGN
  Des Moines, Iowa
designer
  JOHN SAYLES
client
  ADVERTISING CLUB OF DELAWARE

creative firm
CREATIVE SERVICES
New York, New York
art director
GIULIO TURTURO
illustrator
MATT MAHURIN
client
SONY CLASSICAL

creative firm
BATEY ADS (PTE) LTD.
Singapore
designers
GARY KNIGHT, DARREN HOGAN
client
SINGAPORE ANTI-NARCOTICS ASSOCIATION

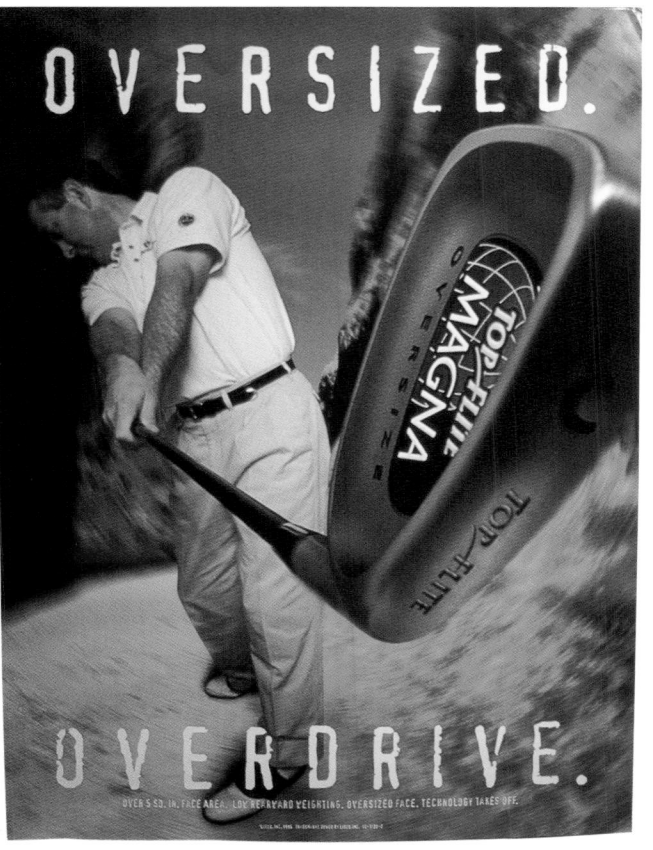

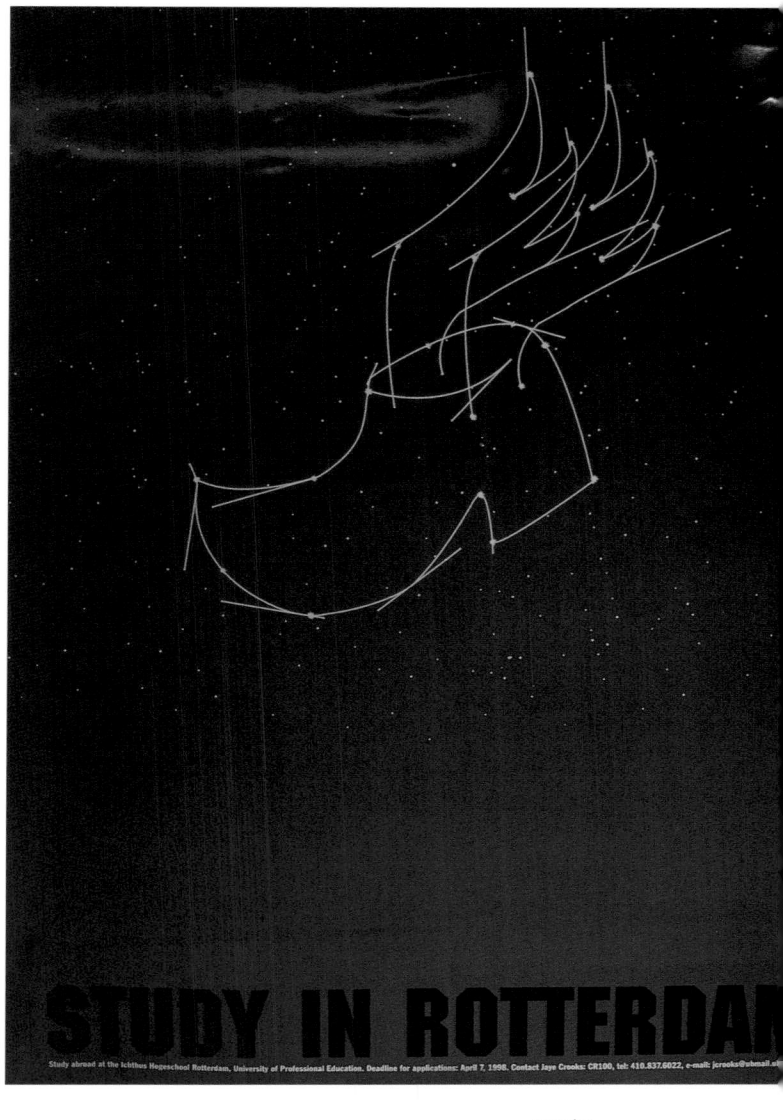

creative firm
THE RIORDON DESIGN GROUP INC.
Ontario, Canada
art director
RIC RIORDON
designer
GREER HUTCHISON
photography
DAVID GRAHAM WHITE
client
COMMUNITY FOUNDATION OF OAKVILLE

RIVERLIFE
PITTSBURGH

creative firm
AGNEW MOYER SMITH INC.
Pittsburgh, Pennsylvania
designers
JOHN SOTIRAKIS, GINA DATRES
client
PITTSBURGH DEPARTMENT OF CITY PLANNING

creative firm
CREATIVE SERVICES
New York, New York
art director, designer
GIULIO TURTURRO
client
SONY CLASSICAL

creative firm
GREG WALTERS DESIGN
Seattle, Washington
designers
GREG WALTERS, RICHARD HESS
client
SEATTLE DESIGN ASSOCIATION

creative firm
  MITHOFF ADVERTISING INC.
  El Paso, Texas
designer
  CLIVE COCHRAN
illustrator
  MELISSA GRIMES
client
  GRAPHIC ARTS SOCIETY OF EL PASO
  AND UNIVERSITY OF TEXAS AT EL PASO

creative firm
  DESIGN MACHINE
  New York, New York
creative director, art director, designer
  ALEXANDER GELMAN
client
  FIVE FIFTY FIVE GALLERY

creative firm
  CAHAN & ASSOCIATES
    San Francisco, California
designer
  BOB DINETZ
client
  WESTERN ART DIRECTORS CLUB

creative firm
  ESTUDIO RAY
    Phoenix, Arizona
art directors
  CHRISTINE RAY, JOE RAY
designers
  JOE RAY, LESLIE LINK
client
  MARICOPA COMMUNITY COLLEGES

creative firm
  AFTER HOURS CREATIVE
    Phoenix, Arizona
client
  MARICOPA COMMUNITY COLLEGE DISTRICT

1999 OUTSTANDING PERFORMERS COMPETITION

Categories: Piano, Jazz Combo, Guitar, Instrumental, Vocal, Chamber Ensemble Deadline for Entries: 3 February, 1999 Contact Your Campus Music Department or Ruth Yandell at 461-7574

creative firm
  SAGMEISTER, INC.
    New York, New York
designer
  STEFAN SAGMEISTER
client
  AIGA

creative firm
  CREATIVE SERVICES
  New York, New York
art director, designer
  GIULIO TURTURRO
photographer
  EDWARD STEICHEN
client
  SONY CLASSICAL

creative firm
  MULLER + CO.
  Kansas City, Missouri
creative director
  JOHN MULLER
art director, designer
  JANE HUSKEY
client
  KANSAS CITY BLUES + JAZZ FESTIVAL

creative firm
  LEOPARD COMMUNICATIONS
  Boulder, Colorado
designers
  BRENDAN HEMP, RICH LOPEZ
client
  IBM PRINTING SYSTEMS COMPANY

"Printing is the only product of civilization necessary to the existence of free men."

Charles Dickens

*info*Print

IBM

TheaterWorks
Steve Campo, Executive Director
presents

valley·song
BY ATHOL FUGARD

"Vivid, haunting...a complex play, simply and beautifully done."
NEW YORK TIMES

Directed by Rob Ruggiero

May 23 through June 22, 1997

TheaterWorks
The Huntsky Theater
233 Pearl Street
Downtown Hartford

For tickets call (860)527-7838

BankBoston

creative firm
  KEILER & COMPANY
  Farmington, Connecticut
designer
  JAMES PETTUS
client
  THEATERWORKS

What is Death?

creative firm
  SIBLEY PETEET DESIGN
  Dallas, Texas
designer
  DAVID BECK
photographer
  DUANE MICHAELS
client
  DUANE MICHAELS

creative firm
  TOM FOWLER, INC.
  Stamford, Connecticut
art director, designer, illustrator
  THOMAS G. FOWLER
client
  CONNECTICUT GRAND OPERA & ORCHESTRA

THE CONNECTICUT GRAND OPERA & ORCHESTRA PRES...

AnAllCzech
OPERA CONCERT

LAURENCE GILGORE, GENERAL DIRECTOR

creative firm
  ATLANTA COLLEGE OF ART
  Atlanta, Georgia
designer
  PETER WONG
client
  ATLANTA COLLEGE OF ART

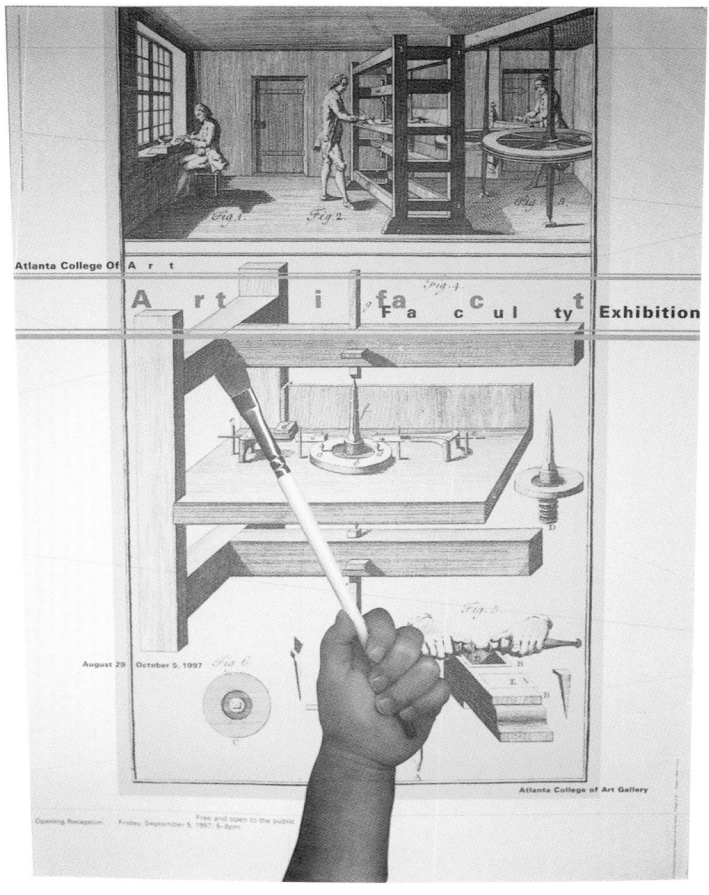

creative firm
  SHIELDS DESIGN
  Fresno, California
designer
  CHARLES SHIELDS
photography
  CAMERAD, INC.
client
  FRESNO DESIGN COMMUNITY

creative firm
  GARDNER DESIGN
  Wichita, Kansas
art directors
  BILL GARDNER, BRIAN MILLER
designer
  BRIAN MILLER
client
  KANSAS SPEECH-LANGUAGE-HEARING-ASSOCIATION

creative firm
  FUSION ART INSTITUTE
  Shizuoka-ken, Japan
art director
  HYOMON FUMIHIKO ENOKIDO
designers
  KOSHI OGAWA, HIDEAKI ENOKIDO
photographer
  TORU KINOSHITA
client
  SADOYAₑₜC⁻ᴵᴱ

creative firm
  GARDNER DESIGN
  Wichita, Kansas
art directors, designers
  BILL GARDNER, BRIAN MILLER
illustrator
  C.B. MORDAN
client
  SEDGWICK COUNTY ZOO

creative firm
  GARDNER DESIGN
  Wichita, Kansas
art director, designer
  BRIAN MILLER
client
  PRINTING HOUSE CRAFTSMAN

creative firm
MIRES DESIGN, INC.
San Diego, California
designers
SCOTT MIRES, DEBORAH HOM
illustrators
SCOTT MIRES, DAVE ADEY, MIGUEL PEREZ
photographer
CARL VANDERSCHUIT
client
JABRA CORPORATION

creative firm
MITHOFF ADVERTISING INC.
El Paso, Texas
designer
CLIVE COCHRAN
client
EL PASO PRO-MUSICA

creative firm
  TOM FOWLER, INC.
    Stamford, Connecticut
art director, designer, illustrator
  THOMAS G. FOWLER
client
  CONNECTICUT GRAND OPERA & ORCHESTRA

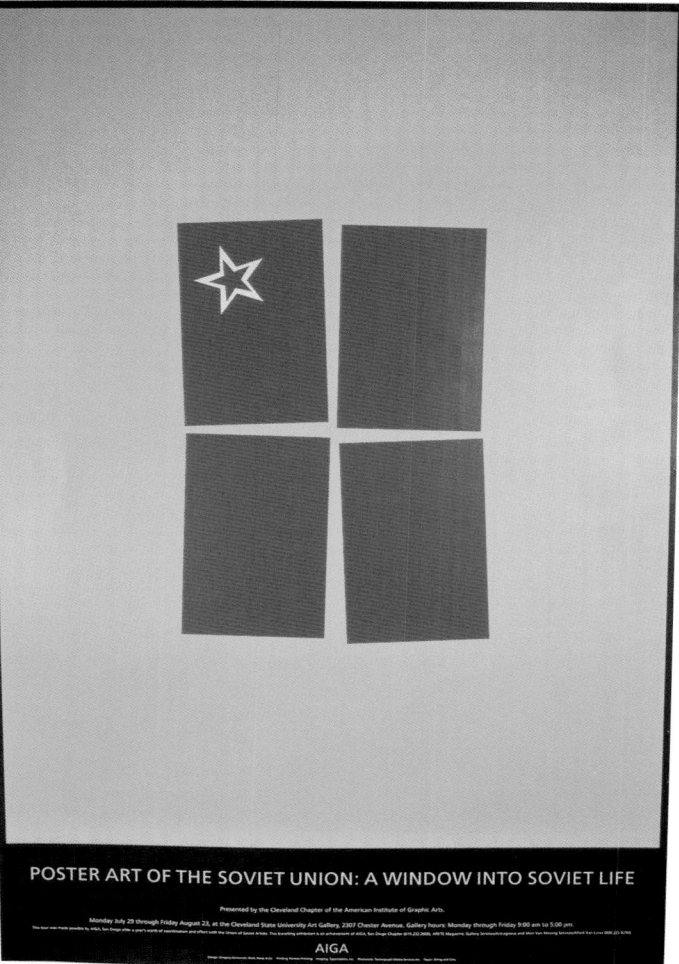

POSTER ART OF THE SOVIET UNION: A WINDOW INTO SOVIET LIFE

AIGA

creative firm
  WATT, ROOP & CO.
    Cleveland, Ohio
designers
  GREG OZNOWICH, JEFF PRUGH
client
  AIGA/CLEVELAND CHAPTER

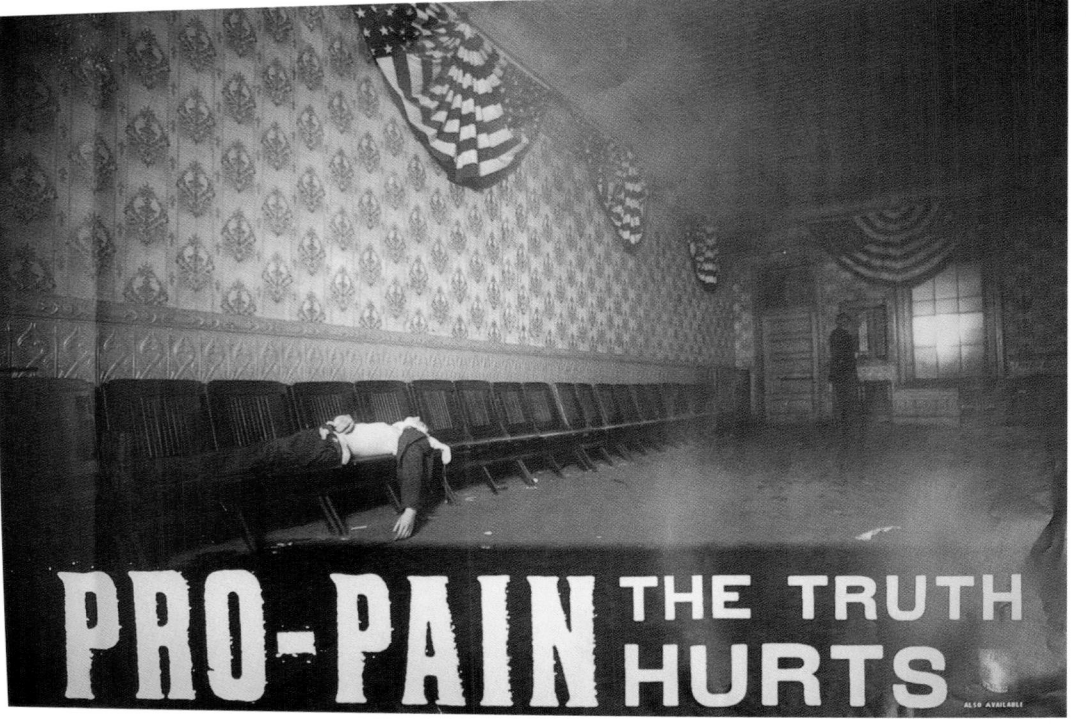

creative firm
SAGMEISTER INC.
New York, New York
designers
STEFAN SAGMEISTER, VERONICA OH
client
ENERGY RECORDS

creative firm
CAHAN & ASSOCIATES
San Francisco, California
designer
CRAIG CLARK
client
SAN FRANCISCO CREATIVE ALLIANCE

creative firm
  ASHER STUDIO
  Denver, Colorado
designers
  CONNIE ASHER, TRISH CUMMINGS
client
  MCI TELECOMMUNICATIONS

creative firm
  THE VISUAL MAFIA
  New York, New York
designers
  MATTHEW McGUINNESS, MORGAN SHEASBY,
  NICK BILTON, CHRIS GARVEY
client
  SOCIAL AWARENESS

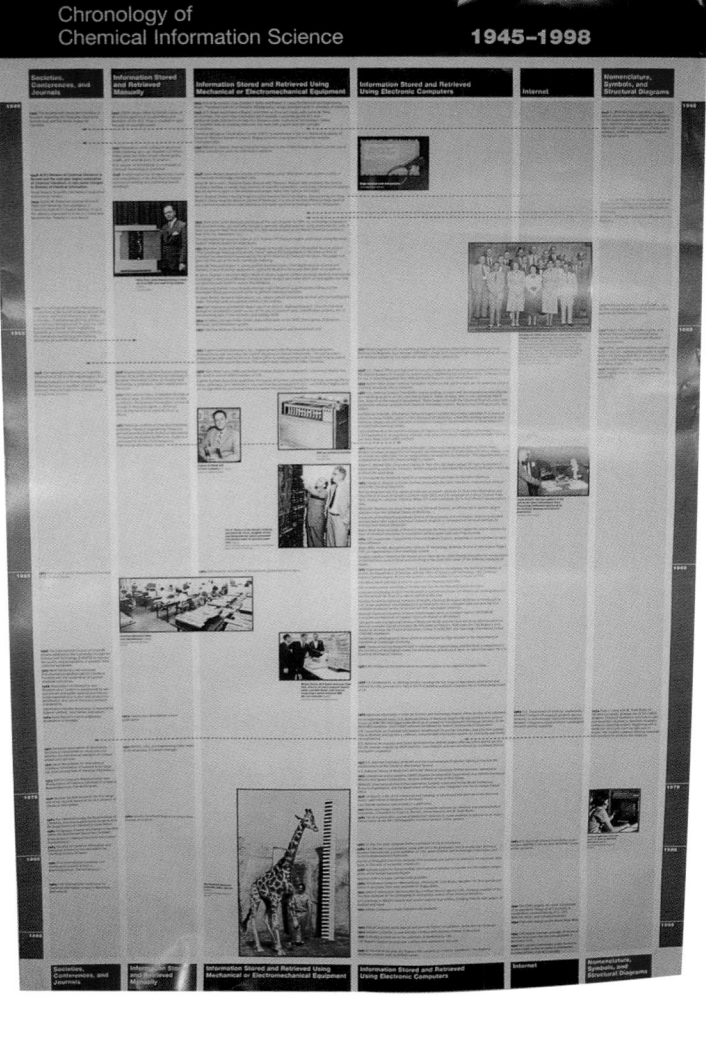

creative firm
JOEL KATZ DESIGN ASSOCIATES
Philadelphia, Pennsylvania
creative director, designer
JOEL KATZ
client
CHEMICAL HERITAGE FOUNDATION

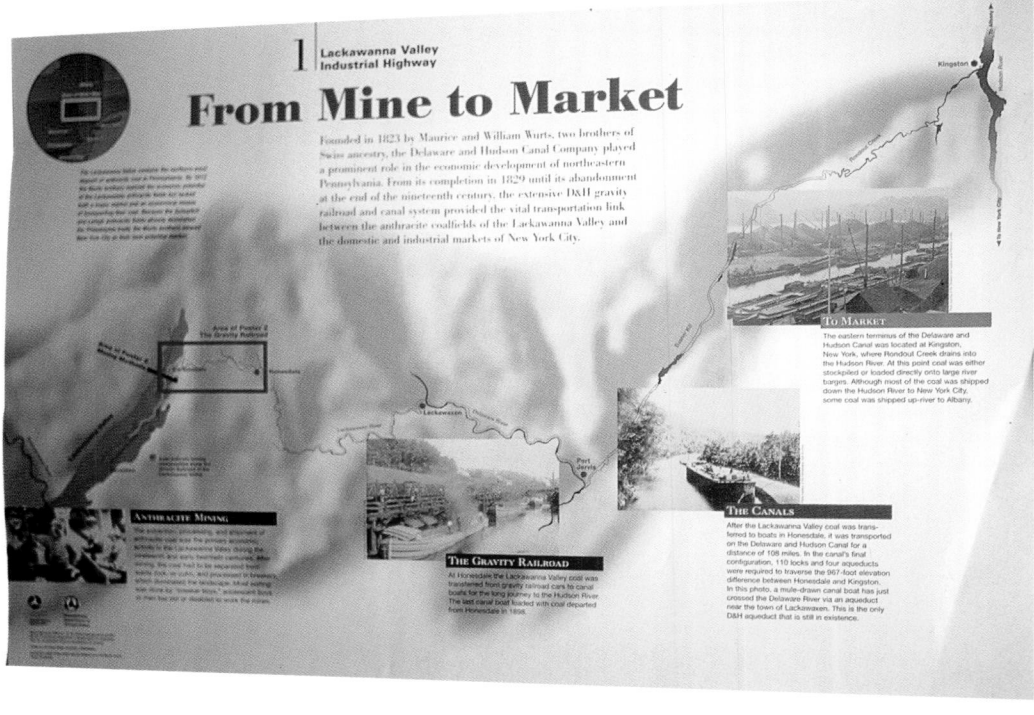

creative firm
JOEL KATZ DESIGN ASSOCIATES
Philadelphia, Pennsylvania
creative director
JOEL KATZ
designer, illustrator
DAVE SCHPOK
client
PENNSYLVANIA DEPARTMENT OF TRANSPORTATION

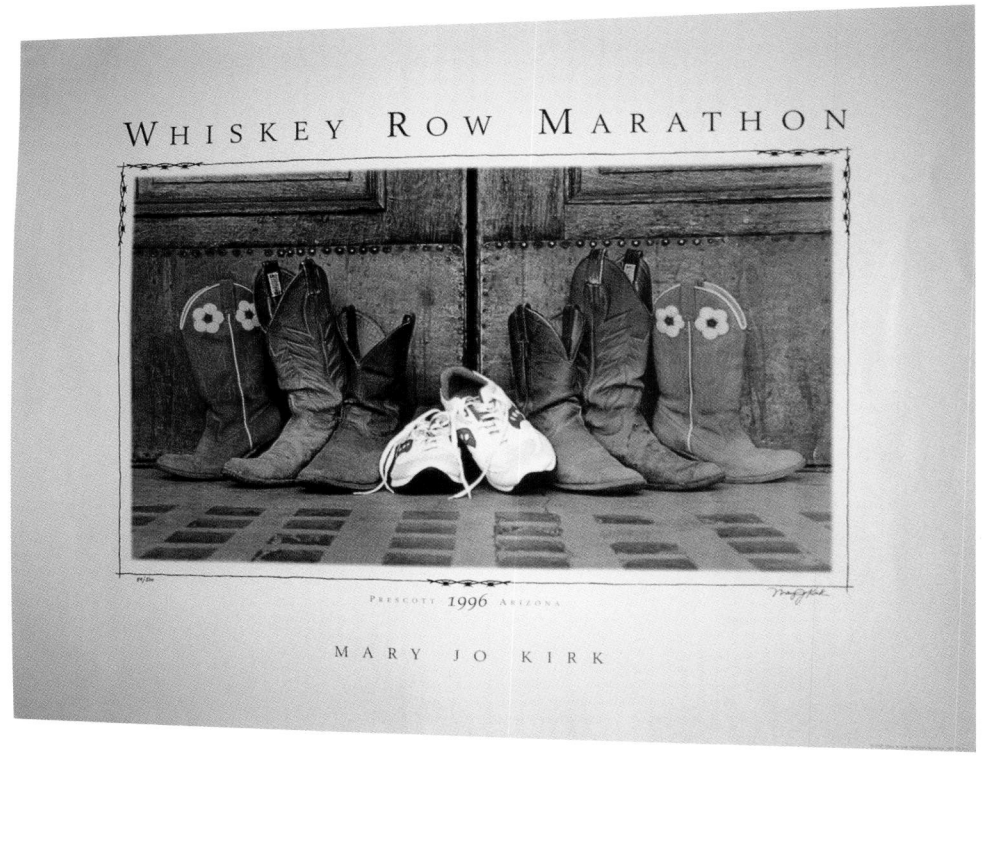

WHISKEY ROW MARATHON

PRESCOTT 1996 ARIZONA

MARY JO KIRK

creative firm
  KIRK DESIGN
  Prescott, Arizona
designer
  MARY JO KIRK
client
  WHISKEY ROW MARATHON 1996

WHISKEY ROW MARATHON

PRESCOTT 1997 ARIZONA

MARY JO KIRK

creative firm
  KIRK DESIGN
  Prescott, Arizona
designer
  MARY JO KIRK
client
  WHISKEY ROW MARATHON 1997

creative firm
   POWELL TATE CREATIVE GROUP
   Washington, D.C.
designers
   LEE JENKINS, DAN CAVEY
client
   NATIONAL PARK FOUNDATION

creative firm
   SULLIVAN SCULLY DESIGN GROUP
   Flagstaff, Arizona
designers
   PJ NIDECKER, JULIE SULLIVAN
client
   PETRIFIED FOREST NATIONAL PARK

creative firm
MULLER + CO.
Kansas City, Missouri
creative director
JOHN MULLER
art director
MARK BOTSFORD
designer
JANE HUSKEY
illustrator
MIKE REGNIER
copywriter
ROB HOLMES
client
MISSOURI DIVISION OF TOURISM

creative firm
MULLER + CO.
Kansas City, Missouri
creative director
JOHN MULLER
art director
MARK BOTSFORD
designer
JANE HUSKEY
illustrator
MIKE REGNIER
copywriter
ROB HOLMES
client
MISSOURI DIVISION OF TOURISM

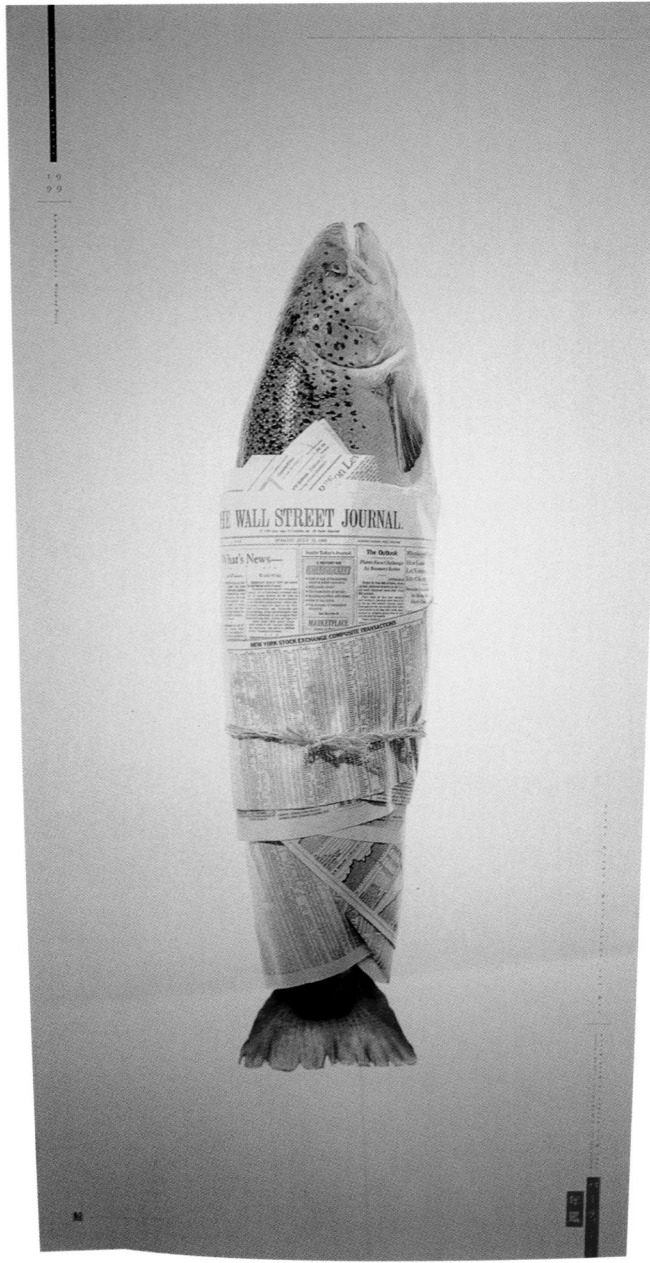

creative firm
  SQUIRES & COMPANY
  Dallas, Texas
designer
  BRANDON MURPHY
client
  SQUIRES & COMPANY

creative firm
  BBK STUDIO INC.
  Grand Rapids, Michigan
creative director
  KEVIN BUDELMANN
designer, typesetter
  ALISON POPP
photographer
  BILL LINDHOUT
calligrapher
  MATT RYZENGA
client
  BBK STUDIO INC.

WOOD

WORK

creative firm
   KEITH WOOD PHOTOGRAPHY INC.
      Portland, Oregon
designers
   EISENBERG & ASSOCIATION
client
   KEITH WOOD PHOTOGRAPHY INC.

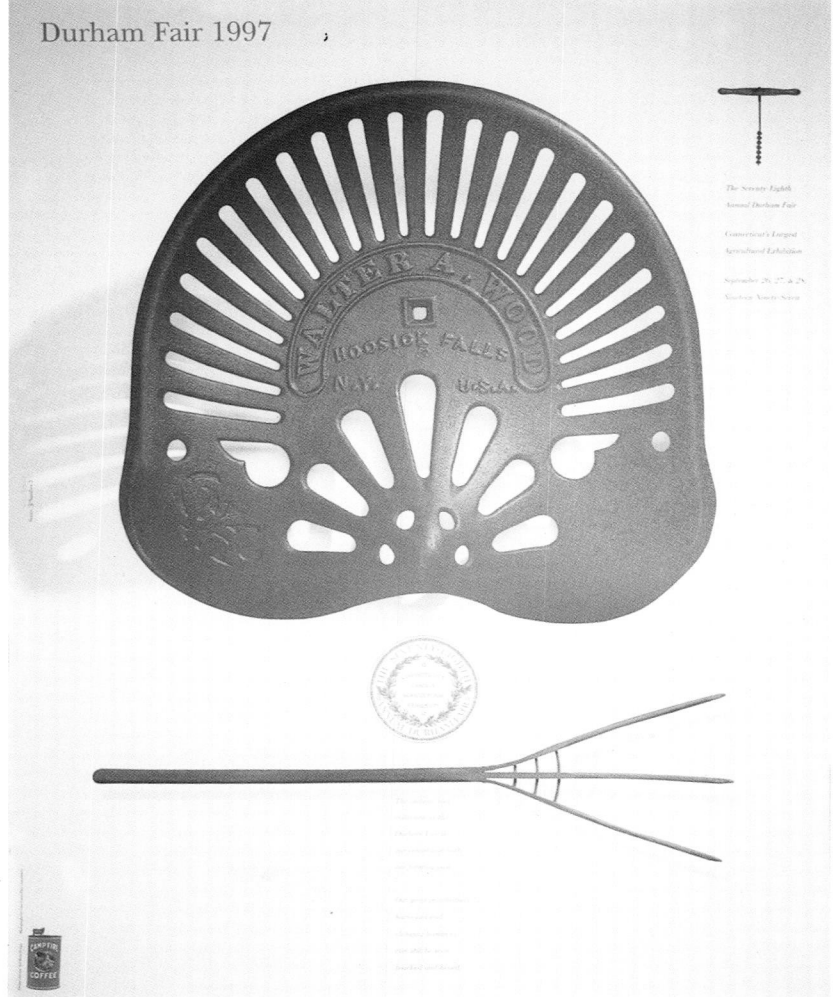

Durham Fair 1997

creative firm
   TED BERTZ GRAPHIC DESIGN, INC.
      Middletown, Connecticut
designers
   TED BERTZ, MARK TERRANOVA
photographers
   GLEN CURTIS, JOHN GIAMMATTEO
client
   THE DURHAM FAIR ASSOCIATION

Rock and Roll Hall of Fame and Museum

Groundbreaking

Monday June 7 1993

Cleveland, Ohio

creative firm
WATT, ROOP + CO.
Cleveland, Ohio
designer
GREG OZNOWICH
client
ROCK-N-ROLL HALL OF FAME GROUNDBREAKING

TRENDS ALWAYS STOP; THE CURVE ALWAYS STRAIGHTENS OUT.

10   AUSTIN DALLAS FORT WORTH HOUSTON SAN ANTONIO WASHINGTON, DC MEXICO CITY www.haynesboone.com

haynes boone

creative firm
GREENFIELD/BELSER LTD
Washington, D.C.
art director
BURKEY BELSER
designer
TOM CAMERON
client
HAYNES AND BOONE

creative firm
  GRETEMAN GROUP
  Wichita, Kansas
creative director
  SONIA GRETEMAN
art directors
  SONIA GRETEMAN, JAMES STRANGE
designer
  JO QUILLIN
client
  WICHITA HUMANE SOCIETY

creative firm
  DESIGN TEAM ONE, INC.
  Cincinnati, Ohio
designer
  DAN BITTMAN
client
  THE CINCINNATI BALLET COMPANY

creative firm
  MULLER + CO.
  Kansas City, Missouri
creative director
  JOHN MULLER
art director, designer
  MARK VOSS
client
  KANSAS CITY BLUES & JAZZ FESTIVAL

creative firm
  THE PETERSON GROUP
  New York, New York
design director
  ALEX PENNINGTON
client
  FUJIFILM COMPUTER PRODUCTS

creative firm
  FUSION ART INSTITUTE
  Shizuoka-ken, Japan
art director
  HYOMON FUMIHIKO ENOKIDO
designers
  KOSHI OGAWA, HIDEAKI ENOKIDO
photographer
  TORU KINOSHITA
client
  JAGDA

creative firm
  DISNEY DESIGN GROUP
  Lake Buena Vista, Florida
creative director
  MICHELE KEATING
art director
  DAVID WHITAKER
designer, illustrator
  ROBERT VANN
client
  WALT DISNEY ATTRACTIONS MERCHANDISE

creative firm
CAHAN & ASSOCIATES
San Francisco, California
designer
KEVIN ROBERSON
client
SAN FRANCISCO CREATIVE ALLIANCE

creative firm
CLEVER LITTLE BOY DESIGNS
Richmond, Kentucky
designers
GRAHAM ALLEN, AMY CAMPBELL
client
GILES GALLERY (EASTERN KENTUCKY UNIVERSITY)

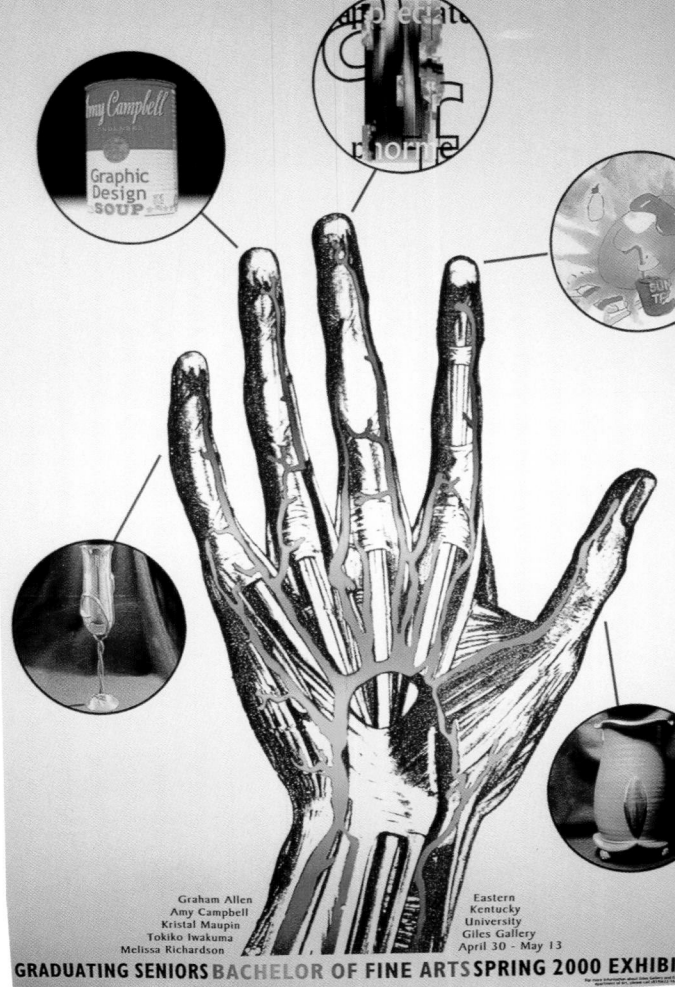

Alcohol. Don't make an
exhibition of yourself

Planning a great night out?
Avoid embarrassing yourself
and your friends:

• eat if you are going to drink
• try a low-alcohol alternative
• have an alcohol-free drink
  as a spacer

Great times with friends are
even better when you can
remember them.

alcohol
go easy

creative firm
    BUTLER KEMP DESIGN
    North Adelaide, Australia
art director
    DEREK BUTLER
designers
    HELLEN KIPRIZLOGLOU, JULIE KEMP
photographer
    RICHARD LYONS
client
    DRUG & ALCOHOL SERVICES COUNCIL

creative firm
    THE ARTIME GROUP
    Pasadena, California
creative director
    HENRY ARTIME
art director
    DENVER MINNICH
designer
    LISA SARKISSIAN
client
    AMERICAN CANCER SOCIETY

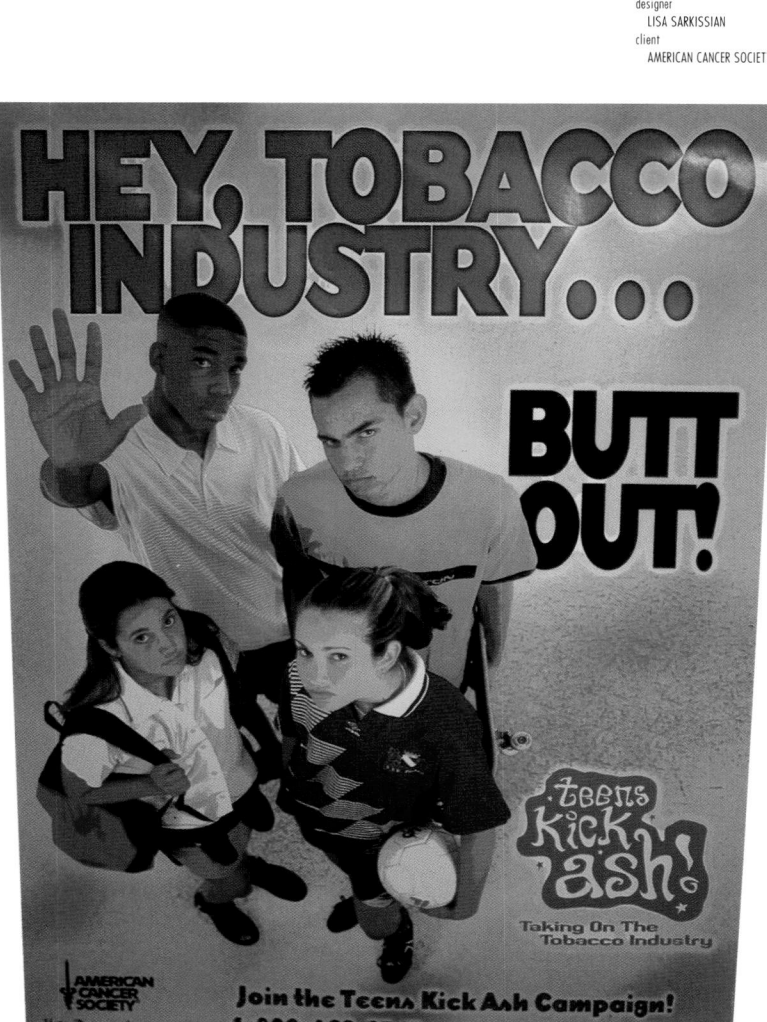

HEY, TOBACCO INDUSTRY...

BUTT OUT!

teens Kick ash!

Taking On The
Tobacco Industry

AMERICAN
CANCER
SOCIETY

Hope.Progress.Answers.

Join the Teens Kick Ash Campaign!
1-800-ACS-2345 • www.cancer.org/ca

1997 Pulitzer Prize Finalist

Collected Stories

By Donald Margulies
Directed by Jacques Cartier

They changed my life
so how can they be
solely your stories
anymore?

They stopped being
your stories
when you
told them to me

Huntington
THEATRE COMPANY

264 Huntington Avenue, Boston
Boston's Leading Professional Theatre,
in Residence at Boston University

Box Office
(617) 266-0800
Ticketmaster
931-ARTS

March 6 –
April 5,
1998

Peter Altman
Producing Director

Michael Maso
Managing Director

creative firm
KOR GROUP
Boston, Massachusetts
designers
ANNE CALLAHAN, CHRIS RICHARD
client
HUNTINGTON THEATRE

creative firm
MITHOFF ADVERTISING INC.
El Paso, Texas
designer
CLIVE COCHRAN
client
UNIVERSITY OF TEXAS AT EL PASO

UTEP
ART
FACULTY
EXHIBIT
OPEN
JAN.23-
FEB.10.

Main Gallery, Third Floor,
Fox Fine Arts Center,
University of Texas at El Paso.

Opening Reception:
Thursday, January 23, 7-9pm.

Gallery Hours:
8:30-4:30 Mon-Fri
Open Thursday from 5-9pm.

The reception and exhibit
are free and open to the public.

creative firm
KOR GROUP
Boston, Massachusetts
designers
ANNE CALLAHAN, JIM GIBSON
client
HUNTINGTON THEATRE

creative firm
FRANK BASEMAN DESIGN
Jenkintown, Pennsylvania
designer
FRANK BASEMAN
client
ZEITGEIST FILMS

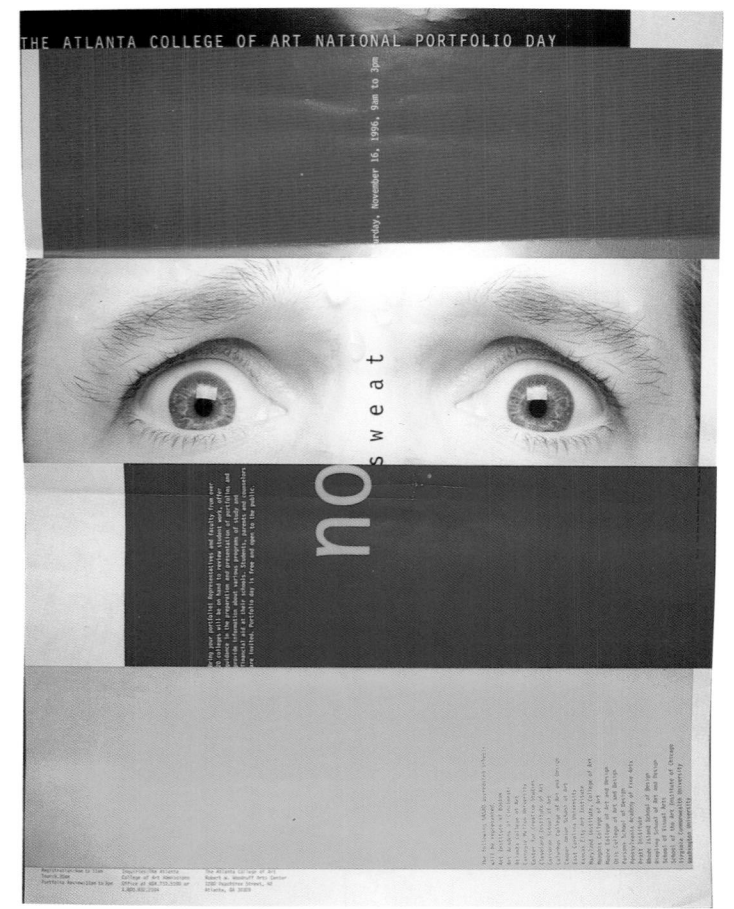

creative firm
ATLANTA COLLEGE OF ART
Atlanta, Georgia
designer
PETER WONG
concept
PETER WONG, MARK ROKFALUSI
client
ATLANTA COLLEGE OF ART

creative firm
ATLANTA COLLEGE OF ART
Atlanta, Georgia
designer
PETER WONG
design assistant
DOUGLAS EVANS
client
AMERICAN CENTER FOR DESIGN

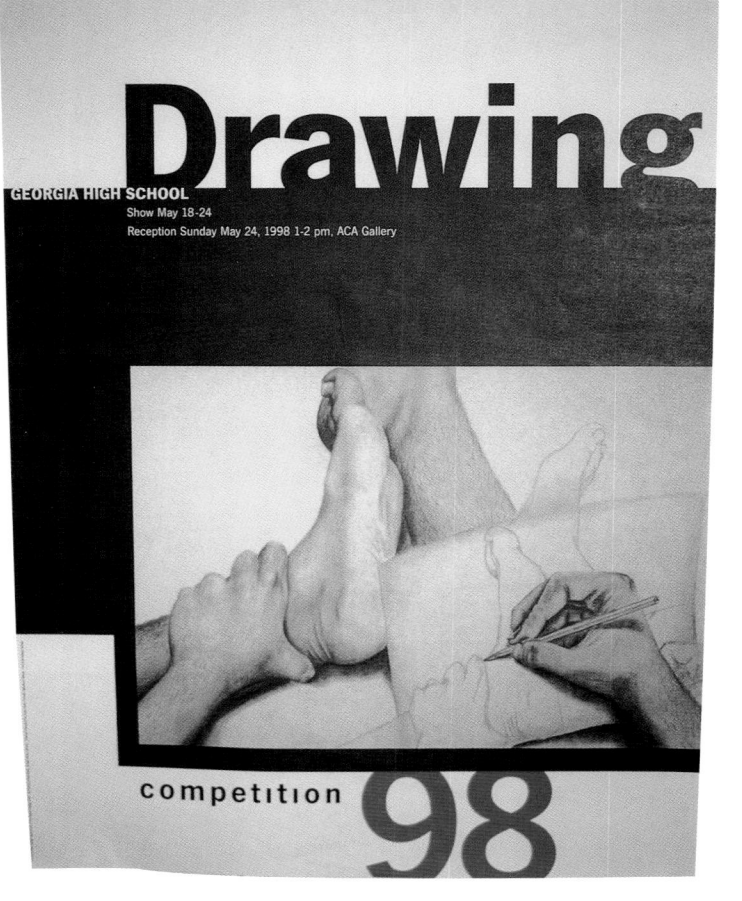

creative firm
  ATLANTA COLLEGE OF ART
  Atlanta, Georgia
art director
  PETER WONG
designer
  JASON LEHRMAN
client
  ATLANTA COLLEGE OF ART

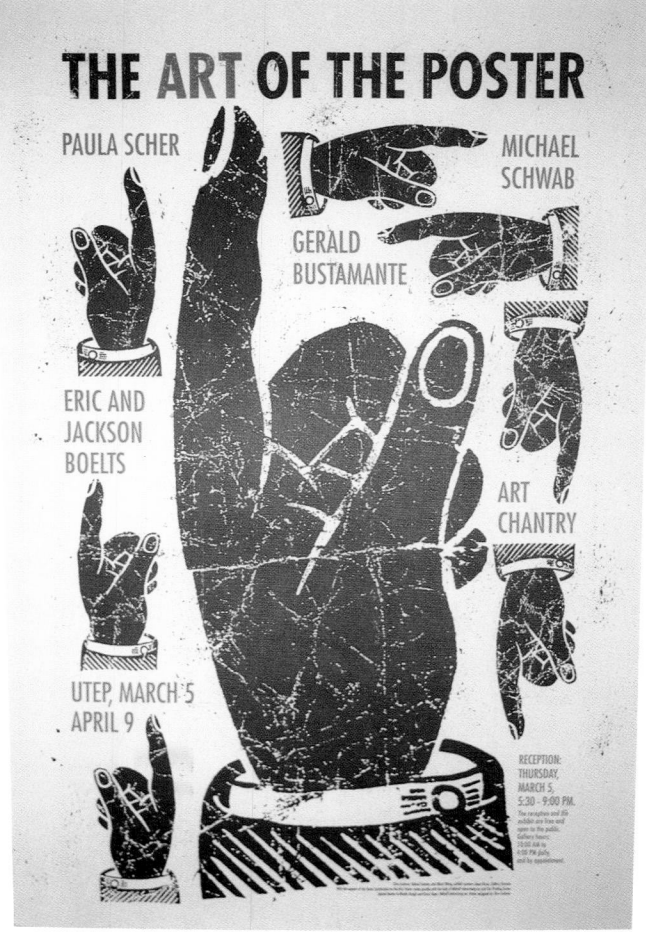

creative firm
  MITHOFF ADVERTISING INC.
  El Paso, Texas
designer
  CLIVE COCHRAN
client
  UNIVERSITY OF TEXAS AT EL PASO

creative firm
  GREG WALTERS DESIGN
  Seattle, Washington
designer
  GREG WALTERS
client
  PIONEER SQUARE BUSINESS IMPROVEMENT AREA

creative firm
  GREG WALTERS DESIGN
  Seattle, Washington
designer, illustrator
  GREG WALTERS
client
  PIONEER SQUARE BUSINESS IMPROVEMENT AREA

creative firm
  DESIGN MACHINE
  New York, New York
creative director, art director, designer
  ALEXANDER GELMAN
client
  GOLDEN BEE BIENNALE

creative firm
 KRISTINE HERRICK DESIGN
  Albany, New York
designer
 KRISTINE HERRICK
client
 TEMPLE UNIVERSITY SOCIOLOGY

creative firm
 NAKATSUKA DAISUKE INC.
  Tokyo, Japan
designers
 DAISUKE NAKATSUKA, TOM NAKATSUKA,
 HIROMI YAMADA, MARIKO ABE
client
 TOKAMACHI REGIONWIDE-AREA

creative firm
 KO DESIGN INSTITUTE
 Tachikawa-shi, Japan
art director, designer
 KOSHI OGAWA
calligrapher
 TSUYOSHI RYU
client
 JAGDA, KOSHI OGAWA

creative firm
 KO DESIGN INSTITUTE
 Tachikawa-shi, Japan
art director, designer
 KOSHI OGAWA
calligrapher
 TSUYOSHI RYU
client
 JAGDA, KOSHI OGAWA

creative firm
 KO DESIGN INSTITUTE
 Tachikawa-shi, Japan
art director, designer
 KOSHI OGAWA
calligrapher
 TSUYOSHI RYU
client
 KOSHI OGAWA

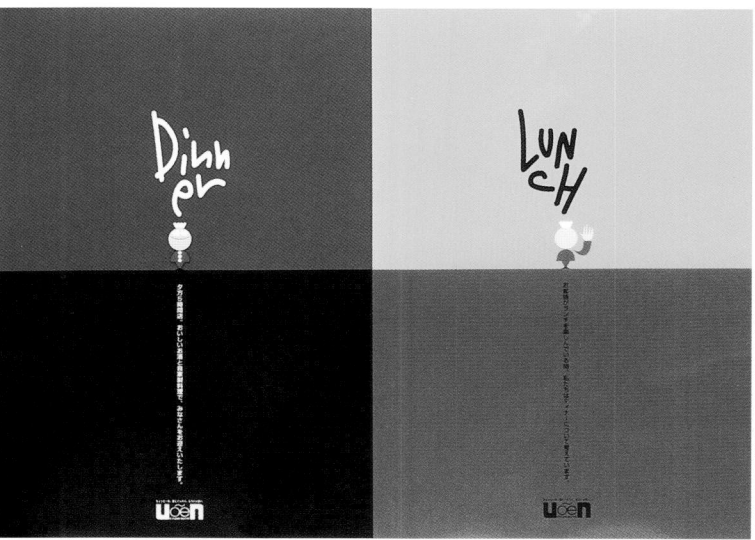

creative firm
  KO DESIGN INSTITUTE
  Tachikawa-shi, Japan
art director, designer
  KOSHI OGAWA
calligraphers
  TSUYOSHI RYU, SHIN OTANI
client
  HAJIME HIROSE

creative firm
  KO DESIGN INSTITUTE
  Tachikawa-shi, Japan
art director, designer
  KOSHI OGAWA
calligrapher
  TSUYOSHI RYU
client
  KOSHI OGAWA

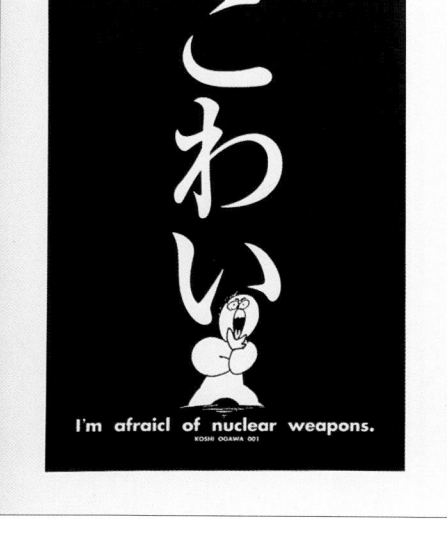

creative firm
  KO DESIGN INSTITUTE
  Tachikawa-shi, Japan
art director, designer
  KOSHI OGAWA
calligrapher
  TSUYOSHI RYU
client
  KOSHI OGAWA

creative firm
KO DESIGN INSTITUTE
Tachikawa-shi, Japan
art director, designer
KOSHI OGAWA
client
KOSHI OGAWA

creative firm
KO DESIGN INSTITUTE
Tachikawa-shi, Japan
art director, designer
KOSHI OGAWA
client
KOSHI OGAWA

creative firm
SQUIRES & COMPANY
Dallas, Texas
designer
BRANDON MURPHY
client
INTERFAITH HOUSING COALITION

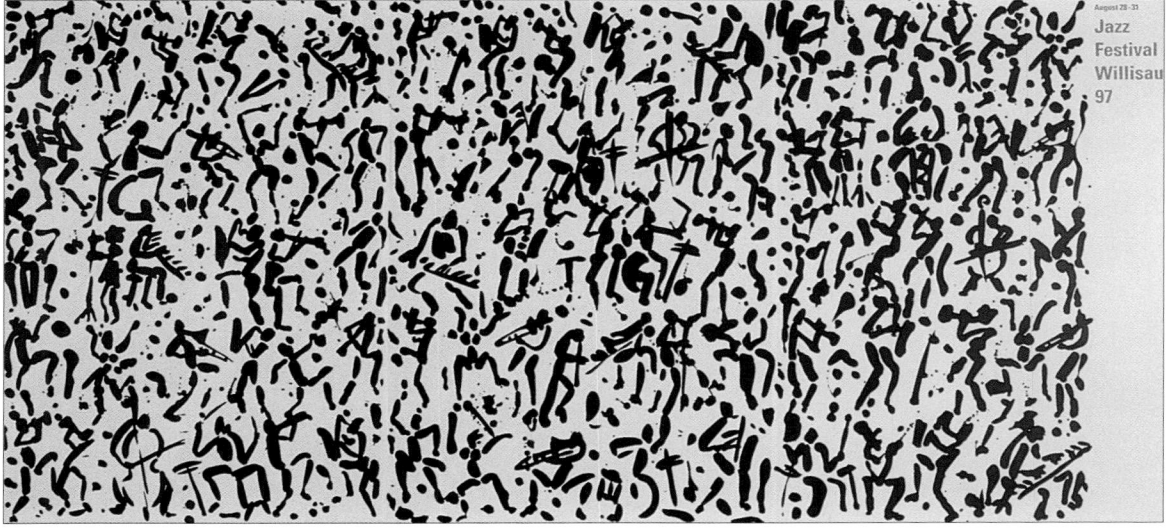

creative firm
  NIKLAUS TROXLER DESIGN
  Willisau, Switzerland
designer, illustrator, typographer
  NIKLAUS TROXLER
client
  JAZZ IN WILLISAU/SWITZERLAND

creative firm
  NIKLAUS TROXLER DESIGN
  Willisau, Switzerland
designer, illustrator, typographer
  NIKLAUS TROXLER
client
  JAZZ IN WILLISAU/SWITZERLAND

creative firm
  NIKLAUS TROXLER DESIGN
  Willisau, Switzerland
designer, illustrator, typographer
  NIKLAUS TROXLER
client
  FILM KUNST FEST SCHWERIN

creative firm
  NIKLAUS TROXLER DESIGN
    Willisau, Switzerland
designer, illustrator, typographer
  NIKLAUS TROXLER
client
  INTERNATIONAL LOGO FESTIVAL BEIJING/CHINA

International Logo Festival 98   Beijing
Sept. 13 - 16 1998   Beijing Exhibition Center

The Capital Corporation Image Institution (CCII)

International Trademark Exhibition   International Trademark Festival Design Award   Seminar of "Corporation Image and Brand Image in the 21st Century"

creative firm
  NIKLAUS TROXLER DESIGN
    Willisau, Switzerland
designer, illustrator, typographer
  NIKLAUS TROXLER
client
  JAZZ IN WILLISAU/SWITZERLAND

creative firm
  MINALE TATTERSFIELD + PARTNERS
    Richmond, Surrey, United Kingdom
creative director
  MARCELLO MINALE
designer
  LEE NEWHAM
client
  MINALE TATTERSFIELD + PARTNERS

25. Jazz Festival Willisau '99
Aug 26-29

creative firm
  TEAMWORK DESIGN LTD.
  Chai Wan, Hong Kong
design director
  GARY TAM
designers
  JOEL ONG, ALEX CHAN, IVY WONG
client
  NUANCE-WATSON (H.K) LTD.

creative firm
  BOLDRINI & FICCARDI
  Mendoza, Argentina
art director
  LEONARDO FICCARDI
designers
  VICTOR BOLDRINI, PABLO AGAPITO
photographers
  FIGUEWA & STALLARD
client
  INSTITUTO PROVINCIAL DE CULTURA

creative firm
  SAYLES GRAPHIC DESIGN
  Des Moines, Iowa
art director, illustrator
  JOHN SAYLES
client
  ADVERTISING PROFESSIONALS OF DES MOINES

REFINED
SCULPTURAL
STUNNING

watering can $24.99

tripod frame $12.99

$39.99 toaster

thermometer $19.99

teakettle $34.99

candleholder $16.99

cook's tools $3.99 each

ice bucket $29.99

clock $19.99

MICHAEL GRAVES
DESIGN

World-renowned architect and designer Michael Graves
has designed a line of products exclusively for Target. Each
piece is an inspired balance of form and function, at once
sensible and sublime. Michael Graves creates useful objects,
which carry their own weight while lifting our spirits high. TARGET

creative firm
  DESIGN GUYS
  Minneapolis, Minnesota
art director
  STEVEN SIKORA
designer
  ANNE PETERSON
client
  TARGET STORES

to label nobody gets me.
but myself.

offensive? that's the way
i like it.

creative firm
  UKULELE DESIGN CONSULTANTS PTE LTD
  Singapore
design director
  KIM CHUN-WEI
designer
  LEE SHIN KEE
copywriter
  EVELYN TENG
client
  MCILHENNY COMPANY

think of it as a
"do not
disturb"
sign.

the fiery bond
of brotherhood.

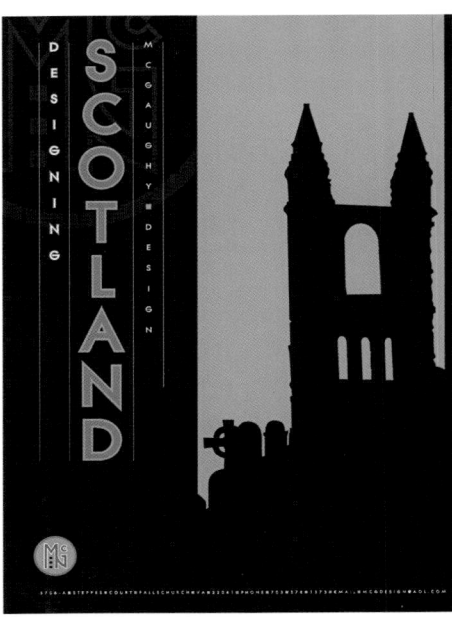

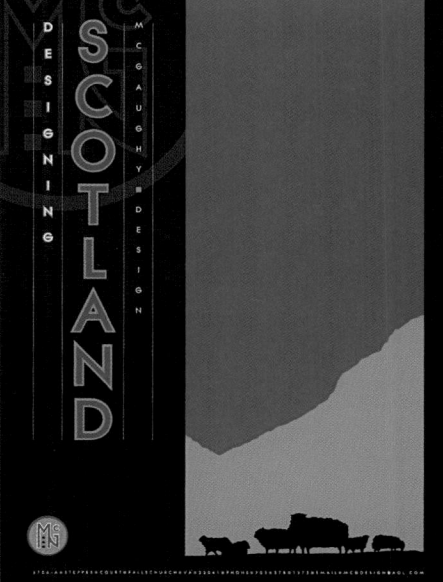

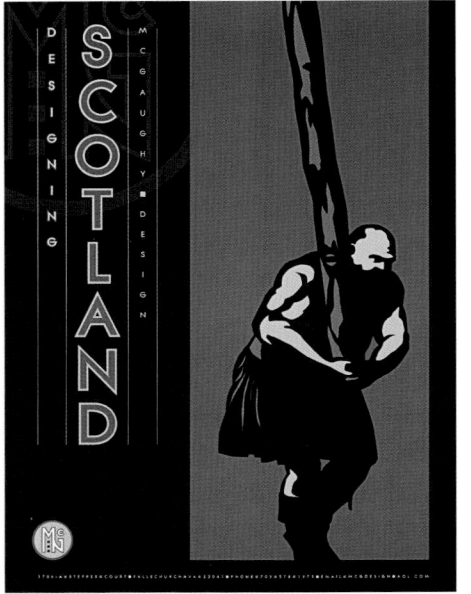

creative firm
McGAUGHY DESIGN
Falls Church, Virginia
designer
MALCOLM McGAUGHY
client
McGAUGHY DESIGN

creative firm
MITHOFF ADVERTISING INC
El Paso, Texas
designer
PETER FRAIRE
client
ACCUBRAPA CORPORATION

creative firm
DESIGN MACHINE
New York, New York
creative director
ALEXANDER GELMAN
art directors, designers
ALEXANDER GELMAN, KAOM SATRE
client
THE ART DIRECTORS CLUB NY

creative firm
MITHOFF ADVERTISING INC
El Paso, Texas
designer
CLIVE COCHRAN
client
UNIVERSITY OF TEXAS AT EL PASO

creative firm
  SAYLES GRAPHIC DESIGN
  Des Moines, Iowa
art director, illustrator
  JOHN SAYLES
client
  HOECHST MARION ROUSSEL "2000 EXCELLENCE IN LEADERSHIP"

creative firm
  GREG WALTERS DESIGN
  Seattle, Washington
designer
  GREG WALTERS
illustrator
  ADAM ROGERS
client
  PIONEER SQUARE PUB CLUB

creative firm
  SAYLES GRAPHIC DESIGN
  Des Moines, Iowa
art director, illustrator
  JOHN SAYLES
client
  SAYLES GRAPHIC DESIGN

creative firm
  SAYLES GRAPHIC DESIGN
  Des Moines, Iowa
art director, illustrator
  JOHN SAYLES
client
  SAYLES GRAPHIC DESIGN

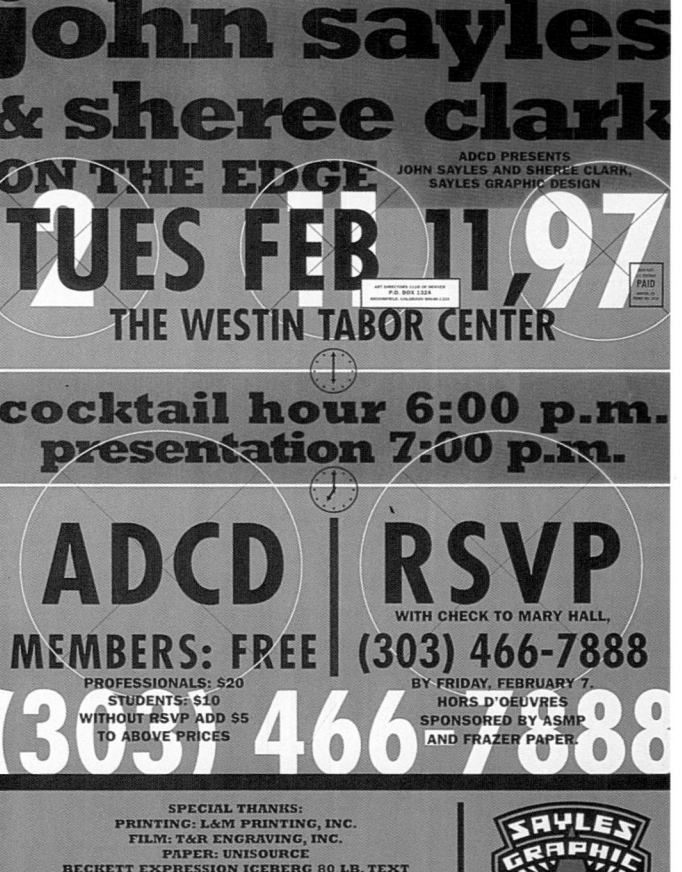

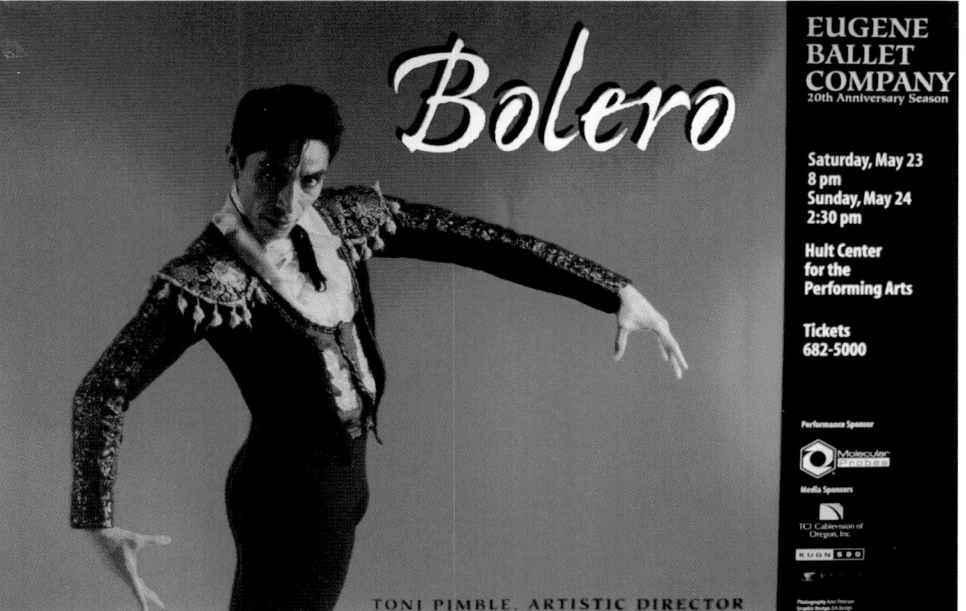

creative firm
  JLN DESIGN
  Eugene, Oregon
art director
  JERRIL NILSON
designers
  JERRIL NILSON, LYNN MARX
photographer
  KENT PETERSON
client
  EUGENE BALLET COMPANY

creative firm
  RGD
  Denver, Colorado
art director
  RICK GRIFFITH
designer
  JUSTIN DOMINGUEZ
client
  MICHAEL D. ROSS, MILLER THEATRE, NY

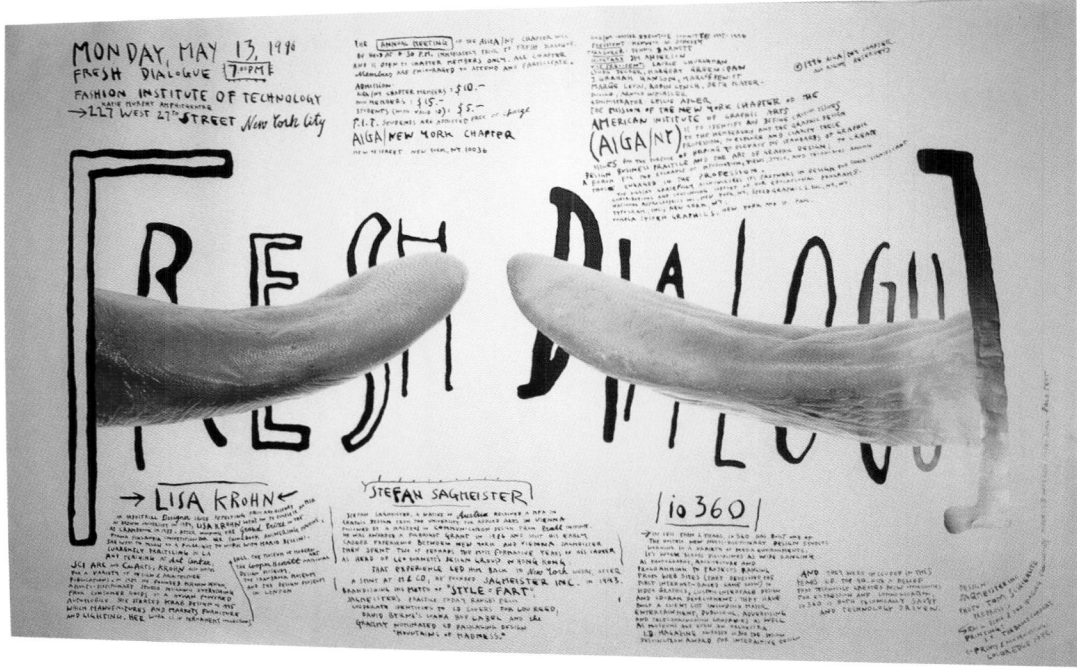

creative firm
  SAGMEISTER INC.
  New York, New York
designer
  STEFAN SAGMEISTER
client
  AIGA NEW YORK

FALL 1999
FACULTY BIENNIAL
Sept 7 - 28
CULTURE FESTIVAL - CHINA
Oct 4 - 26
MURRAY STATE UNIVERSITY
ART FACULTY
Nov 1 - 30
1999 FALL GRADUATING ART
B.F.A. MAJORS
Dec 5 - 18

SPRING 2000
QUILT AS ART
Jan 24 - Feb 15
INVITATIONAL HIGH SCHOOL
ART EXHIBIT
Feb 22 - March 16
ANNUAL STUDENT EXHIBITION
April 2 - 25
2000 SPRING GRADUATING ART
B.F.A. MAJORS
April 30 - May 13

1999 -2000 EXHIBITION SCHEDULE
EASTERN KENTUCKY UNIVERSITY • GILES GALLERY • CAMPBELL BUILDING

creative firm
  CLEVER LITTLE BOY DESIGNS
  Richmond, Kentucky
creative director, designer
  GRAHAM ALLEN
client
  GILES GALLERY (EASTERN KENTUCKY UNIVERSITY)

Giving way
to new ideas
Richard Mellor in Atlanta
14th March 96, 7.30
High Museum, Hill Auditorium
Hosted by Atlanta College of Art

creative firm
    ATLANTA COLLEGE OF ART
    Atlanta, Georgia
designer
    RICHARD MELLOR
client
    ATLANTA COLLEGE OF ART

WINTER CONCERT

OHIO UNIVERSITY

SCHOOL OF DANCE 1995

March 2, 3 and 4 at 8pm
Matinee 2 pm March 4th

BAKER THEATER KANTNER HALL
CALL 614.593-4800 FOR TICKETS
TICKET PRICES $6 evenings $5 matinee $4 seniors & children

creative firm
    ARLYN EVE SIMON
    Santa Fe, New Mexico
designer
    ARLYN EVE SIMON
client
    DEPARTMENT OF FILM/VIDEO AT OHIO UNIVERSITY

creative firm
  ROSS ADVERTISING
  Peoria, Illinois
creative directors
  SKIP DAMPIER, BRIAN BRUSH,
  KEVIN CARROLL
designer
  BRIAN BRUSH
production art
  EDEN SCHWINDENHAMMER
copywriter
  KEVIN CARROLL
client
  STRACK & VAN TIL

creative firm
  ROSS ADVERTISING
  Peoria, Illinois
executive creative director
  SKIP DAMPIER
senior art director
  NICK JIBBEN
copywriter
  JOHN RUEBUSH
client
  STRACK & VAN TIL

creative firm
  ROSS ADVERTISING
  Peoria, Illinois
creative directors
  SKIP DAMPIER, BRIAN BRUSH,
  KEVIN CARROLL
designer
  BRIAN BRUSH
production art
  EDEN SCHWINDENHAMMER
copywriter
  KEVIN CARROLL
client
  STRACK & VAN TIL

creative firm
  MIRES DESIGN INC
  San Diego, California
designers
  SCOTT MIRES, MIGUEL PEREZ,
  NEILL ARCHER ROAN, LAURA CONNORS
illustrator
  MARK ULRIKSEN
client
  ARENA STAGE

creative firm
  MIRES DESIGN INC
  San Diego, California
designers
  SCOTT MIRES, MIGUEL PEREZ,
  NEILL ARCHER ROAN, LAURA CONNORS
illustrator
  MARK ULRIKSEN
client
  ARENA STAGE

creative firm
  MIRES DESIGN INC
  San Diego, California
designers
  SCOTT MIRES, MIGUEL PEREZ,
  NEILL ARCHER ROAN, LAURA CONNORS
illustrator
  JODY HEWGILL
client
  ARENA STAGE

creative firm
  MIRES DESIGN
  San Diego, California
designers
  SCOTT MIRES, MIGUEL PEREZ,
  NEILL ARCHER ROAN, LAURA CONNORS
illustrator
  MARK ULRIKSEN
client
  ARENA STAGE

creative firm
  MIRES DESIGN
  San Diego, California
art director
  SCOTT MIRES
designer
  MIGUEL PEREZ
client
  ARENA STAGE

creative firm
  MIRES DESIGN
  San Diego, California
art director
  SCOTT MIRES
designer
  MIGUEL PEREZ
client
  ARENA STAGE

creative firm
  MIRES DESIGN
  San Diego, California
art director
  SCOTT MIRES
designer
  MIGUEL PEREZ
client
  ARENA STAGE

creative firm
    ODEN
        Memphis, Tennessee
creative director
    BRET TERWILLEGER
designers
    BRET TERWILLEGER, JEFF BLANKENSHIP
copywriter
    KATIE PRICE
client
    INTERNATIONAL PAPER

creative firm
    A TO Z COMMUNICATIONS, INC.
        Pittsburgh, Pennsylvania
creative director
    ALAN BOARTS
senior graphic designer
    AIMEE LAZER
client
    PNC BANK

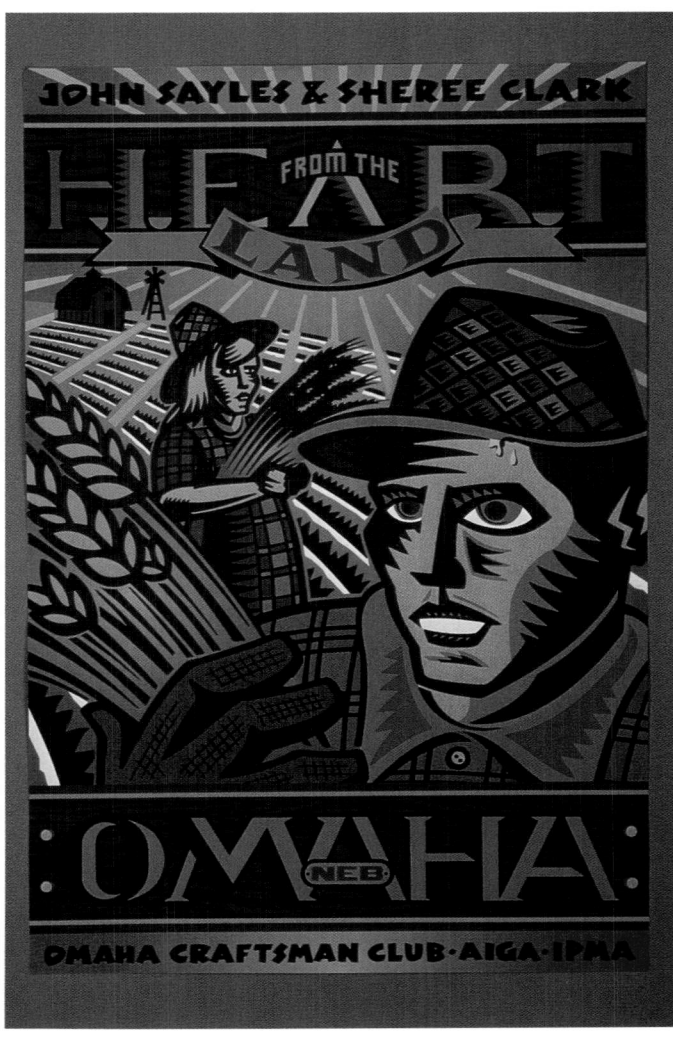

creative firm
  SAYLES GRAPHIC DESIGN
  Des Moines, Iowa
designer
  JOHN SAYLES
client
  CRAFTSMEN CLUB OF OMAHA,
  ART DIRECTORS CLUB OF DENVER,
  ART DIRECTORS ASSOCIATION OF TULSA

creative firm
  SAYLES GRAPHIC DESIGN
  Des Moines, Iowa
designer
  JOHN SAYLES
client
  CRAFTSMEN CLUB OF OMAHA,
  ART DIRECTORS CLUB OF DENVER,
  ART DIRECTORS ASSOCIATION OF TULSA

creative firm
  SAYLES GRAPHIC DESIGN
    Des Moines, Iowa
designer
  JOHN SAYLES
client
  CRAFTSMEN CLUB OF OMAHA,
  ART DIRECTORS CLUB OF DENVER,
  ART DIRECTORS ASSOCIATION OF TULSA

creative firm
  BALDWIN FILTERS
    Kearney, Nebraska
art director, designer
  MICHAEL HINTON
illustrator
  ROBERT CASE
client
  BALDWIN FILTERS

creative firm
FOSSIL DESIGN STUDIO
Richardson, Texas
senior art director
BILL MORGAN
product designer
ROBIN BOSWELL
client
FOSSIL

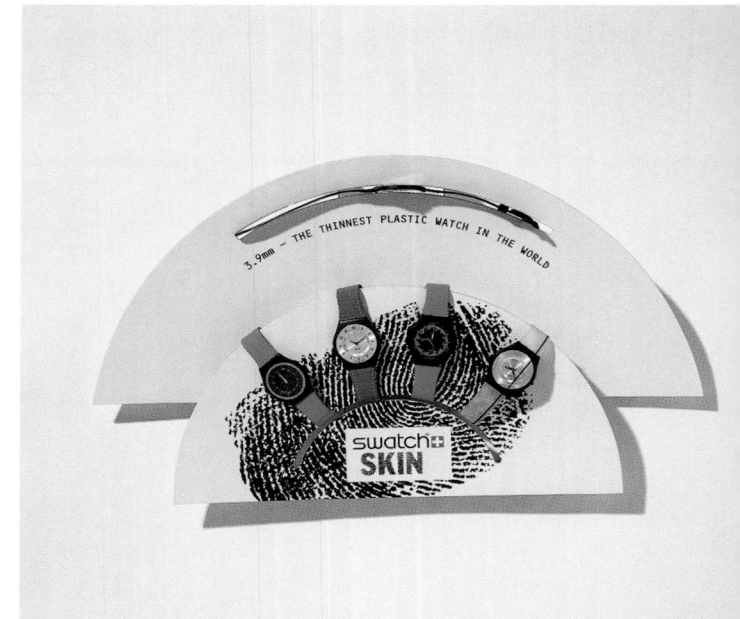

creative firm
RISE AGENCY, INC.
New York, New York
creative director
CAROLINA RODRIGUEZ
art director
ROBERT ZWASCHKA
client
SWATCH

creative firm
FOSSIL DESIGN STUDIO
Richardson, Texas
senior art director
BILL MORGAN
senior product designer
LINDA TSAI
client
FOSSIL

creative firm
   DISNEY DESIGN GROUP
   Lake Buena Vista, Florida
creative director
   MICHELE KEATING
art director, designer
   ALEX SANSO
client
   WALT DISNEY ATTRACTIONS MERCHANDISE

creative firm
   RISE AGENCY, INC.
   New York, New York
creative director
   CAROLINA RODRIGUEZ
art director
   ROBERT ZWASCHKA
client
   SWATCH

creative firm
  DISNEY DESIGN GROUP
  Lake Buena Vista, Florida
creative director
  MICHELE KEATING
art director
  JIM TRONOSKI
designer
  MARK FRANKEL
illustrator
  DAVID WILGUS
client
  DISNEY CRUISE LINE

creative firm
  DISNEY DESIGN GROUP
  Lake Buena Vista, Florida
creative director
  MICHELE KEATING
art director
  DAVID WHITAKER
designer
  MICHAEL COLE
client
  WALT DISNEY ATTRACTIONS MERCHANDISE

creative firm
  FOSSIL DESIGN STUDIO
  Richardson, Texas
senior art director
  BILL MORGAN
product designers
  WILLIAM HO, BROOKE MUDD
client
  FOSSIL

She's on the Web.

Fact is, Heartland GlobalNet can promote your business on the Internet quickly and painlessly, making it easier for customers everywhere to get exposed to your company.

creative firm
ROSS ADVERTISING
Peoria, Illinois
senior art director
NICK JIBBEN
copywriter
JOHN RUEBUSH
client
HEARTLAND GLOBAL NET

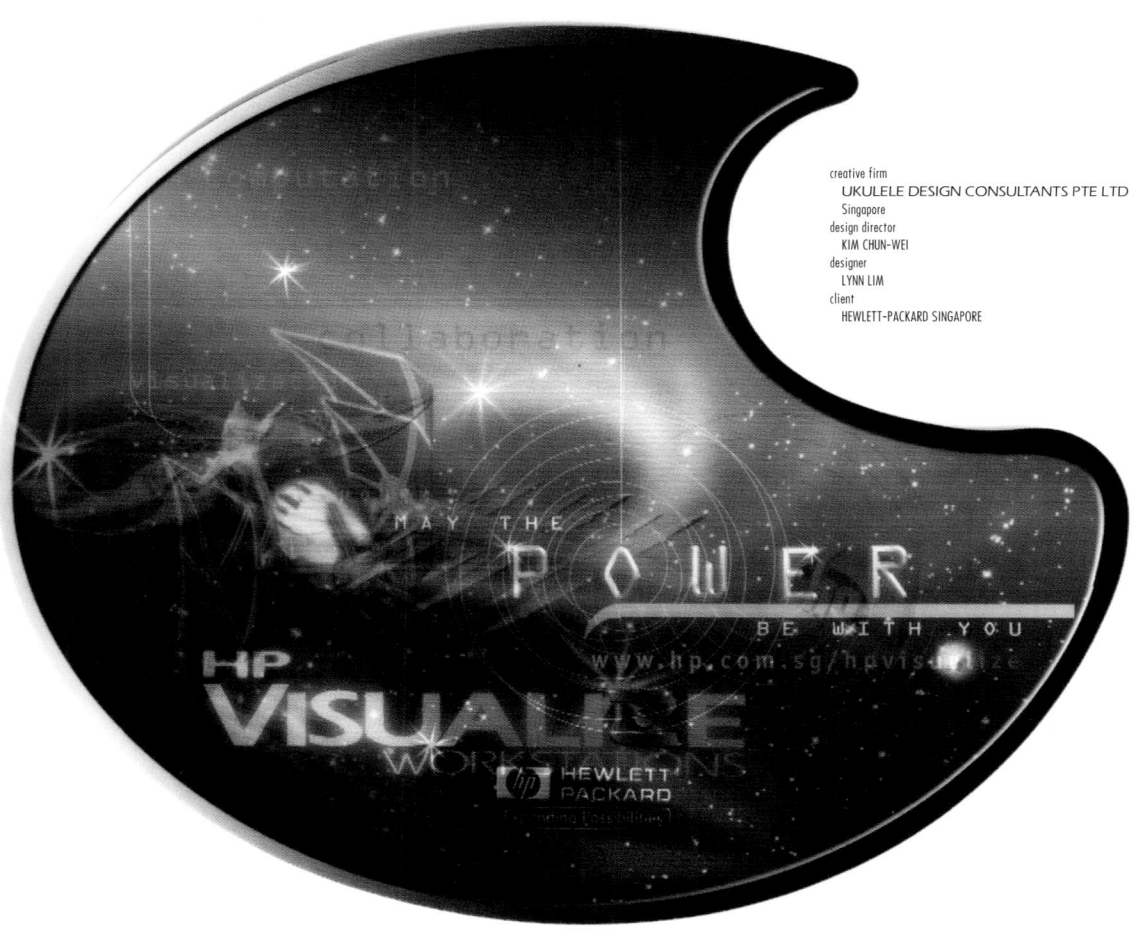

creative firm
UKULELE DESIGN CONSULTANTS PTE LTD
Singapore
design director
KIM CHUN-WEI
designer
LYNN LIM
client
HEWLETT-PACKARD SINGAPORE

creative firm
  BBK STUDIO INC.
  Grand Rapids, Michigan
creative director, designer
  YANG KIM
copywriter
  THE GREYSTONE COMPANIES
client
  THE GREYSTONE COMPANIES

creative firm
  OH&CO IN COLLABORATION WITH IDEO
  New York, New York
creative director
  BRENT OPPENHEIMER
strategy director
  ROBIN HAUETER
design director
  MARY ELLEN BUTTNER
designer
  DAVID SHIELDS
client
  AMTRAK

creative firm
  WONG WONG BOYACK, INC.
  San Francisco, California
designers
  BEN WONG, MICHAEL FRANDY
illustrator
  BEN WONG
copywriters
  PENELOPE WONG, JANA BENDER, BEN WONG
client
  CISCO SYSTEMS, INC.

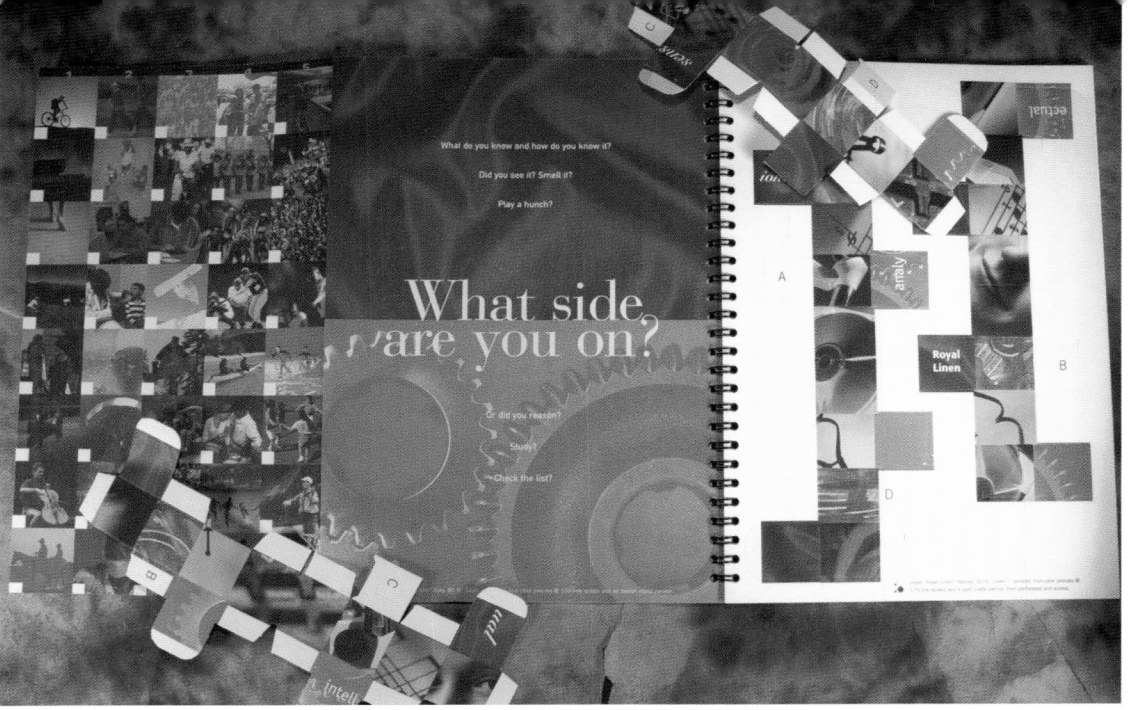

creative firm
    LARSEN DESIGN + INTERACTIVE
    Minneapolis, Minnesota
creative director
    PAUL WHARTON
designer
    TODD MANNES
production
    PAM BORGMAN
copywriter
    PAM POWELL
client
    WAUSAU PAPERS

creative firm
    AIRE DESIGN COMPANY
    Tucson, Arizona
creative director
    CATHARINE M. KIM
art director
    SHARI RYKOWSKI
client
    DESERT WHALE JOJOBA COMPANY

creative firm
    DESIGN GUYS
    Minneapolis, Minnesota
art director
    STEVEN SIKORA
designer
    DAWN SELG
client
    TARGET STORES

GIUSEPPE VERDI'S

RiGOLETTO

Truly one of the operatic masterpieces of the past millennium, Verdi's Rigoletto was a turning point in operatic history. The passion and tragic beauty of the perennially popular piece ensures it will endure for the next hundred years.

MARINA VYSKVORKINA **GABRIEL GONZALES** **STEPHEN KECHULIUS**

Laurence Gilgore, Conductor

**John Pascoe, Director,
Scenic and Costume Designer**

For Subscriptions
Call: 203.359.0009
For Single Tickets Stamford
Call: 203.325.4466
For Single Tickets Bridgeport
Call: 203.359.0009

SATURDAY
NOV 13, 1999, 8 PM
THE KLEIN MEMORIAL
AUDITORIUM
BRIDGEPORT
■
SATURDAY
NOV 20, 1999, 8 PM
THE PALACE THEATRE
STAMFORD

Sung in Italian with USTitles (english supertitles)

creative firm
 TOM FOWLER, INC.
 Stamford, Connecticut
art director, illustrator
 THOMAS G. FOWLER
designers
 THOMAS G. FOWLER, KARL S. MARUYAMA
client
 CONNECTICUT GRAND OPERA & ORCHESTRA

to the ➡
Future

creative firm
 DESIGN MACHINE
 New York, New York
creative director
 ALEXANDER GELMAN
art directors, designers
 ALEXANDER GELMAN, KAORU SATO
client
 JANOU PAKTER INC.

creative firm
 THE PETERSON GROUP
 New York, New York
graphic designer
 MAY LOUIE
client
 FUJI FILM COMPUTER PRODUCTS

creative firm
  MacVICAR DESIGN + COMM.
  Arlington, Virginia
art director, designer
  CATHY BROADWELL
client
  INTER. BOTTLED WATER ASSOC.

creative firm
  GRETEMAN GROUP
  Wichita, Kansas
creative director
  SONIA GRETEMAN
art directors
  SONIA GRETEMAN, JAMES STRANGE
designer
  JAMES STRANGE
client
  LEARJET

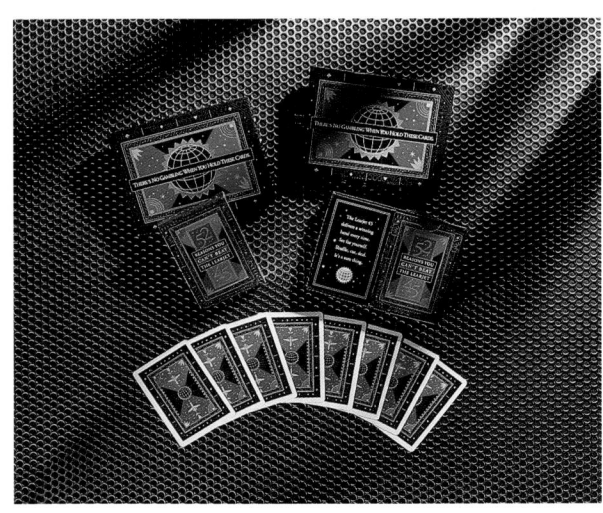

creative firm
  SAYLES GRAPHIC DESIGN
  Des Moines, Iowa
art director, illustrator
  JOHN SAYLES
client
  HOECHST MARION ROUSSEL

creative firm
  SAYLES GRAPHIC DESIGN
  Des Moines, Iowa
art director, illustrator
  JOHN SAYLES
client
  1998 AMERICAN CANCER SOCIETY

creative firm
  SHEILA HART DESIGN, INC.
  Strongsville, Ohio
art director
  SHEILA HART
client
  MERGERSHOP, INC.

open

MERGER SHOP INC

creative firm
  THE RIORDON DESIGN GROUP
  Oakville, Canada
art director
  CLAUDE DUMOULIN
designer
  DAN WHEATON
client
  CARLSON MARKETING GROUP (MAZDA)

creative firm
  SQUARE ONE DESIGN
  Grand Rapids, Michigan
designers
  MIKE GORMAN, GRANT CARMICHAEL,
  JOHN TOTTEN, MARTIN SCHOENBORN
client
  HAWORTH

creative firm
  GILL FISHMAN ASSOCIATES, INC.
  Cambridge, Massachusetts
creative director
  GILL FISHMAN
designer
  ALICIA OZYJOWSKI
client
  SCHOOL OF THE MUSEUM OF FINE ARTS

creative firm
  A TO Z COMMUNICATIONS, INC.
  Pittsburgh, Pennsylvania
creative director
  ALAN BOARTS
senior graphic designer
  JOE TOMKO
client
  ALCOA

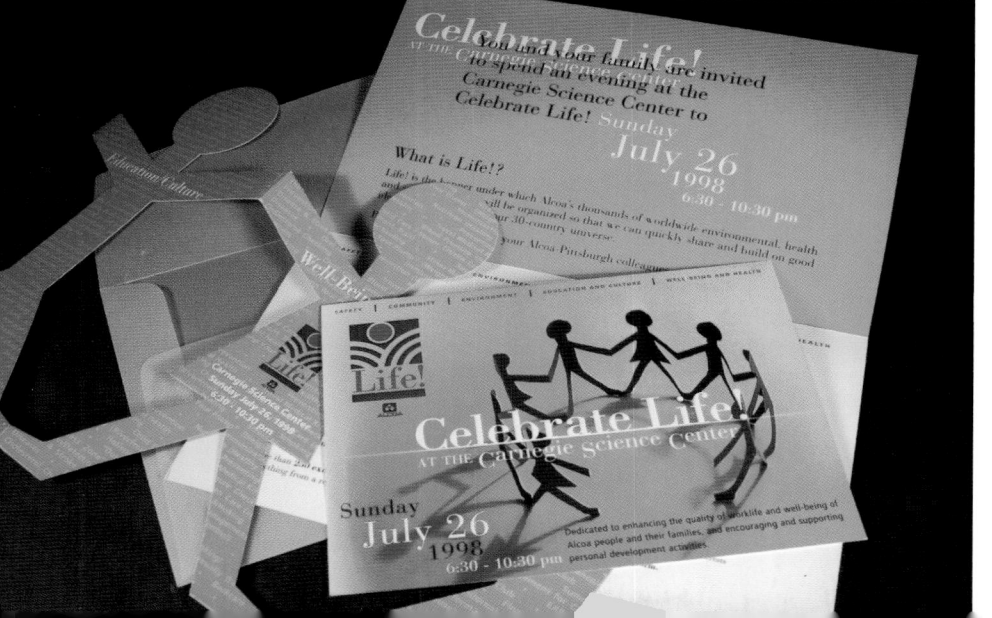

creative firm
  FROST DESIGN LTD
  London, England
creative director
  VINCE FROST
client
  PHOTONICA

creative firm
  GRETEMAN GROUP
  Wichita, Kansas
creative director
  SONIA GRETEMAN
art directors
  SONIA GRETEMAN, JAMES STRANGE
designer
  JAMES STRANGE
client
  COSTA RICA

creative firm
  HORNALL ANDERSON DESIGN WORKS
  Seattle, Washington
art director, designer
  JACK ANDERSON
directors
  HEIDI FAVOUR, BRUCE BRANSON-MEYER, MARY HERMES
client
  MAHLUM ARCHITECTS

creative firm
  GRETEMAN GROUP
  Wichita, Kansas
creative director
  SONIA GRETEMAN
art directors, designers
  SONIA GRETEMAN, JAMES STRANGE
client
  HWS HORSE THERAPY

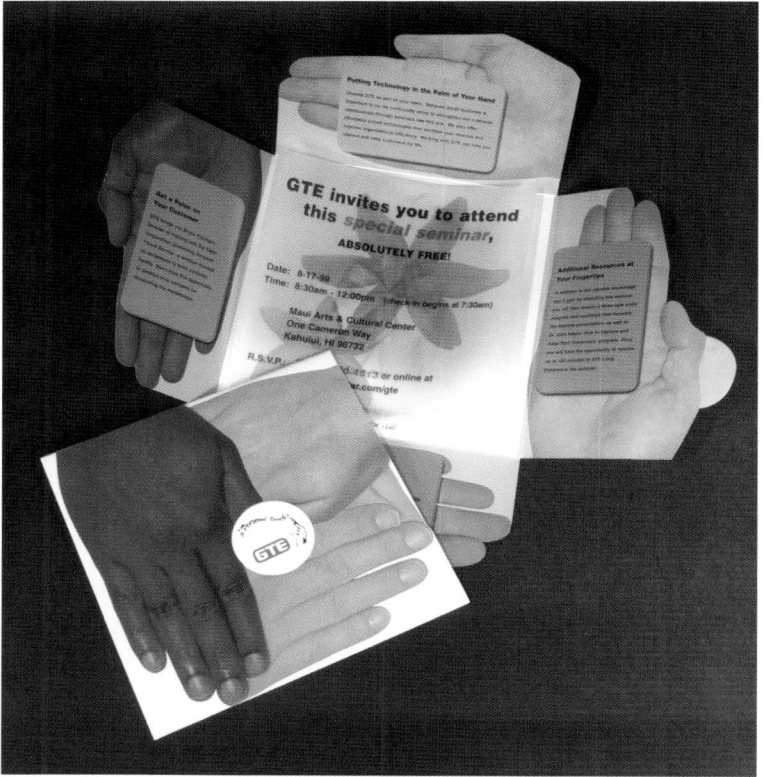

creative firm
  GRETEMAN GROUP
  Wichita, Kansas
creative director
  SONIA GRETEMAN
art directors
  SONIA GRETEMAN, JAMES STRANGE
designer
  JAMES STRANGE
client
  FLEXJET

creative firm
  JA DESIGN SOLUTIONS
  Coppell, Texas
designer
  JEAN ASHENFELTER
copywriter
  LINDA CAPRIOTTI
photography
  JACK WILSON
client
  GTE EVENT MARKETING

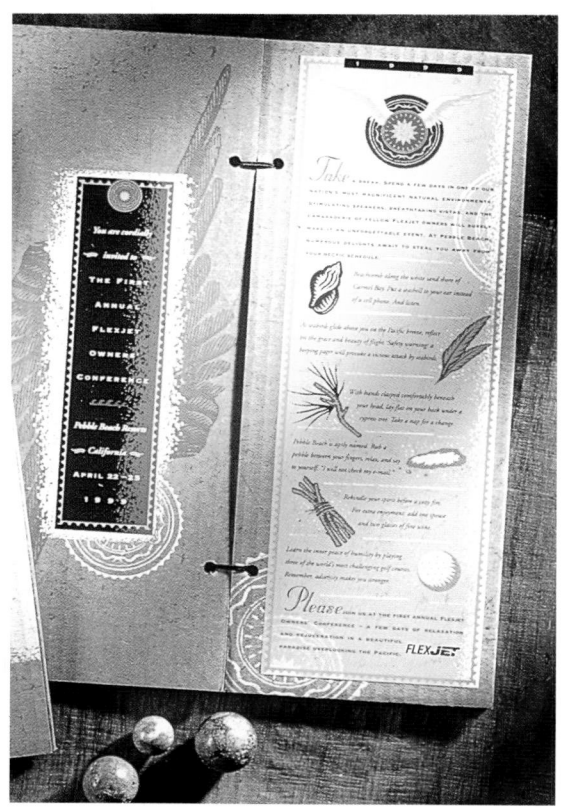

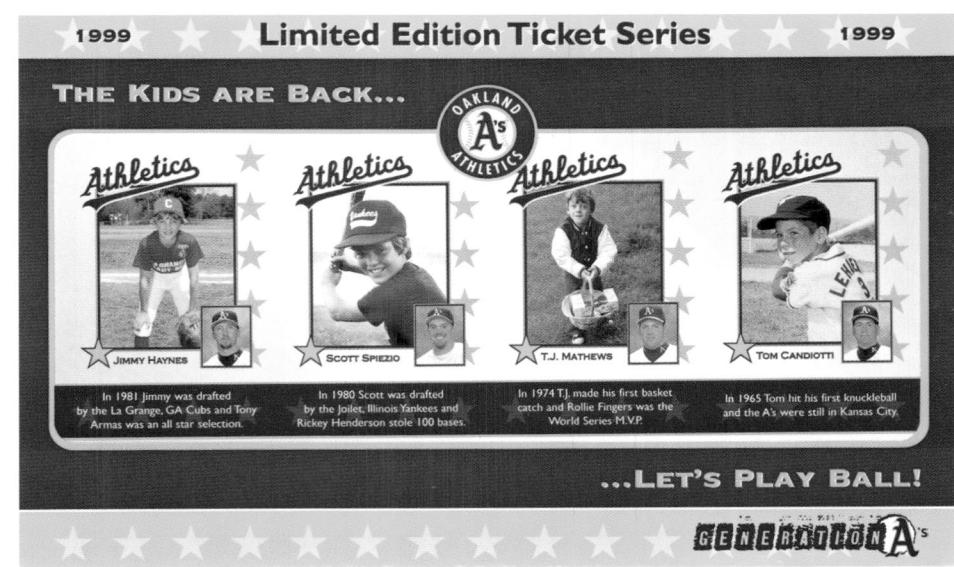

creative firm
STRATFORD DESIGN ASSOCIATES
Brisbane, California
designer
JOHN F. MORGAN
photography
MICHAEL ZAGARIS, MOM'S
client
OAKLAND ATHLETICS

creative firm
MULLER + CO.
Kansas City, Missouri
creative director
JOHN MULLER
art director, designer
MARK VOSS
client
KANSAS CITY BLUES & JAZZ FESTIVAL

creative firm
NBBJ GRAPHIC DESIGN
Seattle, Washington
designer
RODDY GRANT
client
INTERNATIONAL INTERIOR DESIGN ASSOC.

THE ART OF INVESTING

direction   strategy   portfolio   communication

Regions Bank

creative firm
    A TO Z COMMUNICATIONS, INC.
    Pittsburgh, Pennsylvania
creative director
    ALAN BOARTS
senior graphic designer
    RICHARD HOOPER
client
    FEDERATED INVESTORS REGIONS BANK CAPABILITIES BROCHURE

holiday | A day on which custom dictates a halting of general business activity to commemorate or celebrate a particular event

creative firm
    SHOOK DESIGN GROUP, INC.
    Charlotte, North Carolina
graphic designer
    STEVE FENTON
client
    HM WHITE SITE ARCHITECTS

Just saw the suite

Just visited the Cupboard

Just saw the potential

VALUE

JUST FORGOT
ABOUT HIS
BUDDY'S LATEST
BUSINESS DEAL

creative firm
    GRETEMAN GROUP
    Wichita, Kansas
creative director
    SONIA GRETEMAN
art director, designer
    JAMES STRANGE
client
    CANDLEWOOD

creative firm
  GRETEMAN GROUP
  Wichita, Kansas
creative director
  SONIA GRETEMAN
art director
  JAMES STRANGE
designer
  CRAIG TOMSON
client
  RAYTHEON

Happy Holidays!
From the pee-ple at …

We're taking your whiz, we're checking it twice,
we're gonna find out who's naughty or nice.

SECON
The Drug Screening Company

In honor of our customers and your contribution to our success, SECON has made a contribution to the Salvation Army.

creative firm
  SIDES & ASSOCIATES
  Lafayette, Louisiana
creative director
  LARRY SIDES
designer
  WILL BAILEY
copywriter
  DARYL McGRATH
client
  SECON

creative firm
  ELLEN BRUSS DESIGN
  Denver, Colorado
designer
  G. CARR
client
  UNISOURCE

| PMS 130C
0c 30m 100y 0k | PMS 280C
100c 70m 0y 10k |
| PMS 116U
0c 30m 100y 0k | PMS 280U
100c 70m 0y 30k |

A bright, clean color palette complements the blue and gold corporate signature.

Washington Mutual

The preferred two-color signature: yellow square, blue "W" and type

Washington Mutual

The preferred reverse two-color signature: blue background, yellow square, blue "W", white type

| PMS 362C
80c 0m 100y 0k | PMS 199C
0c 100m 60y 0k |
| PMS 369U
60c 0m 90y 0k | PMS 199U
0c 95m 65y 0k |

| PMS 021C
0c 69m 100y 0k | PMS 2665C
94c 94m 0y 0k | PMS 877C/U
metallic silver | PMS 2746C
100c 94m 0y 0k |
| PMS 021U
94c 91m 0y 0k | Pantone Violet U
94c 91m 0y 0k | | PMS2746U
100c 87m 0y 0k |

8 9

creative firm
HORNALL ANDERSON DESIGN WORKS
Seattle, Washington
art director
JOHN HORNALL
designers
JOHN HORNALL, KATHA DALTON, HOLLY CRAVEN
client
WASHINGTON MUTUAL

creative firm
THE RIORDON DESIGN GROUP INC.
Oakville, Canada
art director
RIC RIORDON
designer
SHARON PECE
client
TMN (THE MOVIE NETWORK)

creative firm
BUTLER KEMP DESIGN
North Adelaide, Australia
art director
DEREK BUTLER
designer
HELLEN KIPRIZLOGLOU
client
EDUCATION ADELAIDE

creative firm
  ODEN
  Memphis, Tennessee
creative director
  BRET TERWILLEGER
designer
  JEFF BLANKENSHIP
copywriters
  KATIE PRICE, SHEPERD SIMMONS
client
  BOYS & GIRLS CLUBS OF GREATER MEMPHIS

New day in Boston: **August 1, 1999**

creative firm
  GREENFIELD/BELSER LTD
  Washington, D.C.
art director
  BURKEY BELSER
designer
  JEANETTE NUZUM
copywriter
  GEORGE KELL
client
  KILPATRICK LOCKHART

creative firm
  ID, INCORPORATED
  Portland, Oregon
designer
  KAREN WIPPICH
copywriter
  JON LEE
client
  BRIDGETOWN PRINTING

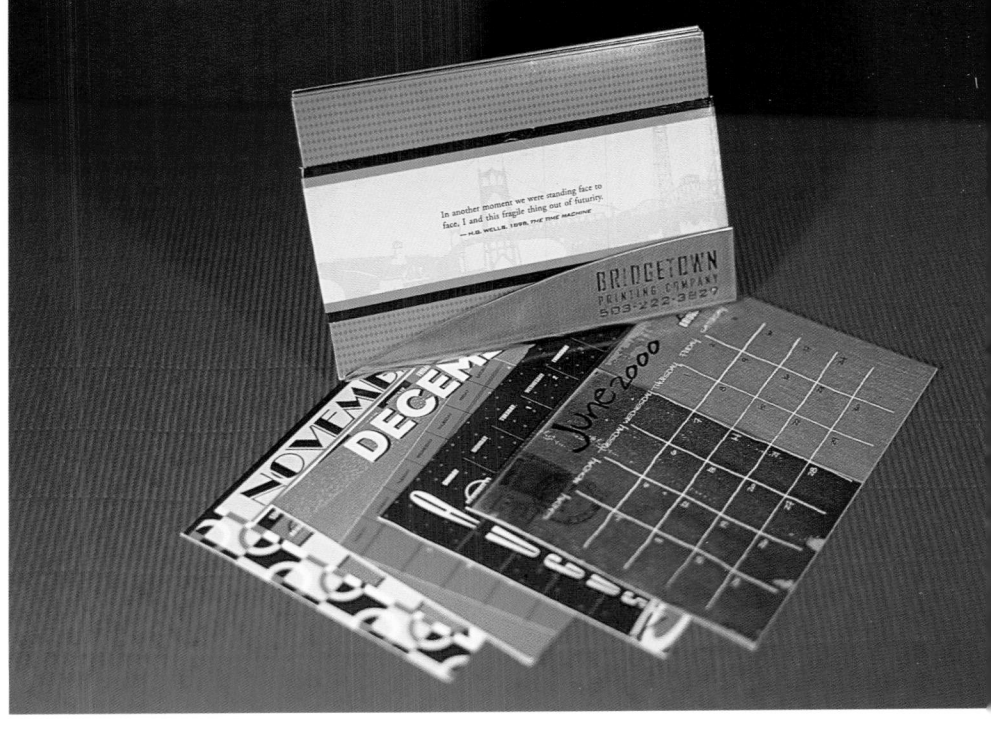

creative firm
DOMINIC JANNAZZO DESIGN
Indianapolis, Indiana
designer
DOMINIC JANNAZO
client
MELISSA KRISANDA PHOTOGRAPHY

creative firm
AIRE DESIGN COMPANY
Tucson, Arizona
creative director
CATHARINE M. KIM
art director
SHARI RYKOWSKI
client
ARIZONA-SONORA DESERT MUSEUM

creative firm
GARDNER DESIGN
Wichita, Kansas
art director, designer, illustrator
BRIAN MILLER
client
PRINTMASTER

creative firm
  MULLER + CO.
    Kansas City, Missouri
creative director
  JOHN MULLER
art director, designer
  JANE HUSKEY
client
  KANSAS CITY BLUES & JAZZ FESTIVAL

creative firm
  TRICKETT & WEBB LTD
    London, England
designers
  LYNN TRICKETT, BRIAN WEBB, HEIDI LIGHTFOOT
paper engineer
  CORINA FLETCHER
client
  ROYAL SOCIETY OF ARTS

creative firm
  UKULELE DESIGN
  CONSULTANTS PTE LTD
  Singapore
design director
  KIM CHUN-WEI
designer
  STEPHANIE TAN
client
  HEWLETT-PACKARD SINGAPORE

creative firm
  TEAMWORK DESIGN LTD.
  Hong Kong, China
design director
  GARY TAM
designers
  JOEL ONG,
  ALEX CHANG, IVY WONG
client
  PEAK TRAMWAYS CO. LTD.

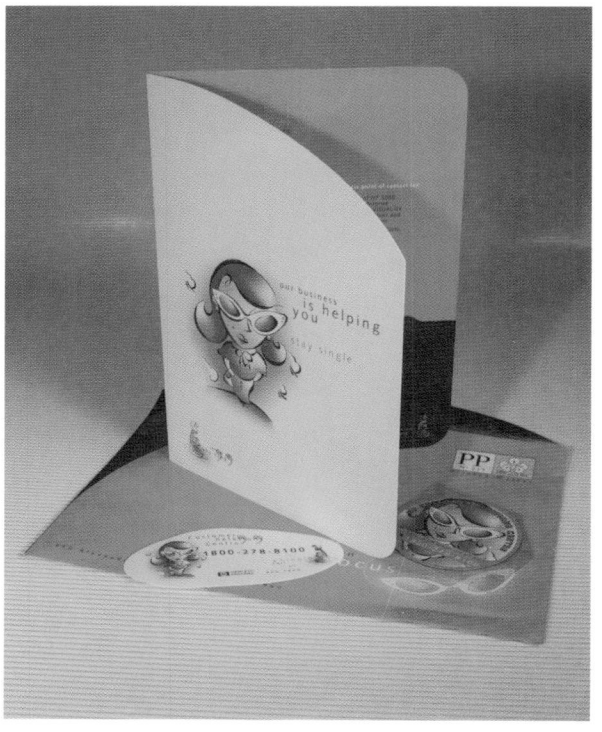

creative firm
  SHOOK DESIGN GROUP, INC.
  Charlotte, North Carolina
graphic designer
  STEVE FENTON
client
  THE SUNSET CLUB

creative firm
  JULIA TAM DESIGN
  Palos Verdes, California
client
  HOULIHAN LOKEY HOWARD & ZUKIM

creative firm
  ROBERT MEYERS DESIGN
  Fairlawn, Ohio
designer
  ROBERT MEYERS
client
  MARK & MYRNA MASON

Please join us
for an evening of

cocktails

and

dinner

on Friday, June 12th
at 7:30 p.m.
1129 Beechwood Blvd.

Myrna &
Mark

rsvp weekdays:
Trudy 261-1500

creative firm
  DISNEY DESIGN GROUP
  Lake Buena Vista
creative director
  MICHELE KEATING
designer
  DARREN WILSON
illustrator
  MICHAEL MOJHER
client
  WALT DISNEY WORLD SALES & MARKETING

creative firm
  CYD DESIGN
  Milwaukee, Wisconsin
art director, designer
  CORY DEWALT
photographer
  PORTRAITS ON PILGRIM,
  STENTEN ROWE STUDIOS
client
  YOUR WEDDING

creative firm
  McELVENEY + PALOZZI DESIGN GROUP, INC.
  Rochester, New York
creative director
  WILLIAM McELVENEY
art director
  EMPIRE FORSTER
designer
  GRETCHEN BYE
client
  EMPIRE FORSTER

creative firm
  BARBOUR DESIGN INC.
  New York, New York
art director
  AVA BARBOUR
designer
  MALI COHEN
copywriter
  JOE WOJTOLA
client
  ESPN MAGAZINE

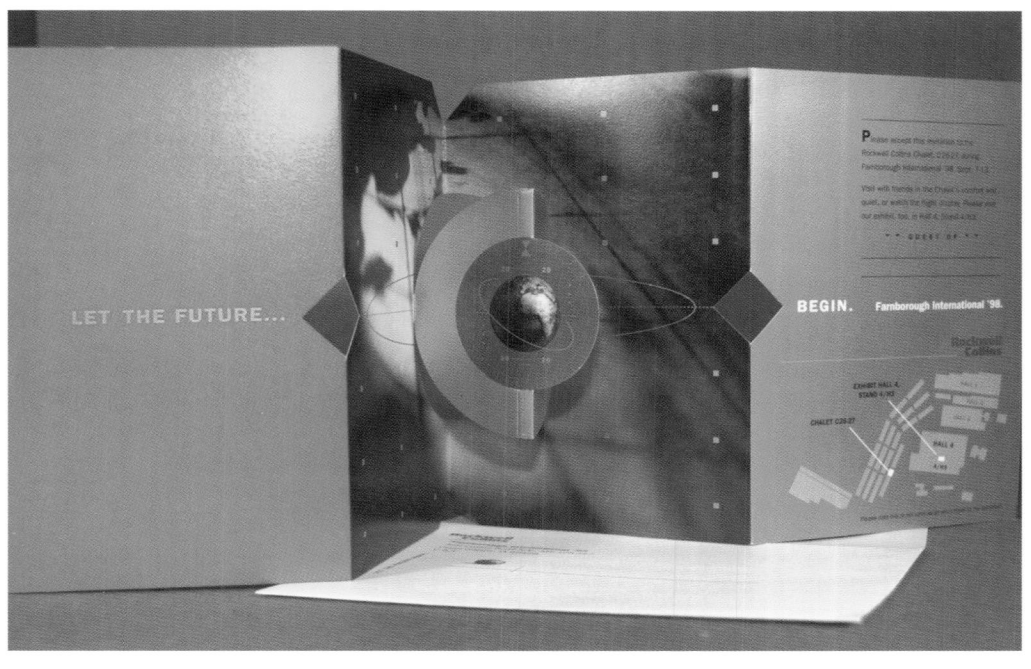

creative firm
GRETEMAN GROUP
Wichita, Kansas
creative director
SONIA GRETEMAN
art directors
SONIA GRETEMAN, JAMES STRANGE
designer
JAMES STRANGE
client
ROCKWELL COLLINS

creative firm
HORNALL ANDERSON DESIGN WORKS
Seattle, Washington
art directors
JACK ANDERSON, LISA CERVENY
designers
JACK ANDERSON, LISA CERVENY, MARY HERMES,
JANA NISHI, JANA WILSON ESSER, VIRGINIA LE
client
MOHAWK PAPER MILLS

creative firm
HORNALL ANDERSON DESIGN WORKS
Seattle, Washington
art directors
JACK ANDERSON, LISA CERVENY
designers
JACK ANDERSON, LISA CERVENY, HEIDI FAVOUR, MARY CHIN HUTCHISON
client
STIMSON LANE

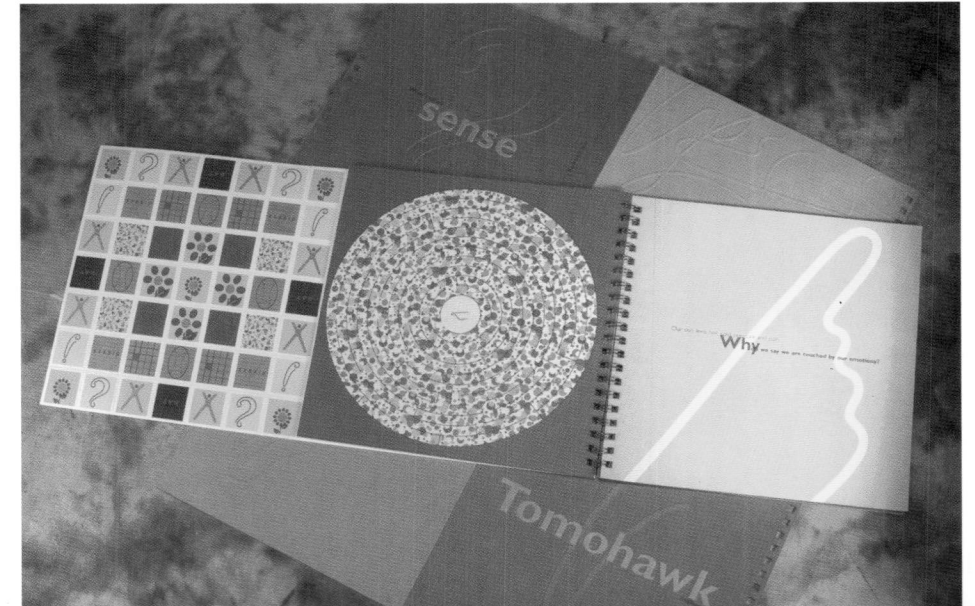

creative firm
  GRAPHICULTURE
  Minneapolis, Minnesota
designer
  BETH MUELLER
client
  CLICK MODELS

creative firm
  TRICKETT & WEBB LTD
  London, England
designers
  LYNN TRICKETT, BRIAN WEBB,
  KATJA THIELEN
illustrator
  JEFF FISHER
client
  TOUCHSTONE

creative firm
  SACKETT DESIGN ASSOCIATES
  San Francisco, California
creative director
  MARK SACKETT
designers
  JAMES SAKAMOTO, WENDY WOOD, GEORGE WHITE III
photographers
  MICHAL VENERA, MARTIN ZEITMAN, CATHERINE BUCHANAN
client
  SAN FRANCISCO INTERNATIONAL AIRPORT

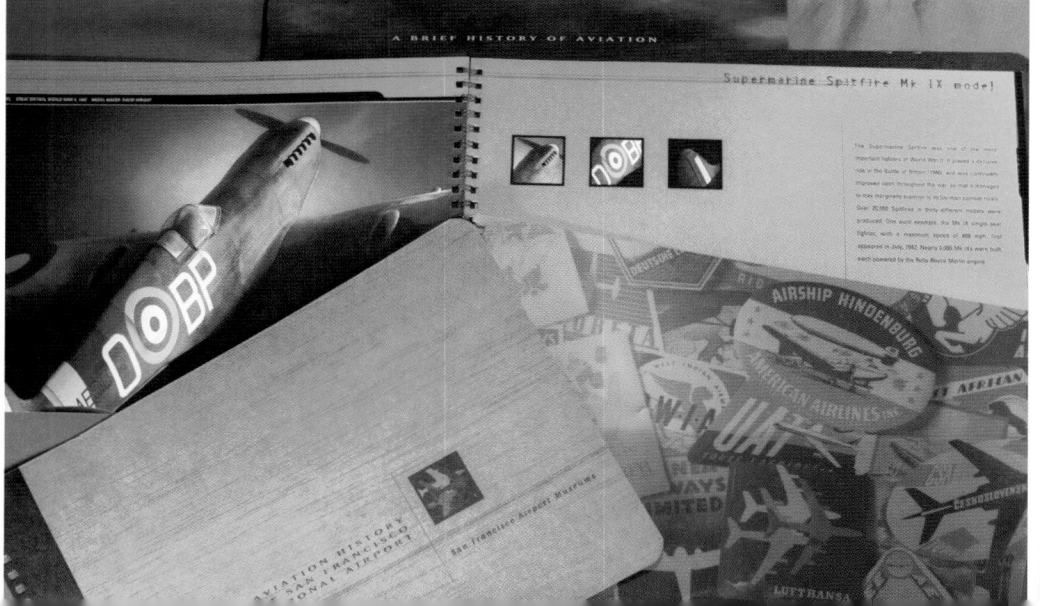

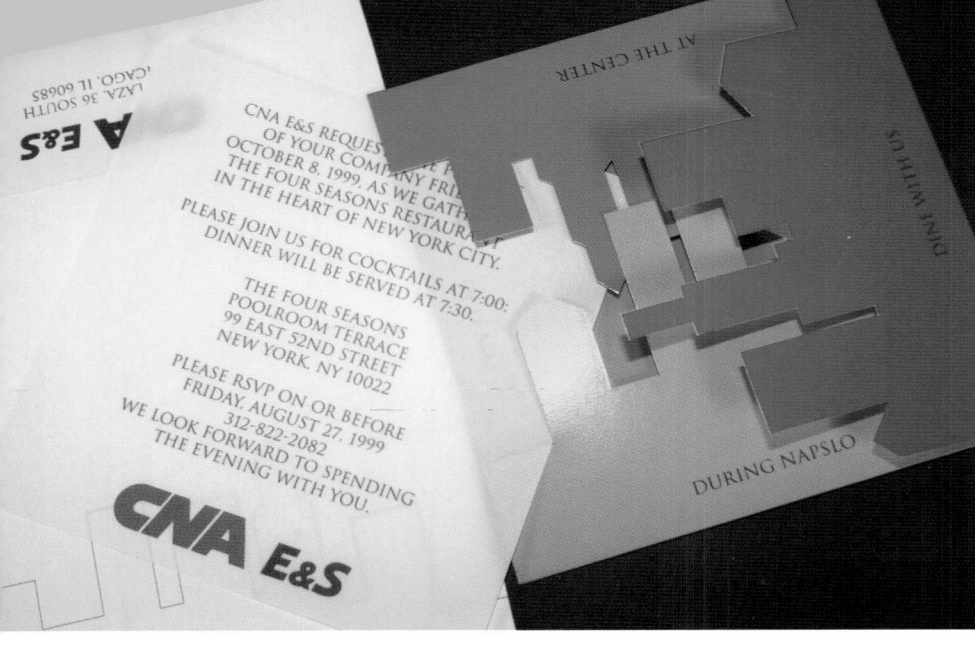

creative firm
  MEYERS DESIGN, INC.
  Chicago, Illinois
designer
  KEVIN MEYERS
client
  CNA—E+S

creative firm
  BELYEA
  Seattle, Washington
art director
  PATRICIA BELYEA
designer
  RON LARS HANSEN
client
  CRUISE WEST

creative firm
  STRATFORD DESIGN ASSOCIATES
  Brisbane, California
art director
  TIM GEROULD
designer
  SILVIA STEPHENSON
client
  PACIFIC FARMS

creative firm
 FIVE VISUAL COMMUNICATION & DESIGN
 Westchester, Ohio
designers
 RONDI TSCHOPP, DENNY FAGAN
client
 CONTEMPORARY ARTS CENTER

creative firm
 5D STUDIO
 Malibu, California
art director
 JANE KOBAYASHI
designer
 ANNE COATES
client
 UNISOURCE + NEW OJI PAPERS

creative firm
 BBK STUDIO INC.
 Grand Rapids, Michigan
creative director
 STEVE FRYKHOLM
designer
 YANG KIM
typesetter
 KIM LAPP
copywriter
 CLARK MALCOLM
client
 HERMAN MILLER INC.

creative firm
   D4 CREATIVE GROUP
   Philadelphia, Pennsylvania
art director
   WICKY W. LEE
client
   ANDY & SAMANTHA CHAN

creative firm
   SAYLES GRAPHIC DESIGN
   Des Moines, Iowa
art director, illustrator
   JOHN SAYLES
client
   CDW

creative firm
   ROSS ADVERTISING
   Peoria, Illinois
executive creative director
   SKIP DAMPIER
art directors
   NICK JIBBEN, BRAD PASCUAL
copywriter
   JOHN RUEBUSH
client
   GRIDIRON

creative firm
EMERSON, WAJDOWICZ STUDIOS
New York, New York
creative director
JUREK WAJDOWICZ
senior art director
LISA LaROCHELLE
client
DOMTAR, EDDY SPECIALTY PAPERS

creative firm
BBK STUDIO INC.
Grand Rapids, Michigan
creative director, designer, typesetter, copywriter
YANG KIM
illustrator
REBECCA GIBSON
client
THE ETHERIDGE COMPANY

creative firm
MULLER + COMPANY
Kansas City, Missouri
creative director
JOHN MULLER
art director
JEFF MILLER
designers
JEFF MILLER, BROHAN WATKINS
client
THE NELSON ATKINS MUSEUM OF ART

creative firm
  KOR GROUP
  Boston, Massachusetts
art directors
  ANNE CALLAHAN, KAREN DENDY
designers
  ANNE CALLAHAN, KAREN DENDY, JIM GIBSON
client
  FORRESTER RESEARCH

creative firm
  McGAUGHY DESIGN
  Falls Church, Virginia
designer
  MALCOLM McGAUGHY
client
  WRC NBC 4-TV

creative firm
  THE PETERSON GROUP
  New York, New York
design directors
  ALEX PENNINGTON, BOB CRUANAS
client
  FUJI FILM COMPUTER PRODUCTS

creative firm
  THE PETERSON GROUP
  New York, New York
design director
  ALEX PENNINGTON
client
  FUJI FILM COMPUTER PRODUCTS

creative firm
  GRETEMAN GROUP
  Wichita, Kansas
creative director
  SONIA GRETEMAN
art directors
  SONIA GRETEMAN, JAMES STRANGE
designers
  JAMES STRANGE, SONIA GRETEMAN, JO QUILLIN
client
  DUFFINS

creative firm
  THE RIORDON DESIGN GROUP, INC.
  Oakville, Canada
art director
  RIC RIORDON
designer
  SHIRLEY RIORDON
illustrator
  DAN WHEATON
client
  TMN

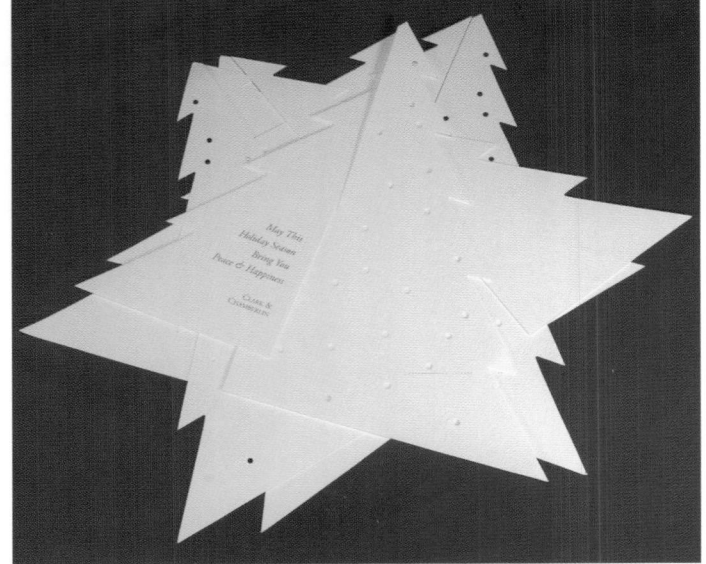

creative firm
ROBERT MEYERS DESIGN
Fairlawn, Ohio
designer
ROBERT MEYERS
client
CLARK & CHAMBERLIN

creative firm
AERIAL
San Francisco, California
designer
TRACY MOON
client
ALVA RESTAURANT, NY

creative firm
DESIGN MACHINE
New York, New York
creative director
ALEXANDER GELMAN
art directors, designers
ALEXANDER GELMAN, KAORU SATO
client
THE ART DIRECTORS CLUB NY

Problem

You now share your business lifeline with 175 million others.

Solution

WatchGuard protects your e-business with live internet security and responsive security experts.

WatchGuard LiveSecurity
SYSTEM

creative firm
  GRETEMAN GROUP
  Wichita, Kansas
creative director
  SONIA GRETEMAN
art director
  JAMES STRANGE
designer
  CRAIG TOMSON
client
  FAIR CHILD DORNIER

creative firm
  HORNALL ANDERSON DESIGN WORKS
  Seattle, Washington
art directors
  JACK ANDERSON, LISA CERVENY
designers
  LISA CERVENY, MARY HERMES, KATHY SAITO,
  MICHEAL BRUGMAN, HOLLY CRAVEN, BELINDA BOWLING
client
  WATCHGUARD

creative firm
  CLEVER LITTLE BOY DESIGNS
  Richmond, Kentucky
creative director, designer
  GRAHAM ALLEN
client
  GILES GALLERY
  (EASTERN KENTUCKY UNIVERSITY)

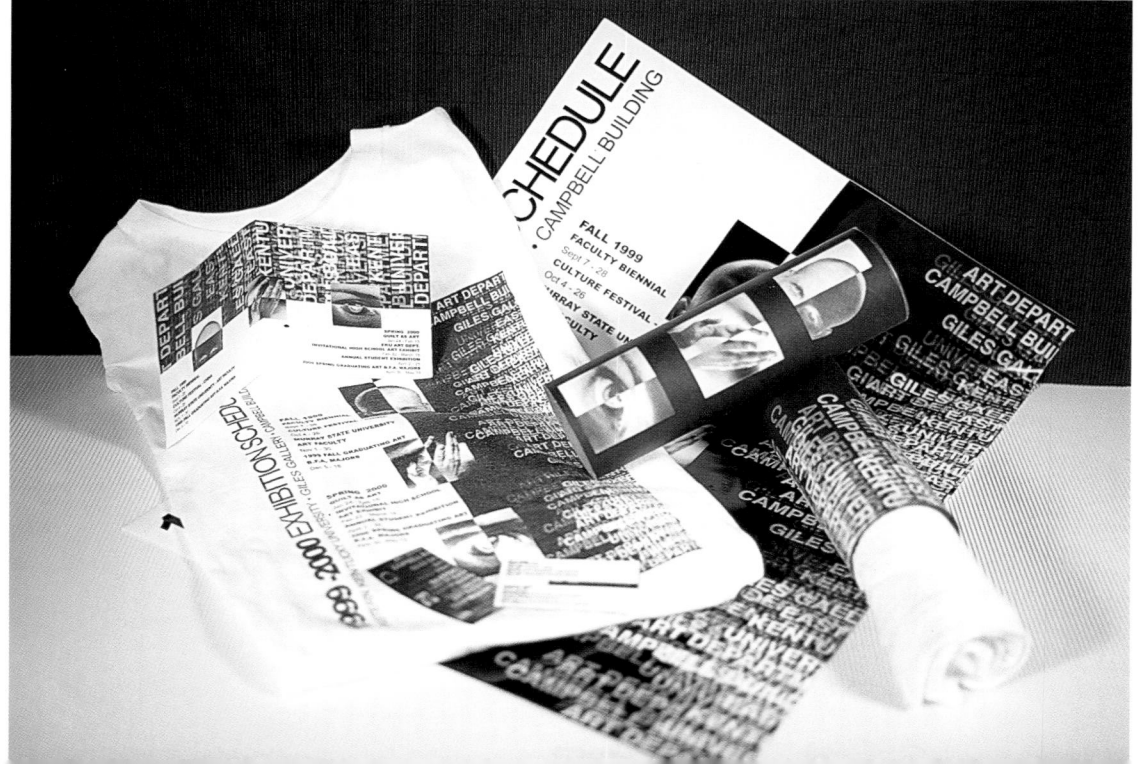

creative firm
  HORNALL ANDERSON DESIGN WORKS
    Seattle, Washington
art director
  JOHN HORNALL
designers
  JOHN HORNALL, JULIE LOCK,
    MARY CHIN HUTCHISON, MARY HERMES, DAVID BATES
client
  NEXTRx CORPORATION

creative firm
  SAYLES GRAPHIC DESIGN
    Des Moines, Iowa
art director, illustrator
  JOHN SAYLES
client
  NATIONAL SOCIETY OF FUND RAISING EXECUTIVES

creative firm
  JA DESIGN SOLUTIONS
    Coppell, Texas
editor
  PATRICIA McWILLIAMS-POWELL
designer
  JEAN ASHENFELTER
composition
  JON MOSIER
copywriter
  LINDA CAPRIOTTI
client
  GTE SUPPLY—LYNN HANDLEY

creative firm
  STAN GELLMAN GRAPHIC DESIGN, INC.
  St. Louis, Missouri
senior designer
  MIKE DONOVAN
client
  UNIVERSITY OF ILLINOIS FOUNDATION

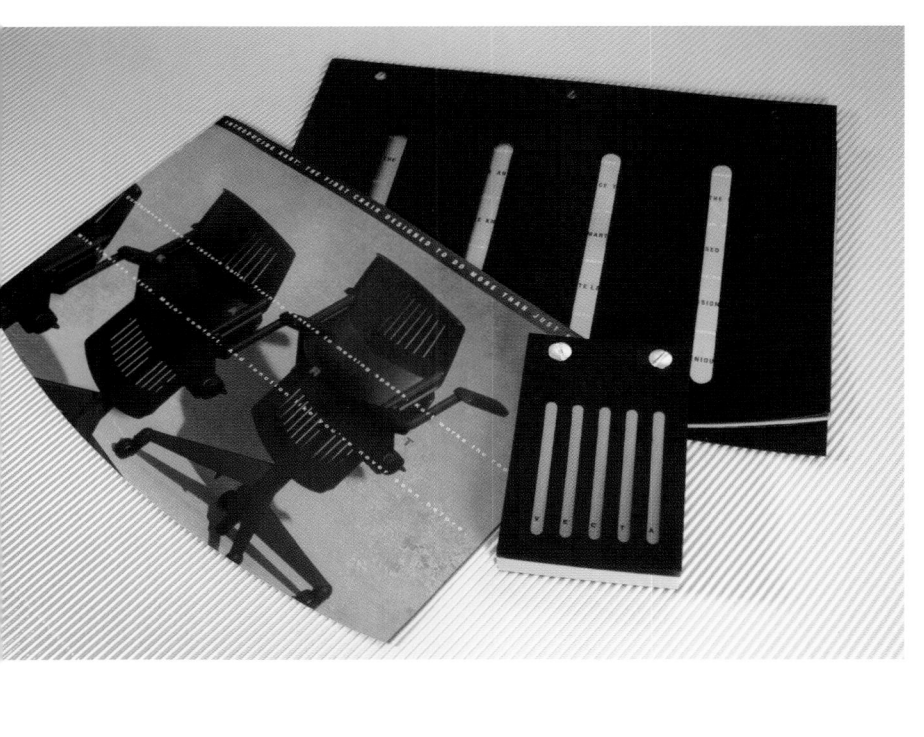

GENERAL MAGIC™

creative firm
  AIRE DESIGN COMPANY
  Tucson, Arizona
creative director
  CATHARINE M. KIM
art director
  SHARI RYKOWSKI
client
  DESERT WHALE JOJOBA COMPANY

creative firm
  HORNALL ANDERSON DESIGN WORKS
  Seattle, Washington
art director
  JACK ANDERSON
designers
  JACK ANDERSON, JANA NISHI, MARY CHIN HUTCHISON
client
  GENERAL MAGIC

creative firm
 MULLER + CO.
 Kansas City, Missouri
creative director
 JOHN MULLER
designer
 BROHAN WATKINS
client
 KANSAS CITY ART INSTITUTE

creative firm
 GREENFIELD/BELSER LTD
 Washington, D.C.
art director
 BURKEY BELSER
designers
 BURKEY BELSER, ERIKA RITZER
client
 LEGAL MARKETING ASSOCIATION

creative firm
 5D STUDIO
 Malibu, California
art director
 JANE KOBAYASHI
designer
 GEOFF LEDET
client
 VECTA

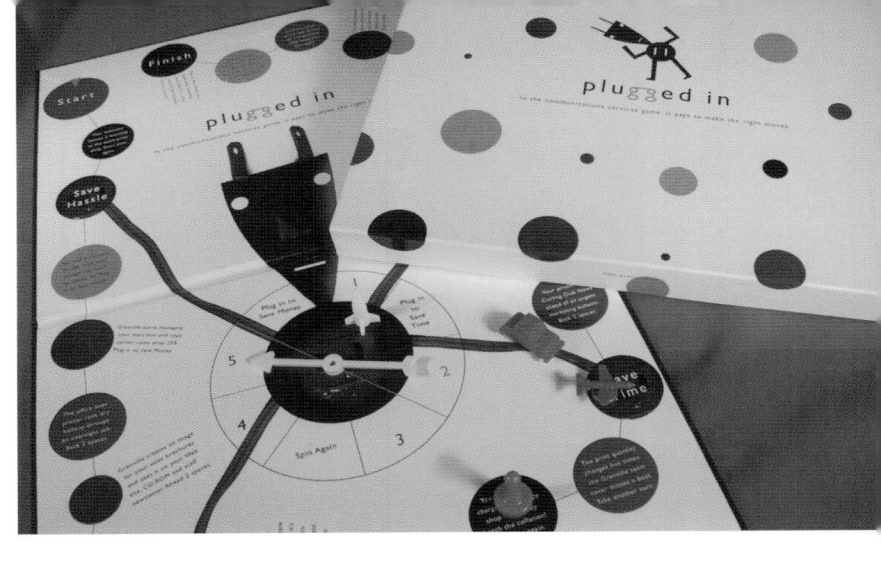

creative firm
  VIVA DOLAN COMMUNICATIONS
  AND DESIGN, INC.
  Toronto, Canada
art director, designer, illustrator
  FRANK VIVA
copywriter
  DOUG DOLAN
client
  GRENVILLE MANAGEMENT SERVICES

creative firm
  GRETEMEAN GROUP
  Wichita, Kansas
creative director
  SONIA GRETEMAN
art directors
  SONIA GRETEMAN, JAMES STRANGE
designer
  JAMES STRANGE
client
  ROCKWELL COLLINS

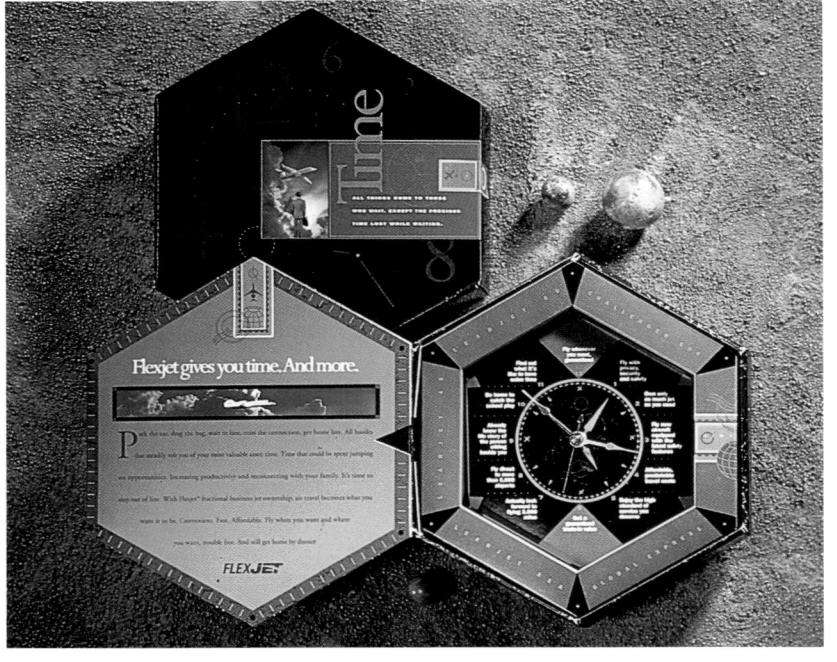

creative firm
  GRETEMAN GROUP
  Wichita, Kansas
creative director
  SONIA GRETEMAN
art directors, designers
  SONIA GRETEMAN, JAMES STRANGE
client
  FLEXJET

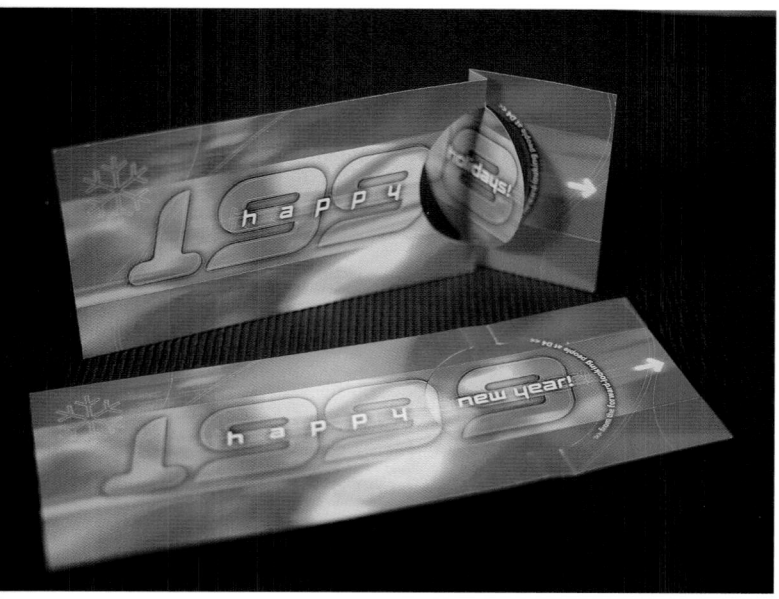

creative firm
  D4 CREATIVE GROUP
    Philadelphia, Pennsylvania
art director, illustrator
  WICKY W. LEE
copywriter
  JERRY SELBER
client
  D4 CREATIVE GROUP

creative firm
  WET PAPER BAG GRAPHIC DESIGN
    Fort Worth, Texas
designer, art director, copywriter
  LEWIS GLASER
client
  WET PAPER BAG GRAPHIC DESIGN

creative firm
  ESTUDIO RAY
    Phoenix, Arizona
art directors
  CHRISTINE RAY & JOE RAY
designers
  CHRISTINE RAY, JOE RAY,
  LESLIE LINK
illustrators
  JOE RAY, FRANK YBARRA
client
  ESTUDIO RAY

creative firm
  TOM FOWLER, INC.
    Stamford, Connecticut
art director
  THOMAS G. FOWLER
designer, copywriter
  ELIZABETH P. BALL
client
  TOM FOWLER, INC.

creative firm
  SAYLES GRAPHIC DESIGN
    Des Moines, Iowa
art director, illustrator
  JOHN SAYLES
client
  SAYLES GRAPHIC DESIGN

creative firm
  VIVA DOLAN COMMUNICATIONS
  AND DESIGN INC.
    Toronto, Canada
art director, designer, illustrator
  FRANK VIVA
photographer
  HILL PEPPARD
copywriter
  DOUG DOLAN
client
  VIVA DOLAN COMMUNICATIONS AND DESIGN INC.

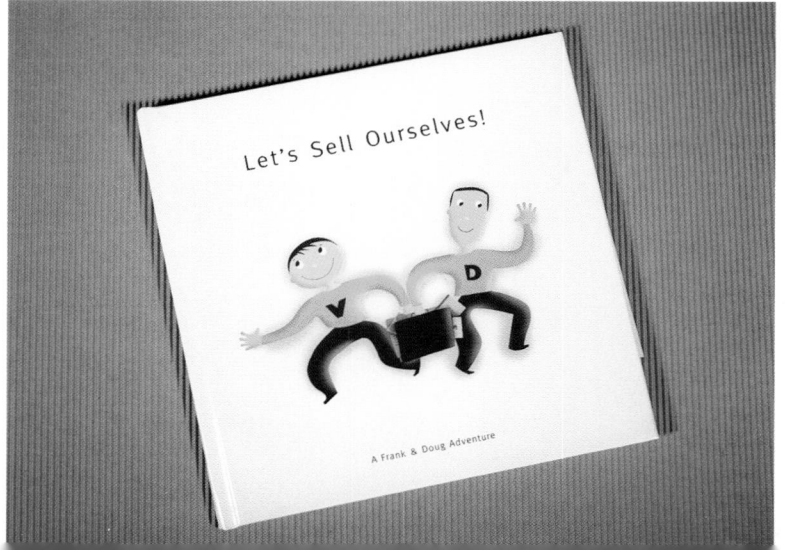

creative firm
  SQUIRES & COMPANY
  Dallas, Texas
designer
  CHRISTIE GROTHEIM
client
  SQUIRES & COMPANY

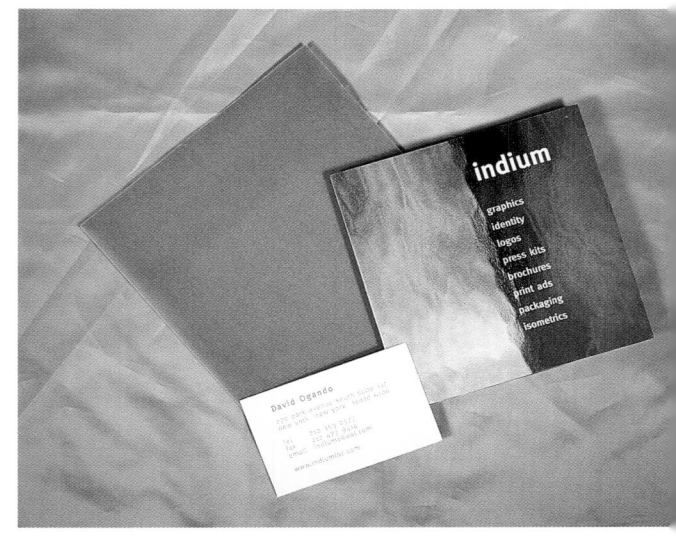

creative firm
  INDIUM
  New York, New York
director
  DAVID OGANDO
photographer
  JUDY JURACEK
client
  INDIUM

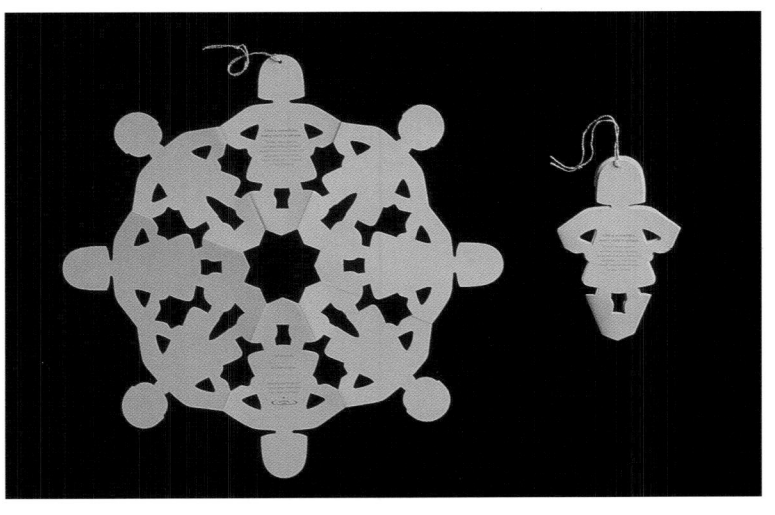

creative firm
  PEARLFISHER
  London, England
creative director
  JONATHAN FORD
designer
  KIM HARDY
client
  PEARLFISHER

creative firm
  LIEBER BREWSTER DESIGN, INC.
  New York, New York
art director
  ANNA LIEBER
designer, photographer
  ANTON GINZBERG
client
  LIEBER BREWSTER DESIGN, INC.

creative firm
  GEORGOPULOS DESIGN
  West Chester, Pennsylvania
designer, illustrator, photographer,
programmer, editor, musical composer
  JONATHAN GEORGOPULOS
client
  GEORGOPULOS DESIGN

creative firm
  SHOOK DESIGN GROUP, INC.
  Charlotte, North Carolina
graphic designer
  STEVE FENTON
client
  SHOOK DESIGN GROUP, INC.

creative firm
O&J DESIGN INC.
New York, New York
art director
ANDRZEJ J. OLEJNICZAK
designer
LIA CAMARA MARISCAL
client
O&J DESIGN INC.

creative firm
30SIXTY DESIGN, INC.
Los Angeles, California
creative director
HENRY VIZCARRA
art director, designer, illustrator
PÄR LARSSON
client
30SIXTY DESIGN,INC.

creative firm
GRETEMAN GROUP
Wichita, Kansas
creative director, art director
SONIA GRETEMAN
designer
JAMES STRANGE
client
GRETEMAN GROUP

creative firm
MIKE QUON/DESIGNATION
New York, New York
designer
MIKE QUON
client
MIKE QUON/DESIGNATION

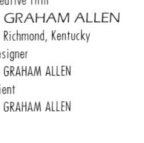

creative firm
GRAHAM ALLEN
Richmond, Kentucky
designer
GRAHAM ALLEN
client
GRAHAM ALLEN

creative firm
SPENCER ZAHN & ASSOCIATES
Philadelphia, Pennsylvania
creative director
SPENCER ZAHN
designers
JOSEPH McCARTHY, ED McHUGH
client
SPENCER ZAHN & ASSOCIATES

creative firm
  BELYEA
    Seattle, Washington
art director, copywriter
  PATRICIA BELYEA
designer
  RON LARS HANSEN
photographer
  JIM LINNA
client
  BELYEA

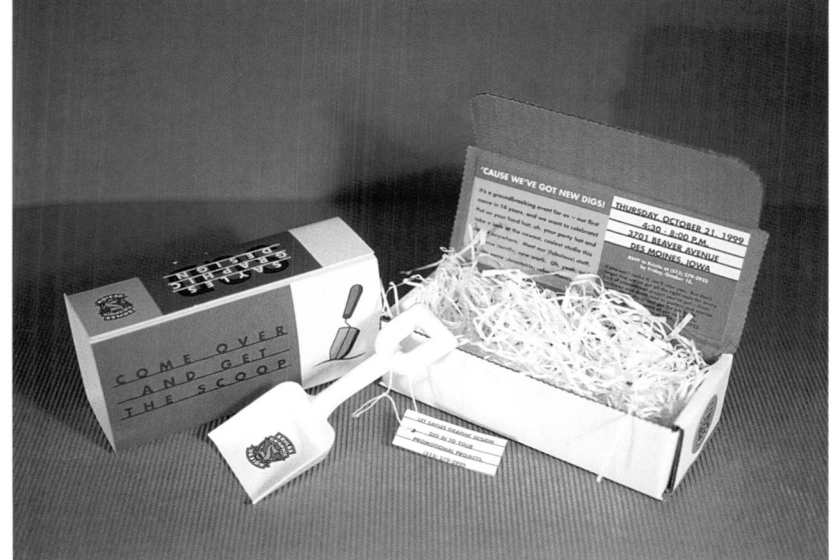

creative firm
  SAYLES GRAPHIC DESIGN
    Des Moines, Iowa
art director, illustrator
  JOHN SAYLES
client
  SAYLES GRAPHIC DESIGN

creative firm
  D4 CREATIVE GROUP
    Philadelphia, Pennsylvania
creative director, copywriter
  DAVID LESSER
art director
  WICKY W. LEE
client
  D4 CREATIVE GROUP

creative firm
GILL FISHMAN ASSOCIATES, INC.
Cambridge, Massachusetts
creative director
GILL FISHMAN
designer
MICHAEL PERSONS
copywriter
SUSAN CONWAY
client
GILL FISHMAN ASSOCIATES, INC.

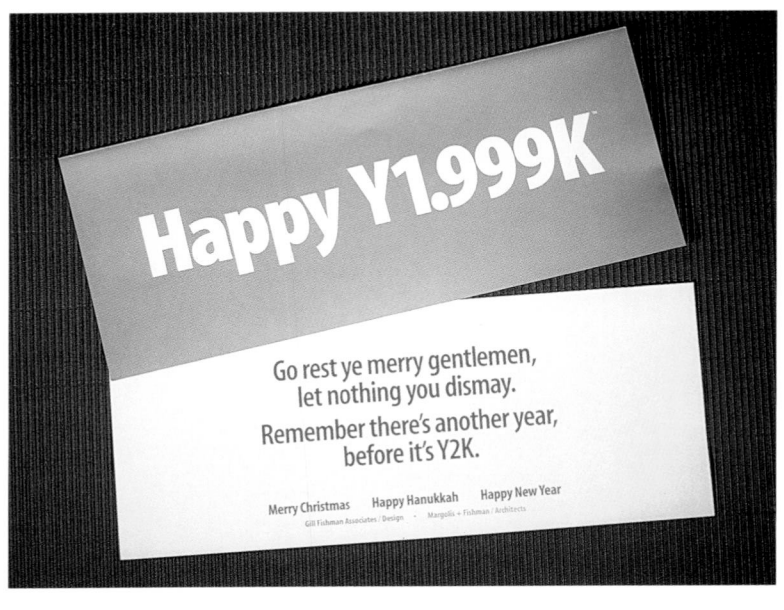

creative firm
GARDNER DESIGN
Wichita, Kansas
art director
BILL GARDNER
designers
BILL GARDNER, BRIAN MILLER
client
BILL GARDNER

creative firm
SWIMMER DESIGN ASSOCIATES
Prospect Heights, Ilinois
creative director
KRISTINE MEYER
client
SWIMMER DESIGN ASSOCIATES

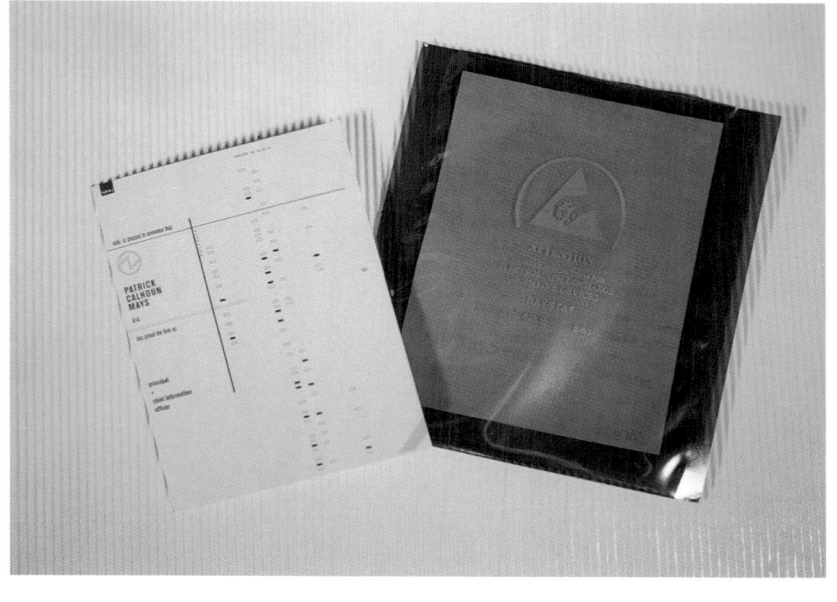

creative firm
  H2D
  Milwaukee, Wisconsin
creative director
  JOSEPH HAUSCH
art director
  ALLAN HAAS
client
  H2D

creative firm
  NBBJ GRAPHIC DESIGN
  Seattle, Washington
designer
  HEATHER HEFLIN
client
  NBBJ GRAPHIC DESIGN

creative firm
  GRAPHICULTURE
  Minneapolis, Minnesota
designer
  CHERYL WATSON
photographer
  JOEL LARSON
client
  JOEL LARSON

creative firm
   GRAPHICULTURE
   Minneapolis, Minnesota
designer
   CHERYL WATSON
photographer
   JOEL LARSON
client
   JOEL LARSON

creative firm
   A TO Z COMMUNICATIONS, INC.
   Pittsburgh, Pennsylvania
creative directors
   ALAN BOARTS, AIMEE LAZER
senior graphic designer
   AIMEE LAZER
copywriters
   ANN HORNAK, DENISE BELIZAR
client
   A TO Z COMMUNICATIONS, INC.

creative firm
   ROSS ADVERTISING
   Peoria, Illinois
creative director
   WENDY BEHRENS
art directors
   JIM JONES, RANDY MARX
illustrator
   LISA LUCAS
copywriter
   JOHN RUEBUSH
client
   ROSS TRAINING AND MOTIVATION

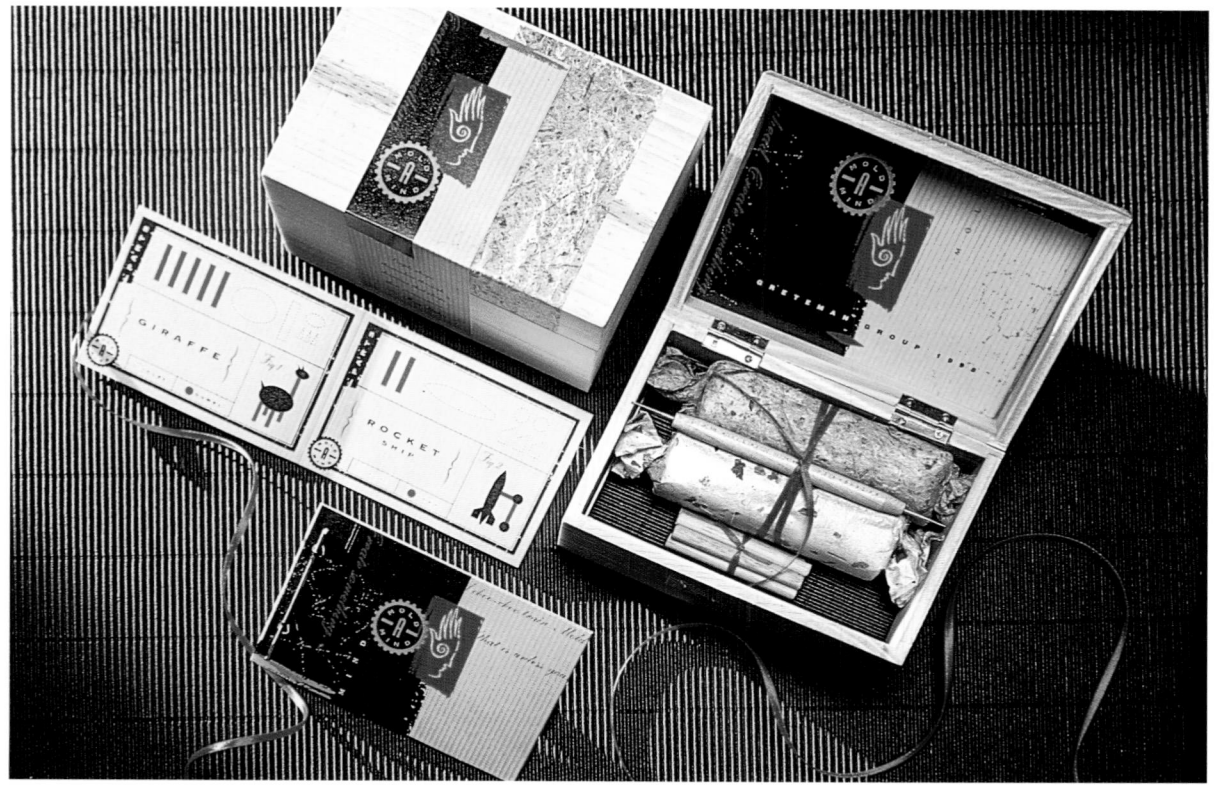

creative firm
GRETEMAN GROUP
Wichita, Kansas
creative director, art director, illustrator
SONIA GRETEMAN
designer
JAMES STRANGE
client
GRETEMAN GROUP

creative firm
BBK STUDIO INC.
Grand Rapids, Michigan
creative director, designer
MICHAEL BARILE
illustrators
MICHAEL BARILE, ALLEN McKINNEY
client
BBK STUDIO INC.

creative firm
FIVE VISUAL COMMUNICATION & DESIGN
West Chester, Ohio
designers
DENNY FAGAN, RONDI TSCHOPP
client
FIVE VISUAL COMMUNICATION & DESIGN

creative firm
GRETEMAN GROUP
Wichita, Kansas
creative director, art director
SONIA GRETEMAN
designer
JAMES STRANGE
client
GRETEMAN GROUP

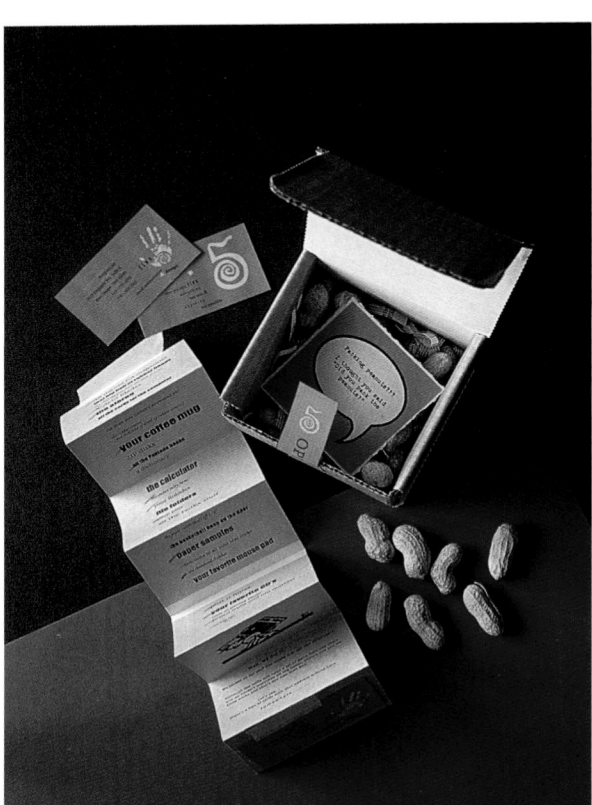

creative firm
FIVE VISUAL COMMUNICATION & DESIGN
West Chester, Ohio
designers
RONDI TSCHOPP, DENNY FAGAN
client
FIVE VISUAL COMMUNICATION & DESIGN

creative firm
  LAZYWOOD PRESS
  Houston, Texas
concept
  PAULA MURPHY
client
  MY TABLE MAGAZINE

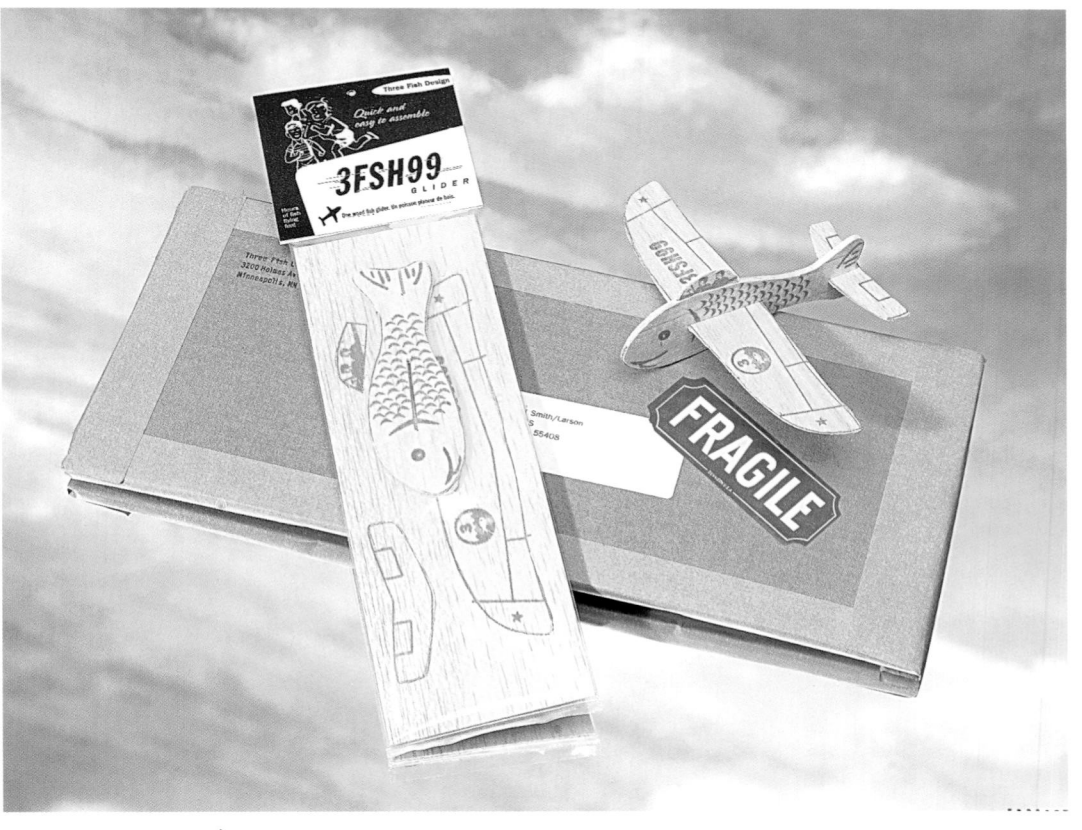

creative firm
  THREE FISH DESIGN
  Minneapolis, Minnesota
art director, designer
  CAROLINE VAALER
production
  ART SERVE
client
  THREE FISH DESIGN

creative firm
  NAKATSUKA DAISUKE INC.
  Tokyo, Japan
designers
  DAISUKE NAKATSUKA, MAYUMI INOUE, SATORU HAMAMURA,
  TOMOKO KANOU, RYOKO YAGITA, GORO ARIZONA
client
  SHU UEMURA COSMETICS INC.

creative firm
  BRUNAZZI & ASSOCIATI/
  IMAGE + COMMUNICATION
  Turin, Italy
art director
  GIOVANNI BRUNAZZI
client
  BURGO

creative firm
  NAKATSUKA DAISUKE INC.
  Tokyo, Japan
designers
  DAISUKE NAKATSUKA, FUMIYO KITAZUME, MASAKUNI FUJIKAKE
client
  SHU UEMURA COSMETICS INC.

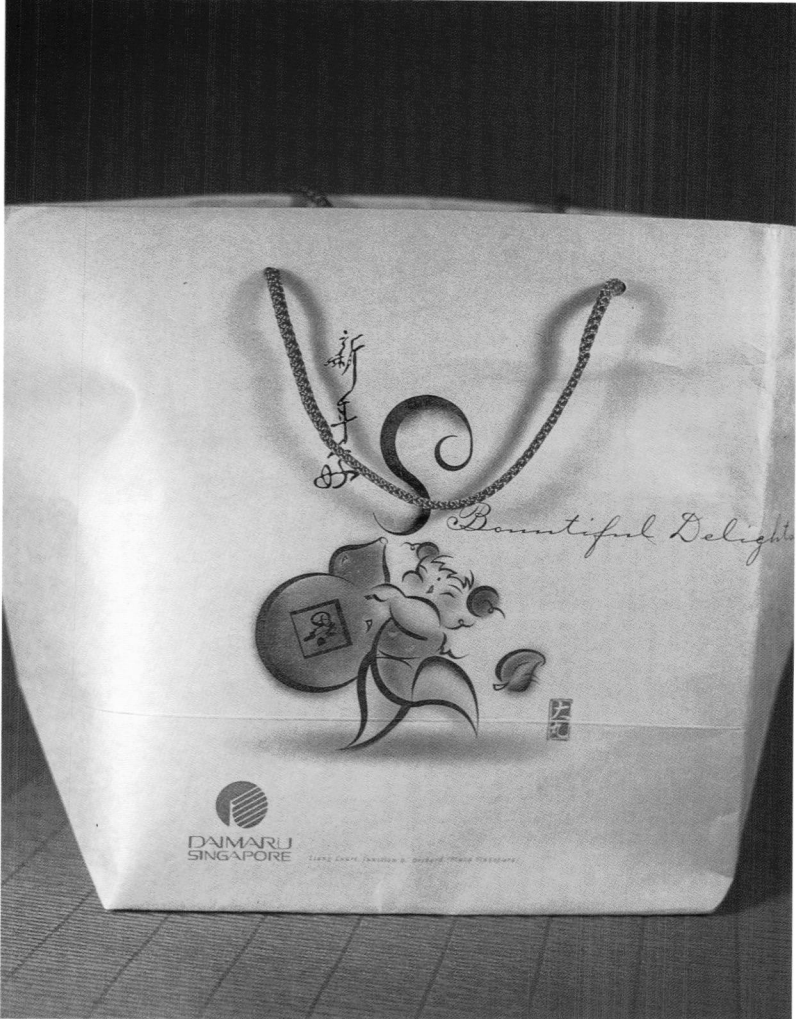

creative firm
  UKULELE DESIGN CONSULTANTS PTE LTD
  Singapore
design director
  KIM CHUN-WEI
designer
  LYNN LIM
client
  DAIMARU SINGAPORE PTE LTD

creative firm
  ADKINS/BALCHUNAS
  Providence, Rhode Island
creative director, designer
  JERRY BALCHUNAS
senior designer
  MICHELLE PHANEUF
client
  THE GROCERIA

creative firm
  SAYLES GRAPHIC DESIGN
    Des Moines, Iowa
art director, illustrator
  JOHN SAYLES
client
  GLAZED EXPRESSIONS

creative firm
  RGB DESIGN
    Rio De Janeiro, Brazil
designer
  MARIA LUIZA GONCALVES VEIGA BRITO,
  MARIA ANGELA LUTTERBACH
client
  MARIA FILÓ FASHION STORE

creative firm
H2D
Milwaukee, Wisconsin
creative director
JOSEPH HAUSCH
client
BRETT FAVRE

creative firm
MIKE QUON/DESIGNATION
New York, New York
designer
MIKE QUON
client
FIELDCREST—CANNON

creative firm
AERIAL
San Francisco, California
designers
TRACY MOON, STEPHANIE WEST
client
TRIBE PICTURES

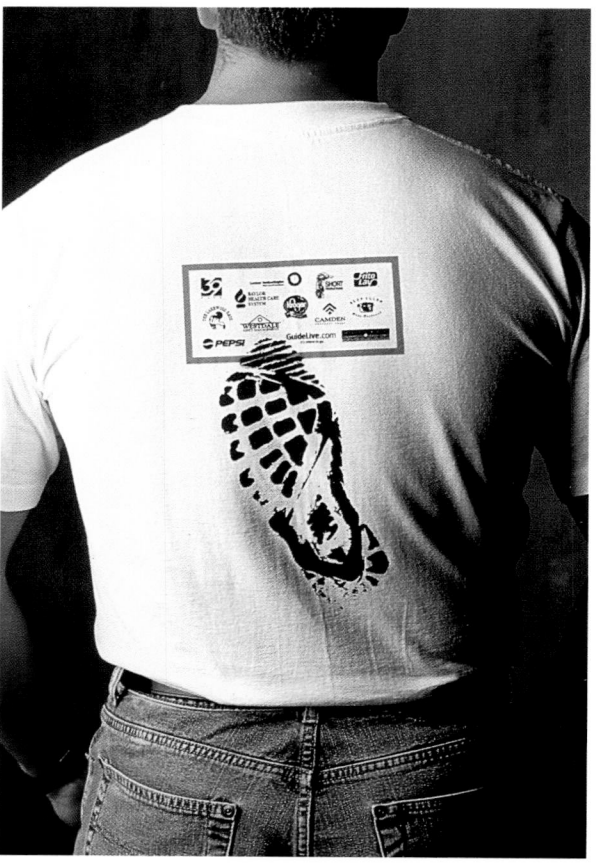

creative firm
SQUIRES & COMPANY
Dallas, Texas
designer
CHRISTIE GROTHEIM
client
DEEP ELLUM DASH

creative firm
  MIKE QUON/DESIGNATION
  New York, New York
art director
  SCOTT FISHOFF
designer
  MIKE QUON
client
  CLAIROL

creative firm
  MIKE QUON/DESIGNATION
  New York, New York
art director
  SCOTT FISHOFF
designer
  MIKE QUON
client
  CLAIROL

creative firm
  H2D
  Milwaukee, Wisconsin
creative director
  JOSEPH HAUSCH
creative specialist
  TONY TABBERT
client
  RALPH MARLIN

creative firm
  MIKE QUON/DESIGNATION
  New York, New York
designer
  MIKE QUON
client
  CHATTAHOOCHEE COUNTRY CLUB

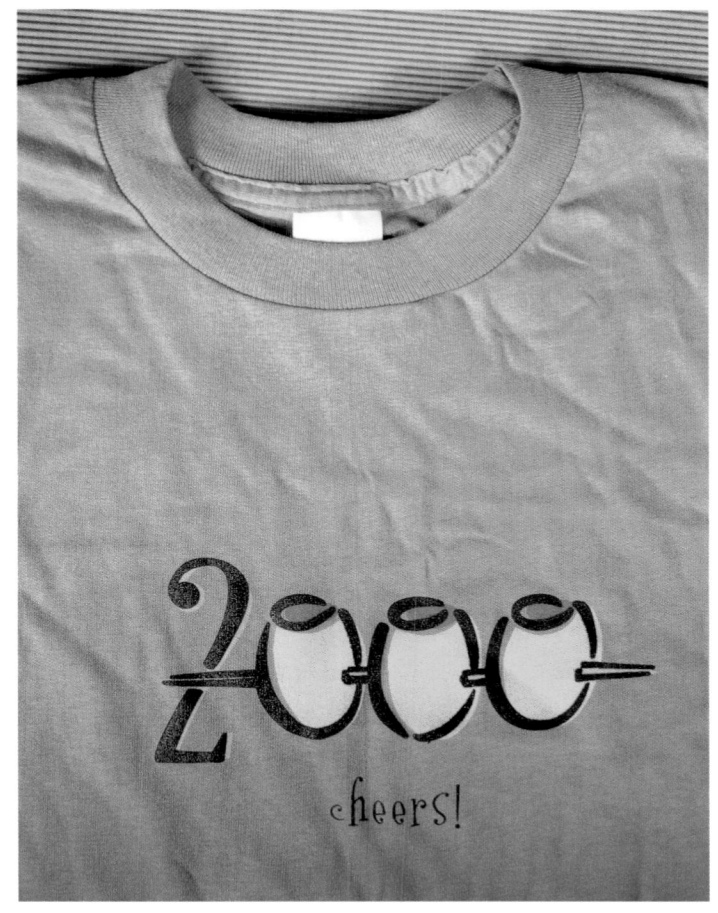

creative firm
AFTER HOURS CREATIVE
Phoenix, Arizona
client
MAX & LUCY

creative firm
MIKE QUON/DESIGNATION
New York, New York
designer
MIKE QUON
client
AMERICAN MUSEUM OF NATURAL HISTORY

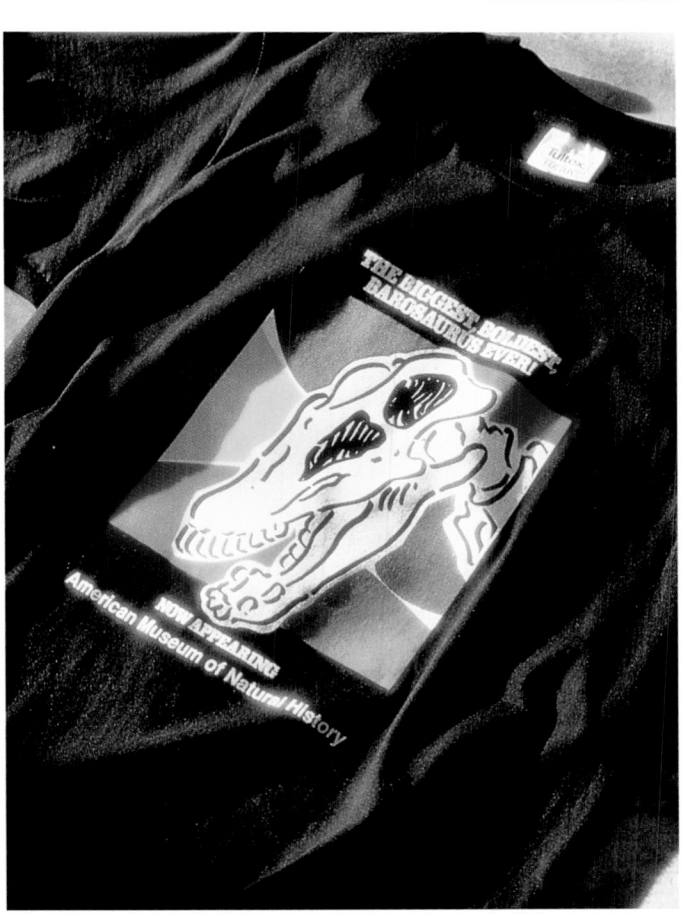

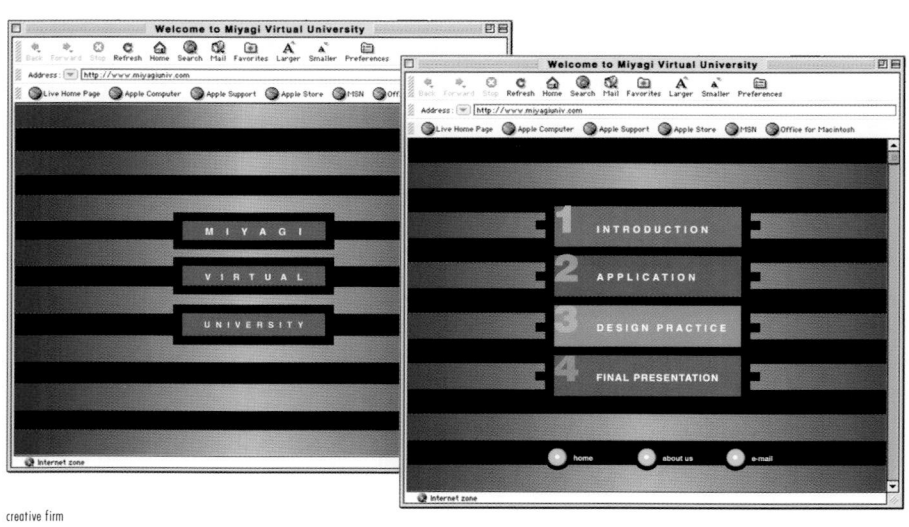

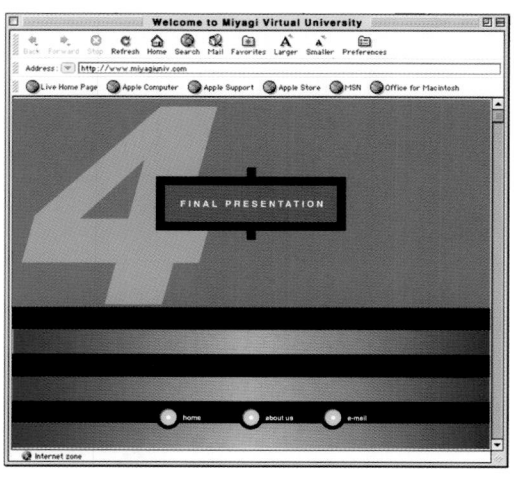

creative firm
 SHIMOKOCHI/REEVES
 Los Angeles, California
designer
 NOBODY LISTED
 BUT SOMETHING FOR YOU
 TO MARK
client
 ROR & MIYAGI

creative firm
 WATERSDESIGN.COM
 New York, New York
design director
 KAYPEE SOH
producer
 KIMBERLY LEASS
designer
 SOO JIN YUM
content
 SHARON TOLPIN
production artists
 KIM NIECE, KARRIE FRYBERG
programmer
 SETH ZALMAN
client
 SOLBRIGHT

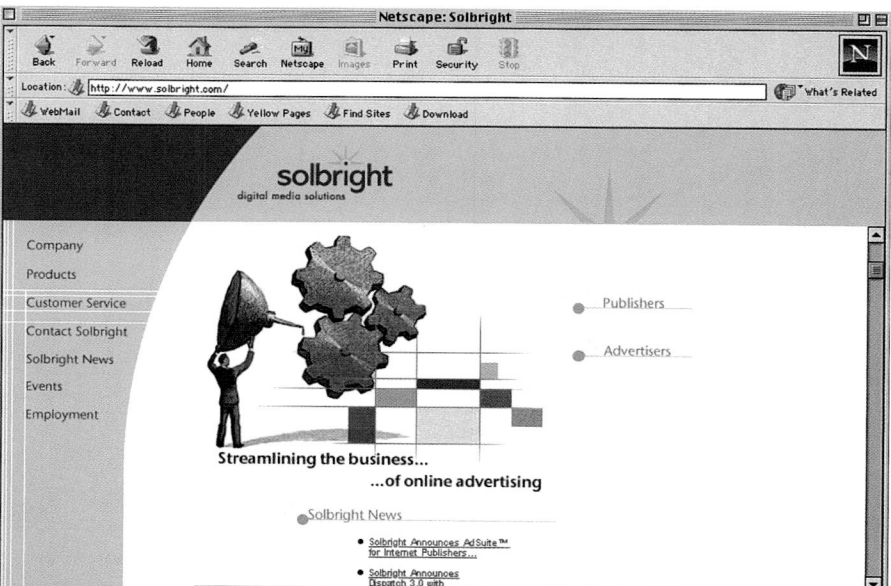

creative firm
 BBK STUDIO INC.
 Grand Rapids, Michigan
art director
 KEVIN BUDELMANN
producer
 LEAH WESTON
designers
 KEVIN BUDELMANN, MIKE CARNEVALE, YANG KIM, ALISON POPP
programmers
 MIKE CARNEVALE, LEAH WESTON, VON NEEL, SCOTT KRIEGER
client
 HERMAN MILLER FOR THE HEALTHCARE

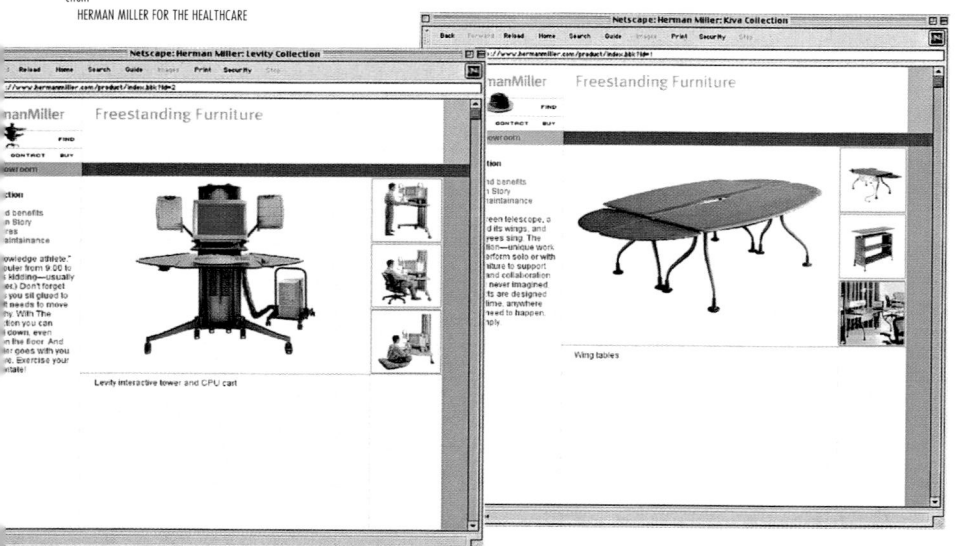

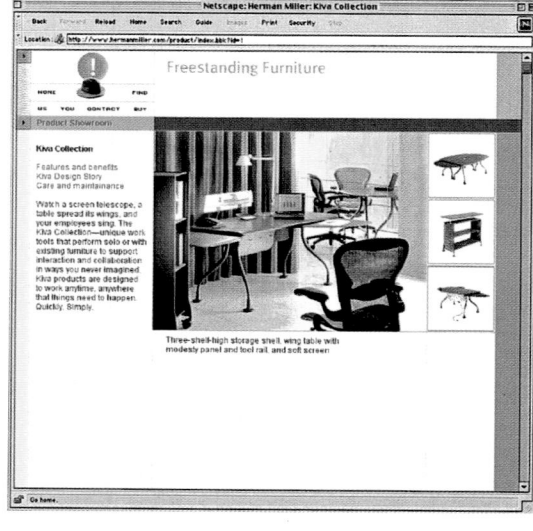

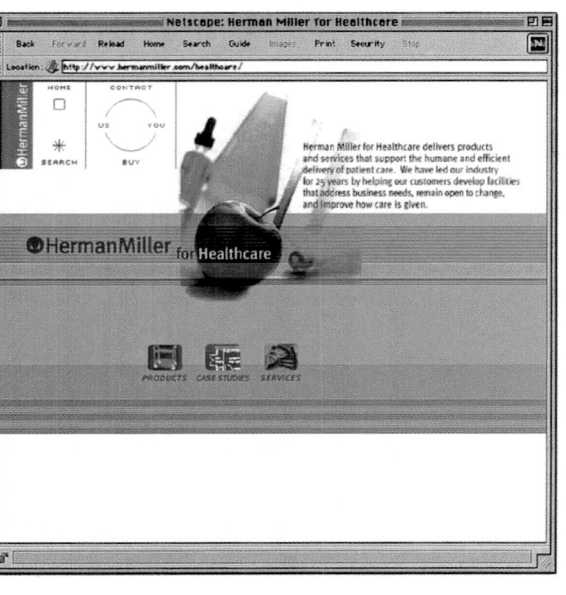

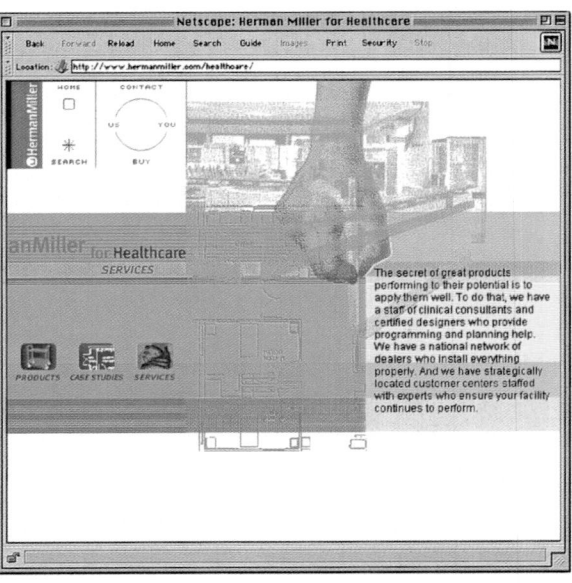

creative firm
   BBK STUDIO INC.
   Grand Rapids, Michigan
art director
   KEVIN BUDELMANN
producer
   LEAH WESTON
designers
   KEVIN BUDELMANN, MIKE CARNEVALE,
   YANG KIM, ALISON POPP
programmers
   MIKE CARNEVALE, LEAH WESTON,
   VON NEEL, SCOTT KRIEGER
client
   HERMAN MILLER FOR THE HEALTHCARE

creative firm
   WATERSDESIGN.COM
   New York, New York
creative director
   JOHN PANOLINI
producer
   KIMBERLY LEASS
designer
   YOSH OSHIMA
content
   DIANA AMSTERDAM
programmer
   NICOLE NEOPOLITAN
client
   TRIBECA PRODUCTIONS

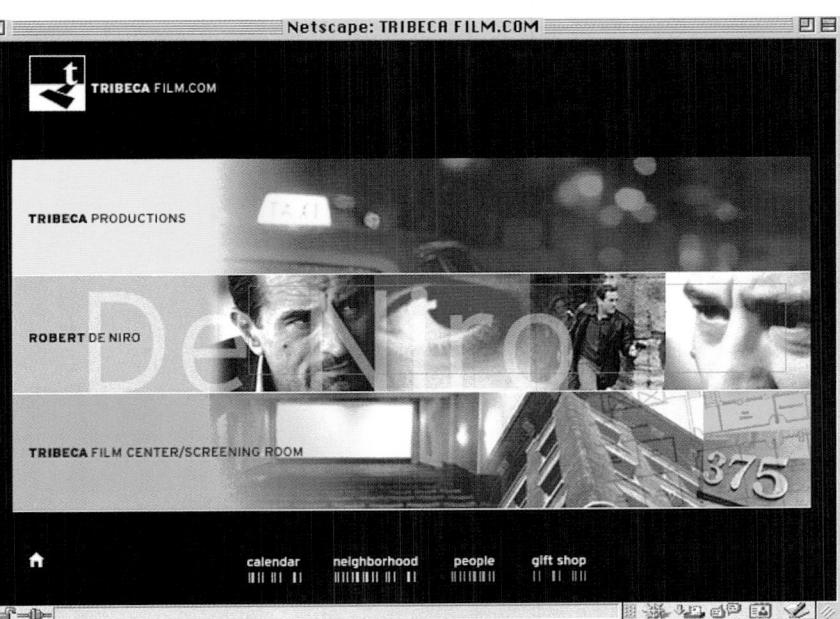

creative firm
   BBK STUDIO INC.
   Grand Rapids, Michigan
art directors
   KEVIN BUDELMANN, YANG KIM
producer
   LEAH WESTON
designer
   KELLY J. SCHWARTZ
programmers
   JEFF SIKKEMA, LEAH WESTON
client
   GUILFORD OF MAINE

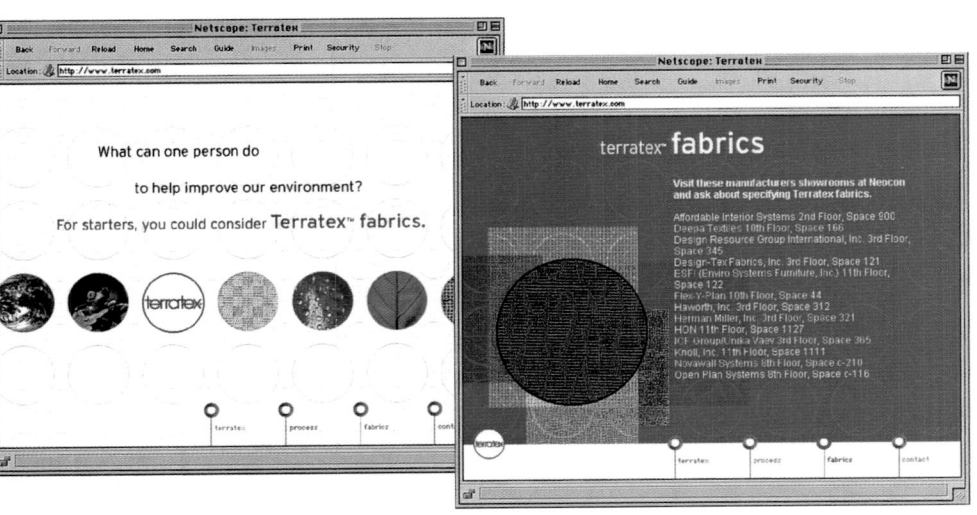

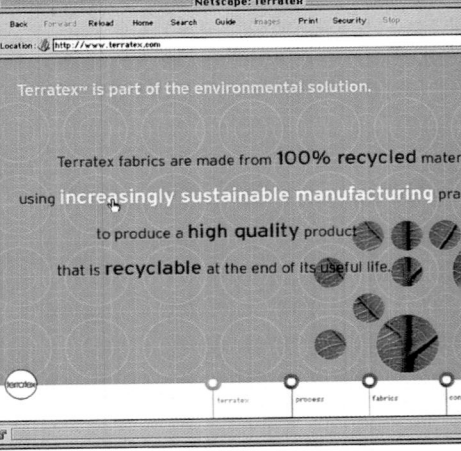

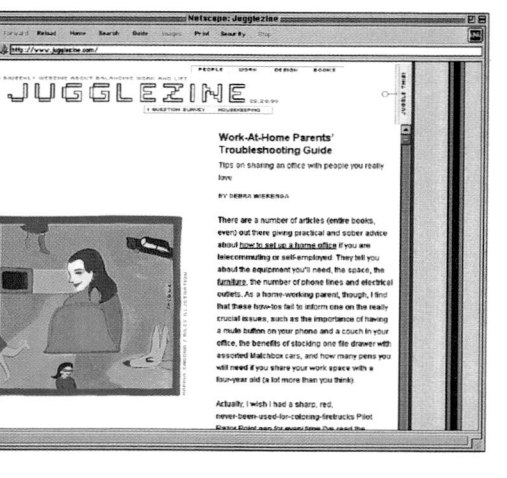

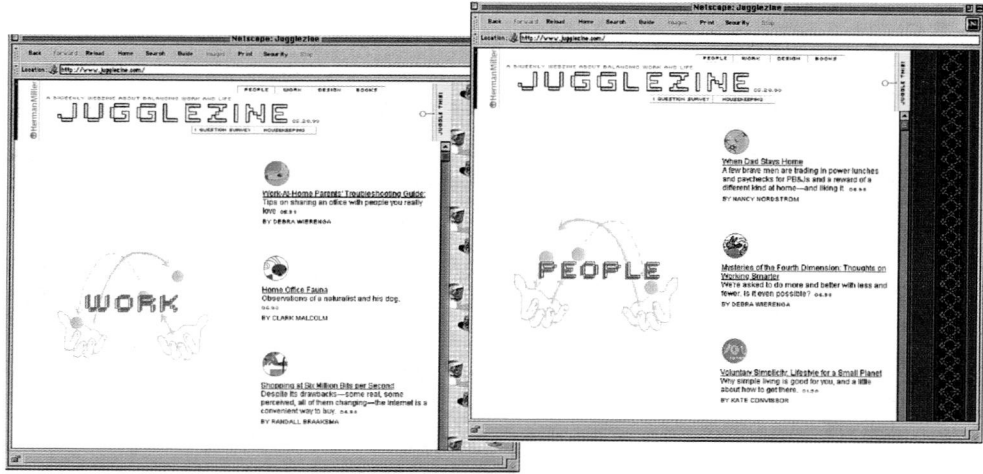

creative firm
BBK STUDIO INC.
Grand Rapids, Michigan
art director
KEVIN BUDELMANN
editor
CHRISTINE MacLEAN
producer
LEAH WESTON
designers
KEVIN BUDELMANN,
ALISON POPP, STEVEN JOSWICK
programmers
VON NEEL, SCOTT KRIEGER,
JEFF SIKKEMA
client
HERMAN MILLER INC.

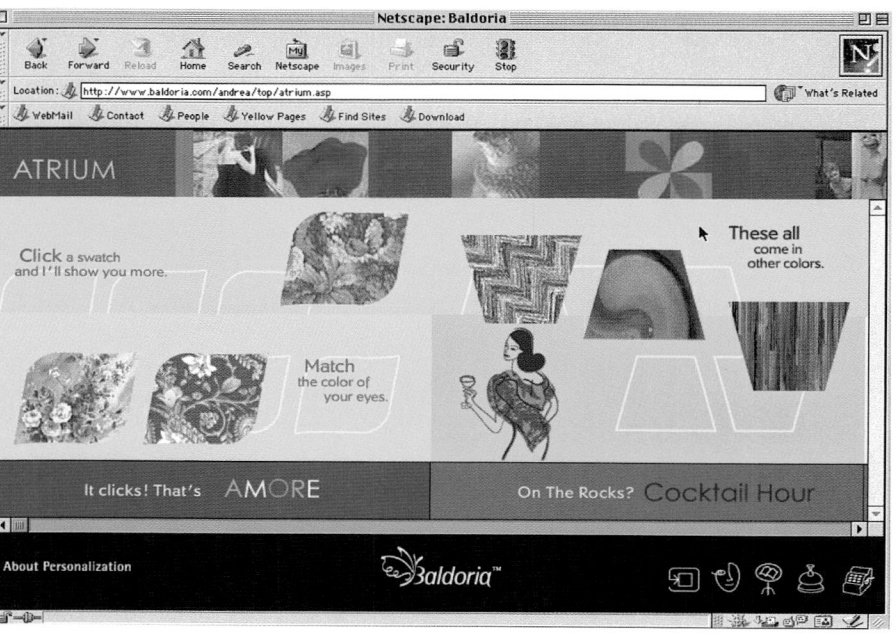

creative firm
WATERSDESIGN.COM
New York, New York
creative director
JOHN PANOLINI
producer
SHEILA DEHNER
designer
YOSH OSHIMA
content
DIANA AMSTERDAM, ANDY AUSTIN
programmer
CAROL ENG
site builders
NICOLE NEOPOLITAN, TYLER RAYNER
client
BALDORIA

creative firm
BBK STUDIO INC.
Grand Rapids, Michigan
art director
KEVIN BUDELMANN
editor
JULIE RIDL
producer
LEAH WESTON
designers
KEVIN BUDELMANN, MIKE CARNEVALE,
YANG KIM, ALISON POPP,
KELLY SCHWARTZ, MATT RYZENGA
programmers
LEAH WESTON, JEFF SIKKEMA,
MIKE CARNEVALE, SCOTT KRIEGER,
VON NEEL
client
HERMAN MILLER INC.

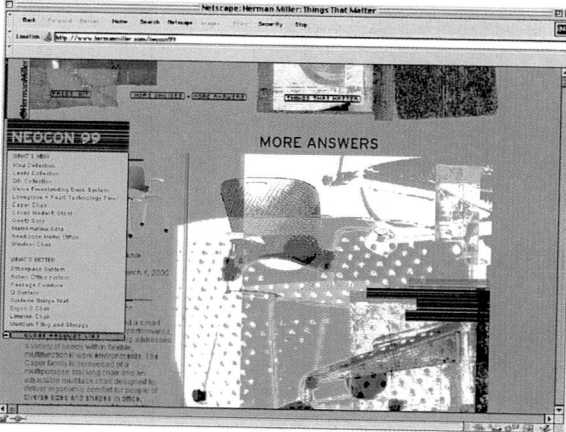

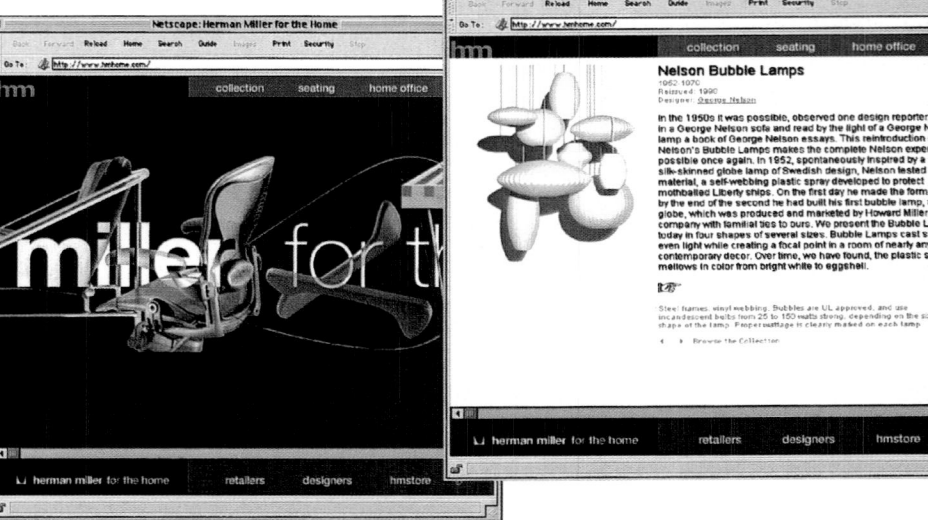

creative firm
  BBK STUDIO INC.
  Grand Rapids, Michigan
creative director
  KEVIN BUDELMANN
producer
  JEFF SIKKEMA
designers
  KEVIN BUDELMANN, ALISON POPP
copywriter
  JULIE RIDL
client
  HERMAN MILLER FOR THE HOME

creative firm
  WATERSDESIGN.COM
  New York, New York
design director
  KAYPEE SOH
producer
  KIMBERLY LEASS
designer
  HENRY KUO
content
  CHRISTOPHER COLLETTE
site builders
  SETH ZALMAN,
  TYLER RAYNER, HENRY KUO
client
  CLICKMAIL

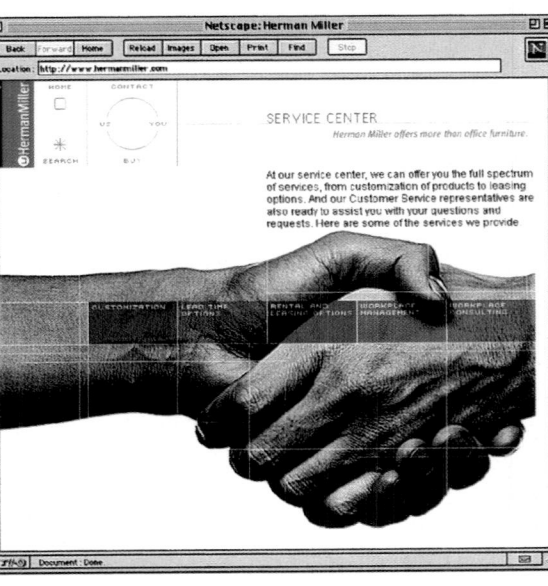

creative firm
  BBK STUDIO INC.
  Grand Rapids, Michigan
art director
  KEVIN BUDELMANN
editor
  JULIE RIDL
producer
  LEAH WESTON
designers
  KEVIN BUEDELMANN, YANG KIM,
  ALISON POPP, MIKE CARNEVALE,
  MATT RYZENGA
programmers
  LEAH WESTON, VON NEEL, JEFF SIKKEMA,
  SCOTT KRIEGER, MIKE CARNEVALE
client
  HERMAN MILLER INC.

creative firm
  SAYLES GRAPHIC DESIGN
  Des Moines, Iowa
art director, illustrator
  JOHN SAYLES
client
  MUSCULAR DYSTROPHY ASSOCIATION
  "LAST DINNER ON THE TITANIC"

creative firm
  GREENFIELD/BELSER LTD
  Washington, D.C.
art director
  BURKEY BELSER
designer
  JEANETTE NUZUM
client
  GREENFIELD/BELSER

creative firm
  BUTLER KEMP DESIGN
  North Adelaide, Australia
art director
  DEREK BUTLER
designer
  SCOTT CARSLAKE
client
  DRUG & ALCOHOL SERVICE COUNCIL
  (drink coasters)

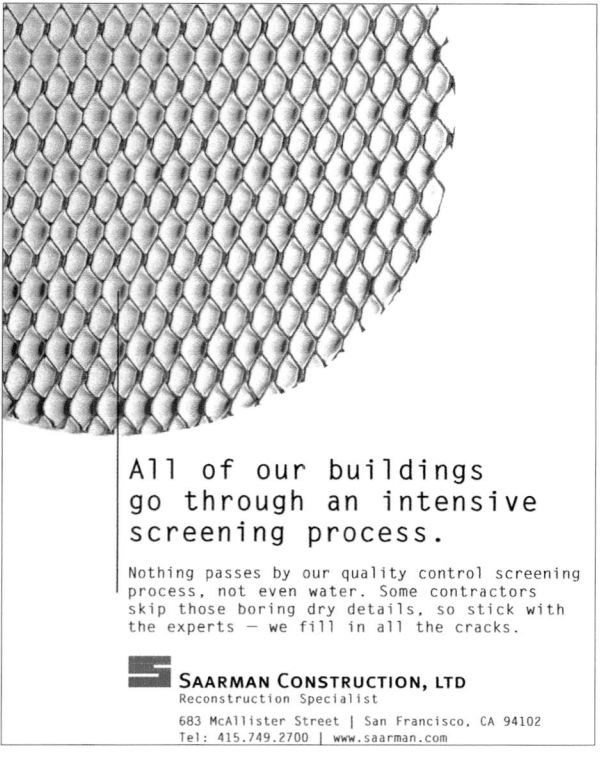

All of our buildings go through an intensive screening process.

Nothing passes by our quality control screening process, not even water. Some contractors skip those boring dry details, so stick with the experts — we fill in all the cracks.

SAARMAN CONSTRUCTION, LTD
Reconstruction Specialist

683 McAllister Street | San Francisco, CA 94102
Tel: 415.749.2700 | www.saarman.com

creative firm
  BRUCE YELASKA DESIGN
  San Francisco, California
art director, designer, copywriter
  BRUCE YELASKA
photographer
  RICHARD GORDON
client
  SAARMAN CONSTRUCTION

When it's raining cats & dogs

It's the leaks you don't see that end up getting you. Be proactive and stop the leaks. Work with Saarman, the specialist in multifamily and commercial defect repair and maintenance. Now you'll never have to worry about falling collies again.

SAARMAN CONSTRUCTION, LTD
Reconstruction Specialist

683 McAllister Street | San Francisco, CA 94102
Tel: 415.749.2700 | www.saarman.com

creative firm
  BRUCE YELASKA DESIGN
  San Francisco, California
art director, designer, copywriter
  BRUCE YELASKA
client
  SAARMAN CONSTRUCTION

creative firm
  SAYLES GRAPHIC DESIGN
  Des Moines, Iowa
art director, illustrator
  JOHN SAYLES
client
  SBEMCO INTERNATIONAL

creative firm
  SAYLES GRAPHIC DESIGN
  Des Moines, Iowa
art director, illustrator
  JOHN SAYLES
client
  SBEMCO INTERNATIONAL

creative firm
  BRUCE YELASKA DESIGN
  San Francisco, California
art director, designer, copywriter
  BRUCE YELASKA
photographer
  RICHARD GORDON
client
  SAARMAN CONSTRUCTION

creative firm
  BRUCE YELASKA DESIGN
  San Francisco, California
art director, designer, copywriter
  BRUCE YELASKA
photographer
  RICHARD GORDON
client
  SAARMAN CONSTRUCTION

Just be happy we're not your dentist.

Ouch! Working with your contractor shouldn't hurt. Like a dentist, we'll fill your building's cavities, while making sure that your construction defect repair and maintenance is a painless experience — every last bit of it.

SAARMAN CONSTRUCTION, LTD
Reconstruction Specialist
683 McAllister Street | San Francisco, CA 94102
Tel: 415.749.2700 | www.saarman.com

Stand back, we're professionals.

At the risk of sounding dull, we're the professionals when it comes to multifamily and commercial construction defect repair and maintenance.

SAARMAN CONSTRUCTION, LTD
Reconstruction Specialist
683 McAllister Street | San Francisco, CA 94102
Tel: 415.749.2700 | www.saarman.com

creative firm
  GARDNER DESIGN
    Wichita, Kansas
art directors, designers
  BILL GARDNER, BRIAN MILLER
client
  WILKINSON

creative firm
  UKULELE DESIGN
  CONSULTANTS PTE LTD
    Singapore
design director
  VERNA LIM
designer
  LYNN LIM
client
  THE PAN PACIFIC HOTEL SINGAPORE

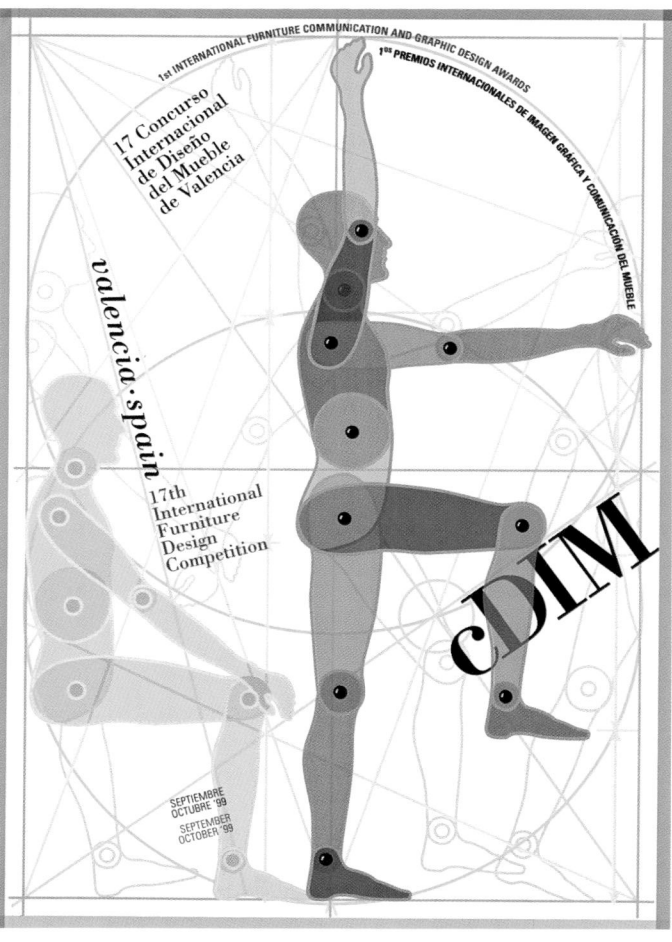

creative firm
PEPE GIMENO—PROYECTO GRÁFICO
Valencia, Spain
designer
JOSE P. GIL
client
FERIA INTERNACIONAL DEL MUEBLE DE VALENCIA

creative firm
SAYLES GRAPHIC DESIGN
Des Moines, Iowa
art director, illustrator
JOHN SAYLES
client
UNITED AIRLINES
"TIME TO OPEN A LITTLE BUBBLY"

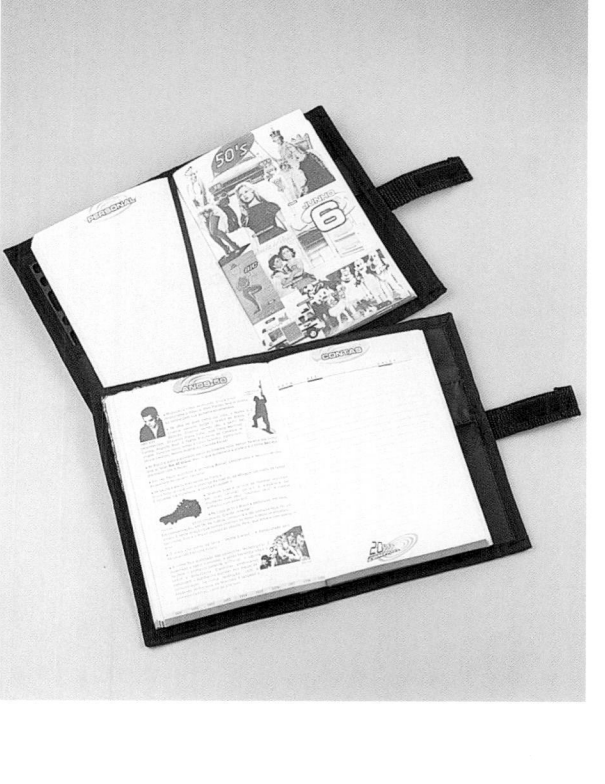

creative firm
  RGB GRAPHIC DESIGN
    Rio De Janeiro, Brazil
designers
  MARIA LUIZA GONÇALVES VEIGA BRITO,
  MARIA ANGELA LUTTERBACH
client
  COMPANY FASHION STORE

creative firm
  BUTLER KEMP DESIGN
    North Adelaide, Australia
art director
  DEREK BUTLER
designer
  JULIE KEMP
client
  DRUG & ALCOHOL SERVICES COUNCIL
    (alcohol Go Easy logo & bar runner)